1994–1995

EDITION

Computers and Information Systems

Sarah E. Hutchinson

Stacey C. Sawyer

IRWIN
Advantage
Series for
Computer
Education

Burr Ridge, Illinois
Boston, Massachusetts
Sydney, Australia

Associate editor: Rebecca Johnson
Project editor: Stacey C. Sawyer
Production: Stacey C. Sawyer, Sawyer & Williams
Designer: Adriane Bosworth
Cover designer: Mercedes Santos
Cover art: Ardon von Haeger
Artists: GTS Graphics
Compositor: GTS Graphics
Typeface: 10/12 Garamond Light
Printer: Wm. C. Brown

ISBN 0-256-14595-4

Printed in the United States of America

3 4 5 6 7 8 9 0 WCB 0 9 8 7 6 5 4

Photo credits are on p. xv

Contents in Brief

Preface

Why We Wrote This Book: Meeting the Needs of Users

Computers and Information Systems: 1994-1995 Edition is written for future computer users—people for whom the computer will be an everyday tool for working with reports, spreadsheets, databases, and the like. It is not intended for specialists who will write programs or design computer systems.

We wrote this book in order to provide instructors and students with the most useful information possible in an introductory computer course. Specifically, we offer the following five important features.

1. Practicality and Completeness

A textbook, we feel, should above all be *practical and complete*. It should give users all the information they need to understand the basics of information systems and to effectively use a microcomputer at work or at home. Thus we try to avoid the weaknesses we've seen elsewhere of stressing software to the detriment of hardware coverage, or of being too brief or too encyclopedic. We try to give users just what they need to know to use a computer competently for business or personal purposes. Some examples:

▼ We present up-to-date PC and Macintosh hardware information and compatibility issues so users can understand the capabilities of the computer systems they are using.

▼ We provide an entire chapter on how to purchase and maintain a microcomputer system, with information on user health and safety.

▼ We give practical information about ethics, privacy, and security.

▼ We offer "bonus" information users may find useful on the job, such as the different RAM requirements of different color monitors

▼ We cover advanced topics such as object-oriented programming, expert systems, virtual reality, and digital convergence—subjects users are sure to encounter in the workplace in the near future.

2. Flexible, Reasonably Priced Software Labs

We realize that students (and instructors) have a great deal of concern about the cost of textbooks. Accordingly, we offer many *reasonably priced*, separately bound software tutorials. These hands-on tutorials from *Irwin's Advantage Series for Computer Education* include the following:

dBASE III Plus	Paradox 3.5
dBASE IV	Paradox 4.0/4.5
DOS 3.3	Quattro 1.01
DOS 5.0	Quattro Pro 3.0
DOS 6.0	Quattro Pro 4.0
Excel for the Macintosh	QBASIC
Excel 3.0 for Windows	System 7.0/7.1 for the Macintosh
Excel 4.0 for Windows	Windows 3.1
Filemaker Pro for the Macintosh	Word for the Macintosh
Lotus 1-2-3 release 2.01 and 2.2	Word 2.0 for Windows
Lotus 1-2-3 release 2.3	WordPerfect 5.1
Lotus 1-2-3 release 2.4	WordPerfect 5.2 for Windows
Lotus 1-2-3 release 3.1	WordPerfect 6.0
Lotus 1-2-3 for Windows release 1.01	

Additional tutorials will be added to the series as the need arises.

3. Avoidance of Clutter

Our market research finds that many instructors have become tired of the cluttered, over-illustrated look and style of many introductory texts. Thus, you will not find margin notes, confusing icons, cartoons, and other such distractions here.

Also, we have attempted to use color to enhance content, not overpower it. We use four specific colors to indicate input (red), storage (blue), processing (gray), and output (yellow).

4. Interesting, Readable Style

We are gratified that reviewers have consistently found our writing style praiseworthy. Our primary goal is to reach students by making our explanations as clear, relevant, and interesting as possible.

5. Effective Pedagogy

We have carefully developed our learning aids to maximize students' comprehension and learning:

▼ *Chapter previews and outlines:* Each chapter opens with a list of chapter objectives, a brief outline of the chapter's content, and an introductory section called "Why Is This Chapter Important?" which explains why the material in the chapter is important to the user.

▼ *Chapter summaries:* Each chapter concludes with a useful summary section to help students review.

▼ *Key terms:* All the important terms covered—and the numbers of the pages on which they are defined—appear in a section called Key Terms at the end of each chapter. All key terms are also listed and defined in the glossary in the back of the book.

▼ *Self-tests and exercises:* Fill-in-the-blank tests, short-answer exercises, and projects test students' comprehension and encourage them to learn more about microcomputers on their own.

▼ *Career boxes:* One- or two-page boxes show students how computers are used in some common and uncommon ways in business and the professions.

▼ *Time-line chart:* This chart, which follows the last chapter, provides an overview of the historical development of information processing and related events from the beginning of recorded history to projected developments in the 21st century.

▼ *Glossary:* All boldface key terms are included, with their definitions, in the comprehensive glossary at the back of the book. We have also listed many terms that are not included among the key terms but that might crop up in students' readings.

Supplements That Work

It's not important how many supplements a book has but whether they're truly useful, accurate, and of high quality. We offer a number of supplements that you will find useful.

▼ *Instructor's Resource Manual with Transparency Masters,* prepared by Phil Koneman, Colorado Christian University (text available also on DOS or Windows disk). This supplement contains:

—Course planning guidelines
—Chapter outlines
—Lecture notes
—Teaching tips
—Suggestions for using transparencies and transparency masters
—Approximately 100 transparency masters

▼ *Color Transparencies*

—65 full-color overhead transparencies of key illustrations and tables are available to qualified adopters.

▼ *Test Bank,* prepared by Anne Breene, Texas A&M

—True/false, multiple choice, fill-in-the blank questions graded in difficulty
  Sample midterm exam
—Sample final exam
—Answers to test questions

▼ *Irwin's Computerized Testing Software: Computest 3*

—This computer-based test bank is available to qualified adopters.

▼ *Videos*

—These 21 videos are from the acclaimed PBS series, Computer Chronicles. Each video is approximately 30 minutes long. The videos cover topics ranging from computers and politics to CD-ROM and visual programming languages.

▼ *Classroom Presentation Software*

—Available for both the PC and Macintosh, Classroom Presentation Software can be used for in-class lecture presentations or in the lab for interactive self-study. Classroom Presentation Software combines text, graphics, and animation with interaction to dynamically illustrate major computer concepts. System requirements for the PC are 640 K RAM and EGA, VGA, or super VGA graphics.

Advantage Custom Editions (ACE)

The preceding supplements are available with Hutchinson/Sawyer, *Computers and Information Systems: 1994–1995 Edition* and/or *Computer Essentials*.

In addition, Irwin is proud to offer adopters an exciting new *customization* program. Now it's possible to order chapters from either text in a sequence that best fits the needs of your course. You may also order a *combination* of chapters from both texts. In addition, you may order an array of lab manuals (see above) from the Irwin Advantage Series to accompany any customized text.

Your custom product will be spiral bound and shipped to your bookstore approximately six weeks from the time you place your order. The only limitation to an order is that the custom text not exceed 1.75 inches. For more information about ACE, please contact your local Irwin representative or Faculty Service at 1-800-323-4560.

Acknowledgments

We're grateful for the assistance of our editor, Rebecca Johnson, who served in an invaluable capacity to guarantee the quality control of this book and to organize the many complicated pieces of a customized publishing program. In addition, we thank Micky Lawler for her careful line-by-line analysis of all our books.

We are also grateful to our many reviewers, who provided helpful comments over the course of several drafts. In particular, we thank the following people, who reviewed portions of this revised edition:

Virginia R. Gibson, University of Maine
Diane Graf, Saint Xavier University
Don Hutchinson, Independent Software Developer
Kenny Jih, University of Tennessee at Chattanooga
William A. Newman, University of Nevada/Las Vegas
Jerry Post, Western Kentucky University
Fred Ramos, Oklahoma City University

In addition, we are appreciative of the efforts of the photo researcher, Judy Mason; the copyeditor, Anita Wagner; and proofreaders Susan Lyon and Patterson Lamb—whose work significantly improved the quality of this book. The staff at GTS Graphics, typesetter and producer of the illustrations—especially Elliott Derman and Daniel Casquilho—are at the top of their field of electronic typesetting and graphics services.

Finally, we thank our cohort in computer book publishing, Brian Williams, for all his expert advice—at least for the advice that we took.

Write to Us

Finally, we need to know: Was this book truly useful to students? We'd like to hear from you about any improvements we might make. Write to us in care of our publisher, Richard D. Irwin.

Sarah E. Hutchinson
Stacey C. Sawyer

Contents in Detail

Photo credits

Page 1.2 (a) © Laima Druskis, Stock/Boston; (b) © Dion Ogust, The Image Works; (c) © J. Pickerell, The Image Works; (d) coutesy of Hewlett Packard; **1.8** © Andrew Popper, Phototake; **1.9** (*top*) (a) Tandem Computers; (b) courtesy of Cray Computers; (*bottom*) © Steve Niedorf, The Image Bank; **1.10** (*top*) courtesy of Digital; (*bottom*) courtesy of International Business Machines Corp.; **1.11** © Walter Bibikon, The Image Bank; **1.14** Apple Computer Corp.; **1.17** courtesy of International Business Machines Corp.; **1.18** Bettmann Newsphotos; **1.25** (a, b) Stacy Pick, Stock/Boston; **1.26** (*top*) (a) © Jonathan Selig, Photo 20-20; (b) © Charles Gupton, Stock/Boston; **1.26** (*bottom*) (a) © Matthew McVay, Stock/Boston; (b) courtesy of Federal Express Corp.; (*bottom*) © Michael Abramson, Woodfin Camp; **2.3** (a) courtesy of Hewlett Packard; (b) © John Thoeming, Richard D. Irwin, Inc.; (c) courtesy of Hewlett Packard; **3.5** © Fred Bodin; **3.7** © Bill Varie, The Image Bank; **3.8** © David Dempster; **3.9** (*top*) courtesy of NCR Corp.; (*bottom*) © Tim Davies, Photo Researchers, Inc.; **3.10** (*top*) © Howard Dratch, The Image Works; (*bottom*) courtesy of Hewlett Packard; **3.13** (a) © Toav Levy, Phototake NYC; (b) © Susan van Etten, Monkmeyer Press; (c) © Valrie Massey, Photo 20-20; **3.14** courtesy of Scantron Corp.; **3.16** © Yoav Levy, Phototake NYC; **3.17** (*top right*) The Complete PC; (*bottom left*) Soricon Corp.; (*bottom right*) Eastman-Kodak Co.; **3.18** Identix Corp.; **3.19** courtesy of International Business Machines Corp.; **3.20** courtesy of AT&T Archives; **3.21** courtesy of Texas Instruments; **3.23** © Joel Grimes, LC Technologies; **3.24** (*top*) Apple Computer Corp.; **3.25** (*left*) Comstock; (*right*) MicroTouch Systems, Inc.; (*bottom*) © Billy E. Barnes, TSW; **3.26** GO Corp.; **4.11** (*top*) AT&T Archives; (*bottom left*) courtesy of Intel Corp.; (*bottom right*) courtesy of Motorola, Inc.; **4.20** © Chris Gilbert; **5.12** courtesy of International Business Machines Corp.; **5.15** (*left*) © Dan McCoy, Rainbow; (*right*) International Business Machines Corp.; **5.21** (*top, bottom*) International Business Machines Corp.; **5.22** (*top bottom*) courtesy of Quantum; **5.23** (*top*) courtesy of Tandon; (*bottom*) courtesy of Quantum; **5.24** (a) © NEC Technologies, Inc.; 5.26 courtesy of Tallgrass Technologies; **5.27** © Jeffrey Dunn, Monkmeyer Press; **5.28** (*top and bottom*) courtesy of International Business Machines Corp.; **6.2** (*top left, top right, and bottom left*) courtesy of International Business Machines Corp.; (*bottom right*) Compaq Computer Corp.; **6.4** Qume; **6.6** Epson Corp.; **6.8** courtesy of Unisys Corp.; **6.10** (*top*) Hewlett Packard; (*bottom*) courtesy of Tektronix; **6.11** courtesy of Tektronix; **6.13** courtesy of Eastman-Kodak; **6.14** (*top*) Costar Corp.; (*middle left and middle right*) courtesy of Houston Instruments; (*bottom*) Versatec; **6.16** courtesy of Minolta Corp.; **6.20** courtesy of International Business Machines Corp.; **6.21** © Chris Gilbert; **6.22** (*top*) NEC Technologies, Inc.; (*left*) courtesy of International Business Machines Corp.; (*middle*) Compaq Computer Corp.; (*right*) Zenith Data Systems; **6.23** (*top*) courtesy of Hewlett Packard; (*middle left*) Grid Systems; (*middle right*) Toshiba America Information Systems; (*bottom*) courtesy of International Business Machines Corp.; **6.25** Kurzweil Computer Products; **7.14** (*top left and right*) Borland International; (*bottom left*) PC Paintbrush; (*bottom middle*) courtesy of International Business Machines Corp.; (*bottom right*) Polaroid Corp.; **7.15** © Peter A. Simon, Phototake NYC; **7.16** (*top*) courtesy of Martin Maritta Corp.; (*bottom a-d*) Gamma Kurita; **8.17** courtesy of Naval Surface Warfare Center, Dahlgren, Ill.; **9.8** (*top*) courtesy of AT&T Archives; (*bottom left and right*) © Fred Bodin; **9.9** © Jean Pierre Pieuchot, The Image Bank; **9.12** (*top*) courtesy of Unisys Corp.; (*bottom*) courtesy of AT&T; **9.14** (*top and bottom*) Hayes Corp.; **9.15** (*right and left*) © Fred Bodin; **9.20** courtesy of AT&T; **9.21** Eastman-Kodak Co.; **9.28** © Fred Bodin; **9.27** (*left*) © James Aronovsky, Picture Group; (*right*) Intel Corp.; **13.3** © Richard Wood, The Picture Cube; **13.5** (*top*) Gregory Heisler, The Image Bank; (*bottom*) © Dan McCoy, Rainbow; **13.6** © Russ Kinne, Comstock; **13.10** © Peter Menzel; **15.5** (*left*) courtesy of International Business Machines Corp.; (*right*) Compaq Computer Corp.; **15.6** (*top and bottom*) Apple Computer Corp.; 15.17 courtesy of International Business Machines Corp.; **15.20** Kinesis Corp.

Computers: Power Tools for an Information Age

The job interview can be a stressful experience for many people. But would you believe that some people actually enjoy interviewing for jobs? The secret, perhaps, lies in being prepared—knowing the job and the company, being certain of your accomplishments, and knowing which questions to ask.

Although most employers do not expect young job seekers to be computer experts, they do expect their potential employees to be prepared to use computers as tools in whatever field or business they choose. Two questions apt to be asked today are "What do you know about computers?" and "What kind of software are you familiar with?" The more you know about how to use the computer as a resource, the more prepared you will be to handle such questions—and to enhance your effectiveness in and enjoyment of whatever activities you choose to pursue.

PREVIEW

When you have completed this chapter you will be able to:

▼ Define who the user is

▼ Explain what a computer system is by focusing on hardware, software, data/information, procedures, and people

▼ Describe the four main types of computer systems and how each might be used in business

▼ Define what it means to be computer literate and describe some of the major events in the development of computers

▼ Name the three main parts of a microcomputer system

▼ List some ways computers are used professionally

The automatic teller machine. The supermarket price scanner. The magic "wand" used in department stores to "read" clothing price tags. A voice on the phone that told you to "Please hang up and dial your call again."

Did you come in contact with one of these special-purpose computer devices today? If not, then you probably encountered something similar, because the average person interacts—directly or indirectly—with a computer several times a day (Figure 1). You, then, are already a user of computer-processed information.

But you want to become more than that. You want to go beyond push buttons and digitized voices and become a true user, someone who can join a business or practice a profession and use the computer as a problem-solving tool. Chapter 1 will start you on your way.

Who Is the User?

To help you better understand who the computer user is, consider the following distinction:

▼ A **computer professional** is a person in the field of computers—for example, a programmer, a systems analyst, or a computer operator—who has had

(a)

(b)

(c)

(d)

FIGURE 1

Computers in daily life. As these commonplace examples show, today it is almost impossible to avoid using a computer. (a) Shopping with a bank card; (b) using a computer to locate books at a New York public library; (c) using an automatic teller machine (ATM); (d) monitoring and analyzing a tennis game.

formal education in the technical aspects of using computers and who is concerned only with supporting the computer's physical functions in producing information for the user.

▼   The **user** is a person perhaps like yourself—someone without much technical knowledge of computers but who makes decisions based on reports and other results that computers produce. The user is not necessarily a computer expert and may never need to become one. Most companies prefer to train new employees in the specific computer uses applicable to their business—and these applications may never require the user to have much technical knowledge.

Keep in mind, however, that the modern computer user is becoming more and more directly involved in the production of reports and other information through the hands-on use of *microcomputers,* often referred to as *personal computers.*

As a person living in what is now often called the Information Age, you know that computers aren't just a passing fad. Business and professional work depend on computers, and you will use computers in your job as well as in the pursuit of private interests. To use them efficiently, you must become computer literate.

Computer Literacy: Why You're Reading This Book

Computer literacy, or **computer competency,** has been a rapidly changing term. In the early 1980s, most computer professionals thought of it simply as "technical knowledge"; to users it usually meant only "computer awareness." Today, however, to be considered computer literate you must have a basic understanding of what a computer is and how it can be used as a resource. You are certainly considered computer literate if you can use a computer, probably a microcomputer, as a tool to assist in producing the information necessary to make intelligent decisions. This change of definition is a direct result of the greatly increased use of microcomputers in business in the past decade. Because many management professionals already know how to use microcomputers, success in the business or professional world—*your* success—depends on mastering this skill, too.

Being computer literate means not only acknowledging the importance of computers and determining to overcome any fears about them, but also actively involving yourself with them. As a computer literate person you should:

▼   Master the terminology used to talk about what a computer is and how to use one

▼   Learn to identify and describe the functions of the various components of a computer and an information system

▼   Learn to use a computer to produce the information you need

The objective of this book is to show you what a computer system is and how to use it—to help you achieve a level of computer literacy that will give you valuable skills in business and in your creative life. But don't be intimidated by the words *computer literacy,* and, by all means, don't be afraid to learn to use a computer! Computers were designed by people, built by people, programmed by people, and do only what people tell them to do.

What Is a Computer System?

The term **computer** is used to describe a device made up of a combination of electronic and electromechanical (part electronic and part mechanical) components. By itself, a computer has no intelligence and is referred to as **hardware.** A computer doesn't come to life until it is connected to other parts of a computer system. A **computer system** (Figure 2) is a combination of five elements:

1. Hardware
2. Software
3. Data/information
4. Procedures
5. People

When one computer system is set up to communicate with another computer system, **connectivity** becomes a sixth system element. In other words, the manner in which the various individual systems are connected—for example, by phone lines, microwave transmission, or satellite—is an element of the total computer system.

Software is the term used to describe the instructions that tell the hardware how to perform a task. Without software instructions, the hardware doesn't know what to do.

The purpose of a computer system is to convert data into information. **Data** is raw, *unevaluated* facts and figures, concepts, or instructions. This raw material is processed into useful **information.** In other words, information is the product of **data processing.** This **processing** includes refining, summarizing, categorizing, and otherwise manipulating data into a useful form for decision making. For instance, Roger Shu records his name on an employee timecard by first entering the letter *R.* This letter, and each of the remaining letters in his name, is an element of data, as are the numbers 12/22 and 5, used to indicate

---

FIGURE 2

A computer system combines five elements: hardware, software, data/information, procedures, and people. Connectivity is a sixth element when two or more separate computer systems are set up to communicate.

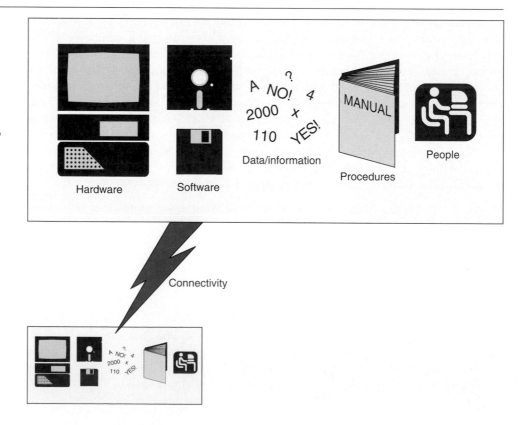

Hardware   Software   Data/information   Procedures   People

Connectivity

the date and the number of overtime hours worked. By themselves, these data elements are useless; we must process them to make them mean something. The report produced when Roger's data is run through a computer-based employee records system gives us information—for example, the amount of money due Roger for his overtime work.

People (sometimes called "liveware"), however, constitute the most important component of the computer system. People operate the computer hardware, and they create the computer software instructions. They also follow certain **procedures** when using the hardware and software. In short, people *use* the computer system to help them make decisions and provide services.

Now we'll discuss the basics of the first part of the typical computer system—the hardware devices that convert data into information.

Computer Hardware

In today's business world, not knowing what computer hardware is and what typical hardware components do is similar to being a taxi driver and not knowing what a car is and that it has components such as an engine, doors, windows, and so on.

Computer hardware can be divided into four categories:

1. Input hardware
2. Processing hardware
3. Storage hardware
4. Output hardware

Figure 3 shows the typical configuration of computer hardware.

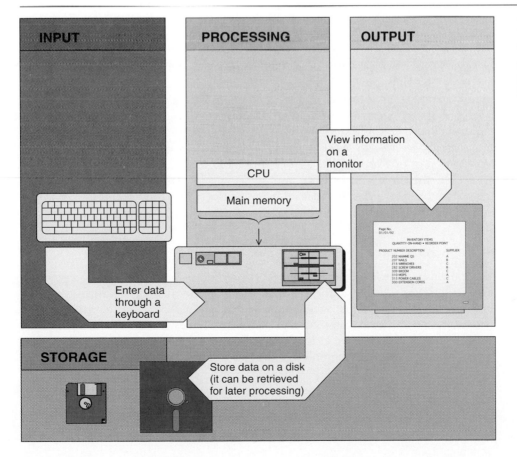

INPUT

PROCESSING

OUTPUT

View information on a monitor

CPU

Main memory

Enter data through a keyboard

Page No.
01/01/92

INVENTORY ITEMS
QUANTITY-ON-HAND • REORDER POINT

PRODUCT NUMBER DESCRIPTION   SUPPLIER

202 MAMME QS   A
207 NAILS   B
213 WRENCHES   C
282 SCREW DRIVERS   B
309 BROOM   C
310 MOPS   A
315 POWER CABLES   C
300 EXTENSION CORDS   A

STORAGE

Store data on a disk (it can be retrieved for later processing)

FIGURE 3

The four categories of computer hardware are input, processing, storage, and output.

In this section, we provide a brief description of the components found in each of these categories so you can see how each component relates to the others. In Chapters 3 through 6 we talk about input, processing, storage, and output hardware in more detail. For now, just focus on the large concepts.

Input Hardware

The purpose of **input hardware** is to collect data and convert it into a form suitable for computer processing. The most common input device is a **keyboard.** It looks very much like a typewriter keyboard with rows of keys in the typical typewriter layout, as well as a number of additional keys used to enter special computer-related codes. Although it isn't the only type of input device available, the computer keyboard is the one most generally used. In Chapter 3, we describe the microcomputer keyboard in detail, along with other types of popular input devices.

Processing Hardware

The purpose of **processing hardware** is to retrieve, interpret, and direct the execution of software instructions provided to the computer. The most common components of processing hardware are the central processing unit and main memory.

The **central processing unit (CPU)** is the brain of the computer. It reads and interprets software instructions and coordinates the processing activities that must take place. The design of the CPU affects the processing power and the speed of the computer, as well as the amount of main memory it can use effectively.

Main memory (also called *random access memory* [*RAM*], *internal memory, primary storage,* or just *memory*) can be thought of as an electronic desktop. The more desk surface you have in front of you, the more you can place on it. Similarly, if your computer has a lot of memory, you can place more software instructions in it. (Some of these instructions and data are retrieved by the computer from storage on disk or tape; others are input directly by the user—for example, through the keyboard.) The amount of memory available determines whether you can run simple or sophisticated software; a computer with a large memory is capable of holding the thousands of instructions that are contained in more sophisticated software programs. In addition, a large amount of memory allows you to work with and manipulate great amounts of data and information at one time. Quite simply, the more main memory you have in your computer, the more you can accomplish. However, the data and instructions in main memory are **volatile**—that is, they are lost when the computer's power is turned off, unless the user has saved them to a storage device.

Storage Hardware

The purpose of **storage hardware** is to provide a means of storing computer instructions and data in a form that is relatively permanent, or **nonvolatile**—that is, the data is not lost when the power is turned off—and easy to retrieve when needed for processing. Storage hardware serves the same basic functions as do office filing systems except that it stores data as electromagnetic signals or laser-etched spots, commonly on disk or tape, rather than on paper.

Output Hardware

The purpose of **output hardware** is to provide the user with the means to view information produced by the computer system. Information is output in either **hardcopy** or **softcopy** form. Hardcopy output can be held in your hand—an example is paper with text (words or numbers) or graphics printed on it. Softcopy output is displayed on a **monitor,** a television-like screen on which you can read text and graphics.

Computer Software

A computer has no intelligence of its own and must be supplied with instructions so that it knows what to do and how and when to do it. These instructions are called *software*. The importance of software can't be overestimated. You might have what most people consider the best computer sitting on your desk. However, without software to instruct the machine to do what you want it to do, the computer will only take up space.

Software is made up of a group of related **programs,** each of which is a group of related instructions that perform very specific processing tasks. Software acquired to perform a general business function is often referred to as a **software package.** Software packages, which are usually created by professional software writers, are accompanied by **documentation**—users' manuals—that explains how to use the software.

Software can generally be divided into two categories:

1. Systems software
2. Applications software

Systems Software

Programs designed to allow the computer to manage its own resources are called **systems software.** This software runs the basic operations; it tells the hardware what to do and how and when to do it. However, it does not solve specific problems relating to a business or a profession. For example, systems software will not process a prediction of what your company's tax bill will be next year, but it will tell the computer where to store and retrieve the data used during processing of that tax bill. Systems software will not process the creation of the animation strip for your next film, but it will manage how it is output.

Applications Software

Any individual instructions or set of related programs designed to be carried out by a computer to satisfy a user's *specific* needs are **applications software.** A group of programs written to perform payroll processing is one type of applications software, as are programs written to maintain personnel records, update an inventory system, help you calculate a budget, or monitor the incubation temperatures at your poultry farm.

Applications software can be purchased "off the shelf"—that is, already programmed, or written—or it can be written to order by qualified programmers. If, for example, a company has fairly routine payroll processing requirements, it can probably purchase one or more payroll applications software programs off the shelf to handle the job. However, if a company has unique payroll requirements, such as a need to handle the records of hourly employees, salaried employees, and commissioned employees, then off-the-shelf software may not be satisfactory. It may be more cost-effective to have the payroll programs written to exact specifications by a computer programmer.

Figure 4 shows a variety of packaged applications software available at computer stores. Many of these products are also available through vendors and mail-order sources.

FIGURE 4

Need help with your budget? Want to design and print some greeting cards or your own newsletter? Want to set up a large bank of cross-referenced, business-related data? Buying off-the-shelf software is almost like buying records, tapes, and CDs. Most computer stores offer a wide variety of applications software packages. But be sure you know what you want to accomplish before you make your selection, and check the hardware compatibility and system requirements listed on the software package.

Types of Computer Systems: What's the Difference?

You should be familiar with the basic differences among computer systems if you want to show a potential employer that you have a working knowledge of computers. Computers come in a variety of sizes and shapes and with a variety of processing capabilities. The earliest computers were very large because of the crude technologies used. However, as technological improvements were made in computer components, the overall size of computers began to shrink. To provide a basis for comparing their capabilities, computers are generally grouped into four basic categories:

1. Supercomputers, which are the powerful giants of the computer world
2. Mainframe computers, which are large, extremely powerful computers used by many large companies
3. Minicomputers, which are the next most powerful
4. Microcomputers, which are the least powerful—but which you most likely will be required to use on the job

It's hard to assign a worthwhile definition to each type of computer because definitions can get bogged down in potentially confusing technical jargon. Nevertheless, the following definitions can suffice:

▼ A **supercomputer** (Figure 5) can handle gigantic amounts of scientific computation. It's maintained in a special room or environment, may be about 50,000 times faster than a microcomputer, and may cost as much as $20 million. As a user in business, you probably would not have contact with a supercomputer. However, you might if you worked in the areas of defense and weaponry, weather forecasting, or scientific research; at one of several large universities; or for the National Aeronautics and Space Administration. For example, Gregory and David Chudnovsky broke the world record for

(a)

(b)

FIGURE 5

Supercomputer. (a) Tandem NonStop Cyclone; (b) Cray supercomputer.

FIGURE 6

Mainframe. The mainframe computer is front left, between two printers. At the back left are disk-drive storage units; tape storage units are at the back and back right. These units, or peripherals, are connected to the mainframe by under-floor cables.

pi* calculations by using two supercomputers to calculate pi to 480 million decimal places (the printout would be 600 miles long). Of course, in the next few years, more and more large industries will start using supercomputers such as the *massively parallel computer*, which has hundreds or even thousands of processors.

▼ A **mainframe computer** (Figure 6) is a large computer, usually housed in a controlled environment, that can support the processing requirements of hundreds and often thousands of users and computer professionals. It is smaller and less powerful than a supercomputer. It may cost from several hundred thousand dollars up to $10 million. If you go to work for an air-

---

*Pi is a commonly used mathematical constant that is based on the relationship of a circle's circumference to its diameter.

line, a bank, a large insurance company, a large accounting company, a large university, or the Social Security Administration, you may have contact—through your individual workstation—with a mainframe computer. However, mainframes are being purchased less frequently now than they used to be. Instead, new, powerful minicomputer and microcomputer systems—often hooked together in networks—are being used in place of mainframes.

▼ A **minicomputer,** also known as a *mid-size* or *mid-range computer* (Figure 7), is similar to but less powerful and smaller than a mainframe computer. It can support 2 to about 50 users and computer professionals. Minicomputers and mainframe computers can work much faster than microcomputers and have many more storage locations in main memory. Minicomputers cost from about $10,000 to several hundred thousand dollars. Many small and medium-sized companies today use minicomputers, which can fit in the corner of a room or on the floor next to a desk.

▼ The **microcomputer** (Figure 8) is the type of computer that you undoubtedly will be dealing with as a user. You may already be familiar with the microcomputer, also known as a *personal computer* (PC). A 1992 survey on microcomputer usage showed that 85% of a sampling of U.S. workers and 88% of Canadian workers use a microcomputer on the job. (These figures compare with 80% of European Economic Community workers and 64% of Japanese workers.)

Microcomputers cost between $500 and about $20,000. They vary in size from small portables, such as *palmtop (hand-held) computers, notebook computers,* and *laptop computers* (Figure 9) that you can easily carry around, to powerful desktop *workstations,* such as those used by engineers and scientists. A microcomputer—which is generally used by only one person at a time but which can often support more—uses a **chip** as its CPU. This chip, with its circuitry, is referred to as the **microprocessor.** As small as 1/4 of an inch square and 1/100 of an inch thick (Figure 10), a chip is made of silicon, a material made from sand. Silicon is referred to as a **semiconductor** because it sometimes conducts electricity and sometimes does not (*semi* means "partly").

Figure 7

Minicomputer. Vax 6000

Figure 8

Microcomputer. The three main components are the monitor, the system unit, and the keyboard. This unit also has a mouse.

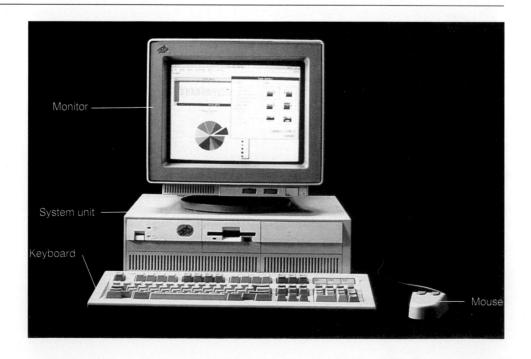

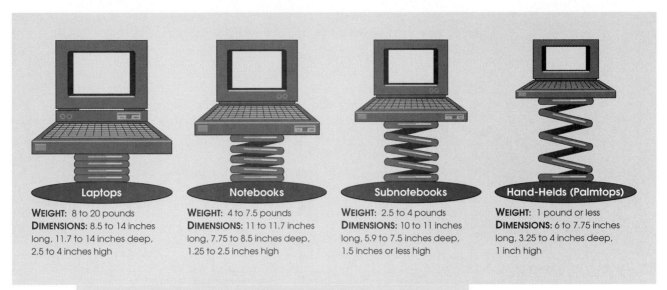

Laptops
WEIGHT: 8 to 20 pounds
DIMENSIONS: 8.5 to 14 inches long, 11.7 to 14 inches deep, 2.5 to 4 inches high

Notebooks
WEIGHT: 4 to 7.5 pounds
DIMENSIONS: 11 to 11.7 inches long, 7.75 to 8.5 inches deep, 1.25 to 2.5 inches high

Subnotebooks
WEIGHT: 2.5 to 4 pounds
DIMENSIONS: 10 to 11 inches long, 5.9 to 7.5 inches deep, 1.5 inches or less high

Hand-Helds (Palmtops)
WEIGHT: 1 pound or less
DIMENSIONS: 6 to 7.75 inches long, 3.25 to 4 inches deep, 1 inch high

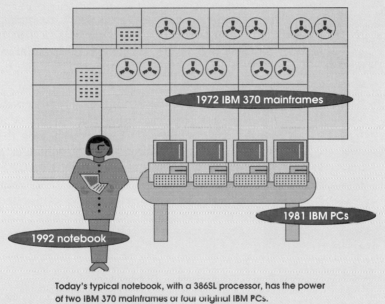

1972 IBM 370 mainframes

1981 IBM PCs

1992 notebook

Today's typical notebook, with a 386SL processor, has the power of two IBM 370 mainframes or four original IBM PCs.

FIGURE 9

Microcomputers come in various sizes: laptops, notebooks, subnotebooks, and palmtops. [Adapted from David Flaherty, Intel.]

FIGURE 10

This photo of a microprocessor gives you an idea of how small a chip is.

Table 1 compares the four basic types of computers. In general, a computer's type is determined by the following seven factors:

1. *The type of CPU*
   As noted, microcomputers use microprocessors, and the microprocessors are usually produced by chip manufacturers in large quantities for sale to various microcomputer manufacturers. The larger computers tend to use custom-made CPUs made up of separate, high-speed, sophisticated components—in other words, the CPU components in a large computer are not all on one chip.

2. *The amount of main memory the CPU can use*
   A computer equipped with a large amount of main memory can support more sophisticated programs and can even hold several different programs in memory at the same time.

3. *The capacity of the storage devices*
   The larger computer systems tend to be equipped with higher capacity storage devices than microcomputers have.

4. *The speed of the output devices*
   The speed of microcomputer output devices tends to be rated in terms of the number of **characters per second (cps)** that can be printed—usually in tens and hundreds of cps. Larger computers' output devices are faster and are usually rated at speeds of hundreds or thousands of *lines* that can be printed per minute.

5. *The processing speed* in **millions of instructions per second (mips)**
   The term *instruction* is used here to describe a basic task that the software asks the computer to perform while also identifying the data to be affected. The processing speed of small computers ranges from 3 to 5 mips. The speed of large computers can be 70 to 100 mips or more, and supercomputers can process from 200 million up to billions of instructions per second. In other words, a supercomputer can process your data a great deal faster than a microcomputer can.

TABLE 1

The Four Kinds of Computers*

	MICROCOMPUTER	MINICOMPUTER	MAINFRAME	SUPERCOMPUTER
Main memory (RAM)	512,000– 32,000,000 characters	8,000,000– 50,000,000 characters	32,000,000– 200,000,000 characters	100,000,000– 2,000,000,000 characters
Storage	360,000– 300,000,000 characters	120,000,000– 1,000,000,000+ characters	500,000,000–? characters	No limitation
Processing speed	700,000– 10,000,000 instructions per second	8–40 mips	30 mips and up	200 mips and up
Cost	$500–20,000	$10,000– $475,000	$250,000 and up	$10,000,000 and up

*The figures in this table represent average approximations. These numbers change rapidly as changing technology blurs the distinctions between categories.

6. *The number of users that can access the computer at one time*
   Most small computers can support only a single user; some can support as many as two or three at a time. Large computers can support hundreds of users simultaneously.

7. *The cost of the computer system*
   Business systems can cost as little as $1,500 (for a microcomputer) or as much as $10 million (for a mainframe)—and much more for a supercomputer.

It's difficult to say exactly what kind of computer you'll be using in the business or professional environment. Some companies use a combination of computers. For instance, a company with branch offices around the country might use a mainframe computer to manage companywide customer data. To access information from the mainframe, the user might use a microcomputer that sits on his or her desktop. In addition to accessing information from the mainframe computer, the microcomputer can be used to perform specialized tasks such as generating invoices or drafting letters to customers. Although it is still relatively easy to find a company that doesn't use a supercomputer, a mainframe, or a minicomputer to process data, it is difficult to locate a company that doesn't use microcomputers for some of its processing. Because microcomputers are generally versatile, increasingly powerful, and more affordable than the other types of computers, they provide a practical tool for the organization that wants to computerize or improve the efficiency and flexibility of an existing computer system.

Chances are that, when you enter the business or professional environment, you will be required to know how to use a microcomputer to perform many of your responsibilities. To use a microcomputer effectively and talk about it intelligently, you must understand the typical components of a microcomputer system. The more you know about them, the more valuable you may be to an employer. In the following section, we concentrate a bit more on microcomputer components.

The Anatomy of a Microcomputer

To understand the tremendous role microcomputers now play in business and the professions, it's helpful to look at how that role has developed. With the introduction of the Apple II and the Radio Shack Model I and II systems in the late 1970s, the business community began to adopt microcomputers. Then a number of additional vendors, including Atari, Commodore, Osborne, and Kaypro, entered the marketplace with computers designed to be used in the office or in the home. The interest in microcomputers grew rather slowly at first for several reasons: (1) The initial cost for some microcomputer systems was quite high, ranging up to $6,000; (2) only a limited amount of software was commercially available, and the average person was not able to write his or her own software; (3) the average person did not have sufficient background in computer-related subjects to use the computer without difficulty; and (4) there were no industrywide standards to ensure the **compatibility**—that is, the usability—of data and software on different types of microcomputer systems.

However, when IBM introduced the IBM PC in 1981, so many businesses adopted the product that an industry standard was set. Most vendors now design their products to be compatible with this standard—these products are referred to as IBM **clones.** The only other relatively successful microcomputer product lines today that have maintained their own unique standards are the Apple II and the Macintosh. The Apple II retains a loyal group of users who have supported it since its introduction in the late 1970s. Although the Apple II has been overshadowed in the business world by IBM-compatible products, the powerful and versatile Apple Macintosh line of microcomputers is now commonly used in desktop publishing operations. (We'll discuss desktop publishing in more detail later.)

The large number of different types of microcomputer systems in the marketplace makes it difficult to select one best system. As a result, our discussion of the microcomputer will center on the three basic hardware devices (Figure 11) found in most desktop microcomputer systems used in business today:

1. The keyboard
2. The monitor
3. The system unit

FIGURE 11

Basic anatomy of a microcomputer. The top part of the illustration shows a Macintosh microcomputer with monitor, keyboard, and system unit with disk drive; on the bottom is a cutaway drawing of the same basic setup.

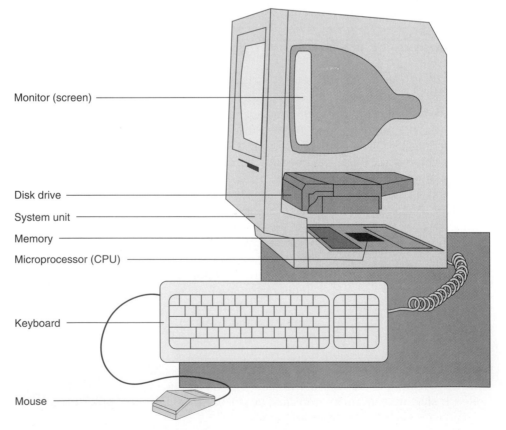

Keyboard

The microcomputer input device that you will use the most—the keyboard—is made up of a circuit board and related electronic components that generate a unique electronic code when each key is pressed. The code is passed along the keyboard cord to the computer system unit, where it is translated into a usable form for processing. The number of keys and their positions on the keyboard vary among machines. You should select a keyboard that is comfortable for you to use. (A mouse is also frequently used to input data, but we will describe the mouse in Chapter 3.)

Monitor

The term *monitor* is used interchangeably with *screen, video display screen,* and *cathode-ray tube* (*CRT*). This output device provides your principal visual contact with the microcomputer system. When you enter commands or data from the keyboard, you see the results on the monitor. A **monochrome monitor** displays text and, in some cases, graphics in a single color—commonly green or amber—usually on a dark background, or in black and white. A **color monitor,** often referred to as an **RGB monitor** (for red, green, blue), can display text and graphics in various colors.

System Unit

The main computer system cabinet, called the **system unit** (Figure 12), usually houses the power supply, the system board, and the storage devices (although some storage devices—disk drives, for example—are often housed in cabinets outside the system unit). These elements can be defined as follows:

1. The **power supply** provides electrical power to all components housed in the system unit. In some microcomputers—such as the Macintosh—it also provides power to the monitor.

2. The **system board,** also known as the **motherboard** or the *logic board,* is the main circuit board of the microcomputer system. It normally includes:

   —The microprocessor chip (or CPU)

   —Main memory chips

   —All related support circuitry

   —The expansion slots where additional components can be plugged in

3. The **storage devices** are usually one or more floppy disk drives and usually a high-capacity hard disk drive. (A "drive" is the equipment that encloses the disk and runs it.) A **floppy disk,** or **diskette,** is a thin plastic disk enclosed in a paper or plastic covering that can be magnetically encoded with data. **Hard disks** are rigid disks capable of storing much more data than a floppy disk. (And hard disk drives access data faster than do floppy disk drives.) Hard disks are more expensive than floppy disks. Since most hard disks are permanently installed in the system unit, floppy disks, which can be carried around, are often used to move data from one computer to another.

4. *Additional components:* The expansion slots on the system board allow users to add new components to their computer systems. The most popular add-on components include:

   —A memory card containing main memory chips that give the user additional main memory

   —An internal modem to facilitate data communications between computers over phone lines and similar cables

FIGURE 12

This illustration shows the basic parts of the microcomputer's system unit. (The system board continues under the diskette drive.)

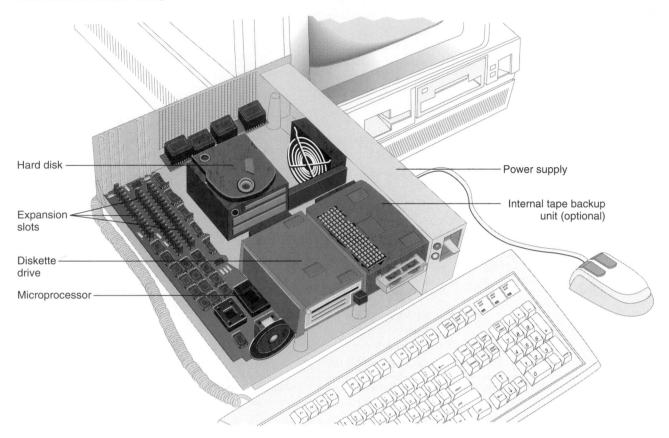

Hard disk

Expansion slots

Diskette drive

Microprocessor

Power supply

Internal tape backup unit (optional)

—A battery-powered clock and calendar mechanism

—Additional printer ports (socket-like hook-ups) that allow you to communicate with several types of output devices

—Specialized processing chips that support (assist) the microprocessor chip

—Video display boards (cards) that enable the user to improve the display capacity of the monitor

Don't worry about remembering what all these components are right now. They will be explained in detail later in the book. Just remember that microcomputers are likely to become an important part of your career. Pay attention to them and focus on what they can do for you.

Brief History of Computer Processing

In the last section, we gave you some historical information about the use of microcomputers in business since the early 1980s so that you could put into perspective their role in business today. In this section, we go back a little farther—almost 5,000 years—to show the tremendous effect that computers have had on data processing in general, which in turn has profoundly affected the society of which you are a part.

Data Processing Before Computers

To record and communicate data and information, prehistoric cave dwellers painted pictures on the walls of their caves, and the ancient Egyptians wrote on a crude form of paper called *papyrus*. Around 3000 B.C., the Sumerians created a device for representing numbers that consisted of a box containing stones. About 2,000 years later, in 1000 B.C., the Chinese took that idea one step further when they strung stones on threads in a wooden frame. The Chinese device was named after their word for box, *baccus*. The *abacus*, as we know it, remains in wide use even today and is still considered a powerful tool for performing mathematical computations.

Over the centuries, people have developed an amazing variety of data processing tools and techniques. Some of the most notable tools in use between the mid-1600s and the early 1900s are described in Figure 13.

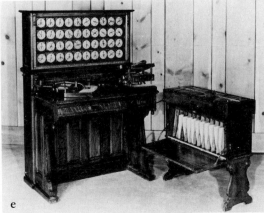

FIGURE 13

Which came first—computers or data processing? Many people think that we have been turning data into information only since computers came into use. The truth is that people have been processing data since prehistoric times. This illustration shows a few of the data processing methods used between the mid-1600s and the early 1900s.
(a) Pascaline calculator (mid-1600s), the first automatic adding and subtracting machine; (b) Leibniz Wheel (early 1700s), the first general purpose calculating machine; (c) Jacquard loom (1801), run by punched cards; (d) Thomas's arithnometer (1860), the first commercially successful adding and subtracting machine; (e) Hollerith's tabulating machine, used in the 1890 U.S. census; and (f) early IBM calculating machine (c. 1930).

The Evolution of Computers

The first large-scale electronic computer, the Electronic Numerical Integrator and Computer (ENIAC) (Figure 14), became operational in 1946. It contained approximately 18,000 electronic vacuum tubes—tubes the size of light bulbs that controlled the flow of electric current. The ENIAC, which weighed 30 tons and occupied about 1,500 square feet of floor space—a huge machine compared to today's standards—was able to perform a scientific calculation involving the multiplication of four numbers in approximately 9 milliseconds (9/1,000 of a second). Since that time, the technology used in the design and production of computers has accelerated at a remarkable pace.

The term **computer generation** was applied to different types of computers to help delineate the major technological developments in hardware and software. To date, computer technology has evolved through four distinct generations and is currently developing into a fifth generation.

First Generation (1944–1958)

In the earliest general-purpose computers, most input and output media were punched cards and magnetic tape, and main memory was almost exclusively made up of hundreds of vacuum tubes—although one computer used a magnetic drum for main memory. These computers were slow and large and produced a tremendous amount of heat. They could run only one program at a time. ENIAC and UNIVAC I—the UNIVersal Automatic Computer, which was used by the U.S. Bureau of the Census from 1951 to 1963—are examples of first-generation computers.

Second Generation (1959–1963)

By the early 1960s, transistors and some other solid-state devices that were much smaller than vacuum tubes were being used for much of the computer circuitry. Magnetic cores, which looked like very small metal washers strung together by

FIGURE 14

ENIAC. The first large-scale electronic computer. ENIAC weighed 30 tons, filled 1,500 square feet, included 18,000 vacuum tubes—and it failed about every 7 minutes.

wires that carried electricity, became the most widely used type of main memory. Removable magnetic disk packs, stacks of disks connected by a common spindle (like a stack of records), were introduced as storage devices. Second-generation machines tended to be smaller, more reliable, and significantly faster than first-generation computers.

Third Generation (1964–1970)

In the third period, the **integrated circuit**—a complete electronic circuit on a silicon chip—replaced transistorized circuitry. The use of magnetic disks became widespread, and computers began to support such capabilities as multiprogramming (processing several programs simultaneously) and timesharing (people using the same computer simultaneously). Minicomputers were being widely used by the early 1970s. The production of operating systems—a type of systems software—and applications software packages increased rapidly. The size of computers continued to decrease.

Fourth Generation (1971–Now)

In 1971, the first electronic computers were introduced that used Large-Scale Integration (LSI) circuits—thousands of integrated circuits on a chip—for main memory and logic circuitry (the circuitry that performs the logical operations of the CPU; different types of chips had different functions). These computers had a much larger capacity to support main memory. This period has also seen increased use of input and output devices that allowed data and instructions to be entered directly through the keyboard. The microprocessor, introduced in 1971, combined all the circuitry for the central processing unit on a single chip. LSI and the microprocessor enabled the development of the supercomputer.

Fifth Generation (Now and in the Future)

Definitions of what constitutes fifth-generation computers do not always agree. Some people think that the new microcomputers with faster operating speeds, greater processing capacity, and virtually unlimited memory should be included. Other people believe that fifth-generation computers will have circuitry based on gallium arsenide. Gallium arsenide offers a fivefold speed increase and uses only one tenth of the power that silicon uses. Scientists are also trying to develop new **superconductors** that can conduct electricity with *no* resistance, thus generating no heat but great speed.

Many fifth-generation computers will also incorporate hundreds or thousands of processors that operate in parallel—that is, simultaneously. Traditional computers use only one main processor or a few processors to work on one problem at a time. **Parallel processing** means that many processors will work on a problem at the same time. This concept promises to provide tremendously more efficient processing than the traditional kind, as will the use of optical "circuitry" that transmits data with light rather than electricity.

What Does All This Mean to the User?

Don't worry if you don't understand all the terms used to describe the sequence of computer generations. As you work through the book, the differences between them will become more clear, and you will gain an understanding of what the general user does *not* need to know.

The net effect of the tremendous increase in processing power provided by the computer is that more data can be processed faster than ever before. This means that all the information you need in your job to make decisions will be quickly available—a necessity in today's rapidly changing business environment.

The catch to all this, however, is that the power of the computer has grown so much that it can often generate more information than we can effectively deal with at one time. Indeed, in this society, knowledge is *the* primary resource for individuals and for the economy overall. As a result, we must be selective about the type of data and information we process. It must be concise, relevant, and accurate so that we avoid getting buried under an avalanche of unnecessary information. And we need to start thinking about the difference between data and information we *really need* and what we *think* we need—especially in our professional lives. Being bogged down by unnecessary details and inaccurate information is frustrating and time-consuming. The problem of being overloaded with information is being discussed more and more in business and computer publications.

The Effect of Computers on Processing Data and Information

New generations of computer technology will continue to affect the processing of data and information. Data collection continues to become easier and easier, data processing is getting faster and faster, mathematical calculations continue to be performed with increased precision, and information is being provided to users in generally more useful forms. And one of the best improvements that new technology brings us is that computers continue to become easier to use.

Data Collection: Hard Labor to Easy Time

Before computers were invented, data was collected and processed by hand in a variety of tedious ways. And the data often had to be copied and recopied more than once before it could be processed into information. Data collection for early computers was often done by transcribing hardcopy data into computer-usable forms such as punched cards or paper tape. The data was recorded by punching a series of holes according to a standardized coding scheme. Technological advancements in data collection have made this cumbersome collection method almost obsolete.

The Production of Information: Faster, Easier, Better (Usually)

It's no wonder that so many businesses have adopted computers so readily. Quick and easy production of accurate information has become a reality to businesspeople and professional people who used to dream about it. The U.S. government was one of the first institutions to benefit from increased data processing speed. In the last century, census taking was one of the most arduous processing tasks ever undertaken in this country. Almost 50,000 people collected data by hand, completing forms for approximately 13 million households. Processing this data by hand usually took more than eight years; no sooner would the population be tallied than the new census would begin. As a result, in 1890 the U.S. Congress authorized the Census Office to hold a competition to select the most efficient new method for recording and tabulating the census. Herman Hollerith won the contest with his system for electric tabulating using data input on punched cards. Although at the time the speed of this data processing method was a major breakthrough—it took Hollerith six weeks to compute an unofficial census—a modern personal computer can process the same amount of data in about half the time, after capturing it in a computer-usable form.

Thanks to the science of **ergonomics** (also called *human engineering*), which designs things to be used easily by people, the convenience of computer use has also improved over the years. Many people have been afraid of computers, but great strides have been made in transforming the computer into a friendlier, less mysterious tool. Input devices have become easier to use, and software is easier to understand than ever before.

In addition to being fast and easy to use, the computer also brings us a math facility that many of us thought was eternally beyond our reach. Have you ever had difficulty balancing your checkbook or creating a budget? Or is your life overshadowed by math anxiety? Many of us find it difficult to consistently perform mathematical calculations accurately by hand. Sooner or later we make a mistake. One of the major advantages of a computer is that, with the proper software, it will perform calculations quickly and accurately, with much greater precision and speed than would be possible manually. Thus math anxiety will not prevent you from providing your employer with, for example, complicated statistical or financial reports.

Information in Usable Forms: For the Computer and for the User

The need for business-related data to be retrieved, manipulated, and analyzed is constant. As we mentioned, in the past data was collected by hand and analyzed manually to produce a report. Then people had to go through the same procedure again if they wanted to use the same data to produce a different report. The computer allows us to capture data in *computer-usable form*—for example, on disk. Once the data is available in this form, the computer can *repeatedly* retrieve and manipulate it to produce information tailored—in people-usable form—to meet specific needs. This flexibility has been welcomed by many people in data-heavy professions such as accounting and banking.

The Effect of Computers on Employment Opportunities

We have seen that computers have revolutionized data and information processing. Computers have also changed some industries and actually created others. The design and manufacture of computer hardware has become an enormous industry, and the need for software by all sorts of businesses—from apple growers to zoo managers—has led to the development of the applications software industry. Major retail sales and wholesale distribution operations have developed to sell these hardware and software products, as well as related products.

All these industries have one thing in common: They need workers. In fact, the growth of the computer information industry has created a vast and varied number of jobs for both computer professionals and computer-literate users. No matter what type of business you go into, you will probably be using computers. Figure 15 shows only a few examples of current job opportunities that are directly related to computers. Each chapter of this book also contains a "Computers and Careers" box that will give you detailed information about how computers are used in various professions that are not directly related to computer hardware, software, and systems businesses. Although the following general career information may not be essential to the understanding of the main topics presented in this chapter, many students find it useful.

Opportunities for Computer Professionals and Information Specialists

Several million people are employed as computer programmers, computer operators, information managers, systems analysts, data entry clerks, database managers, and other technical workers. The growth of the microcomputer hardware and software industries has created a large number of new jobs in the retail sales and marketing of computers as well. Many jobs have also been created by

FIGURE 15

These job ads from real newspapers and magazines represent only a few ways computers are used in business and the professions.

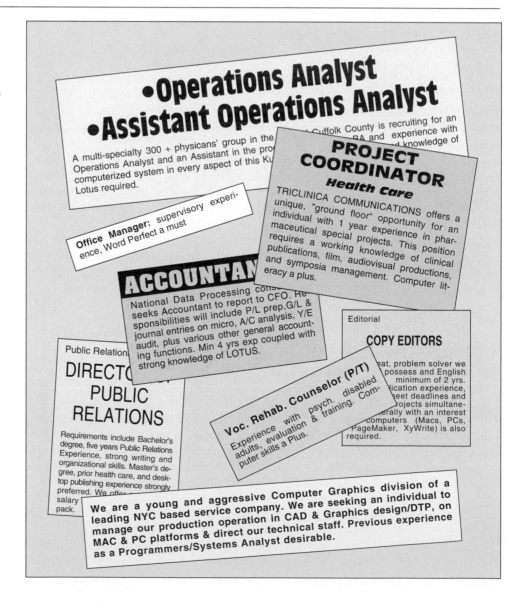

companies that manufacture the various computer components and by companies that specialize in computer repair.

In general, *computer programmers* design, write, test, and implement the programs that process the data in the computer system. *Systems analysts* know programming basics but have broader responsibilities than programmers do. They plan and design not just individual programs but entire systems of programs, including the procedures that users must follow when using the system. The *database administrator* (*DBA*) works with systems analysts on issues relating to the database. He or she must resolve conflicts among users and among technical people working on the database and database management software and administrate the use, maintenance, and security of the database. The *chief information officer* coordinates and gives direction to the database managers, systems analysts, programmers, and various office systems managers. He or she helps people cope with changes in technology and solves problems relating to information needs.

Opportunities for Users

The employment picture for users (you) is good if you have some experience actually using computers. As we've mentioned, many employers now require some degree of computer competency as a prerequisite for employment. Computers are becoming standard business tools for all employees, from the president of the company to the clerks in the typing pool. For example, accounting departments and public accounting firms now seek college graduates who have substantial hands-on microcomputer experience. Many administrative and managerial employees are also using microcomputers or computer terminals in their offices. To meet the demand for computer literacy, many schools offer extension courses or seminars in computer skills.

The most popular courses cover *word processing programs* (designed to create and output professional-looking documents in a short amount of time), *database management system programs* (designed to easily store, update, and manipulate large amounts of data), and *electronic spreadsheet programs* (designed to handle calculations and update complex financial forms). Attendance in these courses by working professionals has increased dramatically in the past few years. An informal survey of several universities has shown that people enroll for training for three reasons:

▼ *To satisfy job requirements.* Some of those surveyed stated that they were strongly encouraged or required by their employers to learn more computer skills.

▼ *To increase job skill and marketability.* Others surveyed said that because microcomputers and related software have become so popular, they felt they needed some additional skills to keep their jobs, to be considered for advancement, or to change to a more desirable job.

▼ *To learn to use a computer as a personal resource.* The remaining people indicated that they wanted to learn to use the computer as a personal resource on the job and at home. These people were not required to use computers on the job but felt computers could help them perform their jobs more efficiently.

But what are some of the specific jobs and activities that involve computer use?

Computers in Business

Different types of businesses commonly use computers to assist with such day-to-day operating activities as:

▼ *Sales order entry:* procedures for handling customer orders, including receipt of the order and verification of availability of ordered stock

▼ *Inventory management and control:* procedures for tracking, counting, and reordering stock items

▼ *Personnel management:* procedures for maintaining employee information (such as hire date, salary, performance rating, and date of last review) for both development and reporting purposes

▼ *Payroll:* procedures for producing paychecks and reports on employee compensation

▼ *Accounting:* procedures for maintaining the company's financial records

▼ *Security:* procedures for controlling who has access to what data and information at what times and where, and who may enter data to a computer-based information system

▼ *Investment and general financial management:* procedures a company institutes, follows, and reviews to guarantee profit and growth

Computers are also being used in business to collect and analyze data, to produce concise information for management in a clear format suitable for making decisions, and to help managers avoid being overloaded with unnecessary information.

To keep up-to-date with detailed information about how computers are being used in the various sections of the business and banking world, consult well-known business publications such as *Business Week, Fortune,* and *The Wall Street Journal,* as well as computer publications such as *PC World, PC Magazine, PC Computing, MacUser,* and *Macworld.*

Computers in Government

Government agencies are among the largest computer users in the world today. It would almost be impossible to collect, tabulate, and categorize the colossal amount of data the U.S. government must deal with daily without the aid of computers. For example, the Internal Revenue Service has 10 huge data centers throughout the country solely dedicated to processing income tax returns. Even so, it takes most of the year to process all of the prior year's tax returns.

To a large extent, the U.S. defense system is based on computer technology. Vast networks of computers work together to coordinate and disseminate strategic information needed to manage and deploy armed forces. Satellites are used to collect and communicate data and information, and the weapons systems have computerized components. Many weapons are now considered "smart" weapons because they can collect data, process it into information, and use it in military strategies. Of course, whether or not *people* are smart enough to use these weapons responsibly remains to be seen.

Computers in the Legal Profession

Law enforcement agencies use computers to collect and analyze evidence. Many agencies are now equipped with data processing facilities that enable them to connect with large, countrywide law enforcement computer systems from which they can obtain and with which they can share information on criminal activities, as well as missing persons. As shown in Figure 16, many police cars are now equipped with computer terminals so that an officer can immediately access information about a suspect or a vehicle.

The criminal justice system uses computers to help manage large amounts of information. The documentation created when a suspect is arrested and tried can easily take up several hundred pages. Without computerized information processing, it would be next to impossible today to collect the data, process it, and keep track of the status of cases. In addition, lawyers can save documents such as wills in a computer system for easy updating in the future and prepare for the defense of a client by referring to similar cases stored in a computer database.

Computers in Medicine

The use of computers in the health-care industry has also grown tremendously. The computer has become a valuable resource in the management of records for physicians, nurses, pharmacists, nutritionists, hospitals, and medical insurance companies, as well as in patient diagnosis and physiological monitoring. Computers are used to process mountains of medical administrative paperwork, including millions of patient insurance claims; patient billing forms; inventory control accounts to track the availability and use of beds; and extensive patient records and histories of test results, treatments, and medicines.

Some computer-related developments in the medical profession involve the use of computer systems to assist in patient diagnosis. CAT and PET scanners (not named after animals, but acronyms from long technical names—computerized axial tomography and positive emission tomography) can take computerized "pictures" of the interior of the brain and other parts of the body (Figure 17). Many of the devices found in intensive care units are also computerized—such as the electrocardiograph system used to record the pulses that cause a patient's heartbeat.

Computers are also used in the education of physicians. Indeed, medical training software is now so sophisticated that medical students and physicians can use the computer to practice certain operations *before* operating on a person.

Computers in Education

In recent years, educators have been involved with computers in three ways: (1) they teach students about computers; (2) they teach students about a variety of subjects such as math, language skills, reading, and grammar using computers (*computer-assisted instruction*); and (3) they use computers as classroom management tools (*computer-managed instruction*). Computer classes have been offered at the college level since the mid-1950s. Today most schools offer

FIGURE 16

Computers in law enforcement. (a) Computers in police cars can be used to check out license plates, drivers' licenses, and registration papers.
(b) Communications center for the Los Angeles Police Department.

(a)

(b)

FIGURE 17

Computers in medicine. (a) CAT scan; (b) critical care nurse receiving training on digitized radiology (X ray) system.

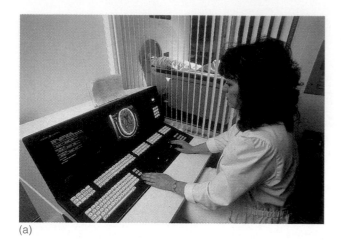

(a)

(b)

FIGURE 18

Computers in industry. (a) Logger using computer to determine free values; (b) sorting packages at a Federal Express station.

(a)

(b)

students some exposure to computers. Most colleges and universities now have their own microcomputer training labs. In addition, their libraries probably use computers to aid in library searches and in management, and their special education departments are probably instructing students in the use of custom-developed programs and hardware to aid in the education of handicapped children and adults. And "electronic universities" are being established to offer all sorts of courses to people who use computers and communications technology to earn educational degrees at home.

Computers in Industry

Many industries are being transformed by the use of computers. You probably already know that automobile and other product manufacturers use computer-based robots to do much of their work. People are involved not only in operating the robots, but in designing them and the systems they are a part of. Engineers and designers are using computer-aided design to construct items from airplanes to zippers (Figure 18).

Publishing is a good example of one industry that has changed dramatically because of computerization. Editing, typesetting, page makeup, photo treatments, creation of illustrations, color work, and film output can all be done electronically now—and much faster than ever before. This means that new types of jobs are being created for people who can combine publishing know-how and/or language expertise with computer experience. Also, computerization has enabled many publishing people to work at home as freelancers, because they can work with almost all the other people in the publishing cycle electronically.

Computers in Entertainment and Sports

Computers have had an amazing effect on such entertainment businesses as movie making and music production (Figure 19). Special effects experts are in demand, as are those who combine musical talent with the ability to operate computer-based musical equipment. People who are trained in video production and modern communications can find work in broadcasting, journalism, advertising, and a number of other fields. And, of course, game companies and software companies are in need of people to develop computer-based games.

FIGURE 19

Computers in entertainment. More and more of the music we hear is created on, modified by, and output by computer.

FIGURE 20

Computers in agriculture. Farmers learning to use computers to manage feed inventory.

In sports, athletes' performances are being analyzed and improved by the use of computers. Sports medicine has also become much more effective through the use of computer systems to analyze and treat injuries.

Computers in Agriculture

Computers are also used professionally by people in animal husbandry (Figure 20)—raising poultry, dairy cattle, or beef cattle—to monitor breeding conditions, diet, and environment, and also to manage accounting and other clerical procedures. New types of disease-resistant plants are being produced through computer-based plant engineering, and computers are being used in farming to monitor weather, water supplies, climate, soil composition, and so on.

Computers in the Home

Computers are such versatile tools that people are bringing them into their homes in increasing numbers. A wide variety of software is available for home use, including (1) educational software for young children, (2) personal financial management software, and (3) entertainment software. Many professionals also use their home computers to do some work-related tasks or even run their businesses from the home, using typical business software packages and modern communications technology.

Of course, many more interesting professions exist that involve the use of computers. The scientific applications alone are astounding—but we can't list all the applications here. To keep up-to-date with changing computer uses in a particular profession, consult professional publications. Your department chairperson or a librarian will be able to help you find those publications.

COMPUTERS AND CAREERS

▼

THE ARTS, SPORTS, AND ENTERTAINMENT

ot planning to make a career in computers and information processing? Think computers will have only the barest presence in your professional life? We're guessing otherwise. In every line of work, computers have become nearly as commonplace as pencil and paper, even in those fields that seem to be mostly rooted in intuition, emotions, and creativity. In this box, the first of many on computers and different career fields, we show how these instruments of logic are used in the arts, sports, and entertainment.

The casting agent is looking for an actor who can speak Spanish, owns cowboy gear, and can shoot a rifle while riding a horse. She turns to her computer and feeds her request into RoleCall, a computerized casting service for film, theater, and television. Almost instantly the computer screen produces the names of 40 actors who fit the bill.

In rehearsals, the director uses a Macintosh computer and a program called TheaterGame to go through the process of staging ("blocking") a scene. The program offers a choice of sets, props (such as furniture, trees), and costumed characters that can be moved around on the screen by using a mouse to direct the cursor. If a chair gets in the way of the action, the director can use the mouse to push it aside. Characters can be manipulated so that they turn their heads to talk, sit, fall down, and so on. Afterward, the director can play back the staging to see how it looks.

In the television studio, there are no longer headphone-wearing operators rolling three or four cameras back and forth. Rather, there are now robotic cameras linked to a central computer called the "cue computer," which prompts the cameras. The cue computer is operated by an engineer, who keeps his or her eyes on several wall monitors to keep each camera in focus. Standard shots, such as an overhead view of the set, can be programmed in advance and called up on the computer as needed.

Examples of how computers can be used in nonscientific ways are found in other artistic fields. Dancers may use computers to choreograph their movements. Musicians may use them to write out musical scores while they compose them on a piano keyboard. Computer artists don't use bristles and pigments but rather metal-tipped styluses, with which they "paint" on slate-like digitizing pads, which in turn transmit their movements and colors to a computer screen. Art dealers may use the Omnivex electronic art catalogue, which stores images of artwork on videodisc and allows dealers to view them by calling them up on high-resolution computer screens.

Viewers of televised sports have become accustomed to seeing all kinds of statistics and percentages flashed on the screen. Now, however, coaches and athletes can receive this kind of computerized analysis even for sports such as tennis, using a program called Computennis. And cyclists can use computer-generated three-dimensional maps, called Terragraphics guidebooks, which give the rider a preview of a planned route. Even people who like to fish can improve their odds with the use of a computerized sonar device, called Specie Select, which uses software based on information from over 1,000 professional anglers and guides to home in on the fish-locating information pertinent to a particular species.

Computers are an important part of all sectors of the entertainment industry. Just one example: Computer-based animation has come of age to produce spectacular new images, from glowing, flying, spinning station call letters to cartoon characters.

▼ Being *computer literate*—being familiar with computers and their uses—is necessary today because it is virtually inevitable that you will be using a computer in your career.

▼ A computer must be part of a system to be useful. A *computer system* has five parts:

1. *Hardware*   4. *Procedures*
2. *Software*   5. *People*
3. *Data/information*

▼ *Hardware* comprises the electronic and the electromechanical parts of the computer system.

▼ *Software* is the instructions—electronically encoded usually on disk or tape—that tell the hardware what to do.

▼ *Data* is raw, unevaluated facts, concepts, or instructions. Through *data processing* data becomes *information,* which is data transformed into a form useful for decision making. Processing can include refining, summarizing, categorizing, and listing, as well as other forms of data manipulation.

▼ *Procedures* are specific sequences of steps, usually documented, that users follow to complete one or more information processing activities.

▼ *People*—the most important part of the computer system—design and develop computer systems, operate the computer hardware, create the software instructions, and establish procedures for carrying out tasks.

▼ Computer hardware is categorized as:

1. *Input hardware*—used to collect data and input it into the computer system in computer-usable form. The keyboard is the most common input device.

2. *Processing hardware*—retrieves, interprets, and directs the execution of software instructions. The main components of processing hardware are the *central processing unit (CPU)*, which is the "brain" of the computer, and *main memory,* the computer's primary storage area, where data and instructions currently being used are stored. These data and instructions are *volatile*—that is, they will be lost when the computer's power is turned off, unless they are saved to a storage device.

3. *Storage hardware*—usually disk or tape devices for relatively permanent (*nonvolatile*) storage of data and instructions for later retrieval and processing.

4. *Output hardware*—provides a means for the user to view information produced by the computer system—either in *hardcopy* form, such as printouts from a printer, or *softcopy* form, such as a display on a monitor, a TV-like screen that can be color (*RGB*) or *monochrome,* usually amber, green, or black and white.

▼ *Software,* which is usually written by professional programmers, is made up of a group of related *programs,* each of which is a group of related instructions that perform specific processing tasks. Software that runs the hardware and allows the computer to manage its resources is *systems software,* software that is written to perform a specific function for the user—such as preparing payroll or doing page makeup for a magazine—is *applications software.* Applications software can be purchased *off the shelf* as a *software package,* or it can be *custom written* to solve the unique needs of one company or business. Software is accompanied by *documentation,* or users' manuals.

▼ Computers are categorized from the largest and most powerful to the smallest and least powerful:

1. *Supercomputer*

2. *Mainframe computer*

3. *Minicomputer*

4. *Microcomputer*

1.29

▼ A computer's type is determined by seven factors:

1. Type of CPU

2. Amount of main memory the CPU can use

3. Storage capacity

4. Speed of output devices

5. Processing speed

6. Number of users that can access the computer at one time

7. Cost

▼ The microcomputer (*personal computer,* or *PC*) is the computer used most by business professionals. Microcomputers range in size from small *palmtops, notebooks,* and *laptops* to powerful desktop *workstations,* which are hooked up to a larger computer. The microcomputer has a small *semiconductor (silicon) chip,* or *microprocessor,* as its CPU.

▼ A microcomputer main system cabinet—the *system unit*—usually houses the *power supply,* the *system board (motherboard),* and some storage devices, such as one or more floppy disk drives and a high-capacity hard disk drive. The system board includes the *microprocessor chip, main memory chips, related support circuitry,* and *expansion slots.*

▼ The term *computer generation* was applied to different types of computers to help delineate the major technological developments in hardware and software. To date, computer technology has evolved through four distinct generations and is currently developing into a fifth generation.

1. *First Generation (1944–1958):* These are the earliest general-purpose computers. Most input and output media were punched cards and magnetic tape, and main memory was almost exclusively made up of hundreds of vacuum tubes. These computers were slow and large and produced a tremendous amount of heat. They could run only one program at a time.

2. *Second Generation (1959–1963):* By the early 1960s, transistors and some other solid-state devices that were much smaller than vacuum tubes were being used for much of

the computer circuitry. Second-generation machines tended to be smaller, more reliable, and significantly faster than first-generation computers.

3. *Third Generation (1964–1970):* During this period, the integrated circuit—a complete-electronic circuit on a silicon chip—replaced transistorized circuitry. The use of magnetic disks became widespread, and computers began to support such capabilities as multiprogramming (processing several programs simultaneously) and timesharing (people using the same computer simultaneously). The size of computers continued to decrease.

4. *Fourth Generation (1971–Now):* In 1971, the first electronic computers were introduced that used Large-Scale Integration (LSI) circuits—thousands of integrated circuits on a chip—for main memory and logic circuitry. These computers had a much larger capacity to support main memory. The microprocessor, introduced in 1971, combined all the circuitry for the central processing unit on a single chip. LSI and the microprocessor enabled the development of the supercom-puter.

5. *Fifth Generation (Now and in the Future):* Some people think that the new microcomputers with faster operating speeds, greater processing capacity, and virtually unlimited memory should be included. Other people believe that fifth-generation computers will have circuitry based on gallium arsenide or other new superconductors. Many fifth-generation computers will support parallel processing—that is, many processors will work on a problem at the same time.

▼ Business has seen many improvements in the area of data processing since the introduction of computers:

1. Data can be collected more easily.

2. Data can be processed with much greater speed.

3. Data can be manipulated over and over again with ease.

4. Calculations are performed not only faster but usually with greater accuracy.

5. Output can be produced in more usable forms.

KEY TERMS

applications software, p. 1.7
central processing unit (CPU), p. 1.6
characters per second (cps), p. 1.12
chip, p. 1.10
clone, p. 1.13
color (RGB) monitor, p. 1.15
compatibility, p. 1.13
computer, p. 1.4
computer generation, p. 1.18
computer literacy (competency),
   p. 1.3
computer professional, p. 1.2
computer system, p. 1.4
connectivity, p. 1.4
data, p. 1.4
data processing, p. 1.4
documentation, p. 1.7
ergonomics, p. 1.21
floppy disk (diskette), p. 1.15

hardcopy, p. 1.7
hard disk, p. 1.15
hardware, p. 1.4
information, p. 1.4
input hardware, p. 1.6
integrated circuit, p.1.19
keyboard, p.1.6
mainframe computer, p. 1.9
main memory, p. 1.6
microcomputer, p. 1.10
microprocessor, p. 1.10
millions of instructions per second
   (mips), p. 1.12
minicomputer, p. 1.10
monitor, p. 1.7
monochrome monitor, p. 1.15
motherboard (system board), p. 1.15
nonvolatile, p. 1.6
output hardware, p. 1.6

parallel processing, 1.19
power supply, p. 1.15
procedures, p. 1.5
processing, p. 1.4
processing hardware, p. 1.6
program, p. 1.7
semiconductor, p. 1.10
softcopy, p. 1.7
software, p. 1.4
software package, p. 1.7
storage device, p. 1.15
storage hardware, p. 1.6
supercomputer, p. 1.8
superconductor, p. 1.19
system unit, p. 1.15
systems software, p. 1.7
user, p. 1.3
volatile, p. 1.6

EXERCISES

SELF-TEST

1. The term _____ is used to describe a device made up of electronic and electromechanical parts.

2. List four categories of hardware:

   a.   c.

   b.   d.

3. Main memory is a software component. (true/false)

4. _____ _____ includes programs designed to enable the computer to manage its own resources.

5. Softcopy output can be displayed on a _____ or TV-like screen.

6. Related programs designed to be carried out by a computer to satisfy a user's

   specific needs are called _____

   _____

7. Computers are generally grouped into one of the following four basic categories:

   a.   c.

   b.   d.

8. You are more likely to use a microcomputer in business than a supercomputer. (true/false)

9. The _____ _____ of a microcomputer usually houses the power supply, the motherboard (system board), and the storage devices.

10. _____ monitors display images only in a single color or black and white.

11. Hard disks have greater storage capacities than diskettes (floppy disks). (true/false)

12. An RGB monitor can display _____

13. Users' manuals that accompany computer hardware and software are referred to as _____

14. Mainframe computers process faster than microcomputers. (true/false)

15. The CPU of a microcomputer is referred to as the _____

16. As a result of data processing, _____ (what you put into the computer) is often processed into useful _____ (what is output by the computer).

17. List the five parts of a computer system:

a.   c.   e.

b.   d.

Solutions: (1) computer; (2) input, processing, storage, output; (3) false; (4) systems software; (5) monitor; (6) applications software; (7) supercomputer, mainframe, minicomputer, microcomputer; (8) true; (9) system unit; (10) monochrome; (11) true; (12) colors; (13) documentation; (14) true; (15) microprocessor; (16) data, information; (17) hardware, software, data/information, procedures, people

SHORT-ANSWER QUESTIONS

1. Describe the function of each of the five main components of a computer system.

2. What does it mean to be computer literate? Why is computer literacy, or competency, important?

3. What is the difference between systems software and applications software?

4. What is the meaning of the term *connectivity*?

5. What is a microprocessor?

6. What is the function of storage hardware in a computer system?

7. What is the purpose of main memory?

8. Why is it better to have a computer with more main memory rather than less?

9. What is the purpose of the system unit in a microcomputer system?

10. How is a computer *user* different from a *computer professional*?

PROJECTS

1. Look in the job opportunities section of several newspapers to see if many jobs require applicants to be familiar with using microcomputers. What types of experience are required? What kinds of computer skills do you think you'll need in your chosen job or career?

2. Many people are afraid of or resistant to learning about computers. Are you one of them? If so, make a list of all the factors that you think are affecting your attitude, then list reasons to refute each point. Keep your list and review it again after you have finished the course. What do you still agree with? Have you changed your mind about computers?

3. Although more new information has been produced in the last 30 years than in the previous 5,000, information isn't knowledge. In our quest for knowledge in the Information Age, we are often overloaded with information that doesn't tell us what we want to know. Richard Wurman identified this problem in his book *Information Anxiety;* Naisbitt, in his books *Megatrends* and *Megatrends 2000,* said that "uncontrolled and unorganized information is no longer a resource in an information society. Instead, it becomes the enemy of the information worker."

   Identify some of the problems of information overload in one or two departments in your school or place of employment—or in a local business, such as a real estate firm, health clinic, pharmacy, or accounting firm. What types of problems are people having? How are they trying to solve them? Are they rethinking their use of computer-related technologies?

The Computer-Based Information System

*N*ow that we have discussed the general development of computers and covered some basic concepts, let us move on to some specific information about how you can use the computer to turn data into useful information.

PREVIEW

When you have completed this chapter, you will be able to:

▼ State what your role might be in a computer-based information system

▼ Describe the four phases of activity of the computer-based information system: input, processing, storage, output

▼ Discuss two basic approaches to inputting and processing data: batch and on-line

▼ Name three methods a company can use to organize its computer-based data processing facility: centralized, decentralized, distributed

*C*an data be turned into information without *the use of a computer? Of course—and it has been, for all the centuries of human history. Whether fingers or pebbles or coins are used to represent quantities, they may be manipulated in all sorts of ways. The main difference between then and now is speed: the computer enormously enhances the rapidity of converting data into information. The invention of computers, however, has created another important difference: what people have to do to data—and to the computer— in order to get information.*

Not all information problems will be best solved using a computer. Right now you may not be in a position to judge when to use the computer, but you will be when you understand what is known as a computer-based information system—the input and processing of data, and the storage and output of information. In the following pages, we will describe exactly what this system is, how it fits into a typical business organization, and what you need to know. But first let's determine where you fit in the overall picture.

Where Do You, the User, Fit In?

Perhaps a secret anxiety of many users like you is the knowledge that computers don't run by themselves—a human presence, *your* presence, is required to make things happen. Indeed, you are a critical part of a computer-based information system, but we will lead you through it step by step so that it won't look quite so fearsome by the time you reach the end of the chapter.

As Figure 1 shows, during normal business activities users interact with the computer system at three points:

1. At the beginning, users *input* data in a form that the computer can use.

2. During *processing*, users may be required to give the computer some direction about how to process the data—that is, users must *interact* with the computer.

3. At the end, users review *output* information. This information is used as a basis for decision making and problem solving.

How users direct the computer during processing depends on the applications software being used. Companies generally train users to use their software, and software users' manuals also give guidance. (We'll get into software use in more detail later.)

The user may also interact with the computer-based information system at yet another point: the development of business software. This doesn't mean that you, the user, have to *write* the software; it means that you may have to help define your business-related requirements in enough detail so that the computer professionals assigned to develop the software understand what is to happen, when it is to happen, and how. For example, if you want the computer to prepare reports on budgeted versus actual sales of bridge paint, your requirements for how the report is to be produced must be carefully thought out. What level of detail do you require? Should reports cover information only on orange bridge paint, or should purple be included? How often do you want reports? When? In what form? and so on. During systems development it often happens that users don't communicate their needs well to the computer professionals who are writing the software for the new system, and so the users end up with a system they dislike—for which they blame the professionals.

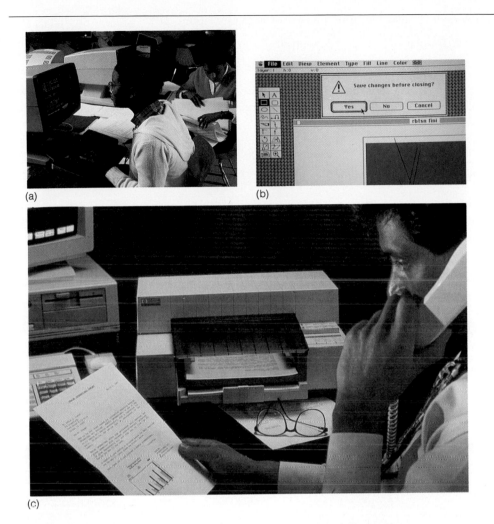

(a)

(b)

(c)

FIGURE 1

At the system's starting point (a), the user inputs data to the computer. During processing (b), the user may be asked to direct the computer. At the system's endpoint (c), the user reviews output information.

Some type of computer hardware is required at every stage of processing. The larger the computer system is, the more removed the users are from the computer hardware. If your company uses a mainframe or a minicomputer system, you may work only with a **terminal** (usually a monitor and a keyboard) connected to the system and never even see the computer. In this case, you will need to learn how to establish communication with the central computer system and to follow the established procedures for requesting that certain programs be run in your behalf. However, if your company has only microcomputers for staff use, you will need to know a great deal more about the hardware.

What Is a Computer-Based Information System?

For our purposes, a system is a method of turning data into information. A system in which a computer is used to perform some of the processing is called a **computer-based information system**. As you have learned, such a system has five components:

1. Hardware
2. Software
3. Data/information
4. Procedures
5. People

However, it also has four phases of activity (Figure 2):

1. Input	3. Output
2. Processing	4. Storage

To help you understand how a computer-based information system works, we will examine how these four activity phases relate to the five components of the system.

Input Phase

During the **input phase** of a computer-based information system, data is "captured" and converted to a form that can be processed by a computer. In this phase people will:

▼ Collect the data, either in document form or verbally

▼ Instruct the computer to begin data input activities (how you do this varies according to the software package used)

▼ Input data (using a keyboard or a mouse, for example) into a device (such as a computer terminal) that captures the data in a computer-usable form—that is, in electronic form and in a code that the computer can "understand"

▼ Supervise the data collection and input process

FIGURE 2

The four phases of a computer-based information system: (1) input, (2) processing, (3) output, and (4) storage. Note that the processing phase can lead to immediate output or to short- or long-term storage for future output.

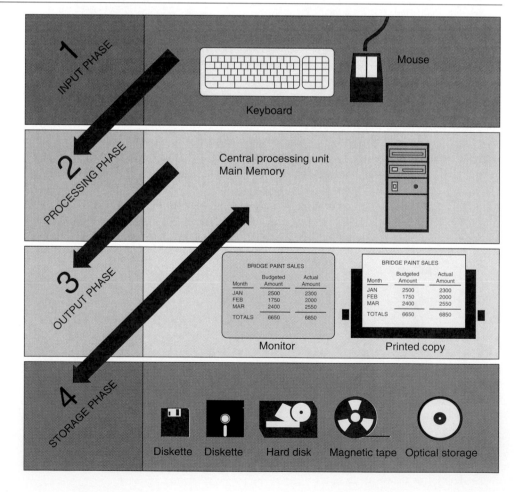

Processing Phase

In the **processing phase** of a computer-based information system, all the number and character manipulation activities are done that are necessary to convert the data into an appropriate form of information. As shown in Figure 3, this includes performing calculations, classifying the input data, sorting the data, summarizing the data, and performing logical processing activities (such as listing information in a particular order or making comparisons).

In a well-designed computer-based information system, people rarely need to do more than issue instructions (by responding to the software's questions and directions) that tell the computer what procedures to perform.

Output Phase

The **output phase** of the system is the result of data processing. It provides the user with all the necessary information to perform and manage day-to-day business activities, as well as *tactical planning* (monitoring current company operations) and *strategic planning* (planning long-range goals for the company). Output can be provided for immediate use or for storage by the computer system

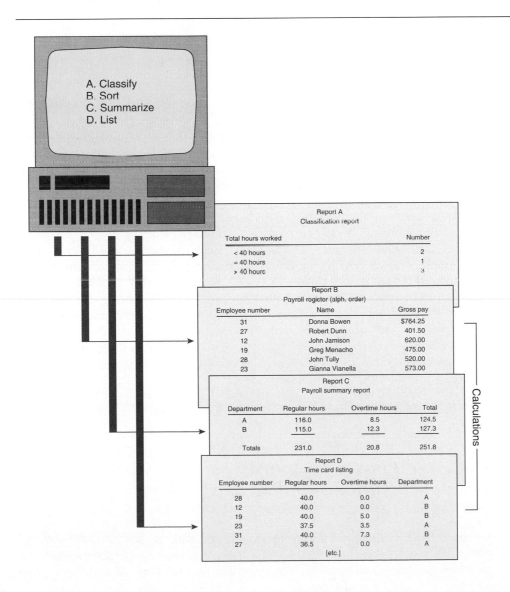

FIGURE 3

Examples of processing activities. Computer processing is useful for organizing different forms of output. For instance, information may be classified, sorted, summarized, or listed in a particular order. Calculations and logical manipulation are often done during such processing.

for future use—either for additional processing or simply for output at a later date.

The form in which information is produced as output will vary according to needs. Some information can be output in *hardcopy* form (generally meaning you can touch the copy)—for example, printed on paper or output on microfilm. Other information may be more useful if displayed immediately in *softcopy* form (generally meaning that you can't actually touch it) on a video display screen. Hardcopy is commonly used for reports and for information that must be seen by many people. Softcopy output is best for information that needs to be viewed only occasionally or only for a few moments and that must be seen by only one person or a few people.

Technological improvements have made it relatively easy and practical to produce both hardcopy and softcopy output that incorporates graphics with text. Sometimes information is also produced in an audio form, such as a telephone number given over the phone by directory assistance.

In the output phase, people usually:

▼ Review the output for "reasonableness"—does it make sense?

▼ Prepare the output for distribution

▼ Distribute the output to the intended recipients

▼ Review the output by analyzing the information, then write reports and make decisions based on the results of the analysis

▼ Use the information to determine what new data to input into the system

Storage Phase

The **storage phase** of a computer-based information system involves storing data, information, and certain processing instructions in computer-usable form for retrieval. There is little need for human involvement in the computerized storage of data. The computer software program directs the computer to store the data in computer-usable form on disks or tapes designated by the user.

People do get involved, however, in the maintenance of computer-based files. (Files are logically related data grouped together into named categories—such as all a store's data on one customer. The user generally determines which category data belongs to and how to name each category, or file.) Files stored, for example, on disk or tape can be retrieved, updated, printed out, stored again, communicated to other computers, or erased. Someone has to monitor how long data should be retained, decide whether backup copies (duplicate disks or tapes kept elsewhere for security reasons) are required, and determine when data should be removed from the system. These activities are normally directed by formal policies and procedures relating to file retention. Indeed, much of the information stored on computers—medical records, for example—must be maintained by law for specified periods of time.

Figure 4 gives you a basic idea of how the five components of the computer-based information system relate to the four phases of activity.

The Four Phases of Activity at Intouch Office Supplies, Inc.

In almost every business it's easy to identify the four phases of activity in the computer-based information system. The user procedures may differ slightly, as may the hardware components; however, the general flow of activities—from

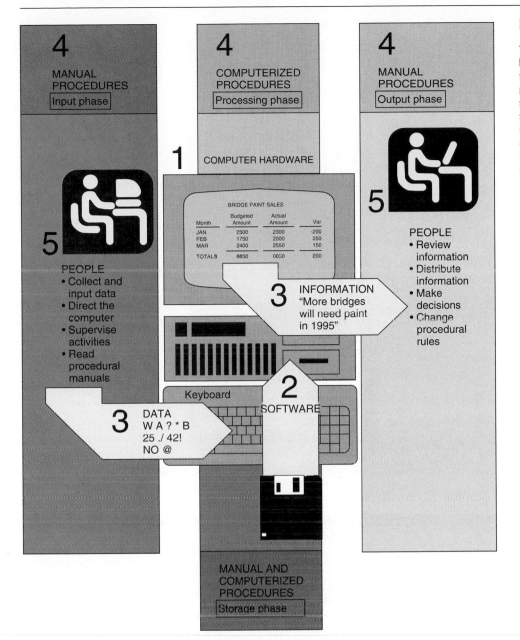

FIGURE 4

This illustration shows the basic relationship between the five components of the computer-based information system—(1) hardware, (2) software, (3) data/information, (4) procedures, (5) people—and its four phases of activity—input, processing, storage, and output.

the input of data into computer-usable form and the processing of data into information to the output or storage of information—remains the same.

In this section we use sales order treatment to illustrate each phase of activity. (Figure 5 shows the process described in this section.)

Intouch Sales Order System: Input Phase

Suppose you were running an office supply store named Intouch Office Supplies, Inc. One of the first things you would need to do in the input phase of dealing with sales orders is to identify the different *types* of input required for processing. Obviously, you have to input data about the price and amount of goods ordered by and sold to customers on a daily basis. In addition, the stock within the store must be replenished, so data about the receipt of goods into stock must also be entered into the computer.

FIGURE 5(a)

Sales order entry. At Intouch Office Supplies, customer order data is taken by phone, mail, and in the store. The data (product numbers plus prices and amount of each item sold) is input to the computer and processed. Processed data is used to update the stored inventory master file, customer files, and sales order files and to output information in the form of invoices and reports.

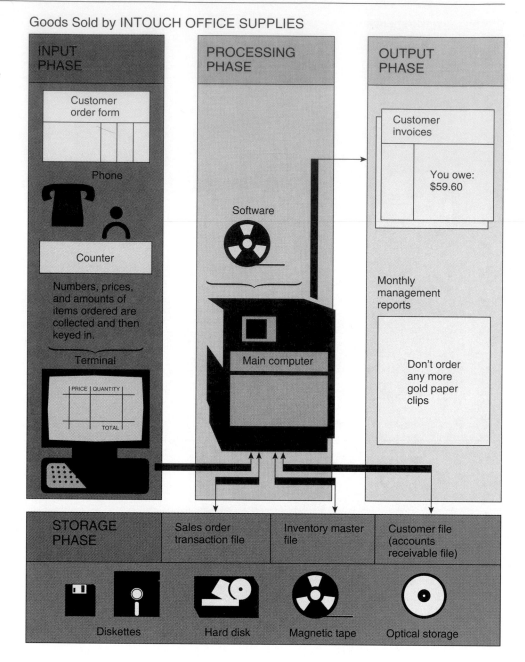

Data related to customer orders can be received in at least three ways:

1. A customer may telephone and place an order.
2. A customer may send an order in the mail.
3. A customer may stop by the store, pick out the needed items from the shelves, and bring them to the cash register.

The input procedures might differ slightly for each circumstance.

When a customer calls on the phone, you might record the order data on an order form (**source document**) for later entry into the computer. As an alternative, if your store is equipped with modern computer processing facilities, you might enter the data immediately into the computer through a keyboard and monitor (called a *point-of-sale terminal*) located near—or combined with—the cash register.

Product Shipments Received by INTOUCH OFFICE SUPPLIES

FIGURE 5(b)

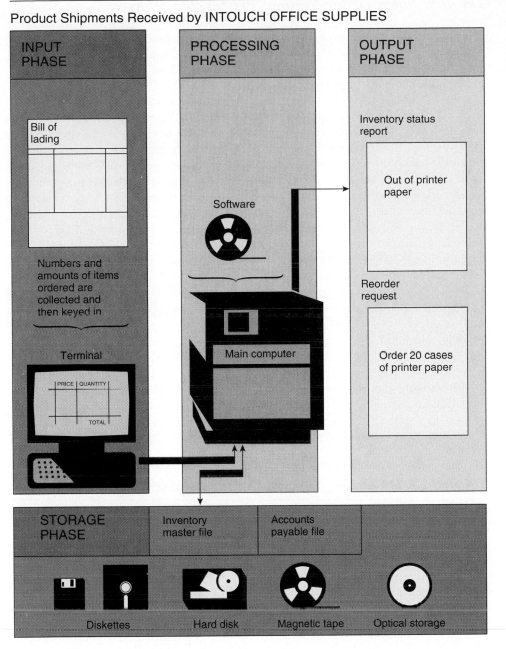

To fill orders effectively, Intouch also needs to process data relating to receipt of product shipments to replenish inventory. Data (numbers and amounts of items delivered, plus their cost) taken from the bills of lading is input to the computer and used to update stored inventory files and to output information in the form of inventory status reports and reorder requests.

The orders received in the mail would probably be collected, grouped into small batches, and entered all at once into the system. (A **batch** is a group of documents intended for input to the computer in a controlled fashion.)

Customer orders placed at the store could be handled in several ways. If all the items in the store have the bar-coded tags we often see at the supermarket, you could use a bar code reading device to automatically scan the product data into computer-usable form. You could also simply use the keyboard on a terminal at the counter to enter the data on the items ordered.

To keep track of the number of items in stock, the data relating to goods ordered and received must also be entered into the computer. The product numbers and number of items received can be taken from the vendor's *bill of lading* (a document identifying the contents of a shipment) and entered directly into the computer.

Intouch Sales Order System: Processing Phase

During the processing phase, the data (now in computer-usable form) is transformed into information. Processing includes performing calculations, classifying the input data, sorting the data, summarizing the data, and performing logical processing activities such as updating files.

At Intouch, Inc., your system probably processes the customer order data in the following fashion. First, the system processes the data about items ordered by customers. The computer verifies the product number for each item by comparing it with the number contained in the inventory master file (stored on disk or tape). Each item's price is retrieved from the master file, as well as the detailed item description. The inventory master file is updated to reflect the number of items ordered and removed from stock. Then all the order data is processed to produce the information necessary to create an *invoice*—the bill for the customer. In the invoice, the quantity of each item ordered is multiplied by its unit price (the price of one item) to produce a line total. All the line totals are added to produce an invoice subtotal. The subtotal, as well as the customer's status, is analyzed to determine what type of *discount*, if any, should be allowed. (For example, customers who owe no money and who order more than 20 gold paper clips at one time get a 5% reduction in price.) The discount amount is computed, as well as any state and local taxes that apply. Finally the invoice total is computed. The last step in processing customer order data is to update the file of unpaid customer invoices (*accounts receivable*, or money owed) with a summary of the invoice-related data.

Processing the bill of lading data (incoming product shipments) involves updating the master inventory file to reflect the number of additional items placed in stock and updating the *accounts payable* file—that is, the file that shows amounts owed to suppliers for shipments.

Intouch Sales Order System: Output Phase

Intouch Office Supplies probably produces two main types of output regularly in its sales order system:

1. Customer invoices, printed out and sent to customers for payment
2. Management reports, produced monthly to summarize and categorize the products sold and the products ordered

In addition, **status reports** of all goods in stock are produced periodically; in other words, the number of items actually on the shelves is compared with the number indicated by the computerized records. **Exception reports** are produced whenever the quantity of an item on hand falls below the minimum stocking level (sometimes referred to as the *reorder point*).

Intouch Sales Order System: Storage Phase

Your office supply company is involved with computer-based storage in three ways:

1. The order data and the data on goods received (to restock inventory) are entered into a temporary storage file (called a **transaction file**) and stored until needed for processing.
2. During processing, information stored in a permanent customer file and an inventory master file is retrieved for use in performing calculations and other processing activities.

3. Information stored in the inventory master file, the accounts receivable file, and the accounts payable file is updated.

In addition, all processing instructions are stored in a permanent form for easy retrieval.

Methods of Input and Processing: If Not Now, When?

We used the sales order system of Intouch Office Supplies to illustrate the activities that might take place in each phase of a computer-based information system; but the activities we described were specific to that example. Any organization that uses computers to process data into information has a computer-based information system. However, the activities of each phase will be different depending on what overall input and processing approach, or combination of approaches, is used.

People in the information management field disagree somewhat about the specific definitions of some input and processing methods. However, for our purposes, we can focus on the two basic approaches an organization might take to input and process data:

1. Batch
2. On-line

In on-line processing, master files are updated as soon as data from individual transactions becomes available; in batch processing, data is entered first to temporary transaction files; processing to update the master files is done later.

Deciding which approach or combination of approaches is best depends on the input, processing, and output needs of the organization.

Batch Approach: Do It Later

An organization that uses batch data collection and **batch processing** collects data in the form of source documents (for example, customer sales orders) and places them into groups (batches). Once all the data has been collected and batched, it is forwarded to a data entry person or group responsible for keying it into computer-usable form (**batch entry**). As the data is keyed in, it may be processed immediately to update master files or stored temporarily in a transaction file for later processing. (In some cases source documents are not used and the data is keyed in as needed and stored in a transaction file.) Data in a transaction file may be stored for only a few hours, but in other cases it may be stored for a week or a month before the regular processing activities are scheduled. At this time each transaction in the batch is processed, one after another, until all related output has been produced and appropriate files have been updated. Figure 6 illustrates the batch approach to a computer-based information system.

Heavy-Duty Batch Input and Processing

Many large organizations that use batch input perform a great number of large-volume, repetitious tasks that would unnecessarily tie up the processing power of a main computer system. This processing, done after regular business trans-

FIGURE 6

Batch. Source documents are collected over a period of time. Then their data is entered into the computer in batches (batch entry). This data can be processed immediately (on-line processing) or stored temporarily in transaction files for later processing (batch processing). Processed data is output as information (reports) and is used to update permanent master files on disk and tape.

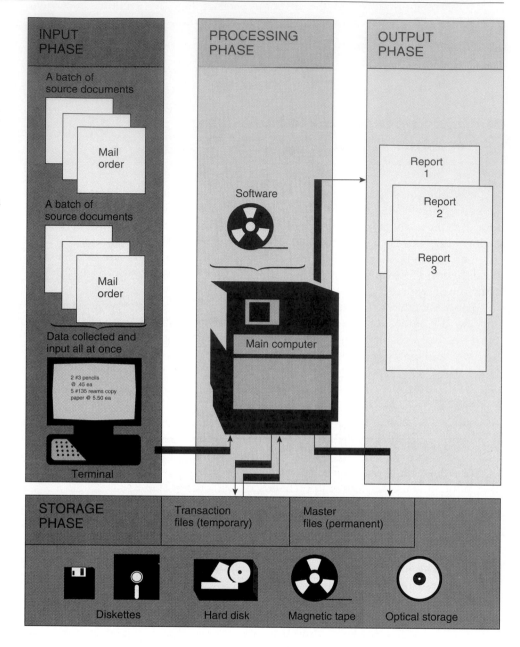

actions have been taken care of, may involve, for example, printing huge numbers of output reports or invoices. For instance, a typical large corporate data processing center may produce 250,000 pages or more per month, and a public utility such as the phone company could easily produce 20 million pages per month of output reports and bills. The input data is stored on disk or tape and then output later—perhaps at night—by special high-speed printers. In some cases, specialized computers "oversee" the output process, thereby freeing up the main computer for other uses.

On-Line Approach: Do It Now

On-line equipment communicates directly with the processing computer. Off-line equipment does not communicate directly. In **on-line processing**, also known as **interactive processing**, data is input immediately as each business transaction occurs, using on-line equipment that allows immediate processing. In other words, instead of collecting manually recorded customer order data into batches

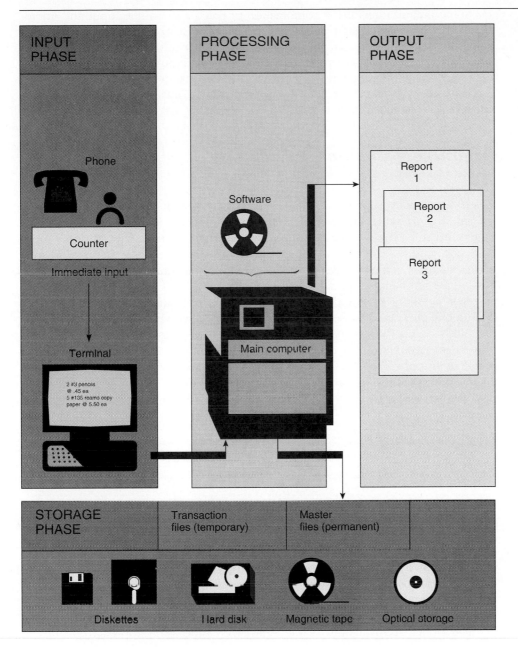

FIGURE 7

On-line. This approach uses no source documents with manually recorded data. Instead, data is input immediately and usually processed immediately.

for later input, a clerk would enter order data immediately, as it came in (Figure 7). The data would be processed right away for output (now or later) and updating of master files. It would not be temporarily stored in a transaction file.

When on-line processing occurs particularly quickly—fast enough to affect the user's activities right away—it is often called **real-time processing**. This approach is used for the most time-sensitive applications to allow decision making to occur as quickly as possible. An airline reservation system is one example of a system that requires real-time processing of transactions; airlines need to use the on-line real-time approach to keep an accurate, up-to-date record of reservations, cancellations, and scheduled flights and flight changes. Some automatic teller transactions are also handled on a real-time basis: When you withdraw your money, your balance is immediately updated and printed on your receipt. Real-time data access is critical to any Wall Street stockbroker. The data that moves across the screen represents stock market factors on which the next decision is made. Any seconds lost in decision-making time could be measured in millions of dollars.

Some organizations use a combination of batch and on-line input and immediate or delayed processing at different points in their operations, depending on whether processing needs are routine or time-sensitive. For example, even though your ATM receipt may have been provided on a real-time processing basis, any paper transactions you made *in* the bank during the same day are probably being batched for after-hours processing. Thus your ATM receipt may not reflect your most current balance.

Organizing Computer Facilities

When a company acquires a large computer system, it also usually sets up a special organizational unit, or department, to operate it. (Because microcomputers are still generally used by only one user at a time, a special department does not need to be set up to operate them—unless, of course, they are hooked up to a larger computer system.) The name of this unit may vary: Data Processing Department, Information Systems Department, or Computer Information Systems Department are common names. The computer system and related equipment plus the area set aside for the employees who staff the department are often called the *computer facility*. How a computer facility functions and how it is used within an organization tend to reflect management's organizational philosophy. You, as a user, should know how your company's computer facility is organized so that you can efficiently perform your job-related activities. Figure 8 diagrams the characteristics of the three types of facilities:

1. Centralized
2. Decentralized
3. Distributed

Centralized Computer Facility: One for All

When an organization has established a *single* computer department to provide data processing and information systems services, this department is often referred to as a **centralized computer facility**. It is called *centralized* because it alone supplies data processing support to all other departments in the company. Entry and retrieval of data can occur either at the central facility or at terminals connected to the central facility through communications lines.

The principal advantages of the centralized processing approach are:

▼ *Cost-effectiveness.* The cost effectiveness of computer hardware resources is increased because equipment is not duplicated at different locations.

▼ *Coordination and control.* Processing activities are easier to coordinate and control in a centralized facility.

▼ *Standards.* The ability to impose and enforce processing standards is easier in a centralized facility.

▼ *Support of users.* Professional data processing personnel are located near users and so can develop a good working relationship with those they support.

In some cases, the centralized approach proved unsatisfactory because of:

▼ *Lack of accountability.* In a large company, it is difficult to track and fairly allocate the costs of the computer processing facility to the many different departments based on individual departmental use. Also, departments at remote locations may feel that their information needs are not being met.

▼ *Unfamiliarity.* The computer specialists responsible for the design of computer applications software ended up being responsible for working in many

CENTRALIZED COMPUTER FACILITY

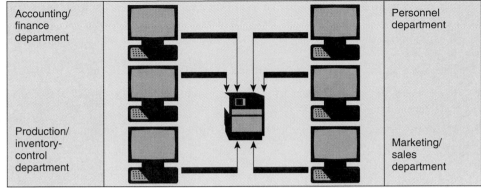

Accounting/
finance
department

Personnel
department

Production/
inventory-
control
department

Marketing/
sales
department

DECENTRALIZED COMPUTER FACILITY

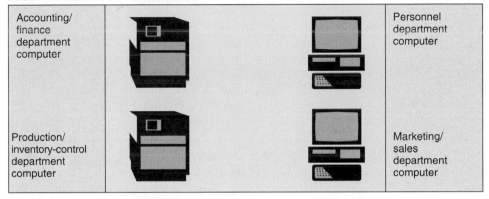

Accounting/
finance
department
computer

Personnel
department
computer

Production/
inventory-control
department
computer

Marketing/
sales
department
computer

DISTRIBUTED COMPUTER FACILITY

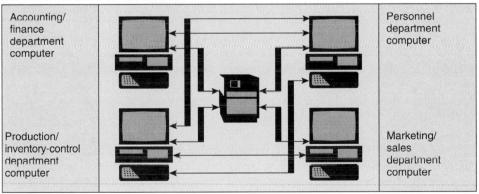

Accounting/
finance
department
computer

Personnel
department
computer

Production/
inventory-control
department
computer

Marketing/
sales
department
computer

FIGURE 8

Companies may organize their computer facilities so that they are centralized, decentralized, or distributed. In the centralized facility, terminals in various departments are hooked up to one main computer system. In the decentralized system, each department has its own computer system, whether microcomputer-based or based on a larger computer. The distributed system has independent processing functions in each department but also connects each department to a larger computer system.

areas of the company with which they were unfamiliar. As a result, the specialists often took a lot of time to understand the processing requirements of a new department. This problem often caused delays in a project and sometimes led to misunderstandings—in other words, some of the software developed failed to meet the needs of the department, or failed to meet them in time.

▼ *Delays.* In many cases the data processing staff in centralized computer facilities had so many demands placed on their time that users had to wait for months (or even years) for their projects to be completed.

▼ *Costs.* Communications hardware and software costs can become high when a company's departments are spread over many distant locations.

Concerns with problems such as these led some organizations to organize their computer facility differently.

Decentralized Computer Facilities: All for One

An organization that uses a separate computer facility to service the needs of each major organizational unit has **decentralized computer facilities**. The size of each facility is determined by the processing requirements of the department it services.

The advantages of using decentralized computer facilities are:

▼ They are better able to meet local departmental information needs than centralized facilities are.

▼ They are better able to match hardware and software to local departmental needs.

▼ They use less sophisticated and less expensive communications hardware and software.

Although this approach solves some problems created by centralized facilities, it also creates new ones.

▼ The decentralized approach makes it difficult to obtain consolidated, companywide management information because each organizational unit has its own key data and information stored on its own computer system, and the various systems are not electronically linked. Because the format and content of data and information are not consistent between organizational units, the data can't be easily accessed or subjected to a simple consolidation procedure.

▼ The duplication of hardware, software, and personnel to run decentralized computer facilities can become an unmanageable expense.

Distributed Computer Facility: Something for Everyone

A combination of centralized and decentralized computer facilities has been used to try to capture the advantages of both while minimizing their weaknesses. In this system, called a **distributed computer facility**, users have their own computer equipment, and one or more computer terminals are connected to a bigger system. With the growth of powerful communications networks and the decline in computer system costs, distributed systems are becoming more common.

To illustrate, let's consider a company with four divisions located in different cities throughout the country with its corporate headquarters on the West Coast. Headquarters has a large mainframe computer system, and each division has a smaller minicomputer to handle its own local processing needs. Individual users in various departments at the division level have microcomputers. The mainframe computer performs all corporate-level processing and passes pertinent data and information to each division as needed through a communications facility built into the computer systems at all locations. In many cases, several departments have microcomputer terminals connected to the minicomputer system.

In a distributed data processing environment, the corporate-level computer facility is ultimately responsible for the control and the coordination of processing activities at all company levels. This is usually accomplished through corporate-level policies and procedures, as well as by direct support from the corporate data processing department, which oversees equipment selection and systems design.

Without careful planning, the compatibility of data files can become a problem when users capture data on a microcomputer and then wish to transfer it to the central computer system. The reverse is also often true. Microcomputers use a different coding scheme for data than many larger computers do. Unless special steps are taken—adding special hardware components and using special software—data cannot be exchanged in either direction. However, when the proper steps are taken, the problem of data file compatibility is eliminated.

The principal advantages of the distributed processing approach are:

▼ *Increased user involvement.* The users are more directly involved in the processing activities than they would be in a centralized structure.

▼ *Easier cost allocation.* Computer processing costs are easier to allocate to different departments than they are in a centralized computer facility.

▼ *Familiarity.* The computer staff is more familiar with the activities and needs of the specific organizational unit they support than they are in a centralized setup.

▼ *Focus on corporate processing needs.* The central computer facility can focus more on corporate processing needs than it can when the organization uses only a centralized facility to support all its departments.

▼ *Fewer personnel.* There is less duplication of hardware, software, and personnel than with the decentralized approach.

▼ *Improved coordination.* There is more coordination between the corporate computer facility and the division-level computer facilities than with other approaches.

Dashboards that talk to you? Instrument panels that look like games? These are the superficial uses of computers in automobiles. We already have electronic systems for engine controls, smart windshield wipers, suspension control, antilock braking, and fuel regulation. And that is only the beginning.

A computer-based navigation system available in Japan uses satellites to plot a vehicle's location. The car's location is indicated on color maps, which are supplied on compact disks. The maps are displayed on a flat 4-inch color screen. A driver can choose from five levels of detail—some maps include the names of thousands of restaurants, hotels, and entertainment facilities and the services they provide. The navigation system can also be used by the drivers of trucks and helicopters; the vehicles can be moving or standing still.

The reverse is also true: managers of fleets of vehicles—trucks, taxis, ambulances, police cars, armored cars, utility repair trucks, and so on—can keep track of vehicles (and even boats and off-road vehicles) located anywhere in the country through the use of satellite or ground-based navigation transmitters. With such position-finding technologies, dispatchers can monitor drivers and give directions when they are needed.

Computer sensor systems are also used to control the roadways. For instance, wire sensors are buried every ½ mile along the Long Island Expressway and convey, to a central computer, information on traffic flow. Engineers monitoring this information are able to tap out messages on their keyboards that are displayed on electric signs at various points over the expressway, warning motorists about possible delays.

Fiber-optic sensors are also being applied to "smart skin" technology, in which networks of fiber-optic sensors embedded in the fuselages of airplanes can alert pilots to small stresses and microscopic cracks.

Air transportation has long been a major user of computer technology. If you fly United Airlines into Chicago's O'Hare airport, for instance, your luggage will be moved through an underground baggage area that is the size of three football fields and that processes up to 480 bags a minute. Whereas once baggage handlers had to read each luggage tag individually, now laser scanning sorters read bar codes and route bags down the appropriate conveyor belts. The airport system receiving a planeload of luggage knows exactly which flights each bag is being transferred to even before the jet lands.

United also uses a computer-based Gate Assignment Display System (GADS) to reduce flight delays. This software, which runs on Texas Instruments workstations, uses an artificial intelligence program that captured the experience and knowledge of United Airlines operations experts. GADS replaces a system whereby gate assignments were handled by airline experts relying on memory and wall-size scheduling boards to chart arrivals and departures.

Airlines also use computers to make fare adjustments. TWA, for instance, has software that can monitor the fares of competitors and can create pricing scenarios flight by flight and determine the profitability of various fares. Continental Airlines can measure bookings against expectations on nearly a half million future flights and can then revise fares and advertising accordingly.

Even ordinary users can take advantage of computers to save on fares. With a microcomputer, modem, communications software, and access to CompuServe or a similar information service ("gateway" network), you can link with different airline reservation services and scan lists of available seats for the best deal.

▼ A *computer-based information system* involves collecting data (input), processing it into information, and storing the information for future reference and output. The system has five basic components:

1. *Hardware*
2. *Software*
3. *Data/information*
4. *Procedures*
5. *People*

▼ A computer-based information system also has four major phases of activity:

1. *Input*
2. *Processing*
3. *Output*
4. *Storage*

▼ During the *input phase*, data is "captured" and converted to a form that can be processed by the computer.

▼ During the *processing phase*, all the number and character manipulation activities are done that are necessary to convert data into information. This includes performing calculations; classifying, sorting, and summarizing data; and performing logical activities.

▼ During the *output phase*, information—the product of data processing—is provided for the user. Information can be in *hardcopy* form (printed on paper) or in *softcopy* form (displayed on a monitor).

▼ During the *storage phase*, the computer stores data, information, and processing instructions in computer-usable form on disk or tape for retrieval.

▼ To accommodate differing processing needs, the computer-based information system can be designed to use one or both of two basic types of processing approaches: *batch* and *on-line*. In batch processing, data recorded manually on source documents is gathered together in batches and input all at one time. In *on-line processing*, data is input immediately, on a case-by-case basis, and is processed immediately. On-line processing used for immediate decision making is often called *real-time processing*.

▼ A *centralized computer facility* has all its equipment in one location. This equipment serves all the company's departments.

▼ A *decentralized computer facility* has separate computer equipment for each department in the company.

▼ A *distributed computer facility* combines aspects of both the centralized and the decentralized facilities: Users have microcomputers with communication programs so that they may switch to the main computer from time to time. They have the choice of working independently or with the central computer.

KEY TERMS

batch, p. 2.9
batch entry and processing, p. 2.11
centralized computer facility, p. 2.14
computer-based information system,
   p. 2.3
decentralized computer facility,
   p. 2.16

distributed computer facility, p. 2.16
exception report, p. 2.10
input phase, p. 2.4
on-line (interactive) processing,
   p. 2.12
output phase, p. 2.5
processing phase, p. 2.5

real-time processing, p. 2.13
source document, p. 2.8
status report, p. 2.10
storage phase, p. 2.6
terminal, p. 2.3
transaction file, p. 2.10

EXERCISES

SELF-TEST

1. A _____ computer facility provides support to all departments in a company.

2. During the _____ phase, data is "captured" and converted to a form that can be processed by a computer.

3. During the _____ phase, all the number and character manipulation activities are done that are necessary to convert data into an appropriate form of information.

4. A distributed computer facility is a combination of centralized and decentralized computer facilities. (true/false)

5. A keyboard and monitor (with no independent processing capabilities) hooked up to a computer system is called a _____.

6. On-line processing is used for immediate decision making. (true/false)

7. During the _____ phase, the user is provided with all the information necessary to perform and manage day-to-day business activities as well as tactical and strategic planning.

8. In a _____ computer facility, each department has a separate computer facility to satisfy its processing needs.

9. With batch processing, data is input and processed immediately, on a case-by-case basis. (true/false)

10. An order form used to collect input data is called a _____ _____.

11. When data is collected from source documents into groups and then given to a data-entry person or group who is responsible for keying it into computer-usable form and placing it in temporary storage for later processing, the processing approach is called _____ _____.

12. A temporary storage file is called a _____ _____.

Solutions: (1) centralized; (2) input; (3) processing; (4) true; (5) terminal; (6) true; (7) output; (8) decentralized; (9) false; (10) source document; (11) batch processing; (12) transaction file

MULTIPLE-CHOICE QUESTIONS

1. People typically interface with a computer-based system when:

   a. information must be output

   b. data must be input

   c. information must be reviewed

   d. the computer needs a direction (or instruction) in order to process data

   e. all the above

2. The following typically happens in the output phase of a computer-based information system:

   a. Data is put into the computer for processing.

   b. Information is produced in hardcopy and/or softcopy form.

   c. Mathematical calculations are performed.

   d. The computer is turned off.

   e. none of the above

3. Which of the following best describes a computer-based information system?

   a. a system in which a computer is used to turn data into information

   b. inputting data

   c. processing data

   d. performing complex mathematical calculations

   e. data is entered into the computer for processing

4. Which of the following is an example of processing activities?

   a. classifying

   b. summarizing

   c. performing calculations

   d. sorting

   e. all the above

5. Which of the following pieces of hardware is used the most in the input phase of a computer-based information system?

   a. printer

   b. diskette

   c. monitor

   d. keyboard

   e. main memory

6. Which of the following statements best describes the batch method of input and processing?

   a. Regardless of whether data is input immediately or collected in batches of source documents and input later, processing is done immediately for immediate updating of master files.

   b. Regardless of whether data is input immediately or collected in batches of source documents and input later, data is stored temporarily in a transaction file for later processing and updating of master files.

   c. Data is input immediately and used for immediate decision making.

   d. Source documents are never used.

   e. none of the above

7. "Computer-usable form" means:

    a. a disk or diskette

    b. hardware

    c. electronically encoded data that a computer can process and store

    d. source documents

    e. on-line processing

Solutions: (1) e; (2) b; (3) a; (4) e; (5) d; (6) b; (7) c

SHORT-ANSWER QUESTIONS

1. Are computers always required to turn data into information? Explain.

2. During which phases of a computer-based information system are users typically involved? How?

3. Why do you think users are more removed from the computer hardware when using a mainframe computer versus a microcomputer?

4. What are the five components of a computer-based information system? The four phases of activity?

5. What are the advantages of the distributed approach to organizing a computer facility?

6. Name some of the different processing activities computers perform.

7. How does batch processing differ from on-line processing?

8. What is the function of a computer facility within an organization? Describe briefly three different methods of organizing a computer facility.

9. When might the delayed input and processing method be used?

10. What is the purpose of a computerized transaction file?

PROJECTS

1. Determine how the computer facility at your school, work, or other business is organized. Who decided how to organize it? Does it meet the needs of the users? How does it use batch and/or on-line data entry and processing? Are there differing opinions relating to the effectiveness of the facility? Why? Why not? Conduct a minimum of two informal interviews.

2. Interview a systems analyst—a computer professional who specializes in setting up computer-based information systems—or a student majoring in systems analysis and design. Find out the many ways users' needs and ability to communicate affect the system they end up with. Report your findings to your class.

3. Based on what you have learned so far, how do you think the four phases of activity in a computer-based system would be represented in your chosen profession? For example, how would data be input? Output? Under what circumstances? What kind of processing activities would take place? What kind of professional computer-related jobs would be necessary to support the users? Would a centralized computer facility be used?

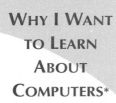
Davina arises from a night of tranquil sleep. She gets her infant from out of his bed and goes to the kitchen. She positions the child in a highchair by a monitor built into the wall. She touches the screen with her finger and then puts the infant's finger on the same spot. After the computer analyzes the data it just received, Davina is informed that she and her child need 500 extra milligrams of vitamin C in their diets to boost their immune systems. It seems that "Cold Virus No. 447" is invading. Davina acknowledges this information, and the selections for breakfast appear. The computer automatically adds grapefruit, tomatoes, and lemon meringue pie to the day's diet to assure that they take in the needed vitamin. As the mother makes her choices, appliances begin to hum behind her as they start breakfast.

Following breakfast, the monitor is checked again. The computer tells Davina the weather conditions and advises her one hour of sunshine and a 20-minute walk to aid her immune system. It also reminds her that a party is scheduled for the day after tomorrow. Some of the food she planned to have needs to be prepared today. She needs to go shopping for some of the items. The computer lists the items needed, their prices at various markets, and waits for the order to be placed. She orders the items and pays for the bill. A message appears, notifying her to pick up her groceries at 1:03 P.M. All that is needed is for her to drive through the market, giving them her order number, and they will load them into her automobile.

Davina and her child get into the automobile. She touches the monitor and the destination is selected. All safety features are turned on. Accidents are a thing of the past, thanks to computers.

As they stroll through the paradise people call "the park," Davina can't help but think back and wonder what life was like 100 years ago when her grandmother was alive. Back then, computers were comparatively new. Her grandmother had a primitive one that she used for typing letters and playing games. In her time, they were using them in automobiles, video cassette recorders, cash registers, and televisions. She wonders what her grandmother would say if she could see how much has been achieved in the world. Why, this park is a marvel. The "Hanging Gardens of Babylon" pale in comparison to this simple park. Computers monitor the soil and environment so the caretaker knows precisely what to do to keep it breathtakingly beautiful all year long.

Back in her grandmother's day, people lived only 70 to 80 years. Now it's not extraordinary to live 150 years. And within the next year, scientists think they will have solved the secret of endless life.

The most priceless thing Davina thinks was invented was the Wisdom Disk. She still doesn't know exactly how it works. She holds a small disk in her hand and meditates on an occurrence she had in her life and the lesson she learned from it. It is recorded on the disk. She gives it to her teenage son. He holds it in his hand and the information is transferred to him. He receives her common sense and so avoids all the silly mistakes in life she made. And the same principle is used in teaching school now.

The world is so much different now as a result of computers. Crime has almost disappeared. People get along with each other. Hideous diseases are found and cured before they occur. The earth is beautiful. Life is satisfying. What would her grandmother think? She probably wouldn't believe it. She can't wait to see her grandmother again and show her all these things. The doctors will be waking her up from death in two months. They have found a cure for the cancer she died of. It will take only about 10 minutes.

---

*By Deborah J. Cook, *PC Novice*, September 1993, p 29.

The preceding story is just a fantasy. But then, going to the moon was a fantasy to my grandmother. There are so many changes taking place in the world today, and all have computers involved in one way or another. I am the grandmother of the girl in the preceding story. I would love to reside in the world I just described. But I fear I won't see it in my lifetime. I do believe that we are on the edge of a new age. A beautiful world awaits us in which computers will be our greatest friends. I positively believe this.

I have a computer. I use it to write letters and play games. But the day is coming when computers will be used in many invaluable ways. Oh, how I wish I could see it. You see, I'm 43 years old. My life is half over. Computers have just emerged. How much different the world will be in 100 years!

I read all the material I can about computers. Much of it I don't understand because it's too technical. I read it anyway, hoping I can pick up at least one thing. Each time I learn seems exciting. Now and then I can aid my friends when they get stumped using their computers. I get a great deal of satisfaction by helping to solve their problems. If I just knew more.

I may never get to live in the world described above. But, I want to learn more about computers so I can get a glimpse of it. I know it will be wonderful. Just let me have a peek at the future!

Input Hardware

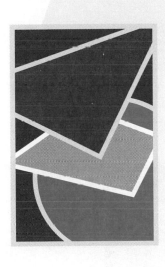

*T*he information you need from a computer system to make decisions is produced by data processing activity. However, before processing can begin, you must first input the necessary data to the system. You do this by using input devices, the topic of this chapter.

PREVIEW

When you have completed this chapter, you will be able to:

▼ Describe the difference between keyboard input and direct-entry input

▼ Identify the most widely used types of input hardware and methods

▼ List the three different types of terminals used for data input and describe some of the ways they are used

▼ Describe the importance of input controls

*A*s a computer user, you will not be able to avoid entering data of some sort into a computer system. However, be glad you are not entering the job market when the principal means of inputting data to a computer system was on punched cards—the so-called IBM cards that a generation of college students were admonished never to "fold, spindle, or mutilate." Although these cards are still in use in some quarters, their numbers are very few compared to the 150,000 tons of them that were used every year in the 1960s— enough, put end to end, to stretch 8 million miles.

Now many different types of input devices exist, all of which are better for some purposes than they are for others. And some input devices have been developed for the use of people with certain disabilities. This chapter will explain what these input devices are and how they are used.

Categorizing Input Hardware

One of the easiest ways to categorize input hardware is according to whether or not it uses a keyboard (Figure 1). We focus special attention on the keyboard

FIGURE 1

Input can be categorized according to whether or not it uses a keyboard.

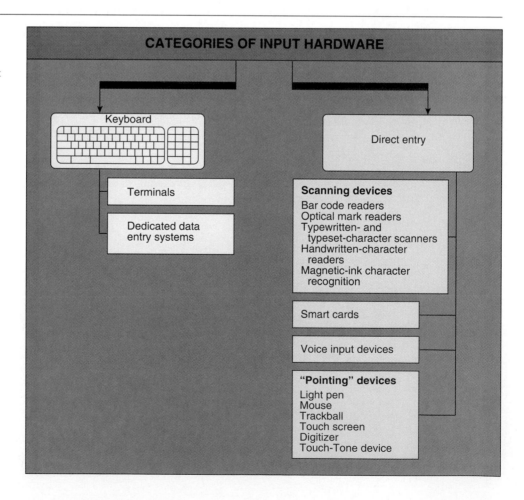

because it will probably be your principal input device. In addition, we describe the following non-keyboard input devices, called *direct-entry devices:* scanners, fax, mice, trackballs, light pens, touch screens, digitizers, pen-based systems, and voice recognition equipment.

Keyboard Input

A computer **keyboard** (Figure 2) is a sophisticated electromechanical component designed to create special standardized electronic codes when a key is pressed. The codes are transmitted along the cable that connects the keyboard to the computer system unit or the terminal (a monitor in front of you that is connected to a system unit in another location), where the incoming code is analyzed and converted into the appropriate computer-usable code. If you can use a typewriter keyboard, you should find it easy to work with a computer keyboard. Except for a few differences, the layout of the keys is similar.

Because a code is sent to the computer every time a key is pressed, in most cases you should only *tap* the keys on the keyboard instead of holding them down. For example, if you press the letter "A" and keep your finger pressed down on the key, you will see something like "AAAAAAAAAAAAAAAAAAAA" on the screen. The same is true of issuing commands. For example, if you are trying to print a document and keep pressing down the keys that initiate the PRINT command, you may be sending multiple print instructions to the printer. As a result, with some computers, multiple copies of your document will print out on the printer.

The Keys

Keyboards come in a variety of sizes and shapes, but most keyboards used with microcomputer systems have a certain number of features in common.

1. Standard typewriter keys
2. Function keys
3. Special purpose keys
4. Cursor-movement keys
5. Numeric keys

You need to understand the purpose of these keys so that you can use the keyboard effectively.

The typewriter-like keys are used to type in text and special characters such as $, *, and #. In general, these keys are positioned in much the same location as the keys on a typewriter. People often refer to this layout as the **QWERTY** layout, because the first six characters on the top row of alphabetic keys spell "QWERTY" (Figure 2a).

The **function keys,** labeled F1, F2, F3, and so on, are used to issue commands (Figure 2). Most keyboards are configured with from 10 to 12 function keys. The software program you are using determines how the function keys are used. For example, using one software program, you would press the F2 key to print your document. However, in a different software program, you would use the F2 key to save your work to disk. The users' manual (documentation) that comes with the software tells you how to use the function keys.

FIGURE 2

This figure shows two common kinds of computer keyboards—(a) an IBM PC keyboard and (b) an enhanced keyboard (which has a numeric keypad separate from the cursor-movement keys).

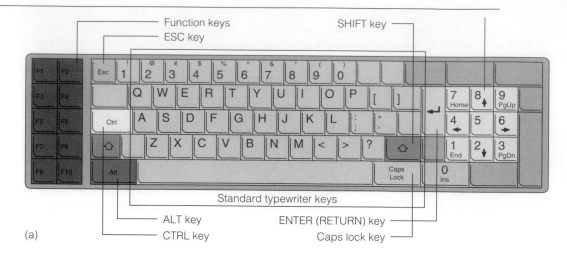

(a)

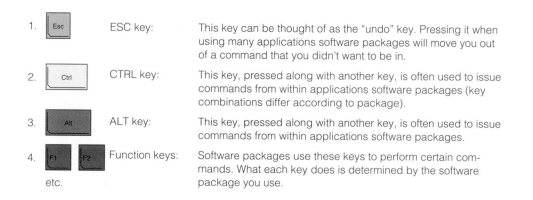

1. ESC key: This key can be thought of as the "undo" key. Pressing it when using many applications software packages will move you out of a command that you didn't want to be in.

2. CTRL key: This key, pressed along with another key, is often used to issue commands from within applications software packages (key combinations differ according to package).

3. ALT key: This key, pressed along with another key, is often used to issue commands from within applications software packages.

4. etc. Function keys: Software packages use these keys to perform certain commands. What each key does is determined by the software package you use.

Computer keyboards also have some special-purpose keys such as Ctrl (Control), Alt (Alternate), Shift, Del (Delete), Ins (Insert), Caps Lock, and Enter. The **Ctrl key,** the **Alt key,** and the **Shift key** are modifier keys. By themselves they do nothing. But when pressed along with another key, they modify the function of the other key.

The **Ins key** and the **Del key** are used for editing what you type. Word processing software uses them frequently to insert and delete text.

The **Caps Lock key** is used to place all the alphabetic keys into an upper-case position (that is, capital letters only). The Caps Lock key affects *only* the alphabetic keys on the computer keyboard.

The **Enter key** is usually pressed to tell the computer to execute a command that has just been input by pressing other keys or using a mouse.

Cursor-movement keys (arrow keys) are used to move the **cursor** around the screen. (The cursor is the symbol on the video screen that shows where data will be input next; see Figure 3.) On the keyboards used with the early IBM PC-compatible microcomputers (which are still used in many businesses today), the keys for cursor movement were combined with the **numeric keypad**—the keys used to enter numbers (Figure 2a). When you turn it on, your microcomputer system "assumes" that the numeric keypad keys will be used for cursor movement. Therefore, you have to remember to press the **Num Lock key** or a Shift key before using these keys to enter numbers.

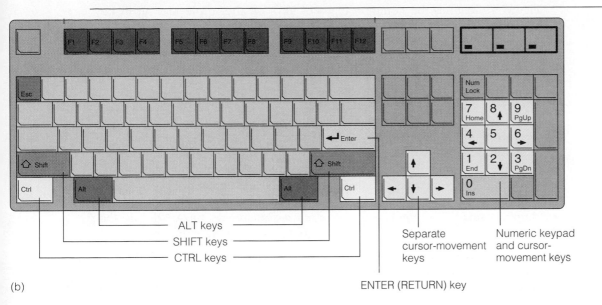

(b)

ALT keys
SHIFT keys
CTRL keys

Separate cursor-movement keys

Numeric keypad and cursor-movement keys

ENTER (RETURN) key

5. SHIFT key: When this is pressed in conjunction with an alphabetic character, the alphabetic character appears as a capital letter. This key works in the same way as the SHIFT key on a typewriter.

6. ENTER key: This key is usually pressed to tell the computer to execute a command.

7. Numeric keypad and cursor movement keys: These keys are used either to enter numbers or to move the cursor around the screen. If the NUM LOCK key has been depressed, when you press these keys, numbers will appear on the screen. Otherwise, pressing these keys will cause your cursor to move around the screen in the direction of the arrows.

FIGURE 3

The cursor shows the position on the screen where the next character, space, or command instruction will be entered. The cursor-movement (arrow) keys are used to move the cursor up, down, right, and left. The cursor can also be moved with a mouse.

Most of today's keyboards have cursor-movement keys that are separate from the numeric keypad keys (Figure 2b). These keyboards are often referred to as *101-key enhanced keyboards*. When a microcomputer system that uses an enhanced keyboard is turned on, it assumes that the Num Lock key is active—that is, the numeric keypad will be used for entering numbers.

Figure 4 identifies the common types of keys on the Apple Macintosh keyboard.

Keyboards are not only used with independent microcomputers; they are often used with terminals and dedicated data entry systems.

Terminals

The **terminal**—typically consisting of a video display screen, a keyboard, and a communications link to hook the terminal up with the main computer system—is used for inputting data to and retrieving data from a remotely located main system. Most terminals are desktop size and are not meant to be carried around; however, some are small enough to be easily portable. Terminals can be "dumb," "smart," or "intelligent" and are used mainly by those who do their work on minicomputers or mainframe computers (or supercomputers).

▼ The **dumb terminal** is entirely dependent for all its capabilities on the computer system to which it is connected. It cannot do any processing of its own or store any data and is used only for data input (by keyboard) and retrieval (data is displayed on the monitor). An airline reservation clerk might use a dumb terminal at a customer check-in station to check flight information stored in the mainframe computer system.

▼ A **smart terminal** can input and retrieve data and also do some limited processing on its own—such as editing or verifying data. However, it cannot be used for programming (that is, to create new instructions). A bank loan officer might use a smart terminal on his or her desk to input data, do some calculations, and retrieve some data before approving a loan. (The data is stored in the mainframe system.)

▼ An **intelligent terminal,** or **workstation,** can input and receive data as well as do its own processing, which means that it can be used as a *stand-alone* device. In addition to the keyboard, monitor, and communications link, this terminal also includes a processing unit, storage capabilities, and software. This type of terminal is actually a microcomputer. Indeed, microcomputers—although much more expensive than dumb or smart terminals—are being used more and more in business as intelligent terminals because they reduce the processing and storage load on the main computer system.

FIGURE 4

The Macintosh extended keyboard

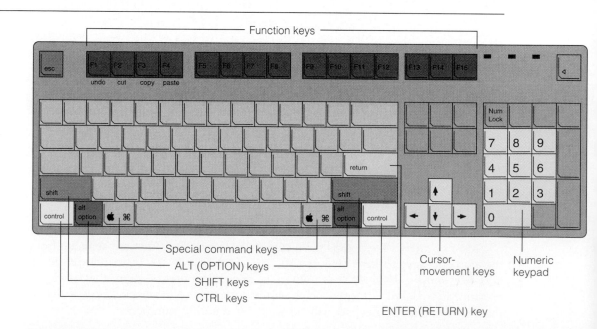

A variety of computer terminals are used to enter data, including the following popular types:

▼   Point-of-sale (POS) terminals

▼   Financial transaction terminals

▼   Executive workstations

▼   Portable terminals

▼   Microcomputers used as terminals

A **point-of-sale (POS) terminal** (Figure 5) is a smart terminal used very much like a cash register, but it also captures sales and inventory data at the time and place of a customer transaction (point of sale) and sends it to the central computer for processing. Many supermarkets have POS terminals that are connected directly to a central computer so that the sales dollars and product-sold data can be immediately recorded. This type of terminal usually displays the price, the product number, and possibly the product description. In addition, this type of terminal is equipped with a cash-register-type keyboard, a cash drawer, and a printer to print the customer's receipt.

A **financial transaction terminal** is used to store data and to retrieve data from a central computer to perform banking-related activities. The two types of financial transaction terminals we see most often are the smart automated teller machines (ATMs) located outside many banks (Figure 6) and the specialized terminals used by bank tellers to retrieve a customer's account balance when he or

FIGURE 5

This point-of-sale terminal is being used at a clothing store. The system updates sales records and inventory files, and it prints out the customer's receipt.

FIGURE 6

The automatic teller machine—a smart terminal—has become more than just a convenience for those who need cash for late-night snack attacks or unexpected emergencies.

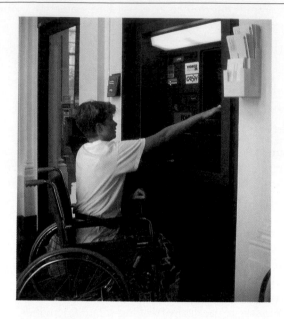

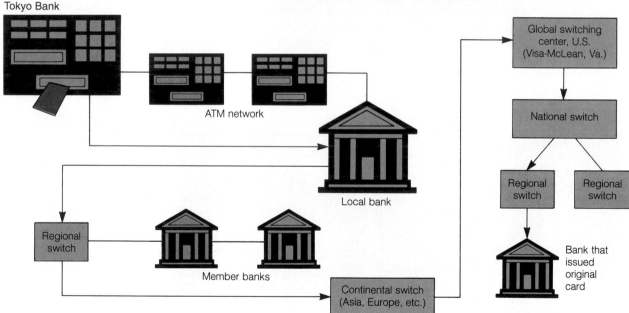

Tokyo Bank

ATM network

Local bank

Global switching center, U.S. (Visa-McLean, Va.)

National switch

Regional switch   Regional switch

Regional switch

Member banks

Bank that issued original card

Continental switch (Asia, Europe, etc.)

When a U.S. resident uses an ATM card in Tokyo: when a bank card is inserted at a Tokyo bank, the local bank's computer determines if that card was issued by that bank. If not, the bank sends the request to the regional switch where a computer sends it to the Cirrus or Plus network. The request then goes to the

network's continental switch—in Europe, for example—then to a global switching center in the United States, next to a national switch, and finally to a regional switch. From there, the request goes to the bank that issued the card. Transaction time: 10 seconds.

she withdraws or deposits money in person. The teller terminals (Figure 7) are usually quite small and specialized. The keyboard has special keys that allow the teller to identify which type of account is being used (savings or checking) and to enter the account number.

Executive (desktop) workstations, or *integrated workstations,* are intelligent terminals used by management professionals to assist them in their daily activities (Figure 8). These workstations can be operated by themselves as stand-alone PCs (personal computers) or in connection with a main computer, and they usually have voice and data communications capabilities, meaning that the terminal includes a phone for regular communication and components for spe-

FIGURE 7

The teller terminals used in banks enable tellers to quickly identify your account and its balance.

cial computerized communication. However, the design and features of this type of terminal tend to vary widely. Executive workstations are not used for high-volume data input. Most have some graphics capabilities (monochrome or color).

A **portable terminal** is a terminal that users can carry with them to hook up to a central computer from remote locations, often via telecommunications facilities. Most portable terminals are connected to the central computer by means of telephone lines. These terminals have components called *modems* built into them that convert the data being transmitted into a form suitable for sending and receiving over the phone lines. If the terminal is dumb, it can do little more than send data to and receive data from the main computer. (Some of the smallest portable terminals can only send data.) If the portable terminal is smart, some data may be entered and edited before the connection to the main computer is made.

Portable terminals are available in a wide variety of sizes and shapes. Most portable terminals include a full typewriter-like keyboard. Some specialized portable terminals are so small they are called **hand-held terminals** (Figure 9). The hand-held terminal weighs up to about 3 pounds and can be used for a variety of purposes, including checking the stock market and identifying cars with many unpaid parking tickets. Like executive workstations, portable terminals are rarely used for high-volume data input.

We have mentioned that **microcomputer terminals** can be used on their own for processing, as well as being used as smart or intelligent workstations; the type of software used determines what kind of terminal the microcomputer "becomes." This flexibility is very attractive to many businesses. Data entry programs can be created for the microcomputer so that data can be input and stored locally—where the user is. When data entry is complete, the microcomputer can then be used as a terminal, and the data can be *uploaded* (transmitted from the microcomputer to the main computer) very quickly. For example, a small editorial production office in San Francisco with a microcomputer equipped with a modem and certain software can arrange with the local telephone company to have telex capabilities activated and a telex number assigned. Then the office

FIGURE 8

The executive (desktop) workstation helps managers take care of daily business through the use of desk management software and communications and data processing capabilities. The workstation can operate on its own as a stand-alone personal computer as well as an intelligent terminal connected to a larger computer system.

FIGURE 9

This engineer is using a hand-held terminal connected to a mainframe computer system.

can input data—page proof corrections, for example—that is telexed to a type-setter in Singapore, who transfers the data into the computerized typesetting system after reading it on a microcomputer screen. In turn, the typesetter can telex data back to the editorial office in San Francisco.

Some microcomputers on the market today have been designed *specifically* to be used both as stand-alone processors (that is, they can operate on their own without being hooked up to a main computer) *and* as terminals. For microcomputers that were not specifically designed to fulfill both functions, manufacturers have produced special hardware that can be purchased and placed into the microcomputer to enable it to communicate with a larger computer.

Dedicated Data Entry Systems

When an organization has high-volume data input requirements, such as the Internal Revenue Service at tax time, it often uses a secondary computer—usually a minicomputer—that temporarily stores previously keyed-in data for later processing by the mainframe computer (Figure 10). This processing usually takes place at night, when the main computer's time is not taken by user requests. The group of terminals connected to the minicomputer that handle data entry and storage are called a **dedicated data entry system**—they do nothing but input and store data, using *key-to-tape, key-to-disk,* or *key-to-diskette* input systems (Figure 11). In the first case, a keyboard connected to a special recorder is used to record data onto magnetic tape reels or cassettes. The tape can then be transported to another area where a tape drive is located. The tape drive reads the data into the main computer. This procedure is similar to key-to-disk and key-to-diskette systems, except that in the latter case, data is recorded on magnetic disks, often available as portable disk packs, or on individual diskettes.

Non-Keyboard (Direct) Entry

Some of the most interesting kinds of input systems don't use a keyboard. For example, did you know that you can touch a video display screen or use a

FIGURE 10

These warehouse employees are using a dedicated data entry system to input product delivery data into the inventory database.

FIGURE 11

Key-to-tape, key-to-disk, and key-to-diskette systems are dedicated data entry systems that use special input hardware to record data on tape or disk. The tape/disk can then be transported to a drive that reads the data into the main computer.

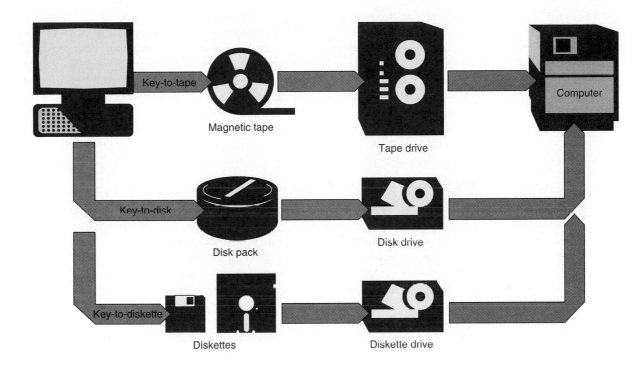

"magic" wand to input data? Talk to a computer? Even use the movement of your eyes to tell the computer what to do? Non-keyboard, or **direct-entry,** data entry systems minimize the amount of human activity required to get data into a computer-usable form. Following are the most commonly used ones:

▼ Scanning devices

    Bar code readers

    Optical mark readers

    Typewritten- and typeset-character readers

    Handwritten-character readers

    Magnetic-ink character readers

▼ Smart cards

▼ Voice input devices

▼ "Pointing" devices

    Mouse

    Trackball

    Light pen

    Touch screen

    Digitizer

    Pen-based systems

▼ Touch-Tone devices

Most direct-entry input devices are used in conjunction with a keyboard because these specialized devices can't be used to input all types of data and instructions. An exception may be the Eyescan Communicator, which translates eye movements into signals for a computer. This innovation—still being refined—allows people who cannot speak or use keyboards to communicate using a computer.

Scanning Devices

So much business-related data and information is recorded on paper that most of us would have difficulty imagining the amount. Before many of our modern input devices and systems were available, a lot of research was devoted to eliminating the expensive and time-consuming step of inputting all this hardcopy data manually by keying it in. As a result, in the 1950s a number of **optical character recognition (OCR)** input devices were developed to read hardcopy (printed) data from source documents into computer-usable form. Today these devices use light-sensitive equipment to scan bar codes, optical marks, typewritten characters, handwriting, and magnetic ink.

Bar Code Readers

By now you have probably become familiar with bar codes similar to the one shown in Figure 12. They're on groceries, cosmetics, paperback novels, and so on. **Bar codes** are recorded on the products by the manufacturers and usually carry the inventory stock number (also called the *product number*). The coding scheme—called the *Universal Product Code*—for recording the data is based on the width of the bars and the space between them. Two types of input scanning devices—**bar code readers**—are used to read the bar codes. The first is a hand-held scanner (Figure 13) that the clerk passes over the tag with the bar code. The wand has a scanning device that analyzes the light and dark bars for width and spacing, translating this data into electrical signals for the computer. The second is found most often in supermarkets and is built into the counter-top (Figure 13) along with a computerized cash register.

Bar code readers have proven to be very valuable as data entry devices for three reasons:

▼ The price and product inventory numbers do not need to be keyed in, eliminating the potential for many keying errors. (Quantities of items, however, *are* keyed in.)

▼ The sales data and inventory status stored on file are kept current.

FIGURE 12

Bar codes such as this Universal Product Code used on many supermarket items contain product data that is read by a scanner and sent to the cash register display and to the main computer.

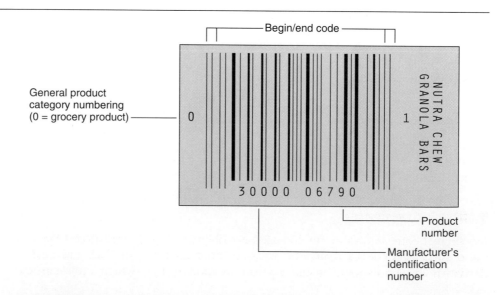

(a)

FIGURE 13

Bar code reading devices can be hand-held, such as this portable scanner used by Federal Express carriers (a), or built into the counter at the checkout stand, like this supermarket scanning equipment (b and c). The clerk moves the product's bar code past the bar code reader, which "reads" it with a light beam and a sensor. The price and the description of the item, which are stored in the computer system, are sent to the POS terminal, where they are printed out as a receipt for the customer. The information from the POS terminal is also used by the store, on the one hand, for accounting purposes and, on the other hand, for restocking store inventory and for analyzing which products sell better than others.

(b)

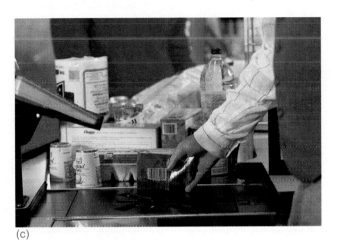

(c)

▼ A complete history can be built and stored for each bar coded item—for delivery services such as Federal Express and UPS, this means that parcels can be traced.

However, when you're checking out at the supermarket, keep your eye on the computerized price and item description display on the register. As we mentioned earlier, the product numbers are recorded in the bar codes on the items you buy, but the corresponding price files must be updated at the supermarket. If someone forgets to enter today's special 50% reduction in cat food prices in the store's computer, you'll end up paying the old price.

One remarkable new use of bar codes has been introduced by Intermec Corp., a manufacturer of bar code hardware, software, and other automated data collection systems. Along with the Washington State Department of Fisheries, they found a way to breed fish that have distinctive bar code patterns in the bones of their ears. They achieved this by manipulating the temperatures of the hatchery ponds in which fish embryos were incubated. This bar code reading technique will be used to track fish populations and conduct other environmental research.

Optical Mark Readers

When you took the College Board SAT (Scholastic Aptitude Test) or similar examination and marked the answers on a preprinted sheet using a no. 2 lead pencil, you worked with the simplest form of optical data recording—**optical**

marks (Figure 14). Data recorded in this form is converted into computer-usable form by an **optical mark reader (OMR)** (Figure 15). The OMR device has a high-intensity light inside that is directed in the form of a beam at the sheets of paper being fed through it. The beam scans the marked forms and detects the number and location of the pencil marks. The data is then converted into electrical signals for the computer.

The optical mark technology is used widely for scoring examinations and inputting raw data recorded on questionnaires. For OMRs to read the data accurately, the forms must be carefully designed and manufactured, and the marks must be carefully recorded.

Typewritten- and Typeset-Character Readers

To help speed up and reduce the cost of converting typewritten and typeset data to computer-usable form, certain manufacturers developed special type fonts (typeface styles) to be read by a scanning device. To assist this process the American National Standards Institute (ANSI) adopted a standard type font called OCR-A for use with special optical character reading devices (Figure 16). OCR-A has

---

FIGURE 14

The College Board examination answer form requires you to mark answers—according to numbers in the test booklet—using a no. 2 lead pencil. The marks are later scanned and tabulated by an optical mark reader and software.

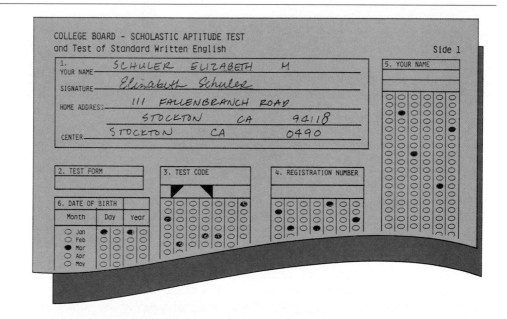

FIGURE 15

This Scantron mark reader can be used with Apple- and IBM-compatible computers.

become the most commonly used typeface for OCR devices. However, the more expensive OCR devices can read a variety of fonts.

In the early 1980s, small-capacity scanners were marketed for use with microcomputers. These were designed to read OCR-A, a variety of other type fonts, and also illustrations. Today the use of scanners with microcomputers is common, including desktop scanners that can input graphics as well as almost all types of typewritten and typeset characters.

A microcomputer **scanning system** (Figure 17) consists of a microcomputer (PC), a scanner, and scanning software. These systems enable users to convert (digitize) a hardcopy picture or a photograph into a computer-usable graphics file that can be understood by desktop publishing software or graphics software. In addition, they enable users to convert hardcopy (printed) text into a text file that can be used by word processing software. Scanned images can be stored in a computer system, manipulated (changed), and/or output in a different form.

The software required to scan graphics is usually packaged with the scanner. The software required to scan characters, or text, called *optical character recognition (OCR) software*, isn't normally packaged with the scanner; you have to buy it separately.

One factor to consider when choosing a scanner is whether you plan to scan graphics and/or text. If you typically scan graphics to be used by a desktop publishing or graphics package, you want your scanner to scan images at a high resolution—*resolution* refers to the clarity of an image. In addition, you want your scanner to support scanning as many shades of gray as possible; this is called **gray-scale scanning.** The more shades of gray that a scanner is capable of scanning, the more natural the scanned image is, which is important if you're working with photographs. Color scanners and slide scanners (Figure 18d) are available for users who are using desktop publishing to produce sophisticated magazines and books.

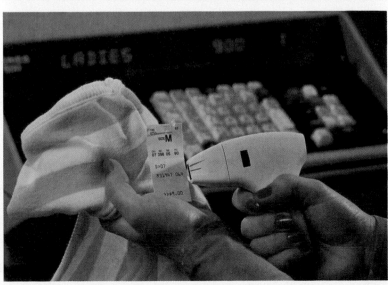

FIGURE 16

The OCR-A type style was designed to be read by a special input scanning device.

FIGURE 17

Simple desktop microcomputer scanning system. The scanner is on the right and the laser printer is in the middle.

Another factor to consider when purchasing a scanner is the physical format of the material you plan to scan. If you will often scan text or graphics from a bound volume, you should consider a **flatbed scanner** (Figure 18). To use a flatbed scanner, the user must hold the material to be scanned in place on a piece of glass while the scanning mechanism, referred to as the *scanhead,* passes over it in a fashion similar to that of a copy machine. If you are working with loose sheets, consider a **sheet-fed scanner** (Figure 18), which uses mechanical rollers to move the paper past the scanhead. Another type of scanner is the **hand-held scanner** (Figure 18), which relies on the human hand to move the scanhead over the material to be scanned.

Scanners are also used for specialized purposes, such as identifying an individual by his or her fingerprints (Figure 19).

A **fax (facsimile) machine** uses a built-in scanner to read text and graphics and transmit them over phone lines to another fax machine or a computer with a fax board in its system unit. (*Fax* is short for *facsimile,* meaning *reproduction.*) One factor to consider before purchasing a fax capability is your need to fax graphics, such as photos. If you do need to fax graphics, make sure the fax scanner can support displaying halftones, or shades of gray—such as in a black-and-white photograph. If you are only faxing text, it doesn't matter if your fax scanner can support shades of gray.

Handwritten-Character Readers

Although the percentage of data recorded by hand has dropped substantially over the last 50 years, quite a bit of data is still recorded this way. As OCR technology advanced, designers felt that it would be possible to also scan handwritten data into computer-usable form in much the same way that typewritten data is. Devices with this capability are the most sophisticated and versatile of the OCR devices. Because handwriting varies widely, specific guidelines must generally be followed so that the OCR reader will "read" (interpret and input) the characters accurately.

FIGURE 18

(a) Flatbed scanner; (b) sheet-fed scanner; (c) hand-held scanner. Photo (b) also shows the documentation that accompanies the software necessary to use the scanner with a computer and the expansion card that must be put in the computer's expansion slot. The computer needs the software and the circuitry on the expansion card to be able to interact with the scanner. (d) Slide scanner.

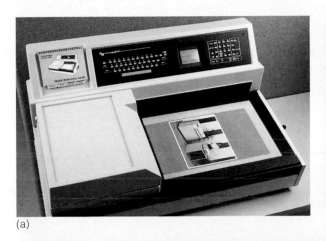

(a)

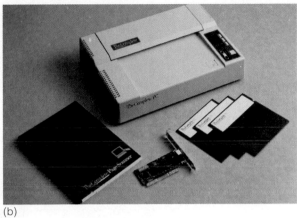

(b)

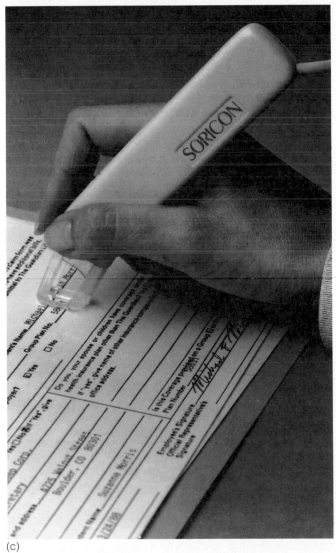

(c)

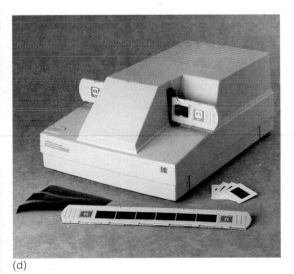

(d)

FIGURE 19

Fingerprint reader—a type of scanner that is used to identify an individual's fingerprint for security purposes. After a sample is scanned, access to the computer or other restricted system is granted if the user's fingerprint matches the stored sample.

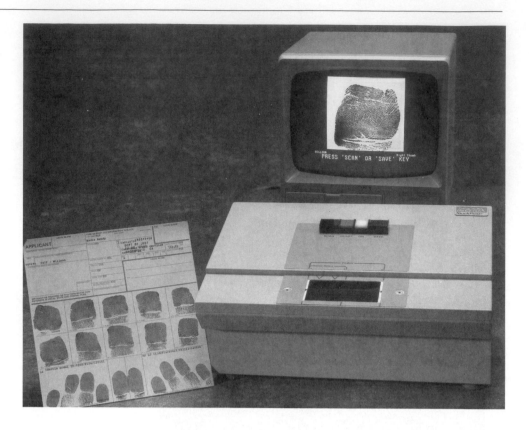

Magnetic-Ink Character Recognition (MICR)

As many as 750 million personal checks are processed each month in the United States. This number does not even include the business checks written each month, which total more than triple the number of personal checks. How does the banking industry handle this mountain of data?

The American Bankers Association (ABA), anticipating this problem in the mid-1950s, adopted the **magnetic-ink character recognition (MICR)** technology as its primary means of data entry for processing checks. This technology involves the reading of numeric characters and a few special symbols printed on checks with magnetic ink. (Alphabetic characters are not used with this technology.) Figure 20 shows the layout of the MICR encoding on a personal check and some MICR recording equipment.

Have you ever noticed a check, returned by your bank with your monthly statement, that had a piece of paper taped to the bottom? That piece of paper contains a duplicate of the MICR encoding on the check. What has happened is that the MICR symbols have been damaged; as a result, the MICR reader rejected your check. So one of the clerks at the bank rekeyed the MICR symbols onto a separate slip of paper and taped it to your check. In 1960, when it became apparent that some standardization was needed in the MICR type font, the ABA adopted a standard character set consisting of 14 symbols (Table 1).

The advantages of the MICR system are that:

Human involvement is minimal, thus the potential for errors is small.

The codes can be read by both people and machines.

It is fast, automatic, and reliable.

However, some human involvement is still required—to encode the check amount in MICR characters—thus, some room for error does remain.

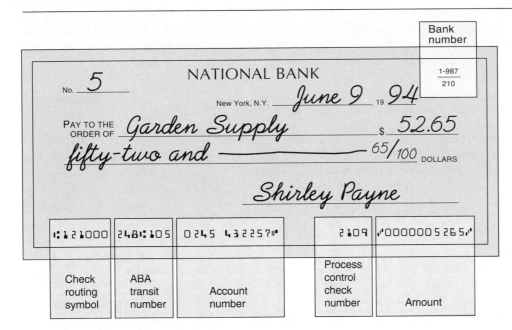

Processing Your Check

1. Checks are fed into large, high-capacity MICR reader/sorter devices.
2. MICR characters on checks are read electronically.
3. Check data is stored on tape or disk for processing.
4. Checks are sorted by bank number and returned to your bank.
5. If you wish, a bank may sort checks by account number and return them to you with the monthly statements.

(a)

(b)

FIGURE 20

Your personal checks are encoded with magnetic ink that is read by MICR equipment. The data is then stored for processing. Note that the printed check amount in the bottom-right corner is encoded by an MICR inscriber. (b) The IBM check-processing system handles 2,400 checks per minute.

TABLE 1

The Standard MICR Character Set

- The numbers 0–9
- An amount symbol (⑊)
- A dash symbol (⑈)
- A transit symbol (⑉)
- An "on-us" symbol (⑇) (tells who is the payer and who is the payee)

Recently, the banking industry has begun to take steps to minimize the amount of paper handling necessary. That is why we are seeing more automated teller machines that use electronic "checks" instead of paper ones and why "smart cards" are becoming more common.

Smart Cards

Smart cards (Figure 21), which were pioneered in the mid-1970s in France, are designed to be carried like credit cards but used like tiny transaction computers. The smart card has a computer chip that provides processing power and an electronic memory that does not lose its data when the power is turned off. To use it, the cardholder inserts the card into a special card-reading point-of-sale terminal and then enters a password on the keyboard. The cards have microchips that can keep permanent records, which are updated each time the card is used. The transaction data stored on the card can later be read into the computer for the user's bank—perhaps via an ATM—to update the user's bank records. In France and Britain smart cards are used to pay bills (while keeping current bank balances on file on the card), buy merchandise, pay highway tolls, make phone calls, buy postal money orders, get exam results from the university, store emergency medical information, and perform other common activities. Electronic card readers have been installed in stores, restaurants, post offices, phone booths, banks, and so on.

The cards are being used to some extent in the United States—by the U.S. Navy, for example, for purchasing procedures—and will become increasingly common. Some manufacturers are already talking about a "supersmart card" that will incorporate a keypad and a display unit along with the memory and processing capabilities. Other manufacturers are developing smart cards to use as "keys" that users must employ to gain access to certain types of computer systems. For now you can use your "unintelligent" bank card with its magnetically encoded strip to pay for gasoline and groceries at some service stations and supermarkets, by electronically transferring funds; the purchase amount is automatically deducted from your bank balance, without any further action from you.

FIGURE 21

Example of a smart card used to pay highway toll. The special card is inserted into a "communicator" mounted to the windshield. The communicator uses radio signals to let special receivers—mounted, for example, in the pavement—know that the toll has been debited to the user's account.

Voice Input Devices

A substantial amount of research has been done in voice recognition—programming the computer to recognize spoken commands and dictated text. **Voice input devices** (Figure 22), or **voice recognition systems,** convert spoken words into computer-usable code by comparing the electrical patterns produced by the speaker's voice with a set of prerecorded patterns. If a matching pattern is found, the computer accepts this pattern as a part of its standard "vocabulary."

Voice input technology is used today in a number of successful applications. NASA has developed experimental space suits that use microprocessors and storage devices to allow astronauts to view computerized displays across their helmet visors. These displays are activated and manipulated by spoken commands—convenient when both hands are busy on a repair job in space! The brokerage house of Shearson Lehman uses a voice input technology called the Voice Trader to enable brokers to communicate trades verbally rather than writing them down on scraps of paper that are often illegible or become lost. The medical industry has also been using voice recognition products to help physicians, hospitals, and clinics minimize the huge quantities of handwritten notes and transcribed reports typed from tape dictation that they would otherwise have to deal with. And people with poor typing skills are starting to use voice-input systems in offices.

Voice technology is also used by people whose jobs do not allow them to keep their hands free and by handicapped people, such as the blind, who may not be able to use traditional input devices. A blind person, for example, can enter commands verbally rather than using the keyboard. In a system with this capability, computer output is typically communicated to the user using text-to-

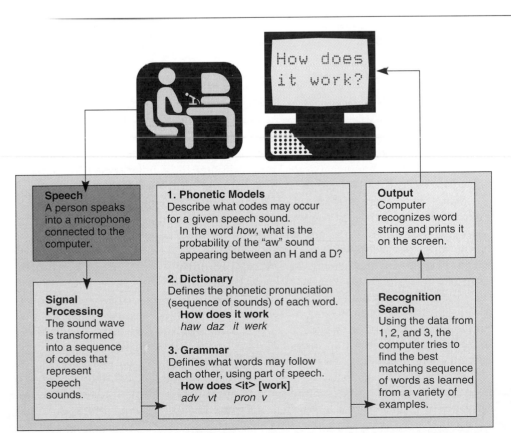

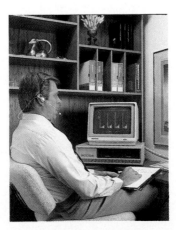

FIGURE 22

Voice recognition. (a) This diagram gives you a basic idea of how voice input works (adapted by permission of Wide World Photos). (b) Texas Instruments voice input system.

(a)

speech capabilities—that is, the computer responds to the user with spoken words. (A blind skipper reportedly used a voice-navigational system to successfully navigate a boat!) For the physically handicapped, the ability to control computers without using a keyboard is crucial. Voice input technology is often used by quadriplegics and people with severe arthritis to control computers, telephones, and other devices.

The biggest problems with voice technology have involved limitations on the size of the computer's vocabulary, pronunciation differences among individuals, and the computer's inability to accept continuous speech. However, research continues at a fast pace, and recent improvements are significant. Several voice input units are currently available for use with microcomputers. IBM Corporation has marketed a voice-activated computer, the Speech Server, which is designed to be shared by a large number of people on a computer network. However, voice recognition systems are still expensive and require significant training to use. In spite of these disadvantages, some voice-input enthusiasts predict that in ten years voice recognition will be a mainstream technology.

Pointing Devices

Data input involves not only typing in text but also entering commands and selecting options. The mouse, the trackball, the light pen, the touch screen, and the digitizer tablet were all developed to make these functions easy. Each of these devices allows the user to identify and select the necessary command or option by, in effect, moving the cursor to (pointing at) a certain location on the screen or tablet and sending a signal to the computer. For this reason they are sometimes called *pointing devices*. Pointing devices are used in **menu-driven** programs—that is, programs that offer varying levels of menus, or choices displayed in lists, to the user.

Some systems enable users to use their eyes to point at the screen to specify screen coordinates. A system that has this capability is typically referred to as a *line-of-sight* system (Figure 23).

Mouse

The **mouse** (Figure 24) is a small, hand-operated device connected to the computer by a small cable. As the mouse is rolled across the desktop, the cursor moves across the screen. When the cursor reaches the desired location, the user pushes a button on the mouse once or twice to signal a menu selection or a command to the computer. (Note: Your computer must have special *driver* software to enable it to "recognize" a mouse connection.)

When mice were first introduced, they functioned mainly as cursor-movement devices that enabled users to choose menu options. Although they are still used this way today, they are increasingly used to create graphics. The technology has improved so that mice can be used to move tiny *pic*ture *ele*ments— called **pixels**—on the screen one by one. In other words, the mouse can be used like a pen or a paintbrush to draw figures and create patterns directly on the video display screen. Used with a monitor capable of displaying high-quality graphics, a sophisticated mouse enables users to generate very complex and precise images. A sophisticated mouse can manipulate extremely small pixels, influencing the clarity of an image. The keyboard, however, is still used to type in characters and to issue some commands, depending on the software.

A type of mouse that may soon become popular is built into a pen-like body. The MousePen works in the same basic way as does the traditional mouse; however, it is shaped like a pen. It's small enough to fit into a shirt pocket and is capable of working on surfaces as small as 3 square inches. As a result, this type of mouse is well suited for use with portable microcomputers.

FIGURE 23

Line of sight. To track the position of the eye's pupil, a video camera is mounted beneath the monitor. These positions are then translated into screen coordinates, thus allowing the eyes to "point." This technology is being used by the handicapped to enable them to direct computer processing.

(a)

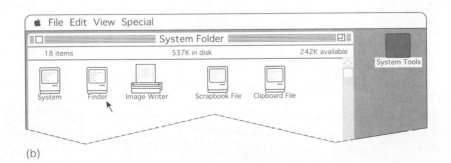

(b)

FIGURE 24

Non-keyboard input control. (a) When the user rolls the mouse around the desktop, the pointer moves correspondingly on the screen. By rolling the mouse to move the pointer to an icon and clicking the mouse button once or twice, the user can select and open the file that the icon represents. By pointing at a particular place on a text line and clicking the mouse button, the user can move the cursor to the desired place. (The use of multiple mouse buttons is determined by the software; the accompanying documentation explains the uses.) (b) Examples of icons.

Trackball

A **trackball** is essentially an upside-down mouse (Figure 25). The ball is held in a socket on the top of the stationary device. Instead of moving the ball by rolling the device around on the desktop, you move the ball with your fingers. Trackballs have become especially popular in offices where crowded desktops are the norm and on airplanes and in cars, where space is limited. Some portable microcomputers have built-in trackballs; the user can also clip some trackball models to the side of the keyboard. One trackball, the Thumbelina, is so small that it can be held in one hand and operated with the thumb.

Light Pen

The **light pen** uses a photoelectric (light-sensitive) cell to signal screen position to the computer (Figure 26). The pen, which is connected to the computer by a cable, is pressed to the video display screen at the desired location. The switch on the pen is pushed to close the photoelectric circuit, thereby indicating the x-y (horizontal and vertical) screen coordinates to the computer. The computer stores these coordinates in main memory (RAM). Depending on the applications software you are using, you can then edit the data stored in RAM and save it onto a disk. Light pens are frequently used by graphics designers, illustrators, and drafting engineers.

Touch Screen

Limited amounts of data can be entered into the computer via a **touch screen** (Figure 27). The user simply touches the screen at the desired locations, marked by labeled boxes, to "point out" choices to the computer. The software determines the kinds of choices the user has. Of course, not all microcomputers have touch screens. Some touch screens are built into the monitor and others can be snapped on to certain kinds of existing monitors.

Digitizer

A specialized method of input that is used in drafting and mapmaking is the **digitizer,** or **digitizing tablet** (Figure 28). The tablets, which come in different sizes, are the working surface. Each is covered by a grid of many tiny wires that are connected to the computer by a cable. (Wacom, Inc. has produced a

---

FIGURE 25

MAC Portable with reversible numeric keypad and trackball. The positions of the numeric keypad and the trackball can be swapped to accommodate left-handed trackball users.

FIGURE 26 (*left*)

Light pen. This user is employing a light pen to design electrical circuits.

FIGURE 27 (*below*)

Touch screen. Making menu choices at a fast-food restaurant.

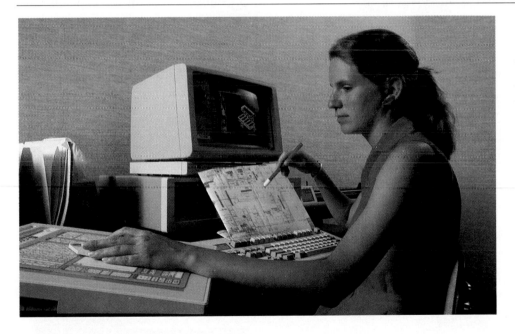

FIGURE 28

Digitizer. This engineer is creating a blueprint using a mouse-like digitizer on a grid with electronic wires that is connected to the computer.

digitizer that is cordless.) Drawings placed over this grid can be traced and entered into the computer by the use of a special pen or a mouse-like device with cross hairs that opens and closes electrical circuits in the grid and thus identifies x-y coordinates. Original drawings also can be entered. As it progresses, the drawing is displayed on the screen; it can later be stored or printed out. Digitizers are also used in design and engineering businesses—such as those that develop aircraft or computer chips.

Pen-Based Computing

Pen-based computing is a recent development by which special software interprets block (not cursive) handwriting done directly on a special type of computer screen (Figure 29). As the computer—such as Go Corporation's PenPoint and Tandy's Grid System—interprets the handwriting, it displays what was written on the screen in a computer typeface. Users can edit what they have entered and give commands by circling words, checking boxes, and using symbols developed by the manufacturer. This type of small computer is used by police officers to record tickets, by salespeople to record sales, and by meter readers, package deliverers, and insurance claims representatives, for instance.

The PenEdit System from Pen Technologies allows editors to edit manuscripts on disk by using an electronic pen to write on the 5-pound computer's magnetic-sensitive screen. The original text is displayed in a traditional typeface

---

FIGURE 29

Pen-based computing. The chart shows 11 basic handwriting gestures used to issue commands and move around on the screen and within files.

 Bracket, left

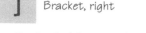 Bracket, right

■ One bracket selects a word to its left or right.
■ A second bracket extends the selection.

 Caret

■ In text, pops up a small writing pad to insert a word.
■ In the Table of Contents, pops up the Create menu to create a new document.

 Check

Displays options for selected text, objects, icons, documents, and tools.

 Circle

Opens an edit pad for a word or selection in text, text fields, and labels.

 Cross out

Deletes a word or selection in text or any object directly beneath the X.

 Flick left

 Flick right

 Flick up

 Flick down

Scrolls documents right, left, down, or up.
■ On the document title line, flick left ⟶ or right ⟶ to turn to the next or previous page.
■ On overlapped tabs, flick up ⎸ or down ⎸ to move the tab up or down. Flick left ⟶ to display all tabs at once.

 Insert space

■ In text, adds a space.
■ In writing and edit pads, adds one or more spaces.

 Pigtail

Deletes a character in a writing or edit pad character box, or an individual character in text.

 Press

■ Begins a move.
■ Begins a drag-through selection.

 Tap

Selects or activates what you touch with the pen.
■ In text, selects one character.

 Tap press

Begins a copy.

PenPoint has eleven basic gestures for commands and navigation. Most gestures have menu equivalents. See the user manuals for more details.

along with the editor's changes in a "handwriting" typeface. In this way, manuscript reviewers can see *both* the original copy and the changes when the manuscript is printed out. A keyboard can be hooked up to this computer to input large blocks of text.

Touch-Tone Device

As you probably know, you can use your **Touch-Tone** phone to send data to a computer—for example, if you want to arrange for Federal Express to come to your home or office and pick up a package, you can call a special 800 number. A computerized voice requests that you touch the numbers for your account number, ZIP code, and number of packages being picked up. The data goes to the central computer system, is checked, and is then retrieved by the appropriate local pickup system, which sends an employee to get your package.

Touch-Tone devices called **card dialers** are also used to run credit card checks in retail stores. After appropriate keys are touched, the device sends data over the phone lines to a central computer, which then checks the data against its files and reports credit information back to the store.

Input Controls: Preserving Data Integrity

No matter how sophisticated your input hardware is and how well thought out your input methods are, you still run the risk of generating inaccurate or even useless information. The completeness and accuracy of information produced by a computer system depend to a great extent on how much care was taken in capturing the raw data that served as input to the processing procedures. An old computer-related saying summarizes this point: "Garbage In, Garbage Out" (GIGO). If you—the user—input incomplete and inaccurate data (Garbage In), then you can expect the information that is produced to be correspondingly incomplete and inaccurate (Garbage Out). How do you ensure that input data is accurate and complete?

Input controls include a combination of manual and computer-based control procedures designed to ensure that all input data has been accurately put into computer-usable form. A variety of control techniques can be used, depending on the design of the computer system and the nature of the processing activities taking place. Systems designers study these techniques and build them into systems.

How important are input controls? Consider the modest-living couple who got a phone bill or a local store's invoice for $450,000 and spent months trying to convince the company it was a mistake. The customer service personnel and the data processing staff were probably trying to identify the glitch in the input control procedures. The computer doesn't make mistakes; the people who input data and monitor input procedures do. Even software writers are not infallible. Without input controls, mistakes might be impossible to detect or correct. Imagine the consequences this could have at the level of international trade, politics, and military activities. Of course, input controls are not the only controls involving data accuracy, completeness, and security.

Y̱ou like the outdoors and you're looking forward to a career in environmental science or wildlife management. It's a good thing, then, that we live in an age of computer technology.

Scientists in Idaho, looking for ways to preserve the nation's diversity of plants and animals, have combined satellite images of topography and vegetation with electronic data on land ownership. The result is a mapping system that identifies habitats rich in wild species that have been poorly managed by state and federal governments. The computerized maps help natural resource administrators save money by determining which tracts of land are highest in biological richness and should be acquired before they become targets of development.

At the University of Rhode Island and Brown University, researchers have used computers to re-create the flying patterns of birds. The work has caught the interest of Federal Aviation Administration officials, who are looking into whether the research might help produce a more efficient air traffic control system.

Using computers and aerial photographs taken over five-year intervals since the 1960s, scientists are attempting to track the past movement of coastal erosion and predict yearly movements of shorelines. With this data, suggests a panel of the National Academy of Sciences, government officials could delineate beach areas with imminent, intermediate, and long-term erosion risk and limit building in those areas.

Long used to help with research in the sciences, computers have also become tools of scholarship in other fields. A few years ago, a computer researcher at New Jersey's Bell Laboratories made a discovery that may be one of the most important in the history of art. Lillian Schwartz juxtaposed a self-portrait painted by Leonardo da Vinci with his world-famous painting of the Mona Lisa and found that the eyes, hairline, cheeks, and nose were identical. From this some scholars concluded that the Mona Lisa was in fact a self-portrait by da Vinci.

An exhibition at the IBM Gallery of Science and Art in New York showed that computer technology could be used to reveal new archeological insights from old ruins and artifacts. The ancient Roman port of Pompeii was buried in A.D. 79 in the volcanic eruption of Mount Vesuvius, preserving many details of everyday life. Recently, computer enhancement techniques were used to resurrect texts from charred papyrus documents found in Pompeii. Computers were also used to restore colors and background images to partially destroyed paintings. From a huge database, experts constructed a large computer-generated map of Pompeii that includes positions and shapes of buildings, baths, and other features.

Finally, computer research has been used to bring the maddeningly complex Chinese writing system into the modern world. With more than 50,000 characters, each composed of at least 1 of 214 root parts plus additional strokes, Chinese ideograms have not been adaptable to typewriters and other office technology. In the last decade, however, researchers have succeeded in designing systems that allow word processors to accommodate characters at speeds averaging 60 per minute.

▼ Input hardware is categorized either as *key-board-based* or *direct-entry* (non-keyboard).

▼ The *keyboard* is the most widely used input device. It includes five basic types of keys:

1. *Standard typewriter keys*—used to type in text and special characters.

2. *Function keys*—used to issue commands.

3. *Special-purpose keys*—Ctrl, Alt, Ins, Del, Caps Lock, and Num Lock, used to modify the functions of other keys. The Enter key is usually pressed to tell the computer to execute a command entered by first pressing other keys.

4. *Cursor-movement keys*—used to move the *cursor,* which marks the position of the next character to be typed, around the screen. The keys for cursor movement are sometimes combined with the *numeric keypad.*

5. *Numeric keys*—used to enter numbers.

▼ The software package dictates how function keys and special-purpose keys are used (check the documentation that comes with the package).

▼ Keyboards are used with *terminals* hooked up to a large computer system. A terminal consists of a video display screen, a keyboard, and a communications link.

▼ Terminals can be "dumb," "smart," or "intelligent."

—A *dumb terminal* is entirely dependent for all its capabilities on the computer system to which it is connected.

—A *smart terminal* can input data to and receive data from the main computer system and also do some limited processing on its own.

—An *intelligent terminal,* or *workstation,* can input and receive data as well as do its own processing. Intelligent terminals are often also used as stand-alone microcomputers.

▼ The following are common terminal types:

—Point-of-sale (POS) terminals

—Financial transaction terminals

—Executive workstations

—Portable terminals, including hand-held terminals

—Microcomputers used as terminals

▼ Keyboards are also used in *dedicated data entry systems,* terminals used only for data entry and storage. The data can be recorded on tape (*key-to-tape*), disk (*key-to-disk*), or diskette (*key-to-diskette*).

▼ Direct-entry (non-keyboard) devices, which are used in conjunction with a keyboard, include:

1. *Scanning devices* that "read" data

2. *Smart cards*

3. *Voice input devices*

4. *Pointing devices*

5. *Touch-Tone devices*

▼ *Scanners* convert (digitize) hardcopy text or graphics into computer-usable code. The text and/or graphics can then be displayed on the monitor and edited, modified, printed, communicated, and stored for later retrieval. Typeset-character scanners can be *flatbed, sheet-fed,* or *hand-held.* They are often used in desktop publishing to input graphics.

▼ A *bar code reader* is a special type of scanner that "reads" Universal Product Codes on products such as grocery items and translates the codes into electrical signals for the computer system. Some bar code readers are hand-held, and others are built into the countertop.

▼ An *optical mark reader* scans pencil marks on special forms into electrically coded data for the computer.

▼ *Handwritten-character readers* can "read" handwriting done according to specific guidelines.

▼ *Magnetic-ink character recognition* (*MICR*) technology is used to encode checks with data that can be scanned by MICR readers and input to a computer system.

▼ A *fax* (*facsimile*) *machine* is a type of scanner that "reads" text and graphics and then transmits them over telephone lines to another fax machine or a computer with a fax board in its system unit.

▼ *Smart cards* are tiny transaction computers on credit-card-like plastic. They are used with special card-reading terminals to make purchases, pay bills, make phone calls, store information, and so on.

▼ *Voice input devices,* or *voice recognition systems,* convert spoken words into computer-usable code by comparing the electrical patterns produced by the speaker's voice with a set of prerecorded patterns. After the computer matches the patterns, it executes the appropriate command.

▼ Pointing devices include:

1. The *mouse*—a small, hand-held device connected to the computer by a cable and rolled around the desktop to move the cursor around the screen. When the cursor is placed at the desired location, the user pushes a button on the mouse once or twice to issue a command or select an option. With appropriate software, the mouse can be used to move the tiny *pixels,* or *picture elements,* on the screen to create graphics.

2. The *trackball*—essentially an upside down mouse. The ball is rolled around in a socket to move the cursor. Trackballs are used where space is limited.

3. The *light pen*—a pen-shaped input device that uses a photoelectric (light-sensitive) cell to signal screen position to the computer. The pen, which is connected to the computer by a cable, is placed on the display screen at the desired location. The switch on the pen is pushed to close the photoelectric circuit, thereby signaling the location to the computer.

4. The *touch screen*—a special display screen that is sensitive to touch. The user touches the screen at desired locations, marked by labeled boxes, to "point out" choices to the computer.

5. The *digitizer*—a tablet covered by a grid of tiny wires that are connected to the computer by a cable. Drawings placed on the tablet can be traced with a special pen or mouse-like device to translate the image into computer-usable code. Original drawings also can be entered.

6. *Pen-based computing* uses special software and hardware to interpret handwriting done directly on the screen.

▼ *Input controls* are manual and computer-based procedures designed to ensure that input data is entered accurately. Without controls, erroneous data can be entered, resulting in unreliable output: "Garbage In, Garbage Out" (GIGO).

KEY TERMS

Alt key, p. 3.4
bar code, p. 3.12
bar code reader, p. 3.12
Caps Lock key, p. 3.4
card dialer, p. 3.27
Ctrl key, p. 3.4
cursor, p. 3.4
cursor-movement keys, p. 3.4
dedicated data entry system,
 p. 3.10
Del key, p. 3.4
digitizer (digitizing tablet), p. 3.24
direct entry, p. 3.11
dumb terminal, p. 3.6
Enter key, p. 3.4
executive (desktop) workstation,
 p. 3.8
fax (facsimile) machine, p. 3.16
financial transaction terminal, p. 3.7

flatbed scanner, p. 3.16
function keys, p. 3.3
gray-scale scanner, p. 3.15
hand-held scanner, p. 3.16
hand-held terminal, p. 3.9
input controls, p. 3.27
Ins key, p. 3.4
intelligent terminal, p. 3.6
keyboard, p. 3.3
light pen, p. 3.24
magnetic-ink character recognition
 (MICR), p. 3.18
menu-driven, p. 3.22
microcomputer terminal, p. 3.9
mouse, p. 3.22
Num Lock key, p. 3.4
numeric keypad, p. 3.4
optical character recognition (OCR),
 p. 3.12

optical mark, p. 3.13
optical mark reader (OMR), p. 3.14
pen-based computing, p. 3.26
pixel, p. 3.22
point-of-sale (POS) terminal, p. 3.7
portable terminal, p. 3.9
QWERTY, p. 3.3
scanning system, p. 3.15
sheet-fed scanner, p. 3.16
Shift key, p. 3.4
smart card, p. 3.20
smart terminal, p. 3.6
terminal, p. 3.6
touch screen, p. 3.24
Touch-Tone, p. 3.27
trackball, p. 3.24
voice input device, p. 3.21
voice recognition system, p. 3.21
workstation, p. 3.6

EXERCISES

SELF-TEST

1. One of the easiest ways to categorize input hardware is whether or not it uses

 a _____.

2. Most keyboards used with microcomputers include the following types of keys:

 a.

 b.

 c.

 d.

 e.

3. What determines what the function keys on a keyboard do?

4. Cursor-movement keys are used to execute commands. (true/false)

5. The Ctrl key, the Alt key, and the Shift key are modifier keys. (true/false)

6. A _____ enables users to convert hardcopy text and graphics into computer-usable code.

7. List three common categories of direct-entry (non-keyboard) input devices.

 a.

 b.

 c.

8. List four pointing devices commonly used with microcomputer systems.

 a.

 b.

 c.

 d.

9. A picture element on the screen is called a *pixel*. (true/false)

10. An input device commonly used in mapmaking is the _____.

11. Trackballs are used to input data when the user has a great deal of space to work in. (true/false)

12. A _____ terminal is entirely dependent for all its processing activities on the computer system to which it is hooked up.

13. The most popular input hardware device is the _____.

14. QWERTY describes a common keyboard layout. (true/false)

15. Scanners cannot scan color images. (true/false)

16. _____ _____ are designed to ensure the accuracy of input data.

17. Function keys are used the same way with every software application. (true/false)

18. Newer keyboards have cursor-movement keys that are separate from the numeric keypad. (true/false)

19. A code is sent to the computer *every* time a keyboard key is pressed. (true/false)

20. Pointing devices were developed to make the functions of entering commands and selecting options easy. (true/false)

Solutions: (1) keyboard; (2) standard typewriter keys, function keys, special-purpose keys, cursor-movement keys, numeric keys; (3) software program or applications software; (4) false; (5) true; (6) scanner; (7) scanning devices, voice input devices, pointing devices; (8) mouse, trackball, light pen, touch screen, digitizer tablet; (9) true; (10) digitizer tablet; (11) false; (12) dumb; (13) keyboard; (14) true; (15) false; (16) input controls; (17) false; (18) true; (19) true; (20) true

SHORT-ANSWER QUESTIONS

1. What are the two main categories of input hardware?

2. What is a fax machine?

3. What is a mouse and how is it used?

4. What do a mouse, a light pen, and a digitizer have in common?

5. What direct-entry devices are commonly used in conjunction with the microcomputer keyboard?

6. What is a workstation?

7. How and where are Touch-Tone devices used to input data?

8. What are function keys, and what determines what happens when you press one of them?

9. What is a light pen? How does the use of a light pen differ from pen-based computing?

10. What is a voice recognition system?

PROJECTS

1. Research scanning technology. What differentiates one scanner from another? Is it the clarity of the scanned image? Price? Software? If you were going to buy a scanner, which do you think you would buy? Why? What do you need to run a color scanner? How do you think scanners are used in your chosen profession?

2. During the next week, make a list of all the input devices you notice—in stores, on campus, at the bank, in the library, on the job, at the doctor's, and so on. At the end of the week, report on the devices you have listed and name some of the advantages you think are associated with each device.

Processing Hardware

*W*hen you look at a computer, you can see and even touch most of the input, output, and storage equipment—the keyboard or the mouse, the video display screen, the printer, the disk drive doors or the tape cartridge. But you cannot actually see the equipment that does the processing—the electronic circuitry inside the cabinet of the computer itself. Although you have no need to puzzle through wiring diagrams and the like, you should have some understanding of processing hardware, because the type of processing hardware used affects how much the computer can do for you and how quickly it can do it.

PREVIEW

When you have completed this chapter, you will be able to:

▼ Briefly describe how data is represented in a computer system

▼ Identify the two main parts of the central processing unit and discuss their functions

▼ Describe how the computer carries out instructions that the user gives it

▼ Describe the importance of and distinguish between random access memory and the different types of read-only memory

▼ Briefly state the differences between expanded memory and extended memory

▼ Describe the factors that should be considered to evaluate the processing power of a computer

*Y*ou may never have to look inside a computer—although if a computer technician comes to your office to fix your microcomputer, we recommend that you look over his or her shoulder and ask the technician to identify some of the internal components, just so you can get a general idea of what's going on inside. But the essential question is why do you need to know anything about the processing hardware and activities—any more than you need to know how the engine of a car works? We think there are two reasons:

▼ Just as some people like to work on their own cars, you may decide, for example, that it's economical for you to do some work on your microcomputer. For instance, you may find that some new software programs are too sophisticated for your computer—that your computer cannot hold enough data or instructions or process them fast enough—and that you need to add some more random access memory. This may well be something you can do yourself.

▼ More likely, you will some day need to make a buying decision about a computer, either for yourself or for an organization. And, just as when you buy a car, you should learn something about the topic first. It is important to understand processing facts and trends so you can purchase a computer that indeed meets your needs and avoid purchasing a machine that will be obsolete in the near future.

Data Representation: Binary Code

Before we proceed with our discussion of processing hardware, we need to briefly discuss *what* computers process. "Data," you say. Yes—but in what form?

When you begin to write a document, you have a large collection of symbols to choose from: the letters A–Z, both upper- and lowercase; the numbers 0–9; and numerous punctuation and other special symbols, such as ?, $, and %. People understand what these characters mean; computers cannot. Computers deal with data converted into the simplest form that can be processed magnetically or electronically—that is, binary form. The term *binary* is used to refer to two distinct states—on or off, yes or no, present or absent, 1 or 0. For example, a light switch can be either on or off, so it can be viewed as a binary device. When data is processed, it is represented as the presence or absence—"on" or "off"—of electrical pulses.

To understand this principle better, look at these powers of 2:*

$2^0 = 1$
$2^1 = 2$
$2^2 = 4$
$2^3 = 8$
$2^4 = 16$
$2^5 = 32$
$2^6 = 64$

---

*This example is from *The Secret Guide to Computers*, 16th ed., © 1992 by Russ Walter, 22 Ashland St. #2, Somerville, MA 02144-3202.

Now try an experiment. Pick your favorite integer, and try to write it as a sum of powers of 2. (An integer is a whole number—that is, not a fraction.)

For example, suppose you pick 45; you can write it as 32 + 8 + 4 + 1. Suppose you pick 74; you can write it as 64 + 8 + 2. Suppose you pick 77; you can write it as 64 + 8 + 4 + 1. *Every* positive integer can be written as a sum of powers of 2.

Let's put those examples in a table:

ORIGINAL NUMBER	WRITTEN AS SUM OF POWERS OF 2	DOES THE SUM CONTAIN . . .						
		64?	32?	16?	8?	4?	2?	1?
45	32 + 8 + 4 + 1	no	yes	no	yes	yes	no	yes
74	64 + 8 + 2	yes	no	no	yes	no	yes	no
77	64 + 8 + 4 + 1	yes	no	no	yes	tes	no	yes

To write those numbers in the binary system, replace "no" by 0 and "yes" by 1:

DECIMAL SYSTEM	BINARY SYSTEM
45	0101101
74	1001010
77	1001101

To process and store data in binary form, a way of representing characters, numbers, and other symbols had to be developed. In other words, *coding schemes* had to be devised as standardized methods of encoding data for use in computer processing and storage.

A scheme for encoding data using a series of binary digits is called a **binary code.** A **binary digit (bit)** is either the character 1 (on) or the character 0 (off). It represents one of two distinct states expressed magnetically, electrically, or optically. All data inside the computer is coded in the form of bits:

PART OF THE COMPUTER	WHAT A 1 BIT IS	WHAT A 0 BIT IS*
electric wire	high voltage	low voltage
punched paper tape	a hole in the tape	no hole in the tape
punched IBM card	a hole in the card	no hole in the card
magnetic drum	a magnetized area	a nonmagnetized area
flashing light	the light is on	the light is off

It usually takes 8 bits—known as one **byte**—to form a character. Data processing and storage capacity is measured in bits, bytes, **kilobytes (K)**, **megabytes (MB)**, **gigabytes (GB)**, and **terabytes (TB)** (see Table 1).

Bit	A binary digit; 0 or 1	
Byte	8 bits, or 1 character	
Kilobyte (K, or KB)	1,024 bytes	
Megabyte (MB)	1,024,000 bytes	
Gigabyte (GB)	1,024,000,000 bytes	
Terabyte (TB)	1,024,000,000,000 bytes	

TABLE 1

Units of Measurement for Disk Storage

---

*This example is from *The Secret Guide to Computers,* 16th ed., © 1992 by Russ Walter, 22 Ashland St. #2, Somerville, MA 02144-3202.

FIGURE 1

An early binary code. Samuel F. B. Morse, developer of the Morse code, showed that data elements (characters) could be represented by using two "states"—long and short, otherwise known as dash and dot.

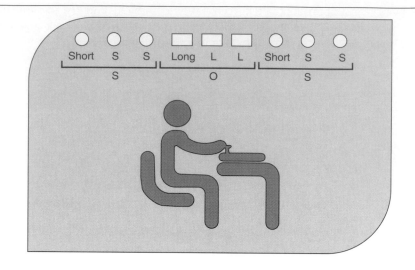

FIGURE 2

ASCII and EBCDIC. This chart shows some of the printed character codes according to the two most commonly used binary coding schemes for data representation. ASCII originally used 7 bits, but a zero was added in the left position to provide an 8-bit code (more possible combinations to form characters). The ASCII-8 code has enabled the use of many more special characters, such as Greek letters, math symbols, and foreign language symbols.

Character	ASCII-8	EBCDIC	Character	ASCII-8	EBCDIC
A	0100 0001	1100 0001	N	0100 1110	1101 0101
B	0100 0010	1100 0010	O	0100 1111	1101 0110
C	0100 0011	1100 0011	P	0101 0000	1101 0111
D	0100 0100	1100 0100	Q	0101 0001	1101 1000
E	0100 0101	1100 0101	R	0101 0010	1101 1001
F	0100 0110	1100 0110	S	0101 0011	1110 0010
G	0100 0111	1100 0111	T	0101 0100	1110 0011
H	0100 1000	1100 1000	U	0101 0101	1110 0100
I	0100 1001	1100 1001	V	0101 0110	1110 0101
J	0100 1010	1101 0001	W	0101 0111	1110 0110
K	0100 1011	1101 0010	X	0101 1000	1110 0111
L	0100 1100	1101 0011	Y	0101 1001	1110 1000
M	0100 1101	1101 0100	Z	0101 1010	1110 1001
0	0011 0000	1111 0000	5	0011 0101	1111 0101
1	0011 0001	1111 0001	6	0011 0110	1111 0110
2	0011 0010	1111 0010	7	0011 0111	1111 0111
3	0011 0011	1111 0011	8	0011 1000	1111 1000
4	0011 0100	1111 0100	9	0011 1001	1111 1001
!	0010 0001	0101 1010	;	0011 1011	0101 1110

Two people contributed greatly to the coding scheme used to record and process data in computer-usable form: Herman Hollerith (1860–1929) and Samuel F. B. Morse (1791–1872). Herman Hollerith, of U.S. Census fame, developed a binary coding scheme for representing data on paper cards through patterns of punched holes. Morse is responsible for the development of one of the earliest forms of electronic data communication—the telegraph. His dream was to break down the information to be communicated into a coding scheme based on electrical pulses. The code for each letter and number was formed by a combination of long and short electrical pulses. A short pulse was a "dot," and a long pulse was a "dash" (Figure 1).

The combined contributions of Morse and Hollerith (and others) laid the foundation for the storage and processing of data in magnetic and electrical form. Several coding schemes for the computer have been adopted that rely on the binary representation. Two commonly used codes are ASCII (pronounced "as-key") and EBCDIC (pronounced "eb-see-dick") (Figure 2).

ASCII

The acronym **ASCII** stands for the **American Standard Code for Information Interchange,** which is widely used to represent characters in microcomputers and many minicomputers. Because microcomputers operate on data in 8-bit groups, ASCII uses 8 bits to represent a character. For example, the character A in ASCII is 01000001.

EBCDIC

The acronym **EBCDIC** refers to **Extended Binary Coded Decimal Interchange Code,** which is the most popular code used for IBM and IBM-compatible mainframe computers. In EBCDIC, A is 11000001.

As you can see in Figure 2, characters are coded differently in ASCII and EBCDIC. Because of these differences, transferring data between computers using different coding schemes requires special hardware and software.

Unicode

Unicode is a new standard binary code that encompasses all written human languages and that may become the equivalent of ASCII in the world community. Unicode uses 16-bit character sets instead of 8-bit sets. Although Unicode is not yet used much, many software developers hope it will become the international standard for encoding data.

Parity Bits

The term *computer error* is often used when a mistake is caused by a person—inputting data incorrectly, for example. However, errors can be caused by other factors, such as dust, electrical disturbance, weather conditions, and improper handling of equipment. When such an error occurs, the computer may not be able to tell you exactly what and where it is, but it can tell you that there is an error. How does it do this? By using **parity bits,** or **check bits** (Figure 3). A parity bit is an extra bit attached to the end of the byte. If you add the number of 1 bits in a byte, you will have either an odd number of 1s or an even number of 1s (for example, ASCII A has two 1s, so it's even). Computers are designed to use either an *odd-parity scheme* or an *even-parity scheme.*

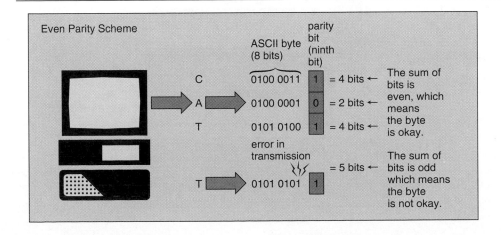

FIGURE 3

Parity schemes. This computer was designed to use an even-parity scheme, which means that the computer expects the total number of 1s (in the binary code) to always add up to an even number. In an even-parity scheme, a transmission error is signalled by the computer when the number of 1s adds up to an odd number. (The opposite is true when an odd-parity scheme is used.)

In an odd-parity scheme, the ninth bit, 0 or 1, is added to make the total number of 1s equal an odd number. If any byte turns up with an even number of 1s in an odd-parity scheme, the computer signals an error message on the screen. Similarly, if a byte turns up with an odd number of 1s in an even-parity scheme, an error message appears.

As a user, you won't have to determine whether to use an odd- or even-parity scheme. The computer manufacturer determines this, and the system software automatically checks the parity scheme. However, you will have to learn what to do when your computer signals an error. If your computer signals an error in the parity scheme, a message such as "Parity Error" will appear on the screen. If this happens to you, have your computer serviced to determine what is causing the problem.

Central Processing Unit

The **central processing unit (CPU)** is the "brain" of the computer system. Among other things, its configuration determines whether a computer is fast or slow in relation to other computers. The CPU is the most complex computer system component, responsible for directing most of the computer system activities based on the instructions provided. As one computer generation has evolved to the next, the size of the CPU has become smaller and smaller, while its speed and capacity have increased tremendously. Indeed, these changes resulted in the microcomputer that is small enough to fit on your desk, on your lap, or in your hand. As we mentioned earlier, the CPU circuitry of a microcomputer—called a **microprocessor**—fits on a chip about the size of your thumbnail, or even smaller.

The CPU has two main parts:

1. Control unit
2. Arithmetic/logic unit

The parts of the CPU are usually connected by an electronic component referred to as a **bus,** which acts as an electronic highway between them (Figure 4). To temporarily store data and instructions, the CPU has special-purpose storage devices called **registers.**

FIGURE 4

Buses, a kind of electronic transportation system, connect the main components of the central processing unit and memory.

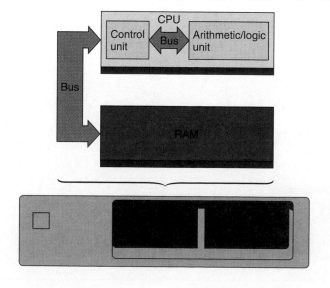

Control Unit

The **control unit,** a maze of complex electronic circuitry, is responsible for directing and coordinating most of the computer system activities. It controls the movement of electronic signals, including the signals between main memory and the input/output devices and the signals between main memory and the arithmetic/logic unit.

The control unit (and the entire CPU) can deal only with instructions written in **machine language** (Figure 5). When programmers write programs, they use high-level (human-language-like) languages. But before the programs can be used by the computer, the programmer must convert them into machine language by using a language processor—a type of systems software. In machine language, data and instructions are represented in binary form—that is, as 0s and 1s. Each type of computer—microcomputer, minicomputer, or mainframe—responds to a unique version of machine language. Once the instructions have been converted into this form, they can be interpreted by the control unit (sometimes referred to as *decoding*). According to each specific instruction, the control unit issues the necessary signals to other computer system components as needed to satisfy the processing requirements. This could involve, for example, directing that data be retrieved from a disk storage device, telling the printer to print the letter you just wrote, or simply directing the arithmetic/logic unit to add two numbers.

Arithmetic/Logic Unit (ALU)

Without the **arithmetic/logic unit (ALU),** you wouldn't be able to perform any mathematical calculations. In fact, without the ALU, computers would not be able to do most of the tasks that we find useful. The ALU performs all the arithmetic and logical (comparison) functions—that is, it adds, subtracts, multiplies, divides, and does comparisons. These comparisons, which are basically "less than," "greater than," or "equal to," can be combined into several common expressions, such as "greater than or equal to." The objective of most instructions that use comparisons is to determine which instructions should be executed next. The ALU also controls the speed of calculations.

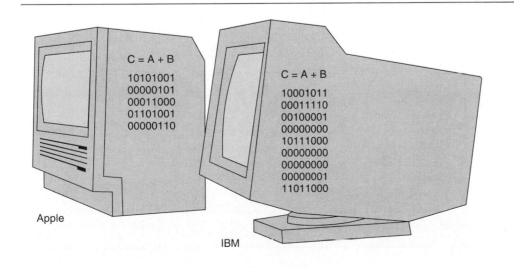

C = A + B

10101001
00000101
00011000
01101001
00000110

Apple

C = A + B

10001011
00011110
00100001
00000000
10111000
00000000
00000000
00000001
11011000

IBM

FIGURE 5

Machine language. This illustration shows the Apple and the IBM instructions for adding two numbers. IBM computers are incompatible with Apple computers because their processors use different versions of machine language instructions. Software written for one machine cannot be used on the other without special conversion software.

Registers

A **register** is a special temporary storage location within the CPU. Registers very quickly accept, store, and transfer data and instructions that are being used *immediately* (random access memory or main memory, to be discussed shortly, holds data that will be used *a little bit later*). To process an instruction, the control unit of the CPU retrieves it from main memory and places it into a register. The typical operations that take place in the processing of instructions are part of either the instruction cycle or the execution cycle (Figure 6).

The **instruction cycle,** or I-cycle, refers to the retrieval of an instruction from memory and its subsequent decoding (the process of alerting the circuits in the microprocessor to perform the specified operation). The time it takes to go through the instruction cycle is referred to as *I-time*. The **execution cycle,** or E-cycle, refers to the execution of the instruction and the subsequent storing of the result in a register. The time it takes to go through the execution cycle is referred to as *E-time*. The instruction cycle and the execution cycle together, as they apply to one instruction, are referred to as a **machine cycle** (Figure 6). The CPU has an internal **clock** that synchronizes all operations in the cycle. The speed is expressed in **megahertz (MHz):** 1 MHz equals 1 million cycles per second. Generally, the faster the clock speed, the faster the computer can process information. Old IBM PCs had a clock speed of 4.77 MHz; an IBM PS/2 Model 50 SX has a clock speed of 16 MHz; the Mac IIci's clock speed is 25 MHz; and the Compaq Deskpro 386/33 has a clock speed of 33 MHz. Some newer microprocessors have a clock speed of 50–66 MHz, and a 100 MHz CPU has been introduced by MIPS Computer Systems.

The number and types of registers in a CPU vary according to the CPU's design. Their size (capacity) and number can dramatically affect the processing power of a computer system. In general, the "larger" the register, the more bits can be processed at once. The size of a register is referred to as **wordsize.** Some personal computers have general-purpose registers that hold only 8 bits; others hold 16 bits; newer microcomputers have 32-bit registers. Computers that handle a 32-bit wordsize can process data twice as fast as those that handle a 16-bit wordsize.

FIGURE 6

The machine cycle—the instruction cycle and execution cycle as they apply to the processing of one instruction

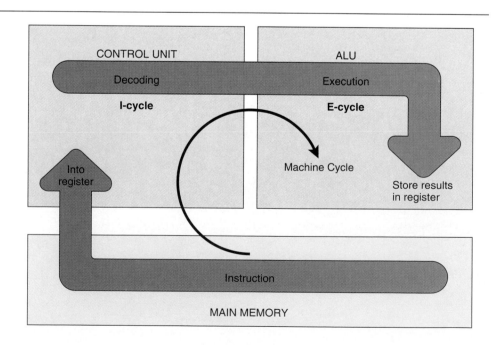

Bus

The term **bus** refers to an electrical pathway through which bits are transmitted between the various computer components. Depending on the design of a system, several types of buses may be present. For the user, the most important one is the **data bus,** which carries data throughout the CPU. The wider the data bus, the more data it can carry at one time, and thus the greater the processing speed of the computer. The data bus in the Intel 8088 microprocessor is 8 bits wide, meaning that it can carry 8 bits—or one character—at a time. In contrast, the data buses in the Motorola 68030 processor (in the Macintosh IIci microcomputer) and the Intel 80486SX processor (in the IBM PS/2 Model 90G and Model 95G microcomputers) are 32 bits wide—they can move four times more data through their data buses than the Intel 8088 bus can. Intel's new Pentium chip is its first 64-bit processor. Some supercomputers contain buses that are 128 bits wide.

Coprocessors

Additional microprocessors are often used inside a computer to handle some of the CPU's overload. These "pinch hitters," called **coprocessors,** help speed up the operation of the computer. For example, a math coprocessor chip can be installed in a socket on a microcomputer's motherboard to perform complex numerical calculations. This kind of chip can speed up the processing of financial and scientific applications. It can also be used to speed up the calculations a computer uses to display complex graphics on the screen and print them out.

The Microprocessor: More about Chips

Chips are designed according to their functions.

▼ Basically, if a chip is designed to "think" (like the microprocessor), it's called a *processor chip* or a *logic chip.* Microcomputers use one or more microprocessor chips, and large computers use several microprocessor chips as well as hundreds or thousands of specialized processor chips.

▼ If it's designed to provide memory, it's called a *memory chip.*

▼ If it's supposed to help devices communicate with one another, it's called an *interchip chip.*

▼ If it's a "helper" chip, it's called a *support chip.*

Other types of specialized chips also exist.

The manufacture of the CPU on a tiny chip—also called a *semiconductor* or an *integrated circuit*—revolutionized the computer industry and created the business market for microcomputers, basically providing the reason why you are reading this book now. How is this chip—the microprocessor—made? Basically, a drawing of circuits is photographed and reduced. The tiny photograph is etched (traced) on silicon with metal and other materials to form circuits.

The microprocessor contains at least a control unit and an ALU. The microprocessor chips in early microcomputer systems weren't nearly as powerful as the CPUs in large computers, but with each technological advance—which seems to occur almost every day—microprocessors are becoming more and more powerful. Some of today's microcomputers, equipped with powerful microprocessor chips, rival the processing power found in many of today's minicomputers.

As we mentioned earlier, large wordsize and data bus width—that is, the number of bits that a computer can process at once and that a data bus can carry at once—translate directly into high processing speed. An 8-bit computer can do anything a 32-bit computer can, just slower. And an 8-bit microprocessor costs a lot less than a 32-bit microprocessor, because its circuitry is much less sophisticated. Table 2 shows a comparison of wordsize, bus width, and clock speed of common microprocessors. The higher the number, the faster the chip.

A microprocessor's circuitry may be as small as a ¼-inch, or even ⅛-inch, square. Hundreds of microprocessors can be produced on a single disk—called a *wafer*—sliced from an ingot of silicon, a nonmetallic element that, after oxygen, is the most common in the earth's crust. A wafer is about ⁴⁄₁₀₀₀ of an inch thick; an ingot is about 2 feet long and 6 inches in diameter (Figure 7). As we mentioned above, chips are made to do different things in addition to being a CPU—for example, to expand a computer's ability to handle numeric compu-

TABLE 2

Comparison of Several Microprocessors

COMPANY	MICRO-PROCESSOR	DATA BUS CAPACITY	REGISTER SIZE (WORDSIZE)	CLOCK SPEED (MHz)	MIPS (MILLIONS OF INSTRUCTIONS PER SECOND)	MICROCOMPUTERS USING THIS CHIP*
MOS Technology	6502	8	8	4		Apple IIE Atari 800 Commodore 64
Intel	8086	16	16	5–10	0.33	Some IBM-compatibles Compaq Deskpro
Intel	8088	8	16	5–8	0.33	IBM PC and XT HP 150 touch screen Compaq Portable
Intel	80286	16	16	8–12	1.2	IBM AT IBM PS/2 Model 50 Compaq Deskpro 286
Motorola	68000	16	32	8–16		Apple Macintosh SE Commodore Amiga
Motorola	68020	32	32	16–33		Macintosh II
Motorola	68030	32	32	16–50		Macintosh IIcx NeXT computer
Motorola	68040	32	32	25–33		Hewlett-Packard workstations
Intel	80386SX	16	32	16–33	2.5	NEC PowerMate SC/20 Compaq Deskpro 386s/20
Intel	80386	32	32	16–33	6	Compaq Deskpro 386 IBM PS/2 Model 80
Intel	80486	32	32	20–50	16.5–20	IBM PS/2 Model 70 Compaq Systempro
Intel	i486 DX2-66	32	32	50–66	40	Compaq Deskpro 66i Dell 486P/66
Intel	Pentium ("586")	32	64	60–100	112	[none yet]

*This table includes a partial list of the microcomputers using each chip.

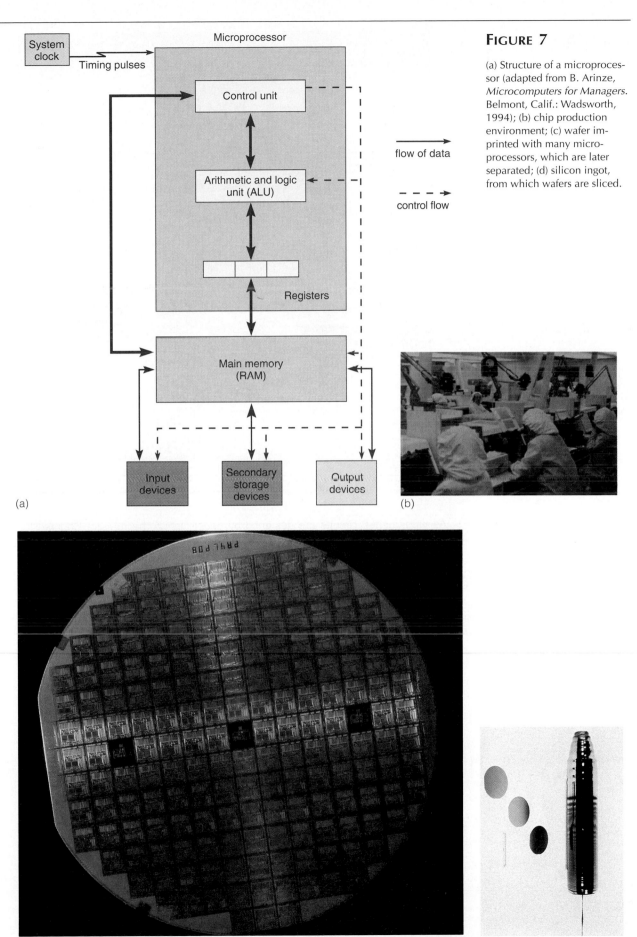

(a)

(b)

(c)

(d)

FIGURE 7

(a) Structure of a microprocessor (adapted from B. Arinze, *Microcomputers for Managers*. Belmont, Calif.: Wadsworth, 1994); (b) chip production environment; (c) wafer imprinted with many microprocessors, which are later separated; (d) silicon ingot, from which wafers are sliced.

FIGURE 8

Chip production cycle

1. All fundamental circuits are designed by people using the rules of Boolean logic. After they have been designed, they reside in disk libraries in the computer system waiting to be selected by the designer.

2. The chip designer selects the appropriate circuits from the library, and the computer generates the physical circuit paths.

3. The circuit paths are refined by a designer. The final results are further inspected to ensure that all the components are aligned properly.

4. The circuitry is turned into several photomasks that will transfer the circuitry design onto chips.

tation (numeric coprocessor) or graphics (graphics coprocessor) and to expand a computer's memory. As a user, you will probably be interested in finding out what types of chips are available to improve your computer system.

Figure 8 gives you more information about how chips are made.

Main Memory (RAM)

CPUs, ALUs, registers, buses, instructions . . . what good are they if you have no data to work with? You wouldn't have any if it weren't for **main memory** (also called *primary storage, memory,* and **random access memory [RAM]**), the part

FIGURE 8

(continued)

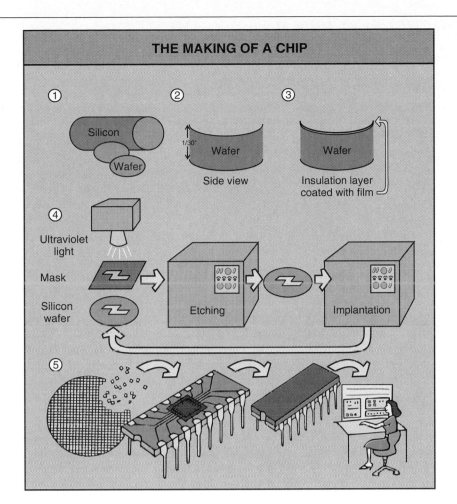

THE MAKING OF A CHIP

1./2. Silicon, the raw material of chips, is refined from quartz rocks and purified. It is fabricated into salami-like ingots from 3 to 5 inches in diameter. The ingots are sliced into wafers approximately 1/30th of an inch thick.

3. The wafer is covered with an oxide insulation layer and then coated with film.

4. A design is transferred onto the wafer by exposing it to ultraviolet light through a mask. Wherever light strikes the film, the film is hardened along with the insulation layer exposing the silicon below. The next step is an implantation process that forces chemicals into the exposed silicon under pressure, creating electricity altered elements below the surface.

Through a series of masking, etching, and implantation steps, the circuitries for many chips are created on the wafer.

5. The finished wafer is tested, and the bad chips are marked for disposal. The wafer is sliced into chips, and the good ones are placed into their final spider-like package. Tiny wires bond the chip to the package's "feet." Each chip is then tested individually. The number of chips that make it through to the very end can be less than the number that don't.

of the processing hardware that temporarily holds data and instructions needed shortly by the CPU. (Remember, registers hold data and instructions that are to be used *immediately*.) (The name *random access memory* is derived from the fact that data can be stored and retrieved at random—from anywhere in the electronic RAM chips—in approximately equal amounts of time, no matter what the specific data locations are.)

Brief History of Main Memory (RAM)

For many years main memory was one of the most expensive computer components to manufacture. However, technology has revolutionized main memory components over the past 40 years or so. Their size has been drastically reduced, and they have become less expensive as the manufacturing materials have changed from vacuum tubes to magnetic cores to transistors and finally to chips.

The earliest form of main memory was based on vacuum tubes. Today's technology can put 256 K or 1 or 2 MB on a single main memory chip; the equivalent main memory capacity would have required a shelf of vacuum tubes more than a mile long. And tubes were not reliable: their power requirements were high, they generated heat, they failed frequently, and they were slow. The transistor, invented in 1947, was a much smaller and more reliable provider of main memory. It also had smaller power requirements and failed less frequently than vacuum tubes. Magnetic cores were smaller still.

However, the main memory of almost all computers today is based on semiconductor chip technology. Chips are very small and relatively inexpensive to manufacture, and they do not consume as much power as older forms of main memory. The use of chips has greatly increased the memory capacity of computers. In 1979 a microcomputer with 64 K of main memory was considered to be a satisfactory system. Today a microcomputer system with less than 640 K of main memory is considered underpowered, and many users are expanding their microcomputer's main memory to 4–8 MB or more.

Function of Main Memory (RAM)

The principal function of RAM is to act as a buffer between the central processing unit (CPU) and the rest of the computer system components. It functions as a sort of desktop on which you place the things with which you are about to begin to work. The CPU can use only those software instructions and data that are stored in main memory.

RAM is an electronic, or volatile, state. When the computer is off, RAM is empty; when it is on, RAM is capable of receiving and holding a copy of the software instructions and data necessary for processing. Because RAM is a volatile form of storage that depends on electric power and the power can go off during processing, many users save their work frequently onto nonvolatile secondary storage devices such as diskettes or hard disks. In general, RAM is used for the following purposes:

▼ Storage of a copy of the main systems software program that controls the general operation of the computer. This copy is loaded into RAM when the computer is turned on (you'll find out how later), and it stays there as long as the computer is on.

▼ Temporary storage of a copy of application program instructions (the specific software you are using in your business) to be retrieved by the central processing unit (CPU) for interpretation and execution.

▼ Temporary storage of data that has been input from the keyboard or other input device until instructions call for the data to be transferred into the CPU for processing.

▼ Temporary storage of data that has been produced as a result of processing until instructions call for the data to be used again in subsequent processing or to be transferred to an output device such as the screen, a printer, or a disk storage device.

Figure 9 shows the banks (a group of usually nine chips arranged in a row) of RAM chips on a microcomputer system board (motherboard). RAM chips are often called *dynamic RAM (DRAM)* chips or *static RAM (SRAM)* chips, based on the style of the electric circuits.

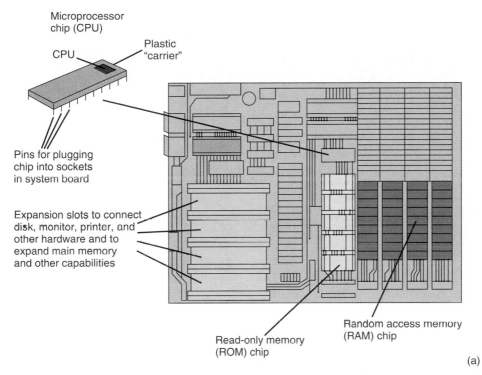

Microprocessor chip (CPU)

Plastic "carrier"

CPU

Pins for plugging chip into sockets in system board

Expansion slots to connect disk, monitor, printer, and other hardware and to expand main memory and other capabilities

Read-only memory (ROM) chip

Random access memory (RAM) chip

(a)

FIGURE 9

(a) Banks of RAM chips on a system board and expansion slots, where cards with more RAM chips can be inserted; (b) two common types of RAM chips; (c) RAM chips on an expansion card that will be inserted in an expansion slot on the system board.

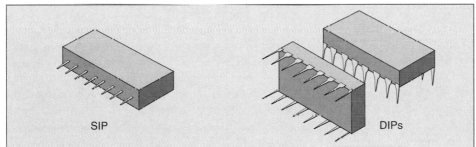

SIP

DIPs

(b)

You will find DRAM (dynamic random-access-memory) chips on your computer's motherboard. DRAMs come in several forms: Single Inline Packages (SIPs) fit into sockets with a single row of holes; Dual Inline Packages (DIPs) fit sockets with a double row.

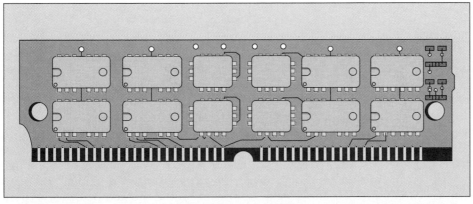

(c)

DRAM also comes in the form of chip modules called SIMMs (Single-Inline Memory Modules). This module card, or board, is inserted into an expansion slot.

Main Memory (RAM) for Microcomputers

The amount of random access memory you have in your microcomputer directly affects the level of sophistication of the software you can use. Sophisticated, or powerful, programs take up a lot of space in RAM. Most of today's software programs require a *minimum* of 640 K to run; many programs require more. In general, the greater your machine's memory capacity, the better because:

▼ It can receive and use much larger programs.

▼ It can hold copies of more than one program in main memory to support the sharing of the computer by more than one user at a time.

▼ It can operate faster and more efficiently.

▼ It will be able to use new, sophisticated software.

▼ It can hold images for creating graphics and animation.

▼ It can work with and manipulate more data at one time.

Early microcomputer systems were not equipped with very much RAM by today's standards: they were able to directly access and control only up to 64 K RAM. Today users can expand memory to over 48 MB. In addition, the price of RAM chips was much higher than it is now.

The software available for microcomputers did not require much RAM until certain new products began to appear on the market around 1984. With the introduction of special software, called *spreadsheets,* to handle large financial reports, the need for increased RAM grew rapidly. Now, for a microcomputer to effectively use many of the new software products, it should have from 640 K to 4 MB or more of RAM.

But what if you, like many users, are faced with the need to expand your computer's RAM capacity to be able to use some new software? For instance, what if your microcomputer is not brand new and has a RAM capacity of only 256 K or 512 K? Unfortunately, you cannot simply pull out two of the 64 K chips and replace them with 256 K chips to increase the amount of main memory available to 640 K. The component that prevents you from doing this is the *dynamic memory access (DMA)* controller. In most older microcomputer systems, the DMA chip was designed to work with only one size of memory chip. However, in newer systems the DMA controller is designed to allow a mix of banks of 64 K, 256 K, 1 MB, 2 MB, and 4 MB memory chips. The DMA chip or module is responsible for managing the use of all main memory. It keeps track of which memory locations are in use (and by what) and which are available for use.

Two basic types of memory are used to increase memory beyond the conventional 640 K limit (Figure 10). The type used is influenced by the sophistication of the microprocessor in your machine.

Expanded Memory

Expanded memory is used in 8088, 8086, 80286, and 80386 (older) microcomputers to increase memory beyond the **conventional memory limit** (or *base memory unit*) of 640 K. Users of early microcomputer systems couldn't increase the amount of RAM directly wired into the motherboard beyond 640 K because of limitations imposed by the systems software (programs designed to allow the computer to manage its own resources). This situation led to the development of a wide variety of new products allowing RAM to be increased through the use of an **add-on memory board,** or **expansion card** (Figure 11). This board is simply pressed into an expansion slot on the motherboard. An **expansion slot** is a plug-in spot specifically meant to support add-on components

Types of RAM: conventional, expanded, extended. Most systems have 384 K of space called *upper memory* above the conventional memory area of 640 K. Upper memory is not considered part of the total memory of your computer because programs cannot use upper memory to store data. This memory is normally reserved for running your system's hardware.

FIGURE 10

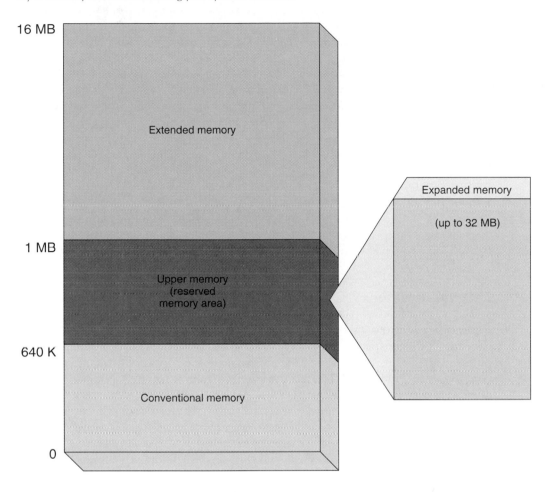

16 MB

Extended memory

Expanded memory

(up to 32 MB)

1 MB

Upper memory
(reserved
memory area)

640 K

Conventional memory

0

FIGURE 11

Expanded/extended memory board and software required for a computer to use it.

(Figure 12). This slot connects the add-on board with the power supply for the computer and links the board with the buses for moving data and instructions.

For your computer to know you've added memory, you must also follow special software instructions that come with the board. To use expanded memory, you must run applications such as Lotus 1-2-3 (a spreadsheet) that are specifically tailored to address expanded memory. These software packages use the *expanded memory manager (EMM)* program agreed on by the Lotus, Intel, and Microsoft companies.

We do need to mention here that add-on boards or cards can be inserted only in computers with **open architecture**—that is, computers built to allow users to open the system cabinet and make changes. Computers with **closed architecture,** such as the Macintosh SE, do not allow the user to add expansion cards. Thus, you can see that a computer's architecture may become important to the user if he or she wants to upgrade the system—not only to increase RAM but also to add disk storage, graphics capabilities, and certain communications capabilities, or to change from a monochrome display screen to a color screen. If you are buying a microcomputer system and think you might want to upgrade it at a later time, make sure you purchase a microcomputer with open architecture (or a new type of Macintosh that allows expansion through sockets on the back without opening up the cabinet).

Extended Memory

Extended memory also refers to memory increased above 640 K; however, it runs faster than expanded memory and can be used only in newer microcomputers with 80286, 80386, or 80486 microprocessors. Extended memory is also composed of RAM chips that are attached to a board that is plugged into an expansion slot, or, in the case of some 386 and 486 microcomputers, inserted directly into sockets on the motherboard. With extended memory, a machine can use up to 16 MB of memory. Like expanded memory, extended memory can be used only by software that recognizes it, such as the *extended memory manager* in Microsoft Windows. The applications software documentation will

---

FIGURE 12

Buy an add-on memory board to plug in an expansion slot and increase RAM. (The expansion card is at the far left.)

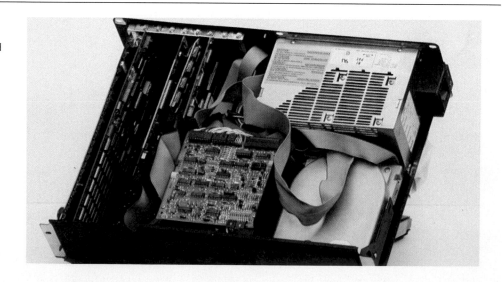

specify whether the software is compatible with one or both of these types of memory. (Users should keep in mind that relatively old software programs and microprocessors will not be able to use extended RAM. For some microcomputers, users can buy both expanded RAM and extended RAM and thus run older software, as well as brand-new, memory hungry software.)

Cache Memory

Although its definitions differ, basically **cache** (pronounced "cash") **memory** is a special high-speed memory area that the CPU can access quickly. Cache memory is sometimes used with 386 and 486 microprocessors. A cache chip is a small, dedicated chip that is associated with a computer's main RAM chips. A copy of the most frequently used data and instructions is kept in the cache chips so the CPU can look there first, which makes the computer run faster. Cache chips are faster but much more expensive than main RAM chips, and each can hold only a small amount of data. Therefore, they are used mainly in large computers and high-priced microcomputers. These cache microcomputers are often used for processor-intensive programs such as computer-aided design (CAD) software. (The heavy workload of such programs could severely slow down a computer system without a cache.)

Virtual Memory

Some microprocessors can also use **virtual memory,** which allows the processor—under control of special software that "chops" your program into little pieces—to use disk storage as an extension of RAM. In other words, the virtual memory program puts as many pieces into RAM as possible and runs them while putting the remaining pieces on disk—which are retrieved when appropriate. For example, virtual memory allows an IBM AT microcomputer to use up to 1 GB (1 billion bytes) of virtual memory. Thus you can run a 4 MB program even if you have only 2 MB RAM.

Read-Only Memory (ROM)

Now you know what RAM (main memory) does: it holds the data and instructions you are about to work with. But what kind of memory gets your computer running properly after you turn it on? How does the computer know to check out its hardware components (such as the keyboard or the monitor) to see that they have been connected correctly? Instructions to perform such operations, which are critical to the operation of a computer, are stored permanently on **read-only memory (ROM)** chips (Figure 13) installed inside the computer by the manufacturer. ROM chips, also called *firmware,* retain instructions in a permanently accessible, nonvolatile form, which means that when the power in the computer is turned off, the instructions stored in ROM are not lost.

ROM chips in a typical microcomputer, as mentioned, contain instructions that tell the CPU what to do first when the power is turned on. (Turning the computer on is called *booting* the computer because it starts the ROM instructions that enable the computer to "pull itself up by its own bootstraps" and get going.) ROM chips also contain instructions that help the CPU transfer information from the keyboard to the screen and printer. Those instructions are called the *ROM operating system,* or the *ROM basic input/output system (ROM BIOS).*

FIGURE 13

ROM chips, installed by the manufacturer on the computer's system board, contain instructions that are read by the computer. Since they cannot usually be rewritten, they are called read-only memory.

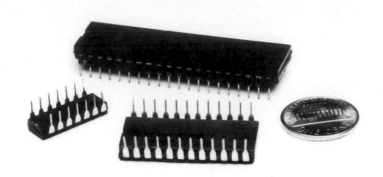

Having basic instructions permanently stored in ROM is both necessary and convenient. For example, if you are using a microcomputer with diskette drives, the more instructions in ROM, the fewer diskettes you may have to handle in order to load instructions into the computer. If you could have all the program instructions you'll ever need to use in ROM, you would have everything you need for processing data and information at your fingertips—always.

Unfortunately, until recently the process of manufacturing ROM chips and recording data on them was more expensive than the process of producing other types of memory chips. As a result, manufacturers tended to record in ROM only those instructions that were crucial to the operation of the computer. However, in recent years improvements in the manufacturing process for ROM chips have lowered their cost to the point where manufacturers are beginning to include additional software instructions.

PROM, EPROM, EEPROM

Three additional kinds of nonvolatile memory ROM-type chips are used in some microcomputer systems—namely, PROMs, EPROMs, and EEPROMs. **PROM** stands for **programmable read-only memory.** This type of memory functions in the same way a regular ROM component does, with one major exception: PROM chips are custom-made for the user by the manufacturer. In other words, the user determines what data and instructions are recorded on them. The only problem with PROM chips is that, like ROM chips, once data is recorded on them, it can't be changed.

Erasable programmable read-only memory (EPROM) chips were developed as an improvement over PROM chips. EPROM functions exactly the same way as PROM; however, with the help of a special device that uses ultraviolet light, in approximately 15 minutes the data or instructions on an EPROM chip can be erased. Once erased, a device generically referred to as a PROM burner is used to reprogram the chip. Unfortunately, to change instructions on an EPROM chip, the chip first must be taken out of the machine and then put back when the changes have been made. This task is one most computer users would prefer to avoid. The alternative to erasing and rerecording an EPROM chip is to replace it with a new EPROM that features the new program code. This is a task best performed by a trained computer professional.

Electrically erasable programmable read-only memory (EEPROM), the latest addition to the ROM family of chips, avoids the inconvenience of having to take chips out of the computer to change data and instructions. Unlike EPROM chips on which changes must be made optically, EEPROM chips allow changes to be made electrically under software control. In other words, they do not need to be taken out of the computer. The only disadvantage of EEPROM chips is they currently cost substantially more than regular ROM chips and disk storage devices. However, Intel and other manufacturers are planning high-volume production, which should push the prices down.

Measuring the Processing Power of a Computer

The proliferation of microcomputers in our society means that more and more people are becoming familiar with the processing power of computers in general. Many individuals are considering the purchase of a microcomputer on their own, with the result that more and more people are asking, "How do you determine how powerful a computer is?"

This question is fairly easy to answer. However, understanding the answer requires knowledge of a few more computer fundamentals.

Addressing Scheme

The **addressing scheme** is a computer design feature that directly determines the amount of RAM that can be controlled by the CPU at any one time. (Memory addresses are designed when a computer is manufactured.) Early microprocessors were limited to 64 K of memory-addressing capability. The popular IBM PC-compatible computers have a memory-addressing capability of 1,024 K. The IBM PS/2 Model P70 uses the 80386 microprocessor, which allows access to approximately 4 GB RAM—equal to the addressing capability of current minicomputers. Some "super" minicomputers can access even more than that. Mainframes usually have an addressing scheme that allows access to between 32 and 128 MB RAM or more.

Register Size

Computers have a number of registers that are used for a variety of purposes, including the temporary storage of results of arithmetic operations. The more of these registers you have and the larger they are, the more processing power you have. The registers in early microcomputers could hold only 8 bits each. Registers in newer microcomputers hold 16 or 32 bits each. Each 32-bit general-purpose register can process twice as much data in each machine cycle per register as a 16-bit register can.

The registers in minicomputers are usually 32 bits. Mainframes generally have registers that are at least 64 bits.

Data Bus Capacity

As you learned earlier, the data bus is like a pipeline used to move data and instructions among RAM, the CPU, and other computer system components, including peripheral devices such as monitors and disk drives. The size of the data bus controls the amount of data that can travel along the pipeline at one time and thus can significantly affect a computer's performance. A microcomputer's data bus is constructed to carry 8, 16, or 32 bits. The hardware and software must be specifically designed for the type of bus used.

Three basic bus designs, or architectures, are found in IBM and IBM-compatible microcomputer systems.

1. *The Industry Standard Architecture (ISA)* bus system (introduced in 1981) is used with the Intel 8088, 80286, and 80386 microprocessors and is capable of passing 8 bits (when using the 8088) or 16 bits (when using the 80286 or 80386) through the data bus.

This slower bus design doesn't fully utilize the 80386 microprocessor—which is capable of supporting 32-bit chunks of data in the data bus. As a result, in 1988 the following two bus systems were introduced that enable 80386- and 80486-based machines to pass 32 bits through the data bus:

2. *IBM's Micro Channel Architecture (MCA)*
3. *Extended Industry Standard Architecture (EISA)*

There is much debate among industry observers about which of the last two bus designs is better. A side-by-side comparison of the two designs reveals more similarities than differences.

In order to bypass existing standard bus systems—in other words, to connect peripheral computer components directly to the microprocessor—some microcomputer companies have recently started adding what are called *local bus extensions* to new machines. For example, if you buy a microcomputer with local bus video, it means that the video circuitry has been installed right next door to the microprocessor, connected by its own private (local) bus. Thus everything on the computer screen seems to move faster, because the data being transmitted back and forth between the microprocessor and the video circuitry does not need to travel along the regular standard (busy) bus system. The principle is like taking a back road to avoid heavy traffic on the main highway.

Unfortunately, users still will have to make a choice about which bus system to adopt in their computer, because the bus systems aren't compatible— that is, hardware and software must be designed specifically for the bus setup that will be used.

Clock Speed

The clock, mentioned in the section on the instruction execution cycle, is the part of the CPU that synchronizes and sets the speed of all the operations in the machine cycle. Early microcomputers operated at speeds of around 1 MHz. This means that those computers had approximately 1 million processing cycles available per second to perform useful work. Today microcomputers are operating at speeds of 20, 33, 50, and 66 MHz.

Instruction Set

The early 8-bit microprocessors were extremely slow when performing mathematical operations. They were designed to handle only addition and subtraction; a more sophisticated operation (such as division or multiplication) had to be performed by a series of special program instructions, often called *subroutines.* For example, to multiply 5 times 3, a subroutine would add the number 3 together 5 times. The more powerful 32-bit microcomputers use additional instructions that handle mathematical operations in a single processing cycle. The 16-bit microprocessors also use single *blocks* of instructions (called *instruction sets*) that can cause whole blocks of data to be moved from one place to another. With the 8-bit microcomputers, this type of operation would also have to be handled by a number of subroutines (lots of "small" individual instructions).

How a microprocessor chip is designed affects how fast it can process. Most microprocessor chips today are designed using the **Complex Instruction Set Computing (CISC)** approach. A multitude of software applications written for use with this chip design are being used in the business environment today. A newer approach to chip design, called **Reduced Instruction Set Computing (RISC),** allows microcomputers to offer very high speed performance by simplifying the internal design and reducing the number of instruction sets. The RISC design enables a computer to process about twice as fast as one based on the CISC design. In the new Pentium (80586, or P5) microprocessor from Intel, "pipelining"—a RISC technology—is used to allow the microprocessor to complete more than one instruction in a single clock cycle. It decodes one instruction while another is retrieved and a third is executed. This technology significantly speeds up processing time.

Checklist

In general, keep these points in mind when you are trying to determine the processing power of a microcomputer:

▼ *Addressing scheme:* The larger the addressing capability, the more RAM the computer can control.

▼ *Register size:* The larger the general-purpose registers, the more data the microprocessor can manipulate in one machine cycle.

▼ *Data bus:* The larger the data buses, the more efficiently and quickly data and instructions can be moved among the processing components of the computer.

▼ *Clock speed:* The faster the clock speed, the more machine cycles are completed per second and the faster the computer can perform processing operations.

▼ *Instruction set:* The more powerful the instruction set, the fewer instructions and processing cycles it takes to perform certain tasks.

Processing the Future

Microcomputers

A CPU of the 1940s weighed 5 tons, took up six rooms, processed about 10,000 instructions per second, and cost about $5 million. Today it is about 5 millimeters square, about ½-inch thick, can process about 4–100 million instructions per second, and costs less than $5. This revolution in computer processing was caused by the development of the microprocessor. Today a microcomputer priced at about $5,000 has essentially the same power as an IBM mainframe of more than 10 years ago—but that machine cost $3.4 million at the time. If the automobile industry had advanced this fast since 1982, said Edward Lucente, the head of IBM's Information Systems Group, "Today we'd have cars that go zero to 60 in three seconds, circle the globe on a tank of gas, and cost half as much as they did six years ago. Of course, they would be difficult to get into, because they would be only half the size."

In general, current developments in the microcomputer industry indicate that the next generation of personal computers will change not so much in the way the hardware looks—although hardware components will continue to decrease in size—but in the way the computers work; that is, main memory capacity will increase, operating systems will change, secondary storage will increase, and software will become more sophisticated and easier to use. In fact, microcomputers will have so much power that they will be able to devote 75% of their time to running software that improves interaction with the user and still calculate faster than current machines.

Of course, many of these improvements relate to microprocessor developments. The speed and power of microprocessors will continue to grow until the microcomputer is no longer a uniprocessor system; that is, the microcomputer will have specific processors for such functions as communications, graphics, and artificial intelligence. Also, serial, or linear, processing—whereby instructions are executed one at a time—may become a thing of the past; true *parallel processing*—whereby many processors attack separate components of a problem simultaneously—will eventually be available on microcomputers as it is now on larger computers. Gallium arsenide, which works at least three times faster than silicon as a semiconductor, may be used in combination with silicon to manufacture chips—that is, if other types of potentially cheaper and faster superconductor materials currently under research don't grab the spotlight.

Superconductor materials being examined by some scientists include special ceramic/metal compounds, bismuth- and thallium-based compounds, and a special type of plastic film that will allow chip circuits to be etched by light rays, which will greatly simplify chip production and reduce its expense. However, many of the materials under investigation are superconductive only at temperatures too low to be practical for the user, and thallium is a deadly poison! Other researchers are currently developing a neural-network computer chip with 256 processors, or "neurons," and 65,536 interconnections, or "synapses." In traditional processors, electrons travel along miniaturized metal-wire circuits engraved in silicon. However, instead of having thousands of circuits engraved onto one chip, the neural-network chip has packets of electrons injected directly into the silicon. The electrons are guided from one neuron to another, enabling each of the chip's processors to exchange data with every other processor in a continually updated circuit. Researchers suspect that neural-network chips will be useful in speech recognition, which requires high-speed processing. If future neural networks are patterned closely on the human brain, "thinking" computers may do just that.

Still other scientists are researching the use of genetically engineered organic materials to be used as *biochips*. Others are doing more work with the RISC (reduced instruction set computer) chip, which simplifies chip architecture and instruction sets—thereby enabling chips to become yet smaller and faster. Another line of research is *optical computing,* which would use light-activated microprocessors. AT&T has already developed the prototype of a digital optical processor that uses light (photons) instead of electricity (electrons) to process data. Optical processors hold the promise of running at clock speeds measured in gigahertz. AT&T officials hope to ready a miniaturized optical processing unit for inclusion in commercially available processors by the year 2000.

Yet one more development in chip production involves increased processor capability across different types of computer systems (called *platforms*) and so-called *scalability,* the ability to build the same chip into anything from a small palm-top PC to a big multimillion-dollar mainframe.

How much the user gets out of the explosion in microprocessor power and speed will depend on what the software industry does with it, for more powerful hardware will require more sophisticated programming to produce useful applications.

Minis, Mainframes, and Supercomputers

The two basic approaches to developing a supercomputer differ in terms of the number of central processing units employed. In the first approach, a moderate number of very fast processors are linked together to perform *linear* processing—each processor typically works on a separate task. The second approach involves the use of a large number of processors to perform *parallel* processing. This is the approach of the current supercomputers. (Some experts say that parallel processing will be used in *all* sizes of computers by the year 2000.) In supercomputer parallel processing, as many as 65,500 processors with a complexity of connectedness that begins to approach biological complexity operate simultaneously to solve problems.

We know that developments in supercomputer-related technologies will lead to tremendous improvements in computer processing power. Many of these improvements will filter down and be used in the minicomputers and micro-computers that are used in business to manage day-to-day activities.

COMPUTERS AND CAREERS

▼

POLITICS AND GOVERNMENT

Using 70 Macintosh SE terminals located at nine campus polling places, Stanford University's student government held the first totally computerized election in California history in April 1985. Some 6,500 students cast ballots for the next year's Council of Presidents. Ironically, when none of the three slates won the top office, students returned to the polls a few weeks later and made their final choice using old-fashioned paper ballots.

Nevertheless, the first election was so revolutionary that it drew observers from local county registrars of voters and from the state capital. County election officials were concerned about possible fraud in electronic voting systems, but Stanford's terminals were not linked into a network, and buzzer alarms were written into the software to deter prospective hackers. To tally the results, election officials transferred the data voters recorded on the Macintosh hard disks onto floppy disks; the data was then tabulated at a single location. The biggest advantages of computerized balloting were the reduced costs of printing paper ballots (only a few were on hand for computerphobes) and the increased speed in tabulating returns.

Electronic voting may be the wave of the future, but computers are already being used extensively in politics and government. Political parties have long used computers for campaign purposes, primarily for fund-raising. Anyone who has ever contributed to a candidate or political party is sure to be in some database. Computers are also used to aim direct-mail pieces with very specific messages at selected audiences. Another use is to identify certain voter groups, such as those who tend to vote in presidential elections but not in off-year congressional elections, in order to urge them to the polls.

Computers also came in for heavy use following the 1990 census, when state legislators used them to redraw boundaries of new election districts in ways that would most favor the party in power. For instance, in one system, a legislator could use computer graphics to call up his or her district on a screen, then shift the boundaries and get instant numbers of what the voting behavior, racial composition, and other population characteristics would be in the new district.

Census Bureau data is available not only to politicians, however. The bureau developed a computer map system called TIGER (for *T*opologically *I*ntegrated *G*eographic *E*ncoding and *R*eferencing system) that, when used with a database such as the 1990 census results or a company's own customer files, provides a detailed cartographic profile. TIGER can produce a map with 26 million street intersections and every city block, river, railroad line, or governmental entity in the country. The entire map comprises 16 billion lines.

▼ In a computer system, data is represented by *binary code,* a system of combinations of *binary digits* (*bits*). There are only two binary digits: 1 ("on") and 0 ("off"). During processing, 1 is represented by a pulse of electrical current, and 0 is represented by the absence of electricity (or by low current).

▼ Two common binary coding schemes are the *American Standard Code for Information Interchange* (*ASCII*) and the *Extended Binary Coded Decimal Interchange* (*EBCDIC*). ASCII is typically used to represent data for microcomputers, and EBCDIC is used on larger computers.

▼ It typically takes 8 bits to represent a character, or *byte,* of data. A *kilobyte* (*KB*) = 1,000 (actually 1,024) bytes; a *megabyte* (*MB*) = 1,000,000 bytes; a *gigabyte* (*GB*) = 1,000,000,000 bytes; a *terabyte* (*TB*) = 1,000,000,000,000 bytes.

▼ The *central processing unit* (*CPU*) is the "brain" of the computer. It has two main parts:

1. *Control unit*—directs and coordinates most of the computer system activities.

2. *Arithmetic/logic unit* (*ALU*)—performs all arithmetic and logical (comparison) functions and controls the speed of calculations.

▼ The CPU of a microcomputer, the *microprocessor,* is a ¼-inch to ⅛-inch square *semiconductor chip* that contains complicated circuitry. The power of the microprocessor chip is indicated by its number—generally, the higher the number (for example, 80286, 80386, 80486), the greater the power.

▼ The parts of the CPU and other computer components are connected by *buses,* or electronic pathways. The most important bus is the *data bus,* which carries data throughout the CPU.

▼ The more bits a computer's buses and registers can handle at once (8, 16, or 32), the faster the computer.

▼ *Registers* temporarily store data and instructions that will be used immediately by the CPU.

▼ The CPU understands only *machine language,* in which data and instructions are represented by 0s and 1s—the off and on states of electrical current.

▼ Software instructions are converted into machine language by a *language processor* program. Each type of computer uses a unique machine language.

▼ To process an instruction, the control unit of the CPU retrieves it from memory and places it into a register. The *instruction cycle* (*I-time*) refers to the retrieval of the instruction from memory and its subsequent decoding. The *execution cycle* (*E-time*) refers to the processing of the instruction and subsequent storing of the result in a register. Together, the instruction cycle and the execution cycle are called the *machine cycle.*

▼ The microprocessor has an internal *clock* that synchronizes all operations of the machine cycle. Its speed is measured in *megahertz* (*MHz*). The faster the clock speed, the faster the computer can process information.

▼ *Random access memory* (*RAM*), also called *main memory, primary storage,* and just *memory,* refers to the part of the processing hardware that temporarily holds data and instructions needed shortly by the CPU. RAM is volatile—unless the data and instructions in RAM have been saved (for example, to disk), they are lost when the power is turned off.

▼ RAM—sort of a "desktop"—acts as a buffer between the CPU and the rest of the computer system components. The CPU can use only those software instructions and data that have been placed in RAM.

▼ A copy of the main systems software is stored in RAM when the computer is turned on; it controls the general operation of the computer and stays there as long as the computer is on. A copy of the specific software you are using (applications software) is also temporarily stored in RAM.

▼ The amount of RAM you have in your computer determines the level of software sophistication your computer can handle because, with more RAM:

1. It can receive and use larger programs.

2. It can hold more copies of more than one program in RAM to support sharing of the computer by more than one user.

3. It can operate faster and more efficiently.

4. It can hold images for creating graphics and animation.

▼ Most modern microcomputers need *at least* 640 K RAM to run today's software. Some software programs require even more RAM—4–8 MB. A user can increase a microcomputer's RAM by inserting *add-on memory boards,* also called *expansion cards,* into one of the computer's *expansion slots.*

▼ Increased memory comes in the form of either *expanded memory* or *extended memory.* The main difference between the two types of memory is the microprocessor models with which each type can be used. Extended memory can be used only with machines that use at least an 80286 microprocessor and that have been designed to use extended memory.

▼ Memory expansion cards can be used only by those computers with *open architecture,* which allows users to open the system cabinet and make changes. Computers with *closed architecture* do not generally allow such changes.

▼ *Cache memory* comprises small, high-speed, expensive chips associated with main RAM. The CPU looks there first for frequently used data and instructions—thus making the computer run faster. Larger computers and high-priced microcomputers may use cache memory.

▼ *Virtual memory* allows the CPU—under control of special software—to use disk space to simulate a large amount of RAM.

▼ Many basic computer instructions are stored in *read-only memory (ROM),* a chip installed by the manufacturer inside the computer. ROM is nonvolatile—the data and instructions are not lost when the power is turned off.

▼ Data and instructions in ROM generally cannot be altered. However, special ROM chips exist that allow users to modify ROM.

1. *Programmable read-only memory (PROM)* allows the user to determine what data and instructions the manufacturer records on the chip—to customize the chip. However, once the data is recorded, it cannot be changed.

2. *Erasable programmable read-only memory (EPROM)* not only allows users to determine what data and instructions are recorded on the chip, but it also allows them to erase the data with a special ultraviolet device. Then a trained technician uses a *PROM burner* to reprogram the chip.

3. *Electrically erasable programmable read-only memory (EEPROM)* allows users to reprogram the chip electrically, under software control.

▼ The processing power of a computer can be measured in terms of:

1. *Addressing scheme*—determines the amount of RAM that can be controlled by the CPU at any one time. The larger the addressing capability, the more RAM the computer can control.

2. *Register size*—The larger the general-purpose registers, the more data the CPU can manipulate in one machine cycle.

3. *Data bus*—The larger the data buses, the more efficiently and quickly data and instructions can be moved among the processing components of the computer. In some microcomputers, standard bus architecture (such as *ISA, MCA,* and *EISA*) can be bypassed by *local bus extensions.*

4. *Clock speed*—The faster the clock speed, the more machine cycles are completed per second and the faster the computer can perform processing operations. Clock speed is measured in *megahertz (MHz).*

5. *Instruction set*—The more powerful the instruction set, the fewer instructions and processing cycles it takes to perform certain tasks. The design (for example, *CISC* vs. *RISC*) of the chip affects how instruction sets—or blocks of instructions—are processed.

KEY TERMS

EXERCISES

SELF-TEST

1. The _____ _____ _____ performs all the computer's arithmetic and logical functions.

2. In machine language, data and instructions are represented with 0s and 1s. (true/false)

3. The _____ is the CPU of a microcomputer. Its circuitry fits on a very small semiconductor _____.

4. The _____ _____ directs and coordinates most of the activities in the computer system.

5. The speed of a microprocessor is measured in _____

6. The more bits a computer's buses and registers can handle at once, the faster the computer. (true/false)

7. Read-only memory is a nonvolatile form of storage. (true/false)

8. A _____ connects the different components in the CPU.

9. A _____ _____ also called _____ _____ temporarily holds data and instructions needed shortly by the CPU.

10. Microcomputer users generally increase their RAM capacity in two ways: _____ and _____.

11. Expansion cards, or add-on boards, can be used only in computers with _____ architecture.

12. The _____ the data bus, the more efficiently and quickly data can be moved among the processing components of the computer.

13. List three types of ROM chips:

    a.

    b.

    c.

14. Extended memory can be used only in newer microcomputers. (true/false)

15. The instruction cycle and the execution cycle together are called the _____ .

16. A _____ is composed of 8 _____.

17. _____ _____ comprises small, expensive chips used in association with main RAM chips to speed up obtaining data and instructions for main memory.

18. Data and instructions in RAM are lost when the computer is turned off. (true/false)

19. Data and instructions in ROM are lost when the computer is turned off. (true/false)

20. The processing power of a microcomputer can be measured in terms of:

    a.

    b.

    c.

    d.

    e.

Solutions: (1) arithmetic/logic unit; (2) true; (3) microprocessor, chip; (4) control unit; (5) megahertz; (6) true; (7) true; (8) bus; (9) main memory, random access memory; (10) expanded memory, extended memory; (11) open; (12) larger [or wider]; (13) PROM, EPROM, EEPROM; (14) true; (15) machine cycle; (16) byte, bits; (17) cache memory; (18) true; (19) false; (20) addressing scheme, register size, data bus, clock speed, instruction set

MULTIPLE-CHOICE QUESTIONS

1. Which of the following are the two main components of the CPU?

    a. control unit and registers

    b. registers and main memory

    c. control unit and ALU

    d. ALU and bus

    e. bus and registers

2. Which of the following is used for manufacturing chips?

    a. control bus

    b. control unit

    c. parity chips

    d. semiconductors

    e. transistors

3. Which of the following processing hardware components does the computer manufacturer design to check for processing errors?

    a. ROM chip

    b. microprocessor chip

    c. parity chip

    d. EPROM chip

    e. coprocessor chip

4. Which of the following are used to quickly accept, store, and transfer data and instructions that are being used *immediately* by the CPU?

   a. microprocessors

   b. registers

   c. ROM chips

   d. data buses

   e. RAM chips

5. Which of the following terms is the most closely related to main memory?

   a. nonvolatile

   b. permanent

   c. control unit

   d. temporary

   e. elephantine

Solutions: (1) c; (2) d; (3) c; (4) b; (5) d

SHORT-ANSWER QUESTIONS

1. List and describe the main factors that affect the processing power of a microcomputer.

2. What is the difference between a computer with closed architecture and one with open architecture?

3. What is the function of the ALU in a microcomputer system?

4. What would be a good indication that two computers are incompatible? Why is knowing this important to you?

5. What is the function of a bus in a microcomputer system? How might one bus be better than another?

6. What does the addressing scheme in a microcomputer system affect?

7. Describe why having more RAM in your computer (as opposed to less) is useful.

8. What is a machine cycle and how does it relate to the term *megahertz*? Why would a user be interested in a computer's megahertz rate?

9. What is a coprocessor and what can it be used for?

10. What led to the development of add-on memory boards?

PROJECTS

1. Research the current uses of and the latest advances in ROM technology. How do you think ROM technology will affect the way we currently use microcomputers?

2. Advances are made almost every day in microprocessor chip technology. What are some of the most recent advances? In what computers are these chips being used? How might these advances affect the way we currently use microcomputers? Research the latest advances by reviewing the most current computer magazines and periodicals.

3. Visit a well-equipped computer store and, with the help of a salesperson, decide what microcomputer might be the best one for you to use based on your processing requirements (if necessary, pick a hypothetical job and identify some probable processing requirements). Use the checklist on page 4.23 to describe the microcomputer you would choose and explain why. Compare this microcomputer to the others you were shown.

4. What does it mean for a microcomputer and related equipment to be "IBM compatible"? Look through some computer magazines and identify advertised microcomputer systems that are IBM compatible. What are their clock speeds? microprocessor model numbers and manufacturers? RAM capacities? register (often called *wordsize*) and data bus capacities? Do you think there are any risks involved in buying an IBM-compatible system instead of an IBM PC?

5. Look through magazines about Apple Macintosh computers and PCs or go to a computer store. Compare the Apple Quadra 950 microcomputer and the IBM PS/2 90 microcomputer according to:

    microprocessor model: _____ .

    clock speed (MHz): _____ .

    cache? (yes/no) _____ If yes, how much?

    _____

    RAM capacity: _____ (upgradable to:

    _____)

    uses extended memory? _____

    data bus capacity: _____

    local bus extension? _____

    register (wordsize) capacity: _____

    cost: _____

    Which computer appears to be more powerful? Based on what you know so far, which machine would you prefer?

Storage Hardware

A great deal of business has to do with keeping score, with record-keeping. Indeed, very few businesses can operate without keeping a running account of daily transactions: who owes what to whom, who collected what, when something is scheduled to happen, and so on. We have already described the fundamentals of the computer-based information system and how data is input and processed. Now let us consider how this computerized data is stored and retrieved.

PREVIEW

When you have completed this chapter, you will be able to:

▼ Describe the difference between primary and secondary storage, and how data is represented in each

▼ Explain what is meant by the data hierarchy

▼ Describe different types of files and file organization

▼ List three data storage and retrieval methods

▼ Describe the common computer storage devices

WHY IS THIS CHAPTER IMPORTANT?

*N*ot understanding the concept of computer storage is like not understanding the concept of a car's gasoline tank. Without using a gasoline tank, you'll get nowhere in your car because, of course, without the tank, you can't use gasoline. Similarly, if you don't use a storage device with your computer, you won't have the capability to store the data that will make your computer useful.

In this chapter we describe the different storage devices you should be familiar with to use a computer efficiently. We focus on how they work, as well as their speed and capacity.

Storage Fundamentals

As you learned in the previous chapter, the data you are working on—such as a document—is stored in RAM in an electrical state during processing. Because RAM exists through electricity, when you turn off the power to your computer, data in RAM disappears. Therefore, before you turn your microcomputer off, you must save your work onto a permanent storage device that stores data magnetically—such as a diskette or a hard disk—rather than electrically. When stored on a magnetic storage device, your data will remain intact even when the computer is turned off. (Optical storage, which we will cover later, is also an option.)

In general, data is stored in a computer system for three principal reasons.

1. *Current input data needs to be held for processing.* For example, daily sales data might be held in a temporary transaction file until it is processed at the end of the day to produce invoices.

2. *Some types of data are stored on a relatively permanent basis and retrieved as required during processing.* For example, to produce a customer invoice, you need data from the customer file: customer's name, address, billing instructions, and terms.

3. *Data is stored to be periodically updated.* For example, the accounts receivable file (reflecting what customers owe) needs to be updated to reflect the latest purchases.

In addition to all this data, the computer software instructions must be stored in a computer-usable form because a copy of these instructions must be placed into RAM from a storage device before processing can begin.

Before we describe the characteristics of the computer storage devices you will likely use in the business or professional environment, you must understand a few storage fundamentals, including:

1. The difference between primary and secondary storage

2. How data is represented in the data storage hierarchy

3. Different types of files

4. The general process of storing data on a storage device

5. Data storage and retrieval methods

Primary and Secondary Storage

The term **primary storage** (main memory) refers to the RAM of a computer, where both data and instructions are temporarily held for immediate access and use by the computer's microprocessor. Although the technology is changing, most primary storage is considered a **volatile** form of storage, meaning that the data and instructions are lost when the computer is turned off. **Secondary storage** (or **auxiliary storage**) is any storage device designed to retain data and instructions (programs) in a more permanent form. Secondary storage is **nonvolatile,** meaning that saved data and instructions remain intact when the computer is turned off.

The easiest way to differentiate between primary and secondary storage is to consider the reason data is placed in them. Data is placed in primary storage only when it is needed for processing. Data in secondary storage remains there until overwritten with new data or deleted, and it is accessed when needed. In very general terms, a secondary storage device can be thought of as a file cabinet. We store data there until we need it. Then we open the drawer, take out the appropriate folder (file), and place it on the top of our desk (primary storage, or RAM), where we work on it—perhaps writing a few things in it or throwing away a few papers. When we are finished with the file, we take it off the desktop (out of primary storage) and return it to the cabinet (secondary storage).

Data Hierarchy

No matter what size or shape computer you work with, you will be working with files. But before we can put data files in their proper perspective, we need to examine the levels of data, known as the **data storage hierarchy.** If you look at Figure 1, at the top of the data hierarchy you'll see the term *file*. A **file** is made up of a group of related records. A **record** is defined as a collection of related fields, and a **field** is defined as a collection of related characters, or bytes, of data. Finally, a byte, or character, of data, as you have learned, is made up of 8 bits. (A bit is 1 or 0.)

To illustrate this concept, let's look at a sample inventory file for a sporting goods store (Figure 2). This particular inventory *file* is made up of a group of *records,* one record for each item in inventory, such as snorkels. Each record contains the same number of *fields* such as: (1) product number, (2) product description, (3) unit price, and (4) quantity on hand. Each field contains a number of *characters,* such as the letter A in the product number. In turn, each character is made up of 8 bits, at the low end of the data hierarchy.

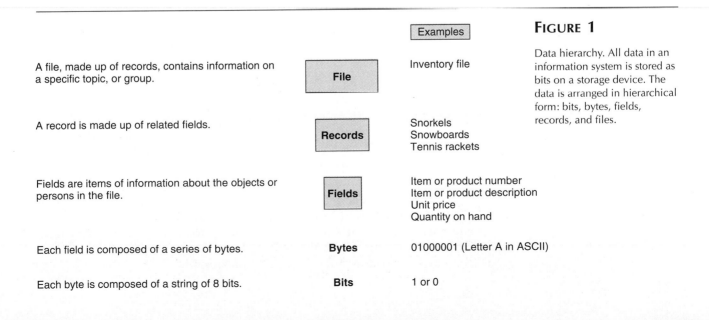

		Examples
A file, made up of records, contains information on a specific topic, or group.	**File**	Inventory file
A record is made up of related fields.	**Records**	Snorkels Snowboards Tennis rackets
Fields are items of information about the objects or persons in the file.	**Fields**	Item or product number Item or product description Unit price Quantity on hand
Each field is composed of a series of bytes.	**Bytes**	01000001 (Letter A in ASCII)
Each byte is composed of a string of 8 bits.	**Bits**	1 or 0

FIGURE 1

Data hierarchy. All data in an information system is stored as bits on a storage device. The data is arranged in hierarchical form: bits, bytes, fields, records, and files.

FIGURE 2

The inventory file contains product records, such as the record for snorkels. Each record contains fields: product number, product description, unit price, and quantity on hand. Each field is made up of characters, or bytes, each of which comprises 8 bits.

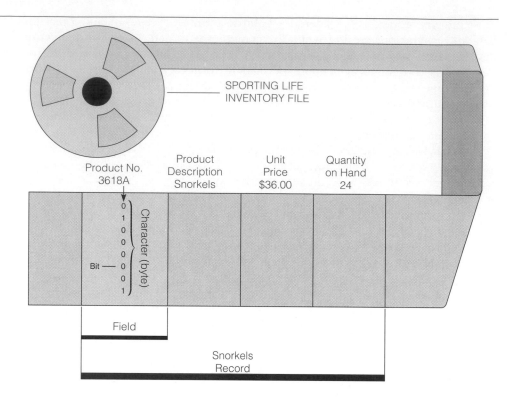

Types of Files

Up to this point, we've described various types of files in general terms, such as master files (used to permanently store data for access and updating) and transaction files (used to temporarily hold data for processing). Now that we've described how data is represented with bits and bytes and how the data hierarchy is structured, we can get a "bit" more detailed in our description of what a file is, what it does, and where it's kept.

Files generally fall into two categories:

1. Files containing data (often referred to generically as *data files*)
2. Files containing software instructions (often referred to generically as *program files*)

Data files, in turn, tend to be categorized according to how they are used (Figure 3):

1. Transaction file   4. Output file
2. Master file   5. History file
3. Report file   6. Backup file

The amount of time that data needs to be stored and the purpose of storing the data vary substantially, depending on the processing objectives. These objectives determine what type of file you'll be storing data in.

You'll recall that some data is input into computer-usable form and then retained only until it is time to process. This type of data is referred to as *transaction data,* and it is stored in an input **transaction file.**

Some data is stored in computer-usable form for lengthy periods of time, after which it is used for retrieval and is updated during processing. A file containing this type of data is referred to as a **master file.**

FIGURE 3

Types of files. How the file is used determines what type of file it is.

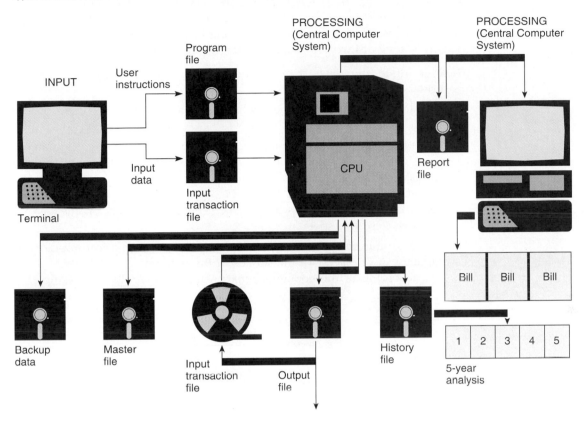

In large computer systems, the volume of reports to be produced is so immense that a special, smaller computer system is set up just to control and coordinate the printing of reports. This is often true of major utility companies that produce millions of customer bills and statements each month. To make this process easier, the data necessary to produce the reports is captured in a **report file,** which is then transferred to the special computer system for printing after it has been processed in the main computer.

Many computer software applications are designed to produce data as output to be used by another program or application at a later time. (An application is usually a group of related programs, such as a payroll application consisting of 14 programs.) A file created for this purpose is referred to as an **output file** at the time it is produced. However, it becomes an *input transaction file* when it is read into another program for processing.

Many organizations find it useful to produce reports that require analysis of data on past company operations. A file created to collect data for long-term reporting purposes is referred to as a **history file.**

Backup files are copies of other types of files that are made to ensure that data and programs will not be lost if the original files are damaged or destroyed. (Users should always remember to back up their files!) Occasionally data is extracted from backup files to use like data in historical files.

Program files are simply instructions stored on disk or tape. They are usually controlled by the computer operations group and maintained in libraries.

How Is Data Stored?

To store data for later use you need two things: a storage *medium* (plural form = *media*)—the type of material on which data is recorded—and a storage device. The storage device records the data onto the medium, where the data is held until needed. The process of recording data onto media, which is coordinated by software, involves four basic steps (Figure 4):

1. After input, the data to be recorded by a storage device temporarily resides in RAM.

2. Software instructions determine where the data is to be recorded on the storage medium.

3. The controller board for the storage device positions the recording mechanism over the appropriate location on the storage medium. For storage on disk, this mechanism is referred to in most cases as a **read/write head** because it can both "read" (accept) magnetic spots and convert them to electrical impulses and "write" (enter) the spots on the disk; it can also erase the spots.

4. The recording mechanism is activated and converts electrical impulses to magnetic spots placed on the surface of the medium as required to record data according to the coding scheme being used (ASCII, for example).

FIGURE 4

Data recording process. (1) Data enters RAM from an external device, such as a keyboard. (2) Software instructions determine where the data is to be recorded on the disk. (3) The data goes to the disk controller board. (4) From here it flows to the read/write head in the disk storage device and is recorded on the storage medium.

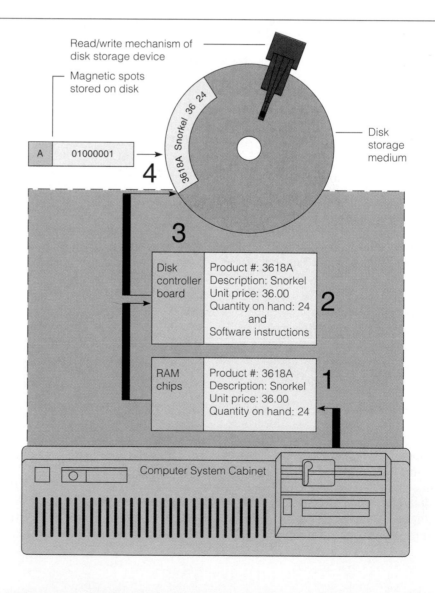

Data Storage and Retrieval Methods

Most of us read a novel from the first page to the end of the book in sequence because we have an interest in following the story in the order that the author intended. However, in a catalog you may wish to locate the information for just a single item. It would take much more time to locate the page you desired if you started at the beginning and read all the pages instead of looking up the item in the index. The same kind of principle applies to the storage and retrieval of data in computer-usable form.

In most cases, when a file cabinet is first organized, the file folders are placed in each drawer in a certain order. For a customer file, the folders are placed into drawers in sequential order by customer number or customer name. If new customers are added later, their folders are inserted into the correct location between the existing folders. When you need to retrieve data from the file cabinet, the way you get it depends on what needs to be done. For example, if you are going to prepare a report on customer status, you will probably review each folder in order. However, if a specific customer calls and asks about the status of one invoice, you will go to the file cabinet and locate and remove that one customer's folder.

In the computer-based environment, a file cabinet is usually thought of as a database (a collection of interrelated files stored together), a file drawer is thought of as a file (master file, transaction file, history file, and so forth), and a folder is thought of as a record. The three principal methods of storing and retrieving the data are based on three types of file organization:

1. *Sequential*—meaning that records are stored and retrieved in sequential order.

2. *Direct,* or *relative* (also called *random*)—meaning that records are not stored or retrieved in any special order.

3. *Indexed*—a combination of the preceding two types, whereby records are stored in sequential order but with an index that allows both sequential and direct retrieval.

Each of these three approaches to computer-based data storage and retrieval is suited to different applications and processing requirements. For most users, the selection of a storage method has been left up to the technical professionals involved in developing the software. However, if you find yourself involved in a project where the requirements for new software are being specified, be sure you tell the information system specialists how you need to store and retrieve data. Users' processing requirements should be used as the basis for selecting the file storage and retrieval method.

Single-File: Sequential File Organization

Sequential storage and retrieval (Figure 5) is ideal for situations in which most of the records in a file need to be accessed for processing—such as producing payroll (because everyone gets a check) or preparing a comprehensive inventory report by part number. In this approach, records are recorded and stored sequentially, one after the other, in ascending or descending order. Records are retrieved in the sequence in which they were recorded on the storage media. They must be accessed (retrieved) one after the other; the user cannot jump around among records. All storage devices support sequential file organization.

FIGURE 5

Sequential file organization. Records are recorded in sequence and accessed one at a time, in the order in which they were recorded. As you can see from this figure, if an airline reservations and flight information system used sequential storage on magnetic tape, it would not be able to get the information it needs very quickly, because the computer would have to read through all the records on the tape prior to the record with the needed information. Because of this disadvantage, such a system would instead use direct access on magnetic disk storage.

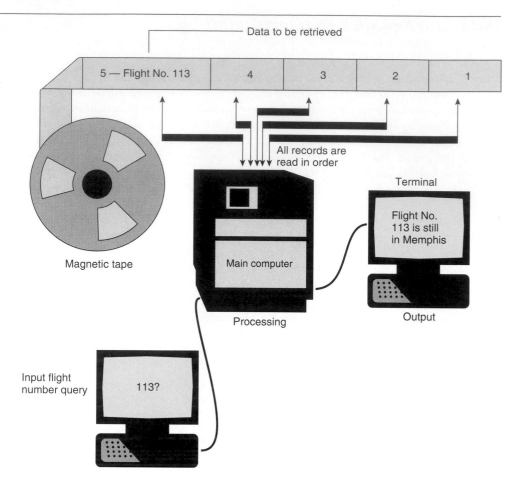

Any Order: Direct (Random) or Relative File Organization

Data in a **direct file,** or a relative file, is recorded and stored according to its disk address or to its relative position within the file. The data is retrieved by the **direct access method**—also called *random access.* This data retrieval method is best suited to situations in which only a few records in a file need to be accessed at one time, and in no particular sequence (Figure 6). Airline reservations systems rely heavily on this method, which uses on-line input/output devices. Because there is no predictable pattern in which customers call to inquire about the status of flights, the individual records containing the status of the flights need to be stored in a fashion whereby they can be directly retrieved in any order—meaning that all the records in front of the record containing status data on your flight No. 113 from Memphis to Cincinnati do not have to be read first.

There are a number of ways to access records directly in no particular order. The most common approach is to use a unique element of data—called a **key field** or **key**—contained in each record as a basis for identifying the record and for determining which storage location on the disk the record should be stored in or retrieved from. To determine where to store a record so it can be retrieved directly, the computer uses a formula and performs a mathematical calculation—called *hashing*—on the key field value. (Hashing is a type of **algorithm,** meaning a problem-solving rule or formula.) This computer operation translates the record's key field directly into an address or a relative location. Obviously, no

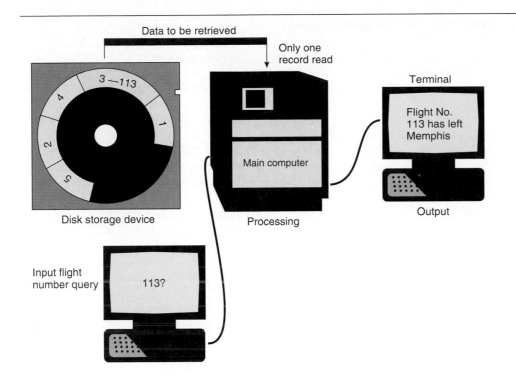

FIGURE 6

Direct, or relative, file organization. Records are recorded, stored, and retrieved in any order. The computer performs a mathematical operation (hashing) on each record's key field to determine where to place that record on the storage medium. A key field contains a unique number or unique group of characters.

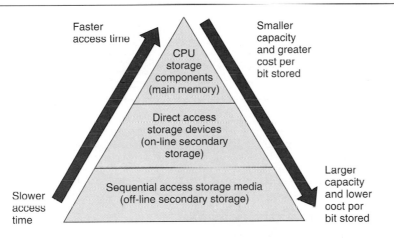

FIGURE 7

Storage methods: Speed and cost. CPU storage components (main memory) generally have the fastest access times, the smallest storage capacity, and the highest cost per bit stored. Secondary storage includes all direct access storage devices and sequential access storage devices.

two key fields should be given the same address on the disk; hashing prevents this by using a mathematical formula that (almost always) produces a unique number.

The direct access storage and retrieval method is ideal for applications like an airline reservations system or the computerized telephone information service, where records need to be retrieved only one at a time and there is no fixed pattern or sequence to the requests for data and records. However, this method cannot be used with magnetic tape, and it is very inefficient in situations that require accessing all records in sequential order: Because the records are not stored in any particular order, following the key sequence in order to retrieve them may involve jumping back and forth around the storage medium, which takes too much time.

In general, sequential storage and retrieval is appropriate for updating master files on a regular basis, inputting a relatively large amount of data. (Sequential storage and retrieval is often used in batch input and processing.) Direct storage and retrieval is better used for irregular updates with only a small volume of input (Figure 7).

Indexed File Organization

In a payroll system, all records are usually accessed in order of employee number—that is, sequentially—when payroll checks are produced. However, occasionally a clerk in the payroll department may need to check on the status of a particular employee. In this case, processing the records sequentially just to access data for a single employee is impractical. To be able to access stored data in *either* a sequential *or* a direct fashion, a third storage and retrieval methodology was developed that uses **indexed file organization** (Figure 8). This method is used almost exclusively with direct access microcomputer storage devices to provide maximum flexibility for processing and has proven to be the most flexible for business applications.

In this approach, each file contains an index of the records stored in it. This index functions somewhat like the index at the back of a book. When you want to look something up in the book, you check the index for the item you want and locate its page number. In the case of computer file storage, the computer checks the file's index, which contains the record's address—location—on the disk. It's also possible to create more than one index for a file, which allows the file to be accessed using different key fields. For example, at least two indexes may be created for a personnel master file: an index by the primary

FIGURE 8

Indexed file organization. Records are stored sequentially but with an index that allows both sequential and direct, random access.

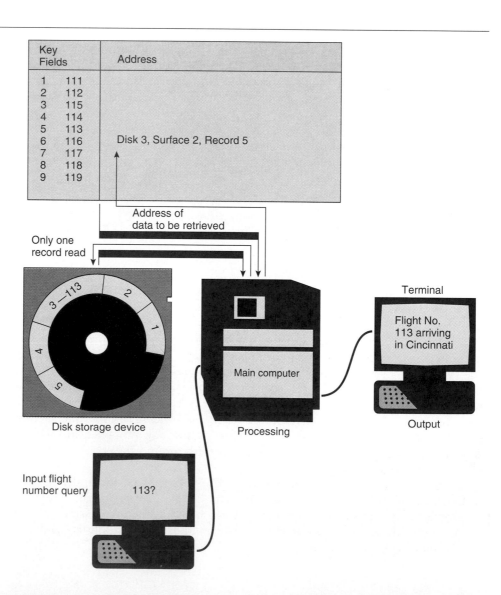

key field (employee number) and a second index by, say, social security number. The first index could be used to provide sequential or direct access by employee number. The second index could be used to process the file to inquire about a specific employee by social security number.

In general, indexed file organization, which cannot be done on tape, allows efficient regularly scheduled processing of large batches of data and irregular updates with only a small amount of input. However, indexed storage and retrieval is slower than direct access, and the hardware and software needed for indexed file organization are more expensive than for sequential or direct access organization. In addition, it makes less efficient use of storage space.

Tape Storage Devices

Magnetic tape is a plastic tape (Mylar) coated with magnetizable iron oxide. The tape is ½-inch wide and is produced in a variety of lengths ranging from 200 to 3,600 feet—the latter weighs about 4 pounds and has a reel about 10½ inches in diameter. Since tape can be carried around, it can be used to easily transport huge amounts of data.

Recording Data on Magnetic Tape

Data is recorded across the width of a magnetic tape in *frames*—rows of magnetic spots; *tracks* or *channels* run the length of the tape. The computer records character codes by writing magnetic spots (1s) and leaving spaces (0s—no magnetic spots) across the frame. Among the coding schemes used on magnetic tape are ASCII and EBCDIC. EBCDIC for standard magnetic tapes involves nine tracks that run the full length of the tape (Figure 9). The nine positions include room for 8 character bits and 1 parity bit. The capacity, or storage density, of a magnetic tape is measured in bits per inch (bpi), or frames per inch.

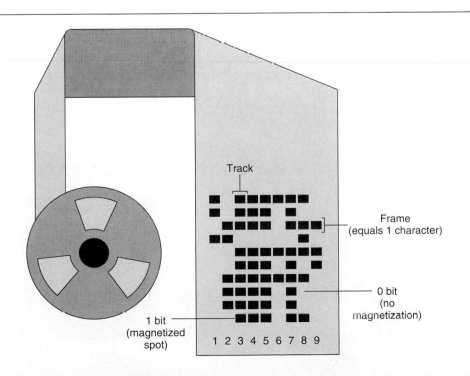

FIGURE 9

This figure shows how characters are recorded in frames across magnetic tape using the 9-track EBCDIC code. The 9 tracks include room for 8 bits plus 1 parity bit.

Track

Frame
(equals 1 character)

0 bit
(no
magnetization)

1 bit
(magnetized
spot)

1 2 3 4 5 6 7 8 9

The Tape Drive Mechanism

Figure 10 shows the components of a magnetic tape storage device. The file reel of tape is placed on the left spindle and locked in place so that it does not come loose as it spins at high speed. The tape is fed through a *drive capstan,* a small cylindrical pulley used to regulate the speed of the tape. Several feet of tape are used as slack and then the tape is run through another capstan called a *stop capstan.* Then the tape is run through the read/write head assembly and the right half of the tape mechanism, which is a mirror image of the left side. The stop capstans work together to hold the tape still long enough for data to be written or read. An empty take-up tape reel is used to temporarily hold the tape after it has been read or written on. The tape moves at speeds approaching 200 inches per second. This translates into an ability to record or read data at an average speed of from 100,000 to 1,250,000 characters per second.

Magnetic Tape Processing Characteristics

Magnetic tape is ideal for applications that require only sequential access to data. Many public utilities still use magnetic tape for storing their enormous customer master files. A file with millions of customer records could easily use close to 100 reels of magnetic tape. Because of the number of tapes to be handled, many companies hire a librarian to manage them. A special room, called a *library,* is often set aside to store the tapes, and procedures are established to control their use.

To ensure that the correct version of a tape is used for processing, an *external label* (Figure 11) is placed on the tape reel and an *internal label* is recorded on the tape magnetically. The internal label is often referred to as a *header label* and is examined by a program before processing begins to ensure it is the correct tape.

FIGURE 10

(b) Magnetic tape storage devices are used by many large companies to provide virtually unlimited storage capacity. (a) This simplified drawing shows the workings of a magnetic tape drive.

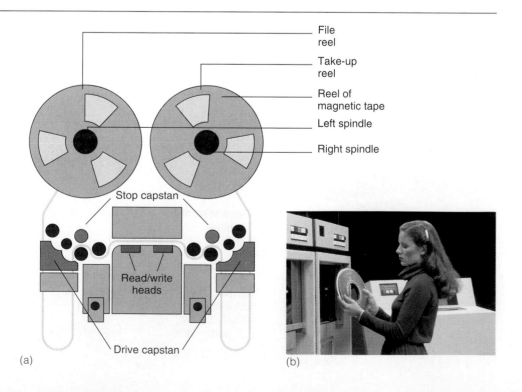

File reel

Take-up reel

Reel of magnetic tape

Left spindle

Right spindle

Stop capstan

Read/write heads

Drive capstan

(a)

(b)

Tapes are protected from being accidentally overwritten by the use of a *file protection ring,* a plastic ring inserted into the back of a tape reel (Figure 11). A tape can be written on or erased only when the ring is in place, so it's the *absence* of the ring that protects the file from changes. When a new master file is created and the tape is stored in the library, the ring is immediately removed to prevent the accidental reuse of the tape.

Limitations of Magnetic Tape

Magnetic tape has two major drawbacks. First, the data recorded on tape cannot be practically altered—that is, it cannot be updated or changed in place. When records need to be changed, added in sequence, or deleted, a completely new tape must be created. Second, the data is recorded on the tape sequentially and can be accessed only sequentially. These limitations make magnetic tape less attractive for applications that require an update-in-place capability and access other than sequential. As the cost of direct access storage devices (disks) dropped, magnetic tape began to lose its popularity. However, despite its limitations, magnetic tape is still used widely today in mini-computer and mainframe computer systems. It remains an ideal medium for making portable backup copies of data stored on disk to enable businesses to recover from a data center disaster.

Direct Access Storage for Microcomputers

The Apple II and Tandy-Radio Shack (TRS-80) Model I personal computer systems were among the first to be made available to the public (1977). These two systems—as well as many of the others that entered the marketplace shortly thereafter—initially offered only cassette-tape storage devices. These devices, much like a personal tape recorder, proved to be remarkably slow and awkward to use. As the microcomputer began to move from the home into the business environment, the need for fast direct access storage and retrieval became a significant issue.

This problem was solved when IBM introduced the diskette as a direct access storage medium. As a result, the microcomputer has dramatically expanded its role in information processing—and continues to do so.

Diskettes

The **diskette,** or **floppy diskette,** is a *direct access storage medium*—meaning that data can be stored and retrieved in no particular sequence. Diskettes are made of a special plastic that can be coated and easily magnetized. Diskettes are often referred to as "floppy" because they are made of flexible material. As Figure 12 shows, the disk is enclosed in a protective jacket—either paper or plastic—lined with a soft material specially treated to reduce friction and static. The disk jacket has four openings:

1. Hub
2. Data access area

FIGURE 11

(a) External labels for a magnetic tape reel. (b) Tapes are protected from accidental changes by the use of a file protection ring that must be inserted in the center of the tape reel before the tape can be recorded on or erased.

(a) External Labels

SUBJECT		DATE WRITTEN
FROM RUN #	INPUT TO RUN #	OPERATOR
REEL NO. OF	JOB NO.	RETENTION

MASTER

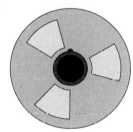

(b) File Protection Ring

File protection ring in place on tape reel

3. Write/protect notch

4. Index hole

To store and retrieve data from a diskette, you must place it into a **disk drive** (Figure 13), which contains special mechanical components for storing and retrieving data.

The *hub* of the diskette is the round opening in the center. When the diskette is placed into the disk drive, the hub fits over a mount, or spindle, in the drive. In some IBM PCs, before you can access any data on the diskette, you must close the **disk drive gate,** or **door,** after you insert the diskette. The act of closing the disk drive gate moves a lever over the drive and clamps the diskette over the spindle of the drive mechanism. Many personal computers

---

FIGURE 12

Diskettes were developed to replace cassette tape as a data storage medium for use with microcomputers. Diskettes provide fast direct access capabilities. IBM PCs and some IBM-compatible microcomputers still use (a) the 5¼-inch diskette; the Macintosh line of microcomputers, as well as most portable IBM-compatible computers and IBM PS/2 series microcomputers, use (b) the 3½-inch diskette.

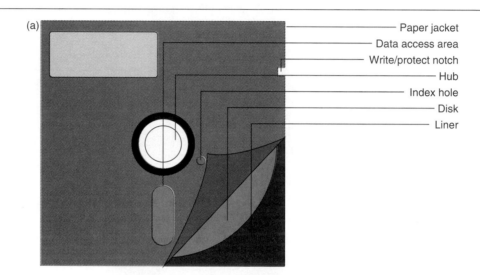

(a)
— Paper jacket
— Data access area
— Write/protect notch
— Hub
— Index hole
— Disk
— Liner

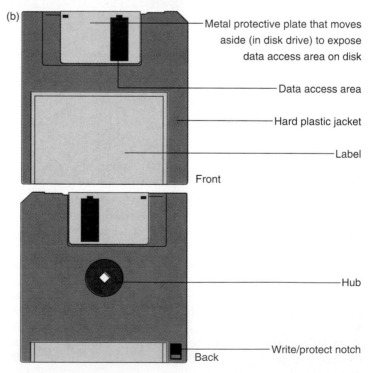

(b)

Metal protective plate that moves aside (in disk drive) to expose data access area on disk

Data access area

Hard plastic jacket

Label

Front

Hub

Write/protect notch

Back

FIGURE 13

(a) These cutaway illustrations show the main parts of a 5¼-inch disk drive and a 3½-inch disk drive for diskettes. (b) Inserting a 5¼-inch diskette in a disk drive. (c) Inserting a 3½-inch diskette in a disk drive.

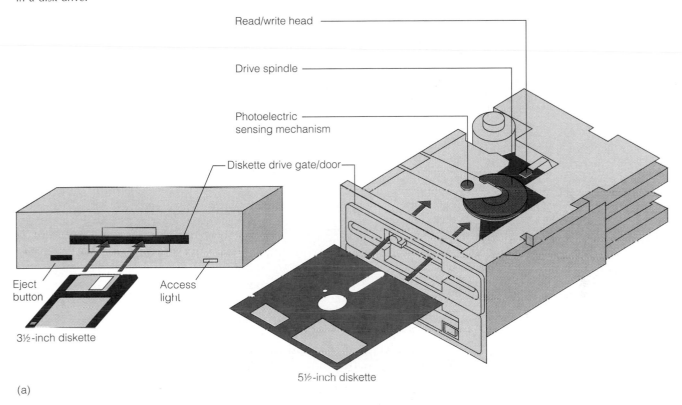

Read/write head

Drive spindle

Photoelectric sensing mechanism

Diskette drive gate/door

Eject button

Access light

3½-inch diskette

5½-inch diskette

(a)

(b)

(c)

today don't have drive doors; the diskette is simply pushed into the drive until it clicks in place. An access light goes on when the disk is in use, and, with many microcomputers, you can eject the disk by pressing the eject button. (In microcomputers without eject buttons, the user simply opens the disk drive door and pulls out the diskette.)

When data is stored and retrieved, the diskette spins inside its jacket, and the read/write head on the actuator arm is clamped on the surface in the **data access area** of the disk. Most disk drives are equipped with two read/write heads so that the top and bottom surfaces of the diskette can be accessed simultaneously. The read/write heads are moved back and forth over the data access area in small increments to retrieve or record data as needed.

Just inside the disk drive unit, a small mechanism checks to determine if the user has covered the disk's **write/protect notch.** If the notch is covered, a switch is activated that prevents the read/write head from being able to touch the surface of the diskette, which means no data can be recorded (Figure 14). This is a security measure: covering the write/protect notch prevents accidental erasure or overwriting of data.

The *index hole* in the jacket is positioned over a photoelectric sensing mechanism in the disk drive. As the diskette spins in the jacket (when data is being recorded or retrieved), the hole (or holes—some diskettes have more than one) in the diskette repeatedly passes over the hole in the jacket, is sensed, and activates a timing switch. The timing activity is critical because this is how the mechanism determines which portion of the diskette is over or under the read/write heads. The diskette spins at a fixed speed of about 300 revolutions per minute (RPM).

Diskette Storage Capacities and Sizes

The **byte** is the unit of measure used most often to determine the capacity of a storage device used with any type of computer (see repeat of Table 1 from Chapter 4). The capacity of a diskette does not necessarily depend on its size. A number of factors affect how much data can be stored on a disk, including:

1. Whether the diskette stores data on only one side (single-sided) or both sides (double-sided)

2. Whether the disk drive is equipped with read/write heads for both the top and the bottom surfaces of the diskette

---

FIGURE 14

(a) The write/protect notch of the 5¹⁄₄-inch disk on the left is open and, therefore, data can be written to the disk. The notch of the 5¹⁄₄-inch disk on the right, however, is covered (the user has put tape over it). Data cannot be written to this disk. (b) Data cannot be written on the 3¹⁄₂-inch disk on the right because the small black piece of plastic is not covering the window in the lower left corner. Plastic covers the window of the 3¹⁄₂-inch disk on the left, so data can be written on this disk.

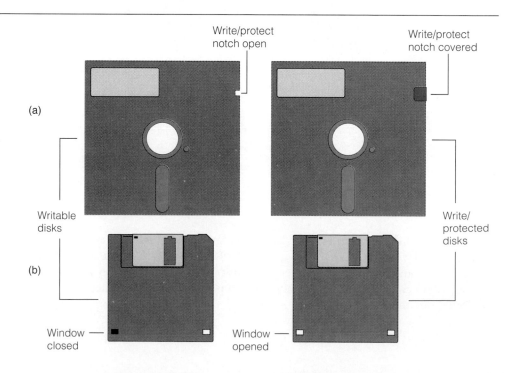

TABLE 1

Units of Measurement for Disk Storage

Bit	A binary digit; 0 or 1	Megabyte (MB)	1,024,000 bytes
Byte	8 bits, or 1 character	Gigabyte (GB)	1,024,000,000 bytes
Kilobyte (K, or KB)	1,024 bytes	Terabyte (TB)	1,024,000,000,000 bytes

3. What the data-recording density is (the number of bits that can be stored per inch)

4. What the track density is (the number of tracks per inch in which data is recorded)

The first diskettes were **single-sided.** But as the need to store more data became a significant concern in the business community, technology produced the **double-sided disk,** which is capable of storing twice the amount of data as a comparable single-sided disk. To take advantage of a double-sided disk, however, you must have a computer with a double-sided floppy disk drive. Double-sided disk drives are equipped with read/write heads for both the top and the bottom surfaces of a disk. This allows data to be read from or written on both surfaces simultaneously. Disk capacity also depends on the recording density capabilities of the disk drive.

Recording density refers to the number of bits per inch (bpi) of data that can be written onto the surface of the disk. Disks and drives are typically rated as having one of three recording densities:

1. **Single-density**

2. **Double-density**

3. **Quadruple-density** (often referred to as *quad-density,* or *high-density*)

The specifications for the exact number of bits per inch for each recording density vary from one manufacturer to another. Disk manufacturers use the recording density designation as a measure of the maximum bpi their diskettes can reliably be expected to store.

A double-sided, double-density 5¼-inch diskette (labeled "DS, DD," or "2S/2D") has a storage capacity of 360 K. The 3½-inch diskettes for the IBM PS/2 series of microcomputers hold from 720 K (single-density) to 1.44 MB (double-density).

The final factor affecting disk capacity is the track density. As pictured in Figure 15, data is recorded on disks in circular bands—similar to grooves on a phonograph record—referred to as **tracks.** The read/write heads are designed to move in small increments across the data access area of the disk to find the appropriate track. Common **track densities** in use today are 48 tracks per inch (tpi), 96 tpi, and 135 tpi. The recording surface of a 5¼-inch disk is slightly less than 1 inch; therefore, there are 40 or 80 usable tracks per inch in most cases.

The use of 5¼-inch diskettes by IBM in their personal computer system in 1981 led to the adoption of this size as the microcomputer industry standard. However, since the Apple Macintosh introduced the 3½-inch diskette and disk drive in 1984 and IBM switched to this size in 1987 in its PS/2 microcomputer systems, the standard has changed. Although they are smaller, the 3½-inch disks are capable of storing more data than 5¼-inch diskettes, and they are also less susceptible to damage because they are covered by a hard plastic jacket rather than a paper jacket. (The care of diskettes is discussed later in this chapter.)

FIGURE 15

Tracks are circular bands on disks on which data is recorded. The tracks are separated by small gaps and are divided into equal areas called sectors. Tracks and sectors are used to determine addresses of fields of data.

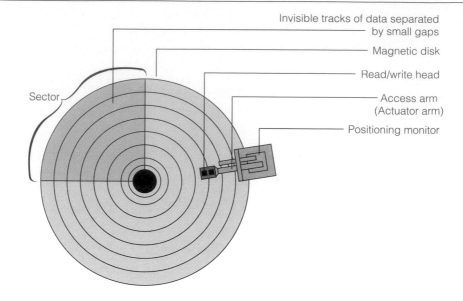

The size and the capacity of the diskette you use depends on the characteristics of the disk drive in your microcomputer system. Some disk drives are intended to store and retrieve data from high-density diskettes, whereas others have been designed to be used with low-density diskettes. Likewise, 3½-inch disk drives are to be used only with 3½-inch diskettes. Don't try putting a 3½-inch diskette in a 5¼-inch disk drive! You could damage the read/write mechanism inside the drive.

Sectors

Typically a disk is divided into eight or nine **sectors,** or equal, wedge-shaped areas used for storage reference purposes (Figure 15). The point at which a sector intersects a track is used by systems software to reference the data location; the track number indicates where to position the read/write head, and the sector number indicates where to activate the read/write head as the disk spins.

Disks and drives are identified as being either hard-sectored or soft-sectored. *Hard-sectored* disks always have the same number and size of sectors, which are fixed by the manufacturer. Today most microcomputer systems use soft-sectored disks. *Soft-sectored disks* are marked magnetically by the user's computer system during a process called **formatting,** or **initializing,** which determines the size and the number of sectors on the disk. Since your diskettes must be adapted to the particular microcomputer and software you are using, you format these diskettes yourself. This is easily done using only a few simple commands on the computer.

Before you proceed to the next section, you need to know how to care for your diskettes—abuse means lost data. Figure 16 shows 5¼-inch diskettes; however, just because the 3½-inch diskettes have hard jackets instead of paper ones does not mean that they cannot be damaged, too!

Access Time

The responsiveness of your computer depends to a great extent on the time it takes to locate the instructions or data being sought and then to load a copy

FIGURE 16

Handle with care! This illustration shows how to avoid disk damage.

into RAM. The term **access time** refers to the average speed with which this is done. The access time of your computer's disk drive is determined by adding up the time it takes to perform each of the following activities:

1. Positioning the read/write heads over the proper track (the time it takes to do this is called the *seek time*)

2. Waiting for the disk to revolve until the correct sector is under or over the read/write heads (this is called *rotational delay,* or *latency*)

3. Placing the read/write head(s) in contact with the disks

4. Transferring the data from the disk into the computer's RAM (at a speed called the *data transfer rate*)

The average access time for diskettes ranges from 150 milliseconds (150/1000 of a second) to 300 milliseconds, depending on the operating characteristics of the drive mechanism. This may not seem like very long, but access time can be a major performance factor for the following reasons: (1) Large applications software packages keep only a portion of the instructions in RAM at one time and must retrieve additional instructions from disk periodically to perform specific tasks. (2) The processing of large files is done only a few records at a time, so a substantial amount of time can be spent going back and forth to the disk to retrieve records.

Hard Disks

The introduction of high-capacity microcomputer **hard disks**—which can store from 20 or 40 MB to more than a gigabyte, or 1,000 MB—solved two serious problems related to the limited storage capacity of diskettes. First, as a business begins to use microcomputers extensively, the amount of software it acquires and data it collects tends to grow substantially. As a result, the number of diskettes it needs to handle increases dramatically. It is not uncommon for one user alone to have a library of 100 or more diskettes. Second, the largest file that can be accessed at one time is limited to the capacity of RAM and the capacity of the storage medium. So, if the capacity of a diskette is 360 K, no file larger than that can be stored on the disk or worked with in RAM.

Hard disks can store much larger files; for example, certain businesses may need to set up an inventory system on a microcomputer that calls for working with a 45,000-item inventory master file. And the 150-page report that didn't fit on one diskette can easily fit on a hard disk. Of course, you could have stored the report in sections in separate files on different diskettes, but that would have been very inconvenient. You would have had to continually swap diskettes, inserting them and ejecting them, to work on your report. The hard disk spares you that trouble.

In some hard disk systems, data is stored in the same way as it is on diskettes. A series of tracks are divided into sectors when the disk is formatted. As their name suggests, hard disks are made out of a rigid substance that is capable of storing a greater amount of data than the soft material used for diskettes. Hard disk drives for microcomputers (Figure 17) can be *internal* (built into the computer cabinet and nonremovable) or *external* (outside the computer cabinet and connected to it by a short cable).

Just a few years ago, one 20 MB hard disk provided enough storage for most users (Figure 18). Today, because of storage-hungry graphical software interfaces (which use pictures and menus to lead users through command options), networking software, and more sophisticated software applications and systems software, hard disk storage capacities of 300 MB and larger are becoming increasingly commonplace and necessary. Hard disk drives can store and retrieve data much faster than can diskette drives. Whereas the average access time for diskettes is approximately 300 milliseconds, the average access time for hard disks ranges from 16–70 milliseconds.

Hard disk units have become increasingly smaller while achieving higher storage capacities. The most popular units today use 3½-inch disks; some units still use 5¼-inch disks. Newer hard disk drives use platters that are 2.5, 1.8, or even 1.3 inches in diameter. (The 1.3 inch, 21 MB, 1 ounce Kittyhawk microdisk is about the size of a half dollar. It also uses sensing technology to stop reading/writing if dropped, enhancing its portability and preventing data loss. These tiny hard disk drives will be used in hand-held computers, because they are much lighter and smaller and less power-hungry than 5¼- and 3½-inch hard disk drives.)

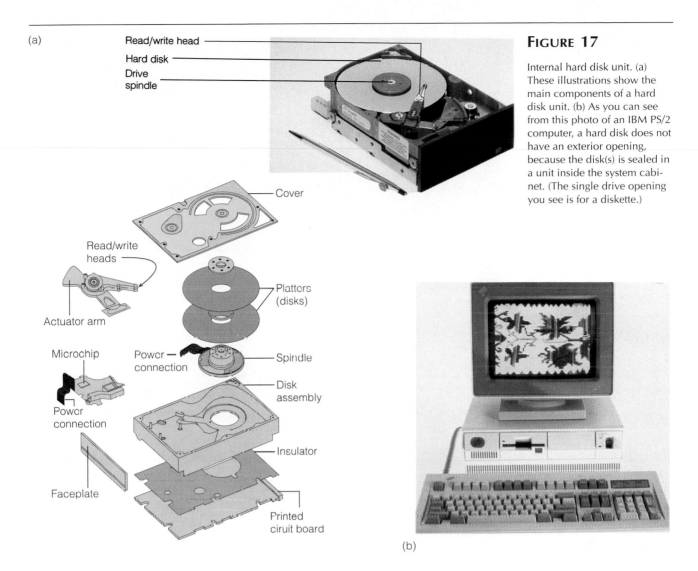

(a)

Read/write head
Hard disk
Drive spindle

Cover

Read/write heads

Actuator arm

Microchip

Power connection

Power connection

Faceplate

Platters (disks)

Spindle

Disk assembly

Insulator

Printed ciruit board

(b)

FIGURE 17

Internal hard disk unit. (a) These illustrations show the main components of a hard disk unit. (b) As you can see from this photo of an IBM PS/2 computer, a hard disk does not have an exterior opening, because the disk(s) is sealed in a unit inside the system cabinet. (The single drive opening you see is for a diskette.)

FIGURE 18

The use of hard disk units on microcomputers has greatly increased their ability to deal with large amounts of data at one time. For example, one 60 MB hard disk holds the same amount of data as 56 double-sided, double-density diskettes.

One double-spaced page of text = 2 K

One DS/DD diskette = 360 K or 180 pages

One high-density diskette = 720 K or 360 pages

One hard disk = 60 MB or 30,000 pages

FIGURE 19

This 1½-inch hard disk drive can be inserted in the computer's system unit to provide the user with high-capacity storage.

FIGURE 20

Hardcard. This hardcard works like a hard disk but plugs into an expansion slot inside the microcomputer cabinet.

The initial 5¼-inch disk drives were approximately 3½ inches high, whereas the new disk drives are just over 1½ inches high; this means that much more disk storage capacity can be put in the same space (Figure 19). Two or more diskette drives can fit where only one used to fit, and two or more hard disk units can occupy the space that one did. This type of configuration—the result of the *miniaturization* trend—provides a powerful system in a small work space.

The alternative to replacing a diskette drive or taking up desk space with an external hard disk drive is to buy a **hardcard** (Figure 20), a circuit board with a disk that plugs into an expansion slot inside the computer. Hardcards store between 40 MB and 240 MB of data. Hard cards are handy for users with no room for additional standard hard disk drives in their computers but with a need for increased storage capacity.

Hard disks have the following characteristics:

1. They are rigid metal platters connected to a central spindle.

2. The entire disk unit (disks and read/write heads) is placed in a permanently sealed container.

3. Air that flows through the container is filtered to prevent contamination.

4. The disks are rotated at very high speed (usually around 3,600 RPM; floppy disks rotate at about 300 RPM).

These disk drives can have four or more (often eight) disk platters in a sealed unit. In most of these disk units (which are often called *Winchester disk drives*), the read/write heads never touch the surfaces of the disks. Instead, they are designed to float from .5 to 1.25 millionths of an inch from the disk surface; because of this characteristic, the design is often referred to as a *flying head* design. Because the heads float so closely to the sensitive disks, any contamination—such as a dust particle or a hair—can cause a *head crash,* also referred to as a *disk crash,* which destroys some or all of the data on the disk. This sensitivity is the reason why hard disk units are assembled under sterile conditions.

Disk Cartridges

Removable hard **disk cartridges** (Figure 21) are an alternative to regular hard disks as a form of secondary storage. Whereas hard disks remain inside the computer or the external disk drive, disk cartridges can be removed and replaced easily. The cartridges usually contain one or two platters enclosed in a hard plastic case that is inserted into the disk drive, much like a music cassette tape. The capacity of these cartridges ranges from 20 MB up to 1.2 GB.

There are many reasons to choose a removable disk drive over a fixed internal hard disk drive. A hard drive has a fixed storage capacity. Once it's full, that's it. With a removable hard disk drive, you just pop a full cartridge out and pop an empty one in. And you can also use cartridges for back-up, instead of a stack of floppy disks or lots of tape. Removable disk cartridges are also handy for transporting large files.

Removable disk drives are available built in on certain microcomputers or as external units that can be hooked up to the computer.

Optical Storage

Because they offer practical solutions to large-scale storage requirements, optical storage technologies are increasingly becoming a rival of magnetic storage. **Optical storage technologies** involve the use of a high-power laser beam to pack information densely on a removable disk (Figure 22).

Optical storage technologies offer users a number of advantages. The primary advantage is storage density. You can fit a lot more data on an optical disk than you can on a comparably sized magnetic disk. Because lasers can be focused with such precision, the tracks recorded on an optical disk are much closer together than those recorded on a magnetic disk. Also, the amount of space required to record an optical bit is much less than that required to record a magnetic bit. As a result, removable optical disk storage capacities range from 128 MB to more than 1 GB. Another advantage of optical storage is that the media on which data is stored is much less susceptible to deterioration or contamination than magnetic recording media. The reason for this durability is that nothing touches the optical disk's surface except for a beam of light. Finally, optical disks are also less susceptible to head crashes than are magnetic disks because the optical head is suspended farther from the surface of the disk. Because the heads are so close to the disk's surface in a magnetic hard disk drive, trying to remove a noncartridge disk would end the life of both the magnetic disk and the drive. Optical disks, however, are easily loaded and removed without risk of damaging either the optical disk or the drive.

Most technologies come with disadvantages; optical storage isn't any different. The primary disadvantage of optical storage is that the time needed to retrieve data, or the average access time, is much greater than with magnetic storage media. In other words, optical disk drives are slow. However, their access speeds are improving.

FIGURE 21

Hard disk cartridges. These cartridges are for external hard disk drives.

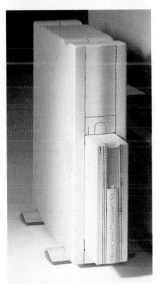

FIGURE 22

(a) Optical disks can store much more data than magnetic diskettes, disks, or tape can. They are also cheaper. Optical storage devices are available for all sizes of computer systems. (b) Diagram of how optical (laser) recording works. (c) NEC W-CDR-74 optical disks and disk drive, plus speakers for outputting sound.

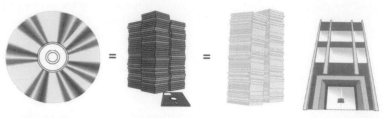

(a)

One CD ROM disc is equal to...

1,800 360K 5¼" floppy disks...

a stack of typewritten pages three stories tall (approx. 300,000 pages).

Reading "1"
The laser reflects off the track surface, sending the light beam to a diode, producing an electric signal = 1.

Reading "0"
The laser beam enters a pit and is not reflected back to the diode. No signal is produced = 0.

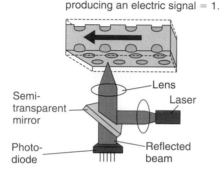
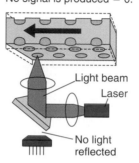

Lens
Laser
Semi-transparent mirror
Photo-diode
Reflected beam

Light beam
Laser
No light reflected

Compact disc
Pits
Acrylic coating

(b)

(c)

Any microcomputer can run an optical disk drive. The drive can be external, connected to the microcomputer by an interface cable, or internal. The internal drive is inserted into a *drive bay* inside the microcomputer. (A bay is a shelf or opening in the computer cabinet, roughly 2 inches high, used for the installation of disk-drive units.)

In the following sections, we describe three types of optical storage disks that are available for use with microcomputers today.

CD-ROM

Compact disk read-only memory (CD-ROM) is the oldest and best-defined optical storage technology. This read-only storage medium is capable of storing 540 to 748 MB of data, images, and sound—the equivalent in storage capacity of about 300,000 pages of text, 1,800 double-density floppy disks, 74 minutes of audio, or thousands of graphic images—all on a disk only 4.72 inches in diameter.

CD-ROMs are imprinted by the disk manufacturer. The user cannot erase or change the data on a CD-ROM or write on the disk—the user can only read the data. The optical disk is used primarily for storing huge amounts of prerecorded information. You will find the following types of information stored on commercial CD-ROMs: (1) encyclopedias, (2) medical reference books, (3) dictionaries, (4) legal libraries, (5) engineering and drafting/design standards, (6) collections of magazine and newspaper articles on specific subjects, (7) graphic images (called *clip art,* grouped according to subject, that can be copied—"clipped"—and used as illustrations in documents produced by desktop publishing or word processing), and (8) large database files, such as telephone directories or ZIP code data.

Some CD-ROMs offer sound effects along with information. For example, Microsoft released a CD-ROM title called *Cinemania,* which has 19,000 capsule reviews, bios of actors and directors, still photos, and sound bites. Microsoft's *Musical Instruments* is an educational disk that recounts the history of instruments from all over the world and illustrates their sounds—a violin, for example, in bluegrass and in a Bach concerto.

WORM

Write Once, Read Many (WORM) technology goes a step beyond CD-ROM. WORM disks are also imprinted by the manufacturer, but the buyer can determine what is written on them. Once the disks have been written on, however, they can only be read from then on—again, no changes can be made. WORM disks have much greater storage capacities than CD-ROM disks. The storage capacity of a WORM disk ranges from 122 to 6,400 MB. WORM disks are ideal for storing custom data that doesn't need to be updated often.

Erasable Optical Disks

Although ideal for certain situations, CD-ROM and WORM drives aren't general-purpose storage devices, because—once written—the data on them can't be changed. The erasable optical disk is the first optical technology to provide to users the capability of changing data under software control.

Erasable optical disks come housed in removable cartridges and store about 281–3,200 MB each. The data access times are between two and six times slower than those of the high-performance hard disk drives. Erasable optical disks are often used in *magneto-optical (MO) disk drives,* which use aspects of both magnetic disk and optical disk technologies. The new MO drives pack up to 256 MB on each removable 3½-inch disk and up to 1 GB on a 5¼-inch disk. No matter how much data a hard disk drive can store, its capacity is limited (for example, to 60 MB or 120 MB). However, MO drives have essentially unlimited capacity—that is, limited only by the number of disks the user buys. A 3½-inch MO disk looks like a 3½-inch floppy disk but is twice as thick. MO drives are available as external or internal units.

MO drives are useful to people who need to save successive versions of large documents, handle enormous databases, work in desktop publishing or graphics, or work with sound and/or video.

Erasable CD technology is also used for *photo CD* storage and retrieval. Photo CD allows photographers and photo agencies to store their photographic images at various resolutions (degrees of definition, or clarity) and easily transport or transmit them to clients. Because complex graphic images—especially photographs—take up an enormous amount of storage space, groups of images could not be stored on regular magnetic disk. (For example, you need about 20 MB of space to store one 8″ × 10″ color photo in digital form.) Also, digital (represented by bits) photography lets you make copies of photos and manipulate photos without any manual labor.

Flash Memory

A new type of nonvolatile direct access memory has become available for new portable computers with *PCMCIA* slots on the system board. (PCMCIA stands for Personal Computer Memory Card International Association, the group that set the standards for the new type of memory.) In these slots are inserted **flash memory cards**—small, lightweight, fast memory circuitry on credit-card-size units—that can take the place of hard disk drives. Their small size and low power consumption will allow portable computers to shrink even more (perhaps to 2 pounds for a complete microcomputer) and run for days on a single battery charge, instead of for hours. Flash memory cards may also be used to simulate RAM.

Backing Up a Microcomputer System

As high-capacity hard disk units increased in popularity, the problem of making backup copies of disk contents became a significant concern. *Users should make backup copies of all stored data files to ensure that they don't lose their data if the hard disk is damaged or destroyed.* Many users neglect this step and live to regret it: How would you feel if two weeks' worth of tax computations turned to dust because your disk storage units were electrocuted by a power surge? But it takes about twenty 3½-inch diskettes to back up the contents of one 20 MB hard disk, and 100 diskettes for a 144 MB disk!

This concern prompted the development of **cartridge-tape units** (also called *tape streamers* and *streaming tape*) to back up high-capacity hard disks (Figure 23). Tape cartridges have a capacity (per cartridge) ranging from 20 MB to 525 MB. The copying speeds of tape backup units vary; it takes approximately 12 minutes to copy the contents of a 60 MB hard disk. (In addition to tape units, hard disk cartridges are also used to back up regular hard disk units.)

FIGURE 23

Cartridge tape units with controlling board (put into expansion slot) and backup management software. Such tape units are used with microcomputers to back up the contents of hard disk units, so that data is not lost if the hard disk units fail.

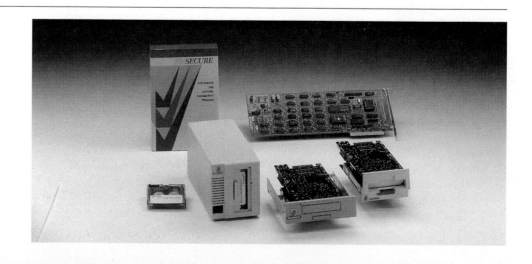

Direct Access Storage Devices for Large Computer Systems

The data storage requirements for large computer systems are enormous compared to the needs of microcomputer-based applications. The access time and the data transfer rate have to be much faster, and the capacity of the disk storage devices must be considerably larger. Early storage devices used with minicomputers and mainframes were limited in storage capacity and were costly. However, modern technology has overcome these problems. Today, two main types of direct access storage devices are used with large computers: (1) removable disk packs and (2) fixed disks.

Removable Disk Packs

In large computer systems, hard disks are sometimes contained in packs that are removable (Figure 24), meaning that they can be removed from the computer and replaced at will. **Disk packs** typically hold 6 to 12 platters that are usually 14 inches in diameter. In disk packs, all tracks with the same track number are lined up, one above the other. All tracks with the same track number make up a **cylinder** (Figure 24). Each disk in the pack—except the top one and the bottom one—has two read/write heads so that both sides of the disk can be read. The cylinder numbers are used by the computer operating system to determine data addresses. (The sector method is used with diskettes and single disks.)

The capacity of removable disk packs varies by manufacturer and ranges from 10 to 300 MB. A minicomputer system with four disk drives can have 1 billion characters of data on line that is, available—at one time for direct access. The total storage capacity could be dramatically increased by having a dozen or so extra disk packs to be interchanged with the packs in the disk drives.

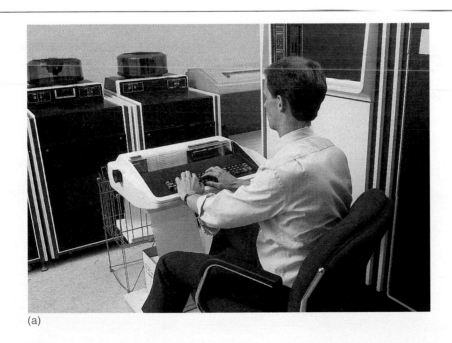

(a)

FIGURE 24

(a) Hard disks used in large computer systems are often contained in removable packs. The same track numbers on all the disks line up vertically—thus all tracks with the same track number form a cylinder (b).

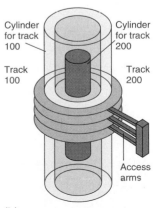

Cylinder for track 100

Cylinder for track 200

Track 100

Track 200

Access arms

(b)

FIGURE 25

This fixed disk unit, with several hard disks, can be installed up to 200 feet away from the processing unit.

Fixed Disks

Fixed disk units (Figure 25) are commonly used with medium-sized and large computers. They are either in the same cabinet as the computer or in their own cabinet. Fixed disks generally are more reliable and have higher storage capabilities than removable disks, but, of course, they are not portable.

Mass Storage Systems

In spite of all the improvements that have been made in magnetic disk storage technology, there still never seems to be enough capacity. Major banks, for example, each do about 600 terabytes worth of check-related processing a year. One terabyte is equivalent to the storage capacity of about 1,250 reels of high-density magnetic tape. Can you imagine trying to manage 750,000 reels of tape in your tape library?

The ability to use both multiple reels of tape and removable disk packs does extend an organization's ability to store a large amount of data. However, as you learned earlier, magnetic tape does not support direct access storage. And removable disk packs provide some flexibility, but the time required to remove a disk pack, retrieve the replacement, mount the replacement, and return the pack to the library just takes up too much time.

Mass storage systems (Figure 26) were developed to remedy this situation. These systems are composed of honeycomb-like "library" cells that hold as many as 2,000 data cartridges, each of which can store 50 MB of data. Each cartridge contains a strip of magnetic tape about 3 inches wide and from 150 to 770 inches long. Each bank of cartridges is serviced by a mechanical unit that retrieves the cartridges individually and positions them under a special read/write head for data transfer.

FIGURE 26

Mass storage. Data is stored on small rolls of magnetic tape and then transferred to disk when needed for processing; afterward, the data is transferred back to the tape, which is stored in a cell. The storage capacity of such a system is in the range of 400 billion bytes. (Each tape cartridge is about 3 inches wide.)

All of us know how to eat. Some of us know how to cook. Numerous enterprising people go into the food and beverage business to try cooking for others. And computers have become as essential for restaurant operators as recipes and menus.

Many small eating and drinking establishments get by with just an electronic cash register, a calculator-like machine with a cash drawer that is not much different from the time-honored cash register. Larger food-service operations, however, may go to a point-of-sale (POS) system. A POS system links three areas: the eating and drinking areas, the kitchen or other food-preparation areas, and the back office.

In the eating and drinking areas—what the industry calls the "front of the house"—there may be POS registers with different cash drawers for different waiters, waitresses, and bartenders. Or, if a cash drawer is shared by several servers, separate cash accountability is maintained by the software. Special-purpose software is also available that tells the host or hostess how many customers came in and when, the size of the order, and which server took the order and when. Some software can help servers be more efficient or helpful—for example, by indicating when a particular food or beverage is out of stock or by cueing servers to ask how an order of beef should be cooked.

So-called cash-taking software is important because often the person taking the order is not the cashier. Cash-taking software consolidates bar and food charges, provides information on discounts and senior-citizen specials, and indicates whether payment is by cash or credit card. Different kinds of printers are available for printing out guest checks: dot matrix or impact printers, which are commonplace but noisy; thermal printers, which require special paper; and laser printers, the most recently developed kind, which are quiet and require no special paper.

Servers in the front of the house may use flat-membrane-type keyboards; touch-screen devices; or, sometimes, hand-held terminals. Hardware in the kitchen must be of a hardier sort, capable of working amid heat, water, and grease. If orders are transmitted electronically by servers from terminals in the front of the house via cable to the kitchen, they may appear on a printer or display screen. Software may process the information sent by the server in a way to assist the preparer. For instance, similar food items might be grouped together, cooking instructions might be put in order, special cooking instructions highlighted, and instructions given on when to begin each part of an order. Software can also indicate that a kitchen is properly stocked to meet demand, based on previous experience.

Depending on the kind of eating establishment, a POS system might be hooked up to outside payment processors for credit card charges and check clearing. Or, if the restaurant is in a hotel, it might link front-of-the-house terminals with the front desk, so that food and beverage charges may be posted to a guest's room bill.

Finally, there is the relationship of the POS system to what is called the "back office," the manager's office or the corporate headquarters. A manager may use the back-office terminal to collect information so that the restaurant can regulate the mix of products, adjust prices, and in general run things more efficiently. If the back-office machine is also a microcomputer, it can be used for other tasks, such as doing spreadsheets, word processing, and telecommunications.

SUMMARY

▼ Data is stored according to a *data storage hierarchy:*

1. *Files*—at the top of the hierarchy. A file is made up of a group of related records.

2. *Records*—second in the hierarchy. A record is made up of a collection of related fields.

3. *Fields*—third in the hierarchy. A field is a collection of related characters, or bytes, of data.

4. *Bytes*—fourth in the hierarchy. A byte is made up of 8 bits.

5. *Bit*—lowest in the hierarchy; 0 or 1.

▼ Files can be categorized as follows:

—*transaction file*　　—*output file*

—*master file*　　　　—*history file*

—*report file*　　　　—*backup file*

▼ The three main types of file organization are

1. *Sequential*—data is retrieved only in the order in which it was stored.

2. *Direct,* or *relative*—data can be retrieved directly without the system having to read all the preceding records.

3. *Indexed*—allows both sequential and direct data access and retrieval through the use of an index that uses *key fields* and storage locations.

▼ The process of storing data involves four steps:

1. After input, the data to be recorded by a storage device temporarily resides in RAM.

2. Software instructions determine where the data is to be recorded on the storage medium.

3. The controller board for the storage device positions the recording device over the appropriate location on the storage medium.

4. The recording mechanism is activated and converts electrical impulses to magnetic spots placed—according to a coding scheme, such as ASCII—on the surface of the medium.

▼ On *magnetic tape,* data is stored only in sequential fashion using either the ASCII or EBCDIC coding schemes. Data put on tape can't be reorganized or altered without creating a new tape. Because of this limitation, *direct access* storage media were developed for microcomputers, including diskettes, hard disks, hard cards, and optical disks. The direct access storage media used with the larger computers include removable disk packs, fixed disks, and disk cartridges.

▼ For disk storage, the recording mechanism is called the *read/write head.*

▼ The *diskette,* or *floppy diskette,* is a storage medium frequently used with microcomputers. Diskettes are made of a flexible plastic that is coated with a material that is easily magnetized. The disk is enclosed in a protective paper or hard plastic jacket.

▼ A diskette jacket has four openings:

1. *Hub*—the round opening in the center, which fits over the center mount, or spindle, in the disk drive.

2. *Data access area*—where the read/write head(s) of the disk drive is positioned. The read/write head(s) moves back and forth over the data access area as the disk(s) spins.

3. *Write/protect notch*—if covered, it prevents the read/write head(s) from touching the surface of the disk(s), thereby preventing accidental erasure or overwriting of data.

4. *Index hole*—repeatedly passes a photoelectric sensing mechanism in the disk drive that activates a timing switch. The timing mechanism determines which portion of the diskette is over or under the read/write head(s).

▼ The *byte* is used to measure the capacity of a storage device:

1. 1,024 bytes = 1 *kilobyte (K)*

2. 1,024,000 bytes = 1 *megabyte (MB)*

3. 1,024,000,000 bytes = 1 *gigabyte (GB)*

4. 1,024,000,000,000 bytes = 1 *terabyte (TB)*

▼ Common diskette capacities range from 360 K to 1.44 MB.

▼ Diskettes are *single-sided* (data is recorded only on one side) or *double-sided* (data is recorded on both sides).

▼ The *recording density* measures the number of bits per inch (bpi) that can be written on the surface of the disk. The higher the density, the more data can be recorded on the diskette. Diskettes are:

1. *Single-density*   3. *Quad-density*

2. *Double-density*

▼ Data is recorded on disks in circular bands called *tracks*.

▼ Track *density* also affects how much data can be stored on a disk. Track density is measured in tracks per inch (tpi).

▼ Diskettes come in two standard sizes: 5¼ inches (with paper jackets) and 3½ inches (with hard plastic jackets).

▼ Diskettes are divided into eight or nine *sectors,* or equal wedge-shaped areas used for storage reference purposes.

▼ *Hard-sectored* disks have the same number and size of sectors, fixed by the manufacturer. *Soft-sectored* disks are marked magnetically by the user with software commands. This process is called *formatting,* or *initializing.* Soft-sectored disks must be formatted before they can be used.

▼ The average speed with which a computer locates instructions or data and loads a copy of it into RAM is called the *access time.* Access time is determined by four factors:

1. *Seek time*—the time it takes to position the read/write head(s) over the proper track

2. *Rotational delay,* or *latency*—the time it takes for the correct sector to rotate over the read/write head(s)

3. The time it takes for the read/write head(s) to contact the disk(s)

4. *Data transfer rate*—the time it takes to transfer the data or instructions from the disk(s) to RAM

▼ *Hard disks* can store more data than can diskettes—from 20 MB to more than a gigabyte of data. Hard disk drives can be *internal* (inside the computer) or *external* (outside the computer, connected to it by a cable).

▼ The interior of a hard disk drive is sealed in order to prevent any contamination, such as dust, from coming between the disk surface and the read/write head(s), which floats about .5 to 1.25 millionths of an inch above the surface. Such an occurrence could cause a *disk crash* and subsequent loss of data.

▼ *Hardcards,* which are inserted into an expansion slot inside the system cabinet, are an alternative to hard disk drive units.

▼ *Hard disk cartridges* are removable cassette-like disk units with one or two platters.

▼ *Optical storage technologies* use a laser beam to pack information densely on a removable disk. Although optical disks can store more data than hard disks or diskettes, their access time is slower.

▼ *Compact disk read-only memory* (*CD-ROM*) is an optical (laser) technology capable of storing huge amounts of data on a disk. The data is prerecorded on the disk by the manufacturer, so the user can only read it.

▼ *Write once, read many* (*WORM*), an optical storage technology, is like CD ROM, except that the user can determine what the manufacturer records on the disk. Once recorded, however, the data can then only be read.

▼ *Erasable optical disks* allow the user both to record data on an optical disk and to erase it. *Magneto-optical* (*MO*) disk drives combine erasable optical disk technology with traditional magnetic disk drive technology.

▼ Users should back up their work. *Cartridge-tape units,* or *streamers,* are often used for backup. (Hard disk cartridges are also used for backup.)

▼ Direct access storage devices for large computer systems include *removable disk packs, fixed disks,* and *mass storage systems.*

KEY TERMS

access time, p. 5.19
algorithm, p. 5.8
backup file, p. 5.5
byte, p. 5.16
cartridge-tape unit, p. 5.26
compact disk read-only memory (CD-ROM), p. 5.25
cylinder, p. 5.27
data access area, p. 5.16
data storage hierarchy, p. 5.3
direct access storage and retrieval, p. 5.8
direct file, p. 5.8
disk cartridge, p. 5.23
disk drive, p. 5.14
disk drive gate (door), p. 5.15
disk pack, p. 5.27
diskette (floppy disk), p. 5.13
double-density, p. 5.17

double-sided, p. 5.17
erasable optical disk, p. 5.25
field, p. 5.3
file, p. 5.3
fixed disk, p. 5.28
flash memory, p. 5.26
formatting, p. 5.18
hardcard, p. 5.22
hard disk, p. 5.20
history file, p. 5.5
indexed file organization, p. 5.10
initializing, p. 5.18
key field, p. 5.8
magnetic tape, p. 5.11
mass storage system, p. 5.28
master file, p. 5.4
nonvolatile, p. 5.3
optical storage technologies, p. 5.23
output file, p. 5.5

primary storage, p. 5.2
quadruple-density, p. 5.17
read/write head, p. 5.6
record, p. 5.3
recording density, p. 5.17
report file, p. 5.5
secondary storage (auxiliary storage), p. 5.3
sector, p. 5.18
sequential storage and retrieval, p. 5.7
single-density, p. 5.17
single-sided, p. 5.17
track, p. 5.17
track density, p. 5.17
transaction file, p. 5.4
volatile, p. 5.3
write once, read many (WORM), p. 5.25
write/protect notch, p. 5.16

EXERCISES

SELF-TEST

1. According to the data storage hierarchy, files are composed of:

   a.   c.

   b.   d.

2. Magnetic tape can handle only sequential data storage and retrieval. (true/false)

3. A backup file should be made only when your original file is very long. (true/false)

4. 1,024 bytes is equal to 1 _____.

5. 1,024,000 bytes is equal to 1 _____.

6. All disks must be _____ before they can store data.

7. Diskettes come in two standard sizes: _____ and

   _____.

8. _____ _____ technologies use a laser beam to store large amounts of data on a removable disk.

9. Diskettes' recording densities can be categorized as one of the following:

   a.   b.   c.

10. Diskettes are often referred to as _____ disks.

11. 1,000,000,000 bytes is approximately 1 _____.

12. Modern storage devices are usually direct access storage and retrieval devices. (true/false)

Solutions: (1) records, fields, bytes (characters), bits; (2) true; (3) write/protect notch; (3) false; (4) kilobyte; (5) megabyte; (6) formatted [or initialized]; (7) 3½ inches, 5¼ inches; (8) optical storage; (9) single-density, double-density, quad-density; (10) floppy; (11) gigabyte; (12) true

Output Hardware

In business, presentation is important—how you present yourself, your product, your information. Although computers may not be able to help you with your wardrobe or your public speaking skills, they can help you create clear and attractive informational presentations quickly. But because computers can produce beautiful, professional, seemingly error-free printouts or exciting colorful graphics on a screen, we are apt to believe that the information is more truthful than the same results scribbled on a yellow pad. In fact, the information that is output—the basis on which you and others will be making decisions—is no better than the quality of the data that was input.

PREVIEW

When you have completed this chapter, you will be able to:

▼ Describe the basic forms of output and categories of output media and hardware

▼ Describe the advantages and disadvantages of the major types of hardcopy and softcopy output devices

▼ Explain why it is important to implement output controls

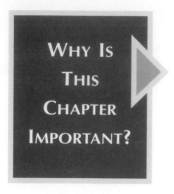
Chapter Topics

*T*he success of a business today can depend to a large extent on how relevant and timely the information is that the computer can produce—that is, the output. Having the right information, in the right hands, in the best form, at the right time—these are the keys to effective decision making (Figure 1).

To be effective, information must be produced in a usable form. To achieve this goal, you may need to use more than one output device and output medium, such as a display on a video screen as well as paper and a printer. Each type of output device has advantages and disadvantages. Is the hardware going to make a lot of noise? What is the quality of the output produced? Is the hardware slow? Is the hardware expensive? Is it compatible with the equipment you already have? Can it handle large volumes of output? Can it handle color? Not all software programs work with all types of output devices. How do you know which output hardware device to use? This chapter will help you learn how to decide.

Output Categories

There are two basic categories of computer-produced output:

1. *Output for immediate use by people*
2. *Output that is stored in computer-usable form for later use by the computer* (and eventually, of course, by people)

FIGURE 1

What form of output is best? As a computer user in the business environment, your output needs will be determined by the kind of decisions you need to make to perform your regular job duties, the type of information that will facilitate those decisions, and the frequency with which you must make decisions.

Output can be in either hardcopy or softcopy form. **Hardcopy** refers to information that has been recorded on a tangible medium (generally meaning that you can touch it), such as paper or microfilm. **Softcopy** generally refers to the output displayed on the computer screen (Figure 2).

The advantages and disadvantages of each output medium must be considered to ensure that outputs are produced in the most usable form.

▼ When computer display devices are not readily available and information has some value over time, it is best produced as hardcopy.

▼ When computer display devices are readily available and information must be quickly accessible by a single user, it is best produced as softcopy.

Hardcopy output tends to have greater value over time, whereas softcopy output is best for displaying information that must be immediately accessible. The principal hardcopy output devices are printers and plotters—the different types and characteristics of these devices are described in detail in the next section. The principal softcopy output devices are cathode-ray tube video screens (CRTs), flat screens, and voice output and sound output systems.

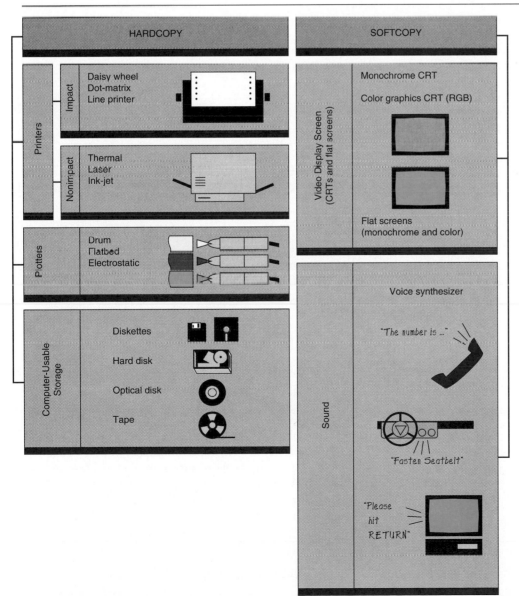

FIGURE 2

Output hardware is categorized according to whether it produces hardcopy or softcopy. Output for immediate use can be in either hardcopy form—such as paper—or softcopy form—such as on a display screen. Output in computer-usable form for later use by the computer is in hardcopy form—such as on disk or tape. This chart shows forms of output commonly used with microcomputers

FIGURE 3

(a) Daisy wheel printer and (b) drawing of how a daisy wheel mechanism works. The daisy wheel spins and brings the desired letter into position. A hammer hits the wedge, which strikes the appropriate spoke against the ribbon, which hits the paper.

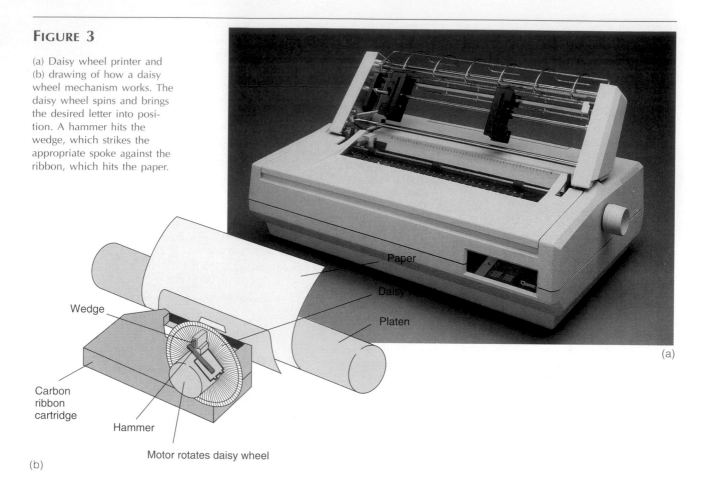

(a)

(b)

Hardcopy Output Hardware

Among the wide variety of hardcopy output devices used with computers, printers and plotters are used the most. A **printer** is capable of printing characters, symbols, and sometimes graphics on paper. Printers are categorized according to whether or not the image produced is formed by physical contact of the print mechanism with the paper. *Impact printers* do have contact; *nonimpact printers* do not. A **plotter** is used most often for outputting graphics because it can produce specialized and free-form drawings on paper. To suit the needs of many different users, different types of printers and plotters are available that have slightly different characteristics and capabilities as to cost, quality, and speed.

Impact Printers

An **impact printer**—also called a *character printer*—makes contact with the paper. It usually forms the print image by pressing an inked ribbon against the paper with a hammer-like mechanism. In one type of impact printer, called a *daisy wheel printer,* the hammer presses images of fully formed characters against the ribbon, just like a typewriter. The print mechanism in another type of impact printer, called a *dot-matrix printer,* is made of separate pin-like hammers that strike the ribbon against the paper in computer-determined patterns of dots.

Daisy Wheel Printers

Daisy wheel printers—often referred to as *letter-quality printers*—produce a very high-quality print image (one that is very clear and precise) because the entire character is formed with a single impact using a print "wheel" with a set of print characters on the outside tips of flat spokes (Figure 3). Daisy wheel printers can print around 60 characters per second (cps). This speed translates into approximately 1 page per minute.

The principal advantage of using daisy wheel printers is that they produce high-quality images. However, they do have some disadvantages, and their sales have declined dramatically as other types of printers have been perfected.

▼ They are too slow for many large-volume output situations.

▼ They are very noisy.

▼ To change the typeface style, the operator must halt the machine and change the print wheel.

▼ They cannot produce graphics.

Dot-Matrix Printers

Dot-matrix printers were developed with two objectives in mind: greater speed and more flexibility. Images are formed by a print head that is composed of a series of little print hammers that look like the heads of pins. These print hammers strike the ribbon individually as the print mechanism moves across the entire print line in both directions—that is, from left to right, then right to left, and so on. They can produce a variety of type styles and graphics without the operator having to stop the printer or change a print wheel. And, because they are impact printers, dot-matrix printers can be used with multipart forms.

Dot-matrix printers can print in either *draft quality* (about 72 dots per inch vertically) or *near-letter-quality* (*nlq*) mode (about 144 dots per inch vertically). Generally, the user determines which mode to operate in by pressing the appropriate button on the front of the printer or by choosing the appropriate software option. It takes longer to print in nlq mode because the print head makes more than one pass for each print line, creating a darker, thicker character (Figure 4). When the dot-matrix printer uses only one pass for each line, it's called *draft quality*. Nlq mode on the dot-matrix printer is used for professional correspondence and other high-quality print needs.

Figure 5 shows how a dot-matrix print head is constructed. The print head of a dot-matrix printer usually has either 9 pins or 24 pins (although other print head configurations are available, they aren't as common).

Following are some of the characteristics that differentiate the two most common types of dot-matrix printers:

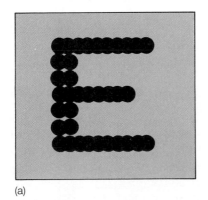
(a)

(b)

FIGURE 4

To produce a near-letter-quality image with a dot matrix printer, the character is printed twice; the second time the print head is positioned slightly to the right of the original image (a). (b) Shows a "real" (daisy wheel) letter-quality character for comparison. (c) Samples of dot-matrix output.

This is a sample of draft quality.

(c) This is a sample of near-letter quality.

FIGURE 5

Dot-matrix print head. Part (a) is an enlarged view of a group of 12 pins, or print hammers, striking the printer ribbon; part (b) shows the print head. The same group of pins can be used to create a variety of characters. The photo (c) shows the Epson LQ-870 dot-matrix printer.

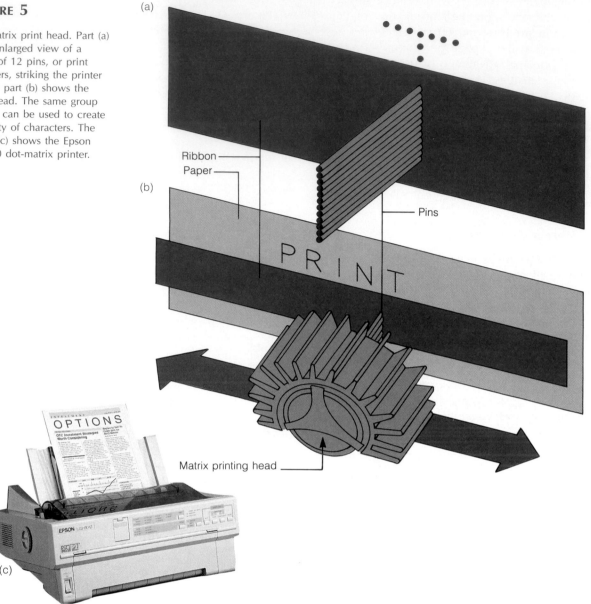

Nine-pin printers:

▼ Are less expensive

▼ Can print between 40 and 130 cps—between 1 and 2 pages per minute—depending on whether they're operating in draft or nlq mode

▼ Are best used for quick draft printing, generating forms, and jobs that don't require a high-quality image

Twenty-four-pin printers:

▼ Are more expensive

▼ Can print between 80 and 260 cps—between 1 and 4 pages per minute

▼ Produce a much more precise image than nine-pin printers—about 360 dpi, or dots per (square) inch

▼ Are best used in a heavy-volume environment where speed and quality are priorities

Although dot-matrix printers are fairly noisy (about 70 decibels; 58 decibels = the sound level of normal talking), new dot-matrix printers run at about 43 decibels.

Table 1 compares daisy wheel and dot-matrix printers.

If you'd like to liven up your business reports with a little bit of color but can't afford an expensive type of color printer, a less expensive color dot-matrix printer may be the one for you. A **color dot-matrix printer** uses the same technology as a monochrome dot-matrix printer, but it uses a color ribbon instead of a black ribbon. Color ribbons usually contain equal bands of black, yellow, red, and blue. Under software control, the colors can be blended to produce up to seven colors. Color ribbons cost up to three times as much as black ribbons.

Line Printers

Several types of high-speed printers have been developed to satisfy the high-volume output requirements of most large computer installations, which cannot be satisfied by dot-matrix or letter-quality printers. These **line printers,** so called because they print a whole line of characters practically at once, instead of a single character at a time, come in several varieties, including **drum printers, band** or **belt printers,** and **chain printers** (Figure 6). Each of these printers has several copies of each printable character on a drum, a belt, or a print chain, with a separate print hammer for each print position across the width of the paper guide. As the drum, belt, or print chain revolves, the hammers are activated as the appropriate characters pass in front of them.

Whereas speed in letter-quality and dot matrix printers is measured in characters per second, the speed of these faster printers is measured in lines per minute. The speed achieved by this type of printer ranges from 200 to 3,000 lines per minute (lpm), which translates into about 5,280 to approximately 79,000 words per minute. Some high-speed printers can print more than 20,000 lines per minute—an astounding 528,000 words per minute! (A highly trained typist can do about 90–120 words per minute on a typewriter.)

Speed is the obvious advantage of this type of printer. Unless your business produces an extremely large volume of hardcopy output, though, you probably will not need to use one. The major disadvantages are noise and relatively poor image quality.

TABLE 1

Comparison of Daisy Wheel and Dot-Matrix Printers

	DAISY WHEEL	DOT-MATRIX
Draft-quality speed	—	80–260 cps
Letter-quality speed	60–100 cps	40–80 cps (near-letter quality)
Image quality	Excellent	Good to very good
Cost	$500 or less	$150–$2,000
Print mechanism	Daisy wheel	9-, 18-, or 24-pin print head
Advantages	Crisp, clear characters	Fast, can do graphics
Disadvantages	Slow, noisy, can't do graphics	Noisy, characters usually less clear
	Cannot print shades of gray	Cannot print shades of gray
	Output photocopies better than dot-matrix output	

Figure 6

High-speed impact line printers. (a) The mechanism of a
drum printer, which can print
up to 3,000 lines per minute;
(b) a belt or band printer
mechanism, which can print
up to 2,000 lines per minute;
(c) a chain printer mechanism, which can print 3,000
lines per minute. Bands and
chains can be changed to use
different typeface styles;
drums cannot. (d) High-speed
Unisys line printer.

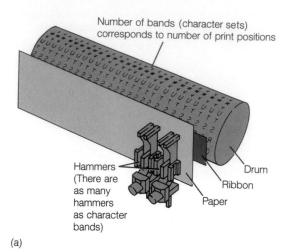

(a)

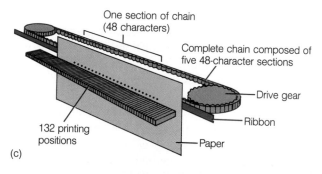

(c)

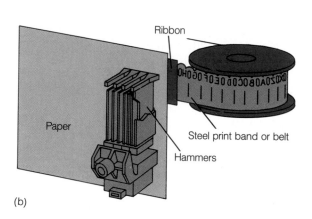

(b)

(d)

Nonimpact Printers

Printers that do not strike characters against ribbon or paper when they print
are **nonimpact printers,** also called *page printers*. The main categories of nonimpact printers are ink-jet printers, thermal printers, and laser printers. These
printers generate much less noise than impact printers. However, if you're using
a nonimpact printer, don't try to print on multiple-part carbon forms: because
no impact is being made on the paper, you'll end up with no copies!

Table 2 compares the various types of nonimpact printers.

TABLE 2

Comparison of Nonimpact Printers

TYPE	TECHNOLOGY	ADVANTAGES	DISADVANTAGES	TYPICAL SPEED	APPROXIMATE COST
Ink-Jet	Electrostatically charged drops hit paper	Quiet; prints color, text, and graphics; less expensive; fast	Relatively slow; clogged jets; lower dpi	1–4 pages per minute	$500–$8,000
Thermal	Temperature-sensitive; paper changes color when treated; characters are formed by selectively heating print head	Quiet; high-quality color output of text and graphics; can also produce transparencies	Special paper required; expensive; slow	.5–4 pages per minute	$5,000–$22,000
Laser	Laser beam directed onto a drum, "etching" spots that attract toner, which is then transferred to paper	Quiet; excellent quality; output of text and graphics; very high speed	High cost, especially for color	4–25 pages per minute	$600–$20,000

Ink-Jet Printers

Ink-jet printers (Figure 7) work in much the same fashion as dot-matrix printers in that they form images (text and graphics) with little dots. However, the dots are formed not by hammer-like pins but by tiny droplets of ink. The text these printers produce is letter quality (rather than near-letter-quality, which is produced by dot-matrix printers). These printers can match the speed of dot-matrix printers—between 1 and 4 pages per minute (ppm), generally 2 ppm—and they produce less noise. Ink-jet printers are often used to produce color proofs of posters, magazine layouts, and book covers, as well as color output for business presentations.

Bubblejet printers, a new type of ink-jet printer, use miniature heating elements to force specially formulated inks through print-heads with 128 tiny nozzles. Tinier than strands of human hair, the multiple nozzles print fine images at high speeds and good color registration. This type of printer is available for IBM and compatible PCs, as well as Macintoshes. Both regular ink-jet and bubblejet printers require specially coated paper.

Thermal Printers

Thermal printers use colored waxes, heat, and special paper to produce images (Figure 8). No ribbon or ink is involved. For users who want the highest-quality desktop color printing available, thermal printers are the answer. However, they are also expensive, and they require special, expensive paper, so they are not generally used for high-volume output.

Laser Printers

Laser printer technology is much less mechanical than impact printing (that is, no print heads move, no print hammers hit), resulting in much higher printing speeds and quieter operation. The process resembles the operation of a photo-

FIGURE 7

Ink-jet printer. Both free-form graphics and text can be produced using a color ink-jet printer like these Hewlett-Packard PaintJets.

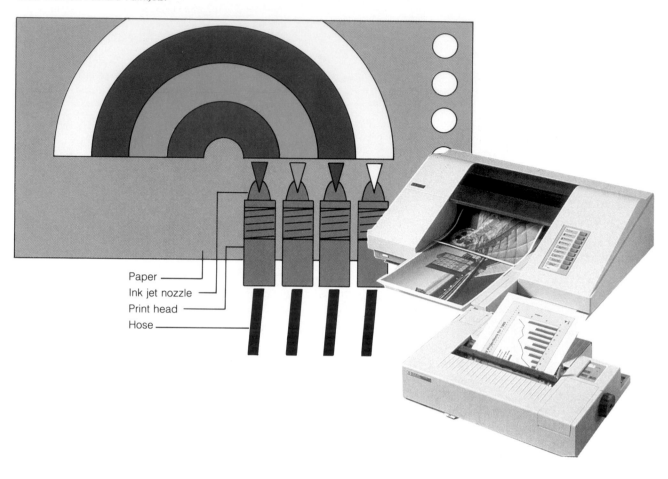

Paper ———
Ink jet nozzle ———
Print head ———
Hose ———

FIGURE 8

Thermal printers produce images by using colored waxes and heat to burn dots onto special paper. (Colored wax sheets are not required for black-and-white output because the thermal print head will register black dots on special paper.)

Thermal
print head

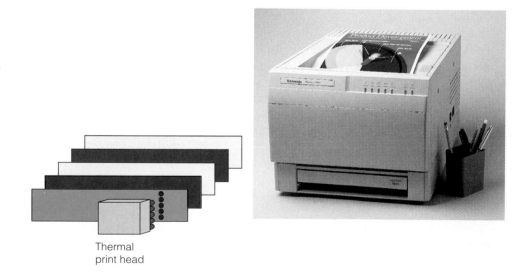

copy machine (Figure 9). A laser beam is directed across the surface of a light-sensitive drum and fired as needed to record an image in the form of a pattern of tiny dots. The image is then transferred to the paper—a page at a time—in the same fashion as a copy machine transfers images, using a special toner.

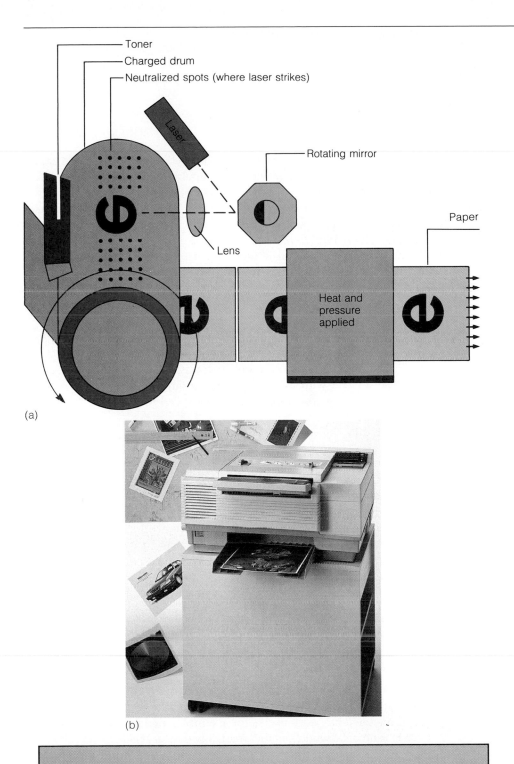

- Toner
- Charged drum
- Neutralized spots (where laser strikes)

Laser

Rotating mirror

Lens

Paper

Heat and
pressure
applied

(a)

(b)

FIGURE 9

Laser printing. (a) A micro-processor controls a small laser beam that is bounced off a mirror millions of times per second onto a positively charged drum. The spots where the laser beam hits become neutralized, enabling a special toner (containing powdered ink and powdered rosin, an adhesive) to stick to them and then print out on paper, through the use of heat and pressure. The drum is then recharged for its next cycle. Part (b) shows the Tektronix Phaser III color laser printer (on top of a supply cabinet); part (c) is actual hardcopy laser output.

"I think there is a world market for about five computers."
--- Thomas J. Watson, founder of IBM (1943)

*"I think there is a world market for about five computers."
--- Thomas J. Watson, founder of IBM (1943)*

(c)

The major advantages of laser printers are:

▼   Very high speed

▼   Low noise level

▼   Low maintenance requirements

▼   Very high image quality (near-typeset-quality)

▼   Excellent graphics capabilities

Laser printers can also generate text in a variety of type sizes and styles (called **fonts**), providing a business with the capability of outputting professional-looking near-typeset-quality reports and publications. Figure 10 shows examples of just a few of the types of fonts that can be generated using a laser printer. Most laser printers are capable of outputting a specific set of fonts that come with the printer (*internal fonts*) or that can be inserted on a font cartridge that contains fonts on ROM chips (*cartridge fonts*). However, laser printers that include a built-in **page description language,** such as Adobe PostScript, provide greater flexibility by enabling users to generate fonts in almost any size and to produce special graphics effects. (Users can increase their font choices by purchasing "soft fonts" on diskettes and storing them on the hard disk to download—load into RAM or the printer—whenever they want. However, their laser printer must be compatible with this technology.)

A variety of laser printers, each different in terms of cost, speed, and capabilities, are available for use with microcomputers today. In general, laser printers can be viewed as falling into three categories: (1) low end, (2) high end, and (3) color.

The laser printers that fall into the low-end category are the least expensive and can print between 4 ppm and 11 ppm. With printers in this range, 300-dpi images are common.

More expensive high-end laser printers can be purchased that are three to five times faster than low-end printers and generate clearer images (400–600 dpi). Printing between 12 and 25 ppm, these printers are appropriate in a networked environment where many users are sharing one printer.

Color laser printers are now available for less than $10,000—a recent breakthrough—and are frequently used in desktop publishing, especially in the magazine and newspaper businesses.

A new laser-based printer, called a *hydra* printer, has recently become available. This machine combines the capabilities of laser printing, scanning, faxing, and photocopying.

Portable Printers

Portable printers (Figure 11) are becoming more and more popular as portable computing using laptop computers has gained in popularity in the business environment. Many portable computer users, for example, need to print out sales reports or service estimates while on the road. So that a business traveler can carry both a 10-pound computer and a printer, **portable printers** are compact in size and typically weigh under 5 pounds. Nine-pin and 24-pin dot-matrix portable printers are available, as well as ink-jet, bubble jet, and thermal printers.

In Japan, IBM has released a laptop computer with a *built-in* Canon bubble-jet printer. This "Thinkpad" can accept up to 10 sheets of paper at a time. The paper is inserted in a slot in front; the printhead can handle both text and graphics.

Specialty Printers

If your office has a printer dedicated to printing labels, or if your printer has a permanently attached label or envelope feeder, then you may not need a spe-

FIGURE 10

A set of characters and symbols in a particular size and style is called a *font*. This is a partial list of fonts as generated by the Hewlett-Packard LaserJet Series II.

FONT ID	NAME	POINT SIZE *	PRINT SAMPLE
S01	Dutch	10	ABCDEfghij#$@[\]^'{|}~123 ÀÂ°ÇÑ¡¿£§êéàèëöÅØåæÄÜßÁÐÒ
S02	Dutch BOLD	14	ABCDEfghij#$@[\]^'{|}~123 ÀÂ°ÇÑ¡¿£§êéàèëöÅØåæÄÜßÁÐÒ
S03	Dutch BOLD	18	ABCDEfghij#$@[\]^'{|}~ ÀÂ°ÇÑ¡¿£§êéàèëöÅØåæÄÜß
S04	Dutch BOLD	24	ABCDEfghij#$@[\] ÀÂ°ÇÑ¡¿£§êéàèëöÅØ
I00	COURIER	12	ABCDEfghij#$@[\]^'{|}~123 ÀÂ°ÇÑ¡¿£§êéàèëöÅØåæÄÜßÁÐÒ
I01	COURIER	12	ABCDEfghij#$@[\]^`{|}~123 íó|┤╡╢╖╕╣║╗╝╜╛┐└┴┬├─┼╞╟╚╔╩╦╠═╬▀απΦ

* 12 points = 1 pica, and 6 picas = 1 inch

FIGURE 11

Portable printer. This illustration shows a Kodak Diconix 150 Plus.

cialty printer—you'll need only the software necessary to handle labels and envelopes.

However, if your printer is not equipped to handle addressing envelopes and/or labels, you can purchase a special printer that can (Figure 12). Both types of printers can print single addresses, mailing lists, and standard bar codes, and they both come with software for creating labels and storing addresses.

FIGURE 12

Address label printer

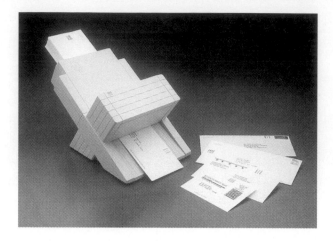

FIGURE 13

This illustration shows (a) drum plotters, (b) a flatbed plotter, and (c) an electrostatic plotter.

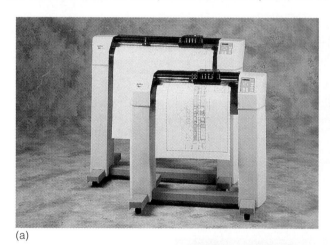

(a)

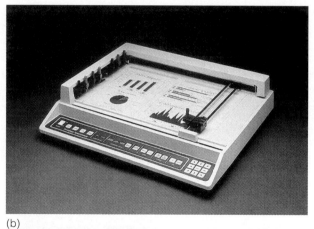

(b)

(c)

Plotters

A **plotter** (Figure 13) is a specialized output device designed to produce high-quality graphics—especially in the areas of drafting and design—in a variety of colors. There are two basic types of plotters: those that use pens and those that don't. Drum plotters and flatbed plotters use pens. Electrostatic plotters do not.

In a **drum plotter,** the paper is mounted on the surface of a drum. The drum revolves and the plotter pens (which are similar to felt-tip pens) are horizontally positioned over the target area. When the paper has rotated to the correct point, the pens are dropped to the surface and moved left and right under program control across the paper as the drum revolves. When the image is complete, the pens are raised from the surface. **Flatbed plotters** are designed so that the paper is placed flat and one or more pens move horizontally and vertically across the paper. **Electrostatic plotters** use electrostatic charges to create images out of very small dots on specially treated paper. The paper is run through a developer to allow the image to appear. Electrostatic plotters are faster than pen plotters and can produce images of very high resolution.

Figure 13 shows a drum plotter, a flatbed plotter, and an electrostatic plotter. The cost of a plotter can range from about $1,000 to more than $100,000, depending on the machine's speed and ability to generate high-resolution images. Several 2- to 8-pen flatbed plotters are available for microcomputer systems, as are some small drum plotters; large plotters, used with large computer systems, can produce drawings up to 8 feet by 8 feet, or sometimes even larger.

Computer Output Microfilm/Microfiche (COM) Systems

The volume of information produced by computers is staggering. If we were limited to regular hardcopy output, it is likely that most Americans would be knee-deep in paper by now. However, what do you use when you don't want to take up space with regular hardcopy output, but softcopy output on display screens is inappropriate?

Computer output systems may be an answer. The two most popular systems capture computer output on **microfilm** or **microfiche.** The principal advantages of this technology are:

▼ *Speed.* COM systems can easily handle output at a rate in excess of 30,000 lines per minute. This is about 50% faster than most large laser printers.

▼ *Size.* The output is condensed in size (compared to hardcopy output) by a factor ranging from 20 to 100.

▼ *Cost.* The cost per page of printed material is less than that of regular hardcopy output methods.

The major disadvantage of COM systems is that, because of the reduced visual size of the output, special equipment must be used to read the output that has been stored. Figure 14 shows microfilm/microfiche reader and output equipment. Because of the high cost of computer output systems (they can exceed $100,000), companies may not buy very many readers, so users may have to share them or go to another department to find one, which may be inconvenient. Microfilm and microfiche are most widely used by libraries for records and reference materials.

Softcopy Output Hardware

Softcopy output generally refers to the display on a monitor, the output device that many people use the most. The two main types of monitors are the cathode-ray tube (CRT) and the flat panel.

FIGURE 14

Computer output microfilm/microfiche equipment outputs information and data on microfiche sheets or microfilm rolls (a). The user needs special equipment to read the microfilm/fiche. Some COM equipment can also enlarge microfilm/fiche and print output on paper. This Minolta Integrated Information and Image Management System (b) can call up and reproduce microfilmed documents in seconds and print them out.

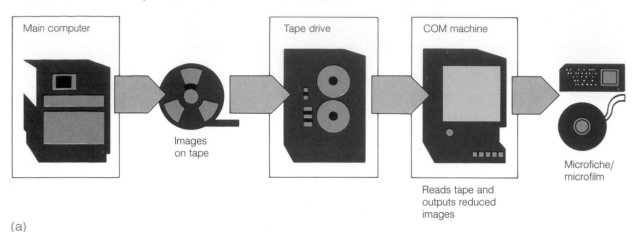

(a)

(b)

Cathode-Ray Tubes (CRTs)

The **cathode-ray tube (CRT)** (Figure 15) is the most common softcopy output device used with computer systems. The CRT's screen display is made up of small picture elements, called **pixels** for short. A pixel (Figure 16) is the smallest unit on the screen that can be turned on or off or made different shades. The smaller the pixels and the closer together they are (the more points that can be illuminated on the screen), the better the image clarity, or **resolution.** A screen resolution of 320 × 320 means the screen has horizontal and vertical rows of 320 pixels each to form images. This is medium resolution. Most users prefer higher resolutions, such as 640 × 480 or even 1,024 × 768. (Screen resolution is also referred to as *dots per inch,* or *dpi.* The higher the number of dots per inch, the better the picture. *Dot pitch* refers to the size of the dots, or pixels. The smaller the dot pitch, the sharper the image.)

CRTs have some disadvantages that recent technology has been trying to overcome, most notably:

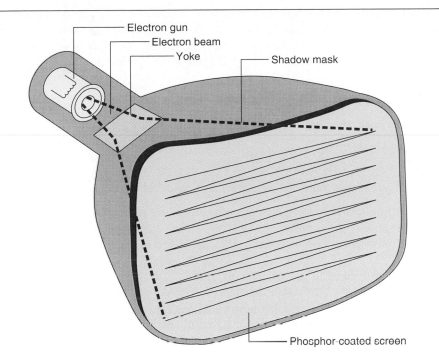

FIGURE 15

The CRT's electron gun emits a beam of electrons that, under the control of the yoke's magnetic field, moves across the interior of the phosphor-coated screen. The phosphors hit by the electrons emit light, which makes up the image on the screen. The distance between the points of light is fixed by the shadow mask, a shield with holes in it that is used to prevent the dispersion of the electron beam.

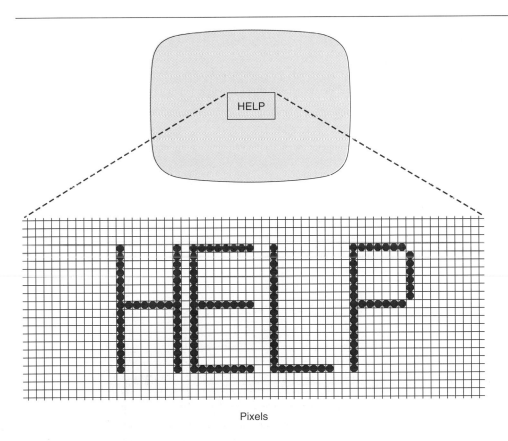

Pixels

FIGURE 16

Each character on the screen is made up of pixels, or picture elements.

1. Large size

2. High power consumption

3. Fragility

The CRT is rather large and bulky because of the need to separate the electron gun from the screen by a particular distance, so it is unsuitable as a display screen for portable computers. The CRT also tends to use a substantial amount of electric power, again making it unsuitable for use with portable computers, which occasionally need to run on batteries. Finally, as with a television, the CRT's glass tube and screen can be damaged if not handled carefully.

Monochrome and Color Monitors

A **monochrome monitor** displays only a single-color image.

1. A *paper-white* monitor displays black and white.
2. An *amber* monitor displays black and yellow.
3. A *green-screen* monitor displays black and light green.

A monochrome monitor and an **RGB color monitor** (RGB stands for *red, green, blue*) differ in two principal ways. First, they have different numbers of electron guns. A monochrome monitor has only one electron gun; however, as shown in Figure 17, an RGB color monitor has three electron guns. Second, the screen in an RGB color monitor is coated with three types—or colors—of phosphors: red, green, and blue. The screen of a monochrome monitor is coated with only one type of phosphor, which is often either green or amber in color.

The operational principles of both monitors are almost exactly the same. However, each pixel in an RGB monitor is made up of three dots of phosphors, one of each color. The three electron guns direct their beams together. Each gun is aimed precisely so that it can hit a specific color dot in each pixel. A wide variety of colors can be created by controlling—through software instructions—which guns fire and how long a burst they project at each dot. As you might expect, the control circuitry and software to direct the operation of an RGB monitor are somewhat more sophisticated and expensive than the corresponding components for a monochrome monitor.

FIGURE 17

RGB monitor. The workings of an RGB color monitor are similar to those of a monochrome CRT, except that the types of phosphors—red, green, and blue—are hit by three electron beams. Each pixel has three color dots that are activated to different degrees to produce a wide range of colors.

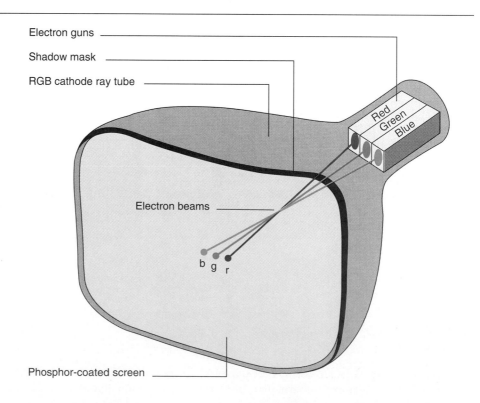

Character-Mapped Displays

Character-mapped display screens, such as the IBM monochrome monitor, can display only characters. (Note: As described in the next section, a character-mapped display screen may be able to display graphics if a video adapter card is plugged into the motherboard.) The patterns of pixels used to represent the standard characters displayed on a monitor (the alphabetic characters, numbers, and special symbols) in character-mapped displays are drawn from prerecorded templates (guides) stored in a video display ROM chip. When the user's software sends a request to display, for example, the letter at a specific location, the template for that pixel pattern is looked up in the video display ROM chip. The electron gun then uses this pattern when it fires at the phosphors in the appropriate *character box.* The screen of a personal computer has 25 lines with 80 characters per line; this means that there are 2,000 positions on the screen where a predefined character can be placed.

Bit-Mapped Displays

Because most software written today requires that the monitor be capable of displaying graphics, different types of video adapter cards were developed (Table 3). With appropriate software, sufficient RAM, and compatible monitors, these cards are plugged into the motherboard of a microcomputer to enable monitors to display **bit-mapped graphics.** To create the variety of images necessary to produce graphics, the computer needs to be able to direct each electron beam individually at each pixel on the screen, not just superimpose a template over a character box. This approach requires more sophisticated control circuitry, software, and RAM than is required by character-mapped displays.

Following are the common video graphics adapters (Figure 18):

▼ *CGA (Color Graphics Adapter)*—IBM PC video display circuit board that provides low-resolution text and graphics. (This was the first color display.) CGA requires an RGB color display monitor and supports 4 colors at a resolution of 320 × 200. This standard has been superseded by EGA, VGA, Super VGA, and XGA.

▼ *EGA (Enhanced Graphics Adapter)*—IBM PC video display circuit board that provides medium-resolution (640 × 380) text and graphics and requires an

---

TABLE 3

PC Graphics Standards (Some RAM requirements for using particular color monitors at particular resolutions are also included.)

	COLORS	RESOLUTION (PIXELS)	RAM REQUIRED
CGA (Color Graphics Adapter)	(1 bit/color) 4	320 × 200	
EGA (Enhanced Graphics Adapter)	(4 bits/color) 16	640 × 350	
VGA (Video Graphics Array)	(8 bits/color) 256	320 × 200	
	(4 bits/color) 16	640 × 480	150 K
Super VGA	(8 bits/color) 256	800 × 600	469 K
	(8 bits/color) 256	1,024 × 768	768 K
XGA (Extended Graphics Array)	(8 bits/color) 256	1,024 × 768	768 K
	(16 bits/color) 65,536	1,024 × 768	1,536 K
	(24 bits/color) 16,777,216	1,024 × 768	2,304 K

FIGUR

Compari

FIGURE 20

Four laptop computers that use a liquid crystal display: (a) NEC Prospeed 80386; (b) IBM PS/2 CL57 9X color LCD display; (c) Compaq SLT 386s/20; (d) Zenith Turbosport 386.

(a)

(b)

(c)

(d)

Electroluminescent Display

Electroluminescent (EL) display (Figure 21) uses a thin film of solid, specially treated material that glows in response to electric current. To form a pixel on the screen, current is sent to the intersection of the appropriate row and column; the combined voltages from the row and the column cause the screen to glow at that point.

EL displays provide very high image resolution and excellent graphics capability. Several manufacturers are currently working on the development of electroluminescent displays with full-color capability. Most experts have predicted that this technology will soon match or even surpass all of the capabilities of the traditional CRT. Like LCD technology, the major limitation of this technology has been cost.

FIGURE 21

Electroluminescent display. This Hewlett-Packard Integral computer uses an EL flat-panel display.

(a)

(b)

(c)

FIGURE 22

Gas plasma display. These laptop computers use gas plasma display: a) GRiDCase 1500 Series; (b) Toshiba T5100; (c) IBM PS/2 P75 486.

Gas Plasma Display

The oldest flat screen technology is the **gas plasma display** (Figure 22). This technology uses predominantly neon gas and electrodes above and below the gas. When electric current passes between the electrodes, the gas glows. Depending on the mixture of gases, the color ranges from orange to red.

The principal advantages of gas plasma display are:

▼ The images are much brighter than on a standard CRT.

▼ The resolution is excellent.

▼ Glare is not a significant problem.

▼ The screen does not flicker as it does on some CRTs.

The main disadvantages are:

▼ Only a single color is available (reddish orange).

▼ The technology is expensive.

▼ It uses a lot of power.

▼ It does not show sharp contrast.

Voice Output

Voice output systems are relatively new and can be used in some situations in which traditional display screen softcopy output is inappropriate. Voice output technology has had to overcome many hurdles. The most difficult has been that every individual perceives speech differently; that is, the voice patterns, pitches, and inflections we can hear and understand are different for all of us. It is not always easy to understand an unfamiliar voice pattern. At this point, two different approaches to voice output have evolved: (1) speech coding and (2) speech synthesis.

Speech coding relies on human speech as a reservoir of sounds to draw from in building the words and phrases to be output. Sounds are codified and stored on disk to be retrieved and translated back as sounds. Speech coding has been used in applications such as automobiles, toys, and games.

Speech synthesis relies on the use of a set of basic speech sounds that are created electronically without the use of a human voice.

Researchers are continuing to develop and improve voice output technologies for use with microcomputers. Many new products using voice output are expected to appear in the marketplace during the next decade. The largest application to date for the speech synthesis approach to voice output—converting text into "spoken" words—has many potential uses, including in reading machines for the blind (Figure 23). And, of course, sound output does not have to be in voice form; it can be music or special-effects sounds, such as the sound accompaniment for computer animation.

Sound Output

PC audio is just entering the mainstream, primarily because of the increasing use of **multimedia**—the computer-based output of text, graphics, sound, and animation combined. To add sound capabilities to a microcomputer, you can purchase a sound card to insert into an expansion slot of a compatible PC, or you can purchase an external sound device and plug it into a socket (*port*) on the back of the computer. (*Note:* Laptop computers have no expansion slots for sound cards.) Sound cards range from $200 to $1,000, based on their capabilities. To use a sound card, you must also have the appropriate software and speakers or headphones.

Newer Macintosh computers come with some sound capabilities built in.

FIGURE 23

Xerox/Kurzweil Personal Reader, a breakthrough in technology for people who are blind, visually impaired, or dyslexic. The Personal Reader uses an optical scanner to convert typeset and typewritten material into speech. It can also be used to write and store information.

Output Controls

We have emphasized that the information a computer-based information system produces must be very reliable, because important business and professional decisions are made on the basis of it. You have learned that data you enter must be accurate and complete and that input control methods have been designed to ensure just that. You also learned that some input and processing methods can produce information more quickly than others, thus affecting the timeliness of the information you are dealing with.

In addition, measures need to be taken to protect stored data so that not just anyone can get to it; this precaution should also be taken with sensitive output. Output information should be checked for completeness and accuracy, information should be accessible only to authorized personnel, and output that contains sensitive information should be destroyed when it is no longer needed.

Some examples of typical output controls are:

▼ Balancing output totals with input and processing totals

▼ Auditing output reports

▼ Providing distribution lists for all reports, so that only those people on the list receive the information

▼ Requiring signatures on a predetermined form from those people who receive reports

▼ Providing delivery schedules for reports so that people expecting them can follow up if the reports do not arrive on time

▼ Requiring users to enter passwords when attempting to obtain softcopy output on the video display screen

▼ Providing guidelines on how, when, and where to destroy reports after they are no longer needed

▼ Securing sensitive data and information in an inaccessible location when it is not being actively reviewed

The degree to which output control measures are taken must be determined by the needs of the business and both the people who run it and those who work there. Obviously, the extent of the controls is directly related to the value and the sensitivity of the information. In any case, the *user* has the responsibility for checking output reports for accuracy.

COMPUTERS AND CAREERS

CRIME FIGHTING

Crime rates have increased, but they might have increased more were it not for the presence of computer technology.

Consider home security. At one time, home-security systems were expensive and notoriously unreliable, with over 90% of alarms triggered being false. Often the alarms were caused by user error, such as a homeowner accidentally tripping a system and forgetting how to deactivate it, but they were also caused by equipment malfunction. Today's computerized home-security systems allow one to turn off some alarms (such as those inside) and turn on others (such as door and window alarms). They can also detect and isolate malfunctioning sensors, eliminating many false alarms.

Police departments, of course, have been using computers for some time, as when an officer in a patrol car calls up on a dashboard-mounted computer the license numbers of suspicious vehicles to check whether they have been stolen. More creative uses of computers have followed. Fingerprint identification, which used to require so many hours of an officer's time that it was virtually not attempted except in the most serious cases, has proved to be extraordinarily successful in those urban police departments that have moved their fingerprint files to a computerized database. The old-fashioned police artist's pad and pencil have been replaced by a software program containing more than 100,000 facial features, allowing officers with no artistic talent to create remarkably professional composite drawings of wanted suspects.

Computers have also helped increase productivity in prosecutors' offices and make the judicial system function better. For instance, a computer system may be used to log all incoming letters and phone calls; the district attorney heading the prosecutor's office can then scan the printouts and find out which callers require return calls and which assistant D.A.s must be reminded to respond to backlogged correspondence. Confidential data can be kept on various cases, and the system can be used to create appropriate legal documents to advance cases through the court system. Weekly calendars of active cases are provided to help prosecutors avoid scheduling conflicts and alert them to necessary actions they must take.

Some prosecutors' offices have a computer system that tracks cases from arrest to disposition. For example, in the Brooklyn, N.Y., district attorney's office, a system called FACTS (Facility for Accurate Case Tracking System) begins to pick up a case when the suspect is first brought to central booking at the police station, where the charges are keyed into a terminal. For misdemeanor cases, a terminal informs the judge about a suspect's prior record, outstanding charges, and the names of prosecuting attorneys. For felonies, the system is used to schedule the first grand jury hearing to determine if the evidence justifies an indictment. Other data includes names of witnesses, bail records, and the like.

Even the U.S. Supreme Court has acquired computer technology. The system is designed to transmit the court's opinion within minutes of its announcement.

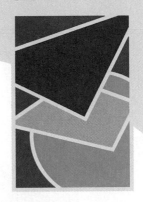

▼ Users must decide what *kinds* of output they require—based on the kind of information they need—before deciding which output hardware and media to use. They should also consider:

1. How much noise the output equipment makes

2. How fast it works

3. How expensive it is

4. Whether it is compatible with the equipment they already have

5. How easily it can be upgraded

▼ The two basic categories of computer-produced output are:

1. Output for immediate use by people

2. Output stored in computer-usable form for later use by the computer (and people)

▼ Output is available in two forms:

1. *Hardcopy*—refers to information that has been recorded on a tangible medium (you can touch it), such as paper or microfilm. When computer display devices are not readily available and information has some value over time, it is best produced as hardcopy.

2. *Softcopy*—refers to the output displayed on the computer screen. When computer display devices are readily available and information must be quickly accessible, it is best produced as softcopy.

▼ Paper is the most widely used hardcopy output medium.

▼ The video display image on the computer screen is the most widely used form of softcopy output.

▼ Common hardcopy output devices used with microcomputers are:

1. *Printers*—capable of printing characters, symbols, and occasionally graphics on paper. Printers are either:

   a. *Impact printers*—the image is produced by physical contact of the print mechanism with the paper. Only impact printers can be used to produce output on multipart forms with carbon layers.

   b. *Nonimpact printers*—no contact with the paper by the print mechanism is required to form the image.

2. *Plotters*—used most often for outputting graphics because they can produce specialized free-form drawings on paper.

▼ Commonly used impact printers are:

1. *Daisy wheel* (*letter-quality*) *printers*—produce a high-quality print image because the entire character is formed with a single impact by a print wheel with a set of characters on the outside tips of the wheel's spokes. Daisy wheel printers produce letter-quality output, but they are being phased out in favor of less expensive and more flexible printers.

2. *Dot-matrix printers*—produce images with a print head composed of a series of little print hammers (usually 9 or 24) that look like the heads of pins.

▼ Although daisy wheel printers produce high-quality images, they also have several disadvantages:

1. They are too slow for many large-volume output situations.

2. They are noisy.

3. To change the typeface style, the operator must halt the machine and change the print wheel.

4. They cannot produce graphics or color output.

▼ Dot-matrix printers are more flexible, quieter, and faster than daisy wheel printers, and they can also produce graphics output. In addition, they can produce a variety of type styles without the operator having to stop the machine. However, their image quality is not as high as that produced by daisy wheel printers.

▼ Dot-matrix printers can print in *draft quality* (one pass of the print head for each line) or *near-letter-quality* (*nlq*) (two or more passes of the print head for each line).

▼ 24-pin dot-matrix printers are more expensive and faster than nine-pin printers, and they produce better-quality images. They are best used in a heavy-volume environment where speed and quality are priorities.

▼ *Color dot-matrix printers* use a multicolor ribbon instead of a black one.

▼ The main types of nonimpact printers are:

1. *Ink-jet printers*—form images by spraying tiny droplets of ink (black or colors); text is letter quality and graphics can be output. These printers are about as fast as dot-matrix printers, and they are quiet.

2. *Thermal printers*—use heat to produce images on special chemically treated paper. No ribbon or ink is involved. Although thermal printers are expensive, they produce excellent color output by using wax.

3. *Laser printers*—use a laser beam to produce images in a process similar to that used by photocopiers. Laser printers are fast, quiet, have low maintenance requirements, and produce high-quality images, including graphics. They can also output text in a variety of fonts—type sizes and styles. Laser printers that have a built-in *page description language* (such as PostScript by Adobe Systems) provide greater flexibility to produce different fonts and special graphics.

▼ Laser printers are:

1. *Low end*—less expensive, slower, produce lower-quality images

2. *High end*—more expensive, faster, produce higher-quality images

3. *Color*—expensive but effective

▼ *Portable printers* (9- and 24-pin dot-matrix, ink-jet, and thermal) have been developed for businesspeople to take on the road.

▼ *Plotters* are used for specialized output, such as blueprints of architectural designs.

▼ The *flatbed plotter* is the type of plotter most commonly used with microcomputers. It is designed so that the paper is placed flat and one or more pens move horizontally and vertically across the paper. Plotter output is available in color.

▼ *Computer output microfilm/microfiche* systems are often used by companies that don't want to collect a lot of paper output but have needs not met by softcopy output.

▼ The *cathode-ray tube* (*CRT*) is the most popular softcopy output device used with microcomputers. The CRT's screen is made up of *pixels* (*picture elements*); the smaller the pixels and the closer together they are, the better the image clarity, or *resolution*. The pixels are illuminated under software control by electron guns to form images.

▼ CRTs are:

1. Large

2. Power hungry

3. Fragile

▼ CRTs can be *monochrome* or *RGB* (*red, green, blue*).

▼ Some CRTs, such as the IBM monochrome monitor, are *character-mapped displays*—they can display characters only, and only according to template grid information stored in a video display ROM chip. Other CRTs are *bit-mapped displays*. They can display characters *and* free-form graphics because the electron beam can illuminate each individual pixel.

▼ *Color Graphics Adapter* (*CGA*), *Enhanced Graphics Adapter* (*EGA*), *Video Graphics Array* (*VGA*), *Super VGA,* and *Extended Graphics Array* (*XGA*) cards are available to upgrade a character-mapped monochrome monitor to display color bit-mapped graphics. (The card is inserted into an expansion slot in the system cabinet.) However, the resolution is determined by the monitor.

▼ *Flat screens,* used with laptop computers, have been developed to overcome the disadvantages of the CRT: large size, high power consumption, and fragility.

▼ The three main types of flat screen technologies are:

1. Liquid crystal display (LCD)

2. Electroluminescent (EL) display

3. Gas plasma display

▼ *Voice output systems*—including *speech coding* and *speech synthesis*—are a relatively new form of output used when traditional output is inappropriate.

▼ *Sound output* is becoming a common part of multimedia presentations.

▼ Care must be taken to ensure that output is responsibly generated, shared, and disposed of. Output controls should be established to ensure that only authorized users see sensitive output and that output is properly secured.

KEY TERMS

band (belt) printer, p. 6.7
bit-mapped graphics, p. 6.19
cathode-ray tube (CRT), p. 6.16
chain printer, p. 6.7
character-mapped display, p. 6.19
color dot-matrix printer, p. 6.7
computer output microfilm/
    microfiche system, p 6.15
daisy wheel printer, p. 6.4
dot-matrix printer, p. 6.5
drum plotter, p. 6.15
drum printer, p. 6.7
electroluminescent (EL) display,
    p. 6.22

electrostatic plotter, p. 6.15
flatbed plotter, p. 6.15
flat screen, p. 6.21
font, p. 6.12
gas plasma display, p. 6.23
gray-scale monitor, p. 6.20
hardcopy, p. 6.3
impact printer, p. 6.4
ink-jet printer, p. 6.9
laser printer, p. 6.9
line printer, p. 6.7
liquid crystal display (LCD),
    p. 6.21
monochrome monitor, p. 6.18

multimedia, p. 6.24
nonimpact printer, p. 6.8
page description language,
    p. 6.12
pixel, p. 6.16
plotter, p. 6.4, 6.14
portable printer, p. 6.12
printer, p. 6.4
resolution, p. 6.16
RGB color monitor, p. 6.18
softcopy, p. 6.3
thermal printer, p. 6.9
voice output system, p. 6.24

EXERCISES

SELF-TEST

1. Output is available in two forms: _____ and

   _____.

2. _____ printers produce images with a print head composed of a series of little print hammers.

3. Printers are either _____ or _____.

4. _____ are used most often for outputting specialized graphics such as blueprints.

5. The most commonly used impact printers are _____ printers.

6. The video display image is the most widely used softcopy output. (true/false)

7. _____ use heat to produce images on special chemically treated paper.

8. The _____ is the most popular softcopy output device used with microcomputers.

9. Portable printers have been developed that can easily be taken on the road. (true/false)

10. Laser printers that have a built-in _____ provide increased flexibility to produce different fonts and special graphics.

11. The image on a CRT is made up of _____, short for

    _____.

12. CRTs can be _____ or _____.

13. CRTs are large, power-hungry, and fragile. (true/false)

14. Three main types of flat screen technologies are:

    a.

    b.

    c.

15. Screen resolution is measured by vertical and horizontal lines of pixels. (true/false)

16. Voice output technology has advanced so far that most microcomputers are configured with voice output capabilities. (true/false)

17. The _____ plotter is the type of plotter most commonly used with microcomputers.

18. Some computer screens can display more than 16 million colors. (true/false)

19. Super VGA cards are used in Macintoshes. (true/false)

20. The more pixels that can be displayed on the screen, the better the

    _____ of the image.

Solutions: (1) hardcopy, softcopy; (2) dot-matrix; (3) impact, nonimpact; (4) plotters; (5) dot-matrix; (6) true; (7) thermal printers; (8) cathode-ray tube; (9) true; (10) page description language; (11) pixels, picture elements; (12) monochrome, color; (13) true; (14) liquid crystal display, electroluminescent display, gas plasma display; (15) true; (16) false; (17) flatbed; (18) true; (19) false; (20) resolution

MULTIPLE-CHOICE QUESTIONS

1. Which of the following is used to insure the high quality of computer output?

    a. voice output systems

    b. output controls

    c. computer output microfilm

    d. liquid crystal display

    e. ROM

2. Which of the following can be output by a computer?

    a. graphics

    b. voice

    c. text

    d. computer-usable data or information

    e. all the above

3. Output hardware is often categorized according to whether it:

    a. is expensive

    b. requires a large amount of electricity to work

    c. produces hardcopy or softcopy

    d. can fit on a desktop

    e. is fast

4. Large computer systems typically use:

    a. dot-matrix printers

    b. daisy wheel printers

    c. ink-jet printers

    d. line printers

    e. portable printers

5. Which of the following printers will you be sure not to use if your objective is to print on multicarbon forms?

    a. daisy wheel

    b. dot-matrix

    c. laser

    d. thimble

    e. line

Solutions: (1) b; (2) e; (3) c; (4) d; (5) c

SHORT-ANSWER QUESTIONS

1. What advantages does the laser printer have over other printers?

2. In what ways do daisy wheel and dot-matrix printers differ? Which printer is used more?

3. What are the principal differences between how an image is formed on a monochrome monitor and on an RGB monitor?

4. What is the difference between a character-mapped display and a bit-mapped display?

5. What were the main reasons for developing flat screen technologies?

6. What is the difference between hardcopy and softcopy? When might each be needed?

7. What must you consider before purchasing output hardware?

8. What is the difference between a character printer and a page printer?

9. What determines how many colors your monitor will display? What determines the monitor's resolution?

10. What is the main difference between a laser printer with a page description language and one without?

PROJECTS

1. Prepare an outline that indicates all the factors a user should consider when he or she is preparing to buy a printer.

2. If you could buy any printer you want, what type (make, model, etc.) would you choose? Does the printer need to be small (to fit in a small space)? Does it need to print across the width of wide paper (11 × 14 inches)? In color? On multi-carbon forms? Does it need to print graphics and typeset-quality text? Analyze what your needs might be and choose a printer (if necessary, make up what your needs might be). Review some of the current computer publications for articles or advertisements relating to printers. What is the approximate cost of the printer you would buy? Your needs should be able to justify the cost of the printer.

3. Visit a local computer store to compare the output quality of the different printers on display. Then obtain output samples and a brochure on each printer sold. After comparing output quality and price, what printer would you recommend to a friend who needs a printer that can output resumes, research reports, and professional-looking correspondence with a logo?

4. Explore the state of the art of computer-generated 3-D graphics. What challenges are involved in creating photo-realistic 3-D images? What hardware and software are needed to generate 3-D graphics? Who benefits from this technology?

5. At a computer store, compare the display quality of the following monitors: EGA, VGA, Super VGA, XGA, 16-bit Macintosh or Quadra, 24-bit Macintosh or Quadra. Which has the highest resolution? Displays the most colors? What size is the monitor you like best? How much does it cost and with what kind of microcomputer system is it compatible?

Applications Software and Systems Software

*W*hy can't you simply buy a diskette with the software program you need, put it into your microcomputer's disk drive, start it up, and have it run? Unfortunately, it's often not that easy; buying software is not like buying an audio cassette of your favorite music and slapping it into a tape deck, or renting a movie to play on your VCR. Computer software comes in two forms: applications software and systems software. Because different systems software is made for different purposes, and some applications software is not compatible with some systems software, it is important for users to understand the fundamental concepts and features of these two types of software and to learn to effectively evaluate software.

PREVIEW

When you have completed this chapter, you will be able to:

▼ Explain why you should try to evaluate your applications software requirements before your hardware and systems software requirements

▼ Describe what applications software is and categorize the types of applications software

▼ List and describe three types of systems software

▼ Explain the basic functions of an operating system and utilities

▼ Name the most common operating systems available for microcomputers

▼ List some points to consider when purchasing microcomputer applications or systems software

Can you use a daisy wheel printer to print out a portrait of Abraham Lincoln? Can you use an RGB monitor to show the colors of the rainbow? With your knowledge of hardware, you know the answers to these questions. Different equipment has different uses. Likewise with software: a software program designed to handle text may not necessarily be used to draw charts and graphs or to manipulate rows and columns of numbers.

No such thing as software existed in the earliest computers. Instead, to change computer instructions, technicians would actually have to rewire the equipment. Then, in the 1950s, computer research began to use punched cards to store program instructions. In the mid-1950s, high-speed storage devices that were developed for ready retrieval eliminated the need for hand-wired control panels. Since that time, the sophistication of computer hardware and software has increased exponentially.

The appearance of the microcomputer in the late 1970s made computer hardware and software accessible to many more people because they became more affordable, easier to use, and flexible enough to handle very specific job-related tasks. Because of this accessibility, a large pool of applications software has been created since then to satisfy almost any user's requirements. In other words, you do not have to be a specialist to use computer software to solve complicated and tedious problems. However, you will be entering the job race without your running shoes if you do not understand the uses of—and the differences among—types of software.

What Software Is Available, and How Good Is It?

To help you begin to understand the differences among types of software, let us repeat the definitions we gave back in Chapter 1 for applications and systems software.

▼ **Applications software** is a collection of related programs designed to perform a specific task—to solve a particular problem for the user. The task or problem may require, for example, computations for payroll processing or for maintaining different types of data in different types of files.

▼ **Systems software** "underlies" applications software; it starts up the computer and functions as the principal coordinator of all hardware components and applications software programs. Without systems software loaded into the RAM of your computer, your hardware and applications software are useless.

Every application works through "layers" in the computer to get to the hardware and perform the desired result. Think of the applications software layer as what the computer is doing and the systems software as how the computer does it. Both systems software and applications software must be purchased by the user (systems software is sometimes included in the price of a microcomputer).

Many people will buy an applications software program just because it was recommended by a friend. They do not bother to evaluate whether the program offers all the features and processing capabilities necessary to meet their needs. It's much easier in the short run to simply take the friend's recommendation, but, in the long run, a lot of extra time and money will be spent. Knowing what software is available—and how to evaluate it—is vital to satisfy processing requirements.

For large computer systems, the choice of systems software tends to be made by computer specialists, and the applications software is usually custom-designed for the system **(custom software).** For microcomputers, the user generally receives systems software along with the computer he or she purchases or uses at work. New versions of microcomputer systems software and applications software can be bought at computer stores.

If you are starting from scratch, you should choose your applications software first, after you identify your processing needs. Then choose compatible hardware models and systems software that will allow you to use your applications software efficiently and to expand your system if necessary. By choosing your applications software first, you will ensure that all your processing requirements will be satisfied. You won't be forced to buy a software package that is your second choice simply because your first choice wasn't compatible with the hardware or systems software already purchased.

When you go to work in an office, chances are that the computer hardware and systems software will already be in operation; so if you have to choose anything, it will most likely be applications software to help you do your job. If you do find yourself in a position to choose applications software, make sure not only that it will satisfy the processing requirements of your job, but also that it is compatible with your company's hardware and systems software.

There is much more applications software to choose from than systems software. Applications software can be purchased off the shelf of a computer store to satisfy almost any business requirement; this software is often referred to as **off-the-shelf software.** Deciding what applications program to use therefore requires very careful analysis.

Applications Software

After the days of rewiring computers had passed, only two sources existed for basic applications software: (1) software could be purchased from a computer hardware vendor, or (2) if you were a programmer, you could develop your own. Today, computer software has become a multibillion-dollar industry. More than a thousand companies have entered the applications software industry, and they have developed a wide variety of products. As a result, the number of sources of applications software has grown. Applications software can be acquired directly from a software manufacturer or from the growing number of businesses that specialize in the sale and support of microcomputer hardware and software. Most independent and computer chain stores devote a substantial amount of shelf space to applications software programs; some businesses specialize in selling only software.

If you can't find off-the-shelf software to meet your needs, you can develop—or have someone else develop—your own. If you don't know how to do it yourself, you can have the computer professionals within your own organization develop the software, or you can hire outside consultants to do it. Unfortunately, hiring a professional to write software for you usually costs much more than off-the-shelf software.

Just as the subject matter of a book determines what literary category it falls into (such as history, gardening, cooking, or fiction), the capabilities of an applications software program determine how it is categorized. Applications software falls into the following common categories:

- ▼ General business management
- ▼ Industry-specific
- ▼ Special disciplines
- ▼ Education
- ▼ Personal/home management
- ▼ General-purpose software for the user

Types of Popular Applications Software

So many different types of applications software packages have come into the market that deciding which ones to buy requires some investigation. Applications software is generally expensive. You can easily spend between $100 and $700 for a single package. In fact, individuals and companies typically spend much more on software than on hardware.

General business management software, the largest group of applications software, includes products that cover the vast majority of business software needs, including accounting, inventory control, finance and planning, personnel, office administration, project management, and many others. However, some industries have very specialized applications software requirements; specific software is designed to meet these needs. Typical industries requiring special products include specialized accounting services, advertising, agriculture and farm management, architecture, banking, construction, dentistry, engineering, legal services, leasing and rental companies, personnel agencies, property management, publishing, and others.

Special discipline software is a category set aside for such hobbies and special-interest areas as amateur radio, astrology, geography, mathematics, music, sports and leisure, visual arts, and others. *Education applications software* products focus on administration of educational institutions, computer-aided instruction (CAI), and special education. *Personal/home management software* includes products that relate to education, entertainment, finance, or home management.

This chapter highlights the types of **general-purpose applications software** you are likely to use in the business or professional environment. Specifically:

- ▼ Word processing
- ▼ Desktop publishing
- ▼ Electronic spreadsheets
- ▼ Database management systems
- ▼ Graphics
- ▼ Communications
- ▼ Integrated programs
- ▼ Computer-aided design, engineering, and manufacturing
- ▼ Applications software utilities
- ▼ Creativity software

Don't worry if you don't know all these terms; you will by the end of the chapter. However, before we discuss the different types of general-purpose applications software, we need to go over some of the features common to most kinds of applications software packages.

Common Features of Applications Software

This is a cursor. ▮

Cursor—This is the blinking symbol that shows you where data—a character, a space, a command—will be entered next. It can be moved with the cursor-movement keys or with a mouse.

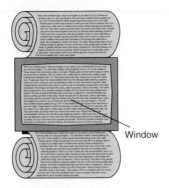

Window

Scrolling—This is the activity of moving images up or down on the display screen, so you can move to the beginning and the end of a document, for example. The portion of the file displayed on the screen is called a window. You can scroll by moving the cursor, using the PgUp and PgDn keys, using the mouse to point at and "click" on (select by pressing the mouse button) specified parts of the screen, or by using certain commands specified in the application package's documentation.

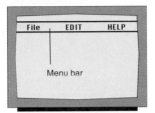

Menu bar

Menu bar—This is a row of command options displayed across the top or the bottom of the screen.

Pull down menu

Pull-down menu—This is a list of command options, or choices, that are displayed from the top of the screen downward when its title is selected from the menu bar. Pull-down menus can be opened by keystroke commands or by "clicking" (pressing) the mouse button while pointing to the title and then dragging the mouse pointer down.

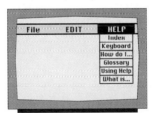

Help screen—This is on-screen instruction regarding the use of the software. The Help menu or options are accessed by clicking the mouse on the Help menu bar title or by using a specified function key (usually F1). The user then chooses the option he or she needs help with—such as printing a document.

Dialog box—This is a box on the screen that contains a message requiring a response from the user.

Word Processing Software

Word processing software offers capabilities that greatly enhance the user's ability to create and edit documents. It enables the user to easily insert, delete, and move words, sentences, and paragraphs—without ever using an eraser. Word processing programs also offer a number of features for "dressing up" documents with variable margins, type sizes, and styles. The user can do all these manipulations on screen, before printing out hardcopy.

Table 1 provides a list of some of the common features of word processing software packages. Figure 1 shows screens from the WordPerfect word processing program and Microsoft Word for the Macintosh. Besides WordPerfect and Microsoft Word, some popular word processing packages are WordStar, Multi-Mate Advantage, PC-Write, OfficeWriter, XyWrite III Plus, and Ami Professional.

Some word processing packages, including WordPerfect, Microsoft Word, and Ami Professional, provide desktop publishing features that enable users to integrate, or combine, graphics and text on a professional-looking page. Compared to dedicated desktop publishing packages (described shortly), word processing packages lack the ease with which different elements in a document can be placed and rearranged. However, the line that differentiates word processing packages and desktop publishing packages is blurring.

TABLE 1

Some Common Word Processing Software Features

Correcting: Deleting and inserting. You simply place the cursor where you want to correct a mistake and press either the Delete key or the Backspace key to delete characters. You can then type in new characters. (Many packages offer shortcuts to deleting and inserting—for example, deleting many lines of text at one time by hitting a special sequence of keys.)

Block and move (or cut and paste): Marking and changing the position of a large block of text; this can be done even between different documents, not just within the same document.

Check spelling: Many packages come with a spelling checker program that, when executed, will alert you to misspelled words and offer correct versions.

Thesaurus: Thesaurus programs allow the user to pick word substitutions. For example, if you are writing a letter and want to use a more exciting word than *impressive*, you can activate your thesaurus program and ask for alternatives to that word—such as *awe-inspiring* or *thrilling*.

Mail merge: Most word processing programs allow the user to combine different parts of different documents (files) to make the production of form letters much easier, faster, and less tedious than doing the same thing using a typewriter. For example, you can combine address files with a letter file that contains special codes where the address information is supposed to be. The program will insert the different addresses in copies of the letter and print them out.

Scrolling: This feature allows the user to "roll" text up or down the screen; you can't see your long document all at once, but you can scroll the text to reach the point you are interested in. Most packages allow you to "jump" over many pages at a time—for example, from the beginning of a document straight to the end.

Search and replace: You can easily search through a document for a particular word—for example, a misspelled name—and replace it with another word.

Footnote placement: This feature allows the user to build a footnote file at the same time he or she is writing a document; the program then automatically places the footnotes at appropriate page bottoms when the document is printed.

Outlining: Some packages automatically outline the document for you; you can use the outline as a table of contents.

Split screen: This feature allows you to work on two documents at once—one at the top of the screen and one at the bottom. You can scroll each document independently.

Word wrap: Words automatically break to the next line; the user does not have to press Return or Enter.

Font choice: Many packages allow you to change the typeface and the size of the characters to improve the document's appearance.

Justify/unjustify: This feature allows you to print text aligned on both right and left margins (justified, like the main text in this book) or let the words break without aligning (unjustified, or ragged, like the text at the right side of this table).

Boldface/italic/underline: Word processing software makes it easy to emphasize text by using **bold**, *italic*, or underlining.

File format exchange: A file format is the structure that defines the way a file is stored and the way it appears on the screen or in print. In addition to text, word processing files also contain these formatting codes. Every word processing program has a different format. To exchange word processing files (for example, to work on a document in WordPerfect that was originally written in Microsoft Word), you use the program's file format conversion feature.

Desktop Publishing Software

Desktop publishing (DTP) is a combination of hardware—usually microcomputer, hard disk, laser printer, and scanner—and software that together provide near-typeset-quality output in a variety of sizes, styles, and type fonts. This technology can integrate graphics and text on a professional-looking page (Figure 2). Well-known desktop publishing software packages are Aldus PageMaker, Ready-Set-Go, Ventura, and Quark XPress. Desktop publishing software allows the user to combine, into one file or output report, the elements from different files that have been generated using different software programs (Figure 3).

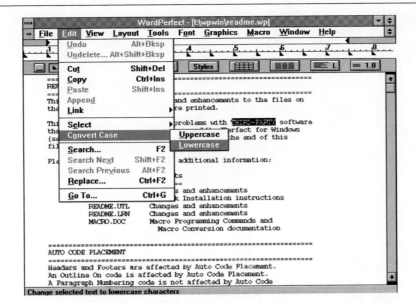

FIGURE 1

Most word processing packages provide a number of different menus to use for editing your documents. Shown here are a PC WordPerfect Edit menu (top) and a Macintosh Microsoft Word screen (bottom) showing the Fonts pull-down menu. (Different type sizes are listed at the top of the pull-down menu, and different type styles are listed at the bottom.)

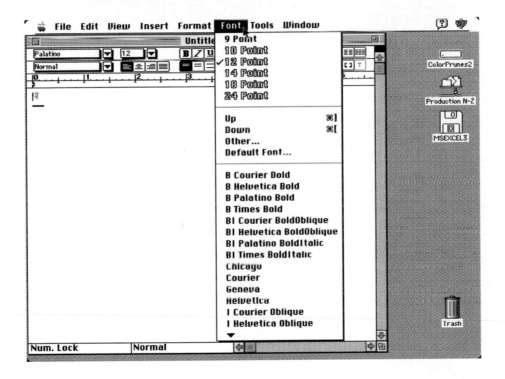

Desktop publishing software takes advantage of both the increased processing power and storage capacities of today's microcomputers and the flexibility in terms of output that a laser printer provides. For a laser printer to effectively combine text and graphics on a single page, a *page description language,* such as Adobe's PostScript, must be stored in the printer's memory and be usable by the software.

Desktop publishing software, often referred to as **page description software,** enables users to combine text and graphics in an organized format on a single page. Page description software falls into two categories—code-oriented and "what-you-see-is-what-you-get" (WYSIWYG). With a **code-oriented page description software** (Figure 4), formatting instructions are embedded (keyed) into a document in the form of codes. Code-oriented packages provide the user with more sophisticated desktop publishing options, compared to the WYSIWYG

FIGURE 2

Do it yourself! This ad was done in a short time using a microcomputer-based desktop publishing system.

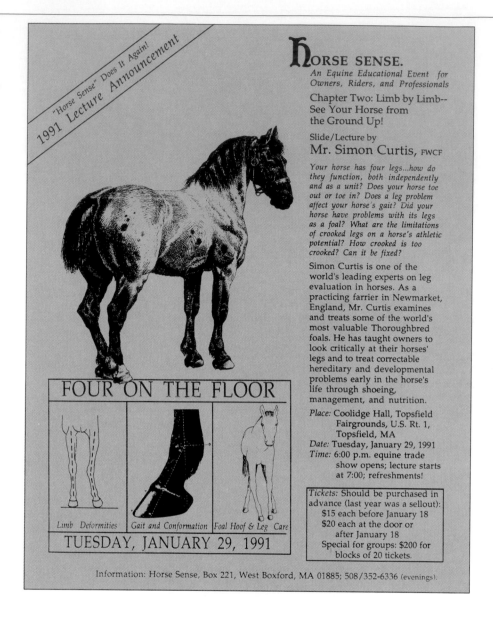

packages, and are based on traditional typesetting techniques, which also use formatting codes. There are two disadvantages to using this type of package. First, because of its high degree of sophistication, the user should have some typesetting experience before attempting to use the package. Second, the user can't see the final output until it's printed out. A user who is unfamiliar with how certain codes will affect the report may have to perform countless revisions. However, these programs usually require less RAM, less processing power, and less storage capacity than the WYSIWYG programs. Among the code-oriented packages being used today are SC-LaserPlus, from Graham Software Corporation, and Deskset, from G.O. Graphics.

WYSIWYG programs (PageMaker, Ventura Publisher, and Quark XPress) allow the user to see the report on the screen as it will appear when it is printed out (Figure 5). For this reason, many people prefer the WYSIWYG programs over the code-oriented programs; users don't have to wait until they print to see what a document will look like. With a WYSIWYG program, the user chooses from lists of menu options to format the text. This type of desktop publishing software is more power-, memory-, and storage-hungry than code-oriented software.

(a)

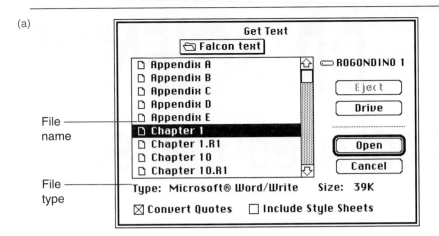

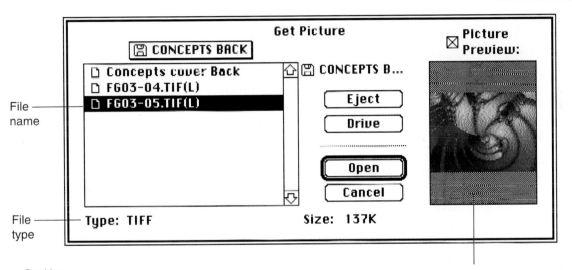

FIGURE 3

(a) Aldus PageMaker desktop publishing screens. The top screen shows that a text file is being imported into the desktop publishing program from a word-processing program (Microsoft Word). The bottom screen indicates that a graphics file is being brought in to be put on a page (TIFF = tagged image file format, a common bit-mapped format for storing graphic images). (b) This diagram shows how DTP software uses files from other applications to produce documents with text and graphics.

File name

File type

File name

File type

Preview of illustration

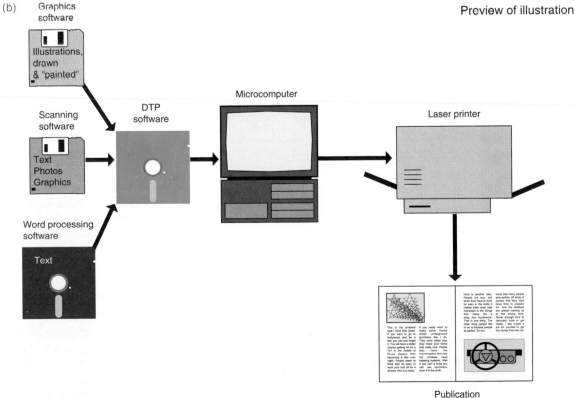

Publication

FIGURE 4

Code-oriented page description software. The top two lines (a bumper sticker) were printed according to the partial listing of codes shown below it, which is what the user would have seen on the screen. The output was not displayed before it was printed.

DR. SCIENCE

He's not a real comedian

```
%!
/paperheight 11 72 mul def
/paperwidth 8.5 72 mul def
/width paperheight def
/height paperwidth 2 div def
/margin .375 72 mul def
/xcenter paperwidth 2 div def
/ycenter paperheight 2 div def

%xcenter ycenter translate
%.25 .25 scale
%xcenter neg ycenter neg translate
```

FIGURE 5

WYSIWYG document. The printed restaurant menu shown at the bottom was displayed on the computer screen (top) before it was printed out. The software documentation explains what the option symbols on the left and bottom sides of the screen mean.

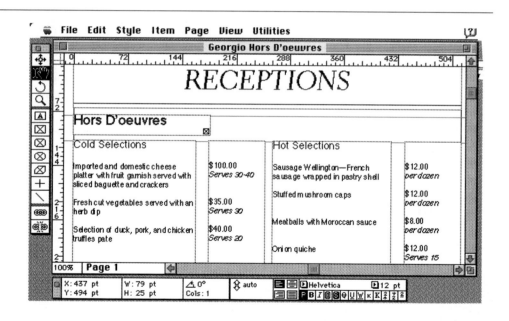

RECEPTIONS

Hors D'oeuvres

Cold Selections

Imported and domestic cheese platter with fruit garnish served with sliced baguette and crackers	$100.00	*Serves 30-40*
Fresh cut vegetables served with an herb dip	$35.00	*Serves 30*
Selection of duck, pork, and chicken truffles pate	$40.00	*Serves 20*

Hot Selections

Sausage Wellington—French sausage wrapped in pastry shell	$12.00	*per dozen*
Stuffed mushroom caps	$12.00	*per dozen*
Meatballs with Moroccan sauce	$8.00	*per dozen*
Onion quiche	$12.00	*Serves 15*

Because it can lead to tremendous savings, desktop publishing can significantly affect any user who currently sends text or graphics out to a professional typesetter. Instead of hiring a typesetter to format documents and graphics into reports, which can be costly, with a desktop publishing system you can design the document yourself—*once you have been trained to do it properly*. Desktop publishing can offer several advantages:

▼ *You save money.* Sending a report, a newsletter, or a brochure out to a professional typesetter can easily cost a few hundred dollars.

▼ *You save time.* Using a desktop publishing system can cut the time spent on preparing documents by nearly 50%. Because you are preparing the report yourself electronically using a desktop publishing system, you can make any needed revisions immediately. The turnaround time necessary to make revisions when you are using a typesetter can easily add days onto a production schedule.

▼ *You maintain control.* You are in charge of the final output and production schedule.

A typical desktop publishing system, including a microcomputer with mouse, a laser printer, and page description software, costs around $8,000–$10,000. This may sound like a lot of money, but when you consider that you might easily spend that much having just a few projects professionally designed and typeset, the cost doesn't look so bad. The cost of a desktop publishing system increases when certain other peripherals are included in the overall system; for example, an optical scanner for inserting drawings and photos into a report and a mouse and graphics tablet for drawing specialized images.

Spreadsheet Software

With **spreadsheet software,** based on the traditional accounting worksheet, the user can develop personalized reports involving the use of extensive mathematical, financial, statistical, and logical processing. Its automatic calculation abilities can save the user almost a lifetime of tedious arithmetic. The small spreadsheet shown in Figure 6 was created by a beginner in less than an hour. This spreadsheet is designed to calculate expense totals and percentages. Some of the terms you will encounter when using spreadsheets are listed in Table 2. Figure 10 shows a window (screen-size working area) of a Lotus 1-2-3 electronic spreadsheet.

One of the most useful functions of spreadsheet software is the performance of *"What if" analyses.* The user can say: "What if we changed this number? How would future income be affected?" and get an immediate answer by having the spreadsheet software automatically recalculate *all* numbers based on the one change. Some spreadsheet packages, including versions 2.2 through 3.4 of Lotus 1-2-3, enable you to *link* spreadsheets together—this is called *dynamic file linking.* If a number, such as an expense amount, is changed in one spreadsheet, the change is automatically reflected in other spreadsheet files that might be affected by the change.

Along with Lotus 1-2-3, popular off-the-shelf spreadsheet packages are Microsoft Excel, Quattro, and Quattro Pro.

Database Management System Software

Database management system (DBMS) software allows the user to store large amounts of data that can be easily retrieved and manipulated with great flexibility to produce reports. With database management system software, also called a *database manager,* you can compile huge lists of data and manipulate, store, and retrieve it without having to touch a single file cabinet or folder. Table 3 lists some common functions of database management software.

FIGURE 6

Electronic spreadsheets (b) look much like spreadsheets created manually (a). However, when a number is changed in an electronic spreadsheet, all totals are automatically updated—certainly not the case when you work with a spreadsheet by hand!

(a)

EXPENSE	JAN.	FEB.	MAR.	TOTAL
TEL	48.50	51.00	37.90	137.40
UTIL	21.70	30.00	25.00	76.70
RENT	465.00	465.00	465.00	1,395.00
AUTO	35.00	211.00	42.00	288.00
MISC	120.00	93.00	41.43	254.43
TOTAL	$690.20	$850.00	$611.33	$2,151.53

(b)

```
A1: [W14]                                                        READY

          A          B         C         D         E         F
  1
  2   EXPENSE TYPE     JAN       FEB       MAR      TOTAL    PERCENT
  3   ----------------------------------------------------------------
  4   TELEPHONE      $48.50    $51.00    $37.90    $137.40     6.39%
  5   UTILITIES      $21.70    $30.00    $25.00     $76.70     3.56%
  6   RENT          $465.00   $465.00   $465.00  $1,395.00    64.84%
  7   AUTOMOBILE     $35.00   $211.00    $42.00    $280.00    13.39%
  8   MISCELLANEOUS $120.00    $93.00    $41.43    $254.43    11.83%
  9   ----------------------------------------------------------------
 10   TOTAL         $690.20   $850.00   $611.33  $2,151.53   100.00%
 11
 12
 13
 14
 15
 16
 17
 18
 19
 20
 23-Feb-93  02:36 PM            UNDO                         CAPS
```

TABLE 2

Common Spreadsheet Terminology

Cell pointer (cursor): Indicates the position where data is to be entered or changed; the user moves the cursor around the spreadsheet, using the particular software package's commands.

Column labels: The column headings across the top of the worksheet area.

Row labels: The row headings that go down the left side of the worksheet area.

Cell: The intersection of a column and a row; a cell holds a single unit of information.

Value: The number within a cell.

Cell address: The location of a cell. For example, B3 is the address of the cell at the intersection of column B and row 3.

Window: The screen-size area of the spreadsheet that the user can view at one time (about 8 columns and 20 rows). Most spreadsheets can have up to 8,192 columns and 256 rows; some have as many as 10,000 columns and more than 300 rows (AppleWorks).

Formula: Instructions for calculations; these calculations are executed by the software based on commands issued by the user.

Recalculation: Automatic reworking of all the formulas and data according to changes the user makes in the spreadsheet.

Scrolling: "Rolling" the spreadsheet area up and down, and right and left, on the screen to see different parts of the spreadsheet.

Graphics: Most spreadsheets allow users to display data in graphic form, such as bar, line, and pie charts.

TABLE 3

Common Functions of Database Management System Software

Create records: Group related data concerning one unit of interest—for example, one employee. A company's database would have one record for each employee.

Create fields: Group units of data within a record. A field might contain one employee's name, for example.

Retrieve and display: When the user issues database commands (determined by the particular DBMS program) and specifies the record and field needed, the DBMS program retrieves the record and displays the appropriate section of it on the screen. The user can then change data as necessary.

Sort: Data is entered into the database in a random fashion; however, the user can use the sort function of the DBMS program to output records in a file in several different ways—for example, alphabetically by employee last name, chronologically according to date hired, or by ZIP code. The field according to which the records are ordered is the *key field*.

Calculate: Some DBMS programs include formulas that allow the user to calculate, for example, averages or highest and lowest values.

Interact: Many DBMS programs can be integrated with other types of applications software—for example, with a spreadsheet program. In other words, the data in the DBMS program can be displayed and manipulated within the spreadsheet program.

Two main categories of DBMS software exist:

▼ Flat-file systems

▼ Relational systems

Flat-file database management systems (also called **file management systems**) can deal with information in only one file at a time. They can't establish relationships among data stored in different files. **Relational DBMSs** can establish links by referring to fields that store the same type of data in different databases. These links enable users to update several files at once or generate a report using data from different database files. Although flat-file DBMSs are perfectly suited for generating mailing labels, most business applications require the use of a DBMS with relational capabilities.

Popular off-the-shelf DBMS packages include dBASE III Plus, dBASE IV, Paradox, Q&A, and Filepro.

Graphics Software

One picture is often worth a thousand words. Thus reports and presentations that include graphics can be much more effective than those that don't. **Graphics software** enables users to produce many types of graphic creations.

In general, **analytical graphics** are basic graphical forms used to make numerical data easier to understand. The most common analytical graphic forms are bar graphs, line charts, and pie charts—or a combination of these forms (Figure 7). The user can view such graphics on the screen (color or monochrome) or print them out. Most analytical graphics programs come as part of spreadsheet packages.

Presentation graphics are fancier and more dramatic than analytical graphics, and so the software that produces them is more sophisticated (Figure 8). Presentation graphics allow the user to function as an artist and combine freeform shapes and text to produce exciting output on the screen, on paper, and on transparencies and film (for slides and photos). Of course, the user can also produce output using bar graphs, line charts, and pie charts. Popular presentation graphics programs are Harvard Graphics, PC Paintbrush, Adobe Illustrator, CorelDRAW, Hollywood, and Persuasion.

FIGURE 7

Analytical graphics. Bar, line, and pie charts are commonly used to display spreadsheet data in graphical form.

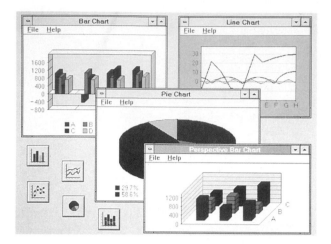
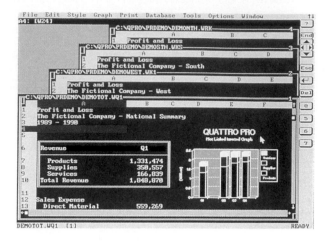

FIGURE 8

Presentation graphics software and software drawing tools provide the user with the means of producing sophisticated graphics.

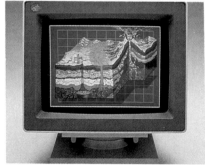
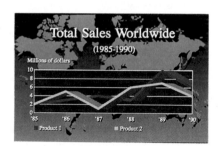

Communications Software

Communications software allows users to access software and data from a computer in a remote location and to transmit data to a computer in a remote location—in other words, to establish *connectivity.* For example, the traveling business professional in Seattle, Washington, who needs to access client information daily from the company's main computer in San Diego, California, needs some communications software and a modem to enable his or her laptop computer to communicate long-distance. Popular microcomputer communications programs are ProComm, Smartcom II, Smartcom III, and Crosstalk XVI.

Communications software and hardware have become important to the computer user. Through systems connectivity the microcomputer is now able to share resources and services previously available only to users of large computer systems.

Integrated Software

Integrated software represents the industry's effort to combine all the software capabilities that the typical user may need into a single package with a common set of commands and rules for its use. The objective is to allow the user to perform a variety of tasks without having to switch software programs and learn different commands and procedures to run each one. Integrated software combines the capabilities of word processing, electronic spreadsheets, database management systems, graphics, and data communications (using telephone lines, satellites, and other communications technology to transmit data and information) into one program.

Microsoft Works is a well-known integrated software package; others are Framework III and Framework IV, Enable, and PFS: 1st Choice. SmartSuite for Windows integrates Lotus 1-2-3 spreadsheet software with Ami Pro word processing software, Freelance Graphics software, and cc:Mail messaging software.

Computer-Aided Design, Engineering, and Manufacturing

Industry, especially manufacturing, has probably experienced the greatest economic impact of computer graphics. Mechanical drawings that used to take days or weeks to complete can now be done in less than a day. Among other things, the drawings can be three-dimensional, rotated, shown in detailed sections or as a whole, automatically rendered on a different scale, and easily corrected and revised. But the use of computer graphics has evolved beyond the rendering of drawings; it is now used to help design, engineer, and manufacture products of all kinds, from nuts and bolts to computer chips to boats and airplanes.

Computer-aided design (CAD) shortens the design cycle by allowing manufacturers to shape new products on the screen without having to first build expensive models (Figure 9). The final design data and images can be sent to a **computer-aided engineering (CAE)** system, which subjects the design to extensive analysis and testing that might be too expensive to do in the real world (Figure 10). From there, the product design may be sent to a **computer-aided manufacturing (CAM)** system, which makes use of the stored computer images in automating the machines (unintelligent robots) that manufacture the finished products. Computer simulation in industry has increased productivity enormously and made previously expensive procedures affordable.

FIGURE 9

CAD. This illustration shows front car-doors designed to resist impact.

FIGURE 10

CAE. This national test facility is using a computer system to simulate and test space technology.

FIGURE 11

Computer-aided research and reconstruction. (a) Actual (wrapped) head of an ancient mummy; (b) (c) (d)—three stages in computer-based reconstruction of the person's face.

(a)

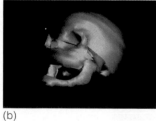

(b)

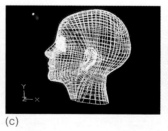

(c)

(d)

CAD and CAE software is also used in special research and reconstruction programs, such as determining what an ancient mummified Egyptian looked like when alive (Figure 11).

Applications Software Utilities

Many different types of **applications software utilities**—inexpensive programs that perform some basic "office management" functions—are available for purchase. These programs can be categorized as follows:

▼ Desktop management utilities   ▼ Disk utilities

▼ Add-on utilities

▼ Disk utilities

▼ Keyboard and screen utilities

Depending on their function, the instructions in utility programs reside either in RAM or on disk. A **RAM-resident utility** is designed to be available at any time to the user because it resides in RAM at all times while the computer is on, even when the utility is not being used. In other words, once such a program is loaded into your computer (for example, from a diskette), a copy stays in RAM, "underneath" any applications software programs you may be using, until you turn the power off. As long as the power is on, you do not have to put the software disk back in the drive to use the utility program—you simply access it from RAM with certain keystrokes.

A **desktop management utility,** which is usually RAM-resident, allows the user to computerize many routine activities, including using a calculator, organizing an appointment calendar (Figure 12), taking notes, looking up words in a dictionary to make sure they are spelled correctly, and many more. The bottom line is that desktop manager software can save the user time. Sidekick and Pop-Up Windows are two popular desktop management packages. Desktop management utilities are also called *PIMs—Personal Information Managers.*

Add-on utilities are usually RAM-resident and are used in conjunction with popular applications software packages. For example, to print wide electronic spreadsheets lengthwise on continuous-form paper (instead of across the width of the paper), many users use a program called Sideways. Allways, from Funk Software, is an add-on utility that is sold with versions 2.2 and 3.0 of Lotus 1-2-3. This utility greatly enhances the way a spreadsheet appears in printed form through the use of stylized fonts in different sizes.

Disk utilities are usually purchased on floppy disks and then stored on hard disk. They provide users with a number of special capabilities, including:

▼ Recovering files that have been accidentally erased

▼ Retrieving damaged files

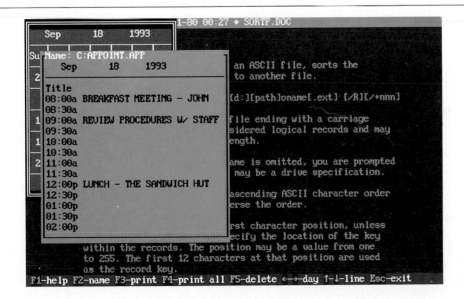

FIGURE 12

This desktop manager software utility allows the user to computerize many routine activities, such as keeping track of appointments.

▼ Making automatic backup copies of a hard disk

▼ Organizing a hard disk by means of a menu system

▼ Compressing existing files on hard disk in order to free up room for additional files

▼ "Parking" the internal hard disk drive's actuator arm with the read/write heads in preparation for moving the computer; this way, disk damage can be avoided (not all computers need to have their disks parked before they are moved)

▼ Defragmentation (When you constantly add and erase files from your hard disk, the space that you free up will frequently be filled up with parts of large files. When this happens, the hard disk must work longer and harder dealing with fragmented files, resulting in delays.)

Keyboard utilities, such as Cursorific, are usually RAM-resident and enable you to change the way the cursor appears on the screen—usually by making it larger—so it is easier to see.

Screen utilities are used to increase the life of your screen. If your microcomputer is turned on and you don't use it for a period of a few minutes, a screen utility will automatically make the screen go blank or display moving graphics, such as "fireworks" or Mowin' Man, who engages in a never-ending battle to keep a screen of growing grass mowed. This saves your screen from having an image permanently burned onto the screen (which leaves a "ghost"). When you press a key, the screen will again display the image that was showing previously.

We have mentioned only a few of the many utilities available. If your applications software package can't do something you want it to, there may be a utility that can. You can find out by phoning a computer software store.

Creativity Software

Dr. Edward Land, inventor of the Polaroid camera, described creativity as "the sudden cessation of stupidity." But what if you, like many of us, have trouble coming up with new, original ideas? If you're a computer user, you can try an idea-generating software package, such as Idea Generator Plus, IdeaFisher MindLink Problem Solver, or Brainstorm. Such programs can assist you through the idea-generation process and help you to explore factors and variables that you might have overlooked or thought unimportant or obvious, as well as to think through solutions from different perspectives.

Some of these programs, like IdeaFisher, ask you questions about your problem and give you dozens of ideas based on the information you provide. (Idea Fisher is credited with a number of successful advertising slogans, including Kentucky Fried Chicken's "Come Home to Roost at KFC.")

Hypertext and Multimedia

Two kinds of sophisticated applications software that do not easily fit into any of the preceding categories are hypertext and multimedia. **Hypertext** software— such as HyperCard, used on the Macintosh microcomputer, and Linkway, used on IBM PCs and PS/2 microcomputers—links basic file units comprising text and/or graphics with one another in creative ways. In HyperCard (Figure 13), a screen of information forms a record called a *card;* related groups of cards are organized into files called *stacks.* The user can work with the cards and stacks provided by the software program (for example, all the information in an encyclopedia) or create cards and stacks of text and graphics at will and combine them in all sorts of ways by using a mouse to click on "buttons" on the

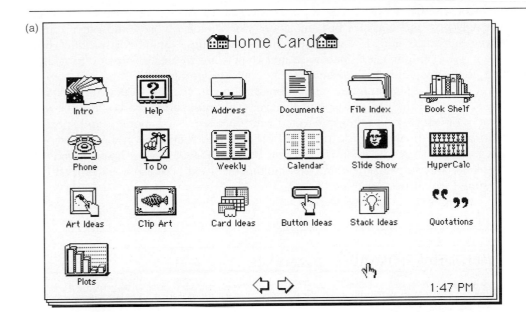

FIGURE 13

HyperCard software provides a new kind of "information environment" for the Apple Macintosh computer. It stores information about any subject in the form of words, charts, sounds, pictures, and digitized photographs. Any "card" (piece of information) in any "stack" (related cards) can connect to any other card. (a) The Home card is the starting place for moving around in HyperCard. The various icons represent stacks for the user to click on, using a mouse. (b) An example of how HyperCard works.

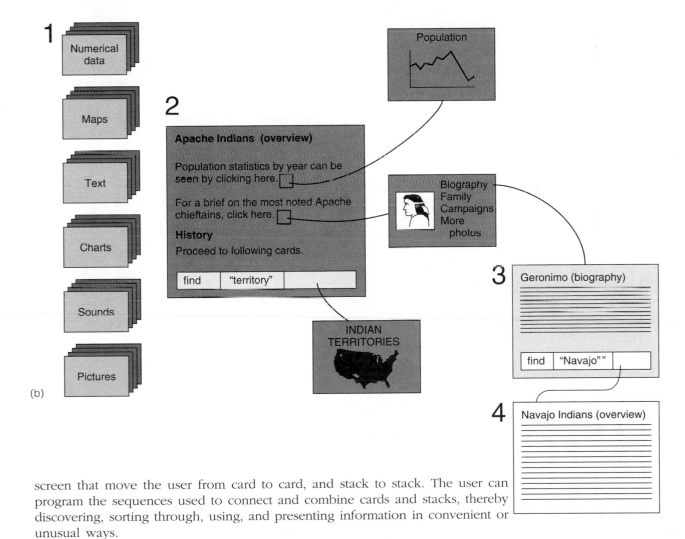

screen that move the user from card to card, and stack to stack. The user can program the sequences used to connect and combine cards and stacks, thereby discovering, sorting through, using, and presenting information in convenient or unusual ways.

Stackware, software packages that are collections of information created and used with HyperCard, is available at computer stores on such varied topics as amino acids, vitamin structures, galaxies, the ear, DNA structures, and the moons of Jupiter.

Multimedia is even more sophisticated than hypertext because it combines not only text and graphics but animation, video, music, voice, and other sound effects as well (Figure 14). In creating and presenting a multimedia product, one might, for example, use a Macintosh and HyperCard to create software programs that could integrate input data. The data could be input in the form of text and graphics through a scanner, animation through a special video camera, and sound through the use of a sound digitizer. The integrated data could be stored on a CD-ROM disk and then presented later on a television monitor and speaker that can run an optical disk; or stored on tape and then run on a VCR; or output from a microcomputer with a sound board, CD-ROM drive, head phones or speakers, and software that supports multimedia. Text could also be printed out or stored on diskette or tape.

FIGURE 14

(a) Multimedia information (adapted from Eric Jungerman, *San Francisco Chronicle*, Dec. 7 1992, p. B1); (b) multimedia equipment requirements (adapted from R. Schultheis and M. Summer. Homewood, Ill.: 1992, p. 144—and *PC World*, March 1990, p. 195).

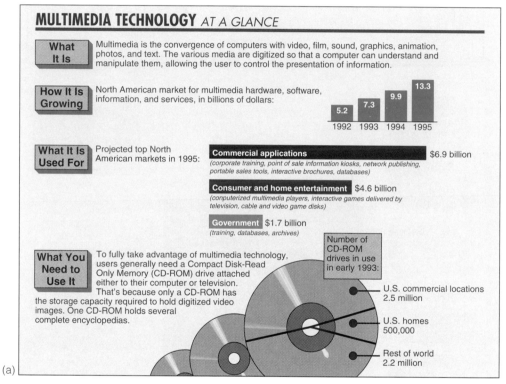

(a)

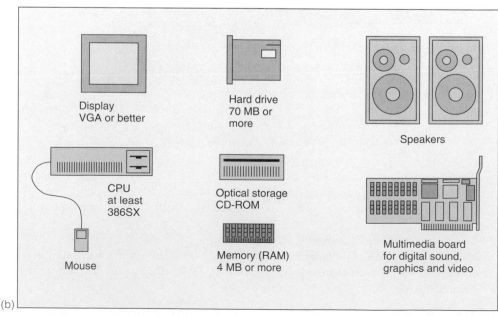

(b)

Among other programs, multimedia sounds are available on disk for users with a Macintosh microcomputer, 2 MB of RAM, HyperCard, and applications software for sound management (such as HyperComposer). For example, Desktop Sounds version 1 includes the following sound effects: aircraft, animals, automotive, combat, comedy, crowds, household, and more. PC users can also enjoy multimedia packages—such as the one tucked in the back of a coffee-table book, *From Alice to Ocean,* by photojournalist Rick Smelan. Packed with narration, music, animation, video, and 300 color photographs not included in the printed version, the CD-ROM disks allow viewers to fully experience one woman's solitary 7½-month camel journey across the Australian wilderness.

Some major publications are starting to use the CD-ROM format. For example, *Newsweek* became the first general-interest magazine to publish an ongoing version on multimedia compact disk. The CDs mix text with still photography, video, animation, and sound.

Multimedia programs are selling well to large corporations, which use them to reduce the time needed for employee training courses by 40% and cut the cost by 30%. However, among general users the number of computers equipped to handle multimedia is still relatively small. Acceptance is further limited because there is no single standard for personal computers using sound and video.

Applications Software Versions

Many software developers sell different versions of the same software application. Each version is usually designated by a different number—generally, the higher the number, the more current the version and the more features included with the package. For example, Lotus 1-2-3 is available in versions 2.2 through 3.4; WordPerfect for the PC in 4.2, 5.0, 5.1, 5.2, and 6.0; Microsoft Windows in 3.0 and 3.1—and so on. In some cases, different versions are written to be used with particular microcomputer systems such as IBM compatibles or Macintosh microcomputers. If you buy a software package, make sure you have the version that goes with your microcomputer.

A user who buys a certain version of a software application may after a few months find that a later version of the same application is now available. This user has two choices: Either stay with the purchased version or upgrade (usually for a fee) to the later version. Because many users want the "latest," they will spend the extra amount for the most recent version of a software package, even if their current version satisfies all of their processing requirements.

If you want to try to keep track of all the software available, you can read software catalogs and directories. For example, magazines such as *Compute, PC World, PC Sources,* and *PC Computing* (all for the IBM PC and clones) and *Macworld* and *MacUser* (for the Macintosh) provide general users with reviews of many different kinds of software. *PC Magazine* and *InfoWorld* (Figure 20) also provide valuable guides to computer hardware, software, services, and related topics of interest. *Byte* magazine's articles are for the more advanced user. *PC Novice* is a great help to beginning PC users.

Installing Applications Software

Once you have bought your applications software package, you must install it to work with your microcomputer system. **Software installation** usually involves telling the software the characteristics of the hardware you will be using so that the software will run smoothly. When you purchase a software application, check to see that the documentation tells you how to install the software.

Systems Software

Without systems software you won't be able to use any applications software. Systems software tells the computer how to interpret data and instructions; how to run peripheral equipment like printers, keyboards, and disk drives; and how to use the hardware in general. Also, it allows you, the user, to interact with the computer. Systems software comprises a large number of instructions that can be grouped into the following categories:

1. Internal command instructions
2. External command instructions
3. Language processors

Internal and external command instructions are often referred to collectively as the **operating system,** or operating systems software.

As a computer user, you will have to use systems software, so it is important to understand the role it plays in the computer system.

Internal Command Instructions

Internal command instructions, often called *resident commands,* can be thought of as the innermost layer of systems software. These instructions direct and coordinate other types of software and the computer hardware. They are automatically loaded into RAM from disk when you turn on the microcomputer—called **booting**—and they reside in RAM until the computer is turned off (Figure 15). Without these instructions in RAM, a computer can be likened to a race car without fuel for the engine and without a driver to decide where to go and how fast. That is why the primary purpose of the procedures followed in starting up a computer is to load a copy of these operating system instructions into RAM. These instructions are referred to as *internal command instructions* because, in order to be usable, they must be stored on an internal storage device (namely, RAM). Operating instructions stored on an external storage device (such as a diskette or a hard disk) are referred to as *external command instructions* (discussed in the next section). Internal command instructions are so important to the functioning of your computer that they must be directly accessible to the microprocessor in RAM at all times.

FIGURE 15

Certain systems software instructions must be stored in RAM at all times for the user to be able to use applications software.

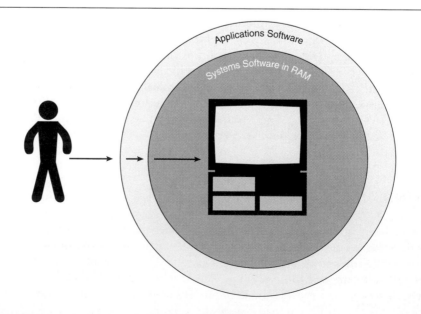

The "captain" of the portion of the operating system that is stored in RAM is often referred to as the **supervisor,** or the **control program.** The supervisor calls in other parts of the operating system (external command instructions) and language processors as needed from secondary storage. The supervisor controls all other programs in the computer. For example, it:

▼ Coordinates processing

▼ Manages the use of RAM

▼ Allocates use of peripheral devices

▼ Checks equipment malfunction and displays error messages

▼ Manages files stored on disk

As we mentioned previously, microcomputer operating systems often come with the microcomputer (usually on diskettes). *If you have decided to use certain applications software packages, you must make sure to choose a computer whose systems software is compatible with those software packages*—or be prepared to buy special hardware and software to make them compatible. We'll describe the most popular types of systems software used on microcomputers at the end of this chapter.

External Command Instructions

External command instructions are general-purpose operating system instructions that take care of what many people call "housekeeping tasks." External command instructions are not needed to run applications software; for this reason, they reside in secondary storage, instead of in RAM, until needed. These instructions are generally provided by the computer manufacturer when you purchase a microcomputer.

Language Processors

You will recall that computers understand only one language—machine language "written" using the digits 1 and 0. Because it is too time-consuming to write programs in machine language, **high-level programming languages** were developed that are easier to learn and use. With high-level languages, programmers don't have to use 1s and 0s to represent computer instructions. Instead, they use everyday text and mathematical formulas, which enable them to use fewer instructions in a program. Programs written using high-level languages—called **source code**—still have to be converted into a machine-language version—called **object code**—before the computer "understands" them (Figure 22).

Programmers use a type of systems software called a **language processor,** or a **translator,** to convert high-level instructions into machine language—for example, the one used by an IBM microcomputer. You will need to use a language processor only if you create a program using a high-level language such as BASIC (*B*eginner's *A*ll-purpose *S*ymbolic *I*nstruction *C*ode), which is commonly taught in university-level courses.

When you purchase an applications software package, the software instructions have already been converted by a language processor into machine language so that you can use the package. Programmers use two types of language processors: *compilers* and *interpreters*.

The **compiler** is a language processor that translates an *entire* high-level language program into a machine-language version of the program in a single process. If no programming errors exist in the source code, the program becomes operative.

FIGURE 16

A language processor translates the high-level language program (source code) into a machine-language version of the program (object code) before the computer can execute the program.

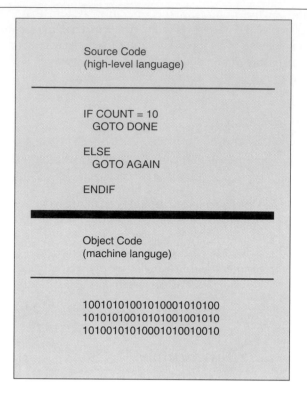

Source Code
(high-level language)

IF COUNT = 10
    GOTO DONE

ELSE
    GOTO AGAIN

ENDIF

Object Code
(machine languge)

10010101001010001010100
10101010010101001001010
10100101010001010010010

The **interpreter** is a language processor that converts and executes high-level language instructions one instruction statement at a time. If an error is detected in the source code, the interpreter displays immediate feedback on the screen. For this reason, interpreters are commonly used with small and simple programs and in educational settings because the user receives immediate feedback.

The most important difference between using compiled or interpreted software is speed. Programs that are compiled tend to execute up to five times faster than programs that are interpreted (such as BASIC). However, if you are working with microcomputers at home or in the office, you won't have to worry about compiling or interpreting—the software packages have already been compiled, and you will not even be able to look at the machine-level language the computer uses.

Other Systems Software Capabilities

Multitasking

As we have mentioned, the first operating systems were designed for computers with limited processing speed and limited RAM and storage capacity. These early operating systems were referred to as *single-user operating systems* because they could accept commands from only a single terminal or other input source and could manage only a single program in RAM at one time. Although most operating systems for microcomputers are considered single-user/single-program operating systems, some microcomputer operating systems are single-user but can also do **multitasking**—that is, they can execute more than one task or program at a time. Multitasking is also known as **multiprogramming.**

In multitasking, a copy of each program to be executed is placed in a reserved portion of RAM, usually called a *partition* (Figure 17). The supervisor

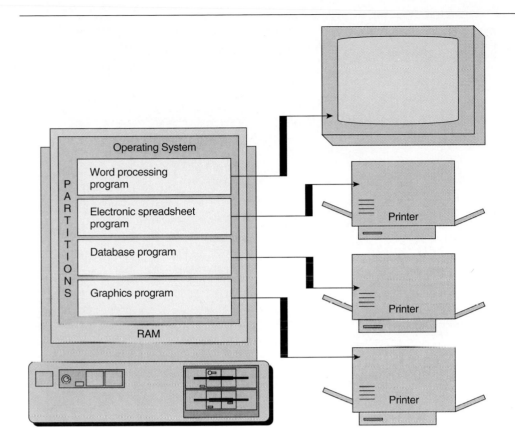

FIGURE 17

Multitasking. An operating system that can execute more than one program at a time (concurrently) is capable of multitasking—in other words, the user can run several different application programs at the same time. Although it may seem as if the programs are being processed at exactly the same time, they are actually being processed one after the other, extremely quickly.

is more sophisticated in an operating system with multitasking capabilities because it coordinates the execution of each program. It directs the microprocessor to spend a predetermined amount of time (according to programmed priorities) executing the instructions for each program, one at a time. In essence, a small amount of each program is processed, and then the microprocessor moves to the remaining programs, one at a time, processing small parts of each. This cycle is repeated until processing is complete. The processing speed of the microprocessor is usually so fast that it may seem as if all the programs are being executed at the same time. However, the microprocessor is still executing only one instruction at a time, no matter how it may appear to users.

Multiprocessing

A multitasking operating system works with only one microprocessor. However, the computer is so fast that, if it spends a little bit of time working on each of several programs in turn, it can allow a number of programs to run at the same time. The key is that the operating system can keep track of the status of each program so that it knows where it left off and where to continue processing. The **multiprocessing** operating system is much more sophisticated; it manages the *simultaneous* execution of programs with two or more microprocessors (Figure 18). This can entail processing instructions from different programs or different instructions from the same program. Multiprocessing configurations are very popular in large computing systems and are becoming practical on UNIX-based microcomputers. (We'll discuss the UNIX operating system shortly.)

Timesharing

A **timesharing** computer system supports many user stations or terminals simultaneously; in other words, the users share time on the computer, based on

FIGURE 18

Multiprocessing. Some computers use two or more microprocessors and sophisticated systems software to process different programs simultaneously.

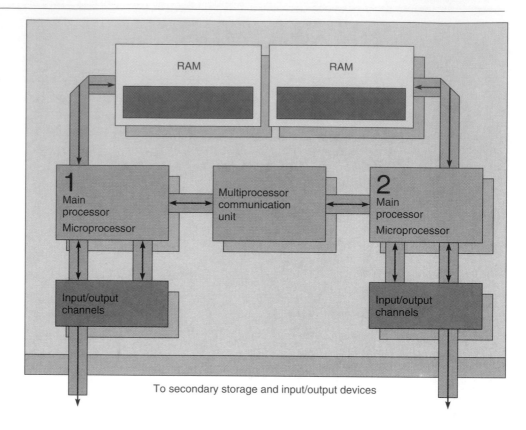

To secondary storage and input/output devices

assigned *time slices*. Timesharing is like multitasking, except that multitasking computers shift tasks based on program *priorities,* whereas timesharing systems assign each program a slice of time and then process the programs in small increments one after the other. The processing requirements of an operating system with timesharing capabilities are great.

In most cases, a computer system that includes timesharing capabilities uses a computer called a **front-end processor,** which is usually a microcomputer or minicomputer, to schedule and communicate to the main computer all the user requests and data entering the system from the terminals. The use of a front-end processor allows the main computer to concentrate solely on processing applications as quickly as possible (Figure 19).

From the user's perspective, timesharing isn't much different from multitasking except that, with timesharing systems, usually more than one user is sharing the processing power of a central microcomputer (main computer) by using terminals connected to it.

Popular Microcomputer Systems Software

In the late 1970s and early 1980s, a number of microcomputer hardware vendors introduced machines that included their own individual, machine-specific operating systems. This individualization created a software compatibility problem because each software applications package was written for a specific operating system and machine—if it worked with one type, it couldn't be used with another. A few operating systems became more popular than others because more software applications were written to be used with them. Software vendors decided to concentrate on developing software for these operating systems—namely, MS-DOS, OS/2, UNIX, and the Macintosh operating system.

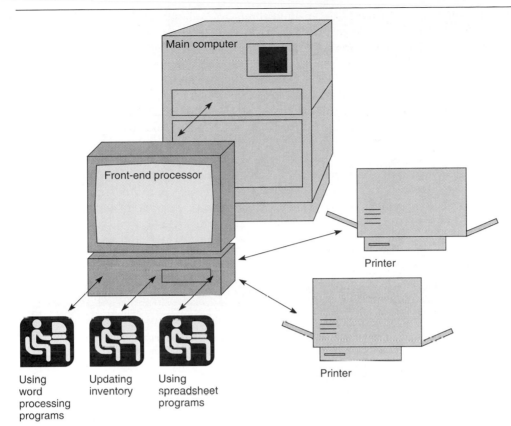

FIGURE 19

In a timesharing environment, the front-end processor schedules and controls users' processing requests. The main computer is thus freed up for processing.

MS-DOS

The development of this microcomputer **disk operating system (DOS)** (pronounced "doss") began in 1978, when Intel Corporation announced the development of a new and much more powerful microprocessor, the Intel 8088 chip. The new processor could use much more RAM and was substantially faster than the older 8080 series of processors.

Because of some differences between the old and the new processors, it became apparent that a new operating system would have to be developed to take advantage of the power of the 8088. In 1979, Tim Paterson of Seattle Computer Products began developing a new operating system called 80-DOS. The rights to distribute 80-DOS were acquired by Microsoft Corporation; Microsoft then entered into an agreement with IBM to make 80-DOS the operating system for the new personal computer IBM had under development. IBM added further program enhancements to 80-DOS and released the product in 1981 as IBM **PC-DOS** (IBM Personal Computer Disk Operating System). The effect of IBM's entry into the microcomputer marketplace was so strong that users and vendors began to indicate a preference for PC-DOS and its generic equivalent, **MS-DOS** (Microsoft Disk Operating System). The main reason for the popularity was that so many quality software applications were being written to be used with PC-DOS. Today, many of the microcomputers manufactured by IBM still use PC-DOS (some IBM microcomputers use OS/2, which is described shortly). Indeed, DOS is installed on approximately 85% of all the microcomputers in the world.

Many hardware manufacturers package systems software with their microcomputer systems. To package MS-DOS, the hardware manufacturer must enter into an agreement with Microsoft. Microsoft owns the source code for MS-DOS and licenses it to hardware manufacturers for a large fee (many thousands of dollars). The hardware manufacturers make slight adaptations to the code so it will run on their systems, give it a new name, and then supply the documentation for the code. (Microsoft doesn't supply the documentation.) Compaq computer licenses MS-DOS from Microsoft and names it COMPAQ DOS. AT&T, Zenith, AST, Toshiba, and NEC also license MS-DOS from Microsoft and call their versions AT&T DOS, Zenith DOS, AST DOS, Toshiba DOS, and NEC DOS, respectively. The modifications these manufacturers make to MS-DOS are very slight so that software written for MS-DOS will run on any of these manufacturers' machines.

Every year or so, Microsoft releases an updated version of MS-DOS, which includes the same capabilities as the previous version plus a few new ones. Version 4.0 was a major improvement over previous versions in terms of ease of use, because it allows users to issue commands by choosing options from a menu (Figure 20). Previous versions required the user to know more of the rules

FIGURE 20

(a) DOS 4.0 opening menu; four choices are listed on the left. (In addition, four choices, including Help, are displayed in the menu bar across the top of the screen.) (b) DOS 5.0 screen with a list of directories (categories under which appropriate files are stored). The directories are listed at left ("Directory Tree"), and the DOS directory is highlighted. At right is the beginning of the list of files stored in the DOS directory (which is located on drive C, the hard disk drive).

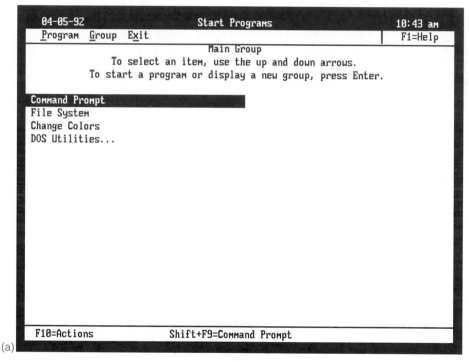

(a)

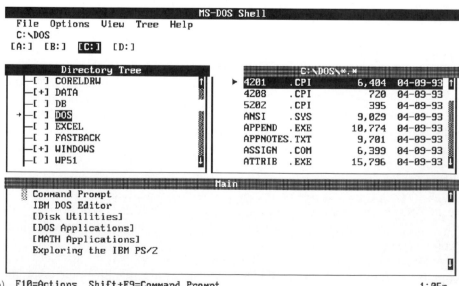

(b)

associated with using each command. The latest version of MS-DOS is 5.0. MS-DOS 6.0 and 7.0 are to be released soon.

When Microsoft releases an updated version, the hardware manufacturers usually upgrade the version of MS-DOS they are selling with their microcomputers. *When you purchase an applications software package, you must make sure it is compatible with the version of DOS you are using.* Some software applications are compatible only with later versions of DOS. The versions of MS-DOS that the application is compatible with are usually listed on the front of the package that the applications software is sold in. For example, the following text is displayed on the box of the popular disk management program called XTREE, from XTREE Company: "Requires IBM PC, XT, AT, PS/2, or compatible. DOS version 2.0 or higher."

DR-DOS (Digital Research DOS) is another version of DOS that is used on some computers.

MS-DOS and Windows

Despite its popularity, the MS-DOS operating system has its limitations. MS-DOS was designed principally to perform a single task for a single user—that is, it can switch back and forth between different applications, but it can't run two or more applications simultaneously. Although it is well suited for microprocessors that have been around for a while (Intel 8088, 8086), it can't fully utilize the capabilities of the more sophisticated microprocessors (Intel 80286, 80386, 80486). In addition, although the 80286 chip is capable of addressing, or using, up to 16 MB of RAM, MS-DOS can use only 640 K (if extended memory has not been installed). And finally, users often complain that MS-DOS is difficult to use. As a result, Microsoft developed **Microsoft Windows,** which is used in conjunction with MS-DOS to make it easier to use and more powerful.

Windows (versions 3.0 and 3.1) creates an operating environment called a *shell* that extends the capabilities of DOS. It supports multitasking, which enables users to run more than one application at a time, to easily switch between applications, and to move data between them. Windows also has a memory manager that enables users to use 640 K of conventional RAM and up to 16 MB of extended memory. Windows also provides users with a **graphic(al) user interface** (**GUI,** pronounced "goo-ey"), which makes IBM-type PCs easier to use (Figure 21). (DOS uses a *character user interface—CUI,* or "coo-ey"—meaning that the user must type words into the computer to get it to perform a function.) Graphic user interfaces enable users to select menu options by choosing pictures, called **icons,** that correspond to the appropriate processing option. To use software that includes a graphic user interface, users typically use a mouse rather than a keyboard to choose menu options.

To use Windows 3.1, you need an 80286 or 80386 PC, a minimum of 640 K RAM, and 4 MB to 6 MB of free hard disk space. All applications written for Windows have a similar graphic user interface, which makes it easier to learn how to use an application—that is, they all provide the user with a similar structure for choosing commands. Windows systems software is very popular; however, some people are waiting for the perfection of potentially more powerful systems software—OS/2.

Windows NT

Microsoft's newest operating system, **Windows NT** ("NT" stands for "New Technology"), promises many advantages over DOS and Windows 3.1. Windows NT blends the operating system and the GUI into a united whole. It supports multitasking and allows new applications to address up to 4 gigabytes (GB) of RAM, which means that users can work with more powerful applications that run faster. Windows NT also provides built-in networking and electronic mail capabilities. Windows NT will run most DOS-based and Windows applications, but

FIGURE 21

Windows' graphic user interface. Most software developed now and in the future will incorporate a graphic user interface that uses many of the components labeled here.

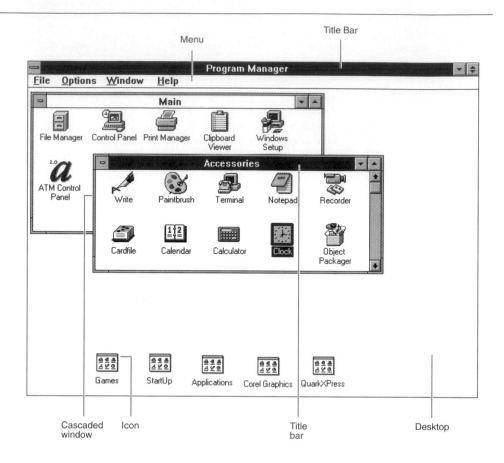

to take advantage of Windows NT's enhanced capabilities, applications must be written specifically for it. Some software applications have already been written specifically for Windows NT, including Harvard Graphics for Windows, Microsoft Excel, and Microsoft Word.

Windows NT will run on a computer that has a minimum of an 80386-SX microprocessor chip, 8 MB of RAM to run itself and several applications, and 30–60 MB of extra space to store Windows NT-related files. These hardware requirements are similar to OS/2's requirements (OS/2 is described shortly).

Since Windows NT has been recently released, we don't yet know how popular it will be. It is expected to be popular in offices that are networked and is viewed as a Windows-compatible alternative to the Unix operating system (Unix is described shortly). The ultimate fate of Windows NT will probably depend on the number and quality of the applications that are written for it.

OS/2

In 1988, IBM and Microsoft introduced **Operating System/2 (OS/2),** which, like Windows NT, is designed to get around some of the limitations imposed by MS-DOS and to take advantage of today's more sophisticated microprocessors (Intel 80286, 80386, 80486). Windows NT and OS/2 are often compared: both support multitasking and will allow new software applications to address 4 GB of RAM, and both have similar hardware requirements. In addition, the popularity of both will depend on the number and quality of the applications that are written for it. OS/2's GUI looks very much like the Macintosh's operating system. OS/2 doesn't include built-in networking or electronic mail support.

OS/2 is expected to be popular in large offices that already have a substantial investment in IBM hardware. OS/2 runs DOS-based microcomputer-to-mainframe software well and also custom applications; most of these applications would have to be rewritten to run on Windows NT.

UNIX

The **UNIX** operating system was developed by Kenneth Thompson at Bell Laboratories, where the earliest version was released in 1971. (UNIX is an abbreviation for "Unics," which stands for "Unified Information and Computing Systems.") This operating system was initially created for minicomputers and provides a wide range of capabilities, including virtual memory, multiprogramming, and timesharing. In 1973, the system was rewritten in a high-level language called C, which allowed it to be used on a wider variety of computers, ranging from the largest mainframe computers to some of the more powerful microcomputers. (Microsoft has invented a slightly improved UNIX version called "Extended UNIX," or XENIX. It runs on the IBM PC and other microcomputers.) UNIX is a popular operating system in universities where a multiuser (networked) environment is needed to support computer science students, programmers, and researchers.

One of the main advantages of UNIX is that it is a *portable* operating system. That means that it can be used on almost any computer. (DOS cannot be used, for example, on a Macintosh; thus DOS is *machine dependent,* and not portable.) However, UNIX is harder to learn than DOS, runs slower, consumes more memory, and costs more. Thus few applications are available for the microcomputer user who wants to use UNIX systems software.

Macintosh Operating System

Apple Computer Corporation introduced its popular Apple II personal computer system in the late 1970s. Because the Apple machines were based on entirely different microprocessors than those used in the IBM microcomputers, their operating systems were incompatible and unable to share data and instructions. The disk operating system used on many Apple computers is called *Apple DOS* and is designed to perform a single task for a single user.

A more powerful disk operating system—referred to as the **Macintosh operating system** (Figure 22)—was designed to be used on the Apple Macintosh computer (based on the 68030 microprocessor), which supports multitasking. The latest Macintosh operating system is System 7, which supports virtual memory, as well as multitasking; it also includes the Apple File Exchange (AFE) software utility, which allows file transfer between the Macintosh and DOS-based

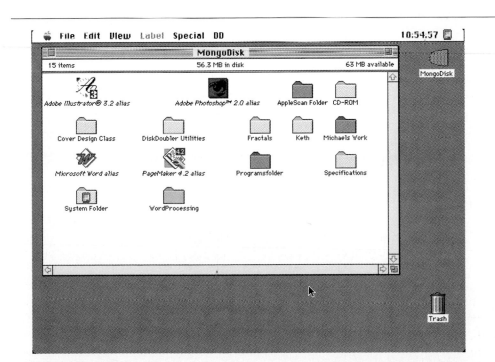

FIGURE 22

This Macintosh operating system screen shows you the directories of files stored on the hard disk ("MongoDisk"). Some of the directories are represented by special applications icons, such as the ones for Microsoft Word and Page-Maker. Other directories are represented by "file folders" such as the ones for Michael's Work and a Cover Design Class. ["Trash" is used to discard (erase) unwanted files.]

PCs. The Macintosh operating system has a refined, easy-to-use graphic user interface that the Windows environment tries to emulate (copy) for the IBM-PC.

Special hardware and/or software must be purchased to allow Apple computers using the Macintosh operating system to share data with PC-DOS/MS-DOS-based microcomputers and OS/2-based microcomputers.

Taligent

A joint venture between IBM and Apple Computer has produced a new operating system called **Taligent.** With this operating system, IBM and Apple hope to challenge Microsoft for leadership in computer operating systems. Microsoft DOS runs on Intel microprocessors, whereas the Macintosh operating system runs on Motorola microprocessors. Taligent runs on both IBM and Macintosh computers. Before Taligent becomes widely used, however, applications software must be written for it. Microsoft hopes to release its own competitor to Taligent; it is developing a new operating system called Cairo.

Making Your Choice

If you ever have to choose a microcomputer, consider carefully the systems software choices available in light of your specific processing needs. There is no right choice for everyone. The choice you make should be determined by:

▼ Type and quantity of compatible applications software you are interested in

▼ Ease of use by both users and programmers

▼ Speed of operation

▼ Capability to support multitasking and multiuser needs

▼ Types of compatible hardware you will need

▼ Availability of trained technical support personnel and manufacturer's hotline support to help you solve problems using your equipment and software

▼ Flexibility for cross-platform use

Table 4 reviews the main systems software used with microcomputers.

Table 4

Microcomputer Operating Systems

PROCESSOR	NT WINDOWS	MACINTOSH OPERATING SYSTEM	MS-/PC-DOS	OS/2	UNIX
M6502					
M68030		X			
Intel 8088			X		
8086			X		X
80286			X	X	X
80386	X		X	X	X
80486	X		X	X	X
Single-user	X		X		
Multitask	X	X		X	X
Multiuser	X				X
Virtual memory	X	X		X	

If medicine isn't quite like this in every locality, it probably won't be long until it is!

Every physician and hospital in town is hooked up by telephone to a medical information system, a specialized database. Doctors can admit or discharge a patient to and from the hospital, without leaving their offices. They can check on how much and what kind of medication a patient has received, what kind of laboratory tests have been run, and whether the patient has been moved from one bed to another. Besides having access to patient records, physicians and other professionals concerned with the patient's health have insurance and Medicare information. When the patient leaves the hospital, the schedule of medication given on discharge will also be available to the on-line physician.

In a significant step toward the future, computers are now being used to help doctors make diagnoses, do surgical procedures, and keep up with rapid changes in medicine. A system called DXplain contains data on thousands of case histories and more than 2,000 diseases, including the latest on AIDS. A physician can build a clinical case description by entering patient signs, symptoms, and lab data; DXplain then presents the physician with a ranked list of diseases that should be considered possibilities. The physician can also ask the system questions, such as why a particular disease does not appear on the list.

Many medical schools are now using computer programs to teach surgical procedures via screen animation. Some schools are using virtual reality techniques to allow medical students to practice these procedures *before* they do them on people.

As costs skyrocket and insurance companies switch to fixed-scale reimbursement for treatment, computerization also helps hospitals to manage their costs. Sacred Heart Hospital in Eau Claire, Wisconsin, installed a 90-terminal electronic information system and found it could save on hiring the equivalent of 50 full-time employees. It was also able to increase the speed of processing doctors' orders from 20 minutes to 5. At Latter-Day Saints Hospital in Salt Lake City, the computer-based system known as the Help Evaluation through Logical Processing (HELP) system can assist physicians in selecting the right medicine mix. At Moses Cone Memorial Hospital in Greensboro, North Carolina, all medical, radiology, laboratory, and pharmacy records are integrated on the same system.

Computers are beginning to find specialized uses in medicine and health not even thought of a decade ago. For instance, plastic surgeons now use computers and videos to show patients what they might look like after a face-lift, breast reduction, or other cosmetic surgery. Robots have been devised to perform tasks for those with physical disabilities. Other devices help the 13 million Americans who have some trouble speaking, reading, or writing. Computers also help children with cerebral palsy, Down's syndrome, and other problems to mitigate their disabilities by helping them to display and improve their skills.

It is possible that some day you will carry a plastic "smart card" that contains your entire medical history. Such a card could be put into a computer at hospitals, physicians' offices, and pharmacies around the country and provide details as to your chronic illnesses, allergies, and adverse reactions.

Applications software is a collection of related programs designed to perform a specific task, such as word processing or payroll management. Applications software is either purchased by the user *off the shelf* at a computer store or from a software outlet, or it is custom written for the user.

Systems software "underlies" applications software; it starts up the computer and coordinates the hardware components and the applications software programs. Systems software usually comes with the microcomputer.

Many categories of applications software exist. The most common are:

1. *General business management*—covers the majority of business software needs—for example, accounting, inventory control, finance and planning, personnel, office administration, and project management.

2. *Industry-specific*—meets needs of specialized businesses—for example, agriculture and farm management, architecture, banking, construction, dentistry.

3. *Special disciplines*—covers hobbies and special-interest areas such as amateur radio, astrology, music, sports, and visual arts.

4. *Education*—focuses on administration, computer-aided instruction (CAI), and special education.

5. *Personal/home management*—covers uses at home relating to entertainment, instruction, finance, and home management.

6. *General-purpose software* for the user—covers the basic types of software that general users are likely to encounter in business and professional life.

The following are common general-purpose software types:

1. *Word processing software*—enables the user to easily create and edit documents, including inserting, deleting, and moving words, sentences, and paragraphs, and to easily alter the appearance of documents through the use of different type sizes and styles and through different text arrangements.

2. *Spreadsheet software* lets users easily develop reports involving the use of extensive mathematical, financial, statistical, and logical processing. When a few numbers are changed, such reports can be automatically recalculated to provide *"What if?"* analyses.

3. *Database management system (DBMS) software* allows the user to input, store, and manipulate large amounts of data to produce reports. The data can be manipulated in different ways, depending on the relationships of the data, which are determined by the software system. *Flat-file management systems (file management systems)* can't establish relationships among data stored in different files. They can deal with only one file at a time. *Relational database management systems* can establish relationships among data in different files by using *key fields* or common identifying characteristics.

4. *Graphics software* gives the user the ability to make reports and other presentations more effective through the use of *analytical graphics,* common graph forms that make numerical information easier to understand, and *presentation graphics,* fancy free-form drawings.

5. *Communications software* allows users to access software and data from and transmit data to a computer in a remote location.

6. *Integrated software* enables the user to perform a wide variety of tasks that typically include creating documents, spreadsheets, databases, and graphs. Most integrated software packages also include communications capabilities.

7. *Desktop publishing (DTP)* uses a combination of hardware and software to enable the user to combine text and graphics on the same page in a professional-looking, publishable

format. The hardware used in a desktop publishing system typically includes a microcomputer, a hard disk, a laser printer, and a scanner. A *WYSIWYG* desktop publishing package lets you view on the screen what your document will look like when printed. To use a *code-oriented* desktop publishing package, the user must embed codes in the document. The effect of these codes can be viewed *after* the document is printed.

8. *Computer-aided design (CAD) software* enables manufacturers to save much time and money because they can design products on the screen without having to construct expensive models. After the designs have been developed, they are sent to a *computer-aided engineering (CAE)* system, which subjects the design to extensive analysis and testing. From there, the product might be created using a *computer-aided manufacturing (CAM)* system, which uses unintelligent robots to manufacture the final product.

9. *Applications software utilities* are inexpensive programs that perform some basic "office management" functions. These utilities are considered *RAM-resident utilities*, because they reside in RAM at all times while the computer is on, even when they aren't being used. These programs can be categorized as *desktop management, add-on, disk, screen,* and *keyboard utilities.*

▼ Applications software must be *installed* by the user before he or she can use it. Installation involves telling the software—through use of one of the software disks that came with the applications package—the characteristics of the hardware that the software will be running. The documentation includes instructions about how to install the software.

▼ While installing software, you will see a list of printers on the screen from which you must indicate the one you will be using. If your printer is not on the list, call the 800 number. The software company may send you a *printer driver* on a disk, which will enable you to use your printer with the applications software, or it may tell you which printer on the list to choose.

▼ Systems software tells the computer how to use the hardware in general, and it allows you to interact with the computer.

▼ Systems software comprises a large number of instructions, which include internal command instructions, external command instructions, and language processors.

▼ *Internal command instructions* are loaded into RAM when you turn on your computer. They direct and coordinate other types of software and the computer hardware.

▼ *External command instructions* are general-purpose operating system instructions that aren't needed to run applications software; instead, they are often used to perform "housekeeping tasks," such as backing up data that is stored on a disk.

▼ The *supervisor* portion of the *operating system* (that is, internal and external command instructions) controls all the programs in the computer, including managing the use of RAM and managing files stored on disk.

▼ Programmers often write programs using *high-level programming languages* because it is too time-consuming to write programs in machine language. Because microprocessors can understand only programs written in machine language, *language processors* are used to convert high-level instructions into machine language before the software can be used.

▼ A *compiler* is a language processor that translates an entire high-level language program, referred to as *source code,* into a machine-language version of the program, called the *object code.*

▼ An *interpreter* is a language translator that converts and executes high-level language instructions, one instruction statement at a time. Programs that have been compiled tend to execute up to five times faster than programs that are interpreted.

▼ Operating systems that can execute more than one task or program at a time are considered *multitasking,* or *multiprogramming,* operating systems.

▼ Operating systems that can manage the simultaneous execution of programs are considered *multiprocessing* operating systems.

▼ The processing requirements of an operating system with *timesharing* capabilities are great. A timesharing computer system supports many user stations or terminals simultaneously.

▼ The operating systems for microcomputers that are given the most attention are *MS-DOS, MS-DOS/Windows, OS/2, UNIX,* and the *Macintosh operating system*.

▼ *MS-DOS* was designed for a single user to perform one task at a time. It is a very popular operating system because so many applications programs have been written to be used with it.

▼ *Microsoft Windows* was developed to be used with MS-DOS to take advantage of more sophisticated microprocessors. Microsoft Windows provides users with a *graphic user interface,* allows users to multitask, and allows users to address up to 16 MB of extended memory.

▼ *Windows NT* is Microsoft's new operating system for microcomputers. It is similar to OS/2.

▼ *Operating System/2 (OS/2)* is designed to get around some of the limitations imposed by MS-DOS. It supports multitasking and will allow new software applications to address directly up to 16 MB RAM. OS/2 also includes a graphic user interface. OS/2, with competition from UNIX, is expected to eventually replace MS-DOS as the standard microcomputer operating system.

▼ The *UNIX* operating system provides a wide range of capabilities, including virtual memory, multiprogramming, and timesharing. It is a popular operating system in universities where a multiuser environment is often needed. However, until UNIX standards are developed, few microcomputer applications using UNIX will be introduced.

▼ The *Macintosh operating system* was designed to be used on the Apple Macintosh computer. This operating system supports multitasking.

▼ Determining what operating system to use on your microcomputer depends on a number of factors, which include:

1. Type and quantity of compatible applications software you are interested in

2. Ease of use

3. Speed of operation

4. Capability of supporting multitasking and multiuser needs

5. Capability of being used with other hardware (compatibility)

6. Availability of technical and hotline support

KEY TERMS

add-on utility, p. 7.17
analytical graphics, p. 7.13
applications software, p. 7.2
applications software utilities, p. 7.17
booting, p. 7.22
code-oriented page description
   software, p. 7.7
communications software, p. 7.14
compiler, p. 7.23
computer-aided design (CAD),
   p. 7.15
computer-aided engineering (CAE),
   p. 7.15
computer-aided manufacturing
   (CAM), p. 7.15
control program, p. 7.23
cursor, p. 7.4
custom software, p. 7.3
database management system
   (DBMS) software, p. 7.11
desktop management utility, p. 7.17
desktop publishing (DTP), p. 7.6
dialog box, p. 7.5
disk operating system (DOS), p. 7.27
disk utility, p. 7.17
external command instructions,
   p. 7.23

flat-file database management
   system (file management system),
   p. 7.13
front-end processor, p. 7.26
general-purpose applications
   software, p. 7.4
graphic(al) user interface (GUI),
   p. 7.29
graphics software, p. 7.13
Help screen, p. 7.5
high-level programming language,
   p. 7.23
hypertext, p. 7.18
icon, p. 7.29
integrated software, p. 7.15
internal command instructions,
   p. 7.22
interpreter, p. 7.23
keyboard utility, p. 7.18
language processor, p. 7.23
Macintosh operating system, p. 7.31
menu bar, p. 7.5
Microsoft Windows, p. 7.29
Microsoft Windows
   NT, p. 7.29
MS-DOS, p. 7.27
multimedia, p. 7.20

multiprocessing, p. 7.25
multiprogramming, p. 7.24
multitasking, p. 7.24
object code, p. 7.23
off-the-shelf software, p. 7.3
operating system, p. 7.22
Operating System/2 (OS/2), p. 7.30
page description software, p. 7.7
PC-DOS, p. 7.27
presentation graphics, p. 7.13
pull-down menu, p. 7.5
RAM-resident utility, p. 7.17
relational DBMS, p. 7.13
screen utility, p. 7.18
scrolling, p. 7.5
software installation, p. 7.21
source code, p. 7.23
spreadsheet software, p. 7.11
supervisor, p 7.23
systems software, p. 7.2
Taligent, p. 7.32
timesharing, p. 7.25
translator, p. 7.23
UNIX, p. 7.30
word processing software, p. 7.5
WYSIWYG page description
   software, p. 7.8

EXERCISES

SELF-TEST

1. _____ _____ is a collection of
   related programs designed to perform a specific task for the user.

2. List four categories of applications software utilities:

   a.

   b.

   c.

   d.

3. _____ _____

   _____ offers capabilities that enable the user to easily

   create and edit documents.

4. Applications software starts up the computer and functions as the principal coordinator of all hardware components. (true/false)

5. _____ _____ enables a computer
   in one location to share data with another computer in a remote location.

6. Programs that reside in RAM at all times are referred to as RAM-resident utilities.
   (true/false)

7. The type of software that enables users to input, store, and manipulate large

   amounts of data so that reports can be produced is _____

   _____ _____.

8. If you need to develop a report that involves the use of extensive mathematical, financial, or statistical problems, what type of software application should you use?

_____.

9. Relational database management systems can't establish links among data stored in different files. (true/false)

10. New applications software must be _____ by the user before it can be used.

11. List four tasks typically performed by disk utilities:

   a.

   b.

   c.

   d.

12. _____ _____ software enables you to combine near-typeset-quality text and graphics on the same page in a professional-looking document.

13. _____ command instructions are automatically loaded into RAM from disk when you turn on the computer.

14. The Macintosh operating system and Windows for the PC both use pictures called

_____ to represent processing functions.

15. A _____ _____ is a file stored on a disk containing instructions that enable your software program to communicate with or print with the printer you are using.

16. Software installation usually involves telling the software what the characteristics are of the hardware you will be using, so that the software will run smoothly. (true/false)

17. List four points you should consider before choosing an operating system to use on your computer.

   a.

   b.

   c.

   d.

18. Microsoft Windows makes using MS-DOS easier to use by means of a

_____ user interface.

Solutions: (1) applications software; (2) desktop management utilities, add-on utilities, disk utilities, keyboard and screen utilities; (3) word processing software; (4) false; (5) communications software; (6) true; (7) database management system (software); (8) electronic spreadsheet software; (9) false; (10) installed; (11) recovering files, making backup copies of a hard disk, organizing a hard disk, compressing files on disk to create more room; (12) desktop publishing; (13) internal; (14) icons; (15) printer driver; (16) true; (17) type and quantity of compatible applications software, ease of use by both users and programmers, speed of operation, capability to support multitasking and multiuser needs, types of compatible hardware needed, availability of trained technical support and hotline access, flexibility of cross-platform use; (18) graphic(al)

MULTIPLE-CHOICE QUESTIONS

1. Which of the following types of software must you have in main memory in order to use your keyboard?

    a. word processing

    b. systems

    c. spreadsheet

    d. applications

    e. CAD/CAM

2. If you want to execute more than one program at a time, the systems software you are using must be capable of:

    a. word processing

    b. virtual memory

    c. compiling

    d. multitasking

    e. interpreting

3. Which of the following is a type of systems software used on microcomputers?

    a. Apple DOS

    b. MS-DOS

    c. PC-DOS

    d. UNIX

    e. all the above

4. Which of the following is not applications software?

    a. word processing

    b. spreadsheet

    c. UNIX

    d. desktop publishing

    e. DBMS

5. Which of the following types of software should you use if you often need to create, edit, and print documents?

    a. word processing

    b. spreadsheet

    c. Presentation Manager

    d. CAD/CAM

    e. applications utility

Solutions: (1) b; (2) d; (3) e; (4) c; (5) a

SHORT-ANSWER QUESTIONS

1. What should you consider before purchasing a particular applications software package?

2. Why does a computer need systems software?

3. What does spreadsheet software do?

4. What is the purpose of communications software?

5. What are applications software utilities?

6. What does the term *booting* mean?

7. What would a good use be for database management system software?

8. What do users need to install software?

9. Why do some people prefer using integrated software to other types of applications software?

10. What do the abbreviations CAD, CAE, and CAM mean?

11. What advantages can desktop publishing software provide?

12. What is the difference between applications software and systems software?

13. What is the list of options displayed across the top or bottom of the screen called? What is it used for?

14. What is an icon? What is it used for?

15. What is a Help screen, and how can the user display it?

16. What is scrolling?

17. What is the operating system most commonly used on microcomputers? Which type of microcomputer uses it?

18. What is the difference between internal and external command instructions?

PROJECTS

1. Locate an individual or a company who is using some custom-written software. What does this software do? Who uses it? Why couldn't it have been purchased off the shelf? How much did it cost? Do you think there is an off-the-shelf program that can be used instead? Why/why not?

2. Attend a meeting of a computer users' group in your area. What is the overall purpose of the group? Software support? Hardware support? In what ways? Does it cost money to be a member? How many members are there? How does the group get new members? If you were looking to join a user group, would you be interested in joining this group? Why/why not?

3. Make a list of all the ways a student could use word processing software to make life easier. Look at Table 1 to get some ideas, read some reviews of word processing software in computer magazines, and read the copy on word processing packages in a computer store.

4. Use current computer publications to research the use of OS/2 in the business environment. On what types of computers is it being used? What types of businesses are using it? Is it easy to use? What do you think the future is for OS/2? How does the use of OS/2 compare to that of UNIX?

5. Go to a large computer store and find out how many microcomputers (and what types) run on which operating systems—MS-DOS, MS-DOS/Windows, OS/2, UNIX, Macintosh operating system, System 7. Ask the salesperson for his or her opinion about which disk operating system is the most powerful and flexible. Ask why.

6. Pen-based computing (Chapter 3) uses its own particular type of systems software. Check some articles in computer magazines to find out what makes this type of systems software different from regular microcomputer systems software. Is pen-based systems software compatible with DOS? How would pen-based systems software limit a traditional microcomputer user?

7. Apple Computer, Inc., has recently introduced At Ease, a software package intended to make the Mac easier to use. This software acts as an extension to System 7, the newest Macintosh operating system software. Obtain a brochure and other information from Apple or from a computer supply store and give a short report on exactly how At Ease makes the Mac easier to use.

Software Development and Programming Languages

*A*t this point, just learning how to use computer hardware and software may seem challenging enough. Yet there often comes a day when users suddenly discover that the ready-made, off-the-shelf programs available to them won't do everything they want. People renovate their houses or modify their clothes for the same reasons that software users fiddle with their programs. Would you ever be able to create applications software yourself? Or be able to help someone else do so? And are you curious about where software comes from—how it is created? In this chapter, we describe ways to develop or modify applications software—through the use of programming languages and techniques and through existing software.

PREVIEW

When you have completed this chapter, you will be able to:

▼ Describe what software development tools exist and which ones you are most likely to use

▼ Describe some of the advantages and disadvantages of using some of the most popular high-level programming languages

▼ Explain how a user could use existing microcomputer software to customize software programs

▼ Identify the responsibilities of the user in the programming process

▼ Name the five basic steps in developing a computer program

▼ Identify some structured programming tools and techniques

▼ Identify the three logic structures used in structured programming

▼ Explain the importance of program testing and documentation

*O*ne day at work you are tinkering with your database management program on your microcomputer when you suddenly realize you can't make it produce a sales report in just the right format. Or perhaps your spreadsheet won't automatically extract all the right data for a particularly useful analysis of an investment strategy. As new computer users gain more experience, they find it easier to identify areas where software can be modified or created to provide more useful and sophisticated processing capabilities above and beyond those of a purchased package. To obtain custom-made software the user can (1) hire an outside computer specialist to develop it; (2) ask the firm's computer specialists to do it; or (3) go it alone. Regardless of the approach you take, you need to understand the process by which software is developed and be familiar with the tools available for you to use.

In addition, users need to understand the basic programming process so that they can effectively deal with programmers who are creating software for them. If users can't specify their requirements properly, they may end up with software they are not happy with.

Just as many tools exist for building a house, many tools are available for creating, or writing, software. These tools include different types of programming languages used to write detailed sets of instructions that enable users to process data into information. Because the topics of software programming and software languages are the subjects of entire courses, the following sections can necessarily offer only the basic principles that users should be familiar with.

Generations of Programming Languages

Software development tools can best be categorized as falling into one of five generations of programming languages (Figure 1). The languages in each successive generation represent an improvement over those of the prior generation—just as the electric saw was an improvement over the manual one. Languages of later generations are easier to learn than earlier ones, and they can produce results (software) more quickly and more reliably. But just as a builder might need to use a manual saw occasionally to cut a tricky corner, professional programmers still need to use some early generation languages to create software.

Compared with later generations, the early-generation programming languages (first, second, and third) require the use of more complex vocabulary and syntax to write software; they are therefore used only by computer professionals. The term **syntax** refers to the precise rules and patterns required for the formation of the programming language sentences, or statements, that tell the computer what to do and how to do it. Programmers must use a language's syntax—just as you would use the rules of German, not French, grammar to communicate in German—to write a program in that language.

In addition to the five generations of programming languages, some microcomputer software packages (such as electronic spreadsheet and database management software) are widely used for creating software. Although these packages generally cannot be categorized into one of the five generations, many people consider some of the database management systems software used on microcomputers, such as dBASE IV, as belonging to the fourth-generation.

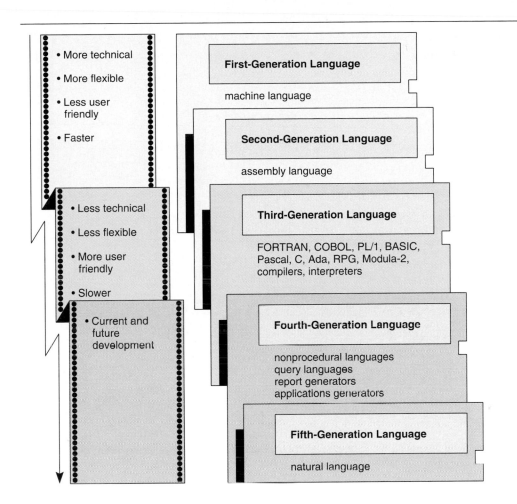

FIGURE 1

The five generations of programming languages

The following sections examine programming languages a bit more closely.

First and Second Generations: Machine Language and Assembly Language

A programmer can use machine language—*first-generation language*—to write software programs. Machine-language programs do not need to be translated before they can be run on the computer. A programmer can also write software programs in higher-level languages; however, these programs must be converted into machine-language form before they can be carried out by the computer. **Machine-language** instructions and data are represented by binary digits (a series of 1s and 0s corresponding to on and off electrical states or on and off magnetic pulses) (see bottom of Figure 2). Because the specific format and content of the instructions vary according to the architecture of each type of computer, machine-language programs can be run only on the type of computer for which they were designed; that is, they are *machine dependent.*

The first step in making software development easier and more efficient was the creation of **assembly languages,** also known as *second-generation languages* (Figure 2). Assembly languages use symbols as abbreviations for major instructions instead of a long combination of binary digits. This means a programmer can use abbreviations instead of having to remember lengthy binary instruction codes. For example, it is much easier to remember L for Load, A for Add, B for Branch, and C for Compare than the binary equivalents—strings of different combinations of 0s and 1s.

FIGURE 2

Down through the generations. An example of a statement in COBOL, part of which is converted first to assembly language and then to machine language. As you can see, the high-level (third-generation) language requires few statements to create a large number of machine-language (first-generation) instructions. (T. J. O'Leary and B. K. Williams, *Computers and Information Systems,* 2nd ed., Redwood City, Calif.: Benjamin/Cummings, 1989.)

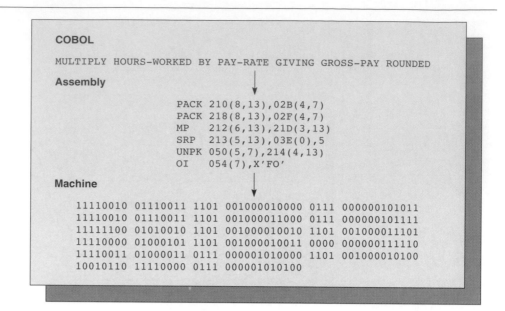

Although assembly languages represented an improvement, they have obvious limitations. They can be used only by computer specialists familiar with the architecture of the computer being used. And because they are also machine-dependent, assembly languages are not easily converted to run on other types of computers.

Third Generation

Third-generation languages, also known as **high-level languages,** are very much like everyday text and mathematical formulas in appearance. They are designed to run on a number of different computers with few or no changes. Unlike machine and assembly languages, then, many high-level languages are *machine independent,* or *portable.* Among the most commonly used high-level programming languages are COBOL, FORTRAN, and BASIC. A large number of additional languages have been developed, each with its own strengths. High-level languages were developed for several reasons:

▼ To relieve the programmer of the detailed and tedious task of writing programs in machine language and assembly language

▼ To provide programs that can be used on more than one type of machine with very few changes

▼ To allow the programmer more time to focus on understanding the user's needs and designing the software required to meet those needs

Most high-level languages are considered to be procedure-oriented languages, or **procedural languages,** because the program instructions comprise lists of steps, or procedures, that tell the computer not only *what* to do but *how* to do it. High-level language statements generate, when translated, a comparatively greater number of assembly-language instructions and even more machine-language instructions (Figure 2). The programmer spends less time developing software with a high-level language than with assembly or machine language because fewer instructions have to be created.

A *language processor* is required to convert (translate) a high-level language program (*source code*) into machine language (*object code*), so that the program will work on the computer. Some languages use translation programs called *compilers,* and others use translation programs called *interpreters.* The basic difference between these two types of translation programs is that with the compiler, a copy of the object code is saved that can be run later. With an interpreter, the object code is not saved; instead it is produced each time the high-level program is run. If you become a programmer, you will learn why each type of translation program has advantages in different situations.

By the early 1960s, most computer manufacturers were working on a version of FORTRAN, the first widely used high-level language, for their computers. Various manufacturers' versions of FORTRAN were similar; however, their efforts to make one package better than the others resulted in a number of small differences. The problems associated with resolving these differences led to the realization that industry standards were needed to ensure complete compatibility of high-level language programs with different computers. The task of establishing such standards was turned over to the American Standards Association, and in 1966 the association released the first FORTRAN standards.

Since the late 1960s, the association—now known as the **American National Standards Institute (ANSI)**—worked with the **International Standards Organization (ISO)** to develop, among other things, standards for all high-level programming languages. All versions of programming languages that developers wish to have designated as meeting the standards must accommodate all the commands, syntax, and processing requirements formulated by the ANSI and the ISO.

Following is a list of the most important high-level programming languages:

▼ FORTRAN

▼ COBOL

▼ PL/1

▼ BASIC

▼ RPG

▼ C

▼ Pascal

▼ Modula 2

▼ Ada

FORTRAN

The **FORTRAN**—short for **FORmula TRANslator** (Figure 3)—programming language was first made available in 1957 by IBM. One of the very first high-level languages, FORTRAN was designed for technical and scientific applications. Its popularity grew rapidly, and by the 1960s a version of the language was avail-

```
IF (XINVO .GT. 500.00) THEN

    DISCNT = 0.07 * XINVO

ELSE

    DISCNT = 0.0

ENDIF

XINVO = XINVO - DISCNT
```

FIGURE 3

FORTRAN. Here, a FORTRAN statement calculates a discount (7% of the invoice amount) if the invoice is greater than $500. Otherwise, no discount is given to the customer.

able for almost all types of computers; however, it is used primarily on minicomputers and mainframes. Because the language was designed to handle research and analytical problems definable in terms of mathematical formulas and relationships, the majority of people using FORTRAN are mathematicians, scientists, and engineers. The newest version of FORTRAN is FORTRAN 90.

ADVANTAGES

▼ It can handle complex mathematical and logical expressions.

▼ Its statements are relatively short and simple.

▼ Programs developed in FORTRAN on one type of computer can often be easily modified to work on other types.

DISADVANTAGES

▼ It does not handle input and output operations to storage devices as efficiently as some other high-level languages.

▼ It has only a limited ability to express and process nonnumeric data.

▼ It is not as easy to read and understand as some other high-level languages.

COBOL

Common Business Oriented Language, or **COBOL** (Figure 4) for short, was released in 1960. The U.S. Department of Defense, which is one of the world's largest buyers of data processing equipment, no longer wanted to commission the development of software in unalterable assembly language, so it funded the development of this programming language for business. The leader of the team that developed COBOL was naval officer Grace Hopper. The concern over the differences among versions of FORTRAN—all machine dependent—led the developers of COBOL to adopt machine independence as one of the primary objectives. The U.S. government then adopted a policy that required a computer to have the COBOL programming language available if the vendor wanted to sell or lease the equipment to the government. In 1968, COBOL was approved as the standard business programming language in the United States; the latest ANSI standards for COBOL were released in 1985.

The commands and syntax of COBOL's instruction statements are like English. As a result, it is much easier for a programmer to read and understand COBOL than FORTRAN. A COBOL program has four divisions: the *identification division,* which contains reference information such as program name and programmer's name; the *environment division,* which describes the type of com-

FIGURE 4

COBOL. This COBOL statement shows the same discount calculation given in Figure 3.

```
OPEN-INVOICE-FILE.
     OPEN I-O INVOICE FILE.

READ-INVOICE-PROCESS.
     PERFORM READ-NEXT-REC THROUGH READ-NEXT-REC-EXIT UNTIL END-OF-FILE.
     STOP RUN.

READ-NEXT-REC.
     READ INVOICE-REC
          INVALID KEY
               DISPLAY 'ERROR READING INVOICE FILE'
               MOVE 'Y' TO EOF-FLAG
          GOTO READ-NEXT-REC-EXIT.
     IF INVOICE-AMT > 500
          COMPUTE INVOICE-AMT = INVOICE-AMT - (INVOICE-AMT * .07)
          REWRITE INVOICE-REC.

READ-NEXT-REC-EXIT.
     EXIT.
```

puter to be used; the *data division,* which describes the data to be processed; and the *procedure division,* which contains the programming logic.

COBOL is used primarily on minicomputers and mainframes but is also available for microcomputer use, and it is the language most used for business applications.

ADVANTAGES

▼ It is machine independent.

▼ Its English-like statements are easy to understand, even for a nonprogrammer.

▼ It can handle many files, records, and fields.

▼ It easily handles input-output operations.

DISADVANTAGES

▼ Because it is so readable, it is wordy; thus even simple programs are lengthy, and programmer productivity is slowed.

▼ It cannot handle mathematical processing as well as FORTRAN.

In spite of the drawbacks, many programmers believe that COBOL will remain the most widely used language for writing business applications.

PL/1

The intended uses of FORTRAN and COBOL were always very clear. However, as the complexity and sophistication of the applications being developed for business increased, a language was needed that would be capable of dealing with computation *and* heavy-duty file handling. For this reason, IBM and two international organizations of computer users began to develop a general-purpose programming language, which was designated Programming Language 1, or **PL/1.** PL/1 was released in the mid-1960s for use on the IBM System 360 series of computers and has since been used primarily on mainframe computer systems. Figure 5 shows an extract from a PL/1 program.

ADVANTAGES

▼ It combines text and mathematical processing capabilities.

▼ It is very flexible—the programmer using it has few coding restrictions.

▼ It automatically identifies and corrects common programming errors.

DISADVANTAGES

▼ It runs more slowly than COBOL and FORTRAN.

▼ It requires a substantial amount of main memory (twice as much as COBOL and four times as much as FORTRAN).

▼ Its list of options is long and difficult to memorize.

▼ It is harder to learn than COBOL.

```
/*CALCULATE DISCOUNT*/

GET LIST (INVOICE);

IF INVOICE > 500 THEN DISCOUNT = INVOICE * .07;

ELSE DISCOUNT = 0;

END;
```

FIGURE 5

PL/1. The discount calculation of Figures 3 and 4 shown in PL/1

BASIC

Beginner's All-purpose Symbolic Instruction Code, or **BASIC,** was developed in the mid-1960s by John Kemeny and Tom Kurtz at Dartmouth College, where the large computer timesharing system supported many student terminals that allowed interactive testing of the new computer language. BASIC was intended to be a programming language that was easy to learn and flexible enough to solve a variety of simple problems. It was used primarily to teach people how to program. BASIC is an *interactive* language—user and computer can communicate with each other during the writing and running of programs.

By the late 1970s and early 1980s, BASIC had become so popular that it was selected as the primary language for implementation on microcomputers, although it can be used on all types of computers. Because of its popularity, a number of extensions have been added to the language to facilitate file creation and handling and the creation of graphics. Figure 6 shows an excerpt from a BASIC program.

The primary advantage of BASIC has been its ease of use. The primary limitation, aside from its normally slow processing speed, used to be a lack of official standardization, although Microsoft's version of BASIC, called MS-BASIC, was accepted as a de facto standard. Each implementation of the language for a particular machine had a few subtle differences that required specific attention when a program was run on a different machine. However, in 1987 the ANSI adopted a new standard for the BASIC language that eliminated portability problems. New versions of BASIC for use on microcomputers, such as Microsoft Quick-BASIC can be compiled as well as interpreted and so are much faster than previous versions.

RPG

The **Report Program Generator,** or **RPG,** language was introduced by IBM in 1964 to help small businesses generate reports and update files easily. RPG is not as procedure-oriented as other third-generation languages but is still often referred to as a programming language. The programmer fills out a number of very detailed coding forms that are easy to learn to use; however, because RPG is designed to be used to solve clear-cut and relatively simple problems, it is much more limited than FORTRAN, COBOL, BASIC, and some other programming languages. RPG is used on a variety of IBM minicomputers and has been *enhanced,* or improved, several times. The first revision, RPG 2, was released in the early 1970s and provided enhanced capabilities for handling tape and disk files. The latest version of the language, RPG 3 (released in 1979), added the capabilities necessary to extract reports from data stored in a database sys-

FIGURE 6

BASIC. Our discount calculation in BASIC

```
10  REM   This Program Calculates a Discount Based on the Invoice Amount
20  REM         If Invoice Amount is Greater Than 500, Discount is 7%
30  REM         Otherwise Discount is 0
40  REM
50  INPUT "What is the Invoice Amount"; INV.AMT
60  IF INV.AMT 500 THEN LET DISCOUNT = .07 ELSE LET DISCOUNT = 0
70  REM       Display results
80  PRINT "Original Amt", "Discount", "Amt after Discount"
90  PRINT INV.AMT, INV.AMT * DISCOUNT, INV.AMT - INV.AMT * DISCOUNT
100 END
```

tem. Figure 7 shows an RPG form with data entered (other forms exist for input, output, and file description specifications). After the data is entered on the form, it is typed into the computer.

The major advantages of RPG are the ease with which reports can be produced with minimal time and effort on the part of the programmer or user and the low number of formal rules for syntax and grammar compared to other high-level languages. However, the first version of RPG had limited computational capabilities and could not be used effectively in scientific or other applications requiring extensive mathematical processing. RPG 2 and RPG 3 substantially corrected some of these limitations.

Today, the use of RPG is declining in favor of newer languages that come with some microcomputer applications, such as dBASE for database management.

C

This programming language was introduced by Brian Kernighan and Dennis Ritchie at Bell Laboratories in the early 1970s for use in writing systems software. **C**, which is quite sophisticated, was used to create most of the UNIX operating system (assembly language was used to create the rest). The recent interest in UNIX as a powerful operating system for microcomputers has sparked interest in converting existing applications software to run with UNIX and in writing new software using C.

Advantages

- ▼ It can be used on different types of computers, including microcomputers.
- ▼ It is fast and efficient.
- ▼ Writing its compiler is easy.
- ▼ It is useful for writing operating systems software, database management software, and a few scientific applications.

Disadvantages

- ▼ It has no input/output routines; these must be imported (brought in) from other programs.
- ▼ It is not good for checking *types* of data—whether it is numeric, characters, etc.

Figure 8 shows an example of the C programming language. Recent versions of C are C++, Microsoft C, and Turbo C from Borland International.

Figure 7

RPG. The discount calculation

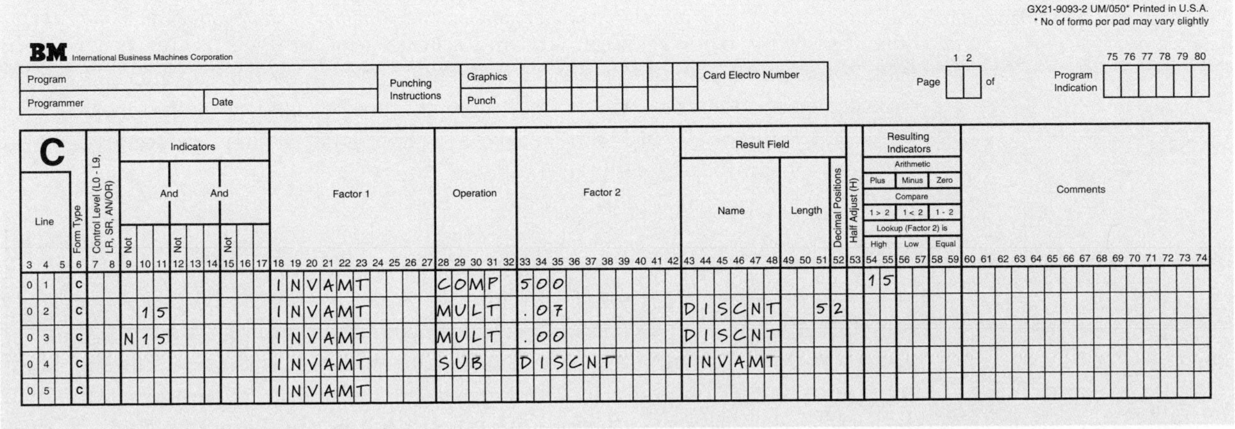

Line	Form Type	Control Level	Indicators	Factor 1	Operation	Factor 2	Result Field Name	Length	Decimal Positions	Half Adjust (H)	Resulting Indicators High	Comments
01	C			INVAMT	COMP	500					15	
02	C		15	INVAMT	MULT	.07	DISCNT	5	2			
03	C		N15	INVAMT	MULT	.00	DISCNT					
04	C			INVAMT	SUB	DISCNT	INVAMT					
05	C			INVAMT								

FIGURE 8

C. The C version of the 7% discount. C has many characteristics of both assembly and high-level programming languages, and, although it is a complex language to learn, it can be used on a variety of machines.

```
if (invoice_amount > 500.00)

   DISCOUNT = 0.07 * invoice_amount;

else

   discount = 0.00;

invoice_amount = invoice_amount - discount;
```

Pascal

The **Pascal** language, named after the 17th-century French mathematician Blaise Pascal, was developed by Swiss scientist Niklaus Wirth and introduced in the early 1970s. Available for both large and small computer systems (Turbo Pascal and Quick Pascal are available for microcomputers), it was developed to teach programming as a systematic and structured activity; Pascal classes are offered at most universities and colleges because of its superior structured programming format. *Structured programming,* which we describe later in this chapter, is based on the principle that any programming procedures can be broken into three parts:

1. Logic that allows a series of operations to be performed in sequence.
2. Logic that allows data elements to be compared and decisions to be made that determine the direction of subsequent processing.
3. Logic that allows procedures to be repeated a controlled number of times (looping).

ADVANTAGES

▼ Pascal can be used for mathematical and scientific processing.

▼ It has extensive capabilities for graphics programming.

▼ It is easy to learn.

The major disadvantage of Pascal is its limited input/output programming capability, which, in turn, limits its business applications. Figure 9 shows an excerpt from a Pascal program.

Modula-2

Developed by Niklaus Wirth as an improvement of Pascal and introduced in 1980, **Modula-2** is better suited for business use than Pascal, and although it's used primarily to write systems software, it can be used as an applications software development tool. Many experts believe that it may become a popular business programming language.

Ada

In 1975, the U.S. Department of Defense began to encourage the creation of a language that would facilitate developing and maintaining large programs that could be used for any type of application—from business to missile launching—and that could be used and modified over a long period of time. This decision was prompted by the results of a study showing that lack of unifor-

FIGURE 9

Pascal. The customer discount calculation shown in Pascal

```
if INVOICEAMOUNT > 500.00 then

    DISCOUNT := 0.07 * INVOICEAMOUNT

else

    DISCOUNT := 0.0;

INVOICEAMOUNT := INVOICEAMOUNT - DISCOUNT
```

FIGURE 10

Ada. The 7% solution in Ada

```
if INVOICE_AMOUNT > 500.00 then

    DISCOUNT := 0.07 * INVOICE_AMOUNT

else

    DISCOUNT := 0.00

endif;

INVOICE_AMOUNT := INVOICE_AMOUNT - DISCOUNT
```

mity in the use of languages resulted in yearly software costs of billions of dollars. These costs were necessary to pay for the large staff of programmers required to support all the different languages used.

The programming language **Ada** was derived from Pascal and named after Augusta Ada, Countess of Lovelace, the daughter of the famous English poet Lord Byron. The Countess of Lovelace worked with the mathematician Charles Babbage in the mid-1800s to develop mechanical computing devices and is considered to be the world's first programmer. This language is intended primarily for use in computer systems that are an integral part of another system for which they act as the control mechanism; that is, they are *embedded* systems. Many military weapons systems and equipment, for example, have embedded computer systems. However, the language can be used for commercial as well as military applications. Ada combines the good qualities of Pascal with improved input/output capabilities. Figure 10 is a sample excerpt of an Ada program.

ADVANTAGES

▼ Extensive support of real-time processing

▼ Automatic error recovery

▼ Flexible input/output operation

▼ Structured and modular design—sections, or "modules," of the program can be created and tested before the entire program is put together

DISADVANTAGES

▼ High level of complexity and difficulty

▼ Large storage requirements

▼ Not as efficient as some other languages

Although Ada has great potential, it is not yet widely used outside of the U.S. Department of Defense.

How Does a Programmer Know Which Procedural Language to Use?

We have discussed only a few of the most popular high-level programming languages—more than 500 programming languages exist for programmers to choose from. However, if a programmer has a good understanding of what a program needs to accomplish—and it is the *users* who must communicate this information to the programmer—then deciding what language to use may not be difficult. The following factors are usually considered when a decision is made:

▼ Does the company already have a standard language that the programmers use?

▼ How easy is it to learn the language?

▼ What other languages are supported on the computer system? How do they need to interface?

▼ Do the processing requirements match the capabilities of the language? For example, FORTRAN is very effective for computations, whereas COBOL is very good at handling large volumes of business information.

▼ Will the program need to run on more than one type of computer system? If so, transportability becomes a consideration; that is, the degree of a language's machine dependence needs to be evaluated. And not all languages are available for all machines.

▼ Are the intended applications using the high-level language oriented toward a batch or an on-line environment?

▼ What are the maintenance requirements? If the program needs to be updated frequently, will that be easy to do in the chosen language?

In general, most microcomputers use BASIC, dBASE, or C. Most minicomputers use BASIC, FORTRAN, COBOL, or C. Most large computers use FORTRAN or COBOL. Pascal is an alternative for all three types of computers.

In most cases, the use of third-generation languages to write applications software is inconvenient for the ordinary user because:

▼ Users require special training to use these languages—thus they need to hire programmers, who may be booked up for a long time in advance. Users may have to wait quite a long time before they can get their applications programs written.

▼ Programmers and other computer specialists, such as systems designers, are expensive.

▼ Users may think they know what they want but after testing the program discover they didn't. Modifications can be costly and expensive—and the programmers might not be immediately available to make them.

How can users sometimes avoid these inconveniences when they need software that is not available off the shelf? By creating their own customized applications software using fourth-generation languages and applications generators. However, we are not suggesting that the ordinary user can undertake complicated programming without training and experience.

Also known as *very-high-level languages* or *problem-oriented languages,* **fourth-generation languages (4GLs)** are as yet difficult to define in general, because they are defined differently by different vendors; sometimes these languages are tied to a software package produced by the vendor, such as a database management system. Basically 4GLs are easier for programmers—and users—to handle than third-generation languages. Fourth-generation languages are **nonprocedural languages,** so named because they allow programmers and users to specify *what* the computer is supposed to do without having to specify *how* the computer is supposed to do it, which, as you recall, must be done with third-generation, high-level (procedural) languages. Consequently, fourth-generation languages need approximately one tenth the number of statements that a high-level language needs to achieve the same result.

Because they are so much easier to use than third-generation languages, fourth-generation languages allow users, or noncomputer professionals, to develop certain types of applications software. It is likely that, in the business environment, you will at some time use a fourth-generation language. Five basic types of language tools fall into the fourth-generation language category:

1. Query languages
2. Report generators
3. Applications generators
4. Decision support systems and financial planning languages
5. Some microcomputer applications software

Query languages allow users (nonprogrammers) to ask questions about, or retrieve information from, database files by forming requests in normal human-language statements (such as English). For example, a manager in charge of inventory may key in the following question of a database:

```
How many items in inventory have a quantity-on-hand that is less than
the reorder point?
```

The query language will do the following to retrieve the information:

1. Copy the data for items with quantity-on-hand that is less than the reorder point into a temporary location in main memory.
2. Sort the data into order by inventory number.
3. Present the information on the video display screen (or printer).

The manager now has the information necessary to proceed with reordering certain low-stock items. The important thing to note is that the manager didn't have to specify *how* to get the job done, only *what* needed to be done. In other words, in our example, the user needed only to specify the question, and the system automatically performed each of the three steps listed above.

Popular query languages are Intellect, generally used on IBM mainframes, and SQL (Structured Query Language), used, for example, in the Oracle database management system.

Report generators are similar to query languages in that they allow users to ask questions of a database and retrieve information from it for a report (the output); however, in the case of a report generator, the user is unable to alter the contents of the database file. And with a report generator, the user has much greater control over what the output (or the result of a query) will look like. The user of a report generator can either specify that the software automatically determine how the output should look or create customized output reports using special report-generator command instructions.

Applications generators do more than query languages and report generators, which allow the user to specify only output-related processing tasks (and some input-related tasks, in the case of query languages). Applications generators allow the user to reduce the time it takes to *design* an entire software application that accepts input, ensures data has been input accurately, performs complex calculations and processing logic, and outputs information in the form of reports. Applications generators basically consist of prewritten modules, or program "building blocks," that comprise fundamental routines that most programs use—such as read, write, compare records, and so on. These modules, usually written in a high-level language, constitute a "library" of routines to choose from. The user must key in the specifications for *what* the program is supposed to do. The resulting specification file is input to the applications generator, which determines *how* to perform the tasks and which then produces the necessary instructions for the software program.

Decision support systems and **financial planning languages** combine special interactive computer programs and some special hardware to allow high-level managers to bring data and information together from different sources and manipulate it in new ways—for example, to make projections, do "what if" analyses, and make long-term planning decisions.

Some *microcomputer applications software* can also be used to create specialized applications—in other words, to create new software. Microcomputer software packages that fall into this category include many spreadsheet programs (such as Lotus 1-2-3), database managers (such as dBASE IV), and integrated packages (such as Framework). For example, in a business without computers, to "age" accounts receivable (to penalize people with overdue account balances), someone has to manually calculate how many days have passed between the invoice date and the current date and then calculate the appropriate penalty based on the balance due. This can take hours of work. However, with an electronic spreadsheet package, in less than half an hour the user can create an application that will calculate accounts receivable automatically. And the application can be used over and over.

Another example of microcomputer software that is used to create new programs is HyperCard for the Macintosh. This package is a database management program that allows users to store, organize, and manipulate text and graphics; but it is also a "programmable program" that uses the programming language called *HyperTalk* to allow ordinary users to create customized software by following the "authoring" instructions that come with the package.

Fifth Generation

Natural languages represent the next step in the development of programming languages—*fifth-generation languages*. Natural language is similar to query language, with one difference: it eliminates the need for the user or programmer to learn a specific vocabulary, grammar, or syntax. The text of a natural-language statement very closely resembles human speech. In fact, one could word a statement in several ways—perhaps even misspelling some words or changing the order of the words—and get the same result. Natural language takes the user one step farther away from having to deal directly and in detail with computer hardware and software. These languages are also designed to make the computer "smarter"—that is, to simulate the human learning process. Natural languages already available for microcomputers include Clout, Q&A, and Savvy Retriever (for use with databases) and HAL (Human Access Language) for use with Lotus 1-2-3. By the turn of the century, you should be able to phrase commands and questions any way you'd like to a large number of computers.

The use of natural language touches on *expert systems,* computer-based collections of the knowledge of many human experts in a given field that are applied to solving problems, and *artificial intelligence,* independently smart computer systems—two topics that are receiving much attention and development and will continue to do so in the future.

Programming: Five-Step Production

For a number of important reasons, the user should understand the basic steps a computer programmer follows to create software. For example, the user may have to evaluate software vendors' claims about what their programs can do. More important, if the user fails to communicate clearly and precisely to the programmer the processing procedures and logic to be incorporated into a program, the programmer will have to make assumptions about what exactly should be done. If the assumptions are wrong, the user will probably end up with reports that contain erroneous information or reports that simply do not have the necessary information.

In addition, as we mentioned earlier, some users today are using existing software packages such as electronic spreadsheets and database management systems to customize their own software applications. If you are one of these people, you should be aware of a few facts. First, no matter how easy a software development tool is to use, you must understand the principal steps to "custom-tailor" an application. Second, the processing logic required for the procedures to be performed must be carefully mapped out. Third, you must understand the importance of testing and documenting the software to ensure it is doing exactly what is expected. Many users do not take this third step seriously, and, as a result, the software they develop often produces incorrect information.

Suppose your boss asks you to create an electronic spreadsheet that will produce information to be considered in making a multimillion-dollar bid for a new project. If you do not proceed carefully, you may end up with problems such as:

▼ A formula for computing costs does not include all the required values; as a result, the cost estimate will be too low.

▼ An estimate of the expected revenues from the project is incorrectly specified; as a result, the cash flow during the life of the project will be overestimated.

With millions of dollars at stake, you may quickly find yourself out of a job and your career ruined. An infinite number of problems can be created if you are not careful when using software. Many people assume that the numbers in a computer report are always correct. *They are correct only if the processing procedures have been carefully specified and thoroughly tested.*

The orderly process that an organization goes through when identifying its applications software program requirements is referred to as the *Systems Development Life Cycle (SDLC)*. This section focuses on just a small part of the SDLC—namely, the steps involved in developing an applications software program once the requirements for the program have been identified. As mentioned earlier, you need to understand these steps so that you will be able to tell a programmer, in terms he or she can understand, exactly what your programming requirements are. Although this section on programming is not detailed enough to allow you to communicate on the level of a programmer, it will tell you the basics about what you, as a user, need to understand about programming.

Step 1—Define the problem (Figure 11).

▼ "Think first and program later." Consider all possible ways of solving a problem and specify the objectives of the intended program, including who (which departments) will use the information produced.

▼ Specify output requirements.

▼ Specify input requirements.

▼ Specify processing requirements.

Figure 11

Five steps of program development

1	2	3	4	5
DEFINE THE PROBLEM	**DESIGN A SOLUTION**	**CODE THE PROGRAM**	**TEST THE PROGRAM**	**FINALIZE THE DOCUMENTATION**
1. Specify program objectives and program users. 2. Specify output requirements. 3. Specify input requirements. 4. Specify processing requirements. 5. Study feasibility of implementing program. 6. Document analysis and objective specification process.	1. Map out program logic. 2. Diagram and document program design using flowcharts, diagrams, data dictionaries, pseudocode, structure charts, and so on. 3. Test design with structured walkthrough.	Write (code) the program using high-level programming language.	Test program using structured walkthrough, desk checking, and sample (test) data to try to "break" the program.	Assemble and finalize all documentation made during all previous steps.

▼ Study the feasibility of the program.

▼ Document the analysis and objective specification process. This may involve using flowcharts, flow diagrams, data dictionaries that catalog and identify the data elements that will be used, sketches of display screen formats and report layouts, and so on.

Step 1 usually involves meetings that include the programmer(s), users, and the systems analyst/designer who designed the system of which the program will be a part. At this point a *make-or-buy decision* is made. If an off-the-shelf program exists that you can buy to solve your problems, you will not have to make (create) your own custom software. However, if you do have to create your own software, you must then proceed to step 2.

Step 2—Map out the program logic and design a solution.

After the problem has been defined, the program must be logically designed. This process is not unlike outlining a long term paper's organization before you actually begin to write it. The programmer must work out **algorithms,** or diagrams of the solutions, before the program is written. The programmer may use a variety of tools to do this, including flowcharts, pseudocode, and structure charts (discussed later in this chapter). You probably won't ever need to use any of these tools, because they are used mostly by programmers mapping out complex logic or by those using third-generation languages. However, you should have a basic idea of how they are used in order to appreciate the detail that is necessary for a programmer to create a program. The more detail you can give the programmer about your processing requirements, the better the resulting program will be.

After the program has been designed, programmers, systems designers, and users check its logic and documentation by means of a "structured walkthrough."

Step 3—Code (write) the program.

Translate the processing requirements of the program into the necessary programming (high-level) language statements and then enter the coded instructions into the computer. (This is usually done on a terminal, and the instructions are stored on disk. The programmer can modify the instructions as necessary.)

Step 4—Test the program.

Review the program carefully to ensure that it is doing exactly what it is supposed to. Repeat "structured walkthroughs," conduct "desk checking" by proofreading a printout of the program, and, using test ("fake") data, review output reports to determine that they are in the correct format and contain all the required information ("logic testing"). The user can play an important role in identifying the "problem areas," or "bugs," in a program by participating in tests to see how it handles the types of tasks it was asked to do—including trying to "break" the program by inputting unusual test data. The programmer can then fix the problems, or "debug" the program (see Figure 12).

Step 5—Collate and finalize the documentation.

Clearly document all the steps, procedures, logic tools, and testing results, as well as the goals of the program and other specific facts. Although listed as Step 5, the activity of *documenting the program actually goes on all the way through the design and coding process.* This documentation, or manual, will tell future program operators, users, managers, and even programmers who may later have to modify the program exactly what the program does and how it does it, and what they need to do to use it. Documentation also helps programmers track down errors. (Users must assume some responsibility to see that the new software is adequately documented.)

The following sections discuss these steps in more detail.

Step 1—Define the Problem

Say your company needs a computer-based payroll processing program. That's the problem. In specifying the objectives of the program you and your employees would list in great detail everything you want the program to do, which means specifying output, input, and processing requirements. For example, do you want both hardcopy and softcopy output? How often? What information must reports and checks include? Do you want to input employee data on-line and process it on-line, or will batch input and processing work better? What will be the source and format of input data? You would also specify who in your company needs to see reports, in what form, and how often.

After you have defined the problem and listed the output, input, and processing requirements, you decide that none of the off-the-shelf programs is ade-

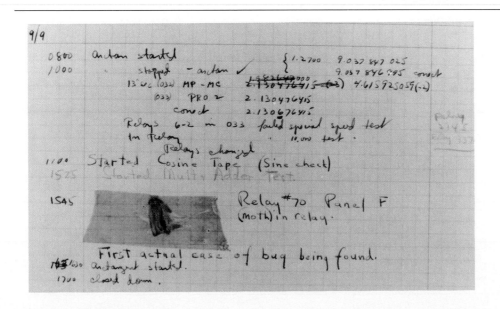

FIGURE 12

Moth found in Mark I computer (1945). The origins of the word "bug," meaning "program error," dates to the discovery of this moth lodged in the computer's wiring. The moth disrupted the execution of the program.

quate; you must have your software custom written. However, you should determine if the project is feasible—in other words, do the apparent benefits of the program outweigh the costs of preparing it? Should you proceed? And, of course, don't forget to continually document everything you do in Step 1, as well as in all subsequent steps.

Step 2—Map Out the Program Logic and Design a Solution

During the programming process, users must know how to express their processing requirements in the detailed terms necessary for the computer specialist to convert them into program logic. It may be easy to describe what you want accomplished to someone who is at least slightly familiar with the working of your department. However, you would be amazed at how much detail is required to communicate to a person unfamiliar with your work exactly what to do, when to do it, and how it is to be done. And exceptions must always be accounted for—a program has to be able to take care of the rare case as well as the routine ones.

A number of tools and techniques have been developed to assist in documenting the logic to be built into programs. We will discuss only program flowcharts, pseudocode, and top-down design, because it's unlikely that, as a general business user, you would come into direct contact with any other programming tools or techniques.

Flowcharts

A **program flowchart** is a diagram that uses standard ANSI symbols to show the step-by-step processing activities and decision logic needed to solve a problem (Figure 13). The flow of logic in a program flowchart normally goes from

FIGURE 13

Standard flowchart symbols. Programmers use plastic templates (b) to trace standard ANSI flowchart symbols when preparing plans for program design (a). (c) Example of a program flowchart.

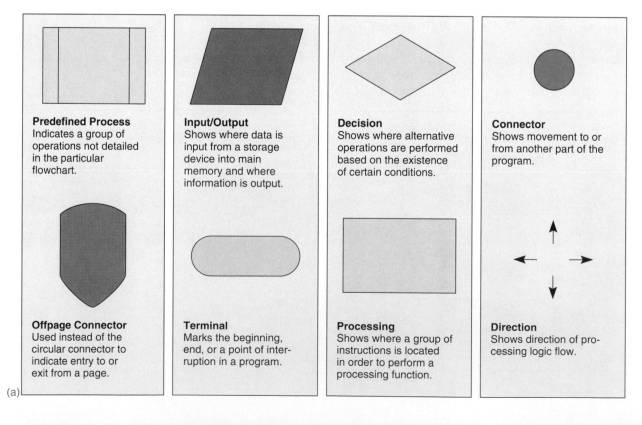

Predefined Process
Indicates a group of operations not detailed in the particular flowchart.

Input/Output
Shows where data is input from a storage device into main memory and where information is output.

Decision
Shows where alternative operations are performed based on the existence of certain conditions.

Connector
Shows movement to or from another part of the program.

Offpage Connector
Used instead of the circular connector to indicate entry to or exit from a page.

Terminal
Marks the beginning, end, or a point of interruption in a program.

Processing
Shows where a group of instructions is located in order to perform a processing function.

Direction
Shows direction of processing logic flow.

(a)

(b)

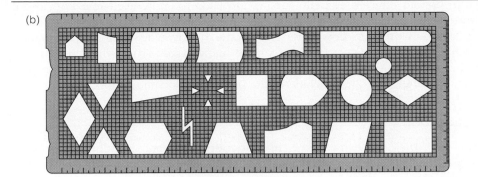

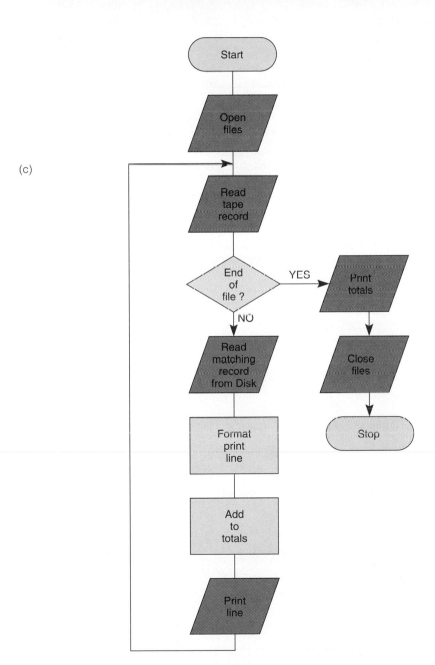

FIGURE 13

(*continued*)

(c)

top to bottom and left to right. Arrows are used to show a change from those directions.

Although program flowcharts have some disadvantages—their preparation may be time-consuming and they can be many pages long—they are considered to be a good tool for documenting the procedures to be used in the program, and they are often included in a program's documentation package.

Pseudocode

The prefix *pseudo* means "fake"; **pseudocode,** therefore, literally means "fake code"—that is, not the code that is actually entered into the computer. Pseudocode uses normal language statements instead of symbols (such as flowchart symbols) to represent program logic. It is more precise in representing logic than regular, idiomatic English but does not follow a specific programming language's syntax. Using pseudocode to document program logic is much less time-consuming than flowcharting because the programmer doesn't have to spend time drawing symbols or boxes. Instead, the pseudocode statements can be composed and edited by hand or by using a typical off-the-shelf word processing program. Some people would argue further that pseudocode is much closer to actual code than are flowcharts, which makes pseudocode more productive than flowcharting. However, some programmers don't like to use pseudocode because it doesn't depict the program logic visually like a flowchart does.

Pseudocode uses four statement keywords to portray logic: IF, THEN, ELSE, and DO. Repetitive processing logic is portrayed using the statements DO WHILE (repeat an activity as long as a certain condition exists), DO UNTIL (repeat an activity until a certain condition is met), and END DO (stop repeating the activity). The processing logic is written out in narrative sentences. The logic statement keywords are capitalized, and several levels of standard indentation are used to show decision processes and subprocesses. Figure 14 gives you an idea of how the keywords, statements, and indentation are used.

FIGURE 14

Using pseudocode to solve a crime

```
        START * murder of Grizzly Beans *

        * Solve murder of Grizzly Beans *

        DO WHILE there are suspects

                IF Roger's fingerprints are on the sword THEN

                        Identify Roger as the murderer

                ELSE

                        Question Matilda

                        IF Matilda has an alibi THEN

                                Grill Captain Murk

                                Give Miss Turtle the third degree

                                Identify fingerprints on sword

                        ENDIF

                ENDIF

                        Arrest murderer

        END DO

        END * murder of Grizzly Beans *
```

Top-Down Design

Program flowcharts, pseudocode, and the rules of a high-level language enable a programmer to design and write software that leads to predictable results that solve a problem. However, for a long time many computer scientists felt that more structure and control were needed to standardize programming and make it more exact—to change it from an art to a science. Thus, in the mid-1960s, the concept of **structured programming** was developed. Structured programming uses top-down design to "decompose" (break down) main functions into smaller ones (modules) for coding purposes.

　　Top-down design starts with the highest level of the program and works its way down to the lowest level of detail. The objective of top-down design is to identify the main processing steps of the program, called **modules.** (In some programming languages, modules are often referred to as **subroutines.**) If possible, each module should have only a single function, just as an English paragraph should have a single, complete thought; this forces a limit to a module's size and complexity. **Structure charts,** also called **hierarchy charts** (Figure 15), are often used to picture the organization and breakdown of modules. A program that is considered modular in design has the following characteristics:

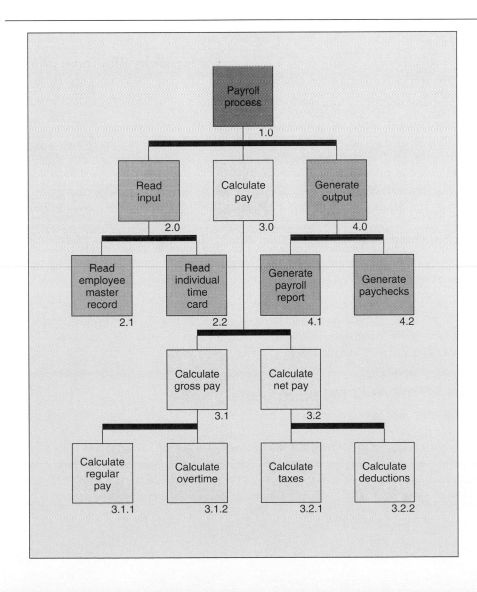

FIGURE 15

Structure chart for top-down design. In a structure chart, to perform the task given in the top of module (1.0), all substructured tasks must be performed first (for example, 2.1 and 2.2 to perform 2.0). Only one task is given each module, which represents a logical processing step.

1. Each module must be of manageable size—have less than 50 program instructions.

2. Each module should be independent and have a single function.

3. The functions of input and output are clearly defined in separate modules.

4. Each module has a single entry point (execution of the program module always starts at the same place) and a single exit point (control always leaves the module at the same place).

5. If one module refers to or transfers control to another module, the latter module returns control to the point from which it was "called" by the first module.

Following are some of the advantages of a modular program:

▼ Complex programs can be organized into smaller and more manageable pieces in a relatively standard way.

▼ Programs can be modified with less effort than nonmodular programs because, when modular programming guidelines are followed carefully, each module is relatively independent and can be changed without affecting all the other parts of the program.

▼ A collection or library of standardized modules can be created to use in various programs (which saves the user money because similar processing tasks don't have to be programmed redundantly and which helps ensure accuracy because the same task is always accomplished in the same way).

▼ Errors in logic can be quickly isolated and fixed.

A structure chart can be used as part of a **hierarchy plus input-process-output** package, also called **HIPO.** The HIPO concept was developed by IBM as a tool for program design and documentation. It includes a visual table of contents, an overview diagram, and a detail diagram.

The **visual table of contents (VTOC)** includes a structure chart, a short description of the contents of the program, and a legend that provides any necessary explanations of symbols used in the overview diagram and the detail diagram.

The **overview diagram** shows, from left to right, the inputs, processes, and outputs for the entire program. The steps in this diagram are cross-referenced to the module numbers in the structure chart.

The **detail diagram** describes in detail what is done within each module.

Neatness Counts

Whether using flowcharts, pseudocode, or structure charts alone or as part of a HIPO package, programmers must be careful to make their logical maps and documentation understandable to other programmers and involved users. Figure 16 lists the rules to remember.

Check Work in Progress

Before the program is written, or coded (Step 3), it should be subjected to initial testing to avoid costly and time-consuming changes "after the fact." This is usually done by a **structured walkthrough**—a group of programmers meet to review the logic and documentation of a program designed by another programmer in order to identify what is not clear or workable and to verify code. Systems designers and users often also attend such meetings.

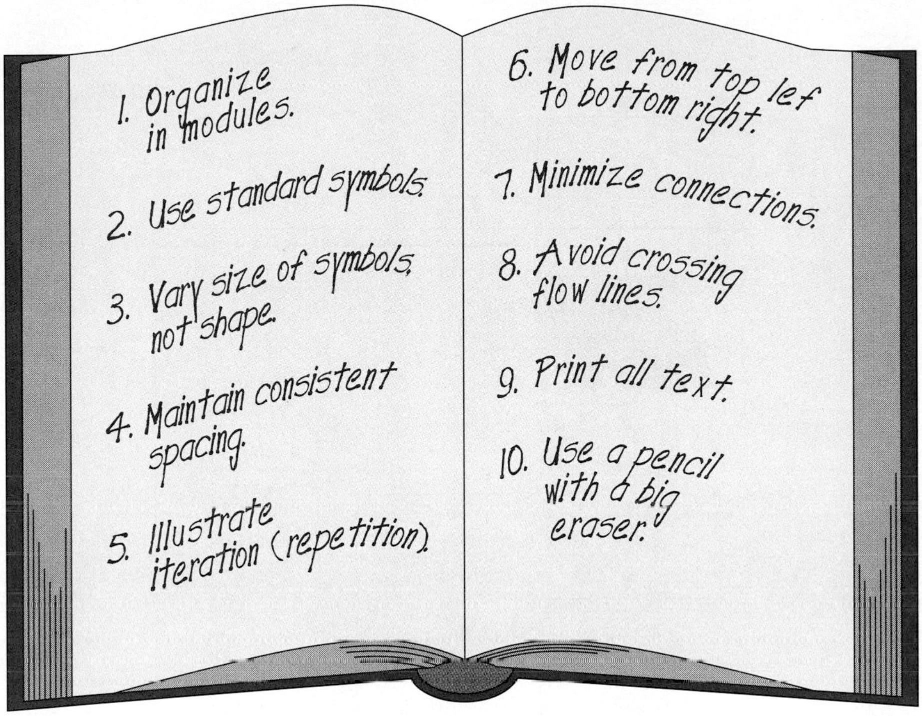

FIGURE 16

Programmers follow these rules in order to produce clear, readable program logic documentation when they are designing a program.

1. Organize in modules.

2. Use standard symbols.

3. Vary size of symbols, not shape.

4. Maintain consistent spacing.

5. Illustrate iteration (repetition).

6. Move from top left to bottom right.

7. Minimize connections.

8. Avoid crossing flow lines.

9. Print all text.

10. Use a pencil with a big eraser.

Step 3—Code the Program

In this step, the programmer actually writes out the program designed in Step 2, using a high-level language. The programmer may write the program out first, using pencil and paper, or he or she may key it in directly. The programmer will follow certain rigid rules and use three logic structures that are part of structured programming: sequence, selection, and iteration.

Sequence

In the **sequence control structure,** when processing begins on any program, each instruction is executed in sequence, one after the other. For example, consider the logic necessary to compute net pay (Figure 17). The first step is to input the number of hours worked, the pay rate, and the deduction percentage (taxes, insurance, and so on). The second step is to compute gross pay by multiplying the number of hours worked by the pay rate. The third step is to compute the deduction amount by multiplying the gross pay amount by the deduction percentage. The fourth and final step is to compute the net pay amount by subtracting the deduction amount from the gross pay amount. These events take place in sequence, one after the other, as specified.

Selection: If-Then-Else

The **if-then-else** control structure (Figure 18) allows a condition to be tested to determine which instruction(s) will be performed next; it allows the sequence control to be shifted depending on the outcome of the test. Thus, the programmer can alter the basic sequence control structure when certain conditions apply. The intent of if-then-else is to determine which of two activities is to be performed—or *selected*—as the result of testing the condition. If the condition

FIGURE 17

Sequencing to get net pay. This example shows the computation of net pay using sequencing. The steps are repeated until the end of the file (EOF) is reached.

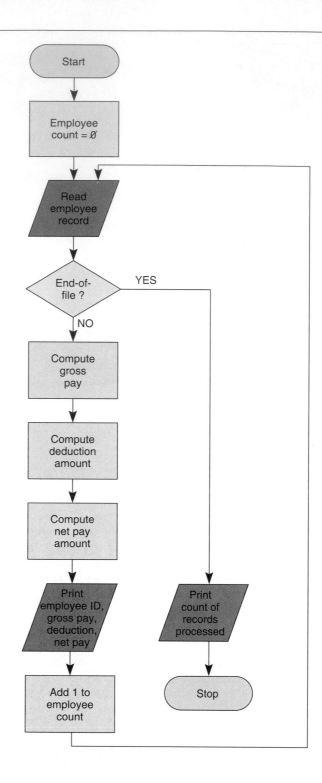

exists—that is, if it is true—a specified event takes place. If the condition does not exist—if it is false—then the event does not take place. In other words, *if* a condition is true, *then* do a particular processing function, (or) *else* do not do it.

Iteration: Do While

The **do while** control structure allows an activity to be repeated (iterated) as long as a certain condition remains true (Figure 19). **Iteration** is often referred

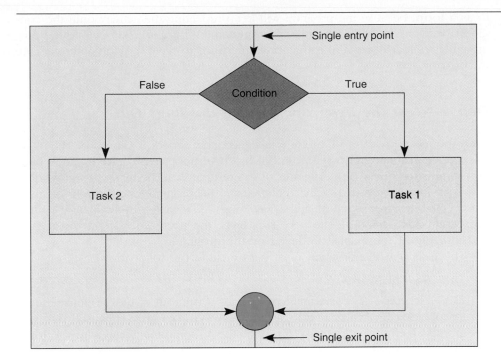

FIGURE 18

If-then-else control structure. If a condition is true, then one event takes place; if the event is false—that is, if it does not exist—then a second event takes place.

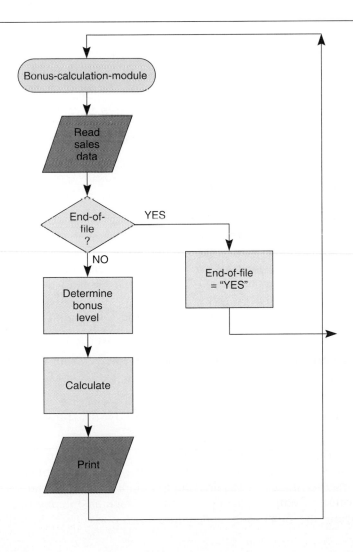

FIGURE 19

Iteration. As long as salespeople are listed for whom bonuses must be calculated, the program repeats the activity—the "loop" shown in the drawing.

to as a **loop,** because the program will keep repeating the activity until the condition becomes false. Loops simplify programming because they enable the programmer to specify certain instructions only once to have the computer execute them many times.

Step 4—Test the Program: Getting the Bugs Out

Even though a program is carefully designed and coded, it cannot be relied on to produce accurate information until it has been thoroughly tested. The object of testing is to "break" the program. If the program can be made to *not* work— that is, if it can be fed data that either halts the program prematurely or gives unexpected answers—that means it has "bugs" that must be eliminated. When a program has passed all the necessary tests, the user can rely on the continued integrity of the results produced by the program.

The tests that the program must pass include the following:

▼ *Structured walkthrough*

▼ *Desk checking*—A programmer proofreads a printout of the program line by line looking for syntax and logic errors. A **syntax error** is caused by typographical errors and incorrect use of the programming language. A **logic error** is caused by not using the correct control structures (sequencing, selection, and iteration) in the proper manner.

▼ *Translation attempt*—The program is run through the computer using a language processor. Before the program will run, it must be free of syntax errors. Any syntax errors will be identified by the translator.

▼ *Sample data test*—After all syntax errors have been corrected, sample data is run through the program to test each program statement.

Of course, all testing procedures and results should be documented. In addition, the documentation that was prepared during program development must be complete and precise enough to allow the testers to test the program in the first place. Users must share in the documentation effort.

Step 5—Collate the Documentation

Program documentation should have been going on since the very beginning of program development. The importance of this step cannot be overemphasized. Without documentation, programmers may not be able to update the program in the future; diagnosis of problems will be difficult; identifying and eliminating any remaining bugs will be nightmarish; and users will have no instructions for using the program.

Program documentation should provide the following:

▼ A permanent record of what the program does

▼ Instructions for program users on how to interact with the program

▼ Instructions for computer operators on how to organize and control the processing of the program

▼ Detailed documentation required to modify the program to meet new requirements

As you can see, program documentation is required at several levels: user documentation, technical documentation, and operator's instructions.

User documentation is required for programs that have the user interacting directly with the computer during operation—such as entering data into the system, directing the processing, and requesting reports. User documentation usually consists of simple step-by-step procedures that describe what the user is to do and how to do it plus report descriptions and sample output.

Technical documentation consists of a number of items prepared during the development of the program including:

▼ A narrative overview of what the program does

▼ A series of flowcharts or paragraphs of pseudocode depicting processing logic (or a combination of flowcharts and pseudocode)

▼ Examples of all reports produced by the program

▼ Examples of any display screen activity such as menus or softcopy reports

▼ A listing of the program language statements

Operator's instructions are required for programs run on large computer systems. These instructions identify what is required for the computer operator to prepare a program to process, and they explain what steps to follow during processing, including what to do about error messages. (For microcomputer applications, such instructions are included in the user documentation.)

As we have stated, the absence of good program documentation can create problems. Users can become frustrated when they try to work with the program. Programmers can have a very difficult time modifying programs they did not create if the documentation is inadequate. If a program is lost, it cannot be reconstructed without good documentation. And the need for good documentation doesn't apply just to custom-written programs: be sure your microcomputer software comes with adequate documentation manuals!

To become a lawyer, you must graduate from law school and pass the bar exam. But to become a computer expert, there's no particular program you must necessarily graduate from, no particular exam to pass, and no particular piece of paper that "proves" you're an expert or even competent.

To become a top computer expert, you must study hard; read lots of computer manuals, textbooks, guidebooks, magazines, newspapers, and newsletters; and practice using many kinds of computers, operating systems, languages, word processing programs, spreadsheets, database management programs, graphics packages, and telecommunications programs. Also, explore the many educational programs for kids. Use many kinds of printers, disk drives, and modems. Study the human problems of dealing with computers. No matter how much you already know, learn more!

When I surveyed computer experts, I found that the average expert still spends two hours per day reading about computers, to fill holes in the expert's background and learn about what happened in the computer industry that day. In addition to those two hours, the expert spends many more hours practicing what was read and swapping ideas by chatting with other computerists.

As a computer expert, you can choose your own hours, but they must be numerous: if your interest in computers lasts just from 9 A.M. to 5 P.M., you'll never become a computer expert.

To break into the computer field, you can use six tools: college, home consulting, home programming, sales skills, job expansion, and on-the-job training.

College

Go to college and get a Ph.D. or an M.A. in computer science (you can specialize, for example, in systems analysis and design, program development, or communications).

Home Consulting

Keep your current job but spend your weekends and evenings helping your neighbors, friends, and colleagues learn about computers. Help them buy hardware and software. Then customize the software to meet their own personal needs. Then train them to use it all.

Home Programming

Write computer programs at home to sell to friends and software publishers.

Sales Skills

Get a job selling computers in a store. As a salesperson, you'll be helping people decide which software and hardware to buy; you'll be acting as a consultant.

Job Expansion

Take a noncomputer job and gradually enlarge its responsibilities so that it involves computers. For example, if you're a typist, urge your boss to let you use a word processor. If you're a clerk, ask permission to use spreadsheet and database management programs to manage your work more efficiently. Or, keep your current job, but expand it to include new skills so you gradually become a computer expert.

On-the-Job Training

Get an entry-level job in a computer company and gradually move up by using the company's policy of free training for employees

---

Adapted from Russ Walter, *The Secret Guide to Computers,* 16th ed., p. 527.

▼ Programming languages can be divided into five generations.

1. *Machine language,* the only language the computer's processor can understand, is first-generation language—the digits 0 and 1.

2. *Assembly language,* easier to work with than machine language because it allows the programmer to use abbreviations, is a second-generation language. (Both machine and assembly language are low-level languages.)

3. *High-level,* or *third-generation, languages* were developed to make writing software programs even easier by using human-language (for example, English-like) statements. Of the hundreds of high-level languages used today, the following are some of the more popular:

   FORTRAN (FORmula TRANslator): the first high-level language, which was formulated for scientific and mathematical applications; this language does not handle the input and output of large volumes of data efficiently. It is not as structured as COBOL.

   COBOL (COmmon Business Oriented Language): its development as a common programming language for business applications was funded by the U.S. government; this language is noted for its machine independence and its data processing and file-handling capabilities.

   PI/1 (Programming Language 1): designed to combine the computational capabilities of FORTRAN and the data processing and file-handling capabilities of COBOL. Although flexible, it is harder to learn than COBOL and requires a great deal of main storage.

   BASIC (Beginner's All-purpose Symbolic Instruction Code): developed at Dartmouth College for instructional purposes, but now used on microcomputers and certain business systems to solve a variety of relatively simple problems.

   RPG (Report Program Generator): introduced by IBM as a program geared to deal with clear-cut problems and produce reports; users can produce reports by filling out special coding forms and then entering the recorded data.

   C: developed by Bell Laboratories as a tool for writing systems software such as UNIX. It works on a variety of different computers, including microcomputers. However, it is not good for checking types of data, and it has no input/output routines.

   Pascal: named for 17th-century French mathematician Blaise Pascal. Developed to teach structured programming. Has strong mathematical, scientific, and graphics-processing capabilities and can be used on large and small computer systems; not used extensively in business.

   Modula-2: an improved version of Pascal; better suited for business; used primarily to write systems software.

   Ada: named for Augusta Ada, Countess of Lovelace (the first programmer), and developed by the U.S. Department of Defense for use as an embedded system in computerized weapons systems.

4. *Fourth-generation languages* do not rely on a long list of detailed procedures that tell the computer *how* to do something. They just use human-language statements to tell the computer *what* to do. The five basic types of fourth-generation language tools are (a) *query languages,* (b) *report generators,* (c) *applications generators,* (d) *decision support systems* and *financial planning languages,* and (e) some microcomputer applications software.

5. *Natural languages,* which some people refer to as *fifth-generation languages,* allow users and programmers to interact with the computer by using human language patterns, including misspellings and mistakes.

8.29

▼ Some microcomputer software packages, including electronic spreadsheets and database management systems, can be used to create customized programs to solve unique needs.

▼ Program development follows five steps:

1. Define the problem.

2. Map out the program logic—that is, work out the necessary *algorithms.*

3. Code the program.

4. Test the program.

5. Document the program.

▼ Many tools and techniques are used to document program logic, including *program flowcharts, pseudocode, structure charts,* and *HIPO packages.*

▼ *Program flowcharts* use standard symbols to represent the step-by-step activities and decision logic needed to solve a processing problem. Logic flow normally goes from top to bottom and left to right.

▼ *Pseudocode* is a "fake" code—that is, human-language statements that use the structure of the programming language statements to describe instructions but without being hard to understand. Pseudocode uses four keywords to portray logic: IF, THEN, ELSE, and DO. Repetitive processing logic is represented by DO WHILE, DO UNTIL, and END DO.

▼ *Structure charts* diagram the hierarchy of program modules, each of which represents one processing step. *HIPO (hierarchy plus input-processing-output) packages* include a structure chart of the program in its visual table of contents along with a program description and a legend. The HIPO package also includes an *overview diagram,* which shows the input-processing-output activities of the program modules, and a *detail diagram,* which shows the steps of each activity in a module.

▼ Programmers use structured programming techniques. *Structured programming* relies heavily on the concept of modularity (*top-down design*) and uses three basic *control structures* to form the program code: (1) *sequence,* (2) *selection* (*if-then-else*), and (3) *iteration,* or *looping* (*do while*).

▼ The *sequence control structure* determines that each program instruction is executed in sequence unless a particular instruction is intended to alter that sequence.

▼ The *selection control structure* allows a condition to be tested (IF) to determine which instruction(s) will be performed next (THEN or ELSE). Using this structure, the programmer can alter the basic sequence structure.

▼ The *iteration control structure* (*looping*) allows an activity to be repeated as long as a certain condition remains true. Loops simplify programming because they enable the programmer to specify instructions only once to have the computer execute them many times.

▼ After a program has been designed, it is tested by a *structured walkthrough* (formal review of a programmer's work by other programmers, systems designers, and users before it is coded). Then, after the program is coded, it must be tested by structured walkthrough, *desk checking* (programmer proofreads a printout of the program), *translation attempt,* and *sample data test.* Testing is done to weed out syntax errors, caused by typographical mistakes and incorrect use of the programming language, and logic errors, caused by incorrect use of control structures (sequencing, selection, iteration).

▼ Program documentation should be done throughout the five steps of program development. User documentation, technical documentation, and operator's instructions provide guidance for all those who must use, maintain, and modify the program.

KEY TERMS

Ada, p. 8.11
algorithm, p. 8.16
American National Standards
   Institute (ANSI), p. 8.5
applications generator, p. 8.13
assembly language, p. 8.3
BASIC (Beginner's All-purpose
   Symbolic Instruction Code), p. 8.8
C, p. 8.9
COBOL (COmmon Business
   Oriented Language), p. 8.6
decision support system, p. 8.14
detail diagram, p. 8.22
do while, p. 8.24
financial planning language, p. 8.14
FORTRAN (FORmula TRANslator),
   p. 8.5
fourth-generation language (4GL),
   p. 8.13

hierarchy chart, p. 8.21
hierarchy plus input-process-output
   (HIPO), p. 8.22
high-level programming language,
   p. 8.4
if-then-else, p. 8.23
International Standards Organization
   (ISO), p. 8.5
iteration, p. 8.24
logic error, p. 8.26
loop, p. 8.26
machine language, p. 8.3
Modula-2, p. 8.10
module, p. 8.21
natural language, p. 8.14
nonprocedural language, p. 8.13
overview diagram, p. 8.22
Pascal, p. 8.10
PL/1, p. 8.7

procedural language, p. 8.4
program flowchart, p. 8.18
pseudocode, p. 8.20
query language, p. 8.13
report generator, p. 8.13
RPG (Report Program Generator),
   p. 8.8
sequence control structure, p. 8.23
structure chart, p. 8.21
structured programming, p. 8.21
structured walkthrough, p. 8.22
subroutine, p. 8.21
syntax, p. 8.2
syntax error, p. 8.26
top-down design, p. 8.21
visual table of contents (VTOC),
   p. 8.22

EXERCISES

SELF-TEST

1. _____ is the high-level language used for creating business applications software.

2. The rules for using a programming language are called syntax. (true/false)

3. Machine language is a _____-generation language.

4. _____ is a high-level language that was developed to help students learn programming.

5. Query languages, report generators, applications generators, decision support systems, and financial planning languages are _____-generation languages.

6. Fifth-generation languages are called _____ languages.

7. A query language allows the user to easily retrieve information from a database using English-like statements. (true/false)

8. A diagram that uses ANSI symbols to document a program's processing activities and logic is called a _____.

9. _____ uses normal human-language statements to represent and record program logic.

10. Third-generation languages are also called _____ languages.

Solutions: (1) COBOL; (2) true; (3) first; (4) BASIC; (5) fourth; (6) natural; (7) true; (8) flowchart; (9) pseudocode; (10) high-level

SHORT-ANSWER QUESTIONS

1. How do third-generation languages differ from first- and second-generation languages?

2. What is natural language?

3. Why is it relevant to users to know what software development tools, or programming languages, are used to create software?

4. What are the main characteristics of machine language?

5. What are the five main types of fourth-generation language tools?

6. What were the reasons behind the development of high-level programming languages?

7. How does a programmer decide what language should be used to write a particular program?

8. What is the difference between procedural and nonprocedural languages?

9. What are the five basic steps of program development?

10. Why is documentation important during program development?

PROJECTS

1. Visit the computer laboratory at your school.

   a. Identify which high-level languages are available.

   b. Determine if each language processor identified is a compiler or an interpreter.

   c. Determine if the language processors are available for microcomputers, larger computers, or both.

   d. Identify any microcomputer-based electronic spreadsheet software and database management systems software available.

2. Scan the employment ads in a few major newspapers and report on the procedural programming languages most in demand. For what types of jobs?

3. If you were a programmer, would you rather work on applications software or systems software? Think of as many reasons as you can to support your choice, and write a brief report.

Communications and Connectivity

Getting from here to there has always fascinated human beings, going farther and doing it faster. Aside from the thrills associated with speed, going places quickly means being able to stay connected with other people, to spread news and information and receive them in return—in other words, to communicate. *Obviously, technology reached the point some time ago of allowing communication to occur without having to transport people from one place to another. But what about more recent developments? And what do they have to do with computers in business and the management of data and information? This chapter will explain how electronic data communications affects the computer user.*

PREVIEW

When you have completed this chapter, you will be able to:

▼ Identify the basic characteristics of data transmission

▼ Describe basic communications hardware in general terms

▼ Explain what a communications network is and describe the typical network configurations

▼ List some of the information services available to personal computer users

▼ Describe the basic operation and uses of a fax machine

▼ Briefly explain what computer viruses are and what can be done about them

*T*he wheel, which is thought to have been invented around 3500 B.C., was a tremendous technological advancement; without it or a similar invention, information probably would still be transported by people on foot or horseback, by smoke signals or drum sounds, by carrier pigeon. By now, however, people have refined the technology of motion to the point where mobility has become a way of life.

The invention of the computer and its introduction into the business environment in the early 1950s marked a similar technological achievement. By the early 1960s, some information needed for business was available in computer-usable form "somewhere"; however, it may have been impossible or impractical to get it if the information needed was only available in a computer 1,000 miles away. Modern electronic communications—the movement of voice and data over long distances through the use of computers and telecommunications channels and equipment—has solved this problem.

You will encounter innumerable situations in the business environment that require data to be sent to, retrieved from, or shared among different locations. For example, you might:

▼ Send electronic "mail" to another user in the company or to a business contact anywhere in the world—and receive electronic mail on your own computer

▼ Send your computer files over telephone lines to another user

▼ Share the same database management software and database with other users

▼ Share hardware such as printers and secondary storage devices with other users

▼ Share processing power—such as a company mainframe—with other users

▼ Access data in a huge commercial subscription database on almost any subject, using your own computer equipment and telephone lines

▼ Participate in teleconferences or multimedia conferences with people scattered around the world

▼ Order equipment or travel services simply by using your computer

▼ Schedule meetings automatically by instructing your computer to consult with other users' computers

To transmit or receive data, you must have special hardware—that is, a transmission method, which we will discuss shortly—as well as access to a telephone line or other transmission medium and special communications software on line at both the sending and receiving locations. Learning to use the hardware and software involved in data communications in normal business situations is not difficult; in this chapter we will explain what they do.

Characteristics of Data Transmission

When you are talking on the phone with another person who is a few houses away, you can probably hear that person clearly and do not need to speak loudly. However, sometimes the farther away you are from the person, the harder it is to hear clearly what is being said on the phone because of static and other noise. A lot of noise increases the chance that parts of your message will be garbled or misheard. This same problem can exist when data is transmitted over phone lines from computer to computer. Although alternative transmission methods and media have been developed that lessen noise problems, including satellite, microwave, and radio wave, they are not without their own limitations, as you will see later on. But before we discuss the various methods of data communications, we need to discuss their common characteristics.

Analog and Digital Signals

When we speak, we transmit continuous sound waves, or **analog signals** (Figure 1), that form what we call the voice. Analog signals could be compared to a fairly steady stream of water coming out of a garden hose. These signals form a single, continuous wave that fluctuates a certain number of times over a certain time period—called the **frequency**, which is measured in cycles per second, or *hertz*. Sometimes our voices sound high (composed of high-frequency sound waves: many wave fluctuations per second), and sometimes our voices sound low (composed of low-frequency sound waves: fewer wave fluctuations per second). Analog signals can also differ in **amplitude**, or loudness: a soft voice is at low amplitude. Most telephone lines are currently an analog communications medium.

In contrast to human voices, computer communication uses **digital signals**, which can be compared to the short bursts of water that shoot out of a timed garden sprinkler. These signals are discontinuous (discrete) pulses over a transmission medium (Figure 1). Computers communicate with each other in streams of binary digits (bits) transmitted in patterns of digital signals—series of on and off pulses. For data to travel from one computer to another across the phone lines, the sending computer's digital data must first be converted into analog form and then reconverted into digital form at the receiving end. This process is called *modulation* and *demodulation*.

Modulation converts digital signals into analog form so that data can be sent over the phone lines. **Demodulation** converts the analog signals back into

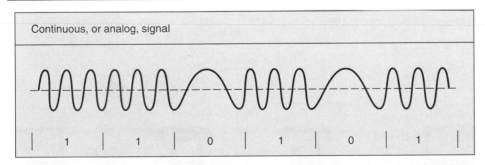

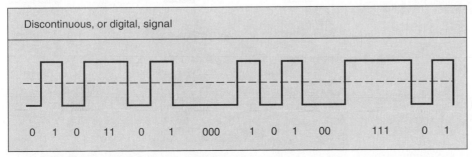

FIGURE 1

Analog and digital signals. Analog signals are continuous waves whose patterns vary to represent the message being transmitted; digital signals are discontinuous, or discrete, bursts that form a transmission pattern. In this figure, the horizontal axis represents time and the vertical axis represents amplitude.

digital form so that they can be processed by the receiving computer. The hardware that performs modulation and demodulation is called a **modem** (*modu*late/*dem*odulate). The sending computer must be connected to a modem that modulates the transmitted data, while the receiving computer must be connected to a modem to demodulate the data (Figure 2). Both modems are connected to the telephone line.

Asynchronous and Synchronous Transmission

When signals are transmitted through modems from one computer to another, patterns of bits coded to represent data are sent one bit at a time. How does the receiving device know where one character ends and another starts? In **asynchronous transmission,** also called *start-stop transmission,* each string of bits that make up a character is bracketed by control bits (start and stop bits) (Figure 3a). In effect, each group of digital or analog signals making up the code for one character is individually "wrapped" in an electronic "envelope" made of a start bit (often symbolized by a 0), an error check bit (or parity bit), and one or two stop bits (often symbolized by a 1). The error check bit is set according to a parity scheme that can be odd or even.

For example, using an even parity scheme, an ASCII *G* would be represented as 00100011101, per Figure 3. The first 0 is the start bit and the last 1 is the stop bit. The nine bits in between are used to represent the code for the character and the parity scheme. In this case, the tenth bit (the parity bit) has been set to 0 to denote an even parity scheme. If an odd parity scheme is being used, then the parity bit (the tenth bit) would be set so that the number of characters between the start and stop bits in the on position would be odd—00100011111.

Users of both the sending and receiving computers must agree on the parity scheme. The scheme chosen is set within a communications software program. For example, if computer A is transmitting to computer B, the users of both computers must first agree on a parity scheme (perhaps by having a telephone conversation), then load the communications software into RAM, and choose the agreed-on parity scheme by selecting the appropriate software option. It doesn't matter which scheme is chosen as long as both computers are using the same one—odd or even.

FIGURE 2

Modems are hardware devices that translate digital signals into analog waves for transmission over phone lines and then back into digital signals for processing.

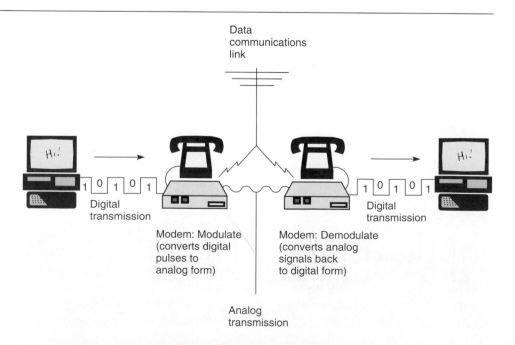

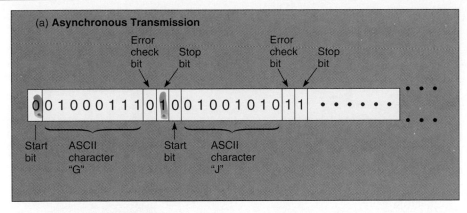

FIGURE 3

Asynchronous and synchronous transmission. So that devices receiving data transmission can decode the beginnings and ends of data strings and check for transmission errors, the character strings are transmitted asynchronously or synchronously. Synchronous transmission takes less time because groups of characters are transmitted as blocks with no start and stop bits between characters.

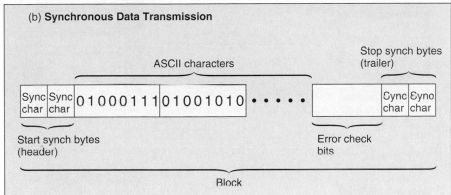

Because asynchronous communication is inexpensive, it is widely used with microcomputers; however, it is also relatively slow, because of the number of parity and error check bits that must be transmitted with the data bits.

In **synchronous transmission** (Figure 3b), characters can be sent much faster because they are sent as blocks, or "packets." Header and trailer bytes are inserted as identifiers at the beginnings and the ends of blocks. In addition, error check bits are transmitted before the trailer bytes. Synchronous transmission is used by large computers to transmit huge volumes of data at high speeds. Expensive and complex timing devices must be used to keep the transmission activities synchronized. Synchronous transmission is rarely used in microcomputer-based communications lines.

Simplex, Half-Duplex, and Full-Duplex Traffic

Besides signal type (analog or digital) and manner of data transmission (synchronous or asynchronous), data communications technology must also consider the *direction* of data traffic flow supported by communications links such as modems. In the **simplex** mode, data can travel in *only one direction at all times* (Figure 4). For example, in some museum rooms, environmental devices send information about temperature, humidity, and other conditions to a computer that monitors and adjusts office environmental settings automatically. However, the computer does not send information back to the devices. The simplex mode is used occasionally in some local area networks, which we will discuss later.

A **half-duplex** communications link can support two-way traffic, but data can travel in *only one direction at one time* (Figure 4). This mode of transmission is similar to using a CB (citizens' band) radio. When you press the transmit button you can talk, but you cannot receive. After you release the transmit

FIGURE 4

Data traffic moves in simplex, half-duplex, or full-duplex modes.

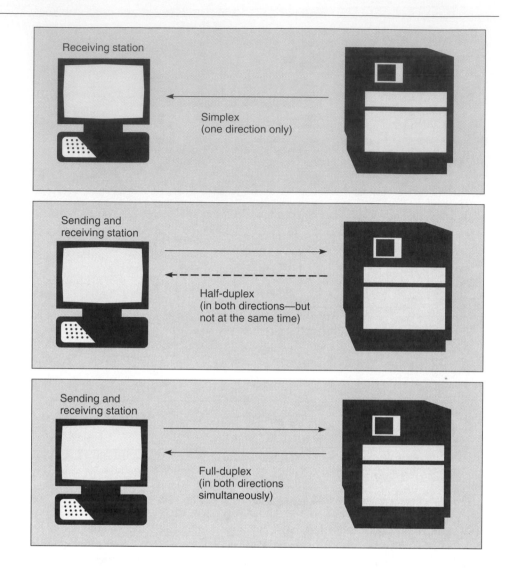

button, you can receive, but you cannot transmit. Transmission of data in this mode over long distances can greatly increase the time it takes to communicate data. This delay is due to three factors: (1) the time needed for device A (at the receiving end) to change from receive to transmit mode, (2) the time required for device A to transmit to device B a request for confirmation that all is ready for transmission, and (3) the time required for device A to receive the confirmation that device B is ready to receive. The half-duplex transmission mode is frequently used for linking microcomputers via telephone lines.

Full-duplex transmission sends data in *both directions simultaneously,* similarly to two trains passing in opposite directions on side-by-side tracks (Figure 4). This transmission mode eliminates the problem of transmission delay, but it is more expensive than the other two modes because it requires special equipment. Full-duplex transmission is used primarily for mainframe communications.

Data Transmission Media (Channels)

To get from here to there, data must move *through* something. A telephone line, a cable, or the atmosphere are all transmission *media,* or *channels.* But before the data can be communicated, it must be converted into a form suitable for communication. The basic forms into which data can be converted for communication are as follows:

1. Electronic pulses or charges (used to transmit voice and data over telephone lines)
2. Electromagnetic waves (microwaves—similar to radio waves but at a higher frequency)
3. Pulses of light
4. Infrared, spread spectrum, or standard radio waves

The form or method of communication affects the maximum rate at which data can be moved through the channel and the level of noise that will exist—for example, light pulses travel faster than electromagnetic waves, and some types of satellite transmission systems are less noisy than transmission over telephone wires. Obviously, some situations require that data be moved as fast as possible; others don't. Channels that move data relatively slowly, like telegraph lines, are *narrowband* channels. Most telephone lines are *voiceband* channels, and they have a wider bandwidth than narrowband channels. *Broadband* channels (like coaxial cable, fiber-optic cable, microwave circuits, and satellite systems) transmit large volumes of data at high speeds.

Electronic Pulses

Telephone Lines

The earliest type of telephone line was referred to as *open wire*—unsheathed copper wires strung on telephone poles and secured by glass insulators. Because it was uninsulated, this type of telephone line was highly susceptible to electromagnetic interference; the wires had to be spaced about 12 inches apart to minimize the problem. Although open wire can still be found in a few places, it has almost entirely been replaced with cable and other types of communications media.

Cable is insulated wire. Insulated pairs of wires twisted around each other—called *twisted-pair cable*—can be packed into bundles of a thousand or more pairs (Figure 5). These wide-diameter cables are commonly used as telephone lines today and are often found in large buildings and under city streets. Even though this type of line is a major improvement over open wire, it still has many limitations. Twisted-pair cable is susceptible to a variety of types of electrical interference (noise), which limits the practical distance that data can be transmitted without being garbled. (To be received intact, digital signals must be "refreshed," or strengthened, every 1 to 2 miles through the use of an amplifier and related circuits, which together are called *repeaters*. Although repeaters do increase the signal strength, which tends to weaken over long distances, they can be very expensive.) Twisted-pair cable has been used for years for voice and data transmission; however, newer, more advanced media are replacing it.

Coaxial Cable

More expensive than twisted-pair wire, **coaxial cable** (also called *shielded cable*) is a type of thickly insulated copper wire (Figure 5) that can carry a larger volume of data—about 100 million bits per second, or about 1,800 to 3,600 voice calls at once. The insulation is composed of a nonconductive material covered by a layer of woven wire mesh and heavy-duty rubber or plastic. Coaxial cable is similar to the cable used to connect your TV set to a cable TV service. Coaxial cables can also be bundled together into a much larger cable. This type of communications line has become very popular because of its capacity and reduced need for signals to be refreshed (every 2 to 4 miles). Coaxial cables

FIGURE 5

Twisted wire (b) is being phased out as a communications medium by coaxial cable (a) and even more sophisticated media such as microwave and fiber optics.

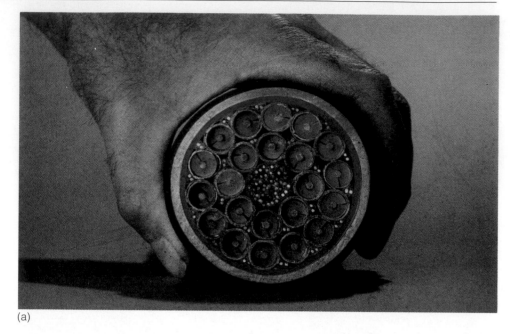

(a)

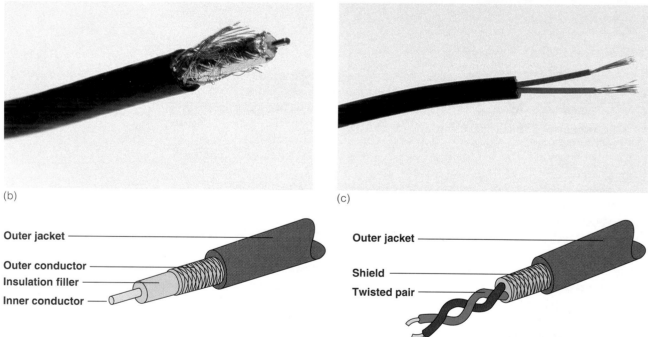

(b)   (c)

Outer jacket
Outer conductor
Insulation filler
Inner conductor

Outer jacket
Shield
Twisted pair

are most often used as the primary communications medium for locally connected networks in which all computer communication is within a limited geographic area, such as in the same building. Computers connected by coaxial cable do not need to use modems. Coaxial cable is also used for undersea telephone lines.

Point-to-Point and Multidrop Lines

Data communications lines can be connected in two types of configurations: point-to-point and multidrop.

A **point-to-point line** directly connects the sending and the receiving devices. If the point-to-point line is a **switched line,** it is a regular telephone line—the telephone company switching stations direct the call on the line they select, just as they do all the other calls they process. After transmission is completed, the line is disconnected. If the point-to-point line is a **dedicated line,** it is always established—that is, it is never disconnected. The dedicated line is available only to the organization that creates it (*private line*) or leases it (*leased line*) from another organization—for example, from the phone company.

A **multidrop line** connects many devices, not just one sending device and one receiving device. The number of devices or terminals that use the line is determined by the experts who design the communications, or network, system. Multidrop lines are usually leased.

Electromagnetic Waves

Microwave Systems

Instead of using wire or cable, **microwave** systems use the atmosphere as the medium through which to transmit signals. These systems are extensively used for high-volume as well as long-distance communication of both data and voice in the form of electromagnetic waves similar to radio waves but in a higher frequency range.

Microwave signals are often referred to as "line of sight" signals because they cannot bend around the curvature of the earth; instead, they must be relayed from point to point by microwave towers, or relay stations, placed 20 to 30 miles apart (Figure 6). The distance between the towers depends on the curvature of the surface terrain in the vicinity. The surface of the earth typically curves about 8 inches every mile. The towers have either a dish- or a horn-shaped antenna. The size of the antenna varies according to the distance the signals must cover. A long-distance antenna could easily be 10 feet or larger in size; a disk of 2 to 4 feet in diameter, which you often see on city buildings, is large enough for small distances. Each tower facility receives incoming traffic, boosts the signal strength, and sends the signal to the next station.

The primary advantage of using microwave systems for voice and data communications is that direct physical cabling is not required. (Obviously, telephone lines and other types of cable must physically connect all communications system points that can't receive atmospheric signals.) More than half of the tele-

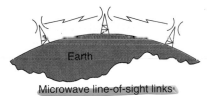

Earth

Microwave line-of-sight links

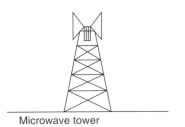

Microwave tower

FIGURE 6

Microwave relay station. Microwaves must be relayed from point to point along the earth's surface because they cannot bend.

FIGURE 7

(*continued*)

(d)

FIGURE 8

Fiber optics. Laser-fired light pulses (representing the "on" state in the binary system of data representation) are fired through very thin glass or plastic fibers.

tial speed for data communications is up to 10,000 times faster than that of microwave and satellite systems. Fiber-optic communications is also resistant to illegal data theft, because it is almost impossible to tap into it in order to listen to the data being transmitted or to change the data without being detected; in fact, it is currently being used by the Central Intelligence Agency. Another advantage to fiber-optic transmission is that electrical signals don't escape from the cables—in other words, the cables don't interfere with sensitive electrical equipment that may be nearby. Given its significant advantages, it is not surprising that fiber-optic cable is much more expensive than telephone wire and cable.

AT&T has developed undersea optical fiber cables for transatlantic use in the belief that fiber optics will eventually replace satellite communications in terms of cost-effectiveness and efficiency. The Japanese have already laid an underwater fiber-optic cable. Sprint uses a fiber-optic communications network laid along railroad rights-of-way in the United States that carries digital signals (analog voice signals are converted to digital signals at company switching stations).

Infrared, Spread Spectrum, and Standard Radio Waves

A new generation of wireless data communications devices is rapidly gaining attention. These devices use three basic technologies: *infrared (IR), spread spectrum,* and *standard radio* transmission.

Infrared is based on the same technology used by TV remote control units. However, transmission devices that use infrared must be within line of sight of one another and so cannot be used for mobile computing (objects may come between the transmission units).

Spread spectrum radio was developed by the U.S. Army during World War II for jam-proof and interception-proof transmissions. This technology is being used in small networks within individual buildings.

Standard radio technology is also being employed for data transmission in networks, but it involves some licensing difficulties. (Standard radio frequencies cannot be used without government licenses.)

We'll discuss these forms of wireless data transmission a bit more in the section to follow on local area networks.

Communications Hardware

Much of the hardware used in data communications is operated by technical professionals and is rarely of immediate consequence to the user unless it stops working—when you're calling from New York and can't reach your division office in London, for example. However, you should become familiar with certain types of common business communications hardware: modems, which were mentioned briefly in the section on analog and digital signals, multiplexers, concentrators, controllers, front-end processors, and protocol converters.

Modems

Modems are probably the most widely used data communications hardware. They are certainly the most familiar to microcomputer users who communicate with one another or with a larger computer. As you learned earlier in this chapter, the word **modem** is actually a contraction of *mo*dulate and *dem*odulate. A modem's basic purpose is to convert digital computer signals to analog signals for transmission over phone lines, then to receive these signals and convert them back to digital signals.

A modem allows the user to directly connect the computer to the telephone line (Figure 9). Modems commonly transmit and receive data at 2,400 or 9,600 or 14,400 **bits per second (bps);** some run at 12,000. Transmitting a 10-page single-spaced report would take about 20 minutes at 300 bps, about 5 minutes at 1,200 bps, and about 2½ minutes at 2,400 bps.

FIGURE 9

Modems. An internal modem (a) is placed inside the computer; an external modem (b) remains outside the computer. In both cases, the phone remains connected for voice communication when the computer is not transmitting.

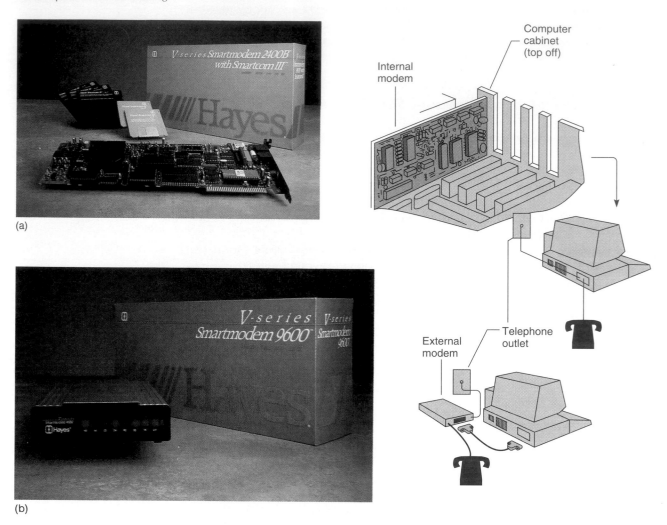

(a)

(b)

Modems are either internal or external. An **internal modem** (Figure 9) is located on a circuit board that is placed inside a microcomputer (actually plugged into an expansion slot). The internal modem draws its power directly from the computer's power supply. No special cable is required to connect the modem to the computer. An **external** direct-connect **modem** is an independent hardware component—that is, it is outside the computer—and uses its own power supply (Figure 9). The modem is connected to the computer via a cable designed for the purpose.

Users who deal with modems and data communications must be sure they are communicating with compatible equipment. Like other types of computer hardware and software, not all modems work with other modems, and not all modems work with the same type of software. In addition, microcomputer communications software packages—such as ProComm, Smartcom II and III, Crosstalk XVI—require users to set their systems at specific "parameters" so that their microcomputer can "talk" to another computer using the same parameters. Parameters include speed of data transmission, parity scheme (error correction), direction of traffic, data compression, and so forth. The software package manual tells users how to set software parameters and how to use a small screwdriver to set certain switches, called *DIP* (*dual inline package*) *switches,* in the external modem cabinet. These software packages allow "smart" modems (with certain types of chips) to do more than simply transmit and receive; for example, you can arrange for automatic dialing and transmission, printing of incoming text, and storage of incoming data on disk.

Serial Ports

Microcomputers have two types of interfaces, or *ports.* A *serial interface,* or *serial port,* is used to plug in devices such as modems that transmit data serially— bit by bit in a continuous stream; *parallel interfaces,* or *parallel ports,* are used to connect devices that transmit data in parallel—along eight separate lines simultaneously (Figure 10). Parallel transmission is used between the computer and the printer.

Multiplexers, Concentrators, and Controllers

When an organization's data communications needs grow, the number of lines available for that purpose often become overtaxed, even if the company has leased one or more private telephone lines—called *dedicated lines*—used only for data communications. *Multiplexing* optimizes the use of communications lines by allowing multiple users or devices to share one high-speed line (Figure 11),

---

FIGURE 10

Serial and parallel
interfaces/ports/cables

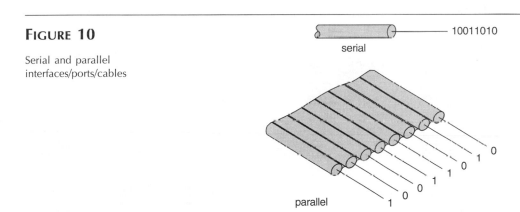

serial   10011010

parallel

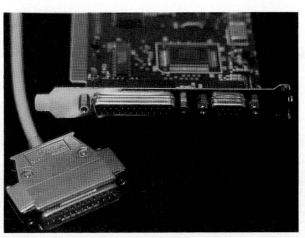

FIGURE 11

This figure shows the basic difference between computer communications with and without the use of a multiplexer.

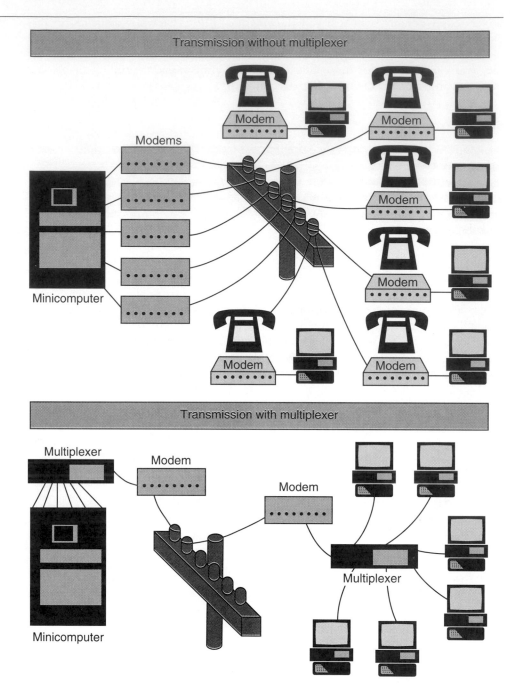

thereby reducing communications costs. Multiplexing can be done by multiplexers, concentrators, or controllers.

Briefly, a **multiplexer** is a data communications hardware device that allows 8, 16, 32, or more devices (depending on the model) to share a single communications line. Messages sent by a multiplexer must be received by a multiplexer of the same type. The devices differentiate individual messages and direct them to their recipients.

A **concentrator,** which also allows many devices to share a single communications line, is more "intelligent" than a multiplexer because it can be programmed to temporarily store some transmissions and forward them later. It is also used to multiplex low-speed communications lines onto one high-speed line.

A **controller** also supports a group of devices (terminals and printers) connected to a computer. It is used in place of a multiplexer and acts to control functions for the group of terminals.

Front-End Processors

In some computer systems, the main computer is connected directly into the multiplexer, controller, or concentrator. In other systems, it is first hooked to a **front-end processor,** a smaller computer that relieves the larger one of many data traffic management and communications functions (Figure 12). In effect, the front-end processor acts as a "mediator" between the network and the main computer, allowing the main computer to concentrate on processing and improving the responsiveness of the system to the user.

Protocols and Protocol Converters

One of the most frustrating aspects of data communications between different types of computers, especially between a microcomputer and a larger computer system, is that they often use different communications protocols. A **protocol** is the formal set of rules for communicating, including rules for timing of message exchanges, the type of electrical connections used by the communications devices, error detection techniques, means of gaining access to communications channels, and so on. To overcome this problem, a specialized type of intelligent multiplexer called a **protocol converter** can be used. Protocol converters are available that even allow a microcomputer operating in asynchronous mode to talk with a large IBM mainframe computer operating in synchronous mode. This type of device is being used by more and more companies that want to establish effective communications between personal computers and the main computer system and with printing devices.

Some groups are working on the establishment of a standard protocol for data transmission. For example, IBM has released the Systems Network Architecture (SNA) for its own machines, and the International Standards Organization (ISO) has released its set of protocol standards, called the Open Systems Interconnection (OSI). However, just because standards exist does not mean that they will be used by everyone or that they can be enforced.

ISDN (Integrated Services Digital Network) is a set of standards put out by the Consultative Committee for International Telegraphy and Telephony (CCITT). The ISDN standards are designed to set rules for a worldwide digital communications network that could simultaneously support voice, data, and video traffic over telephone wires (traditionally an analog communications medium). For ISDN to work, users will have to replace their existing telephones with ISDN telephones and insert an ISDN board in their microcomputers.

All regional Bell operating companies across the United States will be able to support ISDN access by 1996 (or sooner). Several ISDN applications are already quite popular, including video teleconferencing and transmitting data at very high speeds. However, ISDN is not yet supported in rural areas.

Communications Software

Even with the best communications hardware, you won't be able to communicate with another computer without communications software. Most **communications software** packages enable you to perform the basic functions of send-

FIGURE 12

A smaller computer, called a front-end processor, is often used to relieve the main computer of many communications functions.

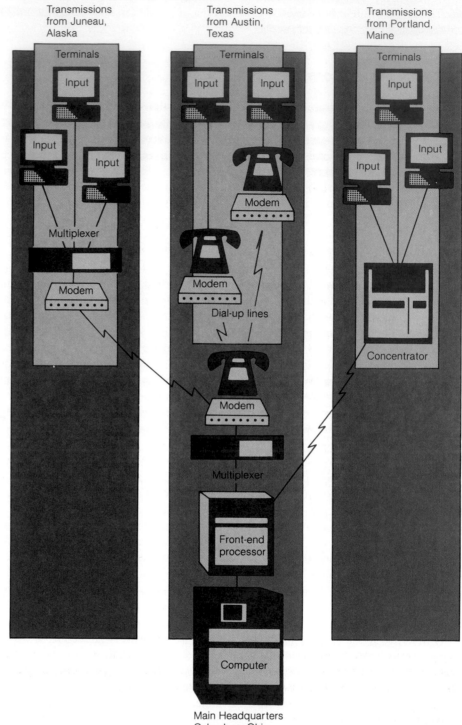

ing files between computers and communicating with a communications service (communications services, systems, and utilities are described shortly). However, most users have business requirements that extend beyond these basic communications tasks. For example, if you want to transmit data only at night to take advantage of low phone rates, your communications software must provide a strong **script language**, like a programming language, that will enable you to automate this process. The most popular microcomputer communications packages include Crosstalk, DynaComm, HyperAccess 5, Mirror III, Procomm Plus, Relay Gold, and Smartcom III.

A useful communications package provides a number of capabilities beyond basic communications functions. The package should provide a wide range of communications protocols (described earlier), or sets of rules, that govern the meaningful transfer of data between two or more computers or services. Most communications programs include protocols for communicating with popular information services such as CompuServe. (Both the sending and receiving party must be using the same protocol in order for data transmission to be successful.) In addition, some communications programs offer protocols that automatically compress a file, or reduce the space it takes up on a storage device, before it is sent, so that the speed of data transmission is lessened. If you often need to send and retrieve complex data such as spreadsheets and programs, make sure your software includes an efficient error-checking protocol.

If you're concerned with speed, make sure your communications software can support sending data at a rate of 9,600 or 14,400 bps. In addition, if you want to perform operations on a remote computer, such as downloading a file to another computer, make sure the communications software supports remote control of communications. If most of your communications tasks involve remote communications, purchase a special program that provides more flexibility for communicating remotely.

Of all the communications software features to be familiar with before purchasing a package, the capabilities and ease of use of the script language can be the most critical to users. The script language enables you to save time when performing tasks particular to your needs. For example, before a vacation, you can use the script language to instruct your computer to send and retrieve data a specified number of times when you're gone. In addition, you can program a script language to simplify the task of establishing communication with complex information systems.

Fortunately, much attention has been given in recent years to improving the user interface of most communications packages so that they are easier to use. Now, most include easy menu systems. In addition, the documentation that accompanies communications software has improved. Helpful illustrations and improved writing make it much easier for the first-time user to communicate.

Communications Networks: Connectivity

Information and resources gain in value if they can be shared. A **network** is simply a collection of data communications hardware, computers, communications software, and communications media connected in a meaningful way to allow users to share information and equipment. The three most common types of networks are private, public, and international.

A **private network** is specifically designed to support the communications needs of a particular business organization. Many organizations with geographically separated facilities and a need for a large volume of data and voice communications implement or install their own private communications networks. The Southern Pacific Railroad was one of the first organizations to develop its own comprehensive microwave communications network to facilitate communication along all its rail lines. Its microwave towers can be seen along any of the major rail lines.

A **public network,** in contrast, is a comprehensive communications facility designed to provide subscribers (users who pay a fee) with voice and/or data communications over a large geographical area (in some cases coast to coast). Public networks such as Bell Telephone and AT&T Communications are sometimes referred to as *common carriers*. Some public communications networks offer **teleconferencing** services—electronically linking several people by phone, computer, and video (Figure 13). Still other communications networks enable users to participate in **multimedia conferences,** during which users can not only see and hear one another but also work on text and graphics projects *at the same time.*

The term **international network** is used to describe a communications network specifically designed to provide users with intercontinental voice and data communications facilities. Most of these networks use undersea cable or satellite communications. Western Union and RCA provide international networks.

Network Configurations

A number of different network configurations, or shapes, are used to satisfy the needs of users in different situations. The basic types of configurations are star (and hierarchical) network, bus network, and ring (and token ring) network. Although each network configuration is actively used today by private, public, and international communications networks, you will most likely come into contact with one in the context of a local area network.

A **local area network (LAN)** is a private communications network, connected by a length of wire, cable, optical fiber or, in some cases, radio/infrared transmission, and run by special network operating software (NOS) that serves a company or part of a company that is often located on one floor or in a single building (Figure 14). (Coaxial cable is used the most.) All computers on the network must have *network interface cards* on the motherboard, or external adapters, to enable them to function as part of the network. A LAN is similar to a telephone system: in the latter, any telephone connected to the system can send and receive information; the same principle is true in the former. Any computer hooked up to the network can send and receive information. The LAN is generally owned by the company that is using it.

Chances are that the microcomputer you will use in your office will be part of a local area network. LANs allow office workers to share hardware (such as a laser printer or storage hardware), to share software and data, and to essen-

---

FIGURE 13

Teleconferencing. These people are participating in a teleconferencing session. They are connected by voice, video, and computer through public network communication facilities.

FIGURE 14

LAN. One of the world's busiest local area networks is at the Hong Kong Stock Exchange. Of course, such a local network can use communications lines to hook up to networks in other parts of the world.

tially make incompatible units compatible. The LAN also provides a communications link to outside communications systems, and it can be connected to other local area networks in different locations, either by public communications lines or by *dedicated lines*—lines leased by the company for its transmission purposes only. Note that modems are not always needed *within* a local area network; special hardware and software are used instead.

As we mentioned earlier in the chapter, LAN hardware and software manufacturers are starting to use infrared and radio-based technologies to transmit data among network stations. These networks, called *WLANs (wireless local area networks)* can offer several advantages over cable LANs. WLANs:

▼ Eliminate cable (especially useful when hard-to-access office areas are involved)

▼ Make computers more mobile (in case of radio transmission) and communicative

▼ Offer a cheap alternative for sharing a printer

▼ Make remodeling the office an easier task than if cable is used

However, wireless computing is still generally slower and more expensive than cable, and interference *between* neighboring WLANs operating on different frequencies can be a problem. Manufacturers are currently working on overcoming these problems, as well as radio-wave licensing problems. (The use of radio-wave frequencies in the United States is controlled by the Federal Communications Commission—FCC.)

A **metropolitan area network (MAN)** links computer resources that are more widely scattered—such as among office buildings in a city. A **wide area network (WAN)** links resources scattered around the country or the world (Figure 15). The communications hardware discussed earlier—modems, multiplexers, and so on—would be used to link various LANs together and to link parts of a MAN or a WAN.

Star Network

The **star network,** a popular LAN configuration, involves a central (hub) unit that has a number of terminals (or workstations) tied into it. These terminals are often referred to as *nodes,* or *clients.* This type of network configuration is well suited to companies with one large data processing facility shared by a

FIGURE 15

WAN. This wide area communications network was used by CBS to transmit the 1992 Winter Olympics from France to the United States. (Adapted from Don Foley, *The Arizona Republic*, February 16, 1992, p. 33.)

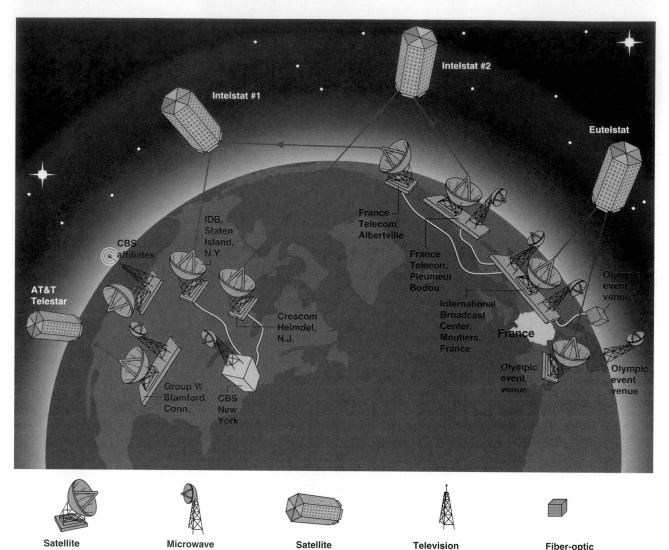

| Satellite transmission | Microwave transmission | Satellite | Television transmission | Fiber-optic communication |

Drawings show how parts of the transmission system relate to each other; their locations are not exact.

number of smaller departments. The central unit in the star network acts as the traffic controller between all the nodes in the system. The central unit is usually a host computer or a **file server** (or simply **server**). The host computer is a large computer, usually a mainframe. A file server is usually a microcomputer with a large-capacity hard disk storage device that stores shared data and programs. The file server acts as the network's "traffic cop."

The primary advantage of the star **client/server network** is that several users can use the central unit at the same time—the star is sometimes used to link microcomputers to a central database. However, its main limitation is that the whole network is affected if the main unit "goes down" (fails to function). In this case, since the nodes in the system are not designed to communicate directly with one another, all communication stops. Also, the cost of cabling the central system and the points of the star together can be very high.

When a number of star networks are configured into a single multilevel system, the resulting network is often referred to as a **hierarchical,** or **tree,** net-

work (Figure 16). In this type of network a single host computer still controls all network activity. However, each (or some) of the computers connected into the main computer in the first level of the star has a star network of devices connected to it in turn.

Hierarchical network configuration is often used by large companies with a main communications center linked to regional processing centers. Each regional processing facility acts as a host computer to smaller offices or branch computer facilities within the region. The lowest-level computer facilities allow the users to conduct some stand-alone applications processing. The regional computer facilities are used to manage large business information resources (usually in the form of regional databases) and to provide processing support that the smaller computers cannot handle efficiently.

Bus Network

The **bus network** is a **peer-to-peer network.** In this network, a number of computers are connected by a single length of wire, cable, or optical fiber (Figure 17). All communications travel along this cable, which is called a *bus* (not the same type of bus as the CPU buses we discussed in Chapter 3). There is

---

FIGURE 16

Hierarchical network. This type of network configuration is basically a star network with smaller star networks attached to some of the nodes.

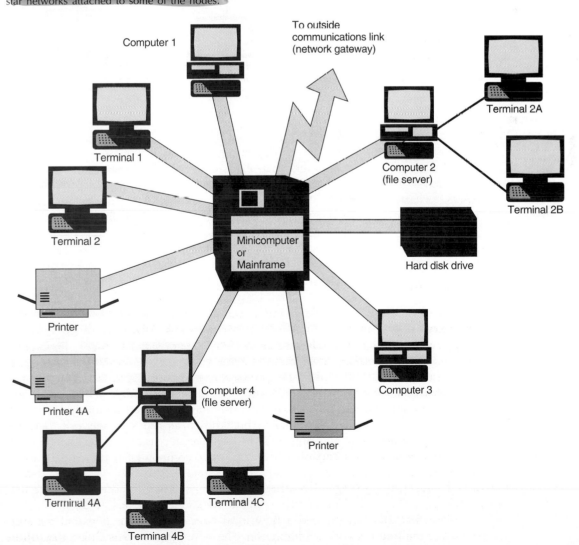

FIGURE 17

Bus network. All messages are transmitted to the entire network, traveling from the sender in both directions along the cable. Each micro-computer or device is pro-grammed to sense uniquely directed messages (one signal out of many). The bus net-work does not necessarily have to be in a straight line; for example, it can be U-shaped.

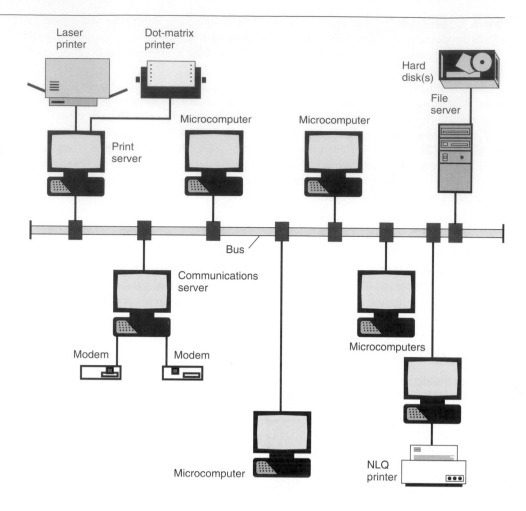

no host computer or file server. The bus network is often used to hook up a small group of microcomputers that share data. The microcomputers are pro-grammed to "check" the communications that travel along the bus to see if they are the intended recipients. The bus network is not as expensive as the star net-work, and if one computer fails, the failure does not affect the entire network. However, the bus peer-to-peer network is not as efficient as the client/server star network.

Ring Network

A **ring network** is much like a bus network, except the length of wire, cable, or optical fiber connects to form a loop (Figure 18). This type of peer-to-peer configuration does not require a central computer to control activity. Each com-puter connected to the network can communicate directly with the other com-puters in the network by using the common communications channel, and each computer does its own independent applications processing. When one com-puter needs data from another computer, the data is passed along the ring. The ring network is not as susceptible to breakdown as the star network, because when one computer in the ring fails, it does not necessarily affect the process-ing or communications capabilities of the other computers in the ring.

Token Ring Network

In early 1986, IBM announced a new local area network for personal comput-ers using the ring network configuration. The new network was called the **token**

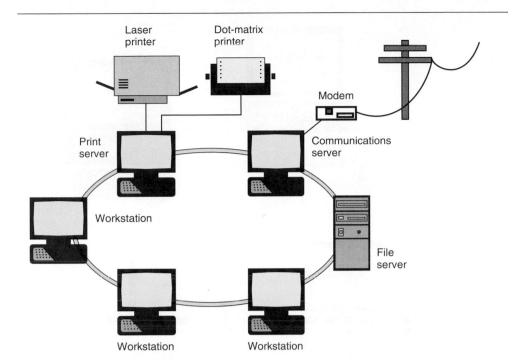

FIGURE 18

Ring network. In this type of network configuration, messages flow in one direction from a source on the loop to a destination on the loop. Computers in between act as relay stations. If one computer fails, it can be bypassed, and the network can keep operating.

ring network (Figure 19). Before the token system was established, existing ring networks used the following approach:

A computer with a message to transmit monitored network activity, waited for a lull, and then transmitted the message. This computer then checked to determine if other computers in the network were trying to transmit a message at the same time. (Overlapping transmission might have garbled its message.) If two or more computers did try to send messages at the same time, then both waited a different random period of time and tried to retransmit their messages.

Obviously, this procedure led to some message garbling and loss of time and productivity. In the token ring network, designed to eliminate these problems, a predefined pattern of bits, or *token*, is passed from computer to computer in the network. When a computer receives the token, it is allowed to transmit its message. Then the token is passed on. This method for transmitting messages (which can also be used in the bus network) prevents two computers from transmitting at the same time. The IBM token ring network is expensive but efficient. It can link up to 250 stations per ring over distances of about 770 yards, and separate rings can be linked to form larger networks.

Communications Services, Systems, and Utilities

If you have a microcomputer, a modem, a telephone, and data communications software, you can hook up to public networks and sell a printer, buy new software, play a game with one or more people, solve a complex problem by researching information in a database or having a conference with several experts, buy stock, book a plane reservation, send flowers, receive mail—all from your desk. Public and academic networks provide users with the vast resources of (among other things) databases, teleconferencing services, information services, electronic stock trading, shopping, and banking.

Figure 19

Token ring network. In this type of ring network, each computer can get exclusive access to the communications channel by "grabbing" a "token" and altering it before attaching a message. The altered token acts as a message indicator for the receiving computer, which in turn generates a new token, freeing up the channel for another computer. Computers in between the sender and the receiver examine the token and regenerate the message if the token isn't theirs. Thus, only one computer can transmit a message at a time.

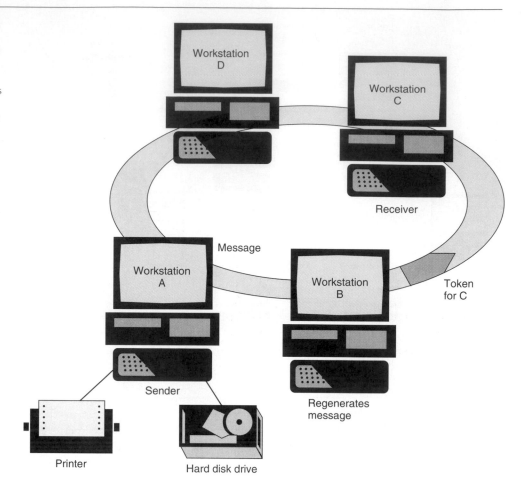

Public Databanks/Information Services

Many industries and professions require access to large volumes of specialized information to conduct business. For example, a law firm must have access to a law library and other specialized legal information. Medical professionals must have access to a tremendous volume of pharmaceutical and research-related information. To serve such needs, **public databanks,** or **information services,** were created by a number of organizations to provide users with access, for a fee, to large databanks, or databases. (In addition to the fee, the user pays regular phone rates for hook-up time.) The user accesses the databank with a terminal or a personal computer through one of the major common carrier networks, like AT&T (telephone lines). The databases contain information that covers a wide range of topics, such as health, education, law, humanities, science, government, and many others.

Some of the largest organizations providing public databases are Mead Data Central, Lockheed Information Systems, Systems Development Corporation, Data Resources, Inc., Interactive Data Corporation, Dow Jones Information Service, and CompuServe. Some specialized 24-hour services do information searches for users to enable them to stay current in their field.

Mead Data Central provides two very extensive public database services: LEXIS and NEXIS. The LEXIS database provides users with access to a tremendous pool of legal information for use in research. It incorporates data from a variety of sources, including federal, state, and municipal court opinions, federal regulations, and a broad collection of recent publications in legal periodicals. The NEXIS database provides users with access to a huge amount of bibliographic data and published articles that have been collected from hundreds of magazines, newspapers, specialized newsletters, and other sources. In addition, NEXIS offers access to the complete text of the *Encyclopedia Britannica*. Students working on term papers and theses can make extensive bibliographic resource searches by using an information service like NEXIS.

Lockheed Information Systems provides a public database service through its Dialog Information Service subsidiary. The Dialog system provides users with access to close to 100 separate databanks covering a variety of areas, including science, business, agriculture, economics, energy, and engineering. Dialog is regarded as the largest supplier of bibliographic data to computer users. To promote the use of the system after normal business hours, a special microcomputer-oriented service (called *Knowledge Index*) is made available at reduced rates.

Systems Development Corporation offers an information service called Orbit Search Service. This service allows users access to over 70 specialized databases. Many of the databases available can also be accessed through the Dialog system.

Data Resources, Inc., and Interactive Data Corporation both offer users access to a variety of statistical databanks covering such industries as banking, economics, insurance, transportation, and agriculture. The sources for their data include Chase Econometric Associates, Value Line, Standard & Poor's, and their own staffs of economists.

The Dow Jones Information Service provides users with access to one of the largest statistical databanks and a news retrieval service. The statistical databanks cover stock-market activity from the New York and American stock exchanges. In addition, a substantial amount of financial data covering all of the corporations listed on both exchanges, as well as nearly a thousand others, is maintained. The Dow Jones News/Retrieval system allows users to search bibliographic data on individual businesses and broad financial news compiled from a variety of sources, including *Barron's* and the *Wall Street Journal.*

Since the early 1980s, several new information services have been created to provide microcomputer users at home with easy access to the statistical and bibliographic databanks and other services. The most popular of these are Prodigy, GEnie, America Online, and CompuServe.

To access Prodigy, you need a microcomputer and a keyboard, a modem, a telephone line, and Prodigy software (which includes written documentation for using the service). The Prodigy software includes communications functions that enable you to communicate with the Prodigy service. If you want to store or print out the information you download from the information service, you also need a secondary storage device (disk drive) and a printer. Prodigy provides access to a wide variety of services, including electronic banking and shopping. In addition, you can obtain the latest news, weather forecasts, and stock quotes, or choose from the many educational and entertaining games that are offered by the Prodigy service (Figure 20). Up to six family members can obtain a password—their own sequence of keystrokes to type in—to the system and can customize it to suit their needs.

Many people would say that Prodigy's greatest attractions are its graphic user interface and its low cost. Most other on-line services assess hourly fees, whereas Prodigy assesses one monthly fee (which is usually lower than one hour on another on-line service). The major disadvantages of Prodigy are its inability to provide lengthy text articles for research and its inability to download financial data into another program, such as a spreadsheet program. Prodigy treats financial data graphically. You can print a graph, but you can't download the data that Prodigy used to generate the graph. In addition, Prodigy keeps track of only current data. Prodigy's market reports contain information from the

FIGURE 20

Prodigy log-in screen

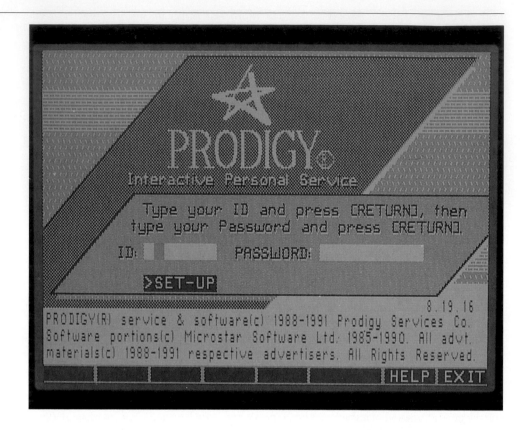

last two trading days on NASDAQ and the New York and American stock exchanges and the past ten business days on the Dow Jones Industrial.

CompuServe provides more in-depth and extensive capabilities than does Prodigy. Among its services, CompuServe keeps track of company and market performance for the past 16 years and enables you to download financial data to another software program. It is also more expensive. As for Prodigy, to use CompuServe you need a microcomputer and a keyboard, a modem, and a telephone line. In addition, you need communications software. Then you have to contact the service through its 800 number and arrange to become a subscriber. As a subscriber, you are assigned two codes, or passwords, to type in when you want to log on to the information service. Like most services, CompuServe provides you with written instructions for using its system's commands. Its on-line service costs about $12.50 per hour at 2,400 bps.

Many information services offer on-line employment information and accept resumes in electronic form. Table 1 gives a sampling of these services, plus tips for writing on-line resumes.

Electronic Shopping

Another type of public network service that is popular with users is **electronic shopping** (Figure 21). To use this service, you dial into a network such as Prodigy or CompuServe (by using your computer keyboard) and select the electronic shopping category. A menu of major categories of items available is presented and you select one. You can then browse through the catalog—shown on the screen—looking for the desired item. When you find the item, you use your keyboard to place an order and enter a previously assigned identification number and perhaps a credit card number (sometimes the credit card number is included in the user ID information). You can even get cost-comparison information for several similar items before you order one.

1. CompuServe Information Service
   5000 Arlington Centre Blvd.
   P.O. Box 20212
   Columbus, OH 43220
   (800) 848-8199

   Offers Adnet Online database, specialized forums such as WORK (job listings and networking for people who work from home), JFORUM (job listings and networking for journalists) and PRSIG (job listings and networking for public relations people).

   Fee: No charge (apart from CompuServe's connect fee) for job seekers to search databases and forums; employers and job seekers placing ads on Adnet pay fees depending on length of listing and amount of time it stays in the system. Searchable by employers and job seekers.

2. Career Network
   Information Kinetics Inc.
   640 N. LaSalle St.
   Suite 560
   Chicago, IL 60610
   (800) 828-0422

   Fee: $50 for three-month enrollment ($150 a year); no extra connect charges; users get 30 free E-mail messages per month and pay 50 cents for each additional message. The company's KiNexus resume database service charges job seeker $19.95 for up to a year (free to recent and pending graduates through college placement center). Searchable by job seekers, employers and college placement officers.

3. Job Bank USA
   1420 Spring Hill Rd.
   Suite 480
   McLean, VA 22102
   (703) 847-1706 (phone)
   (703) 847-1494 (fax)

   Fee: Charges job seekers up to $30 for one-year enrollment in resume database; charges employers up to $100 for each database search. Searchable by Job Bank employees only.

4. National Resume Bank
   c/o Professional Association of Resume Write
   3637 Fourth St. North
   Suite 330
   St. Petersburg, FL 33704
   (813) 896-3694 (phone)
   (813) 894-1277 (fax)

   Fee: Charges job seekers $25 for three-month listing; free to employers. Searchable by employers only.

   (continued)

TABLE 1

On-Line Employment
[Reprinted with permission of *PC Today*.]

```
≡
 File   Edit   Services   Special                    6:23
CompuServe+

SOFTEX Selections

 1 AMBIZ-PAK/IBM          IBM PC  $50.00
 2 Mail List Manager      IBM PC  $35.00
 3 TagCommand! for Ventura P  IBM PC  $79.95
 4 Tally Ho! Financial Calc  IBM PC  $49.95
 5 Teledoll               IBM PC  $49.95
 6 Teledoll-Plus          IBM PC  $89.95
 7 UPMover for Ventura Publi  IBM PC  $49.95
 8 Byte Size Calendar     IBM PC  $21.95
 9 Byte Size Calculator   IBM PC  $21.95
10 Byte Size Mail/Phone List  IBM PC  $29.95
11 Byte Size Stock Portfolio  IBM PC  $29.95
12 Byte Size DOS Shell    IBM PC  $29.95
13 PRNTLABL Label System  IBM PC  $15.00
14 Byte Size General Ledger  IBM PC  $49.95
15 Byte Size Labeler      IBM PC  $39.95


Enter choice or <CR> for more !
F1=Help  F10=Menu bar  F5=Logging [OFF]  F6=Printer [OFF]
```

FIGURE 21

Modems and communications software allow the microcomputer user who subscribes to certain public network services to shop at home. This CompuServe shopping screen displays a partial list of SOFTEX applications software packages for sale to the CompuServe subscriber.

TABLE 1

(*continued*)

5. Prodigy Interactive Personal Service
   445 Hamilton Ave.
   White Plains, NY 10601
   (800) 284-5933
   Offers Adnet Online, TPI Online Classifieds, databases.

   Fee: No charge (apart from $14.95 a month Prodigy subscription fee) for job seekers to search the databases; employers and job seekers pay fees to place ads. Searchable by employers and job seekers.

6. Resumes-on-Computer
   c/o The Curtis Publishing Co.
   1000 Waterway Blvd.
   Indianapolis, IN 46202
   (317) 636-1000 (phone)
   (317) 634-1791 (fax)

   Fee: No charge to job seekers (though resumes must be converted via special software to ASCII text file and sent to Curtis by a quick printer, trade association or other resume-preparation group); employers pay $1.20 per resume retrieved and $1.70 a minute to access the system. Searchable by employers only.

7. Resumes: On-Line
   3140 K South Peoria
   Suite 142
   Aurora, CO 80014
   (303) 337-4818 (modem)
   (303) 337-2420 (phone)

   Fee: $29.95 for job seekers, free to employers during service's introduction. Searchable by Colorado-area employers.

The variety of goods available through electronic shopping has grown rapidly over the past few years and now includes a wide range of name-brand goods at discount prices from nationally known stores and businesses. In fact, users now not only buy products but also make travel reservations through electronic shopping.

Electronic Bulletin Boards

The **electronic bulletin board service (BBS)** (Figure 22) is a popular information service that allows subscribing users to place messages and advertisements into the system and also scan existing messages in the system. For example, suppose you have an item you would like to sell or trade—an automobile, bicycle, motorcycle, sports equipment, or even a microcomputer or some software. After setting up your computer and modem with your communications software, you would dial the information service and select the electronic bulletin board mode. Next you would compose an electronic 3-by-5-inch card describing the item(s) for sale and include an electronic mailbox number to which inquiries can be directed. You can check back for responses over a period of days, or whenever appropriate.

Electronic bulletin boards are also used simply to exchange information between computers in remote locations, such as offices in different parts of the country, or even within a company at one location. As long as the sending and receiving computers have modems attached and have established an account with the same BBS, one user can upload data to the BBS for the other to down-

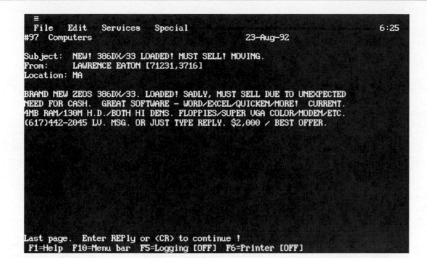

FIGURE 22

Electronic bulletin boards allow users to "post" messages on particular topics, read messages from other people, and reply to messages. This CompuServe bulletin board screen shows a for-sale notice posted by a user from Massachusetts.

load. Since data on a BBS is stored in a basic text format, any microcomputer can read it. This is one method for getting around the problem of moving data between machines that store data in incompatible formats. For example, to convert an IBM file into an Apple Macintosh format (IBMs and Macintoshes use different machine languages), the IBM file could be sent to the BBS, at which point the Macintosh user could retrieve it.

The procedure for scanning the bulletin board is very straightforward. Once you have entered the electronic bulletin board mode, you simply identify the type of item you would like to search for and let the computer do the work for you. You can also scan *all* the messages. Most BBSs also provide *forums* that enable users to conduct on-going conversations, interviews, and debates. These forums are often used for some unusual purposes. For example, the producers of *Sneakers,* the computer-hacker film starring Robert Redford, marketed the film through CompuServe, putting the film's producer on-line to answer questions about the film. And, not too long ago, comedian Jerry Seinfeld logged on to Prodigy to field questions about his TV series.

Figure 23 lists some common BBS terminology you might encounter as a BBS user.

Electronic Mail

Electronic messages can also be sent via **electronic mail,** or **E-mail,** which uses a special communications line rather than a telephone line. Electronic mail is often used within companies to exchange memos, make announcements, schedule meetings, and so forth. Each user has a "mailbox"—an electronic file—with a number and a password to limit access to approved users. To send a message, the user types in the recipient's mailbox number, the password, and then the message. Approximately 12.4 million people are sending 1.2 billion messages via E-mail each year—about a 3,000% increase in ten years. Until recently, there were almost no links between different E-mail systems. However, new developments such as AT&T Mail, cc: Mail, MCI Mail, and ALL-In-1 are making links possible.

FIGURE 23

Common BBS terminology [Reprinted with permission of *PC Novice.*]

The telecommunications field is rife with jargon—technical words, phases, and abbreviations that might have scared off Albert Einstein. Here are some of the more common ones:

Baud — Often used erroneously to mean bits per second (bps). Baud actually refers to the switching of a transmission (phone) line.

BBS — Bulletin Board System. An online system that users can call up with a modem-equipped computer to communicate with others and access information.

Board — Same as bulletin board system; also discussion board, an area within a BBS for discussing a certain topic (also called **SIG** for special interest group, a **conference**, or a **forum**).

bps — bits per second. The number of bits transferred across a communications link per second.

BTW — An online abbreviation meaning By The Way.

Communications parameters— Settings that determine how a telecommunications program interprets incoming and outgoing data.

Download — The transferring of information from the BBS to your computer.

Echo conference — The discussion area that has messages "echoed" to (shared with) other BBSs around the country.

E-mail — Electronic mail. The electronic form of the post office that lets you send and receive private messages.

Emoticon — A sideways facial expression used to express emotion. Also called a **facegram.**

Flamewar — A heated debate on a BBS.

FWIW — An online abbreviation for For What It's Worth.

Handle — An alias or fake name, which people sometimes use on BBSs.

Handshaking — The procedure where two modems get in "sync" with each other and prepare to transfer information.

Host system — A computer that runs the BBS to which you're connected.

IMHO — An online abbreviation for In My Humble Opinion. The statements that precede or follow this are often anything but humble.

Log off — To disconnect from a BBS.

Log on — To connect to a BBS.

Lurk — To read BBS messages without responding.

MNP — Microcom Networking Protocol. A series of proprietary error-correcting and data compression standards.

Modem — A device that connects a computer to a phone and lets it transfer information over the line.

Online — If you are connected to a BBS or other service, you are considered to be online.

Script — A set of commands instructing your telecommunications program to perform a task automatically.

Shareware — Software that's freely distributed on BBSs and elsewhere and that requires a registration fee for continued use.

Sysop — The system operator; the person in charge of running a BBS.

Telecommunicate — To communicate using your computer and a telephone line.

Upload — To transfer from your computer to the BBS.

V.32 — An international standard for modems having modulation speed of 9600 bps.

V.32bis — An international standard for modems having modulation speed of 14400 bps (bis means enhanced).

V.42 — An international error correcting standard.

V.42bis — An international data compression standard.

V.Fast — An international standard for modems having a modulation speed of 28800 bps.

Xmodem — The oldest commonly used file transfer protocol; used to automatically detect and correct errors when uploading and downloading files.

Ymodem — The transfer protocol that allows for the transfer of multiple files.

Zmodem — Considered to be the fastest and most secure file transfer protocol; can be used to transfer multiple files.

Voice Mail

Voice mail systems, or voice-messaging systems, are essentially computer-based answering machines. A recording of the user's voice speaks to callers who then leave messages for the user to retrieve later. Voice mail capabilities are provided by computer systems, or a voice board in a microcomputer, linked to users' phones, that convert the human voice messages to digital bits and store them. These systems can also forward calls to wherever the user is—hotel, home, business, etc. He or she can dictate answers that are recorded and sent out to the appropriate people. Voice mail systems can be set up within a company or within a geographical area. Individual users can obtain voice mail services by calling their local telephone company or by installing a voice board in their PC and purchasing the necessary software.

Electronic Banking and Investing

In the past few years, many major financial institutions have begun to offer customers a new service referred to as **electronic banking.** This service allows customers to access banking and investment services via a terminal or personal computer from the comfort of their offices or homes. The customer just uses the keyboard to dial the local-access telephone number into the electronic service. When the communications link has been established, the user is prompted to enter an identification code. If the code is accepted, the user can request a number of electronic financial services, including:

▼ Viewing the balances in checking and savings accounts

▼ Transferring funds between checking and savings accounts

▼ Directing that certain utility bills be paid directly by the bank

▼ Verifying the latest rates available on certificates of deposit, passbook savings accounts, and other investment options

▼ Following the stock market and entering buy and sell orders for stocks

Computer Viruses

The proliferation of relatively low-cost, high-tech communications devices and powerful microcomputers has created a breeding ground for a new kind of computer bug—the computer virus. More than 1,500 viruses have infiltrated the world's information infrastructure to date, and some experts say that more than 50 new viruses are added to that number each month.

Normal bugs are accidental programmer's errors that are weeded out of a system's software during testing. **Viruses** are *intentional* bugs that are usually created by sophisticated, obsessive computer programmers and users (often called *hackers* or *crackers*) sophisticated programming skills are usually required to create a virus. These viruses consist of pieces of computer code (either hidden or posing as legitimate program code) that, when downloaded or run, attach themselves to other programs and files and cause them to malfunction. Sometimes the viruses are programmed to lie dormant for a while before they become active; thus, they can be spread from disk to disk and system to system before they are detected (Figure 24). The viruses are transmitted by downloading through modems from electronic bulletin boards and networks, and through shared disks (Figure 25). They reproduce themselves over and over again. In recent years, some major companies, universities, and government agencies have had their systems disabled by computer viruses. More than 110 different viruses have been detected to date; because so many critical aspects of modern life depend on computer programs, the destructive potential of viruses has become a threat to all of us.

What exactly do viruses do? Among other things, they can rename programs, alter numeric data, erase files, scramble memory, turn off the power, reverse the effect of a command—or simply display a message without damaging the system. For example, in 1988 the so-called Meta-Virus was unleashed on users of a particular software system. This virus did not actually damage the system; rather, it was intended to create anxiety on the part of the users. The message that popped up on the user's screen said:

> WARNING! A serious virus is on the loose. It was hidden in the program called 1987 TAXFORM that was on this bulletin board last year. By now, it is possible that your system is infected even if you didn't download this program, since you could easily have been infected indirectly. The only safe way to protect yourself against this virus is to print all files onto paper, erase all the disks on your system, buy fresh software disks from the manufacturer, and type in all your data again. FIRST! Send this message to everyone you know, so they will also protect themselves.

FIGURE 24

(a) How a computer virus can spread. Just as a biological virus disrupts living cells to cause disease, a computer virus—introduced maliciously—invades the inner workings of computers and disrupts normal operations of the machines. (Adapted from Knight-Ridder Tribune News/Stephen Cvengros, *Chicago Tribune,* October 6, 1989, Section 1, p. 2.) (b) A screen from Central Point's Anti-Virus software. Note the disk drive designations on the left: A and B represent floppy disk drives, and C is the hard disk drive. F represents an electronic mail connection. At the top of the screen is the title bar, under which you see a menu bar with several options. Under that is a row of "buttons"; the user points to the buttons with the mouse pointer and clicks the mouse button to quickly open up frequently used option files.

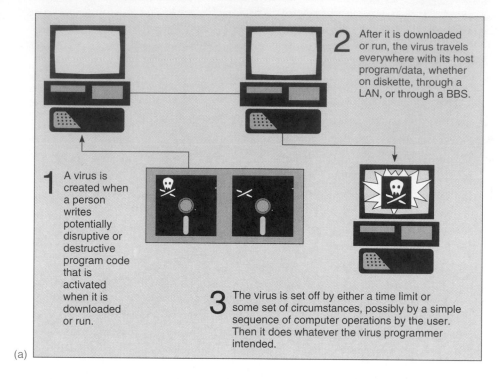

(a)

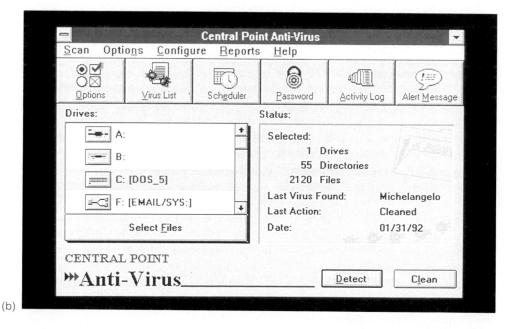

(b)

In early 1992, many PC users were worried about the Michelangelo virus, which was programmed to wipe out hard disk files on the anniversary of the Italian Renaissance artist Michelangelo's birthday, March 6. Many of these users scanned their files with virus-detection software and eliminated this virus before the date arrived (Figure 25).

Other programs are like viruses in that they are created to cause problems for users. *Trojan horses* act like viruses, but they don't reproduce themselves. *Worms* use up available space by rewriting themselves repeatedly throughout the computer's memory.

What can users do to protect themselves? First, they can obtain free or low-cost software programs (called *freeware* or *shareware*) that detect and cure common viruses—for example, FluShot+, Norton Anti-Virus, Integrity Master, Virex,

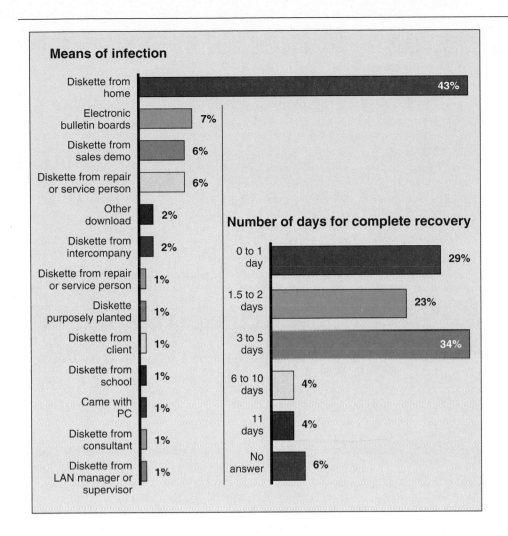

FIGURE 25

Means of virus infection and recovery times [Reprinted with permission from the *San Francisco Examiner*. ©1993 San Francisco Examiner / Joe Shoulak. Source: Dataquest, Inc.]

Interferon, and Symantec Antivirus. Also, some new microcomputer systems software comes with anti-virus programs built in. These programs come with instructions for use. Also, personal computer users should:

▼ Run all disks obtained from another user or service through a virus-checker program before using them on their system. (This procedure is standard in many organizations.)

▼ Buy updated versions of their anti-virus software on a regular basis (to protect against new viruses).

▼ Make backup copies of their data on a regular basis.

▼ Increase the use of the write/protect tabs on their diskettes. With 5¼-inch diskettes, this involves putting a plastic sticker (write/protect tabs are included in every box of diskettes) over the write/protect notch. With 3½-inch diskettes, this involves sliding down a plastic notch on the back of the diskette.

▼ Avoid using master disks by making working copies and storing the masters in a safe place.

▼ Avoid using computer games from bulletin board services.

▼ Avoid downloading from bulletin board services whose programs are not regularly checked for viruses.

▼ Be cautious with whom they network, share data, or share applications software programs, or avoid sharing at all.

Table 2 provides a list of common virus-related terms.

TABLE 2

Virus-Related Terms

Antidotes—Programs that help remove viruses

Bug—Programmer error

Counterhacker—One who is in the business of identifying hackers

Crashing—A term used to describe a computer system that is being halted by a virus

Finger hacker—One who obtains access codes from a service like U.S. Sprint Telephone, using a programmable memory telephone

Hacker—A sophisticated, obsessive computer user who gains unauthorized access to proprietary computer systems. Some sophisticated hackers with programming skills create computer code that acts as a virus to disrupt the accessed computer system.

Password—A code used to gain entrance into a computer system so that data can be accessed

Replicate—To copy or repeat

Scan programs—Used to detect viruses

Vaccines—Programs that prevent machines from being infected with viruses

Virus—An intentional bug created by a computer user (usually a programmer) that can cause harm to data stored in a computer system and cause a computer system to malfunction

Virus strain—A particular virus with its own unique characteristics

Worm—A type of virus that repeats (replicates) itself on a disk, thus destroying critical data and computer code

---

Facsimile (Fax)

Today, the question "what is your fax number?" is almost as common as asking for someone's telephone number. In fact, most business cards today include both a telephone number and a fax number. In what seems like a very short time, many businesses and individuals have adopted the fax (*fax is short for facsimile,* meaning *reproduction*) as the standard communications medium. A **fax** is a copy of a document that is sent using fax hardware (described in the following paragraphs) through the phone lines to another location that has fax hardware. The process of sending or receiving a fax is called **faxing**—faxing a document is faster than sending it through the mail or using an overnight courier service. If you are in charge of bringing the fax capability to your home or office, you have two choices. You can either purchase a stand-alone fax machine or you can purchase a fax board, which fits into an expansion slot in your system unit. Both methods have their advantages.

A stand-alone **fax machine** (Figure 26) is composed of a scanner for input, a thermal printer or a plain-paper printer for output, and a modem so that text and graphics can be sent across the phone lines. (Thermal printers use special paper on rolls; plain-paper fax printers use regular single-sheet paper.) Because the phone line is the transmission medium, each machine is usually given its own fax number, which is used the same way as a telephone number. To send a fax, put the document you want to fax into the fax machine, punch in the number of the fax machine you want to send to, and then press a button to transmit the document. The scanner moves the document through the machine and transmits that data to a receiving fax machine. Some fax machines can also transmit photos, and some have many options for such functions as number storage and automatic dialing, security checks, transaction record, printouts, and voice communication. The more options, the more expensive the fax machine.

A **fax card** (board) (Figure 27) is essentially an internal fax modem that differs from conventional modems in that it can send and receive both text and

FIGURE 26

Stand-alone fax machine. This delicatessen owner accepts faxed food orders.

FIGURE 27

Intel fax board. The board is inserted in an expansion slot on the motherboard.

graphics and can typically send and receive at a faster rate (9,600 or 14,400 bits per second versus 2,400 bps). Since fax cards don't provide users with all the capabilities of the stand-alone fax machines, they typically cost hundreds of dollars less. However, they require special software to function. A microcomputer with a fax board can receive faxed images and display them on the screen. It can also print them out on a printer. It can fax documents to another computer with a fax board or a fax machine.

With a fax card, if you want to match the capabilities of the stand-alone fax machines, you would have to purchase a scanner so that you can fax documents that don't originate in your PC, such as newspaper clippings. The scanner converts paper images into computer-usable files that can then be faxed, using the fax board, to a fax machine in another location or to a PC that is configured with a fax board. The fax board you use must be compatible with the type of scanner you want to use, because not all fax boards drive every scanner. In addition, if you want to print a faxed document, make sure the fax board in your computer is compatible with your printer. If you consider using a fax board, include the added expense of purchasing a scanner and possibly a printer in the total cost of your fax system.

Deciding whether to purchase a stand-alone fax machine or a fax board may depend on the amount of space you have on your desktop (for a fax machine) or whether you have an expansion slot in your PC or notebook computer (for the fax board). Some new pocket-size fax devices can be hooked up to the back of a notebook computer.

Some companies use fax to improve customer services. For example, Borland (a software company) offers callers who have fax capabilities a menu of choices via telephone. The caller punches in responses on the telephone buttons and then receives chosen information faxed automatically within minutes by a computer. (This is called *fax on demand.*)

Telecommuting

Many people are taking advantage of fax and modem capabilities, small notebook-size microcomputers, and even cellular (portable) phones to become telecommuters. *Telecommuting* means working at home—via electronic communications—for an employer located elsewhere. For many people, commuting is almost painful—fighting one's way through crowded highways, riding on packed trains and buses, taking two or more hours just getting to work and arriving "wiped out." Commuting has even made some people sick from stress, exhaustion, and exposure to pollution.

Telecommuting can spare people the stress of commuting. A telecommuter uses modems, faxes, the telephone, and other communications technologies to stay in touch with the employer—and the employer's network—sending and retrieving information as necessary. The telecommuter is fully employed by the company and receives the same salary and benefits as on-site workers. Perhaps the one major drawback of telecommuting, for some people, is the isolation of working alone.

Digital Convergence: "The Mother of All Industries"

A remarkable transformation is coming about that may change everything. It's called the *digital revolution,* or **digital convergence**—the merger of five huge industries: computers, communications, consumer electronics, media/publishing, and entertainment. According to Apple Computer Inc. former chairman John Scully, this convergence—what he calls "the mother of all industries"—could be worth more than $3 trillion by the year 2000.

The blurring of industries will come about, it is predicted, as information, sound, video, text, and images become converted to digital bits—0s and 1s—that can be decoded by similar hardware. Everything is expected to go digital—from the images of photos, graphics, and films to the analog waves of telephone, radio, and television. In time, the electronic world could be a huge melting pot of a new digital order.

In many ways, the Digital Revolution is well along. We have seen digital compact disks supplant vinyl LP records. Recently, digital audiotape (DAT) has proven to be much superior to conventional audiocassettes. Europe and Canada are leading the way toward digital audio broadcasting, bringing the quality and reliability of CDs to radio. Electronic imaging has taken a step forward with the digital camera, which requires no film developing and which allows images to be transmitted as digital files via computer modem to, for example, electronic pictures desks at newspapers. Family photos can now be stored on photo CDs, which in turn can be manipulated on microcomputers as digitized images. This brings to the home market the digital techniques of "morphing," as professional film makers call it, whereby an image can be digitally changed to another by a computer—for example, putting one person's head on another person's body.

Many companies currently send digital information over telephone lines, communicating with digital beepers, for example. As present cellular telephone channels fill up, producing more garbled calls, the cellular telephone industry has geared up to convert to digital transmission in large cities. Just emerging is HDTV—high-definition television—for which the Federal Communications Commission is approving a U.S. digital standard. Although Japan already has HDTV, it is stuck with the old analog wave signal. U.S. broadcasters could be broadcasting digital high-definition signals to home HDTV sets in 1996. HDTV and digital video is expected to make advances in teleconferencing, video telephones, electronic cameras, and interactive education systems.

What's holding up the Digital Revolution? As so often happens in technological matters, the main sticking point is lack of agreement about standards. There is no standard format for digitizing, integrating, and manipulating all the information around us. Yet another problem is how to go about converting older materials, such as newspapers, photographs, and music, into digital form, presently an expensive, time-consuming task. Clearly, if the new digital world is to emerge, it will take a lot of cooperation between hardware, software, and communications companies and perhaps many years.

Still, the prospect of such convergences promises opportunities. For example, ultimately they could lead to a wireless, pocket-size "personal communicator" or "personal digital assistant" somewhat like Apple's Newton. This gadget would combine a personal computer, pager, appointment book, address book, fax machine, and even "electronic book" and pocket CD player—all in a hand-held box operated by a pen or voice commands.

COMPUTERS
AND CAREERS

▼

MOBILE
COMPUTING AT
FIVE MILES PER
SECOND

ore than 200 miles above the Hawaiian islands, bathed in brilliant sunlight, astronaut Rick Hieb and two other spacewalkers, Pierre Thuot and Tom Akers, performed the impossible in May of 1992 when they rescued a wayward 8,960-pound Intelsat communications satellite during a record 8-hour, 29-minute space walk. Their success not only saved the stranded $131 million satellite, now on station over the Atlantic Ocean, but it also vividly demonstrated the power packed into today's mobile computers.

Earlier, as the astronauts left the airlock to begin their daring unplanned space walk, pilot Kevin Chilton used a laptop computer to calculate the distance from the shuttle to the satellite. On screen, he saw an image of the shuttle and the path the spacecraft would have to take to reach the satellite. He passed the information on to Commander Dan Brandstein, who gently eased the shuttle ever closer to the errant satellite.

The program Chilton used was created by Hieb, a computer hobbyist who had written several programs to help with his own work.

Although Hieb created this program on a desktop computer, it could be used on the shuttle's laptops because they run DOS and use the same family of Intel microprocessors.

Laptops first journeyed into space in 1983, when one was added to help the shuttle crew fly the spacecraft and conduct experiments. Today shuttle missions often carry as many mobile computers as astronauts. The mobile PCs supplement on-board computers and provide astronauts with their own data so that they don't always have to rely on mission control.

Today NASA's standard mobile computer is the Payload and General Support Computer, or PGSC. This off-the-shelf Grid Computer System 1530 has a standard 386DX microprocessor, 8 MB of RAM, and a 40 MB hard drive. NASA considers the laptop so versatile that every shuttle mission carries at least two of them—usually more.

The Spacelab Microgravity Laboratory's summer 1992 mission carried six laptops. They served as display terminals for Spacelab computers and as general-purpose tools; the crew used them to control experiments and to transmit and receive data.

During another mission, remembered best for its aborted attempt to reel out an experimental tether to generate electricity, science astronaut Franklin Chang-Diaz used two Grid laptops to collect and store all the data from a host of scientific instruments. "It's kind of a new application," says Chang-Diaz, "a sign of things to come for future science operations on the shuttle, where we control major payloads directly from a portable laptop computer."

Phillip Chien, Intel "Special Report," p. N36.

▼ When people speak, the sound travels as *analog signals*—continuous signals that repeat a certain number of times over a certain period (*frequency*) at certain *amplitudes* (degrees of loudness). Telephone lines carry analog signals. Computers, in contrast, use digital signals— discontinuous (discrete) pulses of electricity (on) separated by pauses (off).

▼ When they communicate, the sending and receiving computers must use *modems* (*mo*dulate/*dem*odulate) to convert the digital signals into analog signals for transmission and then back again into digital signals for reception. Modems can be *internal* (built into the computer or inserted on an add-on card or board) or *external* (connected to the computer and the telephone by cable).

▼ When signals are transmitted from computer to computer, patterns of bits coded to represent data are sent one bit at a time. For the receiving computer to be able to determine where one character of data ends and another starts, data is sent either *asynchronously* or *synchronously*.

▼ In asynchronous transmission, each string of bits that make up a character is bracketed by control bits—a start bit, one or two stop bits, and an error check bit, or parity bit. Most microcomputers use asynchronous transmission.

▼ In synchronous transmission, characters are sent as blocks with flags inserted as identifiers at the beginning and end of the blocks. This type of transmission is used by large computers to transmit huge volumes of data at high speeds.

▼ Data communications technology must also consider the direction of data traffic: *simplex* (one way only), *half-duplex* (two-way traffic but only one direction at a time), or *full-duplex* (two-way traffic passing at the same time).

▼ The media most commonly used for communication are *telephone wire* (*open* and *twisted-pair*), *coaxial cables,* atmosphere (*microwave* and *satellite systems*), and *fiber-optic cables*. Each of these media differs in terms of the form of the transmitted data (electrical pulses, electromagnetic waves, or light pulses), the rate at which data moves through it, and its susceptibility to noise and "eavesdropping."

▼ The hardware typically used to communicate between computers includes *modems, multi-plexers, concentrators, controllers, front-end processors,* and microcomputer *protocol converters*.

▼ Multiplexers, concentrators, controllers, and front-end processors all allow multiplexing— the sharing of one high-speed communications line by multiple users or devices. A concentrator, which is like a multiplexer, is more "intelligent" because it can store and forward transmissions. A controller performs more functions than a multiplexer or a concentrator. A front-end processor, a smaller computer connected to the main computer, not only allows multiplexing but also relieves the main computer of many routine data traffic management and communications functions.

▼ To communicate, the sending and receiving computers must follow the same rules, or *protocols*. In the case of microcomputer communications, the software parameters can be set on both ends to agree. In other cases, *protocol converters* must be used. For example, a protocol converter could be used to allow a microcomputer in asynchronous mode to communicate with a mainframe operating in synchronous mode.

▼ Companies often set up communications *networks,* which are collections of data communications hardware, computers, communications software, and communications media connected in a meaningful way to allow users to share data and information.

▼ Three basic types of networks are private, public, and international. *Private networks* support the communications needs of particular business organizations. *Public networks* provide paying subscribers with voice or data communications over a large geographical area. *International networks* provide users with intercontinental voice and data communications facilities.

▼ Networks can be set up in different shapes: star (and hierarchical) network, bus network, and ring (and token ring) network. The normal business user may encounter one of these network shapes in the context of a *local area network* (*LAN*), which is a private network that serves a company or part of a company that is located on one floor, in a single building, or in offices within approximately 2 miles of each other.

▼ The *star network, a client/server network,* uses a host computer or a microcomputer *file server* connected to a number of smaller computers and/or terminals, called *nodes.* The nodes are not designed to communicate directly with one another, so if the main computer fails, the whole network "goes down."

▼ In a more complicated star network called a *hierarchical,* or *tree, network,* some nodes have devices connected to them in smaller star networks.

▼ In a *bus network, a peer-to-peer network,* a number of computers are connected to a single communications line. In this network, if one computer fails, the others can continue to operate.

▼ A *ring network* is much like a bus network, except that the communications line forms a loop. This network has no central computer, and each computer connected to the network can communicate directly with the others.

▼ In the *token ring network,* predefined patterns of bits, or tokens, are passed from computer to computer. The computer with the token can transmit; the others cannot. This setup prevents the garbling of messages that occurs when more than one computer tries to transmit at the same time.

▼ The business user can benefit from computer-to-computer communications using a number of public services and utilities to access data and information. *Public databanks* provide information about such topics as health, education, law, the humanities, science, and government. To use these databanks, the user pays a fee plus the regular phone charges. *Public information services* also provide the user with such conveniences as *electronic shopping, banking and investing, electronic bulletin boards, electronic mail,* and *forums* for discussion.

▼ More and more offices today have the ability to send and receive faxes by using either a fax machine or a fax board. A *fax machine* is composed of a scanner (for input), a thermal printer (for output), and a modem so that text and graphics can be sent across the phone lines. A *fax card* is essentially an internal fax modem on a board that can be inserted into an expansion slot in your PC. Fax cards can also send and retrieve both text and graphics. If you want to fax images that don't originate in your PC, you must purchase a scanner.

▼ *Computer viruses* are intentional program bugs introduced by a person or persons intending to damage a computer system. They can be downloaded from BBSs, for example, or can spread during disk copying and thus move from system to system. The virus code can rename programs, alter numeric data, and erase files, among other things. Users can buy and install anti-virus software to install that will scan for and eliminate viruses.

KEY TERMS

amplitude, p. 9.3
analog signal, p. 9.3
asynchronous transmission, p. 9.4
bits per second (bps), p. 9.13
bus network, p. 9.23
client/server network, p. 9.22
coaxial cable, p. 9.7
communications software, p. 9.17
concentrator, p. 9.16
controller, p. 9.17
dedicated line, p. 9.8
demodulation, p. 9.3
digital convergence, p. 9.39
digital signal, p. 9.3
electronic banking, p. 9.32
electronic bulletin board service
   (BBS), p. 9.30
electronic mail (E-mail), p. 9.31
electronic shopping, p. 9.28
external modem, p. 9.14
fax, p. 9.36

fax card, p. 9.36
fax machine, p. 9.36
faxing, p. 9.36
fiber optics, p. 9.10
file server, p. 9.22
frequency, p. 9.3
front-end processor, p. 9.17
full-duplex, p. 9.6
half-duplex, p. 9.5
hierarchical (tree) network, p. 9.22
information service, p. 9.26
internal modem, p. 9.14
international network, p. 9.20
local area network (LAN), p. 9.20
metropolitan area network (MAN),
   p. 9.21
microwave, p. 9.9
modem, p. 9.4, 9.13
modulation, p. 9.3
multidrop line, p. 9.9
multimedia conference, p. 9.20

multiplexer, p. 9.16
network, p. 9.19
peer-to-peer network, p. 9.23
point-to-point line, p. 9.8
private network, p. 9.19
protocol, p. 9.17
protocol converter, p. 9.17
public databank, p. 9.26
public network, p. 9.19
ring network, p. 9.24
satellite, p. 9.10
script language, p. 9.18
simplex, p. 9.5
star network, p. 9.21
switched line, p. 9.8
synchronous transmission, p. 9.5
teleconferencing, p. 9.20
token ring network, p. 9.25
virus, p. 9.33
voice mail, p. 9.32
wide area network (WAN), p. 9.21

EXERCISES

SELF-TEST

1. List four transmission media that are used for data communications.

   a.

   b.

   c.

   d.

2. To communicate between computers across wire phone lines, you need a

   _____ at both the sending and receiving locations.

3. Whereas computers "understand" _____ signals, the

   telephone line can usually transmit only _____ signals.

4. For a microcomputer to communicate with a mainframe, it must be configured
   with the necessary hardware and software to allow it to support

   _____ transmission.

5. A _____ communications link can support two-way traffic,
   but data can travel in only one direction at a time.

6. Asynchronous transmission, commonly used in microcomputers, is faster than
   synchronous transmission. (true/false)

7. Pulses of light are sometimes used to represent data so that it can be communicated over a distance. (true/false)

8. List three popular network configurations.

   a.

   b.

   c.

9. _____ optimizes the use of communications lines by allowing multiple users or devices to share one high-speed line, thereby reducing communications costs.

10. _____ transmission sends data in both directions simultaneously, similar to two trains passing in opposite directions on side-by-side tracks.

11. Satellite communications systems transmit signals in the gigahertz range—billions of cycles per second. (true/false)

12. A _____ is a standard set of rules for electronic communications.

13. A _____ is a collection of data communications hardware, computers, communications software, and communications media connected in a meaningful way to allow users to share information and equipment.

14. The term _____ refers to electronically linking several people by phone, computer, and video so that they can hold a meeting.

15. The _____ _____

    _____ _____ is a popular information service that allows subscribing users to place messages and advertisements into the system and also scan existing messages in the system.

16. A _____ consists of pieces of computer code intentionally created by programmers or users that, when downloaded or run, attaches itself to other programs and files and causes them to malfunction.

17. List two hardware devices that you could choose from to bring a fax capability to your home or office.

    a.

    b.

18. _____ _____ technology is expected to revolutionize the communications industry because of its low cost, high transmission volume, low error rate, and message security.

19. In contrast to a private network, a _____

    _____ is a comprehensive communications facility designed to provide subscribers with voice and/or data communications over a large geographical area.

20. _____ _____ is a system often used within companies to electronically transmit memos and announcements and to schedule meetings.

Solutions: (1) telephone lines, microwave, satellite, fiber optics, radio/infrared waves; (2) modem; (3) digital, analog; (4) synchronous; (5) half-duplex; (6) false; (7) true; (8) ring, token ring, bus, star, tree; (9) multiplexing; (10) full-duplex; (11) true; (12) protocol; (13) network; (14) teleconferencing; (15) electronic bulletin board service; (16) virus; (17) fax machine, fax card (board); (18) fiber-optic; (19) public network; (20) electronic mail

MULTIPLE-CHOICE QUESTIONS

1. Which of the following performs modulation and demodulation?

    a. fiber optic

    b. satellite

    c. coaxial cable

    d. modem

    e. protocol converter

2. What type of network would most likely be found in a company that occupies a single building?

    a. WAN

    b. WIDE

    c. LAN

    d. MAN

    e. WAVE

3. Which of the following can a stand-alone fax machine do?

    a. transmit text and graphics over the phone line

    b. dial up other fax machines automatically

    c. scan documents for transmission

    d. receive text and graphics over the phone line and print them out

    e. all the above

4. Which of the following is not a common network configuration?

    a. star network

    b. circle network

    c. bus network

    d. token ring network

    e. tree network

5. Which of the following can a computer virus do?

    a. alter numeric data

    b. turn off the power and erase data

    c. scramble memory

    d. rename programs

    e. all the above

Solutions: (1) d; (2) c; (3) e; (4) b; (5) e

SHORT-ANSWER QUESTIONS

1. When might you encounter electronic communications in the business environment?

2. What are modems used for?

3. What is the function of a multiplexer?

4. Explain the difference between analog and digital signals.

5. What does a microcomputer user need to do in order to communicate synchronously?

6. What is the main function of a front-end processor?

7. What is meant by the term *protocol* as it relates to communicating between two computers?

8. What does the term *digital convergence* mean?

9. Describe the difference between synchronous and asynchronous transmission modes and how they affect the speed with which data can be communicated.

10. What is a communications network? What are the three main types of network?

11. What kind of port is used to connect an external modem to a microcomputer?

12. Name five things you can do to protect a computer system against viruses.

PROJECTS

1. You need to purchase a computer to use at home to perform business-related tasks. You want to be able to communicate with the network at work so that you can use its software and access its data. To do this you need to know what hardware and software exist at work. Include the following in a report:

   ▼ A description of the hardware and software used at work

   ▼ A description of the types of tasks you will want to perform at home

   ▼ The name of the computer you would buy (include a detailed description of the computer, such as the RAM capacity and disk storage capacity)

   ▼ The communications hardware/software you would need to purchase

   ▼ A cost estimate

2. Are the computers at your school or work connected to a network? If so, what are the characteristics of the network? What advantages does the network provide in terms of hardware and software support? What types of computers are connected to the network (microcomputers, minicomputers, and/or mainframes)? Specifically, what software/hardware is allowing the network to function?

3. Using current articles and publications, research the history of ISDN, how it is being used today, and what you think the future holds for it. Present your findings in a paper or a 15-minute discussion.

4. "Distance learning," or "distance education," uses electronic links to extend college campuses to people who otherwise would not be able to take college courses. College instructors using such systems are able to lecture "live" to students in distant locations. Is your school involved in distance learning? If so, research the system's components and uses. What hardware does it use? Software? Protocols? Communications media?

5. With 17 million to 20 million fax machines in the world and with sales growing about 15% annually, this communications technology is becoming a convenient source of information dissemination. For example, ten daily U.S. newspapers are offering or experimenting with weekday fax editions. If you were to start a fax-information business, what group of information buyers would you target? How would you prepare your faxes? How often would you fax? How would you contact and establish your clientele? How much would you charge for your service? How would you get your data, and what type of computer-based system would you set up?

The old rules of presenting yourself might now hurt

Peg Donovan barely bothered to hope when a friend sent her résumé to athletic-shoe maker Nike last April. The 38-year old Beaverton, Ore., woman assumed her credentials would join a vast pile of unsolicited résumés "on file" in a deep black hole. But Donovan soon got a call inviting her in for an interview. Within 10 days, she took a job as assistant to the corporate controller.

Donovan was the beneficiary of the latest trend in corporate hiring. To economize on headhunters' fees and classified advertising, a growing number of companies are now filing the résumés that snow in each year where they might actually do job seekers some good: in an electronic database. In the past, "nobody ever looked at the résumés because they were just too huge," says Karen Cross, an employment specialist at Nike. Since March, when Nike began scanning résumés into a database, it has taken only a few keystrokes to pull up a short list of candidates with the desired qualifications. Other companies are instead turning for the first time to independent résumé databanks. Job seekers store their résumés in these databanks; employers such as AT&T, Avon, and Citicorp call when they have an opening and ask for suitable job applicants.

Job seekers who want their vitae to pop up need to get with the program. Computers react differently than people do to the contents of a résumé, so many time-honored rules of how to best present yourself no longer apply. Elegant italics cannot be scanned easily by an optical character reader, for example, and are decidedly unwelcome. The poor contrast between type and background that often results when blue or gray paper is used also confuses the scanner, so that such a résumé may have to be keyed in by hand. "Unless it is a super résumé, we are not going to spend the time," says Ed Gagen, manager of recruiting for Ortho Pharmaceutical in Raritan, N.J. Ortho's database has been up and running since January [1992].

Old guidelines about content may be passé too. Technical jargon that makes a company recruiter yawn, for example, is often what excites the computer. That's because the database searches rely on key words or phrases in your résumé that indicate specific skills or attributes. A recent search in one of Hewlett-Packard's Atlanta offices for a computer engineering position, for example, plugged in, among other things, "Unix," "X Window" and "Motif," computer operating systems the candidate should be familiar with. Such nouns used to identify your skills are far more important than old standards like "streamlined" and "implemented," which are never used in a search. First-cut lists are often shortened by keying in other factors: past job titles, location, languages spoken, college, type of degree, for example.

Worth trying. Given the growing enthusiasm with which companies are using the independent databanks, anyone who is launching a job hunt should probably consider signing on with one. The cost is fairly low—typically $20 to $50 for a six- to 12-month listing. (Often, applicants are sent a lengthy application form that subs for a résumé.) Some of the databank services are so young, however, that it is virtually impossible to compare their placement track records. A few questions asked upfront should provide a rough indication of how likely your résumé is to actually circulate.

How many employers—and which ones—subscribe? Most databanks, like Job Bank USA (800-296-1872; $30 for 12 months) and SkillSearch (800-258-6641; $49 for a year), work with employers from all over the country and in a wide range of industries. Someone interested in a brokerage will want to

By Margaret Mannix, *U.S. News & World Report,* October 26, 1992, p. 93.

know that brokers in a desirable location make use of the service. But a list of corporate subscribers may be misleading, since sometimes only a particular division has signed on. A call for applicants from the sales division won't help a job seeker interested in the legal department.

One reassurance you definitely want is that your résumé will not land in your boss's in box. Most databanks allow the job seeker to note on the application the companies he does not want the résumé to go to. Others call to discuss an opening before your résumé is passed on.

No one who signs up with a databank should stop bugging other contacts. Four long months passed without a call before Computoservice Inc. of Mankato, Minn., took an interest in Curtis Northrup, a 36-year-old computer programmer who used the National Résumé Bank (813-896-3694; $25 for three months and $40 for six). Northrup ended up a Computoservice hire, but during those four months he also blanketed five states with résumés and phone calls, and even began taking college courses toward a new career—accounting.

Besides Job Bank USA, the National Résumé Bank and SkillSearch (which requires a college degree and two years' experience), first-time job seekers in particular may want to consider kiNexus (800-828-0422) and Peterson's Connexion (800-338-3282). Both are free to many students through their college career centers. KiNexus charges everybody else $19.95 for a six-month listing; Peterson's charges $40 for a year. Other databases target particular employers or applicants. Access, a databank in Westwood, Kan. (800-362-0681, $25 for three months), serves only Kansas City area employers. HispanData (805-682-5843, $15 for 12 months), which markets itself as a source for companies looking to diversify their work forces, specializes in Hispanic professionals who are generally bilingual and have a grade point average of at least 3.0.

Some career experts suggest that even the happily employed should keep an updated résumé on file in a databank—the high-tech equivalent of being open to a headhunter's call. That's the philosophy of the University ProNet database (800-726-0280), which is owned by and serves the alumni of nine colleges and universities, including Carnegie Mellon University and Stanford University. For a lifetime fee of only $25, alums can sit back and let the opportunity come knocking.

Forget the flourishes

A jazzy résumé meant to catch a recruiter's eye will only confuse a computer. According to Resumix Inc., a maker of résumé tracking software, here are the new rules of résumé writing:

▼ Exotic typefaces, underlining, and decorative graphics don't scan well.

▼ It's best to send originals, not copies, and not to use a dot-matrix printer.

▼ Small print may confuse the scanner; don't go below 12-point type.

▼ Use standard 8½ × 11-inch paper and do not fold. Words in a crease can't be read easily.

▼ Use white or light-beige paper. Blues and grays minimize the contrast between the letters and background.

▼ Avoid double columns. The scanner reads from left to right.

▼ Technical jargon is a good idea. A computer search will target key words specific to your profession.

Systems Development

If you choose a descriptive word at random—nervous, planetary, educational—and put it in front of the word system, you immediately suggest something powerful: a collection of separate items or functions that form a whole and serve some purpose more important than the items themselves. Systems are an important concept used with computers in business and other organizations.

No matter what your position in an organization, you will undoubtedly come in contact with a systems development life cycle (SDLC)—the process of setting up a business system or an information system. The user always has a definite role in a systems development life cycle. If you, the user, understand its principles, you will be able to apply them to solving many types of problem, not just business- and/or computer-related ones.

PREVIEW

When you have completed this chapter, you will be able to:

▼ Explain why some systems fail

▼ Identify six phases of a systems development life cycle

▼ List some techniques for gathering and analyzing data describing the current system

▼ Describe the extent to which the requirements for a new information system must be defined before the system is designed

▼ Identify the major factors to consider in designing the input, output, and processing procedures and the storage requirements of a new system, as well as hardware and software requirements

▼ Describe the role of the user in the systems development life cycle

▼ Describe four basic approaches to implementing a new computer-based information system

*A*n **information system** is an arrangement of interdependent human and machine components and procedures that interact to support the information or business needs of an organization and the system's users. Such systems do not come prepackaged like some software applications programs; they must be custom developed.

The extent to which your job brings you in contact with your company's **systems development life cycle (SDLC)**—the formal process by which organizations build computer-based information systems—will vary depending on a number of factors. These factors can include the size of the organization, your job description, your relevant experience, and your educational background in information-processing concepts, tools, and techniques. In large companies the SDLC is usually a formal process with clearly defined standards and procedures. Although the technical aspects of each phase of the cycle will undoubtedly be handled by information specialists, users will always interface with these specialists.

User Participation in Systems Development

Following are some examples of how you, as a user, may participate in systems development:

▼ It may be necessary for you to explain how the current system works in your department: the manual procedures you use or what you do to support an existing computer-based system, as well as the current business terminology and purpose of the system.

▼ You could easily find yourself in a meeting discussing the nature of problems with the current system and how it can be improved.

▼ You may be required to provide the departmental objectives and requirements that the system must meet to systems analysts and designers. For instance, if you expect to have the new system produce useful reports, then you should plan to assist the information specialists in designing how these reports should look and what information or data they should contain.

▼ You may often be involved in the approval of projects and budgets as a member of a special steering committee.

▼ As the development of a new system nears completion, you will probably help evaluate and test it to ensure that it works as expected.

▼ You will have to help prepare some of the documentation that is accumulated during the entire process of system development.

▼ You may attend briefings and training sessions to learn how the new system will affect your job and what its new operating procedures will be.

▼ And last, but certainly not least, you will end up using the new system. This may involve preparing data for input or using information produced by the system.

In a large company the SDLC may seem like a complex process with which you have limited contact; however, your role in it is still important. Although in a small organization you are likely to be involved in more phases of the SDLC, and your role in each phase will tend to be more detailed, you shouldn't assume that the principles of an SDLC apply only to large computer systems and applications. Users often assume that they can purchase a microcomputer and a payroll software package on Monday and have a staff member produce paychecks on Friday. Unfortunately, it just isn't that simple. The basic principles of an SDLC should be followed even at the microcomputer level.

Remember: systems can fail because the components and the functions of the system are not clearly defined in terms of specific objectives and are not controlled tightly enough. In these situations, user requirements are not met, and costs greatly exceed estimates. In some cases, failure occurs because testing was inadequate. For example, recently the U.S. Internal Revenue Service was unable to send tax refunds on time because it couldn't process the tax returns fast enough; the new system had not been tested beforehand in all necessary areas. These problems can be avoided through, among other things, user participation—*your participation*—in the system development process.

Systems Development Life Cycle (SDLC)

Businesses and other organizations are made up of many systems and subsystems, including many manual and automated procedures. Some systems are very simple: an order entry system could be just a set of procedures for taking down a telephone order from a customer and seeing that the order is accurately entered for processing. Other systems are very complicated: a large company's payroll system involves a number of subsystems for tracking employee turnover, pay rate changes, tax exemption status, types of insurance deductions, and pension contributions, as well as overtime rates and bonuses.

In some cases, the systems development effort will be so large that dozens of people will be involved for a year or more. In other cases, a system can be set up in a relatively short time. In both extremes, however, it is equally important to follow a clearly defined process. The degree of complexity of an SDLC and the amount of effort that goes into each of its phases will vary according to the scope of the project. However, in simple and complex systems, people must interact with the system and perform the manual procedures required to feed it raw data, review the information produced, and take appropriate actions.

Why Do Some Systems Development Projects Fail?

The chances are great that a systems development project will fail if a clearly defined SDLC isn't followed. Sometimes, however, even when companies go to the trouble to establish a formal and comprehensive SDLC, projects still fail to achieve their objectives. Why? Most failures can be traced to a breakdown in communications between the users and the data processing group and information specialists. The reasons for failure often include:

▼ *Inadequate user involvement.* Users must assume responsibility for making sure the analyst understands the business applications, requirements, and policies. (For example, a system may fail because major functions weren't included in the design—because users didn't make their needs known.)

▼ *Continuation of a project that should have been canceled.* Often it's tempting to *not* cancel a project because of the investment already made. Analysts should reevaluate the project at various phases to determine if it remains feasible—in other words, multiple feasibility checkpoints should be established throughout the development process.

▼ *The failure of two or more portions of the new system to fit together properly* (called *systems integration*). This often results when major portions of the systems are worked on by different groups of technical specialists who do not communicate well.

Responses to systems failure vary. Project leaders may be fired; usually the systems requirements are reassessed, and the highest-priority requirements are identified to be satisfied by a smaller system that can be more easily controlled.

Wanted: Orderly Development Process

In most large companies, a great deal of money is allocated for information processing functions (hardware, software, and staff support). In such companies, a systems development project that costs more than $1 million is not uncommon. Hundreds, even thousands, of individual tasks may need to be performed as part of the development effort. These tasks may involve many people within an organization, often in several different organizational units. This multiplicity of effort can lead to conflicting objectives and result in a project that is difficult to coordinate. If the process of developing a system bogs down, the final product can be delayed, and the final cost can be more than double the original estimate. To avoid such difficulties, the SDLC is used as a guideline to direct and administer the activities and to control the financial resources expended. In other words, following a structured procedure brings order to the development process. In a small company the amount of money spent on project development may not be much; however, following the steps of the SDLC is no less significant. Some—but by no means all—risks of ignoring these steps include the following:

▼ *The new system does not meet the users' needs.* Inaccurate or incomplete information gathered by systems analysts and designers may result in the development of software that does not do what the users need.

▼ *Unnecessary hardware or too much hardware is acquired.* If personal computers and printers are sitting idle most of the time, then probably far too much money has been invested without a clear definition of how much processing power is needed.

▼ *Insufficient hardware may be acquired.* For example, users may have to wait in line to use printers, or the system may have inadequate storage capacity.

▼ *Software may be inadequately tested and thus may not perform as expected.* Users tend to rely heavily on the accuracy and the completeness of the information provided by the computer. However, if software is not adequately tested before it is given to users, undetected programming logic errors may produce inaccurate or incomplete information.

Different organizations may refer to the systems development life cycle by different names—such as *applications development cycle, systems development cycle,* or *structured development life cycle.* However, the general objectives will always be the same. The number of steps necessary to complete the cycle may also vary from one company to another, depending on the level of detail necessary to effectively administer and control the development of systems. One way to look at systems development is to divide it into six phases:

Phase 1: Analyze current system

Phase 2: Define new systems requirements

Phase 3: Design new system

Phase 4: Develop new system and have users test it

Phase 5: Implement new system

Phase 6: Evaluate performance of new system and *maintain* system; when the system becomes obsolete, a *planning* stage is then entered to start the SDLC over again and develop a new system

Figure 1 diagrams the six phases of the SDLC. Keep in mind that, although we speak of six separate SDLC phases, one phase does not necessarily have to be completed before the next one is started. In other words, the phases often overlap. The degree of overlap usually depends on the project's size and the amount of resources committed to the project. However, work done on a subsequent phase is subject to change until the work of the preceding phase is completed.

Three groups of personnel are usually involved in an SDLC project: (1) the user group staff members *(users)*; (2) representatives of user management, information processing management, and system owners *(management)*; and a technical staff consisting of systems analysts and programmers *(information specialists)*.

The computer professional generally in charge of the SDLC is the head **systems analyst,** or *project leader.* This person studies the needs and problems of an organization and determines how computer technology—data capture, input, processing, storage, and electronic communications—interacts with data, activities, and people to deliver timely and useful information to the people who need it. The analyst often helps design the database. Systems analysts are often called *systems engineers* or *analyst/programmers,* because they usually are

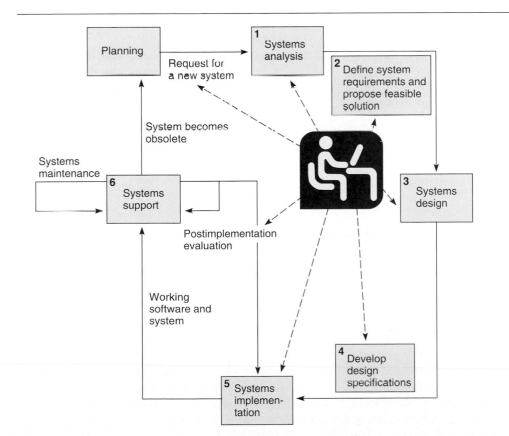

FIGURE 1

Typical systems development life cycle. An SDLC commonly includes six phases. After each of the first four phases, management must decide whether or not to proceed to the next phase. User input and review is a critical part of each phase. [Adapted from J. Whitten, L. Bentley, and V. Barlow, *Systems Analysis and Design Methods,* 2nd ed. (Homewood, Ill.: Richard D. Irwin, 1989), p.7.]

required to do some programming during systems development—that is, to write some of the coded computer programs. Figure 2 shows some of the qualifications and responsibilities of a systems analyst.

Occasionally *steering committees* are formed to help decide how to get started. Steering committees determine which systems development projects to work on first. A steering committee is a group of individuals from each department in an organization. It may hear reports from experts about the advantages, disadvantages, and costs of a particular project. Based on the reports, the committee must decide whether it is in the organization's interest to implement the project. If it decides to go ahead, the systems development life cycle proceeds.

All the detailed processes and tools used in the SDLC phases cannot be covered in one chapter of an introductory text. However, in the following section, we provide the basic principles of the SDLC.

Phase 1: Analyze the Current System

Before a company starts to analyze its current system in detail, a company steering committee may request experts to report on a proposed new systems project. This report, often called a *feasibility study,* can be considered part of the first phase of systems development. The goal of a feasibility study is to identify as quickly as possible whether the benefits of a proposed project appear to outweigh its expected cost and disruption, based on what already is known. Because early feasibility estimates may be overly optimistic, it's usually a good idea to conduct feasibility studies at various times *throughout all phases* of the SDLC to determine whether to continue the project.

Purpose of Phase 1

The main objective of Phase 1 is to gain a clear understanding of the existing system and its shortcomings, to identify existing problems, and to determine where improvements can be made. An analysis of the current system takes place regardless of whether it is manual or computer-based, and each situation *(application)* must be analyzed. Figure 3 shows a few of the problems identified in a sporting goods store's manual accounting system, as well as areas in which a computer-based system could make improvements.

Some aspects of each application within the current system that are studied include:

▼ Inputs (transactions)

▼ Outputs

▼ File structure and storage

▼ Users' requirements

▼ Methods and procedures

▼ Communications needs

▼ Controls

▼ Existing hardware and software (if any)

The systems analyst studies not only these individual components but also how they interact. Those users who are asked to participate in the study of users' requirements can assist the analyst by expanding their thinking about the components being studied. For example, if you were helping a systems analyst study the existing filing system, you would have to describe *everything* used as

FIGURE 2

The job description for a typical systems analyst provides an example of some of the many tasks the analyst must perform and the people and departments he or she must serve. [Whitten, L. Bentley, and V. Barlow, *Systems Analysis and Design Methods*, 3rd ed. (Homewood, Ill.: Richard D. Irwin, 1993).]

JOB TITLE:	Systems Analyst (multiple job levels)
REPORTS TO:	Systems Development Team Manager or Assistant Director of Systems Development
DESCRIPTION:	A systems analyst shall be responsible for studying the problems and needs set forth by this organization to determine how computer hardware, applications software, files and databases, networks, people, and procedures can best solve these problems and improve business and information systems.
RESPONSIBILITIES:	1. Evaluates projects for feasibility. 2. Estimates personnel requirements, budgets, and schedules for systems development and maintenance projects. 3. Performs interviews and other fact gathering. 4. Documents and analyzes current system operations. 5. Defines user requirements for improving or replacing systems. 6. Identifies potential applications of computer technology that may fulfill requirements. 7. Evaluates applications of computer technology for feasibility. 8. Recomends new systems and technical solutions to end users and management. 9. Identifies potential hardware and software vendors, when appropriate. 10. Recommends and selects hardware and software purchases (subject to approval). 11. Designs system inputs, outputs, on-line dialogue, flow, and procedures. 12. Designs files and databases (subject to approval by Data Administration). 13. Writes, tests, and/or supervises applications software development. 14. Trains users to work with new systems and versions. 15. Converts operations to new systems or versions. 16. Supports operational applications.
EXTERNAL CONTACTS:	1. Assigned end users of mainframe computers and applications. 2. Assigned owners (end user management) of mainframe computers and applications. 3. Data Administration Center personnel. 4. Network Administration Center personnel. 5. Information Center personnel. 6. Operations Center personnel. 7. Methodology/CASE expert and staff. 8. Computer hardware and software vendors. 9. Other systems analysis and development managers.
MINIMUM QUALIFICATIONS:	Bachelor or Master's Degree in Computer Information Systems or related field. Programming experience preferred. Prior experience with business applications considered helpful. Prior training or experience in systems analysis and design, preferably structured methods, preferred. Good communications skills—oral and written—are mandatory.
TRAINING REQUIREMENTS:	Analysts must complete or demonstrate equivalent backgrounds in the following in-house training courses: STRADIS Methodology and Standards, Joint Application Design (JAD) Techniques, Systems Application Architecture (SAA) Standards, Fundamentals, DB2 Database Design Techniques, CSP Prototyping Techniques, Excelerator/IS Computer Aided Design Techniques, Project Management Techniques, Microcomputer Software Tools, and Interpersonal and Communications Skills for Systems Analysts.

JOB LEVELS:	Initial assignments are based on programming experience and training results. The following job levels are defined:
	    Programmer/analyst: 30% analysis/design - 70% programming
	    Analyst/programmer: 50% analysis/design - 50% programming
	    Analyst: 70% analysis/design - 30% programming
	    Senior Analyst: 30% management - 60% analysis/design and 10% programming
	    Lead Analyst: 100% analysis/design or consulting

FIGURE 3

Phase 1 analysis of a sporting goods store's current accounting system. These are only a few of the
general problems and objectives that may be identified.

```
Problem Definition--Current Accounting System
The following problems have been detected in the current accounting system:

1. Because files are spread among many filing cabinets in different locations, it
   takes too long to locate the required accounting files in order to update them.
   Often a file has been misplaced, or the file contains information that belongs
   somewhere else.

2. The procedures for updating all accounting files are not clearly defined.
   Mistakes are often made when entering accounting data.

3. The files that need to be updated daily include the General Ledger, Accounts
   Receivable, Accounts Payable, and the payroll files. Because it takes so much
   time to access the files, there is never enough time to get the job done;
   consequently, the job is often done haphazardly and updated only weekly.

4. Because data is filed in several places but under different labels, it is
   difficult to obtain information from the accounting files to generate the
   following types of reports:
        Summary reports about the financial status of the company (daily, weekly,
        monthly, yearly)
        Reports about the projected growth of the company.

Objectives

The new computer-based accounting system should:

1. Reduce by 50% the amount of time required to locate the files that have to be
   updated.
2. Include built-in procedures for the user to follow when updating the accounting
   files.
3. Establish built-in controls to reduce data input errors.
4. Make it easy to update the accounting files daily.
5. Make it easy to obtain information from the accounting files to generate
   reports.
```

a file, including not only files in file cabinets or on disk but also index card
boxes, in/out boxes on your desk, the telephone book, notebook, log sheets,
and materials on your shelf. In other words, anything that is used as reference
for obtaining information to help you make decisions would have to be identified. The analyst will also need to know *how* and *when* you use these refer-
ences/files.

*Note: Users should keep in mind that, although systems analysts may be
experts about computers and their applications, they are not as knowledgeable as
the business users about the business functions they perform. It is the user's
responsibility to make sure the analyst is well informed about the current system.*

Gathering Information

As you can see, the principal activities in this phase involve gathering information about the current system and then analyzing it. The analyst can use a number of techniques, including:

▼ *Conducting interviews:* The analyst interviews staff members who actually perform the work and compares their perceptions of what is being done and how with those of managers, who are also interviewed. In a *structured interview* the analyst prepares outline forms with predetermined questions. If the questions deviate from the predetermined outline, it is called an *unstructured interview.*

▼ *Reviewing policies and procedures:* The extent to which existing policies and procedures have been documented can give the analyst valuable insight into what is going on. The analyst should look over what documentation exists, thereby obtaining a picture of how current system activities are expected to operate. However, all documentation should be compared with the information obtained during interviews to determine if the documentation is up to date. Also, remember that continual new documentation of processes and decisions is necessary throughout the SDLC.

▼ *Collecting sample forms, documents, memos, reports, and so on:* Collecting samples of operating documents can also help the analyst to assemble an accurate picture of current system activities. The term *document* refers to paper on which data has been recorded, including preprinted forms, handwritten forms, and computer-produced forms. The user must be sure to give the analyst copies of *all* documents used for data recording. In addition, the analyst studies the **organization chart** (Figure 4), which shows the organization's management levels and lines of authority.

▼ *Observing operations and office environment:* The information gathered during interviews represents what users *say* is being done. The existing descriptions of procedures (if any) answer the question: what *should* be done and how? Observing operations and the office environment will confirm the analyst's understanding of what actually exists and answers the question: what are the users *actually doing?*

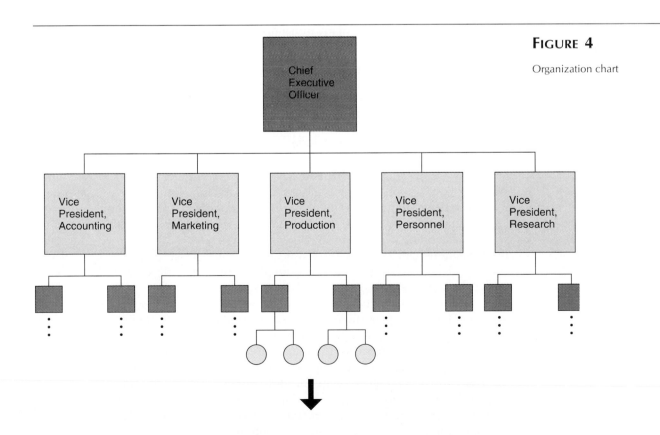

FIGURE 4

Organization chart

▼ *Using questionnaires to conduct surveys:* Analysts find that using questionnaires to take a survey can be useful when information must be collected from a large group of individuals. Although questionnaires take less time than personal interviews, and many responses can be collected, they must be used with care. The questions must be precisely worded so that the user completing the questionnaire understands the instruction and does not need to interpret the questions.

Needless to say, the systems analyst does not necessarily do these activities alone. Users themselves can collect data on a current system using these techniques, perhaps along with the analyst.

Analyzing Information

After the analyst has gathered information about the current system, he or she must analyze the facts to identify problems—including their causes and effects—and opportunities for improvement. Just a few of the things that the analyst determines are:

▼ *Minimum, average, and maximum levels of activity.* For example, when do most sales orders come in?

▼ *Relative importance of the various activities.* This means prioritizing the activities.

▼ *Redundancy of procedures.* For example, are two users entering the same sales order data at different times?

▼ *Unusually labor-intensive and/or tedious activities.* These are manual activities that could be computerized, like filling out forms to record sales data.

▼ *Activities that require extensive (complex and/or repetitive) mathematical computation.* An example is updating customer charge account balances and interest charges.

▼ *Procedures that have become obsolete.* Perhaps your company's licensing requirements have changed, rendering the old procedures useless.

The analyst can use several tools to assist in the analysis. **Modeling tools** enable the analyst to present graphic (pictorial) representations of a system, or part of a system. These tools include, among others, data flow diagrams (DFDs), systems flowcharts, connectivity diagrams, grid charts, and decision tables. Special software packages, such as Excelerator, a computer-aided software engineering (CASE) tool, automate the production of modeling tools.

Data flow diagrams (Figure 5) show the flow of data through a system and diagram the processes that change data into information. They focus on where data originates, where and how it's processed, and where it goes. Data flow diagrams can be used for clarification in any phase of the systems development life cycle. To give you an example of how data flow symbols are used, Figure 6 diagrams one physician's billing system.

Systems flowcharts focus not only on data flow but on all aspects of a system. They use their own special set of ANSI symbols (Figure 7). Figure 8 shows an example of a systems flowchart.

Connectivity diagrams (Figure 9) are used to map network connections of people, data, and activities at various locations. These diagrams are used as the basis for designing the network and communications systems.

Grid charts show the relationship between data on input documents and data on output documents. For example, in Figure 10, you can see that the data on input forms 1 and 3 is included in output forms A and B.

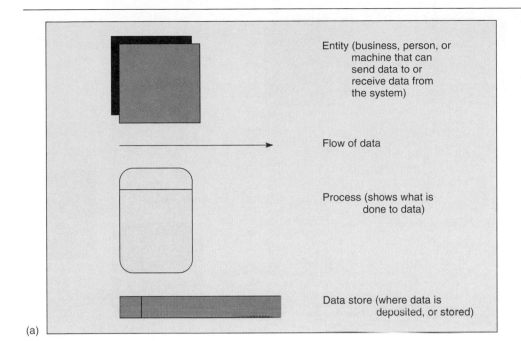

(a)

FIGURE 5

Data flow diagram symbols (a) and sample diagram (b). Systems analysts use these standard data flow diagram symbols to make data flow diagrams throughout the systems development life cycle. [Adapted from K. Kendall and J. Kendall, Systems Analysis and Design, 2nd ed. (Englewood Cliffs, N.J.: Prentice-Hall, 1992).]

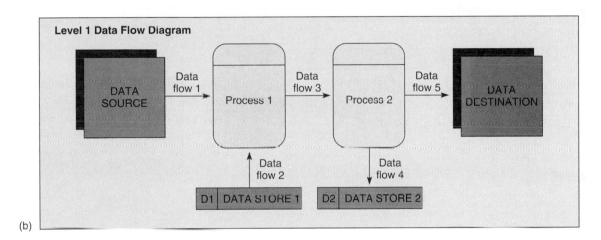

(b)

Decision tables (Figure 10) show the rules that apply when certain conditions occur.

Prototyping is another tool used by systems analysts to help them analyze a system and start building a new one. A prototype is essentially a small working model of the system or some aspect of it. The prototype can be set up during this phase, or a later phase, and then modified and improved during subsequent phases.

The first phase of the SDLC usually concludes with a *detailed study report* to management or the steering committee. The objectives of the Phase 1 report are to provide a clear picture of what the current system does, how it does it, and what the analysis identified as problems, causes and effects of problems, and areas where improvements can be made.

FIGURE 6

General data flow diagram of a physician's billing system. [Adapted from K. Kendall and J. Kendall, Systems Analysis and Design, 2nd ed. (Englewood Cliffs, N.J.: Prentice-Hall, 1992).]

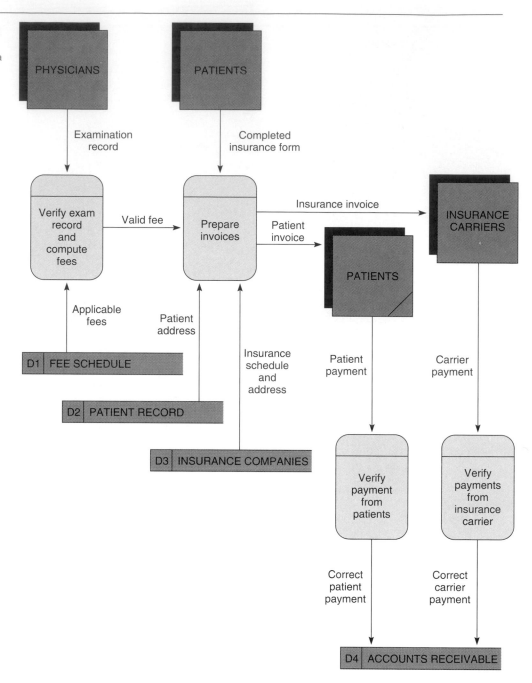

Phase 2: Define New Systems Requirements

In Phase 2 the analyst focuses attention on what he or she—and the users—want the new system to do. But before designing the new system, the analyst has to define the requirements that it must satisfy. And the requirements must be defined very carefully; otherwise the new system might not end up doing what the users hope it will do.

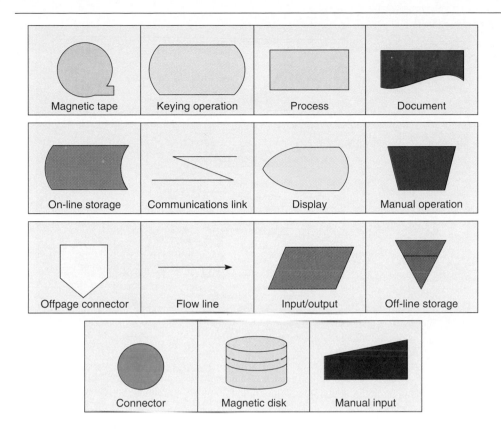

FIGURE 7

ANSI systems flowchart symbols. Systems flowcharts use symbols standardized by the American National Standards Institute.

Purpose of Phase 2

In the second phase of the SDLC, the analyst defines the requirements for the new system in enough detail so both computer professionals and users know exactly what the new system is going to do and how the system is going to do it. Needless to say, these requirements should solve the problems identified in the first phase.

Once the requirements of a system are known, then both manual and computer-based alternatives are evaluated for new and improved systems. Among the factors affecting what alternatives should be implemented are the availability of computer hardware that is technologically suited to the business's requirements and that fits within the budget of the proposed system. Cost becomes a major factor if software must be created from scratch by a professional programmer, instead of being bought off the shelf (the "make or buy" decision).

The systems analyst uses the modeling tools and prototyping mentioned earlier to help define and graphically describe the new system's requirements and suggest ways of fulfilling these requirements.

As we mentioned earlier, a prototype is a small-scale working model of a new system module (or of a small system). Analysts often use computer-aided software engineering and automated design tools, such as Excelerator, to create prototypes (Figure 11). The objective of prototyping is to get feedback from users as soon as possible; by trying out a prototype of a proposed part of a new system, users alert analysts to problems early in the SDLC.

Also, modeling and prototyping will be used throughout the entire SDLC to continually document design and development progress and to try out program and systems modules.

Figure 8

Systems flowchart example.
[Adapted from K. Kendall and
J. Kendall, Systems Analysis
and Design, 2nd ed. (Engle-
wood Cliffs, N.J.: Prentice-
Hall, 1992).]

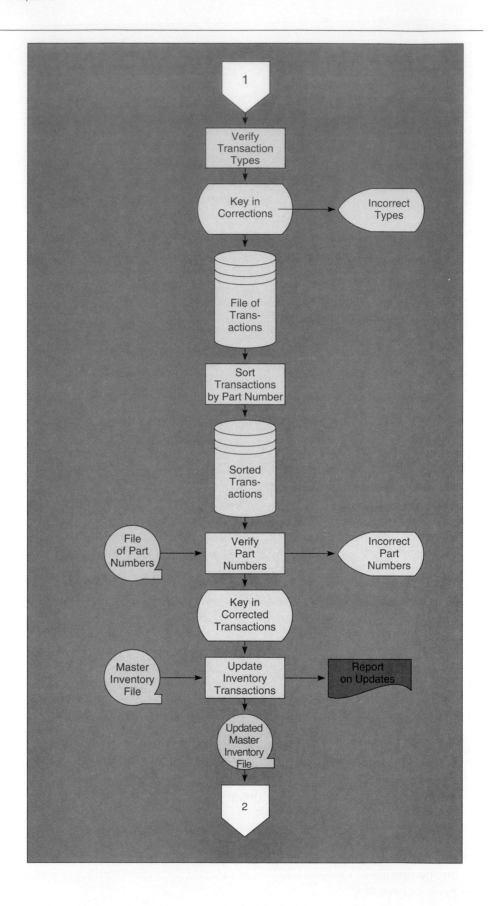

FIGURE 9

Connectivity diagram. [Whitten, L. Bentley, and V. Barlow, *Systems Analysis and Design Methods*, 3rd ed. (Homewood, Ill.: Richard D. Irwin, 1993).]

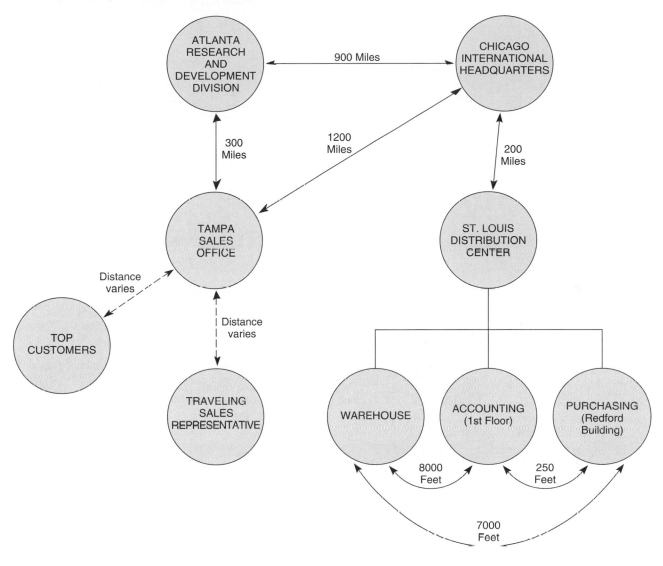

FIGURE 10

(*Left*) Decision table, (*right*) grid chart

	Decision rules				
	1	2	3	4	5
Conditions if . . .	N	Y	Y	Y	N
And if . . .	Y	Y	N	Y	N
And if . . .	Y	Y	N	N	Y
Actions Then do . . .	✓				
Then do . . .			✓		✓
Then do . . .		✓		✓	

Forms (input)	Reports (output)		
	Report A	Report B	Report C
form 1	✓	✓	
form 2			✓
form 3	✓	✓	

FIGURE 11

Prototyping software allows analysts (or users) to quickly generate working models of data forms. (a) Model of a hardcopy report form; (b) model of a softcopy "form" that will appear on screen. In both cases, the user just fills in the appropriate data.

```
   1-10      11-20     21-30     31-40     41-50     51-60     61-70     71-80
123456789012345678901234567890123456789012345678901234567890123456789012345678 9

                                     ABC

                                 CORPORATION

                              PARTS MOVE REPORT
                             -----------------------

        PART-ID    MGR   APPR      LOCATION     QTY-STOCK   QTY-REQUEST   STATUS
       ---------  -----  -------  -------------  -----------  -------------  -------

    1)  999999    XXX    XX       9,999.99     9,999.99      99/99/99      XXX

    2)  999999    XXX    XX       9,999.99     9,999.99      99/99/99      XXX

    3)  999999    XXX    XX       9,999.99     9,999.99      99/99/99      XXX

    4)  999999    XXX    XX       9,999.99     9,999.99      99/99/99      XXX
```

(a)

```
PANEL DEFINITION MENU ********** ********** END PROCESSING PERFORMED
COMMAND ==>

FUNCTION: UP   CR-CREATE     UP-UPDATE    PU-PURGE    SH-SHOW     LI-LIST


ITEM       PI    PI-IMAGE       PD-DEFIN
                                      FD-FIELD      CE-CONSIS      SL-SEGLOOP
                                        (UP)         (CR,UP)       (CR,UP,PU)

MEMBER NAME:
      HEADER TR____
      ID      XXAD_ PRE-CLASS ASSIGN, STUDENT NAME
      DESC    ____________________________________________

ENTER VALUE FOR SPECIFIC ITEM TO BE PROCESSED:
     1. IMAGE     < > + | \ (INPUT OUTPUT OUTIN SELECT LIT-BREAK CHARACTERS)
                  24 080    (LINE-COLUMN IMAGE SIZE)
                  U         (UPPER/LOWER CASE LITERALS)
     2. DEFIN     Y Y Y Y N (INPUT OUTPUT OUTIN SELECT LITERAL FIELDS LISTED)
     3. FIELD     _________ (NAME OR LINE, COLUMN OR "*PANEL")
     4. CONSIS    _________ (TYPE - "XFEDIT", "SEGEDIT", OR BLANK FOR LIST)
                  _________ (NAME - IF TYPE SPECIFIED)
     5. SEGLOOP   _________ (TYPE - "FILE" OR "TABLE")
                  ________  (FROM NAME OR LINE,COLUMN)
                  ________    (TO NAME OR LINE,COLUMN)
```

(b)

Requirements That Affect Software

Once the business requirements have been defined, most systems analysts and designers focus on the *output* the system must produce. The output requirements fall into three general categories:

1. *Hardcopy output* (reports, special forms, and so on)
2. *Softcopy output* (displayed on video screen)
3. *Computer-usable output* (a computer file created during processing for output in one system that is also used as input to another system—for

example, a file produced by the payroll system that is later used in the general ledger system).

To define the requirements for hardcopy and softcopy outputs, the analyst meets with each user who will be using each type of output to carefully identify:

▼ The purpose of the output

▼ The elements of information it will contain

▼ How each element will be used

▼ How often and how fast the output will need to be produced

In many cases, the analyst will use prototyping tools to produce forms for the user to approve.

The storage, processing, and input requirements are closely related to the output requirements. Input requirements are formulated in terms of:

▼ Who will be performing the input procedure

▼ The elements of data that will be entered

▼ The input screens (the information displayed on the screen that tells the user what data elements to enter)

▼ The control procedures to be exercised over the data entry process

Storage requirements are defined in terms of the different files that will need to be created to satisfy the processing and output requirements—for instance, (among other types of files) a master file, an inventory file, an accounts receivable file, an accounts payable file, input transaction and output/report files, and different backup files.

Processing requirements deal with processing schedules—that is, when data is to be input, when output is to be produced, and when files are to be updated—and the identification of logical and computational processing activities.

When all the software-related requirements have been defined, they are usually summarized as a part of the New Systems Requirements Report (described later).

Requirements That Affect Hardware

The new system's software requirements must be defined first to determine what type of computer hardware is needed. This may involve modifying equipment already owned or buying new equipment. Hardware requirements will be discussed in more detail in Phase 4.

Evaluating Alternative Solutions

Once the new system's requirements have been defined, the analyst should examine *alternative* approaches to satisfying the requirements. This step keeps people from jumping to conclusions and gives several options to management. For example, perhaps an expensive conversion to a computer-based system from a manual one is not really necessary! The analyst carefully weighs the advantages and disadvantages of each alternative, including how each might affect the time required to get the new system in place and its estimated cost.

Systems Requirements Report

Phase 2 concludes with the analyst's preparation of a *systems requirements report*. The report provides the basis for the final determination of the completeness and accuracy of the new systems requirements, as well as the economic and practical feasibility of the new system. After everyone has reviewed and discussed the report, a final decision is made about whether to proceed and, if so, which alternatives to adopt. A revised schedule for project completion is also worked out. If the company is going outside its organization to develop a new system, its systems requirements report may also contain a document called a *request for proposal (RFP)*. This document is used when a company wants to get bids from vendors for prices of software, hardware, programs, supplies, or service. It lists the systems requirements and any limitations.

Phase 3: Design the New System

The third phase of the SDLC focuses on the design of the new system. To determine how the new system will be constructed, the analyst analyzes the requirements defined in Phase 2. The activities in this phase are carried out primarily by computer specialists—that is, programmers. Users may have little direct involvement in the design phase; however, their responses are critical when a programmer needs clarification of logical or computational processing requirements. Users should also continue to be involved in the final approval of procedures that provide for user interface with the system—such as what type of dialog will show up on the terminal—and of proposed report forms, both hardcopy and softcopy. After all, the analysts can leave when their job is done; the users must live with the system!

Purpose of Phase 3

Phase 3 involves two main objectives: (1) to design the new system and (2) to establish a sound framework of controls within which the new system should operate. Tools used are, among others, dataflow diagrams, systems flowcharts, program flowcharts (used by programmers writing software programs), structured design and programming, and prototyping.

Computer-aided systems engineering (CASE) tools are also used in Phase 3. These software programs are used in any or all phases of the SDLC (Figure 12). CASE tools provide computer-automated support for structured design techniques; they speed up the design process and improve the quality of systems development and documentation. CASE tools are built around the concept of a *project dictionary,* also called a *repository* (Figure 13), which stores all the requirements and specifications for all elements of data to be used in the new system.

Among other outputs, CASE tools can generate:

▼ Graphics tools such as dataflow diagrams, flowcharts, structure charts, and data models

▼ Reports on file contents, properties of data elements, and rules of logic

▼ Prototypes

▼ Quality analysis reports

▼ Programming code for writing software programs

▼ Project management charts

▼ Cost/benefit analyses

Figure 14 gives you an idea of how these capabilities relate to one another. In addition to Excelerator, CASE tools include Knowledgeware, Framework, AW/DOC, firstCASE, HyperAnalyst, SPQR/20, and System Architect.

FIGURE 12

CASE tools are used across the entire SDLC. [Whitten, L. Bentley, and V. Barlow, *Systems Analysis and Design Methods,* 3rd ed. (Homewood, Ill.: Richard D. Irwin, 1993).]

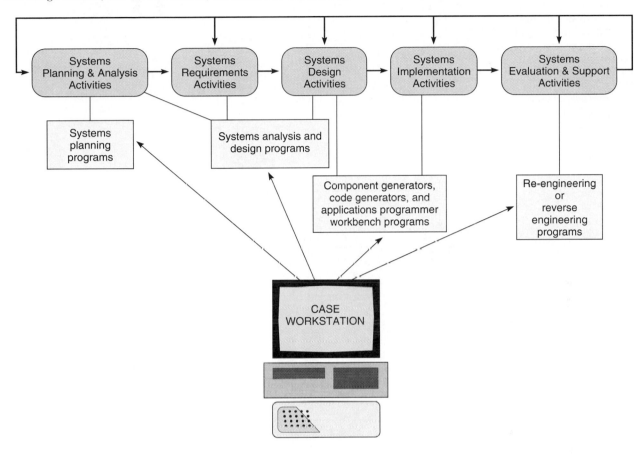

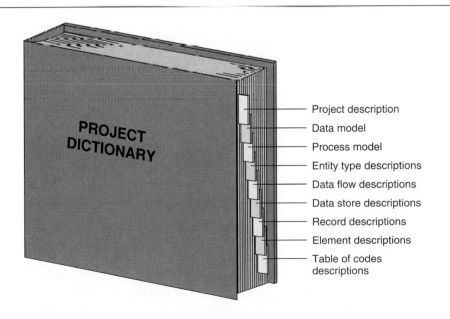

FIGURE 13

Project dictionary organization. A project dictionary forms the base of a CASE tool. The dictionary is maintained on the computer and then ultimately output as documentation.

FIGURE 14

Some computer-assisted software engineering (CASE) capabilities. This figure shows how the capabilities relate to one another and to the people involved in the systems development process. [Adapted from J. Whitten, L. Bentley, and V. Barlow, *Systems Analysis and Design Methods*, 2nd ed. (Homewood, Ill.: Richard D. Irwin, 1989), p. 127.]

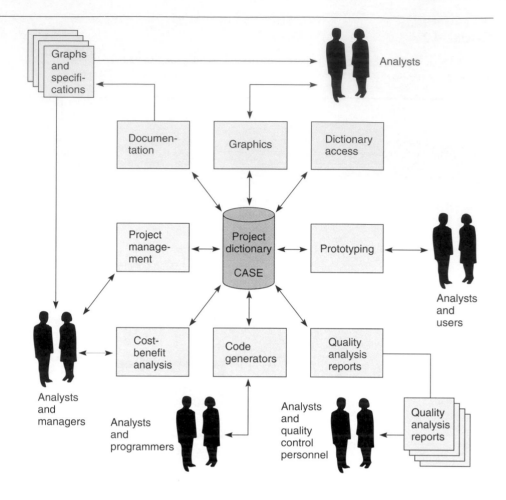

Designing New Systems Controls and Security Functions

New systems must be designed to operate within a framework of controls, a system of safeguards that protect a computer system and data from accidental or intentional damage, from input and output inaccuracies, and from access by unauthorized persons. As computer systems become easier and easier to use, and as software becomes more and more user friendly, the importance of designing adequate security controls into an information system grows. Controls involve the physical environment of the system (for example, limiting access to buildings, rooms, doors, and computer hardware), the manual procedures performed by users and computer specialists (creation of a disaster plan, documentation of procedures for distributing output) and the computer-based processing procedures (access to data, use of software, and standards for data input and verification).

Concluding the Design Phase

At the end of Phase 3, the analysts/designers complete, organize, and assemble the new systems design documentation by using a combination of the tools and techniques discussed earlier in the chapter. The documentation should include:

▼ A complete overview of the new system as a whole

▼ A description (narrative or graphic) of the major processing modules into which the system has been divided for design purposes

▼ Detailed documentation describing the input, processing, and output activities in each module and submodule

▼ Specifications of the storage requirements for the new system; a description of each file to be maintained in the system, including anticipated size and organization scheme/access method to be used

▼ A narrative description of the controls to be used with the new system

Then systems analyst(s), users, and management meet to review the design. A decision is made to approve the design and proceed to the next phase of the SDLC—systems development—or to revise the design before continuing. Although most organizations would decide to discard a project entirely at an earlier phase, it is still possible that the project could be terminated at this time.

Phase 4: Develop the New System and Have Users Test It

A company that is changing from a manual to a computer-based system (or modifying an existing computer-based system) cannot run out and buy hardware in Phase 1 because it doesn't yet know what the new system is supposed to do. The company shouldn't make purchases during Phase 2 either because, although its requirements have been established, the new system has not yet been designed. During Phase 3, the system has been designed but not yet accepted. It's not until Phase 4 that the system is accepted and development begins. Now the company can acquire software and hardware.

Purpose of Phase 4

During Phase 4, four major activities occur:

1. Acquire software
2. Acquire hardware
3. Train the users
4. Test the new system

Acquire Software

If the software is not purchased off the shelf, it must be written by programmers. These programmers use appropriate logic-development tools, programming languages, coding procedures, and testing and documentation methods (discussed in Chapter 8).

Acquire Hardware

Here are some points company representatives consider when buying (or leasing) hardware:

▼ If some computers have already been acquired, determine if additional units need to be compatible.

▼ For a microcomputer-based system, establish the minimum amount of main memory to satisfy the processing requirements. Most software products for microcomputers require a minimum of 640 K; many others require *at least* 1–4 MB or more.

▼ If processing will involve extensive mathematical or graphics calculations, plan to install special math coprocessor chips in some microcomputers.

▼ Determine which video display units will need to be high resolution for certain applications like graphics. If graphics are required, graphics adapter cards and RGB monitors may be required for certain computers.

▼ Analyze carefully the storage requirements to help determine what size system to purchase; consider removable storage media like hard disk packs or cartridges for flexible storage capacities.

▼ Consider the quality, volume, and type of printed output to be produced in order to determine the types of printers required.

▼ Determine the delivery schedules for all equipment.

▼ Determine where the hardware should be installed.

▼ Determine how many users the system will need to support now—and in a year or two.

▼ Determine the amount of multiusing and multitasking required.

▼ Determine the type of operating system that will ensure program compatibility and efficiency.

▼ Evaluate computer network and other communications needs.

If using existing hardware, the new system design must be reviewed to determine if additional hardware is required.

Once hardware needs have been identified, the company must determine which vendor to choose.

Train the Users

The users (and the computer operators) must be trained to use the new hardware and software. This can often be started before the equipment is delivered; for example, the vendor may give training seminars on its own premises or provide temporary training equipment.

Test the New System

Several methods may be used to test the new system. However, a **user-acceptance test** must be done to make sure the system does what users want it to do *before* the new system is implemented. Sample data will be fed into the system to see that it performs correctly. Testing may take several months. Of course, any bugs must be eliminated.

Phase 5: Implement the New System

The process of developing a new system costs a great deal of time, energy, and money. However, even a beautifully designed and developed system can fail to meet its objectives if it is not carefully implemented. In this phase, the company converts from the old system to the new system.

Purpose of Phase 5

The implementation phase, which gets the new system up and running, involves creating the final operating documentation and procedures, converting files, and using the new system.

Final Operating Documentation and Procedures

In the first step in getting ready to implement a new system, the analyst prepares the final operating documentation. The procedures covered include entering data, making inquiries, directing processing activities, and distributing reports. The computer operators must have operating documentation that identifies the processing schedule, files to be used, and programs to be run. The data entry group must have procedures on how the input data is to be entered. The control group must have procedures for monitoring system controls and coordinating the distribution of reports. Figure 15 shows some elements of a documentation package.

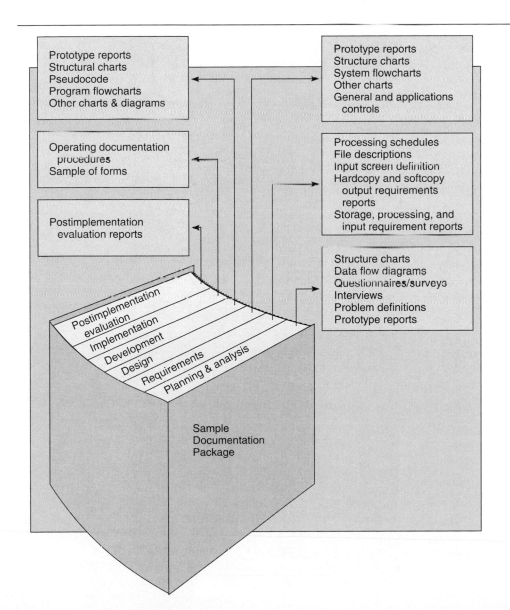

FIGURE 15

Sample documentation package

Converting Files ("Data Migration")

A new computer-based system cannot be used until all the manually recorded data files are converted into computer-usable form—this is sometimes called *data migration*. When a manual system is computerized, file conversion can become a monumental task. The time, effort, and cost required to design appropriate file structures and key in the data are enormous. Outside assistance may be required for large file conversion tasks. If an existing computer-based system is being changed to a new system, the files can be converted by a computer program.

Using the New System

There are four basic approaches to implementing a new system: direct implementation, parallel implementation, phased implementation, and pilot implementation. The concepts behind the four approaches are diagrammed in Figure 16.

FIGURE 16

Four approaches to systems implementation

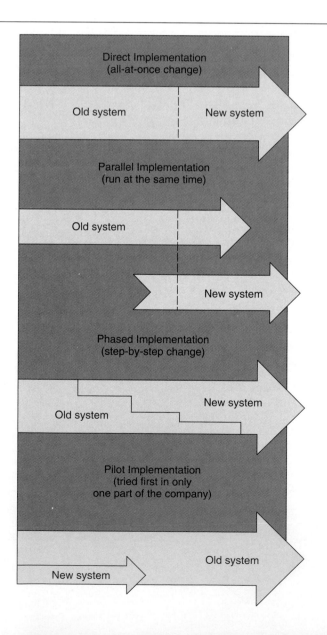

In **direct implementation,** the change is made all at once. The old system is halted on a planned date and the new system is activated. This approach is most often used for small systems or larger systems for which a systems model was previously developed and thoroughly tested. Simply halting the old system and starting up the new system is a very simple approach; however, this method carries some risks. For example, in most large systems, there are far too many variables to be adequately tested. As a result, a few unexpected errors are almost always found during the initial implementation period. These errors are much more disruptive and difficult to correct when the old system has been halted. Normal processing cannot continue until the errors are fixed.

Parallel implementation involves running the old system and the new system at the same time for a specified period. The results of using the new system are compared to the old system. If the performance of the new system is satisfactory, use of the old system is discontinued. This approach is the safest because operations do not have to be shut down if the new system has problems; however, it is by far the most expensive and difficult approach to coordinate. Operating two systems takes much more time and effort. In addition to operating both systems, it will be necessary to compare the output from the new system to the old system and evaluate the results.

When the parallel implementation approach is used, a formal meeting of the project development team and the users is held at the end of the trial period. The performance of the new system is discussed and a decision is reached as to whether the findings are positive enough to warrant discontinuing the operation of the old system.

Some systems are just too broad in scope or are so large that they must be implemented in phases to avoid the traumatic effect of trying to implement all the components at once. Implementation is more easily handled one phase at a time—**phased implementation.**

If a system is to be implemented at many locations in a widely dispersed company, the task can be very difficult to manage all at once. To implement the system at one location at a time—and ensure that it is working correctly before moving on to other locations—is safer. This is called **pilot implementation.**

Phase 6: Postimplemenation Evaluation and Maintenance (Support)

Two very important activities take place after the new system has been implemented: postimplementation evaluation and systems maintenance (systems support). Ongoing **systems maintenance** involves making necessary adjustments and enhancements, or additions, to the system during the years it is used. Adjustments may be needed because, as users gain experience in using the new system, they may discover minor processing errors. Or government reporting regulations may change, creating new requirements for a system to satisfy. Companies must remember to budget funds to pay for maintenance.

Purpose of Phase 6

After a new system has been in operation for several months and any necessary systems maintenance has been done, a formal evaluation—called a **postimplementation evaluation**—of the new system takes place. This evaluation determines either that the new system is meeting its objectives or that certain things need to be done so that it will meet these objectives.

The end of the final step in the SDLC is marked by the preparation of a new systems evaluation report. The report summarizes the extent to which the system meets the original objectives and includes a list of enhancements to be considered for future development and implementation.

After a system has been in operation for an extended period of time, it may become obsolete. That means that the time and money involved in modernizing or altering the system may cost more than developing an entire new and better system. Time to start planning the SDLC all over again.

What Skills Does the User Need?

Figure 17 reviews the points at which you, the user, may interact with the systems development life cycle. Whether or not you will need to use any of the tools and techniques for analyzing and documenting systems and their development depends on the type of organization you're with and the level of expertise you have gained. But, in most cases, you will need only a basic understanding of the life cycle used at your place of business and the objectives of each phase. You will need to develop your ability to communicate effectively with computer specialists to help your company operate efficiently and profitably. If you can't communicate your business needs clearly, your requirements may not be met by the new system.

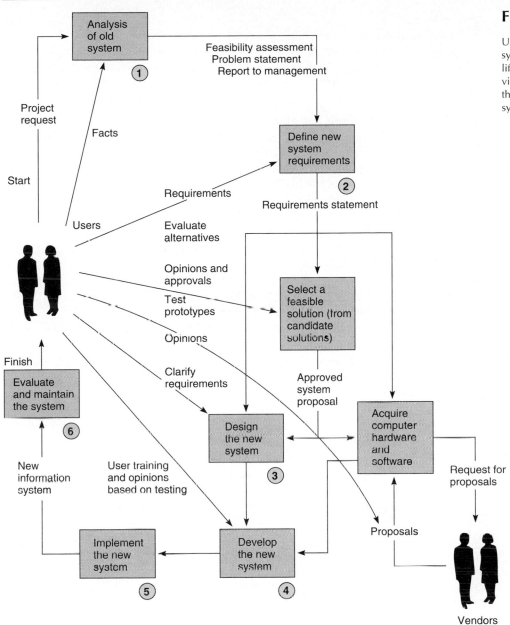

FIGURE 17

User interaction with the systems analysis and design life cycle. This diagram reviews the points at which you, the user, may interact with systems analysts and designers.

COMPUTERS AND CAREERS

▼

INFORMATION

There is a new business breed: "infopreneurs," specialized entrepreneurs moving to exploit opportunities for information products and services provided by advances in computers and communications. The real value of information, it has been pointed out, is when it becomes knowledge. This is where infopreneurs come in.

Infopreneurs transform existing information into new uses. They identify and create new markets by developing new information services and products. Examples are those who have bought the electronic rights to printed lists of names. The Yellow Pages, for instance, appear not only in book form but also in computer form, giving rise to databases that can create different kinds of lists or be sent over communications lines.

Two examples of how information business works are as follows: Dow Jones News/Retrieval takes information collected by the company's news organizations, such as *The Wall Street Journal,* splits it into news, financial data, and stock prices, and sells them separately. An organization that tracks commercial oceangoing ships, Lloyd's Maritime Data Network, sells the information to shippers, who can use it to negotiate better deals with carriers.

Half the electronic information sold in the United States is financial, used for stock trading and the like. However, there are other uses for databases and communications. For instance, instead of using advertisements and personnel agencies, some companies searching for the right person for the right job use computerized files of resumes offered by industry associations, alumni groups, and entrepreneurs such as Computer Assisted Recruitment International of Schaumberg, Ill. Comp-U-Card is a merchandise broker that takes orders from home shoppers—either by telephone or by modem-linked computer—for thousands of products. CheckFree, of Columbus, Ohio, offers home-computer users an automatic bill-paying service, working with any bank you choose.

Nearly all occupations now have their own specialized information services. Most major law firms, for example, use Mead Data Central's LEXIS service, a computer-based research system for lawyers. Mead also owns Micromedex, which sells information on poisons, drugs, and emergency care to several hospitals and poison centers. Many catalog mailers pay Claritas Corp., a marketing consulting firm, to tell them how to reach certain kinds of prospective buyers, whose lifestyles can be identified according to the ZIP codes they live in.

As computer-based information has become more a part of every industry and occupation, investigative journalists have found that being able to sift though electronic databases is as important as a notepad and good shoes. Indeed, some journalists feel that the only way that reporters can monitor enormous organizations such as government agencies is to get access to computer-based files.

Where will this deluge of information end? Reportedly the Library of Congress alone doubles in volume every 10 years. As the Information Society continues to grow, more and more people will specialize in the creating and selling of information.

▼ The *systems development life cycle (SDLC)* is the formal process by which organizations build manual and computer-based information systems. Systems development life cycles may be known by different names and comprise varying numbers of phases, but their principles are basically the same.

▼ Users must participate in the systems analysis and design process because they have to explain to analysts and designers how they use the current system and what they think is wrong with it. Users also must be involved in testing new systems and have to be able to follow the charts, diagrams, and written procedures in the new systems documentation so that they will be able to use the new system effectively.

▼ An SDLC is used as a guideline in directing and administering the activities involved in establishing business system requirements, developing the system, acquiring hardware and software, and controlling development costs. Without a reasoned approach to systems analysis and design, systems development can result in disruption of normal working procedures, acquisition of too much or too little computer hardware, development of inadequate software, misunderstood user needs and requirements, new system problems resulting from inadequate testing, and inadequate documentation for system maintenance and future modification.

▼ An SDLC can be divided into six phases:

Phase 1: Analyze current system

Phase 2: Define new systems requirements

Phase 3: Design new system

Phase 4: Develop new system and have users test it

Phase 5: Implement new system

Phase 6: Evaluate performance of and *maintain* (support) new system

▼ In *Phase 1,* the objective is to gain a clear understanding of the existing system, including its shortcomings, and determine where improvements can be made.

▼ To analyze the current system, analysts and users must gather information about the existing system using such techniques as interviewing; reviewing written policies and procedures; collecting sample forms, reports, and other documents, including *organization charts;* observing operations and office environment; and using questionnaires to conduct surveys.

▼ After information about the current system has been gathered, it must be analyzed. Problems and opportunities to improve the system are identified. Systems analysts use many tools and techniques to study the system and document the analysis. Among these tools are *data flow diagrams, grid charts, decision tables, systems flowcharts, prototyping,* and *computer-assisted software engineering (CASE) tools.* Phase 1 concludes with a report and presentation to management that summarizes the current systems analysis and gives a recommendation about whether or not to proceed.

▼ *Phase 2* of the SDLC involves defining the requirements for the new system—manual as well as computer-based procedures. Requirements should be defined in the areas of input, storage, processing, and output. Defining software requirements focuses first on the output that the users will need. Phase 2 concludes with a systems requirements report.

▼ *Phase 3* of the SDLC focuses on the technical design of the new system, using programming techniques and methods plus CASE tools and continued prototyping. Designing the new systems controls for both manual and computer-based procedures is also an important part of Phase 3.

10.29

▼ Developing the new system, *Phase 4* of the SDLC, involves acquiring software and hardware, training users and operators, and testing the new system *(user acceptance test)*.

▼ *Phase 5* of the SDLC involves implementing the new system. This phase includes three steps:

1. Creating final operating documentation and procedures

2. Converting files ("data migration")

3. Using the system

▼ New systems can be implemented:

1. All at once *(direct implementation)*

2. While the old system is still running *(parallel implementation)*

3. Step-by-step *(phased implementation)*

4. In one section of the company at a time; each section's system must be working before the next section's system is implemented *(pilot implementation)*

▼ *Phase 6* of the SDLC involves postimplementation evaluation and maintenance. The evaluation determines whether or not the new system is meeting its objectives. Maintenance involves ongoing support of the system

▼ One reason why a new system fails is a lack of communication somewhere along the line. Thus users should understand the basics of the systems development life cycle—so that they can intelligently communicate to the information specialists the problems with the current system as it affects their jobs and their requirements for the new system.

KEY TERMS

computer-aided software
  engineering (CASE) tools,
  p. 10.18
connectivity diagram, p. 10.10
data flow diagram, p. 10.10
decision table, p. 10.11
direct implementation, p. 10.25
grid chart, p. 10.11

information system, p. 10.2
modeling tools, p. 10.10
organization chart, p. 10.9
parallel implementation, p. 10.25
phased implementation, p. 10.25
pilot implementation, p. 10.25
postimplementation evaluation,
  p. 10.25

prototyping, p. 10.11
systems analyst, p. 10.5
systems development life cycle
  (SDLC), p. 10.2
systems flowchart, p. 10.10
systems maintenance (support),
  p. 10.25
user acceptance test, p. 10.22

EXERCISES

SELF-TEST

1. The process of building a small, simple model of a new information system is

   called _____.

2. Name three ways of gathering data in Phase 1 of the SDLC.

   a.

   b.

   c.

3. What are the four methods of implementing a new system?

   a.

   b.

   c.

   d.

4. A _____ stores all the requirements and specifications for
   all elements of data to be used in a new system.

5. _____ _____ is when the old sys-
   tem is halted on a given date and the new system is activated.

6. Users are never involved in systems development. (true/false)

7. The modeling tool used by the systems analyst to focus on the flow of data

   through a system is called a _____

   _____.

8. The situation in which the old system and the new system are running at the
   same time for a specified period is called _____
   implementation.

9. The document used by a company when it goes outside its organization to
   develop a new system or purchase parts of a new system is called a

   _____ _____.

10. A _____ supports and usually automates day-to-day

    business operations, whereas an _____ generates informa-
    tion to support decision making by managers.

11. An _____ _____ shows an organi-
    zation's levels of management and lines of authority.

12. Automated systems design and prototyping tools are called

_____   _____

_____ (_____) tools

Solutions: (1) prototyping; (2) conduct interviews, observe operations, conduct surveys, review policies and procedures; (3) direct, phased, parallel, pilot; (4) project dictionary; (5) direct implementation; (6) false; (7) data flow diagram; (8) parallel implementation; (9) request for proposal; (10) business system, information system; (11) organization chart; (12) computer-assisted software engineering (CASE)

SHORT-ANSWER QUESTIONS

1. What is the importance of first defining the output requirements of a proposed system?

2. Briefly describe the six phases of the SDLC.

3. What are some of the techniques used to gather data in the analysis phase of the SDLC?

4. What determines the extent to which your job brings you in contact with your company's SDLC?

5. Why is it important for users to understand the principles of the SDLC?

6. Describe the four basic approaches to implementing a new system.

7. What are computer-assisted software engineering tools used for?

8. Several common tools are used for defining a new system's requirements, including modeling tools. Name some modeling tools. What are they used for?

9. Why is it important for a company to follow an orderly SDLC?

10. Why should users be included in the testing stages of a new system?

PROJECTS

1. Using recent computer publications, research the state of the art of computer-assisted software engineering (CASE) tools. What capabilities do these tools have? What do you think the future holds for CASE tools?

2. Designing system controls. Your company is just beginning the process of computerizing the sales order entry activities. Currently, orders are received by mail, over the phone, and at the counter when customers stop by. The plan is to key the phone orders and counter orders into the computer immediately. The orders received in the mail will be entered into the computer in groups. A typical order contains customer information (such as number, name, and address) and product information (such as product number, description, quantity ordered, and unit price).

   a. Identify possible control techniques that could be designed into the system to ensure that all sales orders are input in their entirety to the computer.

   b. Identify possible control techniques to help ensure all sales order data is accurately entered into the system.

   c. How would the control techniques for phone orders and counter orders differ from the orders received in the mail?

4. Design a system that would handle the input, processing, and output of a simple form of your choice. Use a data flow diagram to illustrate the system.

Database Management Systems

Where does the power come from in a computer-based information system? Although your first answer may be "hardware and the speed with which it can process data," if you think about it a bit longer you will probably realize that the real power comes from the data. From data comes information, and access to information offers power. But the amounts of data being handled by companies with computer-based systems have grown so large in recent years that managing data properly has become a sophisticated operation.

PREVIEW

When you have completed this chapter, you will be able to:

▼ Explain what a database is

▼ Describe the difference between file management systems and database management systems

▼ Describe how database management systems software relates to hardware and the user

▼ Identify the advantages and the disadvantages of the three database models and of database management systems in general

▼ Explain the importance of database administration within an organization

WHY IS THIS CHAPTER IMPORTANT?

*M*anagers and users need information to make effective decisions. Indeed, the lifeblood of any business, no matter how large or small, is its information. The more accurate, relevant, and timely the information, the better informed people will be when making decisions. Now we turn our attention to the organization of the data that makes up the information. In general, database management concepts are the same for large computer systems and for microcomputers. As a general business user, you will most likely be using a microcomputer or a terminal to access data stored in a database. Therefore you need to understand the features of a database and a database management system. Through a better understanding of database systems, you can put them to effective use in your job.

What Is a Database Management System?

A **database** is a large group of stored, integrated (cross-referenced) data elements that can be retrieved and manipulated with great flexibility to produce information. A **database management system (DBMS)** is a comprehensive software tool that allows creation, maintenance, and manipulation of a database to produce relevant business information. By *integrated* we mean that the file records are logically related to one another so that *all* data on a topic can be retrieved by simple requests. The database management systems software represents the interface between the user and the computer's operating system and database (Figure 1).

Picture a typical corporate office with a desk, chairs, telephones, and a row of file cabinets along the wall. A wide variety of business data is stored in file cabinets. If the files have been carefully organized and maintained, then any piece of data that needs to be retrieved can usually be located quickly and removed. However, if the data has not been properly filed, some time and effort will be expended to find it. And, regardless of how carefully the files have been organized and maintained, you will always need to retrieve related pieces of data. For example, suppose you need to review the customer files for all invoices for payments due in excess of $2,500 and prepare a simple report. How would you accomplish this task? First, you would probably go through the customer files in alphabetical order, folder by folder. You would examine each invoice in the folders to determine if the amount is in excess of $2,500 and remove and copy each invoice that meets the criterion. You would then have to refile the copies you removed (and risk misfiling them). When you had examined all the customer folders and copied all the appropriate invoices, you would then review

FIGURE 1

DBMS software as interface. The database management system is the facilitator that allows the user to access and manipulate integrated data elements in a database.

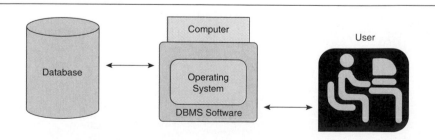

the copies and put together your report. Imagine how much time this could take. If there are a lot of customers, you would need to spend hours, if not days.

Now let's look at the situation in a different way. The environment is the same, except you have, instead of file cabinets, a microcomputer or a terminal and DBMS software that has access to a customer database file (Figure 2). In this file a row of customer data is referred to as a *record.* An individual piece of data within a record, such as a name, is referred to as a *field.* (See Figure 3 and Table 1 for a review of the filing and database terminology introduced in

Customer Name	Date	Item Ordered	Quantity Ordered	Invoice Amount
Arthene Ng	02/12/94	4065	6	2510.67
Pamela Robert	02/13/94	4128	7	1510.62
Jeff Arguello	02/13/94	4111	1	1905.00
Sylvia Arnold	02/14/94	4007	6	2950.93
Richard Mall	02/14/94	4019	1	63.55
Alan Steinberg	02/14/94	4021	3	1393.00
Harry Filbert	02/14/94	4106	2	940.56
Frances Chung	02/15/94	4008	5	2717.00
Bruce Chaney	02/15/94	4007	8	1720.00

Field   Record

File

FIGURE 2

Customer database file. This figure illustrates only a small section of our hypothetical customer file. Data stored electronically in a DBMS can be much more easily retrieved than data stored in filing cabinets.

FIGURE 3

Data hierarchy. The figures show how most of the data terms in Table 1 fit into the data hierarchy (first introduced in Chapter 5).

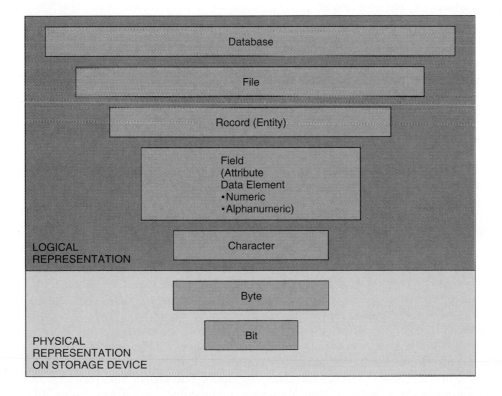

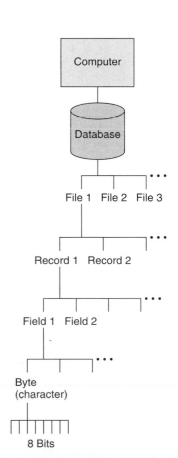

TABLE 1

Database Terminology

Alphanumeric (character) data: data composed of a combination of letters, numbers, and other symbols (like punctuation marks) that are not used for mathematical calculations

Bit: contraction of *binary digit*; either 1 ("on") or 0 ("off") in computerized (digitized) data representation

Character: the lowest level in the data hierarchy; usually one letter or numerical digit; also called byte (8 bits)

Data: the raw facts that make up information

Database: a large collection of stored, integrated (cross-referenced) records that can be maintained and manipulated with great flexibility; the top level in the data hierarchy

Entity: any tangible or intangible object or concept about which an organization wishes to store data; entities have attributes, such as name, color, and price

Field, or attribute, or data element: a group of related characters (*attribute* is also a column of a relation in a relational database, discussed later); the second-lowest level in the data hierarchy

File: a group of related records; the fourth level from the bottom in the data hierarchy

Information: data that has value to, or that has been interpreted by, the user

Key: a unique field within a record that uniquely identifies the record

Numeric data: data composed of numeric digits (numbers); used for mathematical calculations

Record: a group of related fields; the third level from the bottom in the data hierarchy (analogous to a *tuple*, or *row*, in a relational database, as described later)

Chapter 5.) To get the invoice data you need, you would do something like this:

▼ Turn on the computer and the printer.

▼ Start up the DBMS software.

▼ Give the command to "open up" the customer database file stored on your disk, which is similar in concept to manually opening up the customer drawer in a file cabinet.

▼ Give the command to search all the records in the database file and display copies of the records that meet your criterion (that is, the names of people with unpaid invoices greater than $2,500). If you were using dBASE IV, a popular microcomputer DBMS, the command would look something like:

```
LIST FOR INV _AMOUNT > 2500
```

If you were using SQL (Structured Query Language), the command would look like this:

```
SELECT NAME FROM CUSTOMER INV _AMOUNT FROM INVOICE
WHERE INV _AMOUNT > 2500
ORDER BY NAME
```

In response to this command, all the records in the file that have an invoice amount greater than $2,500 will be listed on the screen. (The SQL command would also sort the listing into alphabetical order by name.) This whole procedure would take only a few minutes for thousands of records.

The DBMS is a software tool designed to manage a large number of integrated, shared electronic "file cabinets." You describe the type of data you wish to store, and the DBMS creates the database file(s). The DBMS also provides an easy-to-use mechanism for storing, retrieving, maintaining, and manipulating the data.

In small businesses, databases may be both created and operated by the user. In moderate- to large-size businesses with minicomputer or mainframe computer systems, the corporate database is created by technical information specialists. Business users generate and extract data stored by the database management system.

Data Management Concepts

The DBMS approach to storing and retrieving data in computer-usable form has evolved to allow users to easily retrieve and update data that is in *more than one file*. To better explain the DBMS approach and its significance, we will first describe the traditional system it evolved from—the file management system.

File Management Systems

Computers were placed in commercial use in 1954, when General Electric Company purchased a UNIVAC (Universal Automatic Computer) for its research division. At first, the processing performed was straightforward. Applications software programs tended to be sequentially organized and stored in a single file on magnetic tape that contained all the elements of data required for processing. The term **file management system** was coined to describe this traditional approach to managing business data and information (Figure 4). However, file management systems did not provide the user with an easy way to group records within a file or to establish relationships among the records in different files. As disk storage became more cost-effective and its capacity grew, new software applications were developed to access disk-based files. The need to access data stored in more than one file was quickly recognized and posed increasingly complex programming requirements.

The most serious problems of file management systems involve:

▼ Data redundancy

▼ Updating files and maintaining data integrity

▼ Lack of program and data independence

In the case of **data redundancy,** the same data fields appear in many different files and often in different formats, which makes updating files difficult, time consuming, and prone to errors. For example, a course grades file and a tuition billing file may both contain a student's ID number, name, address, and telephone number. Obviously, if data fields are repeated often in different files, storage space is wasted.

Data redundancy creates a problem when it comes to **file updating.** When a data field needs to be changed—for example, student address—it must be updated in *all* the files in which it occurs. This is a tedious procedure. If some files are missed, data will be inconsistent. Inconsistent data leads to inaccurate information. When data is inconsistent, **data integrity** is not maintained—and reports will be produced with erroneous information. (Data integrity generally refers to the quality of the data—that is, to its accuracy, reliability, and timeliness. If data integrity is not maintained, data is no longer accurate, reliable, and/or timely.)

Another limitation of file management systems has to do with the lack of **program independence** and **data independence.** This lack of independence means that programs must be written by programmers to use a specific file format. This process takes a programmer a large amount of time and costs a company a great deal of money for program and data file maintenance. Program and data independence means that files are organized so that business programs

FIGURE 4

(a) Traditional file management approach. In old file management systems, some of the same data elements were repeated in different files. (b) In database management systems, data elements are integrated, thus eliminating data redundancy.

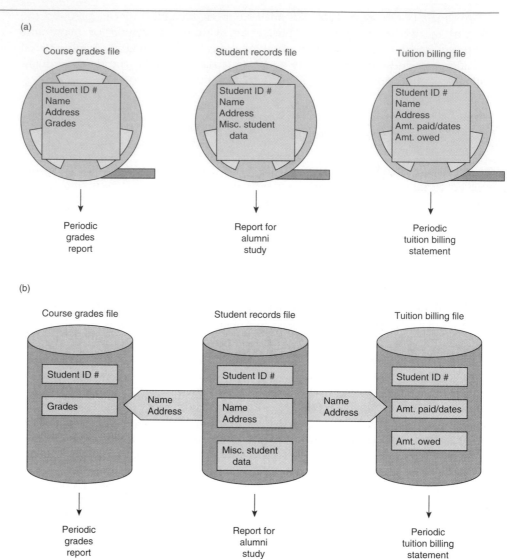

can be written to access data from the multiple files stored in the database. A change can be made in the program without having to change the data and vice versa.

To deal with these problems and the ever-growing demands for a flexible, easy-to-use mechanism for managing data, the concept of a database was developed.

Fundamentals of Database Management Systems

As we mentioned earlier, the term *database* describes a collection of related files that form an integrated base of data that can be accessed by a wide variety of application programs and user requests. In a database management system, data needs to be entered into the system only once. When the user instructs the program to sort data or compile a list, the program searches quickly through the data in memory (or in storage), making available needed data for the business task. The user's instructions do not change the original set of data in any way. Only authorized personnel, such as the database administrator, may change the data in the process of maintaining the database. Accessing data and maintaining the data are possible through the database management system (DBMS).

Hardware: Storage Counts

Storage capacity is crucial to the operation of a database management system. Even the many megabytes of hard disk storage in an efficient, modern microcomputer system can't handle the many gigabytes of data that move through some large corporations. However, not all organizations need minicomputer- or mainframe-based database management systems. Recent advances in the speed and the capacity of hard disk drives for microcomputers—plus the use of CD-ROM drives—have made microcomputer-based database management systems possible for some organizations.

Because database files represent an important business resource, they must be protected from damage, loss, and unauthorized use. The most common way to protect the corporate database from loss or damage is to periodically make backup copies of it. In large database systems, backup copies are usually made on one or more cartridges of magnetic tape. The backup process for large corporate databases requires the involvement of computer operations specialists. The most popular form of backup for microcomputer hard disks is the tape streamer, or streaming tape unit, which is also available in cartridges. These devices are small, fast, and so easy to use that the user can perform the backup operation unassisted.

Software: In Control

A database management system is an integrated set of software programs that provides all the necessary capabilities for building and maintaining database files, extracting the information required for making decisions, and formatting the information into structured reports. It is intended to:

▼ *Make data independent of the applications programs being used, so that it is easy to access and change.* For example, you create a student database with many student records. After some time, you decide to change the structure of the student database to include phone numbers. With a DBMS you can do this and still use the applications program you were using before you changed the database structure. This is possible because the data's organization is independent of the program being used.

▼ *Establish relationships among records in different files.* The user can obtain *all* data related to important data fields. For example, the user can obtain student name and address information from the student file at the same time as viewing the student's course information (course numbers and names) from the registration file because each file has the student's social security number (data field) in it.

▼ *Minimize data redundancy.* Because data is independent of the applications program being used, data needs to be stored only once. For example, the student data file can be accessed by both the billing applications program or the student grade averaging program.

▼ *Define the characteristics of the data.* Databases can be created that have data stored in them based on particular informational needs.

▼ *Manage file security.* For example, the DBMS can "examine" user requests and clear them for access to retrieve data, thus keeping data safe from unauthorized access.

▼ *Maintain data integrity.* Because data redundance is minimized, file updating is made easier and data consistency is improved. The DBMS ensures that updates are properly done.

Using DBMS software, users can request that a program be run to produce information in a predefined format or extract information in a specific way. For example, if you are employed by the school's registration department, you may need to review a report of the classes that currently have space available for registration purposes. For budget purposes, the manager of the school's finance division may want to use the same data to generate a report on courses that have low enrollment.

The easiest way to view a DBMS is to think of it as a layer of software that surrounds the database files (Figure 5). The DBMS software usually includes a query language, report writers, and utilities. Newer DBMS programs also offer graphics capabilities that make it even easier for users to run the program and graphically enhance the appearance of output reports—both hardcopy and soft-copy.

Query Language

Most users find a **query language** for data retrieval to be the most valuable aspect of DBMS software. Traditionally, business personnel and managers rely on the information provided by periodic reports. However, this creates a problem when a decision must be made *now* and the information required to make it will not be produced until the end of the week. The objective of a query language is to provide users with a simple, natural language structure (like English) to select records from a database and produce information on demand. To be effective, a query language must allow the user to phrase requests for information in a flexible fashion. For example, take a request for inventory information. Here are some examples of questions that the user could ask using a query language when a single file is involved:

▼   List all items in the inventory database for which the quantity on hand equals 10. (Immediate orders would have to be placed to restock these items.)

FIGURE 5

DBMS software. The software that comprises the functions of a database management system can be thought of as a layer that surrounds the database files. Among other things, this software provides the user interface, which allows the user to interact easily with the system.

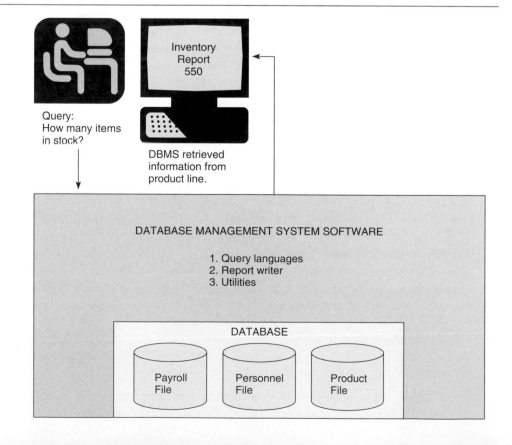

▼ List all items in the database for which the quantity on hand is less than or equal to the reorder point. (This information would be used to process regular orders for restocking inventory.)

Here are examples of questions that the user could ask using a query language when more than one file is involved:

▼ List the names and addresses of all customers who ordered items that were out of stock and now are in stock. (This would involve using the customer order file and the inventory file and would show a listing of all customers who should be notified by mail that the items they ordered are now available for pickup.)

▼ List the phone numbers of customers who ordered items that were out of stock and that aren't going to be restocked. (This would also involve using both the customer order file and the inventory file and would show a listing of all phone numbers of customers who should be notified that the item they ordered will no longer be carried in inventory.)

You, the user, can learn to use a typical query language effectively with about eight hours of instruction and practice. Once you have this skill, you can prepare a special report in a few minutes instead of several days or weeks. Structured Query Language (SQL) is the most commonly used query language in database management systems.

Report Writer

The **report writer** aspect of DBMS software simplifies the process of generating reports after querying the DBMS system for information. The procedure is fairly easy. Report headings, column headings for the items to be included in the report, as well as any totals, subtotals, or other calculations are easily specified (Figure 6). The report form can then be saved for future use.

Some DBMS software also includes **screen generators** to simplify the process of making data readily accessible to users. Screen generators display preformatted "forms" on the screen that users fill in to retrieve, modify, and/or add data.

Utilities

The utilities part of the DBMS software is used to maintain the database on an ongoing basis. This includes such tasks as:

FIGURE 6

DBMS-generated report

```
Page No.     1
01/01/94

            INVENTORY ITEMS
      QUALITY ON HAND < REORDER POINT

PRODUCT NUMBER DESCRIPTION       SUPPLIER

     202 HAMMERS                 A
     207 NAILS                   B
     213 WRENCHES                C
     202 SCREW DRIVERS           B
     309 BROOMS                  C
     310 MOPS                    A
     315 POWER CABLES            C
     300 EXTENSION CORDS         A
```

▼ Creating and maintaining the data dictionary (described in more detail later in the chapter)

▼ Removing records flagged for deletion. (Most DBMSs have built-in protection schemes to prevent users from accidentally deleting records.)

▼ Establishing control of access to portions of the database (protecting the database against unauthorized use)

▼ Providing an easy way to back up the database and recover data if the database is damaged

▼ Monitoring performance

▼ Preventing data corruption when multiple users attempt to access the same database simultaneously

▼ Reorganizing the data in the database into a predefined sort order to make access quicker. This is necessary after a database has had new records added and deleted.

Data Dictionaries and Transaction Logs

Once a DBMS has been implemented, two types of files are constantly in use besides the database files—the data dictionary and the transaction log.

The **data dictionary** is essentially a small database with information about the data and the data structure of a database. The information in the data dictionary varies from one DBMS to another. In general, the data dictionary maintains standard definitions of all data items including:

▼ What data is available

▼ Where the data is located

▼ Data attributes (descriptions)

▼ Who owns or is responsible for the data

▼ How the data is used

▼ Who is allowed to access the data for retrieval

▼ Who is allowed to update or change the data

▼ Relationships to other data items

▼ Security and privacy limitations

The dictionary is used constantly by the DBMS as a reference tool (Figure 7). When an application program requests elements of data as part of a query, the DBMS refers to the data dictionary for retrieving the data. The database administrator, whose job we'll discuss in more detail later, determines what the data dictionary contains.

The **transaction log** (Figure 7) contains a complete record of all activity systems for minicomputers and mainframes usually build the transaction log automatically.

Database Models

Three models are used to organize a database:

1. Hierarchical
2. Network
3. Relational

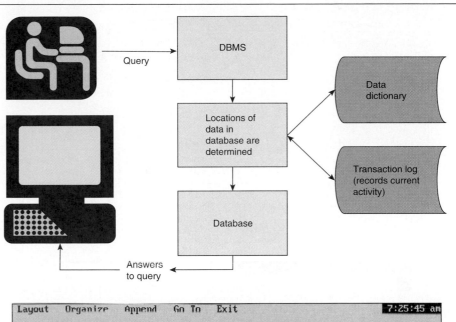

FIGURE 7

Data dictionary and transaction log

These three models have evolved gradually as users and computer specialists gained experience in using database management systems. They differ in terms of the cost of implementation, speed, degree of data redundancy, ease with which they can satisfy information requirements, and ease with which they can be updated.

In use since the late 1960s, the hierarchical and network database models were first developed and used principally on mainframe computers. The concepts behind the relational database model were pioneered in the early 1970s. The relational database model, which takes advantage of large-capacity direct access storage devices, was developed for mainframe and minicomputer systems but is now also used on microcomputers. The relational database model is rapidly replacing the hierarchical and network models.

Hierarchical Database Model

In the **hierarchical database model,** data is organized into related groups much like a family tree (Figure 8). The model comprises two types of records—par-

FIGURE 8

Hierarchical database model for the Moser Corporation. In this database model, which looks somewhat like a family tree, a parent record can have many child records, but each child record can have only one parent record. The root record is the topmost record.

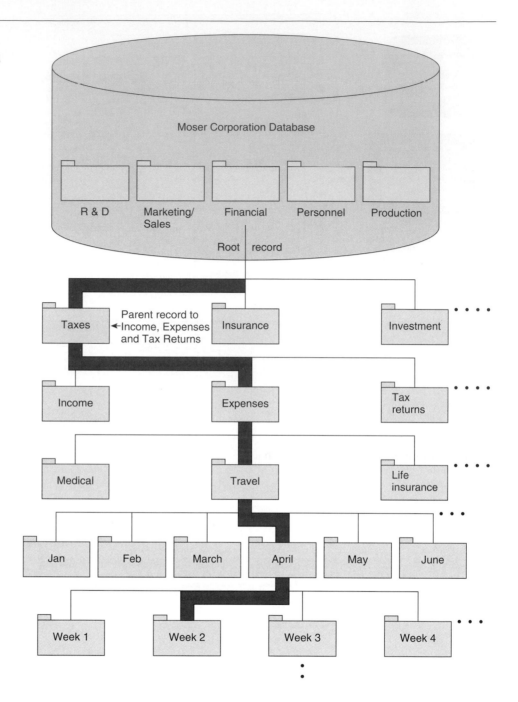

ent records and child records. **Parent records** are higher in the structure of the model than **child records.** Each "child" can have only one "parent"; that is, each record may have only one record above it. When a child becomes a parent, it may have many records below it. The record at the highest level, or top of the "tree," is called the root record. The **root record,** which is the key to the model, connects the various branches.

To store or retrieve a record in a hierarchical model, the DBMS begins at the root occurrence and moves downward through each of the occurrences until the correct record is located. There is no connection between separate branches in this type of model. See, for example, the route that is followed in Figure 8 to locate the record of travel expenses for the second week in April.

The primary advantage of the hierarchical database model is the ease with which data can be stored and retrieved, as well as the ease with which data can be extracted for reporting purposes.

The main disadvantage of this type of database model is that records in separate groups cannot be directly related without a great deal of effort. In Figure 8, for example, medical, travel, and life insurance are separate groups. The Moser Corporation might want to compare by month and by year the different expense amounts of each category to answer such questions as: "What percentage is each yearly expense amount of the total of all expenses for the year?" or "What is the average expense amount for each month and for the year?" But the user is confined to retrieving data that can be obtained from the established hierarchical links among records.

Another disadvantage is deleting all the child records when a parent is deleted from the model.

In addition, modifying a hierarchical database structure is complex and requires a trained and experienced programmer who knows all the physical connections that exist between records. Another restriction is the inability to implement hierarchical models without a great deal of redundancy.

Network Database Model

The **network database model** (Figure 9) is somewhat similar to the hierarchical model, but each record can have more than one parent. This model overcomes the principal limitation of the hierarchical model because it establishes relationships between records in different groups. Any record can be related to any other data element.

Figure 9 shows, as part of a network database model, the expense types and expense periods for the first quarter of a year for the Moser Corporation. With this type of model, it would be easy to compare weekly or monthly expense amounts or to determine what percentage travel expenses are of all expenses for the first quarter.

The primary advantage of the network database model is its ability to provide sophisticated logical relationships among the records. However, as in the hierarchical model, the user is limited to retrieving data that can be accessed using the pre-established links between records. IDMS is an example of a network database model still being used on some mainframes.

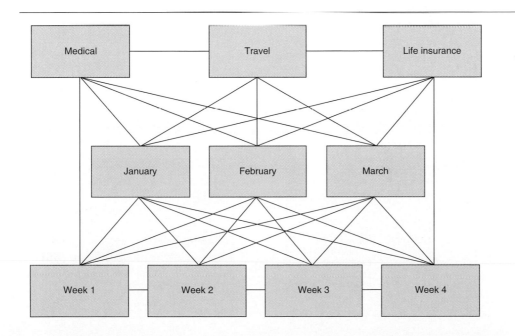

FIGURE 9

Network database model for the Moser Corporation

Relational Database Model

The **relational database model** (Figure 10) is made up of many tables, called *relations*, in which related data elements are stored. The relations—similar in concept to files—are made up of rows and columns, and they provide data to the user about an *entity* class. A row (similar to a record) is called a *tuple*, and a column (similar to a field) is called an *attribute*. All related tables must have a common data item, or key field. A **key field**, or *candidate key attribute*, is an item of data that is assigned to uniquely identify each record, or tuple. Thus, any data stored in one table can be linked with any data stored in any related table. For example, the key used to relate the top two tables in Figure 10 is 1; the key for the bottom two tables is Publicity. The main objective of the relational database model is to allow complex logical relationships between records to be expressed in a simple fashion.

Relational databases are useful because they can cross-reference data and retrieve data automatically. Users do not have to be aware of any "structure" to use a relational database, and they can use it with little effort or training.

The main disadvantage of the relational model is that database searches can be time-consuming. Developed for mainframe and minicomputer systems—DB2 is an example—the relational model has become a popular database model for microcomputer-based database management systems—for example, Paradox.

Designing a Database

Many users in the microcomputer environment will design a database and will actually build and implement it using a microcomputer DBMS. However, users are less involved in database design and development when the database man-

---

FIGURE 10

Relational database model

Division Number / Division Name Pair	
Division Number	Division Name
1	East Coast
2	West Coast
3	North Atlantic
4	Central South
5	Mid-West
6	Southwest
7	North Central

Division Number / Department Letter Pair	
Division Number	Department Letter
1	A
2	B
2	C
3	D
4	E
4	F
5	G
6	H
	I

Department Letter / Department Name Pair	
Department Letter	Department Name
A	Publicity
B	Database Administration
C	Personnel
D	Research and Development
E	Production
F	Order Fulfillment
G	Information Center

Department Name / Employee Name Pair	
Department Name	Employee Name
Publicity	Biggs, Linda
	Cruces, Luis
	Judd, Karen
Database Administration	Ng, Arlene
	Bosworth, Joanne
	Liu, Mark
	Salto, Gilda
	Washington, Carl

agement system is intended to be used in minicomputer and mainframe computer environments. (Users are highly involved in defining what data needs to be stored in the database, though.) In minicomputer and mainframe situations, trained and experienced information system specialists design and develop the systems.

Matching the Design to the Organization

Most users working with microcomputer-based DBMS software focus on a very specific set of objectives and information processing needs—their own. For many small applications this is a satisfactory approach. However, the objectives must be broader when working with a large corporation, a large computer system, and more complex and sophisticated DBMS software. And the plans for the use of the database management system must be integrated with the long-range plans for the company's total information system. The information processing needs of the entire corporation must be considered to build a corporate database that facilitates collecting, maintaining, and sharing data among all organizational units. Once the general information needs have been established, the design process can proceed. This process usually comprises two distinct phases of activity—the logical design phase and the physical design phase.

Logical Design

Logical database design refers to *what* the database is as opposed to *how* it operates; in other words, the logical design is a detailed description of the database model from the users' perspective rather than the technical perspective. The logical design of a database involves defining user information needs, analyzing data element requirements and logical groupings, finalizing the design, and creating the data dictionary. The major focus is on identifying every element of data necessary to produce the required information systems reports and on the relationship among the records.

Physical Design

Once the logical design of the database is ready, the next step is physical design. The **physical database design** specifies exactly *how* the data will be arranged and stored on the direct access storage devices allocated for DBMS use. The objective of the physical design is to store data so that it can be updated and retrieved as quickly and efficiently as possible. DBMS users are not involved in the physical design of the DBMS, since that is determined by the type of DBMS package they have purchased for their microcomputers or that is running on a large computer system.

Database Administration

The effective use of a database within an organization requires a great deal of cooperation and coordination. User requirements and needs throughout an organization need to be frequently reviewed, and the overall security and integrity of the database must be ensured. Organizations working with DBMSs quickly recognized the need for an individual or a group of individuals to coordinate all related database activities and to control the database. A **database administrator (DBA)** undertakes these functions.

Why Administer?

As we mentioned earlier, developing and implementing a corporatewide database is a major task that requires management's complete support, substantial time from designers and users, and often large sums of money. This task needs to be coordinated. In addition, the data in the database often represents the company's most precious resource: it must be managed well, so that it is not misused or damaged.

The Job of the Database Administrator

The responsibilities for administering the database activities within an organization are usually assigned to an individual or a small group, depending on the size of the organization and the scope and complexity of the database. The database administrator has six major responsibilities.

1. *Database design.* The DBA plays a key role in both the logical and the physical design phases. He or she guides the definition of the database content and the creation of the data dictionary, as well as setting data classification and coding procedures and backup and restart/recovery procedures.

2. *Database implementation and operation.* The DBA guides the use of the DBMS on a daily basis. Among other things, this includes adding and deleting data, controlling access to data, detecting and repairing losses, instituting restart/recovery procedures when necessary, and assigning space used on secondary storage devices.

3. *Coordination with users.* The DBA receives and reviews user requests for additional DBMS support that have been forwarded by programming analysts. The administrator establishes feasibility, resolves redundant or conflicting requests, and assists in the process of establishing priorities for the requests. In addition, the DBA is responsible for establishing and enforcing organizationwide DBMS standards for such things as techniques for accessing data, formats in which data elements will be stored, and data element names.

4. *Backup and recovery.* The DBA is responsible for preparing a plan for periodically backing up the database(s) and for establishing procedures for recovering from the failure of the DBMS software or related hardware components.

5. *Performance monitoring.* The DBA constantly monitors the performance of the DBMS using specialized software to calculate and record operating statistics. If a problem occurs, such as slowdown in responsiveness, the DBA must identify the problem and take steps to improve the performance.

6. *System security.* The DBA is responsible for designing and implementing a system that controls users' access to the database files and determines which DBMS operations can be performed, as well as which applications programs can be accessed. This system often involves the assignment of user identification codes and passwords.

Organizations with a well-organized and well-staffed database administration department are much more successful with their database management systems than organizations without such a department.

Advantages and Limitations of the DBMS

The principal advantages of the DBMS approach include:

▼ *Minimization of data redundancy.* More storage becomes available when maintenance of redundant data elements among traditionally separate application files is minimized.

▼ *Easy file updating and maximization of data integrity.* In traditional systems in which the same element of data was kept on several different files, ensuring that all copies of the data element were updated when changes were made was a problem. When a data field needed to be changed, it had to be updated in *all* the files in which it occurred. If some files were missed, data became inconsistent. When data is inconsistent, data integrity is not maintained, and reports will be produced with erroneous information. Data is no longer accurate, reliable, and/or timely. DBMSs make updating files much easier and so improve the consistency of data, thus ensuring data integrity.

▼ *Data independence and simplification of program maintenance.* In a DBMS the programs are much more independent of the data than in traditional file processing systems. Previously, programs had to include a substantial amount of information about the format and structure of the fields and records in each file accessed. In a DBMS, this information is contained in the data dictionary.

▼ *Increased user productivity.* The ability of a DBMS to respond quickly to user requests for additional information without involving the user in technical language manipulation encourages faster and more efficient work. The report generators and query languages associated with database management systems make them easy to use.

▼ *Increased security.* Control of access to and use of the database is easily established. With traditional file processing systems, the data was too fragmented for effective security to be exercised.

▼ *Standardization of data definitions.* Before database management systems, each application program could define similar elements of data with different names. However, the use of data dictionaries standardizes the names and descriptions of data elements.

There are disadvantages to using a database management system:

▼ Database management systems are complex; extensive planning and a substantial amount of technical expertise are needed to implement and maintain a system.

▼ The costs associated with the development and operation of a corporatewide DBMS can be substantial in terms of software and hardware acquisition, technical support personnel, and operations personnel.

▼ The consolidation of an entire business's information resources into a DBMS can create a high level of vulnerability. A natural disaster, a fire, or even a hardware- or software-related problem can cause the loss of the current version of the database files. This could be fatal for a business unless proper precautions are taken. A very thorough framework of policies and procedures must be established to ensure that backup copies of the database files are made on a regular basis, that a transaction log is maintained, and that documentation exists for recovery procedures.

Who Owns the Database?

Before ending this chapter we need to say a few words about who owns a given type of database. Small and large databases can all be classified as individual, company, distributed, or proprietary.

The *individual database* is basically a microcomputer database used by one person. The data is usually stored on a large-capacity hard disk. A sales representative, for example, who is on the road a lot, may build and maintain an individual database of customer and sales information.

The *company database,* or *shared database,* is shared by the users of one company in one location. The company owns the database. The data is usually stored on a minicomputer or a mainframe and managed by a database administrator. Users are linked to the database through terminals or microcomputer workstations.

The *distributed database* is shared by the users of one company, which owns the database, but the data is stored in several locations linked by a variety of communications networks.

The *proprietary database* is a huge database that functions as an information service, such as CompuServe, Prodigy, and Dow Jones News/Retrieval. The proprietor owns the database in this case. To access this type of proprietary database, the user needs a modem to hook the computer up to the service via the phone lines. (Fees are charged by the information service.) Another type of proprietary database can be "licensed" (purchased to use for a specified period of time) by computer users. For example, ABI's Business Lists-on-Disc (LOD) contains data on 9.2 million American businesses. It allows users to search for records by company name, type of business, company size, geographic area, and use of Yellow Pages ads in phone books. LOD comes on CD-ROM and works with MS-DOS microcomputers. Such electronic database directories can be useful for direct mail, telemarketing, directory assistance, and personal sales calls.

FIGURE 11

Popular Microcomputer DBMS packages.

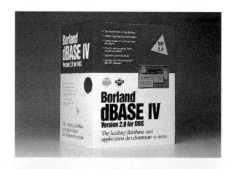
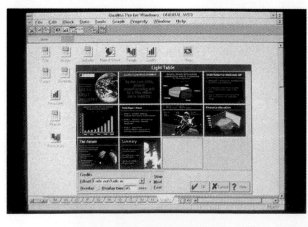
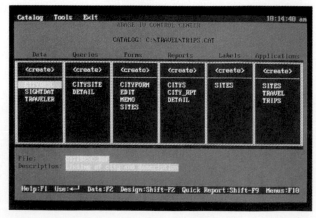

I f you're a white-collar worker who sits behind a desk—or even sits behind a steering wheel making sales calls on your mobile phone—it's fairly certain you'll be using computer technology.

Consider real estate sales. Century 21, an international organization of independent real estate agents, developed a system called Century Net that helps agents move away from slips of paper and lists in notebooks. Listing agents enter names and properties for sale from several directories. Sales agents list likely prospects. This database can then be used to generate lists of prospective buyers and generate personalized form letters. It can also be used to make telephone contacts: the sales agent enters a name, the computer dials the contact's telephone, and the date and time of the call are displayed on the screen. The system can also be used to generate reminders for important dates or follow-up calls. The use of modem-equipped laptops only expands the possibilities. When calling on prospective clients, agents can use the machines to do investment analysis for customers, comparing loan interest rates and showing how buying a home compares with other forms of investment.

Small investors themselves have also turned to computers for assistance. The old-time way of playing the stock market was to get stock prices from the newspapers, read investment newsletters, and place orders by phone to one's stockbroker. Now, using a computer in his or her home office, an investor can obtain up-to-the-minute stock quotes and, through modem and telephone links, press a button to transmit buy and sell orders to a broker. Some investors use their computers to do complex stock analysis. For instance, AIQ Systems distilled the knowledge of several investment experts to devise a series of rules that rate up to 500 stocks on a 1–100, up-or-down scale. When there is a 100 rating on the up side, an investor should definitely buy a stock; the same number on the down side indicates one should sell. Making money means paying taxes, of course. Many taxpayers turn to tax professionals to prepare their tax returns. Most accountants, however, turn to outside computer services for help with calculations and paperwork. Each year, about 20 service bureaus across the country, such as Computax and Accutax, process millions of tax forms. Accountants collect information from their clients, work out the tax strategy, and then send the numbers to the service bureau, which eliminates a lot of the accountant's most labor-intensive work.

Outside auditors—those analysts who go over company accounts to make sure that accounting principles are being followed, that supplies arrive when ordered, and that vendors' bills are accurate—have found that they are no longer "bean counters." With portable computers to gather financial data in hours instead of days, auditors can become helpful business advisors who find areas for cutting costs, spot deadbeat customers, and supply important financial projections to make essential business decisions. For instance, a Peat Marwick auditor performing an annual look at the books for a chain store operator was able to use microcomputers to print out 15 different financing scenarios in one day, thus providing a means for ensuring future operations.

▼ *Database management systems (DBMSs)* are comprehensive software tools that allow users to create, maintain, and manipulate an integrated base of data.

▼ *File management systems* used to be the only way of managing data and files. In these systems, data was stored in a series of unrelated files on tape or disk. The major problems associated with file management systems are:

1. *Data redundancy.* The same data appeared in more than one file.

2. *Tedious updating procedures.* Because the same data appeared in many places, updating files was time-consuming.

3. *Poor data integrity.* If some redundant data elements were missed during file updating, data became inconsistent and caused inaccurate information to be produced.

4. *Lack of data and program independence.* Programmers could not use the data file to develop new programs because the data and the programs were restricted by existing formats. To update either the applications program or the data file became a major task.

▼ DBMSs were developed to:

1. Make data independent of the programs, so that it is easy to access and change

2. Minimize data redundancy

3. Establish relationships among records in different files

4. Define data characteristics

5. Manage file directories

6. Maintain data integrity

7. Provide a means of securing access to the database

8. Make it easier to access data for reports

▼ DBMS software often uses a *query language* as an interface between the user and the system. This interface allows users to easily ask questions of the DBMS and obtain information to answer the questions and produce reports.

▼ DBMS software also includes capabilities to simplify *report writing* and maintain the database (utilities) as well as to allow different application programs to use the database.

▼ During the design of the database, a *data dictionary* is constructed that contains all the data descriptions used by the DBMS to locate and retrieve data.

▼ The DBMS also can include a *transaction log* of current activity. This log can be used to update necessary backup copies of the database in case of failure of or damage to the operating database system.

▼ A DBMS is usually modeled after one of three structures:

1. Hierarchical

2. Network

3. Relational

These models differ in terms of the cost of implementation, speed, degree of data redundancy, ease with which they can satisfy information requirements, and ease with which they can be updated.

▼ The *hierarchical database model* resembles a family tree; the records are organized in a one-to-many relationship, meaning that one parent record can have many child records. Records are retrieved from the hierarchical model by starting at the root record at the top and moving down through the structure. There is no connection between separate branches.

▼ The *network database model* is similar to the hierarchical model, but each child record can have more than one parent record, which allows relationships between records in different groups. Also, access to the database can be made from a number of points—not just from the top.

▼ The *relational database model* is made up of many tables, called *relations,* in which related data elements are stored. The data elements are in rows, called *tuples,* and columns, called *attributes.* The main objective of the relational database model is to allow complex logical relationships between records to be expressed in a simple fashion.

▼ In general, the hierarchical and network models are less expensive to implement and allow faster access to data. However, they are more difficult to update and aren't as effective at satisfying information requirements as the relational model can be. Relational database models are rapidly replacing the other two database models.

▼ Database design usually consists of two phases: logical design and physical design. The *logical design* refers to *what* the database is as opposed to how it operates. The logical design is a detailed description of the database from the users' perspective. The *physical design* specifies exactly *how* the data will be arranged and stored on the storage devices.

▼ The process of database design is usually carried out exclusively by specialists. However, users may have occasion to set up small databases for microcomputers. Users also participate in defining the data during the logical design of a database for a large computer system.

▼ The main responsibilities of a database administrator include:

1. Guiding database design

2. Overseeing database implementation and operation

3. Coordinating users

4. Backing up and recovering files

5. Monitoring performance

6. Setting up and maintaining system security

▼ In general, the main advantages of database management systems are:

1. Minimization of data redundancy

2. Increased ease of file updating

3. Increased data independence and simplification of program and maintenance

4. Increased user productivity and efficiency

5. Increased security

6. Standardization of data definitions

▼ The main disadvantages are:

1. Complexity

2. High cost of implementation and personnel costs

3. Vulnerability of consolidated business data in a central database

KEY TERMS

child record, p. 11.12
database, p. 11.2
database administrator (DBA), p. 11.16
database management system
  (DBMS), p. 11.2
data dictionary, p. 11.10
data independence, p. 11.5
data integrity, p. 11.5

data redundancy, p. 11.5
file management system, p. 11.5
file updating, p. 11.5
hierarchical database model, p. 11.11
key field, p. 11.14
logical database design, p. 11.15
network database model, p. 11.13
parent record, p. 11.12

physical database design, p. 11.15
program independence, p. 11.5
query language, p. 11.8
relational database model, p. 11.14
report writer, p. 11.9
root record, p. 11.12
screen generator, p. 11.9
transaction log, p. 11.10

EXERCISES

SELF-TEST

1. An individual piece of data within a record is called a

   _____.

2. If an element of data in a database needs to be changed, it must be changed in

   all the files in order for data _____ to be maintained.

3. A group of related records is called a _____.

4. *Data redundancy* means that an element of data (field) is repeated in many different files in a database. (true/false)

5. Microcomputers always had the storage capacity to handle database management systems. (true/false)

6. If you have a collection of related records that forms an integrated base of data that can be accessed by a wide variety of applications programs and user

   requests, then you have a _____.

7. DBMS software can manage file access by "clearing" users through the use of passwords. (true/false)

8. The aspect of DBMS software that simplifies the process of generating reports is

   called a _____ _____.

9. The most sophisticated database model that allows complex logical relationships

   among records in many different files is the _____
   database model.

10. A microcomputer-based database owned by one person is called a/an

    _____ database.

11. Key fields, or candidate keys, are used to relate, or link, tables in a relational database. (true/false)

12. Old file-handling methods provided the user with an easy way to establish relationships among records in different files. (true/false)

13. A/An _____ allows the user to phrase requests for information from a database in very flexible fashion.

14. A special file in the DBMS called the _____ maintains standard definitions of all data items within the scope of the database.

15. dBASE III, dBASE IV, and Paradox are popular microcomputer DBMS packages. (true/false)

16. Ensuring backup and recovery of a database is not one of the functions of a database administrator. (true/false)

17. The _____ contains a complete record of all activity that affected the contents of a database during the course of a transaction period.

Solutions: (1) field; (2) integrity; (3) file; (4) true; (5) false; (6) database; (7) true; (8) report writer; (9) relational; (10) individual; (11) true; (12) false; (13) query language; (14) data dictionary; (15) true; (16) false; (17) transaction log

MULTIPLE-CHOICE QUESTIONS

1. Which of the following hardware components is the most important to the operation of a database management system?

    a. high-resolution video display

    b. printer

    c. high-speed, large-capacity storage units

    d. plotter

    e. mouse

2. Database management systems are intended to:

    a. increase data redundancy

    b. establish relationships among records in different files

    c. manage file access

    d. maintain data integrity

    e. achieve data independence

3. Which of the following is a part of DBMS software?

    a. programming language

    b. query language

    c. utilities

    d. report writer

    e. all the above

4. Which of the following contains a complete record of all activity that affected the contents of a database during a certain period of time?

    a. report writer

    b. query language

    c. data manipulation language

    d. transaction log

    e. file management system

5. Which of the following is a serious problem of file management systems?

    a. difficult to update

    b. lack of data integrity

    c. data redundancy

    d. program dependence

    e. all the above

6. Which of the following is not a database administrator's function?

    a. designing database

    b. backing up the database

    c. monitoring database performance

    d. writing the DBMS software

    e. coordinating users

Solutions: (1) c; (2) b, c, d, e; (3) b, c, d; (4) d; (5) e; (6) d

SHORT-ANSWER QUESTIONS

1. Why is a database management system important to many organizations?

2. What are the three main problems with old file management systems?

3. What is a query language in a DBMS?

4. What does the data dictionary in a DBMS provide?

5. What used to be the main limitation to microcomputer-based DBMSs?

6. What is the difference between a distributed database and a proprietary database?

7. Give three main advantages of a DBMS over old file-handling approaches; give three main disadvantages.

8. Name four functions of a database administrator.

9. What is the main difference between the logical design and the physical design of a database?

10. Why are microcomputer DBMS users usually involved in the logical design of the database but not in the physical design?

PROJECTS

1. Interview someone who works with or manages a database at your school or university. What types of records make up the database, and which departments use it? What types of transactions do these departments enact? Which database structure is used? What are the types and sizes of the storage devices? Was the software custom-written?

2. What types of databases do you think would include information about yourself? Prepare a brief summary.

3. Contact TRW Credit, P.O. Box 14008, Orange, CA 92613, and ask for a credit report in your name (the report comes from their huge database). If you are in their database, are there any mistakes in the report? If so, how do you think the incorrect data came to be in your file? (Be sure to inquire about any costs involved before you tell TRW to send the report.)

4. People's resistance to change, sometimes called *social inertia,* may come about simply because change is stressful to many people. Employees in organizations undergoing change from old, familiar procedures to new, computer-based procedures often resist the efforts of trainers and administrators to institute the new programs. If you were a new database administrator in a large company converting to a new computer-based DBMS, what are some things you would tell people to lessen their resistance?

5. Look through magazines such as *PC Computing, PC Magazine, PC World, MacWorld,* and *MacUser* for microcomputer DBMS ads. Make a list of the functions advertised to help the user and also list the hardware requirements mentioned for each one. How do you think you could use a microcomputer DBMS in your profession, job, or other activities?

6. A number of on-line information services provide databases of job openings and also post users' resumes. Users with microcomputers and modems can (for a fee) scan job listings and reply electronically, with their resumes, to the groups offering jobs they are interested in. Following are a few information services that offer this job-hunting assistance.

   Adnet—through Prodigy (800-PRO-DIGY); GEnie (800-638-9636); and Compuserve (800-848-8199)
   Dialog's Career Placement Registry (800-334-2564)
   Job Information Services (JIS) (904-488-9180)
   Capsule Online Job Listing (512-250-8127)
   College Recruitment Database (317-872-2045)

   Contact a few of these information services and request brochures and any other information on their career placement databases. Give a short report on the procedures and potential advantages involved in using such databases.

Management Information Systems

*T*o be functional, systems and databases need to be tied clearly to organizational goals, objectives, and plans. Indeed, data and systems have no meaning until they are put into the context of what an organization or a business does. To be useful as a resource—just as people and money are resources for a company—data and data processing systems must be managed *according to a company's needs. Management information systems provide the means and the methods to manage the components of the computer-based information cycle—hardware, software, data/information, procedures, and people—as well as its four phases—input, processing, storage, output.*

PREVIEW

When you have completed this chapter, you will be able to:

▼ Explain what a basic management information system is and describe its role in the organization

▼ Describe the levels of management, the five basic functions of managers, and the types of decisions typically made at each level

▼ Distinguish among transaction processing systems, management information systems for middle management, decision support systems, and executive information systems

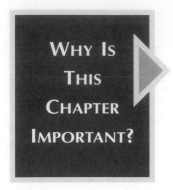

*I*nformation technology can ruin our lives unless we think of ways to get it under control. Without an organized approach to managing information, we may drown in an ocean of available information, unable to make decisions. Do these statements sound farfetched? They may have seemed so only a few years ago, but today, because of the fast pace of computer hardware and software development, they sound accurate. Although knowledge may be power, we must remember that information does not equal knowledge. And, for knowledge to be useful, it must be integrated into a task.

What should managers do to change an information technology into an intelligence technology—to put knowledge to work to assist with decision making and establishing efficient, productive, and high-quality business operations? In other words, how can users of an information system do their jobs better and not just shuffle overwhelming amounts of data and information from input to storage, from storage to processing and back to storage, from processing to output? The answer is: through management information systems. By understanding the principles of information management, users can help exploit technology to accomplish business and professional goals. As more and more hardware, software, and data are shared by multiple users, users are becoming more and more involved in the on-line functioning and management of the entire information system.

Information Systems: What They Are, How They Work

Chapter 2 described the computer-based information system as comprising five parts—hardware, software, data/information, procedures, and people. The fourth component includes manual and computerized procedures and standards for processing data into usable information. A *procedure* is a specific sequence of steps performed to complete one or more information processing activities. In some organizations, these processing procedures are carried out only by the staff; in others they are carried out by a combination of the staff and the computer specialists.

If you walk into a busy discount consumer-products showroom, stand in a corner, and observe what takes place, you will probably see the following kinds of activities: Customers come in and browse around, looking at the display cases. Some customers decide to buy items and begin to fill out order forms. If they are completed properly, the order forms are taken at the counter by a clerk and placed into a *queue*—that is, in line to be processed. If an order form is not complete, the clerk asks the customer questions and completes it. Then a stock person takes the completed order forms into the stockroom or warehouse and returns with the goods. A clerk takes each order form, marks it "filled," and rings up the sale on the cash register. All these activities form a procedure that is part of the *sales order entry system* (Figure 1).

A business is made up of many procedures, grouped logically into systems. The types of information systems found in companies vary according to the nature and the structure of the business. However, the systems commonly found in many businesses include payroll, personnel, accounting, and inventory.

Businesses receive data from a variety of sources, including customers who purchase products or services, vendors from whom supplies are ordered, banks,

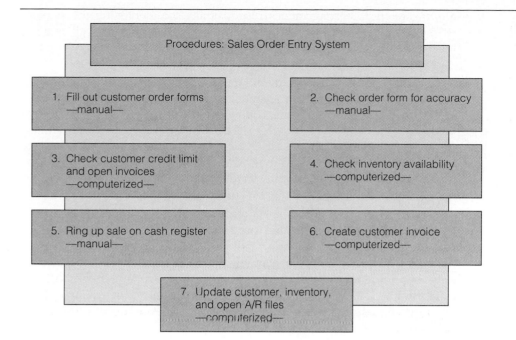

FIGURE 1

This group of related procedures makes up a simple sales order entry system. (A/R = accounts receivable.)

government agencies, and insurance companies—to name just a few. Information systems help organizations process all this data into *useful* and *complete* information. One of the most important purposes of a business's information system, then, is to satisfy the knowledge requirements of management.

What Is Management?

Management often refers to those individuals in an organization who are responsible for providing leadership and direction in the areas of planning, organizing, staffing, supervising, and controlling business activities. These five functions, which are the primary tasks of management, may be defined as follows:

1. *Planning* activities require the manager to formulate goals and objectives and develop short- and long-term plans to achieve these goals. For example, an office manager must work with top management to formulate a plan that satisfies the short- and long-term needs of the organization for office space; the vice president of marketing must take many factors into account when planning short-term advertising campaigns and activities aimed at opening up new long-term markets.

2. Management's responsibility for *organizing* includes the development of an organizational structure and a framework of standards, procedures, and policies designed to carry out ongoing business activities. For instance, top management must decide on the type and number of divisions and departments in the company and evaluate the effectiveness of the structure; it may decide to combine the personnel and the payroll departments to save money. Office managers establish working procedures, such as "Working overtime must be approved by the department supervisor in advance."

3. *Staffing* refers to management's responsibility for identifying the personnel needs of the organization and selecting the personnel, as well as training staff. Many companies have personnel managers to take charge of these activities.

4. *Supervising* refers to management's responsibility to provide employees with the supervision, guidance, and counseling necessary to keep them highly motivated and working productively toward the achievement of company objectives. This includes the recognition of good work, perhaps through certificates or bonuses, and concrete suggestions about how to improve performance. Companywide educational seminars may also be held to upgrade employees' knowledge of the company in general or perhaps to help them deal with stress and improve their health.

5. *Controlling* refers to management's responsibility to monitor organizational and economic performance and the business environment so that steps can be taken to improve performance and profits and modify plans as necessary in response to the marketplace. This includes keeping alert to new opportunities in the marketplace and recognizing new business opportunities. Many new computer software products, for example, have been developed because software companies are ever watchful for potential markets.

Each primary management function involves making decisions, and information is required to make good decisions. Thus, to fulfill its responsibilities, management must set up information systems and subsystems. And these systems must all be designed to manage change and innovation.

What Is a Management Information System?

A **management information system (MIS)** comprises computer-based processing and/or manual procedures that provide useful, complete, and timely information. This information must support management decision making in a rapidly changing business environment. The MIS system must supply managers with information quickly, accurately, and completely.

The approaches that companies take to develop information systems for management differ depending on the structure and management style of the organization. MIS systems enable *information resource management* (*IRM*). However, the scope of an MIS is generally companywide, and it serves managers at all three traditional levels:

1. Low-level (operational) management

2. Middle (tactical) management

3. Upper, or top (strategic), management

The primary objective of the MIS is to satisfy the need that managers have for information that is (1) *more summarized and relevant to the specific decisions that need to be made* than the information normally produced in an organization and that is (2) *available soon enough to be of value in the decision-making process*. The information flows up and down through the three levels of management and is made available in various types of reports.

Levels of Management: What Kinds of Decisions Are Made?

Each level of management can be distinguished by the types of decisions made, the time frame considered in the decisions, and the types of report information needed to make decisions (Table 1 and Figure 2).

TABLE 1

A Comparison of the Information Systems at the Operational, Tactical, and Strategic Management Levels

SUMMARY CLASSIFICATION OF INFORMATION SYSTEMS			
CHARACTERISTIC	OPERATIONAL	TACTICAL	STRATEGIC
Frequency	Regular, repetitive	Mostly regular	Often ad hoc (as needed)
Dependability of results	Expected results	Some surprises may occur	Results often contain surprises
Time period covered	The past	Comparative	Future
Level of detail	Very detailed	Summaries of data	Summaries of data
Source of data	Internal	Internal and external	Internal and external
Nature of data	Highly structured	Some unstructured data (semistructured)	Highly unstructured
Accuracy	Highly accurate data	Some subjective data used	Highly subjective data
Typical user	First-line supervisors	Middle managers	Top management
Level of decision	Task-oriented	Control and resource allocation oriented	Goal-oriented

Adapted from R. Schultheis and M. Sumner, *Management Information Systems: The Manager's View*, 2nd. ed. (Homewood, IL: Richard D. Irwin, 1992), p. 329.

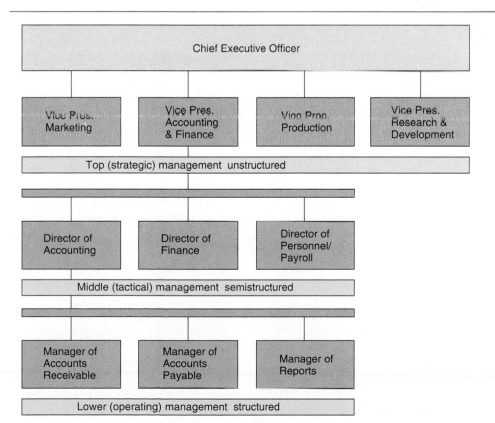

(a)

FIGURE 2

Three levels of management, three kinds of decisions. Different types of decisions are made depending on the level of management. The higher a manager is in an organization's hierarchy, the more decisions he or she must make from unstructured information. The four basic business functions or departments that top managers control are marketing, accounting and finance, production, and research and development. (a) This part of the figure shows the organizational hierarchy from a vertical perspective, focusing on the department of accounting and finance. (*continued*)

FIGURE 2
(continued)

(b) This shows the oraniza-
tional hierarchy as a pyramid,
with fewer managers at higher
levels of management.

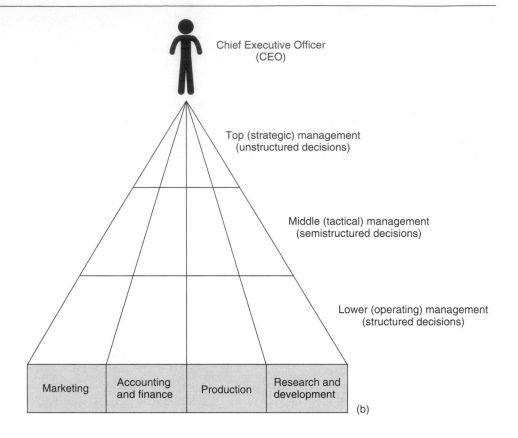

(b)

Operational Management

The lowest—and the largest—level of management, **operational management,** deals mostly with decisions that cover a relatively narrow time frame. Operating management, also called *supervisory management,* actualizes the plans of middle management and controls daily operations—the day-to-day activities that keep the organization humming. Examples of operating managers are the warehouse manager in charge of inventory restocking and the materials manager responsible for seeing that all necessary materials are on hand in a manufacturing firm to produce the product being manufactured. Most decisions at this level require easily defined information about current status and activities within the basic business functions—for example, the information needed to decide whether to restock inventory. This information is generally given to low-level managers in **detail reports** that contain specific information about routine activities. These reports are structured. The form of a structured report can usually be predetermined. Daily business operations data is readily available, so their processing can be easily computerized.

Managers at this level are often referred to as *operational decision makers.* They typically make structured decisions (Figure 3a). A **structured design** is a predictable decision that can be made by following a well-defined set of predetermined, routine procedures. For example, a clothing store floor manager's decision to accept your credit card to pay for some new clothes is a structured decision based on several well-defined criteria:

1. Does the customer have satisfactory identification?

2. Is the card current or expired?

3. Is the card number on the store's list of stolen or lost cards?

4. Is the amount of purchase under the cardholder's credit limit?

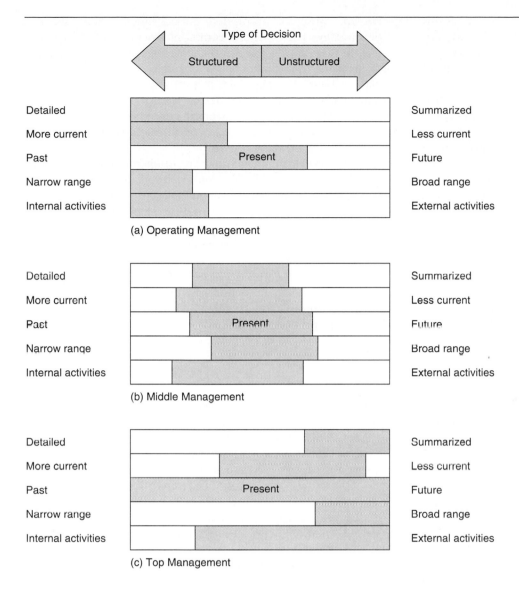

(a) Operating Management

(b) Middle Management

(c) Top Management

FIGURE 3

(a) Structured decisions are typically made at the operating level of management by following clearly defined routine procedures. Operating managers need information that is detailed, focused on the present, and concerned with daily business activities. (b) Semistructured decisions, typically made at the middle-management level, involve information that does not necessarily result from clearly defined, routine procedures. Middle managers need information that is detailed and more summarized than information for operating managers and that compares the present with the recent past. (c) Unstructured decisions, typically made at the upper level of management, are supported by the management information system in the form of highly summarized reports. The information should cover large time periods and survey activities outside (as well as inside) the company.

At this level of management, almost all the data needed to make decisions comes from within the organization. Also, decision makers at this level generally know quickly whether their decisions were correct.

Middle Management

The **middle** level of **management** deals with decisions that cover a somewhat broader range of time and involve more experience. Some common titles of middle managers are plant manager, division manager, sales manager, branch manager, and director of personnel. The information that middle managers need involves review, summarization, and analysis of historical data to help plan and control operations and implement policy that has been formulated by upper management. This information is usually given to middle managers in two forms: (1) **summary reports,** which show totals and trends—for example, total sales by office, by product, by salesperson, and total overall sales—and (2) **exception reports,** which show out-of-the-ordinary data—for example, inventory reports that list only those items that number fewer than 10 in stock. These reports may be regularly scheduled (periodic reports), requested on a case-by-case basis (on-demand reports), or generated only when certain conditions exist (event-initiated reports).

Periodic reports are produced at predetermined times—daily, weekly, monthly, quarterly, or annually. These reports commonly include payroll reports, inventory status reports, sales reports, income statements, and balance sheets. **On-demand reports** are usually requested by a manager when information is needed for a particular problem. For example, if a customer wants to establish a large charge account, a manager might request a special report on the customer's payment and order history. **Event-initiated reports** usually deal with a change in conditions that requires immediate attention, such as an out-of-stock report or a report on an equipment breakdown.

Managers at the middle level of management are often referred to as *tactical decision makers* who generally deal with semistructured decisions. A **semistructured decision** is a decision that includes some structured procedures and some procedures that do not follow a predetermined set of procedures. In most cases, a semistructured decision (Figure 3b) is complex, requiring detailed analysis and extensive computations. Examples of semistructured decisions include deciding how many units of a specific product should be kept in inventory, whether or not to purchase a larger computer system, from what source to purchase personal computers, and whether to purchase a multiuser minicomputer system. At least some of the information requirements at this level can be met through computer-based data processing.

Upper Management

The **upper** level of **management** deals with decisions that are the broadest in scope and cover the widest time frame. Typical titles of managers at this level are chief executive officer (CEO), president, treasurer, controller, chief information officer (CIO), executive vice president, and senior partner. Top managers include only a few powerful people who are in charge of the four basic functions of a business—marketing, accounting and finance, production, and research and development. Decisions made at this level are unpredictable, long-range, and related to the future, not just past and/or current activities. Therefore, they demand the most experience and judgment.

A company's MIS must be able to supply information to upper management as needed in periodic reports, event-initiated reports, and on-demand reports. The information must show how all the company's operations and departments are related to and affected by one another. The major decisions made at this level tend to be directed toward (1) strategic planning—for example, how growth should be financed and which new markets should be tackled first; (2) allocation of resources, such as deciding whether to build or lease office space and whether to spend more money on advertising or the hiring of new staff members; and (3) policy formulation, such as determining the company's policy on hiring minorities and providing employee incentives. Managers at this level are often referred to as **strategic decision makers.**

Upper management typically makes unstructured decisions (Figure 3c). An **unstructured decision** is the most complex type of decision that managers are faced with. Because these decisions are rarely based on predetermined, routine procedures, they involve the subjective judgment of the decision maker. As a result, this type of decision is the hardest to support from a computer-based data processing standpoint. Examples of unstructured decisions include deciding five-year goals for the company, evaluating future financial resources, and deciding how to react to the actions of competitors.

At the higher levels of management, much of the data required to make decisions comes from outside the organization (for example, financial information about other companies). Also, managers at this level may not know for years if they made the correct decisions.

Figure 4 shows the areas that the three levels of management would deal with in a foods-supply business and an insurance company.

FIGURE 4

Areas covered by the three management levels in a foods-supply business (a) and an insurance company (b). [R. Schultheis and M. Sumner, *Management Information Systems*, 2nd ed. (Homewood, IL: Richard D. Irwin, 1992), pp. 332–333.]

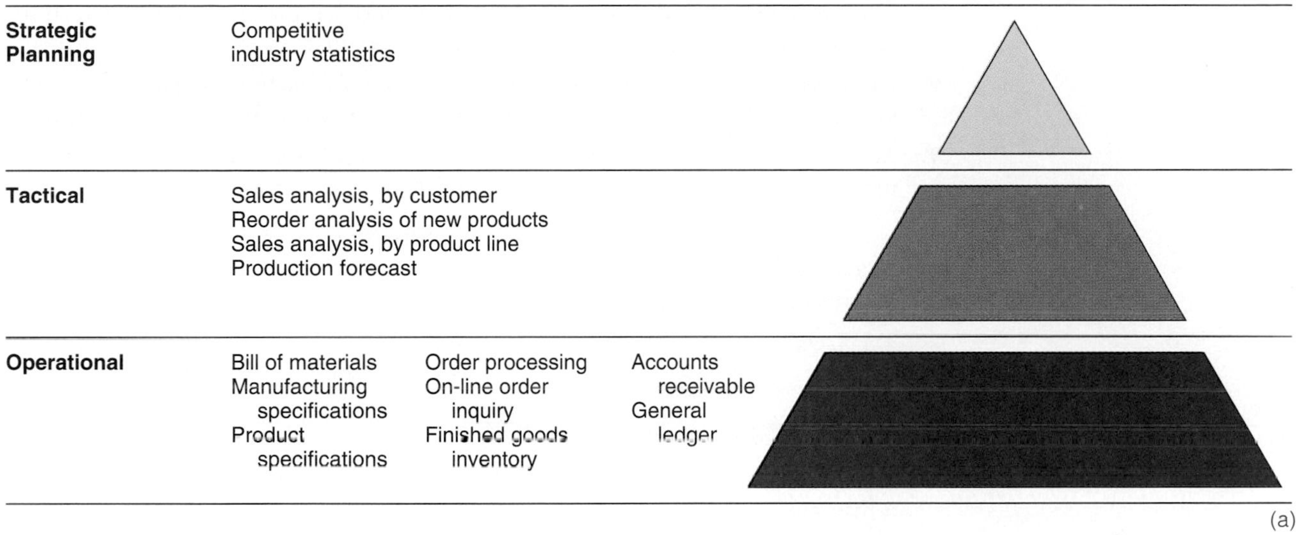

Strategic Planning	Competitive industry statistics		
Tactical	Sales analysis, by customer Reorder analysis of new products Sales analysis, by product line Production forecast		
Operational	Bill of materials Manufacturing specifications Product specifications	Order processing On-line order inquiry Finished goods inventory	Accounts receivable General ledger

(a)

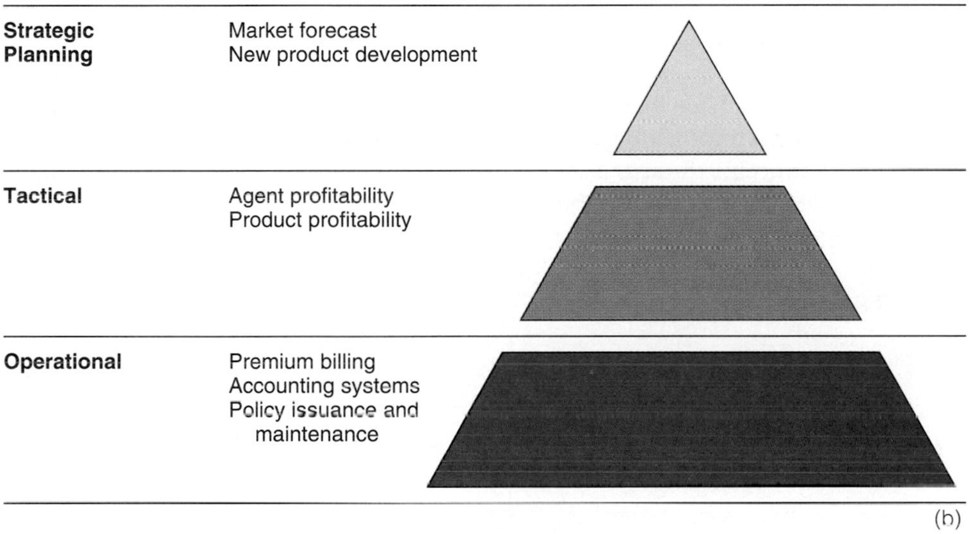

Strategic Planning	Market forecast New product development
Tactical	Agent profitability Product profitability
Operational	Premium billing Accounting systems Policy issuance and maintenance

(b)

The Role of the MIS in Business

Now that you know what we mean by *managers* and understand their need for the right kinds of information, we can go on to describe in more detail the role of the management information system. First, as we have already pointed out, an MIS must provide managers with information (reports) to help them perform activities that directly relate to their specific areas of responsibility. For example, to effectively manage marketing responsibilities, the vice president of marketing needs information about sales, competitors, and consumers. The head of the personnel department needs information about employee performance, work history, and job descriptions, among other things.

Second, a management information system must provide managers with information about the functional areas of the business so that they can coordinate their departmental activities with activities in these areas. These functional areas are usually categorized as:

▼ *Accounting and finance*—keeps track of all financial activities, pays bills, issues paychecks, and produces budgets and financial forecasts

▼ *Production*—makes the product

▼ *Marketing and sales*—handles advertising, promotion, and sales of the product

▼ *Human resources (personnel)*—hires staff and handles sick leave, vacations, retirement benefits, and staff performance evaluation

▼ *Information services (design and support of information systems)*—manages systems analysis, design, and development; provides user support services

▼ *Research and development*—Conducts research regarding product improvement and new products; develops and tests new products

For example, suppose that the accounting department (one functional area) has kept track of all customer invoices produced so far this year by maintaining an invoice history file. The file contains such information as:

1. Customer name
2. Customer address
3. Invoice date
4. Products sold
5. Invoice amount

To better coordinate marketing activities, the vice president of marketing (another functional area) can use this data to produce a variety of information, such as the year-to-date sales by month, a ranking of customers to whom the largest amounts of sales have been made, and an analysis of the months of highest sales. This same information could be passed along to the materials manager in production (another functional area), who can make informed decisions about when inventory levels should be raised or lowered to meet consumer demand.

But *how* do managers use information to make decisions? To understand how an MIS works, you must know something about the decision-making process.

How Does Management Make Decisions?

Management styles vary. Some managers follow their instincts and deal with situations on a case-by-case basis. Other managers use a more systematic and structured approach to making decisions. If we approach decision making systematically, we can view it as a process involving five basic steps, as shown in Figure 5 and described below. Bear in mind that feedback, or review of the gathered information, is analyzed at each step, which may necessitate revisions or a return to a previous step. For example, suppose a company decides in Step 2 to purchase one of two software packages to help with in-house publishing; at Step 3 the company discovers that one of the two software manufacturers has gone out of business. The process must return to Step 2 to evaluate other software alternatives.

Step 1—Problem Recognition and Identification

In the first step of the decision-making process, the manager acknowledges a problem that affects the business. Take, for example, a small business like Bowman, Henderson, and Associates (BH&A), which provides training in the use of

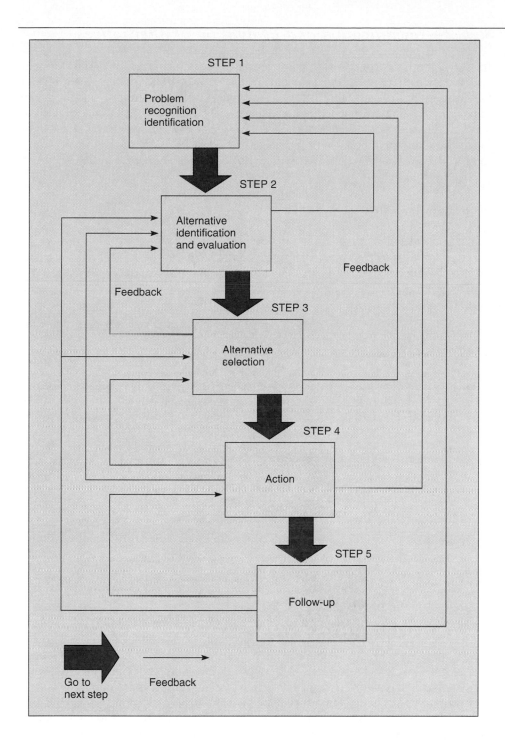

FIGURE 5

Five steps of the decision-making process. At any step, feedback—a review of gathered information—may require returning to any of the previous steps.

microcomputer hardware and software. The demand for training has grown so fast that the staff cannot handle it, and the facilities cannot support an increase in the number of students who can be taught per session. The fact that a problem exists becomes obvious when management notices that the staff is too busy to take a day off and everyone is always running around trying to take care of last-minute details. The seriousness of the problem becomes evident when staff morale begins to drop and potential customers are turned away.

Step 2—Identification and Evaluation of Alternatives

In the second step of the decision-making process, management considers various alternatives to solve the problem. In the case of BH&A, alternatives include (1) adding more staff and offering training in the existing facilities during expanded training hours (perhaps evenings and weekends) and (2) adding more staff, purchasing additional equipment, and leasing additional training facilities. Once the alternative courses of action have been identified, they must be examined and compared in terms of anticipated costs and benefits.

Step 3—Alternative Selection

When each alternative has been carefully explored, the next step is to select the one that appears to best meet the manager's objectives. The logical choice would be the alternative that offers the most benefits for the least cost. However, the manager must ensure that the chosen action is not in conflict with other activities or organizational objectives.

Step 4—Action

Once management has decided how to solve the problem, it must act on the decision. Suppose BH&A management selected the alternative of adding more staff and scheduling the use of existing facilities for additional hours. Implementing this decision would probably involve:

1. Defining specific staff requirements and skills
2. Advertising for additional staff
3. Interviewing prospective staff members
4. Selecting the best candidates
5. Notifying existing customers of the additional staff and expanded hours
6. Scheduling the use of the facility during the new hours of operation

Step 5—Follow-Up

In the final step of the decision-making process, management follows up on its choice of action to determine if it has been successful. Management assesses the degree to which original objectives and anticipated benefits are being achieved and takes corrective action when necessary. If the solution to the original problem has created a new problem, a new decision-making process begins to solve it.

What Kind of Information Does Management Need to Make Decisions?

Because decisions are made on the basis of information, the decision-making process is greatly affected by the scope and quality of the information provided by the MIS. This information is produced by processing data from three sources:

1. Internally generated data (produced by normal data processing systems of the business)

2. Data provided by higher or lower levels of management

3. Externally generated data (produced by sources outside the company)

Information, as required by management, has three distinct properties that vary in significance depending on the organizational level and type of decision being made:

1. Level of summarization

2. Degree of accuracy

3. Timeliness

As we mentioned in the discussion of the three management levels, the degree to which information needs to be *summarized* increases as the level of management goes up. Conversely, the lower the level of management, the more detailed the information needs to be. Top managers do not want to wade through mountains of details to make a decision. They want to be able to identify problems and trends at a glance in summary reports and exception reports; that is, they need only essential information, not nonessential details. Operational managers, however, need details on daily operations to make decisions regarding scheduling, inventory, payroll, and so on.

Of course, information must be *accurate* for wise decisions to be made. (Remember: garbage in, garbage out.) The higher the accuracy of the information, the higher the cost of the processing system. Higher costs are incurred because more controls—both manual and computer-based—must be installed to increase the accuracy of output information. Some areas such as inventory may be able to live with an accuracy rate of 90–95%, but this rate is probably too low for the accounting department, where a 5–10% error rate in dealing with money might mean substantial losses or tax problems, for example.

The *timeliness* of management information involves how soon the information is needed and whether the information is about the past, present, or future. When decisions are time-sensitive (they must be made quickly), the information system must accommodate this need. For example, whether a system is designed to use batch processing or on-line processing might be determined by how fast the information is needed by management. On the one hand, the kind of planning done by top management covers a broad time frame and requires reports that contain information covering past years as well as current performance. This type of decision making is not highly time-sensitive, so batch processing would probably be adequate. On the other hand, decisions related to banking activities may be highly time-sensitive and require on-line processing to provide up-to-date information.

In general, to support the making of intelligent and knowledgeable decisions, information generated at all levels of management must be:

▼ Correct (be accurate)

▼ Complete (include all relevant data)

▼ Current (be timely)

▼ Concise (include only the relevant data)

▼ Clear (be understandable)

▼ Cost-effective (be efficiently obtained)

▼ Time-sensitive (be based on historical, current, and/or future information and needs as required)

Types of Management Information Systems

The more structured the problem, the easier it is to develop computer-based processing support to produce the information needed to solve it. As an organization matures in its use of the computer, the extent to which it uses computers to produce information for decision making grows.

Transaction Processing System (TPS)

Supporting day-to-day business operating activities, or *transactions,* is usually the first and most important objective of an information system. A computer-based **transaction processing system (TPS),** also called an *operations information system (OIS)* or an *electronic data processing (EDP) system,* focuses on the operating level of a business and deals mostly with data from internal sources (Figure 6). The management information produced by transaction information systems usually consists of detail reports of daily transactions (such as a list of items sold or all the accounting transactions that have been recorded in various ledgers and registers) or future transactions (such as lists of items that need to be ordered).

A TPS usually operates only within one functional area of a business. In other words, accounting and finance, production, marketing and sales, and research and development each has its own transaction processing information system. Database management systems were designed to solve the problems involved with sharing computer-based files among the different functional areas.

FIGURE 6

Three information systems for three levels of management.

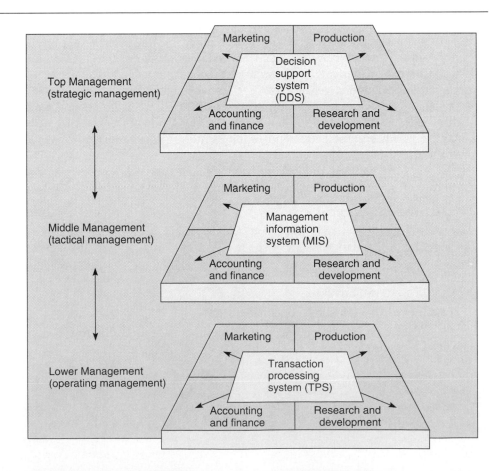

Although the reports generated by a TPS are useful to lower-level managers, they are not generally helpful to middle managers, who need more summarized information. Thus, management information systems were developed to take care of middle management's information needs.

Management Information System (MIS)

Management information systems (MIS), also called *information reporting systems,* provide middle management with reports that summarize and categorize information derived from all the company databases. The purpose of the reports is to allow management to spot trends and to get an overview of current business activities, as well as to monitor and control operational-level activities. (Although the term *management information system* is used to refer to *any* type of information system for managers, it is also used to refer specifically to *middle* management information systems.)

The scope of the reports and the characteristics of their information vary according to their purpose. As you have seen, the reports can be periodic (such as income statements and balance sheets), on-demand, or event-initiated, and they can summarize information or report on exceptional events or conditions. Examples of reports generated by an MIS are sales region analyses, cost analyses, annual budgeting reports, capital investment analyses, and production schedules.

Decision Support System (DSS)

The **decision support system (DSS),** a set of special computer programs, establishes a sophisticated system to provide tools to assist managers in analyzing information from the two lower management levels and from outside the company. The analyses are used for unstructured decision making. DSSs are generally used by top management (although they support all levels of management), combine sophisticated analysis programs with traditional data access and retrieval functions, can be used by people who are not computer specialists, and emphasize flexibility in decision making. They are used to analyze unexpected problems and integrate information flow and decision-making activities. A DSS may use database management systems, query languages, financial modeling or spreadsheet programs, statistical analysis programs, report generators, and graphics programs to provide information (Table 2).

To reach the DSS level of sophistication in information technology, an organization must have established a transaction processing system and a management information system. But these two types of systems are not designed to handle unpredictable information and decisions well. Decision support systems *are* designed to handle the unstructured types of decisions—the "what if" types of decisions and analyses of special issues—that traditional management information systems were not designed to support (Figure 7). Moreover, decision support systems provide managers with tools to help them better model, analyze, and make decisions about the information they have. Indeed, some people regard decision support systems as a separate type of information system altogether, not just an information system for top management.

Although most DSSs are designed for large computer systems, electronic spreadsheet packages and database management packages are used by many business people as tools for building a DSS for microcomputers. Spreadsheet software is popular among managers because it allows them to examine a variety of business situations—that is, to "see what would happen" if business conditions changed—and to make projections, or guesses, about future developments based on sophisticated computer-based data analysis. Decision support

TABLE 2

Software Tools for Decision Support Systems

DATABASE SOFTWARE	MODEL-BASED SOFTWARE	STATISTICAL-SOFTWARE	DISPLAY-BASED (GRAPHICS) SOFTWARE
dBASE IV	Foresight	SAS	ChartMaster
FOCUS	IFPS	SPSS	SASGRAPH
NOMAD II	Lotus 1-2-3	TSAM	TELLAGRAF
RAMIS	Model	1	Presentations
R:base System V	Quattro Pro		
DB2	Mathematica		
Oracle	Excel		
Ingres			
Informix			
Paradox			
Access			

FIGURE 7

Decision support system. These processing questions represent the types of questions a top manager might ask a DSS. (These questions would not be keyed into the computer word by word exactly as you see here; the manager would use a query language, such as SQL.)

1. If we discontinue selling baseball bats, will fewer people come into our stores?

2. If we add a new clothing line, will more people come into our stores?

3. How will offering the customers a 10% discount for all purchases totaling over $35 affect next year's net income?

4. What effect will hiring 50 additional sales employees have on the company's overall performance (i.e., profit)?

5. What effect will modernizing our stores have on sales?

systems designed for large computer systems collect large amounts of data and analyze it in more ways and with greater efficiency than a microcomputer spreadsheet does.

Because a DSS is tailored to meet specific management information requirements, the nonmanagement user would not likely be directly involved with it. However, this type of user might be involved in gathering data to be processed by the DSS and then used as information for management.

Decision support systems generally fall into two distinct categories: general and institutional. A general DSS produces information that can be used in making a wide variety of management decisions. The electronic spreadsheet is an ideal tool for the development of general decision support systems for microcomputers. Large database management systems and natural languages or query languages are used to develop decision support systems for large computer systems. An institutional DSS is much more industry- and function-specific. Examples include a DSS for the medical profession (including hospitals), which supports decision making in the areas of administration, patient diagnosis, determination and monitoring of drug dosages, and medical records, among other things; a DSS for the advertising profession, which supports strategy in presenting products; and a DSS for the transportation industry, which supports traffic pattern analysis.

The users of a DSS must be reasonably comfortable working with the hardware and DSS software to be effective. Many managers develop substantial skills in using some of the microcomputer-based packages such as electronic spreadsheets that can provide decision support. The software used for DSSs on large computer systems is generally too complex for people who are not computer specialists to handle; the manager would use it only on a simple level—to ask questions and obtain reports. (**Executive information systems** are now available that provide executives with all the capabilities of a DSS but that are designed specifically to be easy to use.)

DSS Software

DSS applications software is usually composed of complex instructions. As mentioned earlier, many different types of programs can make up a DSS. In most cases, it can be divided into three levels: database management systems software, query language, and specialized software or languages.

Database management software provides managers with the ability to collect, maintain, manipulate, and retrieve huge amounts of data.

A query language allows people to use software easily without having to learn countless lists of codes and procedures. This "layer" of DSS software helps managers use the database with less difficulty and perform a variety of activities such as basic mathematical operations on fields of data contained in the database, calculation of ratios and various statistical measures, search of the database for records of a certain type, and extraction of records for the preparation of hardcopy reports and graphic representation of data.

Specialized software or languages are used to develop decision-making models. Some organizations purchase industry-specific modeling software for such common activities as financial risk analysis and forecasting (predicting future performance and conditions). However, the most sophisticated DSS users develop their own custom-made business activity and decision-making models.

The following list identifies some of the major differences between a management information system (MIS) and a decision support system (DSS):

▼ MIS users *receive* reports or information from the system, whereas DSS users *interact* with the system.

▼ MIS users can't direct the system to support a specific decision in a specific way, whereas DSS users can.

▼ MISs generate information based on the past, whereas DSSs use information from the past to create scenarios for the future.

▼ MIS activity is initiated by middle management, whereas DSS activity is usually initiated by top management.

Although MISs and DSSs effectively process information to support managerial activities, the quantity of available information continues to grow at an alarming rate and threatens to overwhelm the users. Thus, the search for more efficient information management tools continues.

Developing and Implementing a Management Information System

The task of developing and implementing any type of management information system is a formidable one, requiring a great deal of planning. Business environments change rapidly, so unless management has great foresight (and the support of good specialists and user input), an information system may be obsolete by the time it is implemented.

The successful development of a management information system requires:

▼ A long- and a short-range plan for the company; a company must have plans for the future to be able to decide what to do tomorrow, next week, and next month

▼ A commitment from management to allocate the personnel and resources necessary to get the job done

▼ A staff of technical specialists with the skills necessary to develop the computer-based parts of the system based on user input

The most important step in undertaking the development of an MIS is forming a project development team (to follow the steps of systems analysis, design, and development discussed in Chapter 10). The team should be made up of managers, information system users, and technical information specialists. All the team members should be familiar with the company's business objectives, current activities, and problems. And all the members must come to a general understanding of how the business operates. This task is not easy because many managers understand only how their own departments work and little, if anything, about other departments; many managers have difficulty explaining how their own departments work; and many managers, users, and computer specialists use jargon—special vocabulary and expressions—to explain what they do. Jargon is not generally understood by everyone. In a situation like this, prototyping is often useful.

Developing a comprehensive MIS is a massive undertaking that may take years to carefully plan and coordinate. However, organizations that plan to survive the 1990s must have efficient management information systems to feed management the information it needs to be competitive.

Use of computers in manufacturing is not just for the mammoth Fortune 500 companies. For his daughter who wanted to open a clothing store, a University of Dayton electrical engineering professor devised a computer-based dressmaking program for tailors. An optical scanner "reads" a person's body, producing figures that can be translated into a personalized dress or suit pattern.

Still, the most dramatic uses of computers have been those employed by large organizations. Once, taking inventory at computer-maker Hewlett-Packard's New Jersey division required the equivalent of 120 hours of a person's time, plus an additional two to three weeks to get the information keypunched and tabulated. Today, two people using electronic wands to scan bar codes on each product finish in less than six hours, and the data is ready immediately.

Moving bar codes from supermarkets to warehouses and factories has produced dramatic productivity gains. Indeed, companies now need entirely too much information in their computer systems for it to be keyed in manually. On an assembly line, laser scanners can read bar codes of up to 360 objects per second. The codes enable a company to keep track of individual lots or products, to track production rates, and to do quality control and inventory, all without the need for paper.

Another form of computer technology becoming more frequently used in factories and warehouses is the industrial robot. A Reynolds Metals plastics plant in Virginia uses a robot that stacks a pallet with boxes, then moves it to an automatic pallet wrapper, where it is shrinkwrapped in plastic film. Employees are happier because they are less fatigued at the end of a shift than they were when this work had to be done by hand.

Nowadays the factory is being reinvented from the top down. Computer simulations are used to recreate the factory floor on a computer screen, including machine tools, robots, and materials-handling vehicles. Manufacturing processes can be tried out before a single machine is put in place. With computer-integrated manufacturing (CIM), a new product that is ordered may be available the next day. Using computer-aided design (CAD), the part is designed on a video screen. Then, with computer-aided engineering (CAE), it is analyzed for performance. Finally, with computer-aided manufacturing (CAM), the part is produced by an automated system on the shop floor.

Some of the lessons or ideas developed for the factory floor are now being used in other areas. Unlike factory robots, so-called *field,* or *service, robots* are mobile and are able to work in nonmanufacturing environments that are hazardous or inaccessible to humans. Field robots equipped with wheels, tracks, legs, and fins are being used to clean up hazardous-waste sites, inspect nuclear power plants, do bomb disposal, and perform maintenance on offshore oil rigs.

Management information systems—organized standards and procedures, both computer-based and manual, for processing data into useful information—are used by three levels of management:

1. *Operational management*
2. *Middle (tactical) management*
3. *Upper (strategic) management*

▼ Management information systems are used in the areas of *planning, organizing, staffing, supervising,* and *controlling* business activities in the functional areas (departments) of *accounting and finance, production, marketing and sales, information systems,* and *research and development*.

▼ The types of decisions made differ according to the level of management. Operating management typically makes *structured,* short-term *decisions*. Middle management, or tactical management, generally makes *semistructured decisions* based on information that is less detailed (summarized to some degree). These types of decisions have some nonquantifiable aspects to them and require some subjective judgment on the part of the decision maker. Upper management, or strategic management, typically makes *unstructured decisions,* which are the most difficult to computerize because they are made with the most subjective judgment. Unstructured decisions are broad in scope, long range, and often unpredictable and future-oriented.

▼ Information must be made available to management in the form of reports. Operating management generally uses *detail reports* that are issued on a regular, or periodic, basis. Middle and top management use *summary reports* and *exception reports* that are issued periodically or on demand or that are initiated by an event.

▼ Managers generally follow five steps when making decisions:

1. *Problem recognition and identification*
2. *Identification and evaluation of alternatives*
3. *Selection of alternative*
4. *Action*
5. *Follow-up*

▼ The data that managers use is generated internally (by normal data processing systems), externally (by sources outside the company), or by other levels of management. The information generated by processing the data into reports differs in level of summarization, degree of accuracy, and degree of time sensitivity, according to the management level.

▼ A business can use three general types of management information systems to satisfy management's need for information.

1. A *transaction processing system* (*TPS*) supports the day-to-day operating activities and is used mostly by operating management.

2. A middle *management information system* (*MIS*) (or simply a management information system) supports the decision making of middle management with reports that summarize and categorize information derived from data generated on the transaction level.

3. A *decision support system* (*DSS*) supports the decision making of top management through a sophisticated software setup designed to answer "what if" questions and aid in making projections. Most DSSs are designed for large computer systems, although electronic spreadsheets and database management systems software can be used to build a type of DSS for microcomputers. General decision support systems produce information that can be used to make a wide variety of management decisions. Institutional decision support systems are much more industry- and function-specific. DSS software generally uses a query language to make its use easy and specialized software languages to develop decision-making models; it also provides the manager with the ability to retrieve and manipulate huge amounts of data.

KEY TERMS

decision support system (DSS),
  p. 12.15
detail report, p. 12.6
event-initiated report, p. 12.8
exception report, p. 12.7
executive information system,
  p. 12.17
management, p. 12.3

management information system
  (MIS), pp. 12.4, 12.15
middle management, p. 12.7
on-demand report, p. 12.8
operational management, p. 12.6
periodic report, p. 12.8
semistructured decision, p. 12.8
strategic decision maker, p. 12.8

structured design, p. 12.6
summary report, p. 12.7
transaction processing system
  (TPS), p. 12.14
unstructured decision, p 12.8.
upper management, p. 12.8

EXERCISES

SELF-TEST

1. A _____ is a specific sequence of steps performed to complete one or more information processing activities.

2. What are the five functions of management?

   a.

   b.

   c.

   d.

   e.

3. A _____ _____

   _____ comprises computer-based processing and/or

   manual procedures to provide useful and timely information to support

   management decision making.

4. The lowest level of management is strategic management. (true/false)

5. Operating management deals with structured decisions and needs detailed information. (true/false)

6. Middle management makes _____ decisions.

7. Decision support systems are used mainly by upper management. (true/false)

8. The five steps involved in making a decision are:

   a.

   b.

   c.

   d.

   e.

9. Information has three properties that vary in importance depending on the decision and the decision maker. They are:

   a.

   b.

   c.

10. A transaction processing system supports day-to-day business activities. (true/false)

11. A decision support system provides information analysis tools not regularly supplied by transaction processing systems and management information systems. (true/false)

12. In most companies, there are six functional areas. They are:

    a.

    b.

    c.

    d.

    e.

    f.

Solutions: (1) procedure; (2) planning, organizing, staffing, supervising, controlling; (3) management information system; (4) false; (5) true; (6) semistructured; (7) true; (8) problem recognition and identification, identification and evaluation of alternatives, alternative selection, action, follow-up; (9) level of summarization, degree of accuracy, timeliness; (10) true; (11) true; (12) accounting and finance, production, marketing and sales, human resources (personnel), information systems, research and development

MULTIPLE-CHOICE QUESTIONS

1. Which of the following is generally true about management reports?

    a. Low-level managers need information in the form of detail reports.

    b. Reports can be issued on demand, periodically, or on the occurrence of a specific event.

    c. Only top management can get reports.

    d. Middle managers use exception reports.

    e. Middle managers use summary reports.

2. Which of the following is true of a transaction processing system?

    a. It is used by managers to spot trends.

    b. It supports unstructured decision making.

    c. It usually consists of detailed reports on daily transactions.

    d. It is used by the highest level of management.

    e. It analyzes information.

3. Distinguishing among the different levels of management can be accomplished by analyzing:

    a. types of decisions made

    b. frequency with which decisions are made

    c. time frame considered in making decisions

    d. types of report information needed to make decisions

    e. all the above

4. Which of the following is not usually characteristic of upper management decisions?

    a. Decisions require judgment.

    b. Decisions are structured.

    c. Decisions are long range.

    d. Decisions are unpredictable.

    e. Decisions require experience.

5. Which of the following statements is the most accurate?

   a. The degree to which information needs to be summarized increases as one moves up through the management levels.

   b. Low-level managers make unstructured decisions.

   c. Upper managers make structured decisions.

   d. Low-level managers need general information about operating activities.

   e. Middle managers make unstructured decisions.

6. Which of the following are functional areas found in most companies?

   a. research and development

   b. cafeteria service

   c. production

   d. sanitation

   e. information systems

Solutions: (1) a, b, d, e; (2) c; (3) e; (4) b; (5) a; (6) a, c, e

SHORT-ANSWER QUESTIONS

1. What is a management information system, and what is its role in an organization?

2. What steps should management follow to make decisions?

3. What is a decision support system?

4. For what is a company's human resources department responsible?

5. What is an executive information system (EIS)?

6. What are transaction processing systems typically used for?

7. Describe some differences between a management information system and a decision support system.

8. What is the difference between a structured decision and a semistructured decision, and which type of decision is easier to support from a computer-based data processing standpoint?

9. What is the difference between information and knowledge? How can knowledge be made useful?

10. What does the management function of *controlling* deal with?

PROJECTS

1. Decision support systems often take years to develop. Given this long development period, some experts argue that the system will be obsolete by the time it is complete and that information needs will have changed. Other experts argue that no alternatives exist. By reviewing current computer publications that describe management information systems, formulate an opinion about this issue.

2. Does your university/college have an information systems department that is responsible for developing and supporting all the university information systems? If so, interview a management staff member about the services and functions of the department. Can this person identify the various levels of management within the department? What kinds of user input were requested when the department was being set up? Does it use any sophisticated decision support software? What kinds of services does the department offer to students?

3. The following quote is from "The New Society of Organizations," by Peter Drucker in *Harvard Business Review* (September/October, 1992, p. 96):

> Society, community, and family are all conserving institutions. They try to maintain stability and to prevent, or at least to slow, change. But the modern organization is a destabilizer. It must be organized for innovation, and innovation, as the great Austro-American economist Joseph Schumpeter said, is "creative destruction." And it must be organized for the systematic abandonment of whatever is established, customary, familiar, and comfortable, whether that is a product, service, or process; a set of skills; human and social relationships; or the organization itself. In short, it must be organized for constant change. The organization's function is to put knowledge to work—on tools, products, and processes; on the design of work; on knowledge itself. It is the nature of knowledge that it changes fast and that today's certainties always become tomorrow's absurdities.

How do you think that managers can plan for change? What can they build into their information systems that can help them be innovative? What tools could they use?

Advanced Topics

*I*s it really possible for computers to think like human beings? Not yet, but perhaps that time is coming. Developments in areas such as artificial intelligence, robotics, expert systems, and virtual reality show that computers are indeed becoming increasingly "intelligent." Professionals who are at the forefront of their disciplines make sure they are aware of new developments in computer technology. As an intelligent user, you should, too.

PREVIEW

When you have completed this chapter, you will be able to:

▼ Define *artificial intelligence* and give a few examples of how it is used

▼ Describe how robots are used

▼ Define *natural language* and *fuzzy logic*

▼ Describe what an expert system is

▼ Define *virtual reality* and describe a few of its applications

▼ Explain what object-oriented programming is

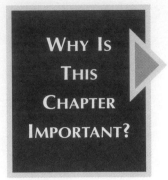
*T*he topics of artificial intelligence, expert systems, and object-oriented programming are receiving widespread attention from researchers, businesses, and the media. In this chapter, we describe why so much interest is focused on these areas and how you can expect to be affected by the research done in these areas now and in the future.

Artificial Intelligence (AI)

For years, researchers have been exploring the way people think, in hopes of creating a computer that thinks like a person. **Artificial intelligence (AI)** is getting a great deal of attention from computer scientists; indeed, it is their main focus for the present and the future. However, existing definitions of artificial intelligence are contradictory. Some experts say that AI is the science of making machines do things that would require intelligence if done by a person. Others state that, if we can imagine a computer that can collect, assemble, choose among, understand, perceive, and know, then we have artificial intelligence. Still others believe that there is no such thing as intelligence that is "artificial" and that, therefore, the term *knowledge-based system* should be used.

Why do the definitions differ? First of all, there is not—and never has been—a single agreed-on definition of human intelligence. Second, agreement on the point at which a machine exhibits intelligence is difficult to achieve. For example, years ago, when a computer could play tic-tac-toe, some researchers considered it to be intelligent because it could choose the next best possible move and could beat its human opponents. Today, most researchers no longer think that a machine's ability to play tic-tac-toe is enough to reflect intelligence. Other characteristics have been added to our definition of *intelligent behavior*—for example, the ability to reason logically and respond creatively to problems.

What Is AI Supposed to Do?

The aim of AI is to produce a generation of systems that will be able to communicate with us by speech and hearing, use "vision" (scanning) that approximates the way people see, and be capable of intelligent problem solving. In other words, AI refers to computer-based systems that can mimic or simulate human thought processes and actions. Some of the primary areas of research within AI that are of particular interest to business users are robotics, natural language processing, expert systems, and virtual reality.

Robotics

According to *Webster's Ninth New Collegiate Dictionary,* a **robot** is an automatic device that performs functions ordinarily ascribed to human beings or that operates with what appears to be almost human intelligence. It derives from the Polish word *robotnik,* which means "slave." In the field of artificial intelligence, there are *intelligent robots* (also called *perception robots*) and *unintelligent robots.*

Most robots are unintelligent; that is, they are programmed to do specific tasks, and they are incapable of showing initiative (Figures 1 and 2). An unintelligent robot cannot respond to a situation for which it has not been specifi-

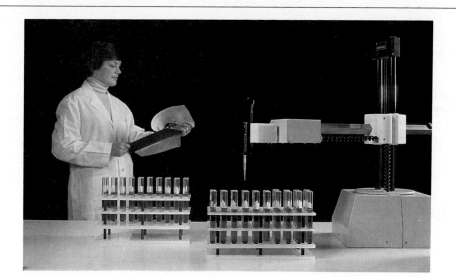

FIGURE 1

Unintelligent laboratory robot

cally programmed. Intelligence is provided either by a direct link to a computer or by on-board computers that reside in the robot. Robotic intelligence is primarily a question of extending the sensory (for example, vision) and mobility competence of robots in a working environment (Figure 3). One future application of intelligent robotics is a machine that is small enough to be swallowed. It will be able to scan intestinal walls with a miniature camera, searching for possible tumors, and send the images to a doctor watching a monitor. Then, under instructions from the doctor, it will take a tissue sample.

In the future, reasoning ability will be incorporated into robots, thus improving their ability to behave "intelligently." For example, robot vision has already been successfully implemented in many manufacturing systems (Figure 4). To "see," a computer measures varying intensities of light of a shape; each intensity has a numbered value that is compared to a template of intensity patterns stored in memory. One of the main reasons for the importance of vision is that production-line robots must be able to discriminate among parts. General Electric, for example, has Bin Vision Systems, which allows a robot to identify and pick up specific parts in an assembly-line format (Figure 5).

Another area of interest is the "personal" robot, familiar to us from science fiction. Existing personal robots exhibit relatively limited abilities, and whether a sophisticated home robot can be made cost-effective is debatable. B.O.B. (Brains On Board) is a device sold by Visual Machines that can speak (using prerecorded phrases), follow people around using infrared sensors, and avoid obstacles by using ultrasonic sound. Software will allow the robot to bring its owner something to drink from the refrigerator. Another type of personal robot is the Spimaster, built by Cybermotion. This security robot patrols up to 15 miles per shift, collecting video images and recording data. If it senses a problem, it heads for the trouble zone and sounds alarms on-site and at security headquarters.

The performance limitations of personal robots reflect the difficulties in designing and programming intelligent robots. In fact, we have just begun to appreciate how complicated such mundane tasks as recognizing a can of Pepsi in the refrigerator can be. Another concern is that, if a robot does in fact become intelligent, what would stop it from deciding that work is something to avoid?

Figure 2

Surgery robot. [Adapted from Steve Kearsley, *San Francisco Chronicle,* November 10, 1992, p. A4.
Sources: Integrated Surgical Systems, *New York Times.* Reprinted by permission.]

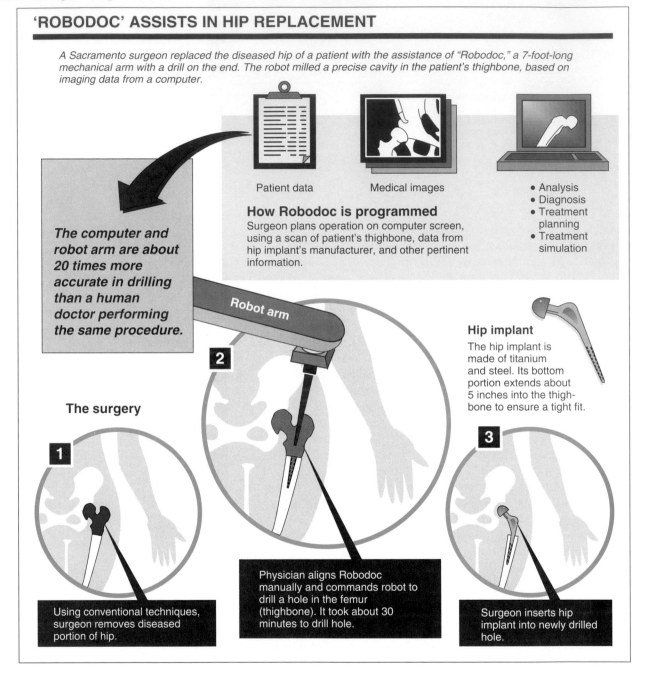

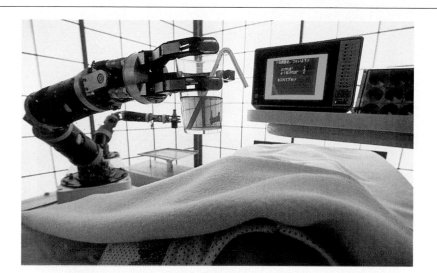

FIGURE 3

Intelligent robot feeding a patient in a Japanese hospital

FIGURE 4

Robot vision

FIGURE 5

Some industrial robots use claws to pick up objects and insert them into various parts of machinery.

Natural Language Processing and Fuzzy Logic

The goal of **natural language processing** is to enable the computer to communicate with the user in the user's native language, for example, English. The primary difficulty in implementing this kind of communication is the sheer complexity of everyday conversation. For example, we readily understand the sentence "The spirit is willing, but the flesh is weak." One natural language processing system, however, understood this sentence to mean "The wine is agreeable, but the meat has spoiled." It also understood the phrase "out of sight, out of mind" to mean "blind idiot." It turns out that the system must have access to a much larger body of knowledge than just a dictionary of terms. People use their world knowledge to help them understand what another person is saying. For example, we know the question "Coffee?" means "Do you want a cup of coffee?" But a computer would have difficulty understanding this one-word question.

Alan Turing, a famous British mathematician, proposed several years ago a method by which the intelligence—or natural language processing capacity—of a computer can be tested. In this test, a person is seated in front of two computer terminals; one terminal is directed by a computer and the other is directed by a human (through a keyboard). The subject is supposed to hold conversations (using a keyboard) with each terminal and then guess which one is run by a human. Hugh Loebner, a New York businessman, with support from the National Science Foundation and the Alfred P. Sloane Foundation, has offered a $100,000 prize for the first computer system that can pass the **Turing test** by fooling the subject into thinking he or she is communicating with a person. In November of 1991 a competition based on the Turing test was held in Boston's Computer Museum. Five out of ten judges were fooled by a computer program called PC Therapist III, from Thinking Software Inc., which won a $1,500 prize. The $100,000 prize is still up for grabs!

The post office is currently using a language-processing system that was developed by Verbex to speed up the sorting and delivery of mail that doesn't include a ZIP code. After the human mail sorter reads the address into a microphone, the computer responds in an electronic voice with the correct ZIP code.

Most existing natural language systems run on large computers; however, scaled-down versions are now available for microcomputers. Intellect, for example, is the name of a commercial product that uses a limited English vocabulary to help users orally query databases on both mainframes and microcomputers. One of the most successful natural language systems is LUNAR, developed to help users analyze the rocks brought back from the moon. It has access to extensive detailed knowledge about geology in its knowledge database and answers users' questions.

One relatively new concept being used in the development of natural languages is fuzzy logic. Classical logic has been based on either/or propositions. For example, to evaluate the phrase "The cat is fat," classical logic requires a single cutoff point to determine when the cat is fat, such as a specific weight for a certain length. It is either in the set of fat cats or it is not. However, "fat" is a vague, or "gray," notion; it's more likely that the cat is "a little fat." **Fuzzy logic** works by allowing partial membership in a set. If the cat weighs 25 pounds, then it probably has 1.00 membership in the set. If it weighs 15 pounds, it may have a partial, 0.70 membership. By allowing for partial membership in sets, fuzzy logic has made controls in electronic products simpler and more efficient.

Artificial intelligence has the potential to solve many problems; however, it may create some as well. For example, some people think that AI is dangerous because it does not address the ethics of using machines to make decisions nor does it require machines to use ethics as part of the decision-making process. In spite of these concerns, AI has been used to develop yet another system— the expert system—to support decision making in many areas, including the business environment.

Expert Systems: Human Expertise in a Computer

Beginning in the mid-1960s, a new type of system, called an **expert system,** began to be developed to support management in the decision-making process. This new type of system, which represents one of the first practical applications of artificial intelligence, is an exciting addition to the kinds of computer systems available to businesses. However, expert systems are designed to be users' *assistants,* not *replacements.*

An expert system solves problems that require substantial expertise to understand. The system's performance depends on the body of facts (knowledge) and the heuristics (rules of thumb) that are fed into the computer. Knowledge engineers gather, largely through interviews, the expert knowledge and the heuristics from human experts in the field for which the computer-based system is being designed to support decisions—fields such as medicine, engineering, or geology. (For example, in the field of medicine, one question that might be asked of an expert system is whether one treatment is better for a patient than another one.) The responses recorded during the interviews are codified and entered into a knowledge base that can be used by a computer. An expert system has the capacity to store the collection of knowledge and manipulate it in response to user inquiries; in some cases, it can even explain its responses to the user.

An expert system has four major program components:

1. Natural (software) language interface for the user

2. Knowledge base (like a database, where the facts are stored)

3. Inference machine (software that solves problems and makes logical inferences)

4. Explanation module (which explains its conclusions to the user)

One of the most famous expert systems—an older system now being replaced by updated ones—is MYCIN, a system that diagnoses infectious diseases and recommends appropriate drugs. For example, bacteremia (bacteria in the blood) can be fatal if it is not treated quickly. Unfortunately, traditional tests for it require 24 to 48 hours to verify a diagnosis. However, MYCIN provides physicians with a diagnosis and recommended therapy within minutes. To use MYCIN, the physician enters data on a patient; as the data is being entered, MYCIN asks questions (for example, "Is patient a burn patient?"). As the questions are answered, MYCIN's inference machine "reasons" out a diagnosis: "IF the infection is primary bacteria, AND the site of the culture is a gastrointestinal tract, THEN there is evidence (0.7) that the identity of the organism causing the disease is Bacteroides." The "0.7" means that MYCIN "thinks" there is a 7 out of 10 chance that this diagnosis is correct. This pattern closely follows that of human thought; much of our knowledge is inexact and incomplete, and we often reason using odds (such as "There's a 40% chance it's going to rain") when we don't have access to complete and accurate information.

Gensym Corporations's G2 Real-Time Expert system is used in Mrs. Baird's Bakery (a large independent bakery in Fort Worth) for scheduling and monitoring the production of baked goods. The system takes care of scheduling such tasks as ingredient mixing and oven operations—don't plan on finding a burned cookie at Mrs. Baird's! The Residential Burglary Expert System (REBES) is an expert system that uses certain rules of thumb to help a detective investigate a crime scene. REBES, which acts like a partner to the detective, might ask "Did the intruder search the entire house? If so, an accomplice might be involved" or "Was valuable jewelry taken but cheaper jewelry left behind? If so, thieves may be professionals/repeaters." Examples of other expert systems are XCON, a system that puts together the best arrangement of Digital Equipment Corporation (DEC) computer system components for a given company; DENDRAL, a system that identifies chemical compounds; PROSPECTOR, a system that evaluates potential geological sites of oil, natural gas, and so on; and DRILLING ADVISOR, a system that assists in diagnosing and resolving oil-rig problems.

Capturing human expertise for the computer is a time-consuming and difficult task. Knowledge engineers are trained to elicit knowledge (for example, by interview) from experts and build the expert system. The knowledge engineer may program the system in an artificial intelligence programming language, such as LISP or PROLOG, or may use system-building tools that provide a structure. Tools allow faster design but are less flexible than languages. An example of such a tool is EMYCIN, which is MYCIN without any of MYCIN's knowledge. A knowledge engineer can theoretically enter any knowledge (as long as it is describable in rules) into this empty shell and create a new system. The completed new system will solve problems as MYCIN does, but the subject matter in the knowledge base may be completely different (for example, car repair).

Expert systems are usually run on large computers—often dedicated artificial intelligence computers—because of these systems' gigantic appetites for memory; however, some scaled-down expert systems (such as the OS/2 version of KBMS, Knowledge Base Management System) run on microcomputers. Negotiator Pro from Beacon Expert Systems, Inc., for IBM and Apple Macintosh computers, helps executives plan effective negotiations with other people by examining their personality types and recommending negotiating strategies. Scaled-down systems generally do not have all the capabilities of large expert systems, and most have limited reasoning abilities. LISP and PROLOG compilers are available for microcomputers, as are some system-building tools such as EXPERT-EASE, NEXPERT, and VP-Expert, which allow relatively unsophisticated users to build their own expert system. Such software tools for building expert systems are called *shells*.

Implications for Business

Expert systems are becoming increasingly important to business and manufacturing firms. However, it is difficult to define what constitutes "expertise" in business. Defining expertise in business is a formidable task because of its general and "soft" nature; that is, "business" (unlike some other areas, notably math, medicine, and chemistry) is not made up of a specific set of inflexible facts and rules. Some business activities, however, do lend themselves to expert system development. DEC has developed several in-house expert systems, including ILPRS (which assists in long-range planning) and IPPMS (which assists in project management). Other examples are TAXMAN, which evaluates the tax consequences of various proposed business reorganization schemes; AUDITOR, which helps auditors assess a company's allowance for bad debts; and TAXADVISOR, which makes tax planning recommendations.

Another issue that inhibits the use of expert systems in business is that businesses want systems that can be integrated into their existing computer systems. Many existing expert systems are designed to run in a stand-alone mode. Furthermore, who will use the expert system? Who will be responsible for its maintenance? Who will have authority to add and/or delete knowledge in the expert system? What are the legal ramifications of decisions made by an expert system? These and other questions will have to be answered before expert systems are fully accepted in the business environment.

Cost is also a factor. Associated costs include purchasing hardware and software, hiring personnel, publishing and distribution costs (if the expert system is used at more than one location), and maintenance costs, which are usually more than the total of any costs already incurred. The costs can easily run into the many thousands of dollars. However, over the last few years, the number of implementations of expert systems has exploded from the hundreds to the thousands as businesses realize the benefits of better performance, reduced errors, and increased efficiency. In addition, less expensive micro-based tools are becoming increasingly powerful and available to businesses.

Virtual Reality

Want to take a trip to the moon? Be a race car driver? See the world through the eyes of an ocean-bottom creature or your cat? Without leaving your chair, you can experience almost anything you want through the form of AI called **virtual reality (VR)** (Figure 6), also known as *artificial reality* and *virtual environments*. In virtual reality, the user experiences a three-dimensional computer-generated environment called **cyberspace;** he or she is inside a world instead of just observing an image on the screen. To put yourself into virtual reality, you need special hardware—a headset called *Eyephones,* with 3-D screens and earphones, and gloves called *DataGloves,* which collect data about your hand movements and recognize commands from hand gestures. The headset includes a head-tracking device to enable the viewpoint to change as you move your head. The hardware uses software, such as Body Electric, that translates data into images and sound.

Aside from entertainment, artificial reality can provide instructional simulation situations to help people learn to exercise skills under varying conditions—skills such as driving, flying, outer space operations, police work, and disaster management, to name but a few. Architects are currently using virtual reality systems to allow clients to "test" their houses—walk through them and try out room sizes and designs—before building plans are finalized. Medical schools are starting to use virtual reality to teach surgical procedures to medical students.

FIGURE 6

(a) Jason Lanier, CEO and founder of VPL Research, wears a black spandex DataGlove with fiber-optic sensors to interact with computer-generated worlds that can be seen in 3-D while wearing the Eyephones seen on top of the monitor. Images from a demonstration world are projected behind him. (b) At VPL, Lou Ellyn Jones wears a data suit she designed; Bea Holster, a VPL electronic technician, makes an adjustment and Asif Ernon, a manufacturing engineer, adjusts the computer connection. Just as the DataGlove enables the user to interact, with hand gestures, in a virtual world, the bodysuit lets the wearer use the entire body to interact with a program. (c) At NASA Ames Research Center, two program developers demonstrate a virtual reality program they developed with a physician. The program enables doctors or students to manipulate the anatomy of a human leg. (d) Gary Reinagle of the Resource Center for the Handicapped takes a virtual reality tour of Seattle. Gary is a quadriplegic.

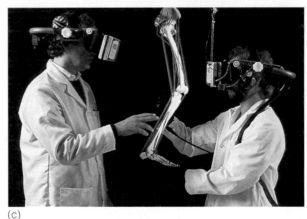

(a)

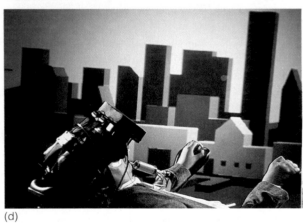

(b)

(c)

(d)

Object-Oriented Programming

Before we describe the fundamentals of the object-oriented approach to programming, we must familiarize you with a few terms and a bit of history. First, a software program, created by a professional programmer, is a group of related instructions that perform specific processing tasks. A group of software programs is referred to as a *software package* or *software application*. The coded instructions contained in most of the software packages in use today were typed by a software programmer one line at a time—usually in a programming language such as BASIC, COBOL, FORTRAN, C, Pascal, or Ada. One of the disadvantages of this traditional approach to creating programs is that much time is spent writing program segments that have already been written. This happens for a few reasons. Programmers don't tend to share their work with other programmers and often will take ownership of the code they develop. Therefore, it is possible that a programmer down the hall or at another location is programming something very similar. In addition, a programmer might have to write the same or slightly modified code over and over again in many different applications. For example, for many of the different applications programs developed, the programmer must write the same instructions for the user interface, or what the user sees on the screen. This process is very time-consuming and can be quite expensive.

To solve the problems of redundancy and time waste in program development, **object-oriented programming** treats each software program segment as an individual unit, or module, called an *object* that can be used repeatedly in different applications and by different programmers (Figure 7). Therefore, programmers won't have to spend time reinventing the wheel.

Imagine for an instant that you are viewing an automobile production line. As a component is moved down the production line, other components, such as seats, doors, windows, and engine, are added to it until a completed car emerges at the end of the assembly line. Each car is made up of individual components, or objects, that are designed to be attached to other components. The individual components were probably manufactured in different parts of the world and were purchased for use in this current line of automobiles.

Object-oriented programming brings production-line efficiency to microcomputer programming. Whereas an object in the production line is an individual component of the automobile, an object in an object-oriented program is a collection of related procedures (software instructions) and data that constitute one component of the entire applications program. The idea behind object-oriented programming is that programmers can pick and choose already-programmed objects to be included in a larger application, just as car makers pick and choose the components they want to include in their car models. For example, if the programmer wants to include a pull-down menu on the screen, he or she can choose the pull-down menu object instead of writing the code for the pull-down menu from scratch.

Clockenspiel's Common View is an object-oriented language that enables developers to use the same objects in applications written for the Microsoft Windows operating environment. Common View includes more than 350 objects for creating user-interface windows on the screen. Borland's C++ is another microcomputer object-oriented programming language for Windows. Taligent—the new microcomputer operating system from IBM and Apple—was written using object-oriented programming.

Conventional Programs

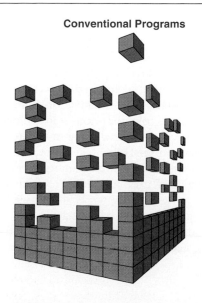

Object-Oriented Programs

FIGURE 7

Object-oriented programming versus traditional programming. Object-oriented programming eliminates the need to start over from scratch every time by allowing programmers to build programs with pre-assembled chunks of code instead of individual pieces. [Adapted from *PC Novice*, November 1992, p. 42.]

Advantages and Disadvantages

A major advantage of using object-oriented technology to develop software applications is that the resulting application is more likely to be error-free than if a traditional programming language and writing process are used. In addition, most new software applications incorporate graphic user interfaces. It is easier to program a graphic user interface by using an object-oriented language such as Smalltalk (developed by Xerox Palo Alto Research Center) or Digitalk Inc.'s Look and Feel Kit than it is to program using the C language, which has in the recent past been the language of choice among sophisticated programmers. In short, object-oriented programming techniques provide the software developer with the following benefits:

▼   Productivity is enhanced.

▼   Number of errors is kept to a minimum.

▼   Source code (actual program instructions) can be reused.

▼   Applications are easier to maintain.

What this means to a business is that, once a programmer becomes familiar with object-oriented techniques, it will take less time for the programmer to generate an initial working application, less time in the future for the programmer to generate additional working applications (because objects from the previous application can be used), and less time to update and maintain existing applications. The bottom line: business can save a lot of money in programming fees.

One drawback to implementing object-oriented technology is that it is initially difficult to learn for the programmer who is accustomed to using traditional programming languages. Traditional programs are code-based; object-oriented languages are object-based (component-based). Furthermore, object technology doesn't keep code and data separate, a fact that requires a programmer to look at a program in an entirely different way. Nonetheless, much excitement has surrounded the topic of object-oriented programming over the past several years, and the momentum behind this new approach to designing software applications is gaining speed.

Why Should Users Be Familiar with Object-Oriented Programming?

If your business needs a new applications program, you should consider employing an object-oriented approach because, as described earlier, your business can save a lot of money in programming fees. Businesses in the computer industry have been focusing on using object-oriented approaches for the past several years and plan to do so in the future. IBM and Apple Computer, Inc. are currently working together on object-oriented programming technologies that would enable networks using different operating environments to interact, or communicate. As this book went to press, Microsoft was planning on releasing an object-oriented version of Windows. In addition, Lotus Development Corporation has been working on modifying and enhancing its Lotus 1-2-3 spreadsheet by using object-oriented programming to update its graphic user interface. The company's main objective is to establish a standard user interface that can be used on different processing platforms.

Experts in the field of object-oriented programming predict that as object-oriented languages become easier to use, users, or nonprogrammers, will be able to develop simple applications by using object-oriented techniques.

*I*nformation technologies will grow far more sophisticated in the next few years, but social acceptance of some information services is likely to lag behind technical capabilities, according to a Delphi poll of experts.

Eleven authorities on technology were asked for estimates of the year in which a particular milestone would take place, as well as the likelihood of its occurrence. The accompanying chart lists mean estimates for these forecasts.

The experts were confident that significant advances in both computer hardware and software would occur in the next ten years or so. Examples include optical computers, automated software production, and computer programs that learn by trial and error. However, information services that would replace social interaction—such as teleconferencing, electronic shopping, and telecommuting—were thought to have a more modest likelihood of acceptance even during the first decade of the next century.

Milestone	Year of Occurrence	Probability (0–1.0)
Sophisticated software programs are developed for personalized teaching, managing medical care, total control of all corporate operations, etc.	1996	.95
Expert systems are commonly used to make routine decisions in business, engineering, medical diagnosis, and other fields.	1998	.88
Access to library materials via computer is more convenient and less expensive than going to the library.	2000	.87
Optical computers enter the commercial market.	2000	.86
Small computers about the size of a writing pad are commonly used by most people to manage their personal affairs and work.	2002	.85
Voice-access computers permit faster, more convenient interaction between humans and machines.	2002	.84
Education is commonly conducted using computerized teaching programs and interactive TV.	2002	.69
Public networks permit anyone access to libraries of data, electronic messages, video teleconferencing, common software programs, etc.	2003	.84
Routine parts of most software are generated automatically.	2003	.82
Parallel processing using multiple CPUs becomes prominent.	2003	.71
Computer programs have the capacity to learn by trial and error in order to adjust their behavior.	2004	.86
Teleconferencing replaces the majority of business travel.	2006	.40
Half of all goods in the United States are sold through computer services such as Prodigy.	2007	.43
Half of all U.S. workers perform their jobs partially at home using computer systems.	2009	.52

*From World Future Society, *The Futurist,* July–August 1992, p. 14; data collected by William E. Halal, David Collins, Tessa Lucero, Janice Parsek, Joseph Shaffner, Joseph Timmins. [7910 Woodmont Ave. #450, Bethesda, MD 20814, 301-656-8274]

S U M M A R Y

▼ *Artificial intelligence* (*AI*) is basically the science of making machines do what humans can do. The following are some of the primary areas of research within AI: robotics, natural language processing, virtual reality, and expert systems.

▼ The *Turing test* is used to determine the "intelligence" of a computer; if an operator is fooled into thinking that he or she is dealing with another human being instead of a computer, the computer passes the test.

▼ A *robot* is an automatic device that performs activities normally performed by human beings. Robots can be categorized according to whether they are intelligent or not. An unintelligent robot can carry out specific tasks, namely those that it was programmed to perform; most robots are unintelligent. An intelligent robot, or perception robot, is capable of showing initiative. Much research in recent years has focused on developing robots that can respond to the spoken word and can see.

▼ The goal of *natural language processing* is to enable a computer or robot to communicate with the user in the user's native language.

▼ *Fuzzy logic* is used along with natural language in artificial intelligence products. This type of logic allows for partial membership in a set, instead of restricting the logic to "either/or" propositions.

▼ *Virtual reality* enables the user to experience a computer-generated environment; in other words, the user feels like he or she is actually experiencing an environment rather than just looking at it on the screen.

▼ *Expert systems,* an application of artificial intelligence, are also used in the business world to aid in the support of decision making. An expert system is a collection of knowledge (and rules for using it, or heuristics) gathered by knowledge engineers from human experts and fed into a computer system.

▼ *Object-oriented programming* uses a programming method that treats individual program segments as *objects* that can be used repeatedly in other applications. Object-oriented programming helps to streamline the programming process by increasing productivity and decreasing the number of programming errors. In addition, applications created with object-oriented programming techniques are easier to maintain over time.

KEY TERMS

artificial intelligence (AI), p. 13.2
cyberspace, p. 13.9
expert system, p. 13.7

fuzzy logic, p. 13.7
natural language processing, p. 13.6
object-oriented programming, p. 13.11

robot, p. 13.2
Turing test, p. 13.6
virtual reality (VR), p. 13.9

EXERCISES

SELF-TEST

1. A _____ is an automatic device that performs functions that are ordinarily performed by a human being.

2. The goal of _____ _____

   _____ is to enable the computer to communicate with the user in the user's native language.

3. An _____ robot cannot respond to a situation for which it has not been specifically programmed.

4. _____ _____, which are based on a body of facts collected from human experts, help to solve problems that require substantial expertise to understand.

5. An _____, in an object-oriented program, is a collection of related procedures, or software instructions, and data.

6. A new concept being used in the development of natural language processing

   is _____ _____, which doesn't base decisions on either/or propositions.

7. A form of AI that lets you experience almost anything, such as viewing the world

   through the eyes of a monkey, is called _____

   _____.

8. An _____ robot is often referred to as a perception robot.

9. The primary areas of research within _____

   _____ are robotics, natural language processing, virtual reality, and expert systems.

10. The _____ approach to programming was developed to solve the problems of redundancy and time waste in program development.

Solutions: (1) robot; (2) natural language processing; (3) unintelligent; (4) expert systems; (5) object; (6) fuzzy logic; (7) virtual reality [or artificial reality]; (8) intelligent; (9) artificial intelligence; (10) object-oriented

SHORT-ANSWER QUESTIONS

1. Why is it so difficult to define *artificial intelligence?*

2. What is natural language processing?

3. What is an expert system?

4. Describe the relationship between the Turing test and research into artificial intelligence and natural language processing.

5. What benefits do object-oriented programming techniques provide? To whom?

6. What are the four main components of an expert system?

7. Why is it so expensive to develop an expert system?

8. What inhibits many companies from using expert systems?

9. What is meant by the terms *virtual reality* and *cyberspace?*

10. What is the difference between an intelligent robot and an unintelligent robot?

PROJECTS:

1. Research virtual reality in current computer magazines and other popular periodicals such as *Time* and *Newsweek*. What do you think of this new technology? What would you use it for? How could it be applied in educational settings?

2. During the 1990s you can expect expert systems to be used for the monitoring and control of a growing number of complex systems. Research what expert systems are currently being used and then focus on one that is of particular interest to you. Who developed the expert system? How long did it take? What are the hardware requirements for supporting the expert system? How is the expert system updated? Who uses the expert system and how is information retrieved from it?

3. Using computer magazines and other periodicals, research the state of the art of object-oriented programming. Who is using object-oriented techniques? What companies have switched from using traditional programming techniques to using object-oriented techniques? Why? Has the transition been difficult?

4. Artificial intelligence professional societies provide a variety of published material as well as symposia, workshops, conferences, and related services and activities for those involved in various AI fields. The societies offer publications and notices intended to keep members up to date on developments in the field. They also lobby elected officials on computer-related issues, provide scholarships, and develop educational videos and television shows. Following are four AI-related societies:

   American Association for Artificial Intelligence (AAAI)—the premier AI society (415) 328-3123

   Association for Computing Machinery (ACM)—for computing professionals of all types (817) 776-6876

   Institute of Electrical and Electronics Engineers (IEEE)—for engineers of all kinds (202) 785-0017

   International Association of Knowledge Engineers (IAKE)—a relatively new group for AI practitioners (301) 231-7826

   Contact these societies and request information on activities, services, and fees. Obtain some of their publications and give a short report. If possible, obtain a video presentation to show to the class.

Ethics, Privacy, and Security

A computer system consists not only of software, hardware, data/information, and procedures but also of people—the users of the computer system. Because computer systems are the products of human effort, we cannot trust them any more than we trust people. People can use computer systems for both good and bad purposes, and they may be comfortable or uncomfortable when they use them. But regardless of how they use them or how they feel about them, most people realize that computers have changed the way we live.

The deeper that computer technology reaches into our lives, the more questions we should be asking ourselves. For example: What are the consequences of the widespread presence of computer technology? Is computer technology creating more problems than it's solving? In the following sections we examine some critical issues related to the widespread use of computers.

PREVIEW

When you have completed this chapter, you will be able to:

▼ Discuss the issue of computers and the unethical invasion of privacy through the use of databases and networks

▼ Name some of the things that credit-reporting bureaus are doing to improve report accuracy and protect data

▼ Discuss the major laws passed in the United States to protect citizens' privacy and prevent the misuse of computers

▼ Define *computer crime* and give some examples of it along with ways to protect computer security

▼ Discuss the major hazards for computer systems

▼ Define *software piracy* and *copyright violation* and describe what freeware, shareware, and public-domain software are

"How did they get my name?" "I've just been denied a job on the basis of an error-ridden credit report!" "My employer got hold of my medical records!" "Someone used my social security number to set up some fraudulent accounts!" "Can XYZ Inc. really sell data on my financial history to that marketing organization?" "Someone took a copyrighted photograph of mine, changed it slightly, and had it printed without my permission in a famous magazine!" "Mary wants to copy my word processing software, since she can't afford to buy her own. Do you think I should let her?"

Such questions and comments are heard frequently these days. Unfortunately, their answers and solutions are heard less often. Indeed, many people are not aware of the extent of the problems relating to the ethical uses of computer technology, let alone the rights and duties they may have in using it. If you are to be a responsible member of the Information Age, you need to know about computers and privacy, hazards, security, and copyright violation.

Computers and Privacy

One definition of **ethics** is that it is a set of moral values or principles that govern the conduct of an individual or a group. People in most countries agree that they are entitled to the right of privacy—the right to keep personal information, such as credit ratings and medical histories, from getting into the wrong hands. The right of privacy from an electronic "invasion" into the realm of personal data has become a serious ethical issue.

Some of the computer-related privacy issues involve the use of large databases and electronic networks, and the enactment of certain laws.

Databases

Large organizations around the world are constantly compiling information about most of us. The number of on-line databases in 1975–1980 was approximately 400; in 1990 the number was 4,465, with 70% of those based in the United States. In the United States, social security numbers are routinely used as key fields in databases for organizing people's employment, credit, and tax records. As part of the billing process, telephone companies compile lists of the calls made, the numbers called, the time the calls were made, and so on. Using a special telephone directory called a *reverse directory* that lists telephone numbers followed by the names of the number holders, governmental authorities and others can easily get addresses of and other details about the persons we call. Credit card companies keep similar records.

Professional data gatherers, or "information resellers," collect personal data and sell it to fund-raisers, direct marketers, and others. In the United States, even some motor-vehicle departments sell the car-registration data they store. From this data database companies have been able to collect names, addresses, and other information about the majority of American households. Some privacy experts estimate that the average person is on 100 mailing lists and in 50 databases at one time. This invasion of privacy raises three issues:

1. How do you feel about personal information being spread without your consent? What if a great deal of information about your shopping habits and your income—collected without your consent—were made available to any small or large business that wanted it? Until they dropped the project in 1990, Lotus Development Corporation and Equifax, Inc. were preparing to do just that.

   On highways and bridges in some states—Texas, Louisiana, and Oklahoma, for example—toll-collecting systems read tags affixed to cars. When a car passes through a toll plaza, a machine records the tag's ID number and then, at the end of the month, bills the driver for tolls. The states say that the system cuts down on traffic and smog. But privacy advocates say the system could also give state government a powerful new tool to monitor its citizens; it will know when they're gone and which way they've traveled.

   What if you discovered that your employer was using your medical records to make decisions about placement, promotion, and firing? A survey done in the United States in 1988 found that half of the Fortune 500 companies were using employee medical records to make these decisions.

2. How do you feel about the spread of inaccurate information? Mistakes made in one computer file may find their way into other computer files. For example, many people find that their credit records contain errors. And even if you get the mistake corrected in one file, it may not be corrected in other files.

   Robert Ellis Smith, a U.S. lawyer, was worried enough about inaccuracy in the collection and dissemination of personal information to do something about it. In the early 1970s, as the use of computers became widespread, he worried that government and businesses could know too much about an individual's life and lifestyle. And what they knew quickly became a commodity for marketers. Smith said: "What I soon discovered was that there was often not any need for the information that was being collected, or respect for its accuracy." Smith has successfully been party in a suit against TRW, Inc., a major U.S. credit-reporting company. The result of the suit is to make it easier for consumers to correct errors in their credit reports. TRW has agreed to set up toll-free numbers for consumers to call with credit report questions. It will also make its reports easier to read and create a set of strict new rules for handling consumer complaints about credit report errors.

   However, credit-reporting companies also do background investigations on individuals for potential employers. Their reports are sometimes incorrect, and the result is that, for no valid reason, the applicant is not hired. To prevent this, consumer groups advocate the following:*

▼ *Improved accuracy:* Credit bureaus should take responsibility for correcting mistakes, no matter where the data came from, and they should inform other credit reporters of errors.

▼ *Free reports:* Consumers are entitled to a free copy of their credit reports once a year, not just when they are denied credit.

▼ *Privacy protection:* Consumers should be given a clear chance to prevent sales of personal data to marketers.

▼ *Improved service:* Credit-denial notices should include a list of consumers' rights. Investigations of errors should take 30 days, tops.

▼ *Better enforcement:* The Federal Trade Commission should be given more power to penalize credit reporters for violating the law.

---

*BusinessWeek, July 29, 1991, p. 70.

Fortunately, U.S. law allows its citizens to gain access to records about themselves that are held by credit bureaus and by governmental agencies (we'll discuss this in more detail later).

3. How do you feel about anonymous individuals and large companies profiting from the personal activities that make up your life? "Whose life is it, anyway?"

Electronic Networks

Imagine you use your company's electronic mail system—or an electronic bulletin board service—to send people a political message that includes some unflattering remarks against a particular group. Later you learn supervisors have been spying on your exchange or that the electronic bulletin board service has screened your messages and not sent them.

In the United States, some legislation has been introduced to control unannounced electronic "spying"—**electronic surveillance**—by supervisors. For example, one proposed law would require employers to provide prior written notice of electronic monitoring and supply some sort of audible or visual signal to alert employees that monitoring was occurring. However, most commercial electronic bulletin board services commonly restrict libelous, obscene, and offensive material through the use of electronic surveillance.

Many people believe that, in a nation linked by electronic mail, there has to be fundamental protection against other people reading or censoring messages or taking action because of their contents. Indeed, in October 1991, in a case involving CompuServe, a federal court in New York ruled that a computer network (information service) company is not legally liable for the contents of the information it disseminates. But some people think that there has to be a limit on the potentially libelous, offensive, or otherwise damaging contents of some messages, in spite of any existing rights to free speech and freedom from censorship. For example, the Prodigy information service network has a policy of prescreening its members' public notes. It warns its members that it won't carry messages that are obscene, profane, or otherwise offensive. But who determines exactly what is "obscene," "profane," or "offensive"?

Major Laws on Privacy

▼ U.S. **Fair Credit Reporting Act of 1970:** This law is intended to keep mistakes out of credit bureau files. Credit agencies are prohibited from sharing credit information with anyone but authorized customers. Consumers also have the right to look at and correct their credit records and to be notified of credit investigations for insurance and employment. However, credit agencies may share information with anyone they reasonably believe has a "legitimate business need." The term *legitimate* is not defined.

▼ U.S. **Freedom of Information Act of 1970:** This law gives citizens the right to look at data concerning themselves that is stored by the U.S. government. However, sometimes a lawsuit is necessary to gain access to the data.

▼ U.S. **Privacy Act of 1974:** This law restricts U.S. governmental agencies in the way they share information about American citizens. It prohibits federal information collected for one purpose from being used for a different purpose. However, some exceptions written into the law permit federal agencies to share information anyway.

▼ U.S. **Right to Financial Privacy Act of 1979:** This act sets procedures that U.S. governmental agencies must follow when examining customer records in a bank. However, the law does not cover state and local governments.

▼ U.S. **Computer Fraud and Abuse Act of 1986:** This law was passed to allow the prosecution of people who gain unauthorized access to computers and databases. However, people with legitimate access can get into computer systems and then create mischief without penalty.

▼ U.S. **Video Privacy Protection Act of 1988:** This act prevents retailers in the United States from selling or disclosing video-rental records without the customer's permission or a court order. (The same restrictions do not apply to more important files, such as medical and insurance records.)

▼ U.S. **Computer Matching and Privacy Protection Act of 1988:** This law sets procedures for using computer data for verifying a person's eligibility for federal benefits or for recovering delinquent debts. People are given a chance to respond before the government takes any adverse action against them. However, computer data can still be used for law-enforcement or tax reasons.

Since the late 1970s, seven European nations have enacted a patchwork of data protection laws. But Italy, Belgium, Spain, Portugal, and Greece have passed none. The matter of data protection and privacy remains one of the many barriers to a Europe that is a truly unified economic entity. If the European nations were to adopt a single privacy standard, however, current thinking is that it could be stricter than U.S. and Canadian laws (Figure 1).

Because many of the records stored by nongovernmental organizations are not covered by existing laws, privacy is still largely an ethical issue, not entirely a legal one. However, many people have indicated that they are concerned about controlling who has the right to personal information and how it is used. The following list summarizes the Code of Fair Information Practice, recommended in 1977. The code has been adopted by many information-collecting businesses in the United States, but many people would like to see it written into law.

1. *No secret databases:* There must be no secret record-keeping systems containing personal data.

2. *Right of individual access:* Individuals must be able to find out what information about them is in a record and how it is used.

3. *Right of consent:* Information about individuals obtained for one purpose cannot, without their consent, be used for other purposes.

4. *Right to correct:* Individuals must be able to correct or amend records of information about them.

5. *Assurance of reliability and proper use:* Organizations creating, maintaining, using, or disseminating records of identifiably personal data must make sure the data is reliable. They must take precautions to prevent such data from being misused.

Computer Hazards

Personal data in a computer database may not be protected if the computer itself is not kept safe from criminals, natural disasters, and other hazards.

Crime and Criminals

A **computer crime** is committed when a person uses computer technology or knowledge of computers in an illegal activity. To catch computer criminals, computers are programmed to do a lot of double-checking; but if the criminal evades the double-checks, he or she may not get caught. Police have a hard time track-

---

FIGURE 1

The privacy furor

The European Commission's proposal would:
▶ Prevent companies from keeping personal data or ID numbers without the person's O.K.
▶ Let consent be withdrawn at any time and permit damage suits if such privacy rights are infringed
▶ Require file-keepers to set up a security system to bar unauthorized access
▶ Ban electronic profiles of individuals based on what they buy or do through computer networks
▶ Bar transmission of data to countries without similar protections

ing down computer criminals because fingerprints and other traditional forms of evidence are irrelevant. Most computers use passwords to try to stop people from fooling around with sensitive data, but some programmers can get around the passwords. Typically, computer criminals who were caught used to be dealt with more leniently in court than other types of criminals—for example, someone who stole $100,000 from an electronic file received a lesser sentence than someone who used a gun and robbed a store of $1,000. But that situation is changing. Computer criminals are being dealt with more harshly than they used to be.

In general, computer criminals are of four types:

1. *Employees:* In this case, the crime can be theft. Of course, it can be theft of physical property, such as equipment and software. But often it is theft of proprietary information, money in electronic accounts, or computer time for private purposes. For example, two Bank of Boston employees were fired in late 1991; one for using the computer system to handicap horse races and the other for using the computer to run his Amway business—which took up 600 MB of memory! In addition, an employee may have a grudge and introduce program bugs into the system.

2. *Other authorized users:* Suppliers or clients may have access to a company's computer system. These authorized users may obtain secret passwords or find other means of committing computer crimes.

3. *"Hackers" and "crackers":* **Hackers** are people who gain unauthorized access to a computer system for fun. **Crackers** gain unauthorized access for malicious purposes—that is, to create trouble. For example, they may steal technical information or introduce a virus into the system.

4. *Professional criminals:* People in organized crime use computers for illegal purposes, such as to record of stolen goods or illegal gambling debts. Counterfeiters and forgers use microcomputer systems to produce checks, drivers' licenses, and other documents.

People are becoming more and more creative in the ways they use computers to commit crimes. Some of the more common types of computer crime are:

▼ *Damage:* Dissatisfied employees sometimes attempt to destroy computers, programs, or files. They may also attempt to infect the computer system with a virus (computer code that can erase or alter data or otherwise damage or shut down a computer system).

▼ *Theft:* Theft may be of hardware, software, data, or computer time. People steal equipment, and they steal data or use (steal) their company's computer time to run a sideline business.

▼ *Unauthorized copying:* Software piracy is the unauthorized copying of software disks for personal use (covered in more detail later in the chapter).

▼ *Manipulation:* Gaining entry into someone's computer network and manipulating, or changing, the data can cause unpredictable damage.

Other Hazards

Other dangers to computers and computer systems include the following:

▼ *Human errors:* Remember the phrase "garbage in, garbage out"? "Garbage" can mean mistakes made in data entry. Perhaps the data entry person's finger slipped while typing—imagine what an incorrectly placed decimal point could do—or perhaps he or she had incorrect data to begin with. Or, it can mean programming errors. Mistakes can also happen if the procedures for data entry are not clear. For example, are time measurements to be entered in minutes or seconds? Are distances to be entered in feet or meters? Can the user input "Y" instead of "yes"? Unfortunately, people tend to regard computer-generated information as gospel, in spite of the sizable potential for input error (Figure 2).

Other types of human carelessness can also have dire consequences for computer systems. For example, the $24 million computer-based security system at New York's Kennedy Airport was jeopardized recently when a computer disk containing classified information about 10,000 airport employees was found in a desk drawer of a Manhattan hotel. The disk was reportedly left behind by a project manager. Security experts now fear the information on that disk could be used by organized crime and terrorists to coerce airport workers into participating in illegal activities.

▼ *Technological failures:* Hardware and software failures can be caused by power surges and power outages. To protect themselves against power changes, many microcomputer users purchase surge protectors and uninterruptible power supply units. Also, users of hard disks should always remember to make backup copies of disk files, on diskettes or tape, in case the hard disk crashes.

▼ *Natural disasters:* Computer systems can be damaged or destroyed by fires, floods, wind, hurricanes, tornadoes, and earthquakes. Even personal computer users must be aware of the importance of storing backup disks of programs and data in safe locations in the event of a natural disaster.

▼ *Civil strife and terrorism:* Wars, revolutions, terrorism, and sabotage are greater risks in some parts of the world than in others, but these occurrences can definitely destroy a computer system. For example, during a period of civil unrest in November of 1991, looters in Zaire destroyed six years of medical data used in AIDS research. The looters stole all the computers and the data had not been backed up.

Computer Security

Controls must be built into computer systems to ensure **security,** the protection of data, hardware, and software from unauthorized use as well as from damage

---

Rex Reed, writer and sometime actor, ordered a bed from a Manhattan department store.

Three months passed. Then came the long-anticipated announcement: the bed will be delivered on Friday.

Reed waited all day. No bed.

Having disposed of his other bed, he slept on the floor.

Next day deliverers brought the bed but couldn't put it up. No screws.

On Monday, men appeared with the screws. But they couldn't put in the mattresses. No slats. "That's not our department."

Reed hired a carpenter to build them; the department store's slats finally arrived 15 weeks later.

Undaunted, Reed went to the store to buy sheets. Two men came up and declared "You're under arrest." Why? "You're using a stolen credit card. Rex Reed is dead." Great confusion. Reed flashed all his identity cards. The detectives apologized—and then tore up his store charge card. Why? "Our computer has been told that you are dead. And we cannot change this."

FIGURE 2

One result of input errors. (From *Time* magazine, reprinted in *The Secret Guide to Computers*, 14th ed., p. 542. © 1990 by Russ Walter, 22 Ashland St. #2, Somerville, MA 02144-3202.)

from intrusions, sabotage, and natural disasters. In general, ensuring computer system security involves:

▼ *Controlling access:* Security professionals are constantly devising techniques to protect computer systems from being accessed by unauthorized persons. Sometimes guards are posted in company computer rooms, to check the identification of everyone who enters. Sometimes locks are put on microcomputers and ID numbers are etched on computer equipment and encoded via software on hard disks and floppy disks. Disks, diskettes, and tapes are kept in locked containers and/or rooms. (Removable hard disk cartridges are easy to lock up.) Passwords may be issued to people to use to gain access to computer files. (Passwords are the secret words or numbers that must be entered into a computer system before it will operate.)

Some security systems use biometrics, the science of measuring individual body characteristics (Figure 3)—using machines that can recognize one's fingerprints, signature, or voice; some can even recognize a face by comparing it with a photograph.

▼ *Forecasting disasters:* Ensuring physical security means protecting hardware from possible human and natural disasters. Data security is involved with

---

FIGURE 3

Computer security: A few ways to keep hackers and crackers out. (Adapted from *Fortune*, December 16, 1991, p. 14.)

Estimates show that U.S. business and government agencies lose more than $1 billion a year to hackers and other high-tech criminals.

Limiting access to files and databases is the key defense. Most Americans use all-too-obvious passwords to log on to their machines, employing such giveaways as their street address, dog's name, or spouse's well-known nickname.

To make access more secure, an increasing number of companies are issuing their employees "tokens," which the user carries. The tokens look like credit cards and display a row of numbers that, through the wonders of modern technology, changes every 60 seconds. To log on to most systems using tokens, the user first types in his or her password then this number. The computer, which is in sync with the numerals, allows entry.

Another mode of computer security involves biometrics. It goes beyond passwords (what you know) and tokens (what you have) to biological features (what you are). See below for how four such systems work.

Voice I.D.

Computer recognizes user's voice. Strength: Completely mobile and makes access from phone possible. Weakness: Expensive; static can block access.

Retinal I.D.

A ray of light looks at map of blood vessels on back of eyeball. Strength: Similar technology can already open doors. Weakness: Eye safety is still a concern.

Fingerprint I.D.

Identification through a "reader" gadget attached to computer. Strength: Fingerprints are unique. Weakness: Limited mobility—user must carry brick-size reader.

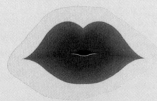

Lip Prints

User kisses screen. Fanciful technology in earliest stages. Strength: Lip patterns are unique. Weakness: Makeup, chapped lips and cold sores can block signal.

protecting software and data from unauthorized interference or damage. Most large organizations have a disaster recovery plan that describes ways to continue operations following a disaster until normal computer operations can be restored. This may include an alternative data center in another location or a "cold site"—an empty facility ready to go as soon as the computer supplier can install the necessary equipment.

▼ *Duplicating data:* If a disaster occurs, computer equipment may be replaced, but data may not be—unless it was backed up. And, the backup files should be kept in a safe place that is in a location different from the location of the original data files (Figure 4). Some companies employ outside services such as Comdisco Disaster Recovery Services, Inc., which maintains client data at a number of centers throughout Canada and the United States.

▼ *Using encryption:* Data transmitted over communications lines can be secured by encryption to prevent eavesdropping. **Encryption** is the encoding of data by converting the standard data code into a proprietary (secret) code for transmission. After transmission, the data is converted back into standard code.

Computers and Copyright Violation

Software Piracy: Don't Copy That Floppy!

Software piracy, or theft, has become a major concern to software writers and manufacturers. For example, the software industry estimates that it lost an additional $2.4 billion of its total 1990 sales of $5.7 billion to software piracy. However, the act of piracy is not quite as dramatic as it sounds. In most cases it simply means illegally copying private domain (copyrighted) software onto blank disks. (It *is* legal for buyers of software to make backup copies on blank disks.) Because much software—from games to sophisticated publishing programs—is expensive, it's tempting to avoid buying an off-the-shelf package by accepting a friend's offer to supply free copies. But, according to the Copyright Act of

---

The following story was related by Russ Walter, who writes and produces a popular guide to computers.

"On my own hard disk, the only file that's critical is TRAN, which contains the details of every transaction that generated income or an order. Since it's too long to copy onto floppies quickly, I copy it instead to a file called TRANBAK on the same hard disk. Copying TRAN to TRANBAK takes just a few seconds, so I do it every day. If I ever lose TRAN, I just tell the computer to rename TRANBAK to TRAN. Simple!

"But what happens if my whole hard disk suddenly goes bad, so that I lose TRAN and TRANBAK simultaneously? To prepare for such a calamity, once a week I copy TRAN onto floppies. I also keep paper records of all transactions that occurred during the week.

"Hard disks are fairly reliable. The only time calamity struck me was when I disobeyed the rules. On a summer afternoon when I was rushing to finish some research, I risked using the computer when the temperature was in the high 90s. I was sorry! The hard disk's outermost tracks—which contain the directory and the fundamental formatting information—burned up. (As we computer junkies say, `The tracks *fried*.') When I tried using the disk the next day, the computer told me the disk didn't exist. After saying a few prayers and other things, I got a new hard disk and restored the previous week's TRAN from floppies."

FIGURE 4

Backup tale. (From Russ Walter, *The Secret Guide to Computers,* 14th ed., © 1990 by Russ Walter, 22 Ashland St. #2, Somerville, MA 02144-3202.)

1976, the Software Copyright Act of 1980, and the Computer Software Piracy and Counterfeiting Amendment of 1983, this practice is illegal. It is also unethical.

Computer programmers and software companies often spend years developing, writing, testing, and marketing software programs—only to lose many royalty dollars to software "pirates." If you spent several years writing a book, only to lose royalties through the distribution of illegally copied volumes, how would you feel? The issue is the same.

What you're really buying when you purchase software is the **license** to use the software (Figure 5). However, vendors include different restrictions with the licenses they sell. When you purchase a software package, make sure that you read the license agreement and send in the registration card, if any, so that you will receive information on new versions and other updates.

If you violate the licensing agreement you may find yourself confronted by the Software Publishing Association (SPA). From July 1, 1991, to June 30, 1992, the SPA collected $3.2 million in fines from U.S. companies. It also filed 33 lawsuits, conducted 75 raids, and sent 561 warning letters. To help companies avoid illegal software copying, the SPA recommends that companies:

1. Appoint a software manager
2. Implement a software code of ethics that all employees sign
3. Establish procedures for acquiring and registering software
4. Establish and maintain a software log
5. Conduct periodic audits of company software

FIGURE 5

This part of a Microsoft software licensing agreement clearly indicates that the product is for a single user; copying for additional users is illegal.

IMPORTANT—READ CAREFULLY BEFORE OPENING SOFTWARE PACKET(S). Unless a separate multilingual license booklet is included in your product package, the following License Agreement applies to you. By opening the sealed packet(s) containing the software, you indicate your acceptance of the following Microsoft License Agreement.

Microsoft License Agreement

(Single-User Products)

This is a legal agreement between you (either an individual or an entity) and Microsoft Corporation. By opening the sealed software packet(s) you are agreeing to be bound by the terms of this agreement. If you do not agree to the terms of this agreement, promptly return the unopened software packet(s) and the accompanying items (including written materials and binders or other containers) to the place you obtained them for a full refund.

MICROSOFT SOFTWARE LICENSE

1. GRANT OF LICENSE. Microsoft grants to you the right to use one copy of the enclosed Microsoft software program (the "SOFTWARE") on a single computer. The SOFTWARE is in "use" on a computer when it is loaded into temporary memory (i.e., RAM) or installed into your permanent memory (e.g., hard disk, CD-ROM, or other storage device) of that computer. However, installation on a network server for the sole purpose of distribution to one or more other computer(s) shall not constitute "use" for which a separate license is required.

2. COPYRIGHT. The SOFTWARE is owned by Microsoft or its suppliers and is protected by United States copyright laws and international treaty provisions. Therefore, you must treat the SOFTWARE like any other copyrighted material (e.g. a book or musical recording) except that you may either (a) make one copy of the SOFTWARE solely for backup or archival purposes, or (b) transfer the SOFTWARE to a single hard disk provided you keep the original solely for backup or archival purposes. You may not copy the written materials accompanying the SOFTWARE.

3. OTHER RESTRICTIONS. You may not rent or lease the SOFTWARE, but you may transfer the SOFTWARE and accompanying written materials on a permanent basis provided you retain no copies and the recipient agrees to the terms of this Agreement. You may not reverse engineer, decompile, or disassemble the SOFTWARE. If the SOFTWARE is an update or has been updated, any transfer must include the most recent update and all prior versions.

4. DUAL MEDIA SOFTWARE. If the SOFTWARE package contains both 3.5" and 5.25" disks, then you may use only the disks appropriate for your single-user computer. You may not use the other disks on another computer or loan, rent, lease, or transfer them to another user except as part of the permanent transfer (as provided above) of all SOFTWARE and written materials.

6. Establish an employee education program

7. Maintain a library of software licenses

8. Take advantage of the benefits of software license compliance that are offered by the software companies (such as free telephone consultation and inexpensive upgrades)

Also, follow the general rule: one machine, one copy.

Some software companies write copy-protect programs into their software to prevent illegal copying; other software authors offer free or inexpensive copies of their programs, called *freeware* and *shareware*.

Shareware, Freeware, and Public Domain Software

Shareware, freeware, and public domain software are all a kind of noncommercial software usually distributed through electronic bulletin board services. Shareware costs something—but much less than commercial software packages—and freeware and public domain software usually cost nothing.

Shareware is distributed on request for an evaluation period, after which the user pays a registration fee or returns the software. After the user pays the registration fee—or licensing fee—he or she is usually sent documentation, and, in some cases, additional support and notification of updates.

Freeware authors do not charge for their software, but they may limit its distribution. Sometimes these authors ask for feedback from users regarding any bugs in and incompatibilities with the program.

Public domain software is entirely in the public domain—that is, it carries no copyrights—and carries no restrictions. Users who use public domain software should keep in mind that software reliability may be an issue. It may have been copied many times and have been altered or tampered with in the process. Also, it may have a virus. Users should install a virus-protection program on their computers and scan all shareware, freeware, and public domain disks before using the programs on those disks.

Electronic Manipulation of Copyrighted Material

Most people are aware that they need to obtain permission to print text and illustrations that are copyrighted by others. Permission to reprint usually involves paying the copyright holder a fee and inserting a credit line—which gives the copyright holder's name—with the reprinted text or illustration. However, now that illustrations, including photos, can be scanned into a computer system and altered using certain types of software, a new type of copyright violation is occurring: the digital alteration of photos and other art without the permission of the copyright holder. Computer users in the field of desktop publishing need to be especially aware of the copyright restrictions of the materials they are working with.

Also, it is unethical for photojournalists to alter photos and then present them to readers as representing reality. The National Press Photographers Association (NPPA) has stated: "Altering the editorial content of a photograph, in any degree, is a breach of the ethical standards recognized by the NPPA."

A Last Word

What are some of the other ethical issues that have arisen as a result of using computers in the workplace and in other aspects of daily life?

Many universities incorporate into their computer science curriculum a course on ethics. For example, in 1990, Polytechnic University in Brooklyn added a course to its curriculum: Information, Society, and Man. This course teaches students that computing professionals have a responsibility to act in an ethical manner. Especially in a networked environment, where many different computers are connected together, professionals maintaining the network have a serious responsibility to hundreds of people they will never see—a responsibility to maintain privacy and accuracy of data, among other things.

Interestingly, although other disciplines have long followed codes of ethics—for example, the goal of a civil engineer is to build public structures that are *safe*—strict codes of ethical standards have not been defined in the world of computing. Computer industry observers predict that users and computer professionals alike will be faced with more and more ethical *dilemmas,* or "gray areas," in the future.

For example, many people focus on the use of computers to free us from repetitive and boring work. This is certainly welcome in many situations, but we must remember that what is boring and routine work to one person may be life-saving employment to another. Traditionally in the United States, many low-level jobs are held by young people and immigrants with language problems. Therefore, what at first seems like an advantage of computerization may really be a disadvantage. McDonald's restaurants came to this conclusion not too long ago when they decided not to eliminate the jobs of people who take orders at the front counters and replace the human order-takers with machines that customers would use to key in their own orders. And maintaining human contact is still better for business.

More and more, information is replacing energy as society's main resource. Many people are concerned that too much emphasis has been put on what the computer can do to streamline business and too little on how it may be affecting the quality of our lives. For example, is it distorting the meaning of thought? That is, is it absurd and dangerous to attribute the capabilities of thinking and creativity to a computer? People have experience, convictions, and cultural traditions. Are these qualities being devalued? If so, perhaps we are heading into an era in which machine-like qualities of speed and problem solving will be valued more highly than what used to be called *humane* qualities. As a result, many people believe computers have the potential to contribute to worker dissatisfaction.

Consider again the potential for using computer-based systems in business to monitor employees. What if computers were (and many already are) programmed to check your speed, the pauses you make, the breaks you take, the rate of keying errors? Would it be fair for the company to do this to make sure it retains only the most efficient workers and thus increase the value of goods and services it has to sell? Or would this detract from your dignity as a human being—your right to do some things better than you do others? And would this type of company get high-quality decisions from its employees—or would the employees be too afraid to work creatively? One major labor union in the United States, the AFL-CIO, has taken the position that electronic surveillance "invades workers' privacy, erodes their sense of dignity, and frustrates their efforts to do high-quality work by a single-minded emphasis on speed."

In addition, a growing percentage of the work force is working at home. Workers can communicate with their offices via a microcomputer and special communications software. In many cases, this arrangement enables workers in metropolitan areas to get work done instead of sitting in traffic. However, how does working at home affect employee morale, efficiency, and motivation? How does the employer maintain control of the employee? With these issues in mind, is the employee who works at home really more productive?

Another important issue relates to the disabled. For most of us, computers make our lives more convenient. But for some—people with disabilities—computers play a much greater role. Computers have the potential of equalizing the workplace by enabling people with mobility, vision, and hearing impairments to do the same work as people who aren't handicapped. Some disabled workers have difficulty holding down more than two keys at once or using a mouse. Blind workers need special translator hardware so they can read text and numbers. Fortunately, many add-on products are available to adapt standard microcomputers to the needs of the disabled, including voice translators for the blind and software that modifies the way the keyboard and the mouse are used. However, products like these vary in sophistication and are usually quite expensive. As a result, very few companies make these purchases. Aren't these companies discriminating against the handicapped? Many legislators are actively working to pass a bill that will make this form of discrimination illegal.

As a close to this topic of privacy, ethics, and security, we invite you to study the code of ethics and professional conduct put forth in December 1992 by the Association for Computing Machinery (ACM) (Table 1), as well as the "Ten Commandments of Computer Ethics" issued by the Computer Ethics Institute (Table 2).

This chapter covered only a few of the many computer-related issues that are being discussed today. Keep an important thought in mind, however: although these problems certainly deserve everyone's attention, they should not obscure the opportunities that will be opened to you if you know how to use computers. In a sense, those of us who embrace technology are ageless. Any and all can participate in computer technology   it knows no age, sex, color, or religious bounds. It's exciting to think that technology can be a force against stereotypes and prejudice.

TABLE 1

Association for Computing
Machinery's Ethics Code

1. General moral imperatives. As an ACM member I will:
   a. Contribute to society and human well-being
   b. Avoid harm to others
   c. Be honest and trustworthy
   d. Be fair and take action not to discriminate
   e. Honor property rights including copyrights and patents
   f. Give proper credit for intellectual property
   g. Access computing and communication resources only when authorized to
   h. Respect the privacy of others
   i. Honor confidentiality

2. As an ACM computing professional I will:
   a. Strive to achieve the highest quality in both the process and products of professional work
   b. Acquire and maintain professional competence
   c. Know and respect existing laws pertaining to professional work
   d. Accept and provide appropriate professional review
   e. Give comprehensive and thorough evaluations of computer systems and their impacts, with special emphasis on possible risks
   f. Honor contracts, agreements, and assigned responsibilities
   g. Improve public understanding of computing and its consequences

3. Organizational leadership imperatives: As an ACM member and an organizational leader, I will:
   a. Articulate social responsibilities of members of an organizational unit and encourage full acceptance of those responsibilities
   b. Manage personnel and resources to design and build information systems that enhance the quality of working life
   c. Acknowledge and support proper and authorized uses of an organization's computing and communication resources
   d. Ensure that users and those who will be affected by a system have their needs clearly articulated during the assessment and design of requirements; later the system must be validated to meet requirements
   e. Articulate and support policies that protect the dignity of users and others affected by a computing system
   f. Create opportunities for members of the organization to learn the principles and limitations of computer systems

TABLE 2

The Ten Commandments of
Computer Ethics (Computer
Ethics Institute, 11 Dupont
Circle NW #900, Washington
DC 20035).

1. Thou shalt not use a computer to harm other people.
2. Thou shalt not interfere with other people's computer work.
3. Thou shalt not snoop around in other people's computer files.
4. Thou shalt not use a computer to steal.
5. Thou shalt not use a computer to bear false witness.
6. Thou shalt not copy or use proprietary software for which you have not paid.
7. Thou shalt not use other people's computer resources without authorization or proper compensation.
8. Thou shalt not appropriate other people's intellectual output.
9. Thou shalt think about the consequences of the program you are writing or the system you are designing.
10. Thou shalt always use a computer in ways that ensure consideration and respect for your fellow humans.

A primary interest of mine is the application of computer technology to the needs of the handicapped. Through the application of computer technology, handicaps associated with the major sensory and physical disabilities can largely be overcome during the next decade or two. I am confident of this development because of the fortunate matching of the strengths of early machine intelligence with the needs of the handicapped. The typical disabled person is missing a specific skill or capability but is otherwise a normally intelligent and capable human being. It is generally possible to apply the sharply focused intelligence of today's machines to ameliorate these handicaps. A reading machine, for example, addresses the inability of a blind or dyslexic person to read, probably the most significant handicap associated with the disability of blindness.

In the early 21st century lives of disabled persons will be far different than they are today. For the blind, reading machines will be pocket-sized devices that can instantly scan not only pages of text but also signs and symbols found in the real world. These machines will be able to read with essentially perfect intonation and with a broad variety of voice styles. They will also be able to describe pictures and graphics, translate from one language to another, and provide access to on-line knowledge bases and libraries through wireless networks. Most blind and dyslexic persons will have them, and they may be ubiquitous among the rest of the population.

Blind persons will carry computerized navigational aids that will perform the functions of seeing-eye dogs, only with greater intelligence than today's canine navigators. Attempts up to now at electronic navigational assistants for the blind have not proved useful. Unless such a device incorporates a level of intelligence at least comparable to that of a seeing-eye dog, it is not of much value. This is particularly true since modern mobility training can provide a blind person equipped only with an ordinary cane with substantial travel skills. I personally know many blind people who can travel around town and even around the world with ease. With the intelligent navigational aids of the future, travel skills for the blind will become even easier.

Ultimately, compact devices will be built that combine both reading and navigational capabilities with the ability to provide intelligent descriptions of real-world scenes on a real-time basis. At that stage of machine evolution they are probably more accurately called *seeing* machines. Such a machine would be like a friend that could describe what is going on in the visible world. The blind user could ask the device (verbally or in some other way) to elaborate on a description, or he could ask it questions. The visual sensors of such a device could be built into a pair of eyeglasses, although it may be just as well to pin it on the user's lapel. In fact, these artificial eyes need not only look forward; they may as well look in all directions. And they may have better visual acuity than normal eyes. We may all want to use them.

The deaf will have hearing machines that can display what people are saying. The underlying technology required is the Holy Grail of voice recognition: combining large-vocabulary recognition with speaker independence and continuous speech. Early versions of speech-to-text aids for the deaf should appear over the next decade. Artificial hearing should also include the ability to intelligently translate other forms of auditory information, such as music and natural sounds, into other modalities, such as vision and touch.

By Raymond Kurzweil, *The Age of Intelligent Machines* (Cambridge, MA: Massachusetts Institute of Technology, 1990), pp. 441–443.

Eventually we may find suitable channels of communication directly into the brain to provide truly artificial sight and hearing. But in any case, there will certainly be progress in restoring lost hearing and sight.

The physically handicapped (paraplegics and quadriplegics) will have their ability to walk and climb stairs restored, abilities that will overcome the severe access limitations wheelchairs impose. Methods to accomplish this will include exoskeletal robotic devices, or powered orthotic devices, as they are called. These devices will be as easy to put on as a pair of tights and will be controlled by finger motion, head motion, speech, and perhaps eventually thoughts. Another option, one that has shown promise in experiments at a number of research institutes, is direct electrical stimulation of limb muscles. This technique effectively reconnects the control link that was broken by spinal cord damage.

Those without use of their hands will control their environment, create written text, and interact with computers using voice recognition. This capability already exists. Artificial hand prostheses controlled by voice, head movement, and perhaps eventually by direct mental connection, will restore manual functionality.

Substantial progress will be made in courseware to treat dyslexia (difficulty in reading for neurophysical reasons other than visual impairment) and learning disabilities. Such systems will also provide richer learning experiences for the retarded.

Perhaps the greatest handicap associated with sensory and physical disabilities is a subtle and insidious one: the prejudice and lack of understanding often exhibited by the general public. Most handicapped persons do not want pity or charity; instead, they want to be respected for their own individuality and intelligence. We all have handicaps and limitations; those of a blind or deaf person may be more obvious, but they are not necessarily more pervasive or limiting. I have worked with many disabled persons, and I know from personal experience that they are as capable as other workers and students at most tasks. I cannot ask a blind person to drive a package across town, but I can ask him to give a speech or conduct a research project. A sighted worker may be able to drive a car, but he will undoubtedly have other limitations. The lack of understanding many people have of handicapped persons is evident in many ways, some obvious, some subtle. By way of example, I have had the following experience on many occasions while eating a meal with a blind person in a restaurant. The waiter or waitress will ask me if my blind friend wants dessert or if he wants cream in his coffee. While the waiter or waitress obviously intends no harm or disrespect, the message is clear. Since there is no indication that the blind person is also deaf, the implication is that he must not be intelligent enough to deal with human language.

A not unimportant side benefit of intelligent technology for the handicapped should be a substantial alteration of these negative perceptions. If the handicaps resulting from disabilities are significantly reduced, if blind people can read and navigate with ease, if deaf persons can hold normal conversations on the phone, then we can expect public perceptions to change as well. When blind, deaf, and other disabled persons take their place beside us in schools and the workplace and perform with the same effectiveness as their nondisabled peers, we shall begin to see these disabilities as mere inconveniences, as problems no more difficult to overcome than poor handwriting or fear of public speaking or any of the other minor challenges that we all face.

▼ The development of computers and large electronic databases has facilitated the collection of information about individuals. In the past, this information has been sold to marketing groups without the individual's consent. Many people believe this is an unethical practice.

▼ The information that is collected about individuals and then transmitted to credit-reporting companies is often error-ridden, causing people to be denied loans and jobs, in addition to causing other problems.

▼ Seemingly private information about individuals—such as medical records—has been disseminated to others—such as employers—and used to make decisions about which the individuals may know nothing.

▼ Consumer groups are trying to correct the problems involving data collection and dissemination and make information sellers more responsible by advocating:

1. *Improved accuracy:* Information sellers must correct mistakes in the data, no matter where it came from.

2. *Free reports:* At the request of an individual, information sellers must provide a copy of the individual's report for free once a year.

3. *Protect privacy:* Companies that sell data must give an individual a clear chance to prevent sales of personal data to marketers.

4. *Improved service:* Credit denial notices should include a list of consumers' rights. Investigations of errors should take no more than 30 days.

5. *Better enforcement:* Credit reporters should be penalized for violating the law.

▼ The use of electronic communications and information networks has also raised ethical concerns about the censorship of some messages and the electronic "spying" on message contents by supervisors in companies and directors of information services.

▼ The United States has passed seven major laws in an attempt to protect individual privacy and regulate the selling of information:

1. *Fair Credit Reporting Act of 1970:* Intended to keep mistakes out of credit bureau files; credit agencies are barred from sharing credit information with anyone but authorized customers; consumers also have the right to review and correct their credit records and to be notified of credit investigations for insurance and employment.

2. *Freedom of Information Act of 1970:* Gives citizens the right to look at data concerning themselves that is stored by the U.S. government.

3. *Privacy Act of 1974:* Restricts governmental agencies in the way they share information about American citizens; prohibits federal information collected for one purpose from being used for a different purpose.

4. *Right to Financial Privacy Act of 1979:* Sets strict procedures that U.S. governmental agencies must follow when they want to examine customer records in a bank.

5. *Computer Fraud and Abuse Act of 1986:* Allows the prosecution of people who gain unauthorized access to computers and databases.

6. *Video Privacy Protection Act of 1988:* Prevents retailers in the United States from selling or disclosing video-rental records without the customer's consent or a court order.

7. *Computer Matching and Privacy Protection Act of 1988:* Sets procedures for using computer data for verifying a person's eligibility for federal benefits or for recovering delinquent debts.

▼ The *Code of Fair Information Practice* was recommended in 1977 and has been adopted by many U.S. businesses. Though not yet law, the code recommends:

14.17

1. *No secret databases*

2. *Right of individual access*

3. *Right of consent*

4. *Assurance of reliability and proper use*

▼ A *computer crime* is committed when a person uses computer technology or knowledge of computers in an illegal activity. It can include:

1. Employee theft of hardware, software, proprietary information, electronic funds, or company time on the computer (for example, by running a private business); a disgruntled employee can also introduce bugs or viruses into a company system.

2. Other authorized users with access to a company's computer system may abuse their privileges by stealing information or funds or by introducing bugs or viruses.

3. Hackers or crackers may gain unauthorized access to a system and steal information or introduce viruses.

4. People in organized crime may use computers for illegal purposes.

▼ In addition to being subject to theft and sabotage, computer systems may be damaged by natural disasters, civil unrest and terrorism, technological failures, and/or human errors. Because of these dangers, computer systems must be made as secure as possible, and all data must be backed up. Ideally, the backup disks or tape should be kept in a different, safe location.

▼ *Computer security* includes:

1. Controlling access to the system by the use of guards and passwords

2. Locking some equipment and rooms and engraving ID numbers on the equipment

3. Using biometrics to identify and clear users

4. Forecasting disasters

5. Duplicating data

6. Using encryption for data transmissions over communications lines

▼ *Software piracy* is the illegal copying of copyrighted software onto blank disks for unauthorized use.

▼ When a user buys software, he or she is really buying a *license* to use that software; he or she is not authorized to make and give copies to anyone else.

▼ *Shareware* is software distributed on request—usually through an electronic bulletin board service—for which the user pays a small fee if he or she wishes to keep it. Shareware carries a copyright.

▼ *Freeware* is free software usually distributed in a limited fashion through an electronic bulletin board service.

▼ *Public domain software* is free software without any copyright and usually distributed through a bulletin board service.

▼ Copyrighted photos and illustrations may not be electronically manipulated without the copyright holder's consent.

KEY TERMS

computer crime, p. 14.6
Computer Fraud and Abuse Act of 1986, p. 14.5
Computer Matching and Privacy Protection Act of 1988, p. 14.5
cracker, p. 14.6
electronic surveillance, p. 14.4
encryption, p. 14.9
ethics, p. 14.2

Fair Credit Reporting Act of 1970, p. 14.4
Freedom of Information Act of 1970, p. 14.4
freeware, p. 14.11
hacker, p. 14.6
license, p. 14.10
Privacy Act of 1974, p. 14.4
public domain software, p. 14.11

Right to Financial Privacy Act of 1979, p. 14.4
security, p. 14.8
shareware, p. 14.11
software piracy, p. 14.9
Video Privacy Protection Act of 1988, p. 14.5

EXERCISES

SELF-TEST

1. _____ is a set of moral values or principles that govern the conduct of an individual or a group.

2. In the United States, it is not possible for someone to use another person's social security number to set up bank accounts and obtain credit cards. (true/false)

3. _____ _____ involves the electronic monitoring by a supervisor of employees' work performance.

4. The U.S. Freedom of Information Act of 1970 gives citizens the right to look at data concerning themselves that is stored by the U.S. government. (true/false)

5. In the United States, video-rental stores can sell customers' video-rental records without the customers' consent. (true/false)

6. A _____ _____ is committed when a person uses computer technology or knowledge of computers in an illegal activity.

7. _____ are people who gain unauthorized access to a computer system for fun; _____ gain unauthorized access for malicious purposes.

8. Computer _____ is the protection of information, hardware, and software from unauthorized use as well as from damage.

9. The encoding of data from a standard code into a secret proprietary code for protection from eavesdropping during data transmission is called

   _____.

10. If a user copies copyrighted software onto blank disks and uses the copies as backup, he or she is committing software piracy. (true/false)

Solutions: (1) ethics; (2) false; (3) electronic surveillance; (4) true; (5) false; (6) computer crime; (7) hackers, crackers; (8) security; (9) encryption; (10) false

SHORT-ANSWER QUESTIONS

1. List five things that consumer groups believe credit-reporting companies should do to better serve customers.

2. List and briefly describe the seven privacy laws enacted in the United States.

3. Define *computer crime* and give a few examples.

4. What does the phrase "garbage in, garbage out" mean?

5. How can users help prevent data damage or loss from natural disasters and technological failures?

6. What is data encryption used for?

7. List at least four ways of ensuring the security of a computer system.

8. Define *software piracy*.

9. What is shareware?

10. What danger might exist in electronically manipulating photos and other illustrations?

PROJECTS

1. What's your opinion about the issue of free speech on an electronic network? Research some recent legal decisions in various countries, as well as some articles on the topic, and then give a short report about what you think. Should the contents of messages be censored? If so, under what conditions?

2. People especially susceptible to electronic surveillance while they are working include those who work for airlines; hotel, rental car, mail-order, insurance, telephone, and credit card companies; or federal, state, and local U.S. government departments and agencies. For example, recently an airline reservation employee took a call from a distraught man who had to book a flight to go to his sister's funeral. The employee purposely spent extra time with the man because he was upset. Later, she was reprimanded by a supervisor who said that her work had been monitored and that she had taken too long with the call, thus losing revenue for the airline.

   Give a short report taking a position for or against the electronic surveillance of employees during work time. Be sure to consider what the opposite position's points would be and refute them.

3. *Privacy for Sale,* by Jeffrey Rothfeder (Simon & Schuster, 1992), catalogs major and minor "horror stories" from the recent annals of America's constantly growing computer state. For example, one man, who did not smoke or drink and who was in good health, was shocked when he was told by an insurance company that he would have to pay an exorbitant premium for disability insurance. Why? Because he was an alcoholic, the insurance company said. The man, who was not an alcoholic, finally discovered that the source of the misinformation was a little-known Massachusetts company that is said to control the largest collection of medical records in the United States.

   Mr. Rothfeder gives some specific suggestions for protecting personal information. Obtain a copy of his book from the library or a bookstore, and prepare a short report on some of the major privacy issues he identifies and his suggestions for protecting privacy.

4. Contact the Software Publishers Association, 1101 Connecticut Avenue #901, Washington, DC 20036 (202-452-1600) and the Adobe Softawareness Hotline (1-800-525-6111). Ask for literature on how to ensure that an organization is "software legal." Give a short report based on the information you receive.

5. Contact Computer Professionals for Social Responsibility, and report on their membership requirements. What is the focus of their activities?

   CPSR
   P.O. Box 717
   Palo Alto, CA 94301
   (415) 322-3778

*M*any Companies Admit Snooping on Workers

Nearly 22 percent of all U.S. employers occasionally dip into the computer files, electronic messages and voice mail of their employees, according to a report released today.

The survey, conducted by San Francisco co-based *Macworld* magazine, suggests that about 20 million U.S. workers are subject to having the boss peak at what many employees believe to be private communications on the job.

But even more employees—at least 30 million—apparently can say whatever they want without worrying about what a supervisor might think. The same *Macworld* survey found that 34.6 percent of all employers believe it's "never acceptable" to monitor their workers electronically.

The results highlight the growing controversy over electronic privacy in the workplace. Widespread use of personal computer networks, voice mail systems and other high-tech innovations provide ample opportunities for managers to surreptitiously keep tabs on their cohorts.

Although there are strict legal prohibitions against opening someone's regular mail, few clear rules apply to electronic communications. Federal rules protect communications as they move from one organization to another, but "the law stops where the office door begins," said Marc Rotenberg, director of a Washington group called Computer Professionals for Social Responsibility.

He said that companies may believe they have legitimate reasons to spy—such as when someone is suspected of selling trade secrets to a competitor. But Rotenberg said employers that go too far risk shutting down the free flow of ideas.

"One of the things that makes communications work is privacy," he said. "If I am talking to you on the phone and your boss is on the line, and my membership is listening along with everybody who has ever disagreed with us, the conversation might be very different."

Earlier . . . Senator Paul Simon, D-Ill., introduced legislation that would set new limits on the right of employers to eavesdrop. Companies still could conduct monitoring, but workers would have to be warned first.

"Many employers see this kind of eavesdropping as a useful tool for quality control," Simon said. "Many workers and consumers see its unbridled use as an invasion of their right to privacy. This bill attempts to strike a balance."

Some employer groups have come out against the measure, saying that advance notice would undermine the effectiveness of the monitoring in such cases as suspected employee dishonesty.

Macworld based its findings on a survey of 301 chief executives and computer-system managers at businesses of various sizes and in a range of industries. Survey results—billed as a reliable indicator of U.S. business practices as a whole within a margin of error of 2.9 percent—are published in the magazine's . . . July issue.

"There is considerable support for these electronic surveillance techniques by employers," said *Macworld's* Charles Piller, a senior associate editor. "Millions of American workers are subject to these kinds of monitoring practices."

Among the survey findings:

▼ About 21.6 percent of employers said they had searched employee "computer files, voice mail, electronic mail or other networking communications." For companies with at least 1,000 employees, the percentage rises to about 30 percent.

▼ Few companies monitor their workers on an ongoing routine basis. Nearly 71 percent said they had rummaged through employee work files only one to five times during the past two years. But 3.1 percent said they had done so more than 100 times.

▼ About 36 percent of the employers said they had a written policy concerning privacy, but only 18 percent said they had any policy about electronic privacy.

▼ Two-thirds of the companies said employees who are monitored are given no advance notice.

▼ The most common reasons cited for monitoring employees is to check on work flow and to investigate thefts and espionage.

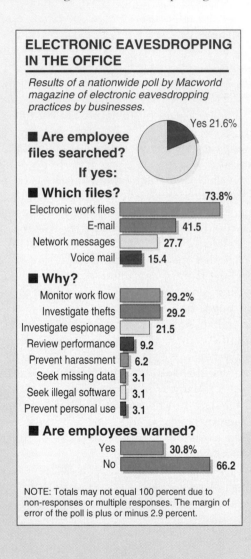

ELECTRONIC EAVESDROPPING IN THE OFFICE

Results of a nationwide poll by Macworld magazine of electronic eavesdropping practices by businesses.

■ **Are employee files searched?**

Yes 21.6%

If yes:

■ **Which files?**

Electronic work files	73.8%
E-mail	41.5
Network messages	27.7
Voice mail	15.4

■ **Why?**

Monitor work flow	29.2%
Investigate thefts	29.2
Investigate espionage	21.5
Review performance	9.2
Prevent harassment	6.2
Seek missing data	3.1
Seek illegal software	3.1
Prevent personal use	3.1

■ **Are employees warned?**

Yes	30.8%
No	66.2

NOTE: Totals may not equal 100 percent due to non-responses or multiple responses. The margin of error of the poll is plus or minus 2.9 percent.

* Article and figure from *San Francisco Chronicle*. Reprinted by permission. By Carl T. Hall; Chronicle graphic source: Macworld.

How to get Your Files

It is possible to find out some of the information that various organizations have been gathering about you and storing away on their databases. In all cases, you should be able to get the same files that are made available to others. Just call or write a letter to the following places, and they'll tell you what to do to get the information:

CREDIT INFORMATION:

Equifax Credit Information Services
Box 740241, Atlanta, GA 30374-0241; 800-685-1111.
Cost: $3 in Maine and Montana, $5 in Maryland, $10 in
Massachusetts, free in Vermont, $8 in all other states.

TRW Consumer Complimentary Report
(This is the address to use if you *have not* been denied
credit in the past 60 days.)
Box 2350, Chatsworth, CA 91313-2350; 214-235-1200 (Dallas HQ).
Cost: Free (one credit report per year).

TRW Consumer Assistance Center
(This is the address to use if you *have* been denied
credit in the past 60 days.)
Box 749029, Dallas, TX 75374; 214-235-1200.
Cost: Free (one credit report per year).

Trans Union Corp.
Box 7000, North Olmsted, OH 44070; 216-779-2378.
Cost: Free if you've been denied credit within the past
60 days; otherwise, $15 for an individual-account
record, $30 for a joint-account.

MEDICAL INFORMATION:

Medical Information Bureau
Box 105, Essex Station, Boston, MA 02112; 617-426-3660.
Cost: Free.

CRIMINAL RECORD INFORMATION:

Federal Bureau of Investigation
(This is the address to use if you *don't have* a criminal
record but think you might have been under FBI
investigation at some point in your life.)
Attn: Freedom of Information Section, 10th St. and
Pennsylvania Ave., NW, Washington, DC 20535; 202-324-5520.
Cost: First 100 pages are free; $0.10 for each additional page.

Federal Bureau of Investigation
(This is the address to use if you *have* a criminal record.)
Identification Div., Rm. 10104, 10th St. and
Pennsylvania Ave., NW, Washington, DC 20535;
202-324-222. Cost: $17.

SOCIAL SECURITY INFORMATION:

Social Security Administration
Wilkes-Barre Data Operations Ctr.
Box 20, Wilkes-Barre, PA 18767-0020; 800-772-1213.
Cost: Free.

From *Self,* December 1992, p. 131.

Purchasing and Maintaining a Microcomputer System

*A*s you can imagine, it's easy to spend a few thousand dollars on a microcomputer system! Given this substantial investment, carefully *consider your processing needs before pulling out your* checkbook. Don't pay for things you don't need, and remember to maintain your microcomputer properly so that it will have a long and problem-free life.

PREVIEW

When you have completed this chapter, you will be able to:

▼ Explain what should be considered before purchasing a microcomputer system

▼ Maintain a microcomputer system on a daily basis so that it can be relied on over time

▼ Explain some of the health concerns associated with frequent computer use, and describe some of the ergonomic options open to users

▼ Describe some of the options open to the environmentally aware computer user

WHY IS THIS CHAPTER IMPORTANT?

*M*any different microcomputers—with different features and processing capabilities—exist on the market today. If you, or your company, are in the market to purchase a microcomputer you should consider carefully your processing needs. Not only should you define your software and hardware requirements clearly before you purchase a microcomputer system, but you should also investigate the company from which you are buying the computer to make sure it will offer support in the long run.

Despite the substantial investment they have made, many users treat their microcomputers no more carefully than they do a desktop calculator or a telephone. For example, microcomputers are very sensitive to temperature changes. But temperature is only one factor that will affect the life of your computer. We'll cover others.

In this chapter we provide you with the basic information that will help you purchase a microcomputer system and maintain it over time.

Purchasing a System: What to Consider

"You need a 120 MB hard disk." "You must purchase a PostScript laser printer." "By all means, purchase *this* word processing package." Purchasing a microcomputer system involves doing some research, listening to a lot of advice, and ultimately making a number of different purchasing decisions. Many people will buy hardware and software solely at the recommendation of a friend. Although recommendations are helpful, if you don't do additional research, you may find yourself spending more for a system that offers features you will never use.

In this section we provide advice on choosing software and hardware to support your processing needs and explain what to consider before you purchase a particular brand of microcomputer or a microcomputer **clone**—that is, a microcomputer that is virtually identical to and compatible with the brand of computer it is copying. In addition, we describe some factors that should affect where you purchase a microcomputer system.

What Software and Hardware Will You Need?

If you are a first-time buyer of a microcomputer, you should choose your applications software *first* (Figure 1), after you identify your processing needs. For example, do you want to generate documents? Budgets? Graphics? In color? Will others use the computer? If so, what are their processing needs? Depending on your needs, you will need to purchase one or more applications software packages.

Once your applications software needs have been determined, choose the compatible hardware models and systems software that will allow you to use your applications software efficiently and expand your system if necessary. (Sometimes the systems software is automatically included with the computer.)

The documentation (user's manual) that accompanies the applications software you purchase will list the minimum hardware requirements necessary to run the software. For example, your microcomputer must have a *minimum* of 640 K RAM to run most of the software programs on the market today—many programs require 2–8 MB. And if your objective is to output graphics, you must make sure that your printer is compatible with your software and will support

Figure 1

Choose your software first, after you have determined processing needs. Then choose hardware that will run your chosen software.

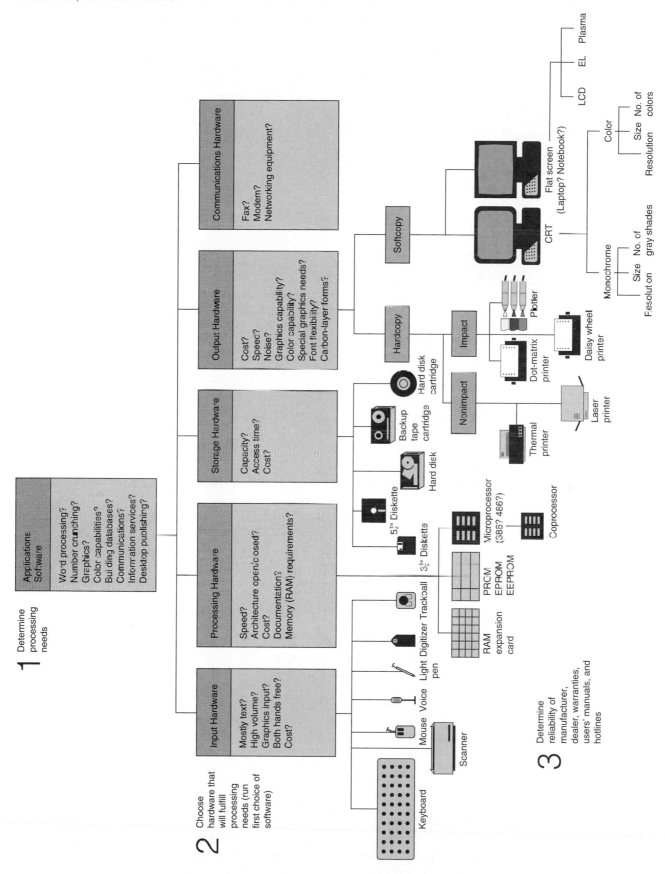

graphics. By choosing your applications software first, you will ensure that all your processing requirements will be satisfied: you won't be forced to buy a software package that is your second choice simply because your first software choice wasn't compatible with the hardware or systems software already purchased.

When you go to work in an office, chances are that the computer hardware and systems software will already be in operation, so if you have to choose anything, it will most likely be applications software to help you do your job. If you do find yourself in a position to choose applications software, make sure not only that it will satisfy the processing requirements of your job, but also that it is compatible with your company's hardware and existing software.

PC Clones: A Good Bet?

It depends. There are good clones and bad clones. But if you ask some important questions before making a purchase, you will end up with a compatible system for a good price.

▼   Is the microcomputer accompanied by proper and adequate documentation? This is extremely important. If your microcomputer needs to be repaired or upgraded, the computer technician will want to look at the technical documentation that accompanies your system. No matter what the price, if the system comes without documentation, you should not buy it.

▼   Is the ROM chip a known PC compatible? If the answer is "yes," then you will be able to run all the software (generally) that is written for the microcomputer your machine is a clone of.

▼   Are the characteristics of the motherboard—the main circuit board—similar to those of the PC's motherboard? If they are, then PC adapter boards (such as expanded memory or video adapter boards) will work in the clone.

▼   Is the system covered by a warranty? The system should be covered by a 6- to 12-month warranty. If something fails during that time, the manufacturer should repair it at no cost.

▼   If the system fails after the warranty period, will parts be available? The manufacturer should service your computer after the warranty period expires. In other words, watch out for fly-by-night manufacturers.

Companies like NCR have conducted studies that prove their computers are 100% compatible with the microcomputer they are cloning. This type of information is useful to the microcomputer clone buyer; ask your dealer about such studies.

Because IBM microcomputers are very popular in the business environment, computer makers often manufacture IBM clones and sell them with their own manufacturing label (Figure 2). Don't think that a microcomputer with an IBM label is better than an IBM clone—clones are sometimes more powerful and typically less expensive than the machines they copy. As a result, IBM clones have become extremely popular and have achieved a niche of their own in the marketplace. When IBM makes a change in its microcomputer line, you can be sure that other compatibles, or clones, will appear that incorporate those changes.

Macintoshes

Since Apple Computer, Inc., introduced the Macintosh microcomputer in 1983, it has remained popular with many people who were impressed with its "user-friendly" graphic interface. In contrast to pre-Windows IBM PCs, the Macintosh

FIGURE 2

The Compaq Deskpro computer on the right is a clone of the IBM computer on the left.

was not command-oriented; in other words, users worked with icons, menus, and the mouse to issue commands instead of having to memorize many DOS commands and type them in on the computer. However, the Macintosh was not—and still is not—used in business as much as the IBM and IBM clones.

Then, with the introduction in 1985 of Adobe's PostScript page description language for the Mac, desktop publishing was essentially invented. Thus the Macintosh line of microcomputers became essential to many types of people in publishing, design, illustration, and typesetting. Although desktop publishing programs—such as Ventura, Quark XPress, and PageMaker—are now available for the IBM, the Macintosh—especially the high-end Quadra 950 (Figure 3)—is still preferred by many people in desktop publishing and related areas.

Basically, the Mac can do anything the IBM can do, and many people still insist it's easier to use than IBM microcomputers (even those with Windows). Although Macs are generally more expensive than IBMs and IBM clones, most of them come with built-in hardware features that are costly extras on IBM clones, including networking capability, sound, and 256-color video. And you can expand most Macs without opening the cover or adding circuit boards: just plug add-on devices into special sockets (interfaces, or ports) on the back of the system unit. Also, it's getting easier to swap files between the two systems— with extra software that costs around $69, all Macs can accept floppy disks formatted on an IBM PC. (Macs with System 7 operating system software include this special software.) Newer Macs have a floppy disk drive called a *Superdrive,* which can handle floppies formatted on an MS-DOS machine. The new Duo Dock Macintosh (Figure 4) functions both as a portable computer and a full-fledged desktop computer.

One possible drawback to using a Mac is that although there's plenty of Mac-compatible software equal to or better than DOS or Windows programs in word processing, spreadsheets, desktop publishing, and graphics, there's comparatively little in some other areas. These include business accounting and programs for creating custom applications.

Where to Go

The following three factors should greatly influence where you purchase a microcomputer:

FIGURE 3

The Apple Quadra 950

FIGURE 4

Macintosh Duo Dock. The Powerbook notebook computer can be used separately, as a portable computer, and as the system unit in a full-size Macintosh computer.

 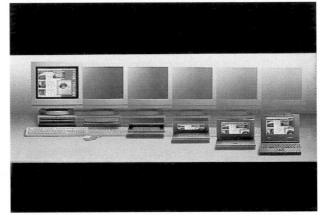

1. The company's reputation
2. The warranty agreement
3. The price

Since each of these factors influences the others, they can't be described independently. If a local computer store has been in business for a few years, you can be reasonably confident that it has tested the waters and won't go out of business. Purchasing a computer from a local computer store offers a number of advantages, including:

▼   Manufacturers generally support warranties on computers sold through dealers. Should anything happen to the computer in 6–12 months, parts and labor are covered by the manufacturer's **warranty,** or agreement between the manufacturer (and sometimes the seller) and purchaser. If a computer has a problem, you will likely experience it in the first 6–12 months anyway, so this warranty is a fair deal. If a computer is sold through someone other than an authorized dealer—computers sold in this way are referred to as *gray-market computers*—many manufacturers ignore the manufacturer's warranty.

▼ Since the computer store is local, you have a convenient place to take the computer if it needs to be serviced.

▼ You can establish personal contacts at the computer store should you have questions about your system.

If you are *very* careful, you can purchase a microcomputer and peripheral equipment from a mail-order company for a substantial discount. Unfortunately, some computer manufacturers don't sell directly to mail-order companies because the mail-order companies don't usually offer support to their customers. Some manufacturers, however, do support their warranties no matter who sells the computer. *Make sure your microcomputer is supported by a warranty before purchasing it.*

Computer magazines such as *Byte, PC World, PC Computing, Personal Computing, InfoWorld, MacWorld,* and *MacUser* all contain advertisements for mail-order companies. Although many mail-order companies have solid reputations, some don't. If you don't do the following homework before making a purchase through a mail-order company, you may be abandoned with little or no hardware, a computer that doesn't work, or one that has no warranty.

▼ Check back issues of the magazine to see if the advertisement has been running regularly. If it has, the company has been paying its bills.

▼ Check the ad for a street address. If no street address exists—only a P.O. box—it is possible that the company may be a temporary operation.

▼ Compare the prices offered by different mail-order companies. If the price you are eyeing is more than 25% lower than the competition, you might be looking at something that is too good to be true.

▼ Make sure the system's price includes all the features and peripherals that you want. For example, make sure the price includes a monitor and a keyboard.

▼ Make sure the system you purchase is covered by a manufacturer's warranty. Many major computer manufacturers don't honor warranties on computers sold through mail-order companies.

▼ Pay by credit card. If you have an unresolved complaint about the product, U.S. federal law says that the credit card company can't bill you if you report your complaint to them promptly.

▼ In addition, you may want to check with the Better Business Bureau or local consumer protection department in the company's area to find out more details about the company.

If everything adds up, you have found yourself a good deal. Of course, you still won't have the personalized support that you get when purchasing a computer from a local store.

Other Practical Considerations

Following are a few more guidelines that will help you in choosing a microcomputer system:

1. Determine the maximum amount of money you can spend. Don't spend money on fancy functions you don't need or may never use!

2. After you decide what you want the system to do for you and have chosen your software, determine what the minimum hardware requirements are to run the software. These requirements are listed in the documentation that accompanies each software program. Pay special attention to RAM requirements.

3. Determine if any of your hardware needs to be portable.

4. To ensure the possibility of upgrading the computer in the future, choose one designed with open architecture or sufficient interfaces (ports) for hooking up the peripheral devices you need.

5. Determine if your system must be compatible with another system—either in your office or in another context—or with software you or your office is already using. If so, be sure to choose compatible hardware, and make sure that any systems software that comes with the computer is compatible also.

6. If possible, buy everything (computer, keyboard, monitor, printer, and so on) at one place, so you have to make only one phone call to ask questions and solve problems.

7. Consider having someone from the computer store or outlet come to your office to set up the system, install the software, and make sure everything is running properly. (Independent professionals can also do this for you.) It's also a plus if the seller offers training classes.

8. Buy a monitor and a keyboard that are comfortable to use; try them out first. Check the RAM requirements of your monitor (Table 1).

9. Determine how much storage you will need and buy accordingly. Consider using removable storage media for essentially unlimited storage capacity.

10. Determine if you need color in either hardcopy or softcopy output.

11. Determine your most common output needs. For example, will you need to print out forms with many carbon layers? Will you be outputting mostly business letters or internal memos? Will you also need to output graphics?

12. Determine your communications needs.

13. Decide what file backup method you will use—floppies? hard disk cartridges? tape?

14. Determine what scanning capabilities you need (Figure 5).

See the end of the chapter for a portable checklist that you can take with you when you decide to purchase a microcomputer. To help you further, Figure 6 interprets a few hardware and software ads to start you on the way to understanding them. Table 2 lists popular computer magazines and periodicals you can consult for more detailed information on buying hardware and software than we can offer here.

TABLE 1

How Much Memory Do You Need to Support Different Color Combinations at Varying Resolutions?

	RESOLUTION		
	640 x 480	800 x 600	1,024 x 768
4 bits per pixel (16 colors)	150 K	234 K	384 K
8 bits per pixel (256 colors)	300 K	469 K	768 K
16 bits per pixel (65,536 colors)	600 K	938 K	1,536 K
24 bits per pixel (16,777,216 colors)	900 K	1,407 K	2,304 K

FIGURE 5

Different scanners for different applications. Desktop publishing, OCR, and other jobs require different scanner features. [Adapted from Patrick Marshall, *PC World,* April 1992, p. 191.]

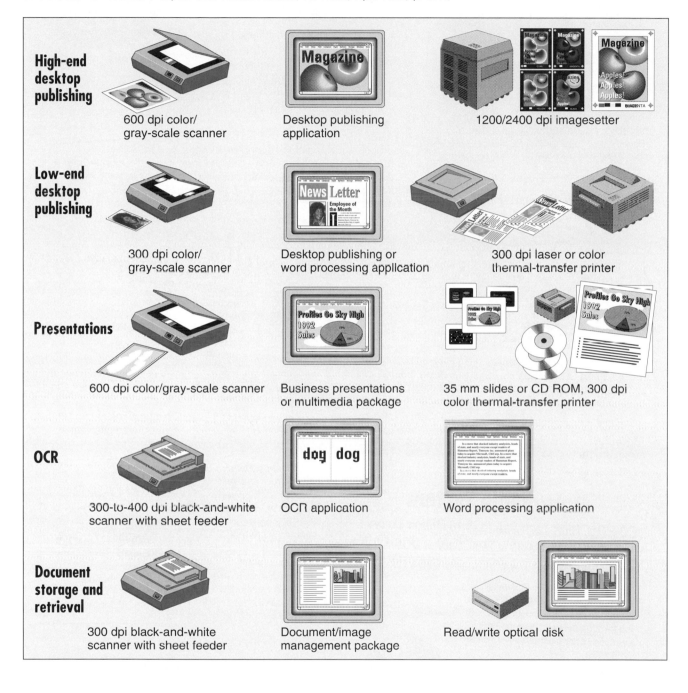

High-end desktop publishing

600 dpi color/ gray-scale scanner

Desktop publishing application

1200/2400 dpi imagesetter

Low-end desktop publishing

300 dpi color/ gray-scale scanner

Desktop publishing or word processing application

300 dpi laser or color thermal-transfer printer

Presentations

600 dpi color/gray-scale scanner

Business presentations or multimedia package

35 mm slides or CD ROM, 300 dpi color thermal-transfer printer

OCR

300-to-400 dpi black-and-white scanner with sheet feeder

OCR application

Word processing application

Document storage and retrieval

300 dpi black-and-white scanner with sheet feeder

Document/image management package

Read/write optical disk

FIGURE 6

AST Premium Exec
386 /25 60MB
- VGA w/32 gray shades
- 4MB RAM
- 60/80MB HD

$1799 80MB $1999

This notebook computer has a 386 microprocessor and a clock speed of 25MHz; it comes with a 60MB or 80MB hard disk, 4MB of RAM and a VGA monitor.

 **486DX-33MHz 64K Cache**
- **4MB RAM** Expandable to 32MB
- 120MB Maxtor
- 1.2MB 5.25" and 1.44MB 3.5" Floppy Drives
- 2 Serial, 1 Parallel, and 1 Game Ports
- 101 Enhanced Keyboard
- High Quality 3 Button Mouse
- 1MB Trident SVGA Card
- WEN 14" 1024x768 SVGA monitor

$1595

This microcomputer system has a 486 microprocessor and a clock speed of 33 MHz. It has 4MB of RAM with 64K of cache memory, a $5\frac{1}{2}$-inch floppy disk drive, several ports for hooking up peripheral devices, a keyboard with a separate keypad, a mouse, a graphics adapter board, and a 14-inch Super VGA monitor with a resolution of 1,024 x 768.

TI PostScript Laser Printer

- PostScript Laser Printer
- 9PPM, AppleTalk Optional
- Small Footprint

This laser printer can print text and graphics on the same page, using the PostScript page description language.

It prints 9 pages per minute, can be used with both Macintosh and IBM computers, and takes up only a small amount of space on the desktop.

Macintosh IIcx 2/40

- 1.4 MB High Density Floppy Drive
- MC8030 Microprocessor
- 16MHz Clock Speed
- 2MB of RAM
- 40MB Hard Drive
- 3 NuBus expansion slots for custom configuration

This Macintosh can be upgraded with expansion cards.

Multimedia System
CD-ROM, High Tech Sound, & 16 Million Colors
24-Bit SVGA! 486-33 w/256K Cache, DOS 5.0 & Windows 3.1 w/Mulitmedia Ext. v1.0

- Intel 486DX CPU, Made In USA Motherboard
- 4 MB (expandable to 64 MB) 8 MB add $180
- 120 MB Maxtor or Conner Hard Drive – 200 MB add $200
- 24-Bit SVGA Card w/1 MB up to 16 Million Colors
- Viewsonic 6 Non-interlaced Super VGA Monitor (1024x768)
- Teac 1.44 MB 3.5" Floppy Drive
- Teac 1.3 MB 5.25" Floppy Drive
- 2 Serial, 1 Parallel, 1 Game Port, I/O Card
- Naxiswitch 101-Key Enhanced Keyboard
- Microsoft Compat. Mouse w/Pad
- DOS 5.0 with Manual
- Windows 3.1 w/Manual & Muitimedia Ext. 1.0
- Sound Blaster Pro Multimedia Kit Including:
  CD ROM
  Sound Blaster Pro
  & 4 CD Software Package

$2745

- 24-bit Super VGA
- 486 microprocessor
- 33MHz clock speed
- 256K cache memory
- DOS 5.0 operating system software
- Windows 3.1 graphic user interface
- Multimedia software
- 4–64MB of RAM
- 120–200MB hard disk
- Monitor resolution of 1,024 x 768
- $3\frac{1}{2}$-inch floppy disk drive
- $5\frac{1}{4}$-inch floppy disk drive
- Various ports for connecting peripherals
- Keyboard with separate numeric keypad
- CD-ROM drive with software and optical disks

EPSON
ACTION LASER II

$695

- **512KB-4MB**
- **6ppm laser engine**
- **HPLJ II Compatible**
- **14 fonts**
- **Accepts HP font cartridge**

This printer is available with 512K–4MB of RAM; it prints 6 pages per minute, is also compatible with microcomputers that use a Hewlett-Packard LaserJet Series II printer, comes with 14 different type styles and sizes, and can use Hewlett-Packard cartridges of additional type styles and sizes.

TABLE 2

Alphabetized List of Popular Computer Magazines and Periodicals

MAGAZINE	PUBLISHER	ISSUE	YEAR	EDITORIAL OFFICE		TOLL FREE
Amiga World	IDG	$3.95	$30	NH	603-924-9471	800-365-1364
Byte	McGraw-Hill	$3.50	$30/$25	NH	603-924-9281	800-257-9402
Computer Language	Freeman	$3.50	$30	CA	415-397-1881	800-451-2248
Computer Monthly	Vulcan	$2.50	$16	AL	205-988-9708	
Computer Shopper	Ziff	$2.95	$30/$22	NY	212-503-3900	800-274-6384
Computerworld	IDG	$2.00	$48/$44	MA	508-879-0700	800-669-1002
Data Based Advisor	DBS	$3.95	$35/$28	CA	619-483-6400	800-336-6060
DBMS	M&T	$2.95	$25/$20	CA	415-366-3600	800-456-1859
Dr. Dobb's Journal	M&T	$3.50	$30/$25	CA	415-366-3600	800-456-1215
Incider A+	IDG	$3.95	$30/$28	NH	603-924-9471	800-289-0619
Infoworld	IDG	$2.95	$110/$0	CA	818-577-7233	
Mac User	Ziff	$2.95	$27/$20	CA	415-378-5600	800-627-2247
Macworld	IDG	$3.95	$30/$24	CA	415-546-7722	800-524-3200
PC Computing	Ziff	$2.95	$25/$15	CA	415-578-7000	800 365 2770
PCM	Falsoft	$3.50	$34	KY	502-228-4492	800-847-0309
PC Magazine	Ziff	$2.95	$45/$30	NY	212-503-5255	800-289-0429
PC Novice	Peed	$2.95	$24	NE	402-477-8900	800-424-7900
PC Sources	Ziff	$1.95	$17/$13	NY	212-503-3900	800-827-2078
PC Today	Peed	$2.95	$24	NE	402-477-8900	800-424-7900
PC Week	Ziff	$3.95	$160/$0	MA	617-375-4000	
PC World	IDG	$2.95	$30/$20	CA	415-243-0500	800-825-7959
Personal Publishing	ABC	$3.00	$24	IL	708-665-1000	800-727-6937
Publish	IDG	$3.95	$40/$24	CA	415-243-0600	800-274-5116
Run	IDG	$2.95	$23	NH	603-924-9471	800-274-5241
WordPerfect Magazine	WordPerf Pub	$3.00	$24	UT	801-226-5555	

From *The Secret Guide to Computers*, 16th Edition, © 1992 by Russ Walter, 22 Ashland St., #2, Somerville, MA 02144-3202, p. 48.

Maintaining a System

A microcomputer system presents a sizable investment—from a few hundred to a few thousand dollars. Even so, many users don't take care of this investment, which leads to system abuse and failures. Most microcomputer problems could have been prevented by regular maintenance. Maintaining a system properly—on an ongoing basis—is easy, and will pay for itself many times over by reducing hardware malfunctions and data loss and increasing the life of your computer.

In this section you will learn how to maintain your microcomputer system by following some simple procedures and words of advice.

Temperature

Computer systems should be kept in an environment with as constant a temperature as possible. In cold climates, where office temperatures are controlled by an automatic thermostat causing warmer temperatures during the day and much cooler temperatures at night, microcomputers tend to have the most system failures. The ideal room temperature for microcomputers ranges from 60 to 90 degrees Fahrenheit when the system is on and from 50 to 110 degrees when the system is off. But maintaining a constant temperature in an environment is more important than the number of degrees.

The following problems can eventually occur if a microcomputer system is subjected to substantial changes in temperature in short amounts of time:

▼   The chips inside the system unit can work their way out of their sockets in the system boards. In addition, the chip connectors can corrode more quickly so that they become brittle and crack.

▼   Hard disks suffer from dramatic changes in temperature, which can cause read/write problems. If a new hard disk drive has been shipped in a cold environment, manufacturers usually recommend that users wait for a few hours to a day before operating the hard disk.

These problems are caused by the expansion and contraction that naturally occurs when materials are heated and then cooled. The bottom line is that changes in temperature are stressful for microcomputer systems. Therefore, don't place your system near heating vents, in direct sunlight, or directly in front of cold-air blasts. If you use removable hard disk cartridges that have been in a cold car, for example, let them—and your computer—return to room temperature before you use them.

Turning the Computer On/Off

Sudden changes in temperature can cause lasting damage to a computer system. When a computer system is turned on, it is subjected to the *most* extreme change in temperature—computers are relatively cool when they are off and become quite warm when they are turned on. For this reason, the fewer times a system has to be turned on, the longer it will remain in good working order. Ideally, a microcomputer's system unit should be kept on continuously—24 hours a day, 7 days a week. However, because of the issue of security during nonbusiness hours and wasteful power consumption, it is unlikely that the typical office worker should keep his or her machine running all the time. A better solution is to keep the system on all day so that it is turned on and off only once each day.

One myth that we would like to dispel is that leaving a microcomputer system on will wear down a hard disk. By running a hard disk continuously, you are greatly reducing any stress on the drive due to temperature variations. This will reduce the potential of any read/write failures that are caused by such variations and increase the life of the drive. If you can't leave your microcomputer system on continuously, at least let the system warm up for 15 minutes or so before reading from or writing to the drive. By remembering this simple rule, you will improve the reliability of the data stored on your disk.

If you do leave your system on for long periods of time without using it, turn the monitor off; otherwise make sure that the screen automatically goes blank after a few minutes if the keyboard or other input device isn't used. Many manufacturers include this feature with their computer systems—if not, special software is available that will do this for you. If your screen doesn't go blank, the phosphors on the screen can burn, leaving a permanent image on the screen (Macintosh computers typically don't show these phosphor burn effects). The monitors in airports that display flight information show these phosphor-burn effects. Some software includes a screen-saver utility; these software utilities may also be purchased separately.

Plugging in the System

Many users plug a number of different system components into one power strip that contains a number of different plug outlets (Figure 7). However, certain types of equipment, including coffee makers, laser printers, and copy machines, can cause voltage *spikes* (surges of electricity), which can do damage to a computer that is connected to the same line. Therefore, it's best to keep your computer on a line separate from other equipment. If you must connect peripheral equipment on the same power line, turn on that equipment *before* turning on the computer. Make sure your circuits will bear the load (Figure 8).

If your computer is in an environment that is susceptible to power surges or power outages, you should plug your system into a surge suppressor or uninterruptible power supply (Figure 9). **Surge suppressors** are devices into which you can plug your microcomputer system, and which in turn are connected to the power line. Costing between $20 and $200, surge suppressors help protect the power supply and other sensitive circuitry in your computer system from voltage spikes. An **uninterruptible power supply (UPS)** is also used to protect your hardware from the damaging effects that a power surge can have on your computer system. In addition, should you lose power, a UPS will keep your system running for around 8–30 minutes, providing you with plenty of time to save your work and shut the system down. The cost of a UPS system is determined by the amount of time it can continue to provide power to your computer system after the power has been cut off. Prices range from about $300 to many thousands of dollars.

Some industry experts say that the electrical distribution infrastructure in North America will be overtaxed by the year 2000. Thus surge suppressors soon will not provide enough protection for computer users against blackouts and brownouts. As a result, UPSs will increase in popularity and perhaps soon will be "bundled" (packaged with) microcomputers and will have longer battery lives than they have now.

Dust and Pollutants

As an experiment, when your computer is on, light a match in front of a diskette drive and notice where the smoke goes. The smoke is inhaled by the system unit!

Most microcomputers are configured with a fan inside the system unit. The fan is mounted near the power supply and causes air to be drawn into the system unit through any possible opening and then blown out. Systems are designed this way to allow even cooling of the microcomputer system. Unfortunately, in this process dust, smoke, and any other pollutants in the air are drawn into the system unit. Over time these particles will insulate the system unit and prevent it from cooling properly. In addition, some of these particles

FIGURE 7

Multiplug extender

FIGURE 8

How many amps does your equipment need? Be sure your circuits will bear your equipment load. (Reprinted with permission of *PC Novice*.)

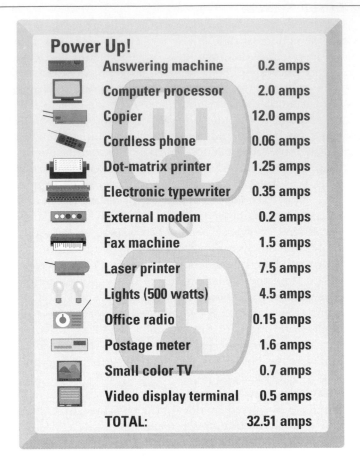

Power Up!

	Answering machine	0.2 amps
	Computer processor	2.0 amps
	Copier	12.0 amps
	Cordless phone	0.06 amps
	Dot-matrix printer	1.25 amps
	Electronic typewriter	0.35 amps
	External modem	0.2 amps
	Fax machine	1.5 amps
	Laser printer	7.5 amps
	Lights (500 watts)	4.5 amps
	Office radio	0.15 amps
	Postage meter	1.6 amps
	Small color TV	0.7 amps
	Video display terminal	0.5 amps
	TOTAL:	**32.51 amps**

FIGURE 9

(a) Uninterruptible power supply (UPS); (b) surge suppressor

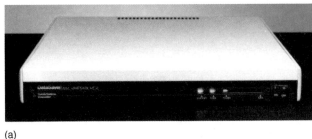

(a)

(b)

can conduct electricity, causing minor electrical shorts in the system. (However, be sure not to block the vents; otherwise the system will overheat.)

Diskette drives are especially susceptible to dust and other pollutants because they provide a large hole through which air flows. The read/write heads in the disk drive won't work accurately if they are contaminated with foreign particles. (Hard disks aren't at risk because they are stored in airtight containers.) For this reason, many companies enforce "No Smoking" policies in rooms where computers are present.

If you want to clean the diskette drives in your computer system (the read/write heads can become dusty over time, and dust can reduce the reliability with which they can store and retrieve data), an easy method does exist. You must first purchase a head-cleaning disk from a local computer store. Head-cleaning disks come in two basic styles—that is, wet or dry. The wet-cleaning disk uses a liquid cleaning agent that has been squirted onto the disk, and the dry-cleaning disk uses an abrasive material that has been put onto the cleaning disk. Most computer professionals recommend using the wet system, because the dry system can actually damage the read/write heads of the disk if it is used too often. To use a cleaning disk, simply put it into the disk drive and run a program (that is stored on the disk) to make the disk spin. When the disk spins in the disk drive, the read/write heads touch the surface of the cleaning disk and are wiped clean. In a clean (smoke-free) office environment, diskette drives should be cleaned about once a year. In a smoking environment, diskette drives should be cleaned every 3–6 months.

The diskette drives aren't the only system components that should be cleaned periodically. If a microcomputer system is operated in a dirty environment, such as on the floor of a lumber shop, it should also be cleaned every 3–6 months. But in most office environments, the cleaning should be done every one to two years. You can either clean the appropriate components yourself or hire a professional to clean them for you. If you aren't familiar with the process of cleaning a microcomputer, hire a professional.

Other Practical Considerations

Shocks and vibrations are bad for computer disk drives. Therefore, you should also keep the following considerations in mind:

▼ Never place an impact printer (dot-matrix or daisy wheel printer) on the same surface as the computer.

▼ Don't drop or throw objects onto the surface on which the computer is located.

▼ If you place your system unit on the floor to free up desk space, make sure it's not in a place where you will accidentally kick it or people will bump into it.

▼ Don't move a laptop or notebook computer when the hard disk drive is working (while the HD light is on).

Backing Up Your Microcomputer System

The scenario: You've stored a year's worth of client information on your hard disk. You are able to retrieve client information easily onto the screen. You have confidence in your computer system—until the hard disk crashes. The read/write heads fall onto the surface of the disk, making the disk unusable and causing the loss of all the data stored on the disk! Well, at least you have a backup copy of your client files. What? You don't?

One of the most important tasks in maintaining a microcomputer system is to make copies, or a backup, of your data files. A popular rule of thumb is to never let the time between backups go longer than the amount of data it represents that you are willing to lose in a disk disaster. Depending on the amount of activity on a system, hard disks should be backed up at the end of each day or each week. All managers should make sure that office policies include backup procedures.

Procedures

You must decide how often you want to back up data. Do you want to back up the entire hard disk or simply the files that have been changed since the last backup? Perhaps you want to make daily copies of the files that have been changed and, at the end of the week, make a backup copy of the entire disk, including software and data files. Whatever the procedures, they should be defined clearly and followed routinely.

Also, remember that backup must be done on **removable media**—storage media that can easily be removed from the system and stored in another place. Some businesses configure microcomputers with two hard disks. The first hard disk is the work disk onto which all the current processing activities and updated files are stored. The second hard disk is used as a backup disk—the contents of the first disk are copied onto the second. This is not advisable. Suppose the microcomputer system is subjected to a massive power surge? The contents of *both* disks will be destroyed. Or suppose the entire microcomputer system is stolen? Once more, you won't have any backup files.

Once data has been backed up, it is important to clearly label and date the backup media.

Note: Wise microcomputer users also back up their operating system software files on floppies and keep them handy in case the hard disk operating system files develop problems. (You can't use your applications software without the system software.) Your systems software documentation will tell you which files to back up and how to do it.

Hardware and Software

Diskettes are still used in some cases as backup media. All microcomputer systems come with at least one diskette drive, so without a substantial hardware investment in a **dedicated backup system**—hardware and software used only for backup purposes—the user can back up the contents of a hard disk onto removable media (diskettes). Backup software for diskette systems is available that assists in the backup process, prompting the user to "insert a new diskette, please" when one diskette becomes full. One such program is called FASTBACK, by 5th Generation Systems. However, using diskettes to back up a hard disk is slow.

Magnetic tape is the more commonly used storage medium for backing up hard disks. With a hard disk of 40 MB or higher, a reliable tape storage unit is a good investment (Figure 10). Tape backup units can easily support up to 120 MB or more per tape and are fast and accurate. Once you decide to purchase a tape backup unit, you must decide on what software to purchase to run the tape system. Many tape backup manufacturers write their own software. In addition to your specific needs, you should be sure that the software offers the following capabilities:

▼ Files can be backed up individually or all at once.

▼ Several backups can be copied onto a single tape.

▼ A backup can span more than one tape.

▼ The backup data can be verified to ensure that it was recorded reliably on the tape.

By paying special attention to the temperature of your system, the number of times you turn it on/off, how it is plugged in, the quality of the air surrounding the system, and routine backup procedures, you will increase the life of your computer system.

FIGURE 10

Magnetic tape is often used for backing up hard disks. This photo shows a portable tape unit; the tape cartridge is inserted in the slot on the front.

Ergonomics: Health Issues

Even though the cost of computers has decreased significantly, they are still expensive. Why have them, then, unless they can make workers more effective? Ironically, in certain ways computers may actually make people less productive. Many of the problems that affect productivity are commonly experienced by people working in data-entry-intensive positions, such as clerks and word processors. However, such problems may also be experienced by anyone whose job involves intensive use of the computer. As a result, interest in ergonomics has been increasing, and greater effort is being made to avoid health risks. Basically, **ergonomics** is the science of human comfort engineering—especially comfort in the area of computer use.

Physical Health

Sitting in front of a screen and using a keyboard for long periods may lead to eyestrain, headaches, back pain, and repetitive strain injury. Of course, adopting such commonsense measures as taking frequent rest breaks and using well-designed computer furniture can alleviate some of the discomfort. However, other suggestions have also proven useful (Figure 11).

1. *Avoid eyestrain and headache.* The use of computer screens requires focusing the eyes on items at a closer range than our eyes are designed for. Focusing on the screen at this close range for long periods of time can cause eyestrain, headaches, and double vision. To avoid these problems, take a 15-minute break every hour or two. Minimize reflected glare on the screen by keeping the screen away from windows and other sources of bright light. (If necessary, purchase an antiglare screen or a glare shield for your existing screen.) The screen should be three to four times brighter than room light. In addition, the computer screen, the keyboard, and anything you are reading while typing should all be positioned at the same distance from your eyes—about 20–24 inches away. Clean the screen of dust from time to time.

2. *Avoid back and neck pain.* Make sure equipment is adjustable. You should be able to adjust your chair for height and angle, and the chair should have good back support. The monitor should be able to tilt and swivel,

FIGURE 11

The ergonomic work office. [From *PCToday,* April 1992, p. 19.]

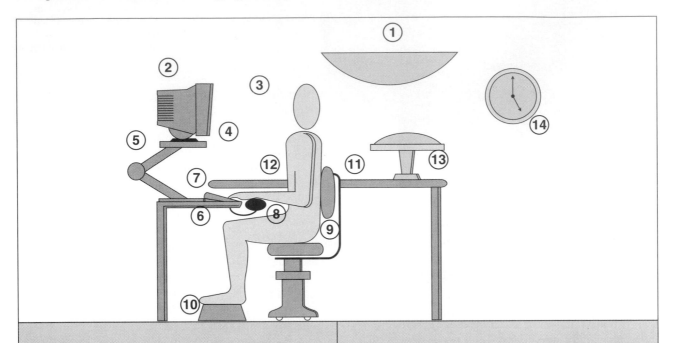

1.   Indirect Lighting — Fixtures that bounce light off ceilings or walls provide a soft light that is less likely than harsh light to reflect off monitor screens and create glare.

2.   Monitor Height — The top of the monitor should be no higher than eye level.

3.   Monitor Distance — 16 to 22 inches is recommended for visual acuity; 24 inches or more is recommended if there are emission concerns.

4.   Monitor Display — High-resolution, noninterlaced screen with dark letters on a light background, with an antiglare screen coating or antiglare filter.

5.   Adjustable Monitor Support — The monitor should move up and down, forward and back, and tilt on its axis.

6.   Keyboard Support — Adjustable from 23 to 28 inches in height. Operator's arm should hang straight down from the shoulder and bend 90 degrees at the elbow and enable the operator to type without flexing or hyperextending the wrist.

7.   Keyboard — Adjustable tilt to enable the typist to keep hands in a straight line with the wrists and forearms.

8.   Wrist Rest — Rounded, padded adjustable support for the heel of the hand or forearm, without constricting the wrist.

9.   Seat Height — Adjustable from 16 to 19 inches. Users should be able to bend their hips and knees at 90 degrees and sit with their feet flat on the floor.

10.   Foot Rest — Keeps user from having to support legs and feet while working.

11.   Back Support — Backrest should adjust up, down, forward, and backward to support the lumbar portion of the spine in the small of the back.

12.   Work Surface Height — A comfortable height for reading, writing, drawing, and other nonkeyboard work.

13.   Reading Light — An independent light source for reading letters, reports, books, etc.

14.   Clock — Schedule regular breaks, preferably 5 minutes per hour.

and the keyboard should be detachable (so you can place it on your lap, for example).

3. *Avoid effects of electromagnetic fields.* VDTs generate electromagnetic field (EMF) emissions, which can pass through the human body. Even though the fact has not been proved, some observers believe that EMF emissions could be involved in miscarriages and possibly some cancers. [In the United States, the Environmental Protection Agency (EPA) and the Federal Drug Agency (FDA) are studying this issue.] For this reason, older

monitors should be replaced with new, low-emission monitors or shielded with special snap-on screen covers.

Also, try to sit 2 feet away from your monitor and at least 3 feet away from any neighboring monitors.

4. *Avoid repetitive strain injury (RSI).* Repetitive strain injury (Figure 12)—also known as *repetitive motion injury* and *cumulative trauma disorder*—is the name given to a number of injuries resulting from fast, repetitive work. RSI causes neck, wrist, hand, and arm pain. The recent publicized increase in RSI problems is mainly the result of increasing computer keyboard use and bar code scanner use (for example, grasping items in the grocery cart and moving them past the bar code scanner mounted in the counter at the supermarket).

An RSI called carpal tunnel syndrome is particularly common among people who use computers and certain types of scanners intensively. This syndrome involves damage to nerves and tendons in the hands. RSI is basically caused by four factors:

▼ *Repetition and duration*—Prolonged, constant, and repetitious movements such as typing irritate tendons and nerve casings, causing them to swell.

▼ *Force*—The harder a person strikes the keys, the more likely he or she is to suffer injury.

▼ *Joint angle*—Flexing, raising, or twisting hands to reach the keys constricts the carpal tunnel (pinches the medial nerve running through the wrist).

▼ *Prolonged constrained posture*—Holding any position without moving puts excessive strain on muscles and tendons.

For some victims, the pain of carpal tunnel syndrome is so intense that they cannot open doors or shake hands. Left untreated, this syndrome can cause atrophied muscles and permanent nerve damage. To avoid RSI, take frequent short rest breaks instead of infrequent long ones. Experts also advise getting plenty of sleep and exercise, maintaining appropriate weight, sitting up straight, and learning stress-management techniques.

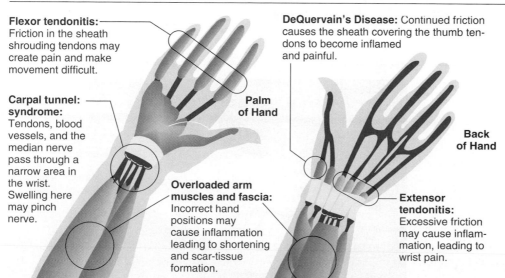

Flexor tendonitis: Friction in the sheath shrouding tendons may create pain and make movement difficult.

Carpal tunnel syndrome: Tendons, blood vessels, and the median nerve pass through a narrow area in the wrist. Swelling here may pinch nerve.

Palm of Hand

Overloaded arm muscles and fascia: Incorrect hand positions may cause inflammation leading to shortening and scar-tissue formation.

DeQuervain's Disease: Continued friction causes the sheath covering the thumb tendons to become inflamed and painful.

Back of Hand

Extensor tendonitis: Excessive friction may cause inflammation, leading to wrist pain.

FIGURE 12

RSI diagram. [Adapted from a drawing by Blumrich for *Newsweek;* source Emil Pascarelli, M.D., Miller Institute.]

You might also try one of the new "ergonomically sound" keyboards like The Vertical, the MI Key, or the DataHand (Figure 13).

Mental Health

Computers often create mental/psychological irritants that can turn out to be counterproductive.

1. *Avoid noise.* Computer users sometimes develop headaches and experience tension from being exposed to noisy impact printers and to the high-pitched, barely audible squeal produced by some computer monitors. Indeed, some people, particularly women, who hear high-frequency sounds better than men do, may be affected by the noise even when they are not conscious of hearing it. Sound-muffling covers are available for some printers. However, to avoid ending up in a high-tension state because of monitor squealing, the advice again is to take frequent short rest breaks.

2. *Avoid stress from electronic supervision.* Research shows that workers whose performance is supervised electronically suffer more health problems than do those watched by human supervisors. For instance, a computer may monitor the number of keystrokes a data entry clerk completes in a day or the time a customer-service person takes to handle a call. Such monitoring may force a pace that may lead to RSI problems and mental stress. One study found that electronically supervised employees reported great boredom, high tension, extreme anxiety, depression, anger, and severe fatigue.

The Environmentally Aware Computer User

These days, we hope everyone is environmentally aware. As you may imagine, computer hardware and software manufacturers use resources that often end up—in one form or another—in a garbage dump. Every year, an estimated 12 million laser printer toner cartridges get dumped in the trash, along with dot matrix printer ribbons, laptop and notebook computer batteries, and paper from fax machines and all types of printers.

FIGURE 13

Ergonomically sound keyboard by Kinesis Corporation

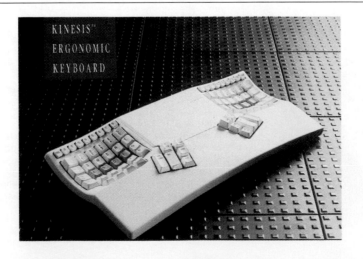

What can you do to help prevent waste and contribute to the recycling effort? For starters, *PC Computing* magazine has a few suggestions, to which we've added some of our own:

▼ *Recycle used printer toner cartridges.* Hewlett Packard (800-752-0900), Canon (800-962-2708), and Lexmark (800-848-9894) all provide postage-paid mailers so you can return your toner cartridges for recycling. Qume (800-421-4326) pays $5 plus shipping per cartridge.

▼ *Consider buying a "green" printer.* Some new laser printers, like the Ecosys from Kyocera, don't use toner cartridges but instead need only to have the toner itself refilled.

▼ *Use a plain-paper fax machine.* Although they are more expensive than the fax machines that use specially coated paper (that tends to curl), fax machines that can print out on regular sheets of paper are better for the environment because their paper can be recycled.

▼ *Refill ink-jet printer cartridges and re-ink dot matrix and daisy wheel printer ribbons.* Once you get the hang of it (or hire someone else to do it), the savings are worthwhile. [Call Computer Friends (800-547-3303) or the International Cartridge Recycling Association (202-857-1154) for information.]

▼ *Reduce paper use, recycle what you use, and purchase recycled paper.* Contact the National Office Paper Recycling Project (202-223-3088) for information about what types of paper are not recyclable.

▼ *Buy CD-ROM reference works* instead of traditional bound reference books like encyclopedias, atlases, etc. (saves paper).

▼ *Don't trash obsolete software.* Contact the manufacturer for permission to give it to a school or to charity. (For example, WordPerfect Corporation will send you a new license that you can give to a school along with your old software. Some 70,000 copies of the WordPerfect word processing program have been donated to schools this way.)

▼ *Recycle hardware.* IBM, Hewlett-Packard (916-785-7124), and Compaq (800-524-9859) will pay postage/freight and recycle many types of computer hardware, including batteries.

▼ Try to buy a computer made of *recyclable plastic* (check the documentation or ask the vendor).

▼ Try to buy computer products with the seal of approval from the *Computer Users for Social Responsibility.*

▼ Buy a computer that has a "sleep mode." This type of computer reduces power consumption by going into a state of "rest" when it is not being actively used (however, it is still on). A PC that uses sleep mode is estimated to use about *half* the power that a regular PC does when both are on all day and turned off at night. Sleep mode microcomputers also run cooler and need no fan—thus they are quieter. (PCs that conserve energy and therefore demand fewer natural resources will be eligible for an Energy Star designation from the U.S. Environmental Protection Agency.)

KEY TERMS

clone, p. 15.2
dedicated backup system,
   p. 15.16

ergonomics, p. 15.17
removable media, p. 15.16
surge suppressor, p. 15.13

uninterruptible power supply (UPS),
   p. 15.13
warranty, p. 15.7

Portable Checklist for Buying a Microcomputer System

Price Range (including peripherals)

_____ up to $1,000   _____ up to $2,000   _____ up to $3,000

_____ up to $4,000   _____ up to $5,000   _____ more than $5,000

Uses (Software Needed)

(*Note: All applications software chosen must run with compatible systems software.*)

_____   Writing letters and reports; preparing professional papers (word processing software)

_____   Personal finance; budgeting and planning; taxes (spreadsheet software)

_____   Programming (programming language, such as BASIC, COBOL, Pascal, C, FORTRAN)

_____   Business applications; finance management, accounting, planning, scheduling, inventory and sales management (spreadsheet, DBMS, and/or graphics software)

_____   Entertainment (software games)

_____   Education (tutorial software)

_____   Mailing lists (word processing software; DBMS software)

_____   Publishing newsletters and brochures (word processing, graphics, desktop publishing software)

_____   Multimedia programs

_____   Information retrieval from public information services (communications software)

_____   Personal record-keeping (desktop management software)

_____   Creating art and graphics for use in published materials (graphics and desktop publishing software)

_____   Communications software

_____   CAD/CAM software

_____   Networking software (_____ needs to be compatible with other networks?)

_____   Anti-virus software

_____   Conversion software for cross-platform use (IBM - Macintosh)

_____   TOTAL projected cost for software $_____

Hardware

(*Check your chosen software's documentation for minimum hardware requirements and compatibility restrictions; when no requirements are given in the documentation, check your own preferences.*)

1. _____   System must be compatible with other systems? (Y/N)

        If yes, what kind: _____

2. _____   Uses what kind of systems software?

3. _____   How much main memory do I need? _____ 640 K RAM;

   _____ 1 MB; _____ 2 MB; _____ 4 MB; _____ 8 MB

4. _____   16-bit processor; _____ 32-bit processor (number of bits that the

   microprocessor needs to handle at once) (check the bus architecture:

   _____ ISA; _____ EISA; _____ MCA; _____ PCMCIA)

5. _____   16 MHz (clock speed); _____ 25 MHz; _____ 33 MHz; _____ 50 MHz;

   _____ other

6. _____   Microcomputer must be portable? (Y/N) (laptop; notebook)

7. _____   Monochrome screen; _____ color screen (_____ RAM requirements;

   _____ low emission?)

8. _____   EGA; VGA; Super VGA (screen resolution, or clarity of image)

9. _____   Number of colors or gray shades

10. _____   Screen can tilt and swivel? (Y/N)

11. _____   Size of screen (appropriate to resolution?)

12. _____   System cabinet can be put on floor to save desk space? (Y/N)

13. _____   Detachable keyboard?

14. _____   QWERTY keyboard; _____ other keyboard

15. _____   Numeric keypad?

16. _____   Number of required function keys

17. _____   Voice input?

18. _____   Single floppy disk drive; _____ dual floppy disk drive; _____ 3½ in. disks;

   _____ 5¼ in. disks; _____ both

19. _____   hard disk: 60 MB, 80 MB; 120 MB; 240 MB; _____ MB

20. _____   Tape backup

21. _____   Surge protector; uninterrupted power supply

22. _____   Mouse; _____ trackball

23. _____   Dot-matrix printer; _____ laser printer; _____ color capability; _____

   graphics capability; _____ multiple-form capability; _____ font availability;

   _____ speed; _____ noise level; _____ quality of text output

24. _____   Modem (_____ internal; _____ external); _____ 2400 bps;

   _____ 9600 bps; _____ 14,400 bps; _____ bps; _____ error

   correction? _____ data compression?

25. _____   Fax (internal; external; handle photos?)

26. _____   Scanner (_____ color? _____ gray-scale? _____ slides?

   _____ photos?)

27. _____   Is system upgradable? How easy is it to upgrade?

28. _____   Any special needs? (e.g., voice output/braille input for a blind person? special keyboards for a disabled person?)

29. _____   Any multimedia hardware needs? Identify: _____

_____

(*Note: If you need sound capability, make sure the sound card is compatible with the software you plan to use. Sound cards use different standards.*)

TOTAL projected cost for hardware $_____

Support

Investigate the following:

1. Manufacturer's reputation and length of time in business
2. Dealer's reputation and length of time in business
3. Warranties
4. Quality of documentation (user's manuals): easy to follow? detailed?
5. Hotline availability to solve problems in emergencies
6. Location and availability of repair services
7. Availability of training
8. Will dealer install?

As a simple guide, *PC Novice* magazine recommends the following minimum requirements for a microcomputer system:

▼ At least 2 MB RAM (4 MB is preferable)

▼ VGA or SVGA monitor

▼ 386SX (20 MHz) or higher CPU

▼ At least 80 MB hard disk drive storage capacity

▼ Mouse

▼ Both 5¼ and 3½ inch floppy disk drives

▼ Modem (fax/modem combination preferable)

▼ Surge protector

▼ Keyboard (usually included)

▼ Extra expansion slots

▼ Upgradable RAM

**DO YOU REALLY
NEED A
COMPUTER?**

*T*here is no point in having computer skills unless you are going to use them. These four episodes will help you do precisely that. These episodes are not "hands-on" tutorials; instead, they are meant to be thought provoking and to be the basis of discussions.

You have started a business in something near and dear to most of us—food. And, since your target market is college students, you opened a pizza parlor near a campus and called it "Professor Pizza."

You, Pat Sanderson, started out the pizza parlor with a small loan from your local banker and have spent a year building a customer base. Paul Robison runs the night shift, which is usually your busiest and most hectic time. Juanita Chavez is your bookkeeper. You additionally have a staff of 15 full- and part-time employees working as cashiers, kitchen helpers, and cooks. Your business is a success, but you have experienced some real growing pains during the past year.

You gross about $750,000 during your 11 A.M. to 2 A.M. business hours. The long hours that your business is open require you to staff two full shifts. You have had a lot of requests for delivery service to the college dorms and near-by student housing, but you are nervous about expanding your business much more at this point, because you are already having trouble keeping up with demand.

Although there is room for more pizza-making tables in the kitchen, the set-up is disorganized, and pizzas often are not made correctly because the cooks can't read the cashiers' handwriting on the orders. Juanita has suggested that most of the problems seem to be with a few specific cooks, and maybe they just want to eat the mistakes. But you currently have no way of tracking who makes each pizza.

Due to the nature of the business, there is a high turnover in employees. To entice employees to stay longer, you offer longevity bonuses. For each six-month period of employment with no absences, the employee will receive a bonus of $200.

Inventory maintenance is out of control. You don't have a method for tracking how much of any particular item you have in stock, and consequently you over- and under-order items. For example, you currently have enough canned tomato sauce to last six months but have run out of fresh mushrooms two of the last five days.

Paul, who is finishing up a computer science major during the day, keeps insisting that a computer could solve all your problems. But Juanita prefers things the old-fashioned way—all manual. You need to weigh all the alternatives and arguments in order to make a decision regarding the future purchase of a computer system for your business.

Current Business

You've now have heard, in a nutshell, about all the basic problems with your business. Now let's examine each of the current practices in a little more depth.

Inventory and Ordering

You personally have had control of all ordering, but this duty often gets neglected until it is too late.

The items you stock comprise three main categories: fresh vegetables, such as onions, tomatoes, green peppers, etc., which have a shelf life of less than one week; fresh meats and cheese, which can be frozen and defrosted as needed; and canned items, such as tomato sauce. You have one main supplier

Many thanks to Mark and Diane Poe for their help with revising these episodes.

for the fresh vegetables, three different suppliers (depending on who has the best price) for the meats and cheeses, and four suppliers for the canned items. You can get better prices for the canned items if you are able to order two weeks before you need delivery. So far, you have not been able to take advantage of this discount very oftcn.

The best way to approach this problem would be to track what quantities of items you use on an average daily basis and then determine future orders to take advantage of discounts. Additionally, by having the night shift take an inventory each night, you could quickly identify items you need to order immediately.

Accounts Payable

Juanita currently pays all bills as soon as she receives them in order to take advantage of any discounts offered for paying promptly. This practice was also helpful when you were first starting your business so that you got a good reputation with your suppliers for paying quickly. But you now would like to pay invoices when they are due (usually 30 days after the invoice date).

You would like to set up a system that will allow you to know when invoices need to be paid and then track them on a daily basis so that you can project cash needs. You approve all invoices before payment since you receive all deliveries and know what has been received.

Payroll and Personnel Information

The weekly payroll and the required federal and state monthly and quarterly payroll reports take a great deal of Juanita's time. Most of the employees are hourly employees, and they are paid according to the hours recorded on their time sheet and initialled as approved by their supervisor. Juanita does all of the payroll manually by filling out payroll cards on each employee. She records the gross wages (hourly wage times hours worked—for example, $4.00/hour $\times$ 8 hours), federal income tax withheld, state income tax withheld, social security tax withheld, Medicare tax withheld, and, finally, the net pay that the employee receives on each individual's payroll card along with his or her name, address, exemptions, and social security number. This information is also recorded on a payroll register that records the name, hours, earnings, deductions, net pay, date paid and check number for each employee paid per pay period (see Figure 1).

FIGURE 1

Payroll Register										
		Earnings			Deductions				Payment	
Employee	Total Hours	Reg.	Overtime	Gross	Fed W/H	FICA*	Medicare	Other	Net	Check #
Juanita Chavez [address] [Social Security number]	40	320.00		320.00	32.00	19.84	4.64	—	263.52	1056
Kim Soong [address] [Social Security number]	25	150.00		150.00	15.00	9.30	2.18	—	123.52	1016
• •	• •	• •		• •	• •	• •	• •	• •	• •	• •

*FICA—Federal Insurance Contribution Act (Social Security)

Each month, Juanita sums up the monthly wages paid to each employee on his or her employee payroll card. She then totals all amounts paid in that month and prepares a report for the state workman's compensation fund based on a percentage of each employee's monthly income. However, only the first $15,000 per employee is taxable. So, she also needs to keep track of how much each employee has been paid each year (see Figure 2).

At the end of each quarter, Juanita also goes through the same procedure to report to the federal government how much federal withholding tax and employees' and employer's share of Social Security Tax and Medicare Tax should be and how much federal unemployment needs to be paid. Also, on a quarterly basis, she reports how much state income tax was withheld and how much state unemployment tax should be paid.

All this reporting takes up a lot of Juanita's time, and sometimes she forgets to pay the employee longevity bonuses. This has created some ill will in the past, and it is a priority for you and Juanita to find a solution to this problem.

Cash Receipts

When customers come into Professor Pizza, they place a pizza order at the cash register. The cashier writes up the order and collects the customer's money for the order. The cashier rings the amount up on the cash register, so there is a record of the amount collected. However, except for the handwritten order, there is no record of what was ordered.

The handwritten order goes from the cashier to the kitchen, where the order is prepared from the slip of paper. As mentioned previously, there is a problem with occasional incorrectly prepared pizzas. This not only wastes food but makes some customers unhappy.

Promotional Materials

You have new competition in the area, and they are sending some slick mailers with coupons to residences around your business. You don't want to invest a lot of money having an advertising agency draw up designs or hiring a printer to print them, so you are interested in what desktop publishing could do for you.

FIGURE 2

Employee Earnings Card

Employee Name __Juanita Chavez__   Social Security Number __111-22-3333__   Employee No. __3__

Address __121 University Row__   Sex: Male ____   Female __xx__   Weekly Pay Rate _____

__College Town, Nevada__   Single ____   Married __xx__   HH ____   Hourly Rate __$8.00__

Date of Birth __04-01-68__   Exemptions __2__   Date Employment Ended _____

Position __Bookkeeper__   Date of Employment __01-01-1993__

1994		Earnings					Deductions			Payment		
Period Ended	Total Hours	Regular	Overtime	Gross	Federal W/H	FICA	Medicare	Other	Net Earnings	Check No.	Cumulative Gross Earnings
09/10	40.0	320.00			32.00	19.84	4.64	—	263.52	1015	11,520.00

3

Cost of Goods Sold: Financial Statements

Juanita is not a full-charge bookkeeper; although she is good at math functions, she is not comfortable preparing some types of financial statements. You know you must be making money because you have money in the bank, but you don't know what kind of profit margin you have on the pizzas or on the beverages. In addition, you have no means for forecasting what the pizza parlor's taxable income will be until after the end of the year, when your CPA (certified public accountant) prepares your annual financial statements and tax return.

What Do You Think?

1. What are the problems and inadequacies in your current system? (Make a list.) At this point, how do you think a computer system could eliminate these problems?

2. What information can the computer give you? What form will the output reports take, and how often will you need the reports?

   a. Inventory—Will you have "trigger" points that tell you when to order items that are being used up?

   b. Accounts Payable—How would you like to see information presented so that you can forecast cash-flow requirements?

   c. Payroll—Besides payroll checks, what other types of payroll-related reports should the system produce?

   d. Pizza Order Forms and Cash Receipts

   e. Promotional Materials—What types of advertising flyers, promotional items, and other forms of desktop publishing could you use for the pizza parlor?

   f. Cost of Goods, Financial Statements—What items do you want to track for costing purposes (for example, labor costs, rent)?

3. How will you physically secure the computer system? What other security concerns do you have? What about controls to ensure data input and information output?

*M*eanwhile, back at the pizza parlor . . .

Professor Pizza has continued to grow. You have not yet purchased a computer or even made a final decision regarding one, largely because everyone is too busy to investigate it further.

Your parlor has added delivery drivers, but you are getting too many complaints about late deliveries and cold pizzas, as well as pizzas with the wrong toppings. Juanita had thought that some of the incorrectly prepared pizzas were for the benefit of the pizza makers, who ate their mistakes. Now, the refused pizzas sit in the delivery cars and arrive back at the parlor cold and generally unappetizing, so you believe that there really is a problem with communication between the order takers and the kitchen.

Your gross sales (sales amounts before deductions are made for taxes, payroll, etc.) have increased, largely due to deliveries, from $750,000 per year to $1,000,000. However, an additional wrinkle has been added because of the deliveries. Your lease with the landlord calls for you to pay a fixed amount for rent and a percentage of gross sales that originate on the premises. Currently, you do not track your sales by type and so cannot subtract the delivery gross sales. Consequently, you are paying your landlord a percentage on the delivery sales—but, according to the terms of the lease, you don't have to do this. This has increased the pressure on Juanita to begin preparing monthly profit-and-loss statements that identify the types of sales.

Additionally, the added staff (now 25 people) has increased Juanita's workload. To help her, you have hired one clerk to prepare payroll and a second clerk to handle accounts payable. Since the personnel is new and a good system of checks and balances does not exist, there are numerous mistakes made in paying invoices and employees. Although you still want to maintain the policy of paying workers longevity bonuses, you generally wait for employees to complain before you pay these bonuses. Juanita now agrees you need a computer system and, in fact, has done the most research into what is available to solve the problems and meet the needs you identified earlier.

As a means of dealing coherently with the needs of the different departments, you have asked Juanita and Paul (night manager) to come up with more detailed "wish lists" of what the computer system could do for them—that is, what they want the software to do. You will also come up with a list. You'll then have a meeting to determine what can best serve all your needs.

HOW WILL THE COMPUTER WORK FOR YOU?

Pat's List (You)

1. I want monthly profit-and-loss (P&L) statements that will tell me how much our food costs are and how much our overhead is. (Overhead is business expenses—like rent, insurance, heating, phone—that are not actual parts of the product—like cheese, mushrooms, etc.) I read an article that said that we should make a bottom-line profit percentage of 2% of total gross sales (income before deductions for costs and overhead) and that cost of foods should be around 25%, with the rest of the cost in overhead. Currently, we don't get that information until a couple of months after the end of the year.

2. We need to be able to identify our types of gross sales—that is, how much of our total sales is made in the store and how much is made from deliveries. Thus we can avoid paying the landlord a percentage of delivery sales.

3. We need a better system to track inventory. By having the night-shift employees take inventory of items on a nightly basis, we do have better control of items in stock than we used to. But, we can't easily get comparative costs on items and don't know if we would be better off ordering large quantities.

4. I really would like to produce our own menus and advertising material. Our system would have to be able to handle text and graphics—a laser printer would be necessary. Could we afford color?

Paul's List

1. It appears to me that my night shift crew is selling most of the pizzas and making most of the deliveries. Yet, we have the same size crew as the day shift. We need more people on the night shift and fewer on the day shift! Is there any way of having a computer-based system that tells us on a daily basis how much in sales each shift has done so that we can staff the shifts appropriately?

2. A lot of my people have been complaining about not getting their longevity bonuses. Can we make this system automatically identify who's eligible and when?

3. Some of the cashiers have horrible handwriting and don't seem to be able to spell. Can we get a computer-based system that prints orders to the kitchen?

Juanita's List

1. I want to computerize our accounts payable so that we can start paying our bills twice monthly. Before writing checks, we will get a printout of all outstanding bills so that we can decide what to pay.

2. I have seen payroll programs that will allow the user to input a lot of data about personnel—such as days missed, start date and birth date, as well as the usual data like hourly wage and hours worked, etc. A standard program like that will do what I need. This program will also give me the information that I need for my payroll reports.

3. We need to also find a way to get the sales information into the accounting system. I have heard of systems that do that directly from the cash register, or we could manually enter sales figures from the cash register tape at the end of the day. Pat and Paul have mentioned different ways they want to track sales and we just need to make sure that we set up the system the way we want.

4. I think that Tao, the accounts payable clerk, and Michelle, the payroll clerk, should have computers (in addition to one for me). We will need a regular dot-matrix printer and probably a higher quality laser printer for correspondence.

After identifying what you want your computer system to do for you—that is, what the software should do for you—you must decide what you need in the areas of input, processing, storage, and output hardware.

What Do You Think?

1. Consider Pat's, Paul's, and Juanita's comments. Do all their requests seem to be practical or realistic? Why or why not?

2. In order to conceptualize how the system would work, you have begun a procedures manual before the actual computer system is in place. What type of back-up should be done on the system? How often and who is responsible for the back-up? What type of storage medium do you want for the back-up? What could happen if you don't back-up your system frequently?

   How could you ensure business recovery if someone broke in and stole the computer equipment?

3. You went down to your local computer store this weekend to begin pricing hardware. A salesperson told you about a two-user network system for $5,300 that has a 486 50 MHz 330 MB server with two workstations; a single-user 486 33 MHz 170 MB system for $3,200; and a 386 25 MHz 120 MB notebook computer for $2,700. What does all that mean?

3

CHOOSING THE SYSTEM

PROFESSOR PIZZA

*O*nward . . .

When we left the last episode, we were pondering the needs of our prospective computer system, and we have finally gotten all the key people behind the idea of purchasing a system. In fact, they're actually enthused about the prospect. Since you and your managers listed your wishes for the new computer system, more questions have been raised. For example, one of the workers in the kitchen wants to put a bar code on the pizza boxes so that you can track the prepared pizzas and scan them when they are delivered. This system would be similar to tracking systems used by many overnight delivery systems, such as Federal Express.

Decisions Made So Far

You have decided to purchase an industry-specific accounting software program instead of an off-the-shelf software package. Although the cost of such software is initially higher (approximately $5,000 compared to about $200 for an off-the-shelf accounting software package), the software will deal with many of the peculiarities of your business. This integrated software program will handle all your accounting data such as sales, accounts payable, payroll, and general ledger as well as inventory and inventory control. It will also provide many useful financial calculations such as labor costs, overhead costs, and average cost of a pizza

Additionally, you have determined that you need point-of-sale cash registers. These registers will allow cashiers to punch a key and easily record the customer's order, as well as produce sales receipts. These registers will also track sales by category for easy summary at day's end. The software that you want to purchase will integrate this sales information easily into the accounting data so that you can easily and quickly analyze what is selling best and what products give you the most profit.

Decisions to Make

What other kinds of software do you need?

▼ *Word processing:* With word processing you can more easily create letters, memos, and reports. Would this be required in your business?

▼ *Spreadsheets:* Do you anticipate a need to further analyze data you receive or present the data in a graphic form? Would you use the computer to prepare "what if" scenarios for your business?

▼ *Database management:* Do you need to create mailing lists, mailing labels, or cross-referenced lists of products with supplier data?

▼ *Communications:* Do you foresee a need to communicate via modem with other computers in other locations? Will you make use of on-line services such as Prodigy or CompuServe for stock quotes, travel plans, or the like?

▼ *Desktop publishing (DTP) and presentation graphics:* Would a high-end word processing package provide enough capabilities for you to create your own menus, fliers, and advertising pieces, or do you want to purchase more sophisticated DTP software and software to create art for very fancy publications?

Of course, you need to purchase hardware that will run your special accounting program plus any additional software you want to use. You must consider cost, compatibility, speed, storage capacity, and convenience. In addition:

▼ Do you need all desktop computers, or do you also need a laptop or notebook computer or two so that you and others can take work home?

▼ Do you need color or monochrome monitors? for which work areas?

▼ What types of printers do you need? Dot matrix printer for printing on multiple forms? Laser printer for high-quality text and graphics output for important correspondence and desktop published items? Do you need to use special paper sizes? Is noise a concern?

▼ What will best serve your back-up needs? Cartridge tape units? (The tapes could be stored in another location.) How can you set up a back-up system to back up all your computer storage units regularly and at the same time?

▼ What kind of peripheral equipment does your business require? Mouse? Special ergonomic keyboards for workers who must do a lot of keyboard data entry? Fax? (Customers could fax you orders to be picked up later!) Could you use a CD-ROM drive?

▼ In what areas should your system have maximum upgrade capacity? Speed? Video capabilities? Communications? Secondary storage capacity? RAM?

Other Future Plans

Business has been so good recently that you want to open a second location within the next year. What special computer system requirements would a second, satellite location of your business have? You have considered linking the second location via modem to your current location so that you can more closely monitor sales. Also, the modem would allow the second store to report directly to the main store and save you (or the manager) time spent traveling between the locations.

At this point, however, you want to keep it small and simple. If you plan well and choose the right hardware, you can always upgrade and add additional software and hardware later. This will help not only keep costs down, but make it easier to adapt to the new system.

Final Considerations

The purpose of the newly automated system is to provide information in a more usable fashion and, of course, to save time and money. But you have heard some horror stories about system "crashes" and realize the importance of having a good support system from your computer dealer and consultant.

▼ Will your dealer provide technical support for a specific length of time? Is there a charge for this support? What is the response time to questions? Does the dealer or manufacturer have a hot line? (If you are a beginner in the world of computers, it is usually more worthwhile for you to pay a little more in order to ensure good technical support. Mail order catalogs can provide cheaper prices, but may provide little or no support.)

▼ Do the manufacturers offer warranties?

▼ Does your dealer offer training classes on site for you and your workers? (You don't want to lose time and money by having confused workers sitting around trying to teach themselves how to use a new computer system.

If your dealer doesn't provide training, you might consider hiring a professional training consultant.)

▼ Can your dealer help with financing or help you find a leasing agent?

▼ Should you purchase a maintenance contract?

▼ Is the dealer's/manufacturer's documentation clearly written and easy to use?

What Do You Think?

1. Make a list of what you have decided to purchase. (Assume $5,000 for your custom accounting software.) Use the purchasing checklist at the end of Chapter 15 as a guide. Include as many categories as you think appropriate, and use computer publications (or a visit to a computer store) to help you determine prices for the various parts of your system. What is your final total cost?

   Compare your list with other students' lists. Have you forgotten anything?

2. What kind of data do you think should be input into the system in each of the following areas? How often should it be entered?

   a. Inventory (what you have in stock)

   b. Accounts Payable (what you owe to suppliers)

   c. Payroll (what you pay your employees and what you owe various agencies in wage-related taxes, insurance, and benefits)

   d. Personnel Records (necessary information about your employees, such as name, address, Social Security number, date of hire, number of dependents, and so on)

   e. Cash Orders and Receipts (what customers order and what they pay)

3. How many computers do you think will be needed? Should they be linked in a network? If so, who should be responsible for maintaining the network system? Would color monitors or extra large monitors be useful? For what?

4. What entries will be made on an on-line system? What type of work would be done as batch entry? Do you need any specialized input devices, or just keyboards and mice?

*T*he Story Continues . . .

It's now one year later, and the new computer system has become fully operational. You still are in one location, and your business has changed very little in the past year. Your sales and profit are still consistent—although cost of goods in general is down, you incurred some additional costs as the result of installing the computer system.

In general, a significant number of business headaches have been minimized or completely eliminated. However, now it's time to begin analyzing your current system for needed changes and upgrades, including any database management needs.

SYSTEM ANALYSIS AND DATABASE MANAGEMENT

Pluses and Minuses

Your completely integrated computer system allows the cashier to input the customer's order at the point-of-sale cash register and simultaneously display the order on a monitor in the kitchen. Thus pizzas are not being incorrectly prepared, customers are happier, and waste has decreased.

The point-of-sale register also tracks sales that can be immediately sent on to Juanita's computer in accounting. However, Juanita still wants better control of the data that goes into the accounting system. (This is a common reaction of new computer users.) Because you respect her concerns—and don't want to make her uncomfortable by pushing her too fast—you have the system set up to batch the sales data and send it to accounting once a day. Juanita (or one of her assistants) then reconciles the paper cash register receipts with the sales recorded and prepares the daily bank deposit.

One disadvantage inherent with batching sales daily is that you don't know which cashiers are making mistakes when the cash-receipts amount is not the same as the recorded-sales amount. Also, by not tracking sales according to the time they occurred (via an on-line system), you don't really have an accurate picture of the times of day when sales are greatest, as well as the times of day different types of sales are greatest. For example, could you close the salad bar at 8 P.M., or do you really need to keep it open all night? Are delivery sales more frequent at a certain time than another? Your system could be upgraded to handle this type of tracking, but you haven't done it yet.

You did try initially to have cashiers log in when they started a shift, but the system became confused when cashiers would forget to log off at the end of their shifts. You wonder if they really understand the importance of logging on and off correctly. Your system currently has degenerated to the point where a few people log in first thing in the morning and whoever is working last logs off.

Your new system does allow you to track overall types of sales. For example, you learned that your salad bar actually made you more money than you realized, so you plan to promote it more prominently. More important, you are able to separate the amount of delivery sales and the amount of in-store sales so that you can properly report the in-store sales for computation of your lease cost. (Remember—your landlord had you locked into a lease that called for a percentage of in-store sales.)

Inventory

You did not automate the inventory. You found that it was too difficult to try to automatically track all supplies as they were used. For example, it would be next to impossible to track each mushroom used in order to decide when you needed to order more! However, you have continued to have the night shift take a physical inventory near the end of the shift. This physical inventory data is then input into a special custom program you created that tells you when and what to order. Currently, the program has trigger points that give you enough lead time for ordering supplies so that you are able to take advantage of special offers from your vendors. You also don't run out of supplies often.

Unfortunately, the radical pizza maker who wanted to put bar codes on the pizza boxes quit in disgust when his idea was rejected as a little too extreme. He is currently back in college, studying Abnormal Psychology.

Payroll and Staffing

One of the smoothest transitions has been with the payroll program implementation. Juanita and Tao experienced a bit of initial frustration while learning the new system, but now they handle payroll smoothly and quickly. You now have access to all kinds of employee information via the system, such as date of hire, pay rate, address, birth date, and days of work missed. This information enables you to use the system to automatically calculate longevity bonuses. The system also prints "Happy Birthday" messages on employees' checks on their birthdays.

The payroll program calculates all the withholding taxes and required federal deposits, and it compiles all the necessary data for easy preparation of quarterly and annual payroll reports. In fact, one payroll clerk, Michelle, has so much free time available that she is working on some advertising flyers. She is using the standard word processing program that you purchased last year, but she is showing so much enthusiasm for creating various types of publications that you are considering purchasing a desktop publishing program and having Michelle trained to use it.

You do not yet have a system for mailing advertising fliers to everyone in town, but you could purchase an electronic mailing list that includes everyone's name and address. The list would be part of a database management program. You could sort the database according to ZIP code or last name and automatically print labels. (Also, with such a database management program, you could track delivery customers according to name, phone number, address, and time of day of order delivery. Perhaps you could offer rebates or discounts to frequent delivery customers and thus encourage repeat business.)

After analysis, you determined that Paul's night shift did indeed have the bulk of the work and have been able to better adjust staffing for the various shifts. However, as mentioned above, you aren't yet using the computer system for tracking when sales occur, so your analysis was a time-consuming manual process and perhaps not as precise as it could have been.

Accounts Payable

Juanita is now doing all the accounts payable. The system automatically calculates when invoices are due and when discounts are available. She issues checks twice a month and is better able to take advantage of "aging" invoices—holding on to invoices for as long as possible—to maximize cash flow.

Financial Statements

The accounting software that you purchased allows you to produce standard financial statements that show a balance sheet and an income statement. The income statement is probably the most useful to you because it shows sales broken down by type and cost of goods for each type, as well as general and administrative (overhead) costs.

However, you have not yet been able to use this information for any type of projections. Your accounting software works only with historic (past) data and does not allow for financial projections into the future. Projections of future cash flows, for example, could be developed based on past average sales and costs so that you could pinpoint potential trouble periods ahead of time or determine when you might have surplus cash for investments. It would also be useful to project taxable income so you know ahead of time approximately how much you'll have to pay the IRS!

These types of projections could be done easily with a spreadsheet program. A spreadsheet program would also provide you with the ability to try our various "what-if" scenarios, which are advisable before making any major business decision.

General Concerns

Juanita—head of accounting—has not yet been able to take a vacation because no one else knows all aspects of the system. Although you do have the standard Users' Guide documentation provided by the manufacturer of your accounting software, you do not have complete written documentation of your business's unique accounting procedures.

In addition, you all admit that you do not consistently back up your system. There is no standard timetable of when to back up, how many back-up versions to keep, or who should be responsible for them.

The employee turnover for cashiers is high. There are frequent errors with new employees on the cash register, because there are no written formal instructions for cash register use.

What Do You Think?

1. Based on the information given in this episode, list the problems you can identify in Professor Pizza's computer system. Now list some alternatives— ways to solve the problems. How would you collect data to identify and analyze a real system's problems?

2. Do you think you could use a database management program? What types of databases would you create? Would maintenance of the database require additional personnel?

3. When you initially purchased your system, you also purchased a modem. Lately, an employee has been using it to access a public bulletin board and has been downloading free software that be useful to the business. Should you be concerned about potential computer viruses? What can you do to protect against them?

Appendix:
Key Dates in the History and Future of Information Processing*

YEAR	EVENT
Less than 100,000 years ago	Homo sapiens begin using intelligence to further goals.
More than 5,000 years ago	The abacus, which resembles the arithmetic unit of a modern computer, is developed in the Orient.
3000–700 B.C.	Water clocks are built in China in 3000 B.C., in Egypt approx. 1500 B.C., and in Assyria 700 B.C.
2500 B.C.	Egyptians invent the idea of thinking machines: citizens turn for advice to oracles, which are statues with priests hidden inside.
427 B.C.	In the *Phaedo* and later works Plato expresses ideas, several millennia before the advent of the computer, that are relevant to modern dilemmas regarding human thought and its relation to the mechanics of the machine.
approx. 420 B.C.	Archytas of Tarentum, a friend of Plato, constructs a wooden pigeon whose movements are controlled by a jet of steam or compressed air.
approx. 415 B.C.	Theaetetus, a member of Plato's Academy, creates solid geometry.
387 B.C.	Plato founds the Academy for the pursuit of science and philosophy in a grove on the outskirts of Athens. It results in the fertile development of mathematical theory.
293 B.C.	Euclid, also a member of Plato's Academy, is the expositor of plane geometry. He writes the *Elements*, a basic mathematics textbook for the next 2,000 years.
c. 200 B.C.	In China artisans develop elaborate automata, including an entire mechanical orchestra.
725	A Chinese engineer and a Buddhist monk build the first true mechanical clock, a water-driven device with an escapement that causes the clock to tick.
1540, 1772	The technology of clock and watch making results in the production of more elaborate automata during the European Renaissance. Gianello Toriano's mandolin-playing lady (1540) and P. Jacquet-Droz's child (1772) are famous examples.
1617	John Napier invents Napier's Bones, of significance to the future development of calculating engines.
1642	Blaise Pascal perfects the Pascaline, a machine that can add and subtract. It is the world's first automatic calculating machine.
1694	Gottfried Wilhelm Liebniz, an inventor of calculus, perfects the Liebniz Computer, a machine that multiplies by performing repetitive additions, an algorithm still used in modern computers.
1726	Jonathan Swift, in *Gulliver's Travels*, describes a machine that will automatically write books.
1805	Joseph-Marie Jacquard devises a method for automating weaving with a series of punched cards. This invention will be used many years later in the development of early computers.
1821	Charles Babbage is awarded the first gold medal by the British Astronomical Society for his paper "Observations on the Application of Machinery to the Computation of Mathematical Tables."
1821	Michael Farraday, widely recognized as the father of electricity, reports his discovery of electromagnetic rotation and builds the first two motors powered by electricity.
1822	Charles Babbage develops the Difference Engine, but its technical complexities exhaust his financial resources and organizational skills. He eventually abandons it to concentrate his efforts on a general-purpose computer.
1829	The first electromagnetically driven clock is constructed.
1832	Charles Babbage develops the principle of the Analytical Engine, which is the world's first computer, it can be programmed to solve a wide variety of logical and computational problems.

* Adapted from Raymond Kurzweil, The Age of Intelligent Machines, Cambridge, Mass.: Massachusetts Institute of Technology, 1990, pp. 465–483.

1835   Joseph Henry invents the electrical relay, a means of transmitting electrical impulses over long distances. The relay serves as the basis for the telegraph.

1837   Samuel Finley Breese Morse patents his more practical version of the telegraph, which sends letters in codes consisting of dots and dashes.

1843   Ada Lovelace, Lord Byron's only legitimate child and the world's first computer programmer, publishes her own notes with her translation of L. P. Menabrea's paper on Babbage's Analytical Engine.

1846   Alexander Bain uses punched paper tape to send telegraph messages, greatly improving the speed of transmission.

1847   George Boole publishes his first ideas on symbolic logic. He will develop these ideas into his theory of binary logic and arithmetic — a theory that is still the basis of modern computation.

1854   An electric telegraph is installed between Paris and London.

1855   William Thomson develops a successful theory concerning the transmission of electrical signals through submarine cables.

1861   San Francisco and New York are connected by a telegraph line.

1864   Ducos de Harron develops a primitive motion-picture device in France.

1866   Cyrus West Field lays a telegraph cable across the Atlantic Ocean.

1876   Alexander Graham Bell's telephone receives U.S. Patent 174,465, the most lucrative patent ever granted.

1879   G. Frege, one of the founders of modern symbolic language, proposes a notational system for mechanical reasoning. This work is a forerunner to the predicate calculus, which will be used for knowledge representation in artificial intelligence.

1885   Boston is connected to New York by telephone.

1886   Alexander Graham Bell, with a modified version of Thomas Alva Edison's phonograph, uses wax discs for recording sound.

1888   William S. Burroughs patents an adding machine. This machine is modified four years later to include subtraction and printing. It is the world's first dependable key-driven calculator and will soon win widespread acceptance.

1888   Heinrich Hertz experiments with the transmission of what are now known as radio waves.

1888   The first commercial roll-film camera is introduced.

1890   Herman Hollerith, incorporating ideas from Jacquard's loom and Babbage's Analytical Engine, patents an electromechanical information machine that uses punched cards. It wins the 1890 U.S. Census competition, with the result that electricity is used for the first time in a major data processing project.

1894   Guglielmo Marconi builds his first radio equipment, which rings a bell from 30 feet away.

1896   A sound film is first shown before a paying audience in Berlin.

1896   Herman Hollerith forms the Tabulating Machine Company, which will become IBM.

1897   Alexander Popov, a Russian, uses an antenna to transmit radio waves, and Guglielmo Marconi, an Italian, receives the first patent ever granted for radio. Marconi helps organize a company to market his system.

1899   The first recording of sound occurs magnetically on wire and on a thin metal strip.

1900   Herman Hollerith introduces an automatic card feed into his information machine to process the 1900 census data.

1900   The entire civilized world is connected by telegraph, and in the United States there are more than 1.4 million telephones, 8,000 registered automobiles, and 24 million electric light bulbs. Edison's promise of "electric bulbs so cheap that only the rich will be able to afford candles" is thus realized. In addition, the Gramophone Company is advertising a choice of five thousand recordings.

1901   Marconi, in Newfoundland, receives the first transatlantic telegraphic radio transmission.

1904   John Ambrose Fleming files a patent for the first vacuum tube, a diode.

1906   Reginald Aubrey Fessenden invents AM radio and transmits by radio waves to wireless operators on U.S. ships off the Atlantic Coast. The transmission includes a Christmas carol, a violin trill, and for the first time the sound of a human voice.

1907	Lee De Forest and R. von Lieben invent the amplifier vacuum tube, known as a triode, which greatly improves radio.
1911	Herman Hollerith's Tabulating Machine Company acquires several other companies and changes its name to Computing-Tabulating-Recording Company (CTR). In 1914 Thomas J. Watson is appointed president.
1913	Henry Ford introduces the first true assembly-line method of automated production.
1913	A. Meissner invents a radio transmitter with vacuum tubes. Radio-transmitter triode modulation is introduced the following year, and in 1915 the radio-tube oscillator is introduced.
1921	Czech dramatist Karel Capek popularizes the term *robot*, a word he coined in 1917 to describe the mechanical people in his science-fiction drama R.U.R. (Rossum's Universal Robots). His intelligent machines, intended as servants for their human creators, end up taking over the world and destroying all mankind.
1923	Vladimir Kosma Zworkin, the father of television, gives the first demonstration of an electronic television-camera tube, using a mechanical transmitting device. He develops the iconoscope, an early type of television system, the following year.
1924	Thomas J. Watson becomes the chief executive officer of CTR and renames the company International Business Machines (IBM). IBM will become the leader of the modern industry and one of the largest industrial corporations in the world.
1925	Vannevar Bush and his co-workers develop the first analog computer, a machine designed to solve differential equations.
1926	The era of talking motion pictures is introduced by *The Jazz Singer*, starring Al Jolson.
1928	John von Neumann presents the minimax theorem, which will be widely used in game-playing programs.
1928	Philo T. Farnsworth demonstrates the world's first all-electronic television, and Vladimir Zworkin receives a patent for a color television system.
1929	FM radio is introduced.
1930	Vannevar Bush's analog computer, the Differential Analyzer, is built at MIT. It will be used to calculate artillery trajectories during World War II.
1932	RCA demonstrates a television receiver with a cathode-ray picture tube. In 1933 Zworkin produces a cathode-ray tube, called the *iconoscope*, that makes high-quality television almost a reality.
1937	Building on the work of Bertrand Russell and Charles Babbage, Alan Turing publishes "On Computable Numbers," his now-celebrated paper introducing the Turing machine, a theoretical model of a computer.
1937	The Church-Turing thesis, independently developed by Alonzo Church and Alan Turing, states that all problems solvable by a human being are reducible to a set of algorithms, or more simply, that machine intelligence and human intelligence are essentially equivalent.
1940	John V. Atanasoff and Clifford Berry build an electronic computer known as ABC. This is the first electronic computer, but it is not programmable.
1940	The 10,000-person British computer war effort known as Ultra creates Robinson, the world's first operational computer. It is based on electromechanical relays and is powerful enough to decode messages from Enigma, the Nazis' first-generation enciphering machine.
1941	Konrad Zuse, a German, completes the world's first fully programmable digital computer, the Z-3, and hires Arnold Fast, a blind mathematician, to program it. Fast becomes the world's first programmer of an operational programmable computer.
1943	The Ultra team builds Colossus, a computer that uses electronic tubes 100 to 1,000 times faster than the relays used by Robinson. It cracks increasingly complex German codes and contributes to the Allies' winning of World War II.
1944	Howard Aiken completes the first American programmable computer, the Mark I. It uses punched paper tape for programming and vacuum tubes to calculate problems.
1945	Konrad Zuse develops Plankalkul, the first high-level language.
1946	John Tukey first uses the term bit for binary digit, the basic unit of data for computers.

1946	John von Neumann publishes the first modern paper on the stored-program concept and starts computer research at the Institute for Advanced Study in Princeton.
1946	John Presper Eckert and John W. Mauchley develop ENIAC, the world's first fully electronic, general-purpose (programmable) digital computer. It is almost 1,000 times faster than the Mark I and is used for calculating ballistic-firing tables for the Army.
1946	Television enters American life even more rapidly than radio did in the 1920s. The percentage of American homes having sets jumps from 0.02% in 1946 to 72% in 1956 and more than 90% by 1983.
1947	William Bradford Schockley, Walter Hauser Brittain, and John Ardeen invent the transistor, a minute device that functions like a vacuum tube but switches current on and off at much faster speeds. It launches a revolution in microelectronics, bringing down the cost of computers and leading to the development of minicomputers and powerful new mainframe computers.
1949	Maurice Wilkes, influenced by Eckert and Mauchley, builds EDSAC, the world's first stored-program computer. Eckert and Mauchley's new U.S. company brings out BINAC, the first American stored-program computer, soon after.
1950	The U.S. census is first handled by a programmable computer, UNIVAC, developed by Eckert and Mauchley. It is the first commercially marketed computer.
1950	Alan Turing's "Computing Machinery and Intelligence" describes the Turing test, a means for determining whether a machine is intelligent.
1950	Commercial color television begins in the U.S.; transcontinental black-and-white television is inaugurated the following year.
1950	Claude Elwood Shannon writes a proposal for a chess program.
1951	EDVAC, Eckert and Mauchley's first computer that implements the stored-program concept, is completed at the Moore School at the University of Pennsylvania.
1952	The CBS television network uses UNIVAC to correctly predict the election of Dwight D. Eisenhower as president of the United States.
1952	The pocket-size transistor radio is introduced.
1952	The 701, IBM's first production-line electronic digital computer, is designed by Nathaniel Rochester and marketed for scientific use.
1955	IBM introduces its first transistor calculator, with 2,200 transistors instead of the 1,200 vacuum tubes that would otherwise be required.
1955	The first design is created for a robot-like machine for industrial use in the U.S.
1955	Allen Newell, J. C. Shaw, and Herbert Simon develop IPL-II, the first AI language.
1955	The beginning space program and the military in the U.S., recognizing the need for computers powerful enough to steer rockets to the moon and missiles through the stratosphere, fund major research projects.
1956	The first transatlantic telephone cable begins to operate.
1956	FORTRAN, the first scientific computer programming language, is invented by John Backus and a team at IBM.
1956	MANIAC I, the first computer program to beat a human being in a chess game, is developed by Stanislaw Ulam.
1956	Artificial intelligence is named at a computer conference at Dartmouth College.
1958	Jack St. Clair Kilby invents the first integrated circuit.
1958	John McCarthy introduces LISP, an early (and still widely used) AI language.
1958–1959	Jack Kilby and Robert Noyce independently develop the chip, which leads to much cheaper and smaller computers.
1959	Dartmouth's Thomas Kurtz and John Kemeny find an alternative to batch processing: timesharing.
1959	Grace Murray Hopper, one of the first programmers of the Mark I, develops COBOL, a computer language designed for business use.
1960	About 6,000 computers are in operation in the United States.
1962	A U.S. company markets the world's first industrial robots.

1962	The first department of computer science offering a Ph.D. is established at Purdue University.
1962	D. Murphy and Richard Greenblatt develop the TECO text editor, one of the first word processing systems, for use on the PDP1 computer at MIT.
1963	AI researchers of the 1960s, noting the similarity between human and computer languages, adopt the goal of parsing natural-language sentences. Susumo Kuno's parsing system reveals the great extent of syntactic and semantic ambiguity in the English language. Kuno's system is tested on the sentence "Time flies like an arrow."
1963	John McCarthy founds the Artificial Intelligence Laboratory at Stanford University.
1964	IBM solidifies its leadership of the computer industry with the introduction of its 360 series.
1964	Daniel Borrow completes his doctoral work on Student, a natural-language program that can solve high-school-level word problems in algebra.
1964	Gordon Moore, one of the founders of Fairchild Semiconductor Corporation, predicts that integrated circuits will double in complexity each year. His statement will become known as Moore's law and will prove true for decades to come.
1964	Marshall McLuhan's *Understanding Media* foresees electronic media, especially television, as creating a "global village" in which "the medium is the message."
1965	Raj Reddy founds the Robotics Institute at Carnegie-Mellon University. The institute becomes a leading research center for AI.
1965	The DENDRAL project begins at Stanford University, headed by Bruce Buchanan, Edward Feigenbaum, and Nobel laureate Joshua Lederberg. Its purpose is to experiment on knowledge as the primary means of producing problem-solving behavior. The first expert system, DENDRAL, embodies extensive knowledge of molecular-structure analysis. Follow-up work, carried out through the early 1970s, produces Meta-DENDRAL, a learning program that automatically devises new rules for DENDRAL.
Mid-1960s	Computers are beginning to be widely used in the criminal justice system.
Mid-1960	Scientific and professional knowledge is beginning to be codified in a machine-readable form.
1967	Seymour Papert and his associates at MIT begin working on LOGO, an education-oriented programming language that will be widely used by children.
1967	The software business is born when IBM announces it will no longer sell software and hardware in a single unit.
1968	The film *2001: A Space Odyssey*, by Arthur C. Clarke and Stanley Kubrick, presents HAL, a computer that can see, speak, hear, and think like its human colleagues aboard a spaceship.
1968	The Intel Corp. is founded. Intel will grow to become the dominant manufacturer of microprocessors in the U.S. computer industry.
1970	The floppy disk is introduced for storing data in computers.
1970	Harry Pople and Jack Myers of the University of Pittsburgh begin work on Internist, a system that aids physicians in the diagnosis of a wide range of human diseases.
1971	Kenneth Colby, Sylvia Weber, and F. D. Hilf present a report on PARRY, a program simulating a paranoid person, in a paper entitled "Artificial Paranoia." The program is so convincing that clinical psychiatrists cannot distinguish its behavior from that of a human paranoid person.
1971	The first microprocessor is introduced in the U.S.
1971	The first pocket calculator is introduced. It can add, subtract, multiply, and divide.
1971	Direct telephone dialing on a regular basis begins between parts of the U.S. and Europe.
1971	Daniel Bricklin and Software Arts, Inc. release the first electronic spreadsheet for PCs, VisiCalc. The program helps launch the personal computing era by showing the convenience with which information can be handled on a desktop.
1973	Alain Colmerauer presents an outline of PROLOG, a logic-programming language. The language will become enormously popular and will be adopted for use in the Japanese Fifth-Generation Program.
1974	The first computer-controlled industrial robot is developed.

1974   Edward Shortliffe completes his doctoral dissertation on MYCIN, an expert system designed to help medical practitioners prescribe an appropriate antibiotic by determining the precise identity of a blood infection. Work to augment this program with other important systems, notably TEIRESIAS and EMYCIN, will continue through the early 1980s. TEIRESIAS will be developed in 1976 by Randall Davis to serve as a powerful information-structuring tool for knowledge engineers. EMYCIN, by William van Melle, will represent the skeletal structure of inferences.

1974   The SUMEX-AIM computer communications network is established to promote the development of applications of artificial intelligence to medicine.

1975   Benoit Mandelbrot writes *"Les objet fractals: Forme, hasard, et dimension,"* his first long essay on fractal geometry, a branch of mathematics that he developed. Fractal forms will be widely used to model chaotic phenomena in nature and to generate realistic computer images of naturally occurring objects.

1975   Medicine is becoming an important area of applications for AI research. Four major medical expert systems have been developed by now: PIP, CASNET, MYCIN, and Internist.

1975   The Defense Advanced Research Programs Agency launches its Image Understanding Program to stimulate research in the area of machine vision.

1975   More than 5,000 microcomputers are sold in the U.S., and the first personal computer, with 256 bytes of memory, is introduced.

1970s   The role of knowledge in intelligent behavior is now a major focus of AI research. Bruce Buchanan and Edward Feigenbaum of Stanford University pioneer knowledge engineering.

1976   Kurzweil Computer Products introduces the Kurzweil Reading Machine, which reads aloud any printed text that is presented to it. Based on omnifont character-recognition technology, it is intended to be a sensory aid for the blind.

1976–1977   Lynn Conway and Carver Mead collaborate on a collection of principles for VLSI design. Their classic textbook Introduction to VLSI Design is published in 1980. VLSI circuits will form the basis of the fourth generation of computers.

1977   Steven Jobs and Stephen Wozniak design and build the Apple computer.

1977   Voyagers 1 and 2 are launched and radio back billions of bytes of computerized data about new discoveries as they explore the outer planets of our solar system.

1977   The Apple II, the first personal computer to be sold in assembled form, is successfully marketed.

1978   Total computer units in the United States exceed a half million.

1979   In a landmark study published in the Journal of the American Medical Association by nine researchers, the performance of MYCIN is compared with that of doctors on 10 test cases of meningitis. MYCIN does at least as well as the medical experts. The potential of expert systems in medicine becomes widely recognized.

1979   Ada, a computer language developed for use by the armed forces, is named for Ada Lovelace.

1979   Pac Man and other early computerized video games appear.

1979   Hayes markets its first modem, which sets the industry standard for modems in years to come.

Early 1980s   Second-generation robots arrive with the ability to precisely effect movements with five or six degrees of freedom. They are used for industrial welding and spray painting.

Early 1980s   The MYCIN project produces NeoMYCIN and ONCOCIN, expert systems that incorporate hierarchical knowledge bases. They are more flexible than MYCIN.

1981   Desktop publishing takes root when Xerox brings out its Star Computer. However, it will not become popular until Apple's Laserwriter comes on the market in 1985. Desktop publishing provides writers and artists an inexpensive and efficient way to compose and print large documents.

1981   IBM introduces its Personal Computer (PC).

1982   Compact-disk players are marketed for the first time.

1982   A million-dollar advertising campaign introduces Mitch Kapor's Lotus 1-2-3, an enormously popular spreadsheet program.

1982   With over 100,000 associations between symptoms and diseases covering 70% of all the knowledge in the field, CADUCEUS, an improvement on the Internist expert system, is developed for internal medicine by Harry Pople and Jack Myers at the University of Pittsburgh. Tested against cases from the New England Journal of Medicine, it proves more accurate than humans in a wide range of categories.

1983   Six million personal computers are sold in the U.S.

1984   Apple Computer, Inc. introduces the Macintosh.

1984   RACTER, created by William Chamberlain, is the first computer program to author a book.

1984   Waseda University in Tokyo completes Wabot-2, a 200-pound robot that reads sheet music through its camera eye and plays the organ with its ten fingers and two feet.

1984   Optical disks for the storage of computer data are introduced, and IBM brings out a mega-RAM memory chip with four times the memory of earlier chips.

1984   Hewlett-Packard brings high-quality printing to PCs with its LaserJet laser printer.

1985   The MIT Media Laboratory creates the first three-dimensional holographic image to be generated entirely by computer.

1985   Aldus Corp. introduces PageMaker for the Macintosh, the first desktop publishing software.

Mid 1980s   Third-generation robots arrive with limited intelligence and some vision and tactile senses.

1986   Dallas police use a robot to break into an apartment. The fugitive runs out in fright and surrenders.

1986   Electronic keyboards account for 55.2% of the American musical keyboard market, up from 9.5% in 1980. This trend is expected to continue until the market is almost all electronic.

1986   Technology for optical character recognition represents a $100-million–dollar industry that is expected to grow to several hundred million by 1990.

1986   New medical imaging systems are creating a mini-revolution. Doctors can now make accurate judgments based on views of areas inside our bodies and brains.

1986   Using image processing and pattern recognition, Lillian Schwartz comes up with an answer to a 500-year-old question: Who was the Mona Lisa? Her conclusion: Leonardo da Vinci himself.

1986   Russell Anderson's doctoral work at the University of Pennsylvania is a robotic ping-pong player that wins against human beings.

1986   The best computer chess players are now competing successfully at the senior master level, with HiTech, the leading chess machine, analyzing 200,000 board positions per second.

1987   Computerized trading helps push NYSE stocks to their greatest single-day loss.

1987   Current speech systems can provide any one of the following: a large vocabulary, continuous speech recognition, or speaker independence.

1987   Japan develops the Automated Fingerprint Identification System (AFIS), which enables U.S. law enforcement agencies to rapidly track and identify suspects.

1987   There are now 1,900 working expert systems, 1,200 more than last year. The most popular area of application is finance, followed by manufacturing control and fault diagnosis.

1988   Computer memory today costs only 10^{-8} of what it did in 1950.

1988   The population of industrial robots has increased from a few hundred in 1970 to several hundred thousand, most of them in Japan.

1988   In the U.S. 4,700,000 microcomputers, 120,000 minicomputers, and 11,500 mainframes are sold in this year.

1988   W. Daniel Hillis's Connection Machine is capable of 65,536 computations at the same time.

1988   Warsaw Pact forces are at least a decade behind NATO forces in artificial intelligence and other computer technologies.

1989   Computational power per unit of cost has roughly doubled every 18 to 24 months for the past 40 years.

1989	The trend from analog to digital continues to revolutionize a growing number of industries.
Late 1980s	The core avionics of a typical fighter aircraft uses 200,000 lines of software. The figure is expected to grow to about 1 million in the 1990s. The U.S. military as a whole uses about 100 million lines of software (and is expected to use 200 million in 1993). Software quality becomes an urgent issue that planners are beginning to address.
Late 1980s	The computer is being recognized as a powerful tool for artistic expression.
Early 1990s	A profound change in military strategy arrives. The more developed nations increasingly rely on "smart weapons," which incorporate electronic copilots; pattern recognition techniques; and advanced technologies for tracking, identification, and destruction.
Early 1990s	Continuous speech systems can handle large vocabularies for specific tasks.
Early 1990s	Computer processors operate at speeds of 100 mips.
1990s	Significant progress is made toward an intelligent assistant, a decision-support system capable of a wide variety of administrative and information-gathering tasks. The system can, for example, prepare a feasibility report on a project proposal after accessing several databases and "talking" to human experts.
1990s	Reliable person identification, using pattern-recognition techniques applied to visual and speech patterns, replaces locks and keys in many instances.
Late 1990s	An increasing number of documents never exist on paper because they incorporate information in the form of audio and video pieces.
Late 1990s	Media technology is capable of producing computer-generated personalities, intelligent image systems with some human characteristics.
1999	The several-hundred-billion–dollar computer and information-processing market is largely intelligent by 1990 standards.
2000	Three-dimensional chips and smaller component geometries contribute to a multithousandfold improvement in computer power (compared to that of a decade earlier).
2000	Chips with over a billion components appear.
2000	The world chess champion is a computer.
Early 2000s	Translating telephones allow two people across the globe to speak to each other even if they do not speak the same language.
Early 2000s	Speech-to-text machines translate speech into a visual display for the deaf.
Early 2000s	Exoskeletal robotic prosthetic aids enable paraplegic persons to walk and climb stairs.
Early 2000s	Telephones are answered by an intelligent telephone-answering machine that converses with the calling party to determine the nature and priority of the call.
Early 2000s	The cybernetic chauffeur, installed in one's car, communicates with other cars and sensors on roads. In this way it successfully drives and navigates from one point to another.
Early 21st century	Computers dominate the educational environment. Courseware is intelligent enough to understand and correct the inaccuracies in the conceptual model of a student. Media technology allows students to interact with simulations of the very systems and personalities they are studying.
Early 21st century	The entire production sector of society is operated by a small number of technicians and professionals. Individual customization of products is common.
Early 21st century	Drugs are designed and tested on human biochemical simulators.
Early 21st century	Seeing machines for the blind provide both reading and navigation functions.
2010	A personal computer has the ability to answer a large variety of queries, because it will know where to find knowledge. Communications technologies allow it to access many sources of knowledge by wireless communication.
2020–2050	A phone call, which includes highly realistic three-dimensional holographic moving images, is like visiting with the person called.
2020–2070	A computer passes the Turing test, which indicates human-level intelligence.

Glossary

access time Average time to locate instructions or data from ~~secondary (auxiliary) storage~~ device and transfer to computer's **main memory (RAM)**.

Ada High-level programming language developed by Department of Defense for military systems; supports real-time procedures, automatic error recovery, and flexible input and output operations.

add-on memory board Circuit board with memory chips plugged into expansion slot on motherboard to increase capacity of microcomputer's main memory.

add-on utility **RAM-resident** software used in conjunction with applications software that is used, for example, to print output lengthwise instead of across the width of the paper or to improve appearance of the output.

addressing scheme Computer design feature that determines amount of main memory CPU can control at any one time.

algorithm Well-defined rules or step-by-step procedures for solving a problem; may include diagrams.

alphanumeric data Data that can include letters, digits, and special symbols such as punctuation marks; it cannot be mathematically manipulated. *Compare* **numeric data.**

alphanumeric monitor (terminal) Screen that displays only letters, numbers, and special characters such as $, *, ?, but no graphics.

Alt key Modifier key on the computer **keyboard**; when a modifier key is pressed along with another key, the function of that other key is modified. The applications software program determines how modifier keys are used.

American National Standards Institute (ANSI) Organization that develops standards for all high-level programming languages.

American Standard Code for Information Interchange (ASCII) Pronounced "*as*-key." Standard 8-bit code used in data communications, microcomputers, and many minicomputers; 128 valid characters can be formulated with ASCII.

amplitude Size of voltage or magnitude of wave form in data or voice transmission.

analog signal Signal that is continuously varying and represents a range of frequencies; the telephone system is based on analog signals. *See* **digital signal.**

analytical graphics Graphical forms used to make numerical data easier to understand; the most common analytical graphics forms are bar chart, line chart, pie chart. Analytical graphics are usually *spreadsheet-based;* that is, they are created using a **spreadsheet** software package. *Compare* **presentation graphics**.

ANSI *See* **American National Standards Institute.**

applications controls Controls to ensure that input and processing of data is accurate, complete, and authorized; (1) input controls, (2) processing controls, (3) output controls, and (4) authorization controls.

applications generator Software system that generates computer programs in response to user's needs. The system consists of precoded modules that perform various functions. The user selects the functions he or she needs, and the applications generator determines how to perform the tasks and produces the necessary instructions for the software program.

applications software Program or programs designed to carry out a specific task to satisfy a user's specific needs—for example, calculate payroll and print out checks. *Compare* **systems software**.

applications software utility Inexpensive program—RAM-resident or retrieved from disk—that performs basic "office management" functions for the user. *See* **add-on utility; disk utility; keyboard utility; screen utility.**

arithmetic/logic unit (ALU) Part of the computer's central processing unit (CPU) that performs all arithmetic and logical (comparison) functions.

arithmetic operations The operations of addition, subtraction, multiplication, division, and exponentiation.

artificial intelligence (AI) Field of study concerned with using computer hardware and software to simulate human thought processes such as imagination and intuition.

ASCII *See* **American Standard Code for Information Interchange.**

assembly language Language using low-level symbolic abbreviations to represent machine-language instructions. Assembly language is specific to different makes and models of computers. Assembly languages are also known as **second-generation languages.** *Compare* **machine language; procedural language.**

asynchronous transmission In data communications, sending one character or **byte** (eight bits) at a time, each byte preceded by a "start" bit and followed by one or two "stop" bits and an error check bit (or parity bit). An inexpensive and widely used but relatively slow form of data communication. Also called *start-stop transmission*.

automated teller machine (ATM) *See* **financial transaction terminal.**

auxiliary storage *See* **secondary storage.**

backup file Copy of file made to ensure data and programs are preserved if original file is damaged or destroyed.

ball printer Letter-quality printer that uses a ball-shaped print mechanism, much like a typewriter ball, to form characters.

band printer *See* **line printer.**

bandwidth (1) Speed at which data can be transmitted on a communications frequency. (2) In determining video screen resolution, the rate at which data can be sent to the electron gun to control its movement, positioning, and firing.

bar code Code made up of a series of variable-width vertical lines that can be read by a **bar code reader.** Bar codes are used to identify retail sales items, such as groceries, books, and clothing.

bar code reader Input scanning device for reading the light and dark bar codes (stripes) on products that represent their inventory stock numbers or product numbers. The scanner analyzes the bars for width and spacing and translates this data into electrical signals for the computer. Two types of scanners are the handheld wand and the countertop scanner.

BASIC (Beginner's All-Purpose Symbolic Instruction Code) High-level (procedural) interactive programming language designed to teach users how to program on microcomputers.

batch Group of documents or transactions intended for input to the computer all at once, in a controlled fashion.

batch entry Technique whereby data is collected over a period of time and then is input at one time for storage or for processing and output.

belt printer *See* **line printer.**

binary code Scheme for encoding data using binary digits.

binary digit (bit) In binary notation, either 1 or 0. The digit 1 represents an "on" electrical (or magnetic) state; the digit 0 represents an "off" state. A group of adjacent bits (usually eight bits) constitutes a **byte**, or single character.

bit *See* **binary digit.**

bit-mapped display (graphics) CRT screen display system in which each possible dot is controlled by a single character in memory. Also known as *dot-addressable* or *all-points addressable* display.

bits per second Unit used to measure data transmission speeds—for example, some modems operate at 2400 bps.

block Group of contiguous records on magnetic tape. Each block is separated on the tape by a gap (interblock gap) to compensate for the tape's acceleration and deceleration as it moves past the read/write head.

block operations By using block operations, it is possible to move, delete, and copy entire sentences, paragraphs, and pages by issuing commands to the software.

boot To turn on the computer and start the automatic loading of software instructions.

bpi Bits per inch; *see* **recording density.**

bps *See* **bits per second.**

bug Programming error.

bus An "electronic highway" or communications path linking several devices and parts of the **central processing unit (CPU).**

bus network Communications **network** in which all messages are transmitted to the entire network (whose ends are not connected to form a circle), traveling from the sender in both directions along the cable until a message reaches the computer for which it was intended. A central computer is not required to control activity.

byte A group of contiguous bits, usually 8 bits, that form a character.

C **High-level programming language** introduced by Bell Laboratories for use in writing systems software. Though complex to learn, C can be used on a variety of machines.

cache memory Special high-speed memory area that the CPU can quickly access; it comprises a small area of RAM created in addition to the computer's main memory (RAM); a copy of the most frequently used data and instructions is kept in the cache so the CPU can look in the cache first—which makes the computer run faster. Cache memory is usually located right on the 386 or 486 microprocessor chip.

Caps Lock key Keyboard key used to place all the alphabetic keys into uppercase position—that is, capital letters only.

card dialer *See* **Touch-Tone device.**

card reader Device that translates the holes in punched cards into electrical signals, which are input to the computer; is also another name for a **Touch-Tone device,** also known as a *card dialer.*

cartridge-tape unit Device that reads **magnetic tape** in cassette form; often used as alternative type of **secondary storage** to **hard disk** and as backup storage for hard disks. The most popular tape cartridges use 1/4-inch tape in reels up to 1,000 feet long. *See also* **streaming tapc.**

CASE *See* **Computer-aided software engineering**

cathode-ray tube (CRT) Electronic screen used with computer terminals to display data entered into a computer and information available from it. Its principal components are an **electron gun,** a **yoke,** a **shadow mask,** and a phosphor-coated screen; also called *video display screen.*

CD-ROM *See* **compact disk/read-only memory.**

centralized computer facility A single computer department in a company established to provide sole data processing support to all other departments.

central processing unit (CPU) The "brain" of the computer; the part of the computer composed of electrical circuitry directing most of the computer system's activities. The CPU consists of the **control unit** and the **arithmetic/logic unit (ALU),** connected by a **bus.**

CGA *See* **color graphics adapter**

chain printer *See* **line printer.**

character *See* **byte.**

character box Fixed location on a video display screen where a standard character can be placed. Most screens can display 80 characters of data horizontally and 25 lines vertically, or 2,000 character boxes (called *character-mapped display*)—the number the electron gun can target. The more **pixels** that fit into a character box, the higher the resolution of the resulting image. Each character box is "drawn" according to a prerecorded template stored in **read-only memory (ROM).**

character-mapped display *See* **character box.**

character printer *See* **letter-quality printer.**

characters per second (cps) Measure of speed of printers and other output devices.

check bit *See* **parity bit.**

child record In hierarchical database, record subordinate to parent record. *Compare* **parent record.**

chip Integrated circuit made of a semiconductor (silicon) and containing electronic components; can be as little as 1/4-inch square.

CISC *See* **complex instruction set computing.**

clock Device in **CPU** that synchronizes all operations in a **machine cycle.**

clone A product or idea that is a duplicate or copy of another; used to refer to a microcomputer that closely resembles the operation of an IBM microcomputer.

closed architecture Attribute of computers that cannot be upgraded by the use of expansion cards; the user cannot open the **system unit.** *Compare* **open architecture.**

coaxial cable Type of thickly insulated copper wire for carrying large volumes of data—about 1,800–3,600 voice calls at once. Often used in local networks connecting computers in a limited geographic area.

COBOL (COmmon Business Oriented Language) **High-level programming language** for business. Its commands and **syntax** use common human language (for example, English). COBOL is most appropriate for business applications.

code-oriented Refers to **desktop publishing;** **page description software** that displays all the formatting codes on the screen, thus preventing the user from seeing what the page will actually look like when it is printed out. *Compare* **WYSIWYG.**

color dot-matrix printer **Dot-matrix printer** that uses multi-colored ribbons to produce color output.

color graphics adapter (CGA) Expansion card plugged into **expansion slot** in **system cabinet** that allows compatible **monitor** to display **bit-mapped graphics;** must be used with appropriate software; monitor displays four colors as well as monochrome images.

color monitor *See* **RGB monitor.**

command syntax *See* **syntax.**

common carrier *See* **public network.**

communications software Programs that allow users to access software and data from a computer in a remote location and to transmit data to a computer in a remote location.

compact disk/read-only memory (CD-ROM) An optical disk whose data is imprinted by the disk manufacturer; the user cannot change it or write on the disk—the user can only "read" the data. *Compare* **erasable optical disk; WORM (write once, read many).**

compatibility Capability of operating together; can refer to different models of computers, different types of hardware peripherals, and various systems and applications software—not all software is compatible with all computers and other types of hardware, and not all types of hardware are compatible with one another. Incompatibility can often be overcome with the use of **modems** and/or special hardware and software.

compiler Computer program that translates a **high-level language** program (**source code**) into **machine-language** instructions (**object code**) all at once. *Compare* **interpreter.**

complex instruction set computing (CISC) Microprocessor chip design used in most of today's **microprocessor** chips. *Compare* **reduced instruction set computing (RISC).**

computer Data processing device made up of electronic and electromechanical components that can perform computations, including arithmetic and logical operations. Also known as **hardware.** By itself, a computer has no intelligence.

computer-aided design (CAD) The use of a computer and special graphics software to design products.

computer-aided engineering (CAE) The use of a computer and special software to simulate situations that test product designs.

computer-aided manufacturing (CAM) The use of computers to control manufacturing equipment; includes **robots**.

computer-aided software engineering (CASE) Software tools used to automate systems design, development, and documentation.

computer-based information system Computer system for collecting data, processing it into information, and storing the information for future reference and output. The system consists of five components: hardware, software, data/information, procedures, and people. It has four major phases of activity: input, processing, output, and storage.

computer generation One of four phases of computer development; the term is used to delineate major technological developments in hardware and software.

computer graphics *See* **analytical graphics; presentation graphics.**

computer literacy Basic understanding of what a computer is and how it can be used as a resource; includes familiarity with some general-purpose applications software like **word processing** and **spreadsheets.**

computer output microfilm/microfiche (COM) system Equipment that captures computer output on microfilm or microfiche.

computer professional Person with formal education in technical aspects of computers—for example, a programmer, a systems analyst, or a computer operator.

computer system System of hardware, software, procedures, and people for converting data into information.

concentrator Communications device that multiplexes (combines) low-speed communications lines onto one high-speed line; it is more "intelligent" than a **multiplexer** because it can store communications for later transmission.

connectivity When one computer is set up to communicate with another computer system, connectivity becomes the sixth system element, after hardware, software, data/information, procedures, and people; it describes the manner in which the systems are connected.

connectivity diagram Chart used in information systems design that identifies parts of a network and shows how they will be connected.

controller Device that allows multiple terminals and printers to share a communications link but that also controls and routes transmissions and performs error checks and other functions; used in place of a **multiplexer.**

control program *See* **supervisor.**

control structure Used in structured programming to solve problems in programming logic. There are three control structures: **sequence**, **selection** (if-then-else), and **iteration** (or looping; do-while).

control unit Part of the **CPU** that reads, interprets, and sees to the execution of software instructions.

conventional memory The first 640 K of RAM (main memory); *compare* **expanded memory** and **extended memory.**

coprocessor chip Special integrated circuit designed to speed up numeric processing. It can be added to a computer after manufacture.

cps *See* **characters per second.**

CPU *See* **central processing unit.**

cracker A programmer who gains access to a system without authorization.

CRT *See* **cathode-ray tube.**

Ctrl key Modifier key on the computer keyboard; when a modifier key is pressed along with another key, the function of that other key is modified. The specific use of modifier keys is determined by the software program.

cursor Indicator on video display screen that shows where data will be entered next.

cursor-movement keys Computer keyboard keys, usually marked with arrows, that are used to move the **cursor** around the video screen.

cylinder All the tracks in a disk pack with the same **track** number, lined up, one above the other. The **read/write heads** in a disk pack move together and so are always on the same cylinder at the same time.

daisy wheel printer **Impact printer** with plastic or metal disk with typeface impressions of characters on outside tips of spokes; the print character is forced against ribbon and paper.

data Raw, unevaluated facts, concepts, or instructions; after processing, data becomes **information.**

data access area Exposed part of a **disk**, through which the **read/write head** inside the disk drive "reads" and "writes" data from and to a disk.

database Large group of stored, integrated (cross-referenced) data that can be retrieved and manipulated to produce information.

database administrator (DBA) Person who coordinates all related activities and needs for a corporation's **database.** A DBA has six major responsibilities: (1) database implementation, (2) coordination with user, (3) backup, (4) recovery, (5) performance monitoring, and (6) system security.

database management system (DBMS) Comprehensive software tool that allows users to create, maintain, and manipulate an integrated base of business data to produce relevant management information. A DBMS represents the interface between the user and the computer's **operating system** and **database.**

database management system (DBMS) software Program that allows storage of large amounts of data that can be easily cross-indexed, retrieved, and manipulated to produce information for management reports.

data bus Electronic communication link that carries data between components of the computer system.

data dictionary Reference **file** in a **DBMS** that stores information about data and information that is essential to the management of that data and information as a resource.

data file *See* **file.**

data flow diagram Graphic representation of flow of data through a system; standard **ANSI** symbols are used to represent various activities such as input and processing.

data independence Attribute of data that is stored independent of applications programs being used, so that it is easy to access and change.

data (information) processing Operations for refining, summarizing, categorizing, and otherwise manipulating data into a useful form for decision making.

data integrity Attribute of data that describes its accuracy, reliability, and timeliness; that is, if data has integrity, then it is accurate, reliable, and timely.

data manipulation language (DML) Program that is part of **DBMS** software and that effects input to and output from the **database** files; the technical instructions that make up the input/output routines in the DBMS.

data processing The computer-based manipulation of raw data to produce useful information; includes such processes as summarizing, classifying, refining, and comparing.

data redundancy Attribute of data that describes how often the same data appears in different files, often in different formats; a high degree of data redundancy makes updating files difficult.

data storage hierarchy The levels of data stored in a computer file: (1) **files** (broadest level), (2) **records**, (3) **fields**, (4) **bytes**, and (5) **bits** (narrowest level).

data transfer rate Time required to transfer data from disk into a computer's **main memory (RAM).**

DBMS *See* **database management system.**

decentralized computer facility Group of separate computer facilities, established to service the needs of each major department or unit in an organization.

decision support system (DSS) A computer-based information system for assisting managers (usually high-level managers) in planning and decision making. A DSS may use **database management systems**, **query languages**, financial modeling or **spreadsheet** programs, statistical analysis programs, **report generators**, and/or **graphics** programs to provide information. A DSS may be general or institutional.

decision table A chart that lists all contingencies to be considered in the description of a problem, with corresponding actions to be taken; sometimes used instead of flowcharts to describe operations of a program.

dedicated data entry system Specialized single-purpose system used for nothing else but entering data; usually **terminals** connected to a **minicomputer** that do nothing but input and direct the storage of data.

dedicated line Communication line created or leased by a company for its own transmission purposes. *See also* **point-to-point line.**

default disk drive The disk drive that is automatically affected by commands unless the user specifies another drive.

demodulation Process of using communications hardware to convert **analog signals** sent over a telephone line into **digital signals** so that they can be processed by a receiving computer.

desk checking Proofreading a printout of a newly written program; part of testing new programs.

desktop computer *See* **microcomputer.**

desktop management utility Software designed to be available at any time to the user by residing in main memory at all times (**RAM-resident**); it provides many routine office support functions such as calendar organization, dictionary, and calculator.

desktop publishing software Programs that enable user to use a **microcomputer**, graphics **scanners**, and a desktop-sized **laser printer** to combine files created by different software applications packages to produce high-quality publications.

desktop terminal A **keyboard** and a **video display screen** connected to a central computer but fitting on top of the user's desk.

detail diagram Part of a **hierarchy plus input-process-output (HIPO) package,** it describes in detail what is done within each **module**; used in programming.

detail report Computer-produced report for **operating** (lower-level) **management** that contains specific information about routine activities; such reports are highly structured and their form is predetermined.

dialog box Interactive message box that appears on the computer screen and that contains a set of choices or questions for the user; appears when the executing program needs to collect information from the user.

digital signal Signal that is discontinuous and discrete; it consists of bursts that form a transmission pattern. Computers communicate with each other in streams of bits transmitted as digital signals—a series of on and off electrical pulses. *See* **analog signal.**

digitizer Input device that can be moved over a drawing or a photograph thereby converting the picture to computerized data that can be stored, printed out, or shown on a video display screen.

direct access storage and retrieval Situation in which records are stored and retrieved in any order. Also called *random access.*

direct-connect modem Modem that directly connects computer to telephone line, resulting in less interference and higher data transmission speeds (300–2400 bps or higher). An internal direct-connect modem is placed inside the computer; an external direct-connect modem is outside the computer.

direct entry Data input that uses nonkeyboard input devices such as **card readers** and **scanning devices.** *Compare* **keyboard entry.**

direct file File in which data is recorded and stored according to its disk address or relative position within the file; the data is retrieved by the **direct access** method. Also called *relative file.*

direct implementation One of four approaches to systems implementation; the change is made all at once, with the old system being halted at the same time the new system is activated. *Compare* **parallel implementation; phased implementation; pilot implementation.**

directory commands Internal command instructions used in microcomputers to create directory structures on a storage device.

disk A revolving platter on which data and programs are stored in the form of spots representing electrical "on" and "off" states.

disk cartridge Form of **secondary storage** consisting of a 5 1/4- or 3 1/2-inch cartridge containing one or two platters and enclosed in a hard plastic case; the cartridge is inserted into the disk drive much like a music tape cassette.

disk drive Device into which a **diskette** (floppy disk), **hard disk**, or **disk pack** is placed for storing and retrieving data.

disk drive gate Door of disk drive, which must be closed for the read/write operation to be performed. (Not all computers' disk drives have gates—for example, the Apple Macintosh.)

diskette Thin plastic (Mylar) disk enclosed in paper or plastic that can be magnetically encoded with data; originally 8 inches in diameter, standard diskettes are now 5 1/4 or 3 1/2 inches. (Diskettes used to be known as *floppy disks,* but now some of them are covered by rigid plastic and are no longer "floppy.")

disk operating system (DOS) Internal command instructions for microcomputers; **MS-DOS** and **PC-DOS** have become the industry standard for IBM PC microcomputers; **OS/2** is used on IBM's PS/2 Series microcomputers; the **Macintosh operating system** is used on the Apple Company's microcomputers; **TRS-DOS** is used on Tandy/Radio Shack microcomputers; **Microsoft Windows** and **Microsoft Windows NT** is used on newer IBM-type microcomputers; **UNIX** is used on larger machines. These disk operating systems are not generally mutually compatible.

disk pack Removable direct access storage medium holding 6–12 magnetic platters usually 14 inches in diameter; capacity is 150–250 MB.

disk utility **Applications software utility** stored on disk; used to recover files that were accidentally erased, to make backup copy of a hard disk, and to organize a hard disk by means of a **menu-driven** system.

distributed computer facility **Centralized computer facility** and **decentralized computer facility** combined; users have own computer equipment, but some computer **terminals** are connected to a bigger computer in a remote location.

DO *See* **pseudocode.**

documentation Written description of a system's or a software package's parts and procedures; can come in the form of a user's manual that tells the user how to operate a piece of hardware or run a particular software program, or it can be a large collection of volumes and printouts to be used by programmers and computer operators.

document cycle Use of **word processing software** for entering, editing, spell-checking, saving and retrieving, and printing a document. The cycle may also include merging text from separate documents into a single document.

DOS *See* **disk operating system.**

dot-matrix printer **Impact printer** using pin-like hammers to strike a ribbon against paper in computer-determined patterns of dots, making possible a variety of type styles and graphics.

double-density *See* **recording density.**

double-sided disk Disk(ette) that stores data on both sides.

double-sided disk drive Disk drive with **read/write head**s for both top and bottom surfaces of a disk.

do while **Pseudocode** logic statement; directs the computer to repeat an activity as long as a particular condition exists. *See also* **iteration**.

drive A (A:) Designation for the first **disk(ette) drive** in a microcomputer; the program diskette is usually inserted in this drive, which is often the left-hand or the upper drive.

drive B (B:) Designation for the second **disk(ette) drive** in a microcomputer; the data diskette is usually inserted in this drive, which is often the right-hand or the lower drive.

drive C (C:) Designation for the **hard disk** drive in a microcomputer.

drive gate *See* **disk drive gate**.

drum plotter Special-purpose output device for reproducing computer-generated drawings. Paper is placed on a drum and stationary pens move across the paper as the drum revolves.

drum printer *See* **line printer**.

DSS *See* **decision support system**.

dumb terminal A **terminal** that is entirely dependent on the computer system to which it is connected; it cannot do any processing on its own and is used only for data input (using the keyboard) and retrieval (data is displayed on the monitor). *Compare* **intelligent terminal; smart terminal**.

EBCDIC *See* **Extended Binary Coded Decimal Interchange Code**.

E-cycle *See* **execution cycle**.

editing Process of changing text—for example, inserting and deleting.

electrically erasable programmable read-only memory (EEPROM) Type of **read-only memory (ROM)** (chip) much the same as erasable programmable read-only memory except that changes can be made to an integrated circuit electrically—new instructions can be recorded—byte-by-byte under software control.

electroluminescent (EL) display Type of **video display screen** with light-emitting layer of phosphor and two sets of electrodes surrounding the phosphor layer—one side forming vertical columns (usually 512), the other side forming horizontal rows (usually 256). To form a pixel on the screen, current is sent to row-column intersection, and the combined voltages cause the phosphor to glow at that point.

electron gun A component of a **cathode-ray tube (CRT)**; it creates an image on the screen by firing a beam of electrons at the inside of the screen, which causes the phosphors to glow. The electron beam is directed across the screen horizontally and vertically by the magnetic field produced by the **yoke** under the control of the computer software.

electronic banking Service enabling customers to access banking activities from home or private office via a terminal or personal computer connected to their telephones.

electronic bulletin board **Information service** that can be reached via computer connected to telephone lines that allows user to place or read messages from other users.

electronic communications Movement of voice and data over short and long distances, such as by telephone or microwave, through the use of computers and communications hardware and software.

electronic mail Transmission and storing of messages by computers and telecommunications.

electronic shopping Service through which users can order merchandise by using microcomputers and electronic communications to browse through products listed on remote databases.

electronic spreadsheet software *See* **spreadsheet software**.

electronic surveillance Use of special hardware and software to monitor people working on a computer system.

electrostatic plotter Special-purpose output device for reproducing computer-produced drawings. The plotter produces images on specially treated paper with small dots of electrostatic charges, and the paper is then run through a developer to make the image appear.

ELSE *See* **pseudocode**.

encryption The conversion of data into a "secret" code to ensure privacy.

enhanced graphics adapter (EGA) Expansion card plugged into expansion slot in **system cabinet** that allows compatible monitor to display **bit-mapped graphics**. Must be used with appropriate software; monitor displays 16 colors at a resolution higher than **CGA** does.

Enter key Computer **keyboard** key pressed to execute a command that was entered by tapping other keys first.

erasable optical disk **Optical storage** disk whose data can be changed and erased. *Compare* **compact disk/read-only memory (CD-ROM); WORM (write once, read many)**.

erasable programmable read-only memory (EPROM) Type of **read-only memory** in which, with the help of a special device using ultraviolet light, the data or instructions on an integrated circuit (chip) can be erased and new data can be recorded in its place.

ergonomics The study of the relationships between people and their work environments; involves the design of products that are easy to use by people; also called *human engineering*.

event-initiated report Report generated for **middle management** only when certain conditions exist, such as changes requiring immediate attention (for example, equipment breakdown).

exception report Report generated for **middle management** that shows out-of-the-ordinary data—for example, inventory reports listing only items numbering fewer than 10 in stock.

execution cycle (E-cycle) Activity in **CPU** that includes execution of instruction and subsequent storing of result in a **register**. *See also* **instruction cycle; machine cycle**.

executive (desktop) workstation *See* **workstation**.

executive information system **MIS** software designed to make gathering information easy for top-level executives.

expanded memory In a microcomputer, main memory (RAM) that has been added to exceed the usual 640 K maximum; it consists of an add-on memory board and special driver software; used only in compatible 8088, 8086, 80286, and 80386 microcomputers.

expansion card (board) Circuit board that plugs into a socket on a computer's **system board** and that adds a new capability or more memory to the computer system.

expansion slot In a microcomputer that has **open architecture**, an area within the **system cabinet** where expansion cards—such as color graphics adapter cards and expanded memory cards—can be inserted and plugged into the computer's circuitry.

expert system Kind of software consisting of knowledge and rules for using it gathered from human experts in a particular occupation. One of the first practical applications of **artificial intelligence**, it consists of (1) a **natural language** interface with the user, (2) a knowledge base, (3) an inference machine to solve problems and make logical inferences, and (4) an explanation module to explain the conclusions to the user.

Extended Binary Coded Decimal Interchange Code (EBCDIC) Pronounced "*eb*-see-dick." The most popular code used for IBM and IBM-compatible mainframe computers.

extended memory In a microcomputer, main memory (RAM) that has been added to exceed the usual 640 K maximum; it consists of an add-on memory board and special driver software; used only in compatible 80286, 80386, and 80486 microcomputers.

external command instructions General-purpose instructions kept in **secondary storage** for "housekeeping" tasks on microcomputers such as the sorting of files and formatting of disks; part of a computer's **systems software**. *See also* **internal command instructions**.

external label Identifying paper label placed on magnetic tape reel.

external modem   **Direct-connect modem** that is outside the microcomputer and uses its own power supply; it is connected to the computer by a cable.

fax   A faxed item. *See* **fax machine**.

fax machine   Short for *facsimile machine,* a type of **scanner** that "reads" text and graphics and transmits them over telephone lines to a computer with a fax board or to another fax machine.

fiber optics   Form of computer communications in which signals are converted to light form and fired by laser in bursts through thin (2,000ths of an inch) insulated glass or plastic fibers. Nearly 1 billion bits per second can be communicated through a fiber optic cable.

field   Group of related characters (bytes) of data. *See* **data storage hierarchy**.

fifth-generation language   *See* **natural language**.

file   Group of related **records**. A file may contain data (data file) or software instructions (program file). *See* **data storage hierarchy**.

file management system   *See* **flat-file database management system**.

filename extension   One to three characters added to a file name to aid in file identification. The file name and the extension are separated by a dot.

filename length   Convention specified by different **operating systems**—for example, DOS specifies one to eight characters in file names.

file protection ring   Plastic ring inserted into back of magnetic tape reel to protect tape from accidentally being written on; a tape can be written on only when the ring is in place.

file server   A computer, usually a microcomputer, with large-capacity storage, that stores data and programs shared by a network of terminals; often the central unit in a **star network**.

file updating   A factor in **data redundancy** and **data integrity**; when an element of data in a **database** needs to be updated (changed), it must be updated in *all* files that contain it.

financial planning language   Special **interactive** business software used by high-level managers to make projections, "what if" analyses, and long-term planning decisions.

financial transaction terminal   **Terminal** used in banking activities to access a central computer. It may be an automated teller machine (ATM) or specialized terminal used by bank tellers.

first-generation language   *See* **machine language**.

fixed disk   Magnetic disk for **secondary storage** that cannot be removed from the disk drive.

flash memory   Small, lightweight, fast memory circuitry on credit-card-size units that can take the place of hard disk drives. Their small size and low power consumption will allow portable computers to shrink even more (perhaps to 2 pounds for a complete microcomputer) and run for days on a single battery charge, instead of for hours. Flash memory cards may also be used to simulate RAM.

flatbed plotter   Special-purpose output device for reproducing computer-generated drawings. Paper is placed flat and pens move horizontally and vertically across it.

flat-file database management system   DBMS software that can deal with data in only one file at a time; cannot establish relationships among data elements stored in different files.

flat screens   Video display screens for laptop computers; the screens are much thinner than a **cathode-ray tube (CRT)**. *See* **electroluminescent display; gas plasma display; liquid crystal display**.

floating point   Scientific form of notation used to handle large numbers; the decimal point is allowed to move around, or "float."

floppy disk   *See* **diskette**.

flowchart   *See* **program flowchart**.

font   A complete assortment or set of all the characters (letter, numbers, punctuation, and symbols) of a particular typeface in a particular size.

footer   Descriptive information (such as page number and date) that appears at the bottom of each page of a document.

formatting   (1) Directing the computer to put magnetic **track** and **sector** pattern on a disk to enable the disk to store data or information. Also known as *initializing.* (2) In **word processing,** the alteration of text by addition of underlining or boldface, change of margins, centering of headings, and so on.

formatting commands   *See* **formatting** (2).

FORTRAN (FORmula TRANslator)   One of the first **high-level languages**; used for technical and scientific applications, primarily on minicomputers and mainframes.

fourth-generation language (4GL)   Nonprocedural programming language that allows nonprofessional computer users to develop software. *See* **applications generator; query language; report generator.** *Compare* **high-level language**.

frame   Row of magnetic spots and spaces (1s and 0s) recorded across the width of a magnetic tape.

freeware   Software provided by a vendor at no charge.

frequency   Number of times signal repeats the same cycle in a second.

front-end processor   Computer used in a computer center to handle data transmission and communications from outside terminals and devices to allow the main computer to concentrate solely on processing applications as quickly as possible.

full-duplex transmission mode   Communications transmitted in both directions simultaneously.

function keys   Specialized keys on a microcomputer **keyboard** for performing specific tasks with applications software; the keys are used differently with each applications package; they are labeled F1, F2, F3, and so on.

gas plasma display   Used as **video display screen** in some **laptop microcomputers**. Gas plasma display uses three pieces of glass sandwiched together. The inner layer has numerous small holes drilled in it. The outer two layers are placed on both sides of the middle one, and the holes are filled with a gas mixture, usually a mixture of argon and neon. Both outer layers of glass have a thin grid of vertical and horizontal wires. A **pixel** appears at a particular intersection when the appropriate horizontal and vertical wires are electrified.

GB   *See* **gigabyte**.

general controls   Organizational controls that apply to overall processing activities of all computer-based systems. They apply to five areas: (1) the organization, (2) system and program documentation, (3) software, (4) physical security, and (5) management practices.

gigabyte (GB)   One billion bytes.

graphic(al) user interface   Software feature that allows user to select **menu** options by choosing an **icon** that corresponds to a particular processing function; makes software easier to use, and typically employs a **mouse**. Examples are **Presentation Manager** and **Microsoft Windows**.

graphics monitor (terminal)   Screen that can display both **alphanumeric data** and graphics; different types can display one-, two-, or three-dimensional graphics. *Compare* **alphanumeric monitor (terminal)**.

graphics software   Programs that allow the user to present information in pictorial form, often with text. *See* **analytical graphics; presentation graphics**.

gray-scale monitor   **Monitor** that can display many shades of gray; 256 shades, for example.

gray-scale scanner   **Scanner** that can "read" many shades of gray—such as those in a black-and-white photograph—and input the data to the computer system.

grid chart   Chart that shows the relationship between documents used for input and documents that are output.

hacker A skilled computer enthusiast who works alone and is obsessed with learning about programming and exploring the capabilities of computer systems.

half-duplex transmission mode Two-way data communications in which data travels in only one direction at a time.

hand-held scanner Small input device used to scan printed documents on a limited basis to input the documents' contents to a computer.

hand-held terminal Small portable **terminal** that users can carry with them to hook up to a central computer from remote locations, often via telecommunications facilities. Most portable terminals are connected to the central computer by means of telephone lines. These terminals have **modems** built into them that convert the data being transmitted into a form suitable for sending and receiving over the phone lines.

hardcard Type of **secondary storage** device consisting of a circuit board with a disk that is plugged into a microcomputer **expansion slot**. A hard card can store up to 40 MB of data.

hardcopy Output recorded on a tangible medium (generally meaning that you can touch it) such as paper or microfilm. *Compare* **softcopy.**

hard disk **Secondary storage** device consisting of a rigid metal platter connected to a central spindle; the entire unit, including the **read/write heads**, is enclosed in a permanently sealed container. Hard disks store much more data than do **diskettes**—40 MB and up.

hard-sectored disk **Hard disk** or **diskette** that always has the same number and size of **sectors**, as determined by the manufacturer. *Compare* **soft-sectored disk.**

hardware Four categories of electronic and electromechanical computer components: input, storage, processing, and output hardware. *See also* **computer.** *Compare* **software**.

header Descriptive information (such as page number and date) that appears at the top of each page of a document.

Help screen On-screen instruction regarding the use of the software.

hierarchical database model Type of **database** organization in which data is arranged into related groups resembling a family tree, with **child records** subordinate to **parent records.** A parent record can have many child records, but each child record can have only one parent record. The record at the highest level, or top of the "tree," is called the *root record.*

hierarchical network **Star networks** configured into a single multilevel system, with a single large computer controlling all network activity. However, a computer connected into the main computer can have a star network of devices connected to it in turn. Also known as *tree network.*

hierarchy chart *See* **structure chart.**

hierarchy plus input-process-output (HIPO) package Programming and systems design tool that uses three types of diagrams: (1) **visual table of contents (VTOC),** which includes a **structure chart,** a short description of the contents of the program, and a legend that explains the symbols used; (2) **overview diagram,** which shows, from left to right, the inputs, processes, and outputs for the entire program; and (3) **detail diagram,** which describes in detail what is done within each **module.**

high-level language Third-generation programming language designed to run on different computers with few changes—for example, **COBOL, FORTRAN**, and **BASIC**. Most high-level languages are considered to be procedure-oriented because the program instructions comprise lists of steps, or procedures, that tell the computer not only what to do but how to do it. Also known as *procedural language.*

HIPO *See* **heirarchy plus input-process-output package.**

history file Data file created to collect data for long-term reporting purposes.

hub Round opening in the center of a diskette, which enables the disk to fit over a spindle in the disk drive.

hypertext Software that links basic file units (text and graphics) with one another in creative ways. The user typically sees index-type "cards" and "card stacks" on the screen as well as other pictorial representations of file units and combination choices; card and stack contents can be determined by the user or supplied in an **off-the-shelf software** package

I-cycle *See* **instruction cycle.**

icon Pictorial representation of a software function or a peripheral device, such as a disk drive or a printer.

IF *See* **pseudocode.**

impact printer Output device that makes direct contact with paper, forming the print image by pressing an inked ribbon against the paper with a hammer-like mechanism. Impact printers are of two types. *See* **letter-quality printer; dot-matrix printer.**

indexed file organization Method of secondary storage file organization whereby records are stored sequentially but with an index that allows both sequential and direct (random) access. Used almost exclusively with random access microcomputer storage devices to provide maximum flexibility for processing. *See also* **direct access storage and retrieval; sequential file organization.**

index hole Hole in protective jacket enclosing **diskette** that enables the disk to be positioned over a photoelectric sensing mechanism. Each time the disk revolves, a hole in the disk passes under the index hole in the jacket and activates a timing mechanism that determines which portion of the disk is over or under the **read/write heads.**

information Raw **data** processed into usable form by the computer. It is the basis for decision making.

information center Department staffed by experts on the hardware, software, and procedures used in the company; the experts help users in all matters relating to computer use. In companies without a mainframe, it is often called a *personal computer support center.*

information reporting system *See* **management information system.**

information service *See* **public databank.**

information system An organization's framework of standards and procedures for processing data into usable information; it can be manual or computer-based. *See also* **computer-based information system.**

initializing *See* **formatting.**

initial program load (IPL) Refers to starting up a mainframe computer.

ink-jet printer **Nonimpact printer** that resembles **dot-matrix printer** in that it forms images or characters with dots. The dots are formed not by hammer-like pins but by droplets of ink fired through holes in a plate.

input controls Manual and computerized procedures to safeguard the integrity of input data, ensuring that all such data has been completely and accurately put into computer-usable form.

input hardware **Hardware** used to input data to a computer system; examples are keyboards and mice, light pens, and digitizers (direct-entry devices).

input/output (I/O) operations Instructions provided by a program for inputting data into **main memory (RAM)** and for outputting information.

input phase First phase of activity in the **computer-based information system**, during which data is captured electronically—for example, via a **keyboard** or a **scanner**—and converted to a form that can be processed by a computer.

input screen On a **video display screen**, a kind of format that is a combination of displayed text and pictorial data that identifies the elements of data to be entered and in which order they are to be entered. Input screens allow data entry operators to verify visually all data being entered.

Insert mode   In **word processing**, the editing mode that allows you to insert text at the position of the cursor without typing over existing text. *Compare* **Typeover mode**.

installation   Use of a special software program provided with applications software for installing the software on the hard disk and configuring it for use.

instruction(s)   Set of characters (code) directing a data processing system to perform a certain operation. *See also* **software**.

instruction cycle (I-cycle)   In the **CPU**, the operation whereby an instruction is retrieved from **main memory (RAM)** and is decoded, alerting the circuits in the CPU to perform the specified operation.

integrated circuit   *See* **chip**.

integrated software package   Software combining several applications into a single package with a common set of commands. **Word processing**, electronic **spreadsheet**, **database management systems**, **graphics**, and data **communications software** have been combined in such packages.

integrated workstation   *See* **executive workstation**.

intelligent terminal   **Terminal** that can be used to input and retrieve data as well as do its own processing; in addition to the keyboard, monitor, and communications link, an intelligent terminal also includes a processing unit, storage capabilities, and software; microcomputers are often used as intelligent terminals. *Compare* **dumb terminal; smart terminal**.

interactive   Describes computer systems or software that actively involve the user in asking and answering on-screen questions and in responding directly to software requests.

interactive processing   *See* **on-line processing**.

interblock gaps (IBGs)   Blank sections inserted between groups or blocks of records on magnetic tape to allow for the acceleration and deceleration of tape through a tape drive.

internal command instructions   **Operating system** software instructions loaded into **main memory (RAM)** when microcomputer is booted where they direct and control applications software and hardware; they remain in main memory until the computer is turned off. *See also* **external command instructions**.

internal label   Label recorded on tape magnetically; it is examined by a program before processing begins to ensure that the tape is the correct one. Also known as *header label*.

internal memory   *See* **main memory**.

internal modem   **Direct-connect modem** that is inside a microcomputer; it is located on a circuit board plugged into an expansion slot and draws power directly from the computer's power supply. No special cable is required.

international network   **Network** providing intercontinental voice and data communications, often using undersea cable or satellites.

International Standards Organization (ISO)   Organization working to develop standards for programming languages, communications, and compatibility among computers.

interpreter   **Language processor** that converts high-level program instructions into **machine language** one instruction statement at a time. *Compare* **compiler**.

interrecord gaps (IRGs)   Spaces left between records when data is written on magnetic tape.

iteration (do-while) control structure   In **structured programming**, the structure that allows an activity to be repeated (iterated) as long as a certain condition remains true. Also known as a *loop*.

justification   In **word processing**, the activity of evenly aligning words on a margin.

K   *See* **kilobyte**.

key   *See* **key field**.

keyboard   Device resembling typewriter keyboard for entering data and computer-related codes. Besides standard typewriter keys, it has special **function keys**, **cursor-movement keys**, **numeric keys**, and other special-purpose keys.

keyboard entry   Inputting data using a **keyboard**. *Compare* **direct entry**.

keyboard utility   **Applications software utility**, usually **RAM-resident**, used to change the way the **cursor** appears on the screen.

key field (key)   Unique element of data contained in each **record** used to identify the record and to determine where on the disk the record should be stored or retrieved using the **direct access storage and retrieval method**.

keypunch machine   Device used to transcribe data from a **source document** by punching holes into cards via a keyboard using a special code.

key-to-disk (diskette) data entry   System of dedicated high-volume data entry in which keyed-in data is recorded on disks (often in disk packs) or diskettes; the disks/diskettes can be stored separately and transported to a different area where the data is input to the main computer.

key-to-tape data entry   System of dedicated data entry in which keyed-in data is recorded as magnetized spots on magnetic tape; the tape can be transported to a tape drive in a different area where the data is read into the main computer.

kilobyte (K)   1,024 bytes.

language processor   Program that translates **high-level languages** and **assembly languages** into **machine language**. Also known as *translator*.

laptop microcomputer   Microcomputer using **flat-screen** technology that is small enough to be held on a person's lap.

laser printer   Output device in which a laser beam is directed across the surface of a light-sensitive drum to record an image as a pattern of tiny dots. As with a photocopying machine, the image is then transferred to the paper a page at a time.

latency period   *See* **rotational delay**.

left justification   Words at the left margin are evenly aligned.

letter-quality printer   **Impact printer** in which, like a typewriter, a hammer presses images of fully formed characters against a ribbon. *See* **daisy wheel printer; thimble printer**.

license   The document that comes with software that authorizes the software purchaser to run the product on his or her computer; *see also* **software piracy**.

light pen   Pen-shaped input device consisting of a light-sensitive photoelectric cell that, when touched to a video display screen, is used to signal the screen position to the computer.

line printer   Nonserial impact output device in which a whole line of characters is printed practically at once. Includes band (belt) printers, drum printers, and print-chain printers, in which a printable character is located on a band (belt), drum, or print chain, with a separate print hammer for each print position across the width of the paper guide. As the band, drum, or print chain revolves around the print line, the hammers are activated as the appropriate characters pass in front of them.

liquid crystal display (LCD)   Used as a flat video display screen in some laptop microcomputers. LCD uses a clear liquid chemical trapped in tiny pockets between two pieces of glass. Each pocket of liquid is covered both front and back by thin wires. When current is applied to the wires, a chemical reaction turns the chemical a dark color, thereby blocking light. The point of blocked light is the **pixel**.

local area network (LAN)   Communications **network** connected by wire, cable, or fiber optics link that serves parts of a company located close to each other, generally in the same building or within two miles of one another. LANs allow workers to share hardware, software, and data.

logical database design   Detailed description of database model from business rather than technical perspective; it involves defining user information needs, analyzing data element requirements and logical groupings, finalizing the design, and creating the **data dictionary**. Every element of data necessary to produce required management information system reports is identified and the relationship among records is specified. *See also* **schema; subschema**.

logical operations   Operations consisting of three common comparisons: equal to, less than, and greater than. Three words used in basic logical operations are AND, OR, and NOT.

logical record   **Record** defined by user according to logic of the program being used; it is independent of the **physical records.**

logic error   In programming, an error caused by incorrect use of **control structures**, incorrect calculation, or omission of a procedure.

loop   *See* **iteration (do-while) control structure.**

low-level programming language   *See* **assembly language.**

machine cycle   In the **CPU** during processing, the **instruction cycle** and the **execution cycle** together, as they apply to one instruction.

machine language   The language the **CPU** understands; data and instructions are represented as **binary digits**. Each type of computer responds to a unique version of machine language. Also known as **first-generation language.**

Macintosh operating system Disk operating system designed by Apple Computers for the Apple Macintosh microcomputer.

magnetic-ink character recognition (MICR)   Data entry technology used in processing checks; it involves the electronic reading of numeric characters and special symbols printed on checks with magnetic ink.

magnetic tape   Plastic tape with a magnetic surface for storing data in a code of magnetized spots; tape storage is **sequential.**

mainframe computer   After the **supercomputer**, the most powerful type of computer; it is usually housed in a controlled environment and can support many powerful peripheral devices and the processing requirements of hundreds of users.

main memory   The primary storage of a computer, where data and instructions are held for immediate access by the **CPU**; main memory is **volatile**—when the power is turned off, all data and instructions in memory are lost unless they have been permanently recorded on a **secondary storage** medium. Also known as *internal memory* and *RAM (random access memory).*

management   Individuals responsible for providing leadership and direction in an organization's areas of planning, organizing, staffing, supervising, and controlling of business activities. Management may be low-level (operating or supervisory), middle-level, and upper-level (strategic). *See also* **middle management; operating management; upper management.**

management information system (MIS)   Computer-based processing and/or manual procedures within a company to provide useful and timely information to support decision making on all three levels of management; at the **middle management** level, also called *information reporting system.*

margins   Space between the right, left, top, and bottom edges of printed text and the edge of the paper.

mass storage system   System for storing enormous amounts of data; it may consist of as many as 2,000 honeycomb-like cells that hold data cartridges with magnetic tape, each of which can store 50 MB of data. Each cartridge may be retrieved individually and positioned under a special read/write head for data transfer.

master file   File used to store data permanently for access and updating. *Compare* **transaction file.**

MB   *See* **megabyte.**

medium (*pl.* **media**)   Type of material on which data is recorded—for example, paper, magnetic tape, or magnetic disk.

megabyte (MB)   1,000 K—approximately 1 million characters.

megahertz (MHz)   One million hertz; a measure of speed at which computers perform operations; clock speed.

memory   *See* **main memory.**

menu bar   List of command options that goes across the top of the screen.

menu-driven   Describes a software program that offers varying levels of menus, or lists of choices displayed on the screen, to the user to lead him or her through the program function; menus may also include small descriptive pictures, or **icons.**

merging   Bringing together information from two different files.

microcomputer   Small, general-purpose computer system that uses a microprocessor chip as its **CPU**. It can usually be used by only one person at one time; can be used independently or as a **terminal**. Also known as *personal computer, desktop computer.*

microprocessor   Integrated circuit (chip) containing the **CPU** circuitry for a microcomputer.

Microsoft Windows   **Graphic user interface** software for DOS-based microcomputers; similar to **Presentation Manager**, used with **Operating System 2 (OS/2).**

Microsoft Windows NT   New microcomputer operating system for recent IBM-type computers; uses a **graphic user interface** and has networking capabilities, among other advanced functions.

microwave system   Communications technology using the atmosphere above the earth for transmitting signals point to point from tower to tower. Such systems are extensively used for high-volume as well as long-distance communication of both data and voice in the form of electromagnetic waves similar to radio waves but in a higher frequency range. Microwave signals are said to be "line-of-sight" because they cannot bend around the curvature of the earth.

middle management   Level of management dealing with decisions that cover a broader range of time and are less structured than decisions made by **operating management**. However, middle management deals with decisions that are more time specific and more structured than decisions made by **upper**, or strategic, **management.**

millions of instructions per second (mips)   Unit of measure for speed at which a computer processes software instructions.

minicomputer   Computer that is similar to but less powerful than a **mainframe computer**; it can support 2–50 users and computer professionals.

mips   *See* **millions of instructions per second.**

MIS   *See* **management information system.**

modeling tools   Program and systems design tools such as **computer-aided software engineering (CASE), pseudocode, structure chart, data flow diagram, systems flowchart, HIPO,** and so on.

modem   Device for translating **digital signals** from a computer into **analog signals** for transmission over telephone lines and then back into digital signals again for processing (a modem must be hooked up at each end of the transmission). Modem stands for MOdulate/DEModulate. *See also* **acoustic coupler; direct-connect modem.**

Modula-2   **High-level** programming **language** that is an improvement of **Pascal**; it is better suited for business use than Pascal and can be used as an applications software development tool.

modulation   Process of converting **digital signals** from a computer into **analog signals** so that data can be sent over a telephone line.

module   In **top-down** programming **design**, a small, easy-to-work-with unit in a program that has only a single function, a single entry, and a single exit point. Also known as *subroutine.*

monitor   Device for viewing computer output. Also known as **cathode-ray tube (CRT); screen; video display screen.**

monochrome monitor   Device for viewing text and in some cases graphics in a single color, commonly green or amber. It has only one electron gun. *Compare* **RGB monitor.**

motherboard   Main circuit board in a microcomputer system. It normally includes the **microprocessor** chip (or **CPU**), **main memory (RAM)** chips, all related support circuitry, and the **expansion slots** for plugging in additional components. Also known as *system board.*

mouse Handheld input device connected to a microcomputer by a cable; when the mouse is rolled across the desktop, the **cursor** moves across the screen. A button on the mouse allows users to make **menu** selections and issue commands.

MS-DOS *See* **disk operating system.**

multidrop line Communications line that connects many devices; usually leased. *Compare* **point-to-point line.**

multimedia Sophisticated software and hardware that combines basic text and graphics along with animation, video, music, and voice.

multiplexer Device that allows several terminals to share a single communications line.

multiprocessing Activity in which an **operating system** manages simultaneous execution of programs with two or more **CPU**s. This can entail processing instructions from different programs or different instructions from the same program. *Compare* **multitasking.**

multiprogramming *See* **multitasking.**

multitasking Activity in which more than one task or program is executed at a time. A small amount of each program is processed, and then the **CPU** moves to the remaining programs, one at a time, processing small parts of each. Also known as *multiprogramming.*

natural language Programming language designed to resemble human speech. Similar to **query language**, it eliminates the need for user to learn specific vocabulary, grammar, or **syntax**. Examples of natural languages are Clout for microcomputers and Intellect for mainframes. Also known as *fifth-generation language.*

network Collection of data communications hardware, computers, communications software, communications media, and applications software connected so that users can share information and equipment. *See also* **international network; private network; public network; ring network; star network; token ring network.**

network database model Type of **database** organization similar to **hierarchical database model** but allowing multiple **one-to-many relationships**; each **child record** can have more than one **parent record**. Access to the database can be from a number of points, not just the top.

nonimpact printer Output device that does not make direct contact with paper when it prints. *See* **ink-jet printer; laser printer; thermal printer.** *Compare* **impact printer**.

nonprocedural language Programming language that allows programmers and users to specify what the computer is supposed to do without having to specify *how* the computer is supposed to do it. *See also* **fourth-generation language.** *Compare* **procedural language**.

nonvolatile storage Type of storage that is relatively permanent—such as data saved to disk or tape; that is, computer instructions and data are not lost when the power is turned off. *Compare* **volatile storage**.

numeric data Data that can be mathematically manipulated. *Compare* **alphanumeric data.**

numeric keys (keypad) The keys labeled 0–9 on the computer **keyboard**; used to enter numbers for mathematical manipulation.

Num Lock key When a computer **keyboard** combines the **numeric keys** with the **cursor-movement keys**, the Num Lock key must be pressed before numbers can be entered via the numeric keys. Then the Num Lock key is pressed again to restore the function of the cursor-movement keys.

object code Program consisting entirely of machine-language instructions. *Compare* **source code.**

off-the-shelf software **Applications software** that can be purchased in a computer store, as opposed to software that is custom-written by a programmer.

on-demand report Report requested by **middle management** on a case-by-case basis.

one-to-many relationship In a **hierarchical database model**, the parent-child relationship between two record types; one **parent record** has many **child records**.

on-line processing Input data processed immediately, not stored temporarily in a **transaction file** for later processing; anything in a computer system that is on-line is linked up to current processing operations.

open architecture Attribute of computers that can be upgraded by the use of expansion cards, such as **expanded memory**; the user can open the **system cabinet** and insert the expansion cards in the computer's **expansion slots**. *Compare* **closed architecture.**

open wire Earliest type of telephone line, composed of unsheathed, uninsulated copper wires strung on telephone poles.

operating management The lowest level of management in an organization; operating managers deal mostly with **structured decisions** covering a relatively narrow time frame, actualizing the plans of **middle management** and controlling daily operations. Also known as *supervisory management.*

operating system (OS) Set of **internal command instructions** or programs to allow computer to direct its own resources and operations; in microcomputers, called a *disk operating system.*

Operating System/2 (OS/2) IBM and Microsoft microcomputer **systems software** intended to take advantage of 80286 and 80386 microprocessors (such as in the IBM PS/2 Series microcomputers) and support multitasking and software applications requiring up to 16 MB of main memory (RAM); used in conjunction with Presentation Manager and Microsoft Windows.

operating system command Internal or external command that allows users to manage disks and disk files. *See* **external command instructions**; **internal command instructions**.

operating systems software Program that starts up the computer and functions as the principal coordinator of all hardware components and applications software programs. *See* **internal command instructions**.

operational decision maker Low-level manager who typically makes **structured decisions** regarding daily business operations.

optical character recognition (OCR) Input device that reads hardcopy data from source documents into computer-usable form; such devices use light-sensitive equipment to read bar codes, optical marks, typewritten characters, and handwriting.

optical mark Mark made by special pencil on form meant to be read by an **optical mark reader.**

optical mark reader (OMR) Device that reads data recorded on preprinted sheets with special pencil and converts into computer-usable form.

optical storage **Secondary storage** technology using a high-power laser beam to burn microscopic spots in a disk's surface coating. Data is represented by the presence and the absence of holes in the storage locations (1s and 0s). A much lower-power laser beam is used to retrieve the data. Much more data can be stored in this way than with traditional storage media and it is faster and cheaper.

organization chart Chart that shows the levels of management within an organization, as well as the functions.

OS/2 *See* **Operating System/2.**

output Computer-produced text, graphics, or sound in **hardcopy** or **softcopy** form that can be used immediately by people, or computer-produced data stored in computer-usable form for later use by computers and people.

output file Data that is processed and then output in the form of a **file** to be used by another person or program at a later time.

output hardware Hardware used to produce **softcopy** output (monitor display) and **hardcopy** output (from printers and plotters, for example).

output phase A phase of activity in the **computer-based information system** during which the user is provided with all the necessary information to perform and manage day-to-day business activities and make decisions. Output can be provided for immediate use or for storage by the computer for future use.

overview diagram Part of a **hierarchy plus input-process-output (HIPO) package,** used as a tool for program design and **documentation**; the overview diagram shows from left to right the inputs, processes, and outputs for the entire program, and the steps in the diagram are cross-referenced to the module numbers in the corresponding **structure chart.**

page description software Part of **desktop publishing software**; it allows the **laser printer** to combine text and graphics from different files on a single page.

page printer *See* **laser printer.**

parallel implementation One of four approaches to systems implementation; the old system and new system are run at the same time for a specified period, then the old system is discontinued when the new system is judged satisfactory. *Compare* **direct implementation; phased implementation; pilot implementation.**

parallel processing Using many processors (**CPUs**) to process data simultaneously, thus speeding up processing.

parent record In **hierarchical database model**, the **record** higher in the structure than a **child record**. Each child can have only one parent—that is, each record may have many records below it but only one record above it, a **one-to-many relationship**. Deletion of a parent record automatically deletes all child records.

parity bit (check bit) An extra (ninth) **bit** attached to the end of a **byte**; it is used as part of an error-checking scheme: Computers are designed to use either an odd-parity scheme or an even-parity scheme, in which the total number of 1s in each byte, including the parity bit, must add up to an odd number or an even number.

Pascal **High-level programming language** for large and small computer systems; developed to teach programming as a systematic and structured activity. It has strong mathematical and scientific processing capabilities.

PC-DOS *See* **disk operating system.**

pen-based computing Recent development by which special software interprets handwriting done directly on a special type of computer screen. As the computer interprets the handwriting, it displays what was written on the screen in a computer typeface. Users can edit what they have entered and give commands by circling words, checking boxes, and using symbols developed by the manufacturer.

periodic report Report for **middle management** produced at predetermined times—for example, payroll report, inventory status report.

personal computer *See* **microcomputer.**

phased implementation One of four approaches to systems implementation: a system is so large it is implemented one phase at a time. *Compare* **direct implementation; parallel implementation; pilot implementation.**

physical database design In design of a **database**, the stage following the **logical database design**. Physical design involves specifying how best to store data on the **direct access storage** devices so that it can be updated and retrieved quickly and efficiently.

physical records *See* **block.**

pilot implementation One of four approaches to system implementation in which, in a widely dispersed company, the system is introduced at one location at a time. *Compare* **direct implementation; parallel implementation; phased implementation.**

piracy *See* **software piracy.**

pixel Picture element, a glowing phosphor on a **cathode-ray tube (CRT)** screen. Small pixels provide greatest image clarity (**resolution**).

PL/1 (Programming Language 1) **High-level**, general-purpose **programming language** for computation and heavy-duty file handling. Primarily used on minicomputers and mainframes.

plotter Output device used to create **hardcopy** drawings on paper in a variety of colors. *See also* **drum plotter; electrostatic plotter; flatbed plotter.**

pointing device Nonkeyboard data entry device that moves cursor and sends command messages to computer—such as a **digitizer, mouse, light pen,** and **touch screen**.

point-of-sale (POS) terminal Input/output device (**smart terminal**) used like a cash register to print sales transaction receipt and to send sales and inventory data to a central computer for processing.

point-to-point line Communications line that directly connects the sending and the receiving devices; if it is a *switched line*, it is disconnected when transmission is finished; if it is a *dedicated line*, it is always established. *Compare* **multidrop line**.

port Electrical interconnection—for example, on a microcomputer, the point where the printer is plugged into the computer.

portable terminal Input/output device that users can carry with them to remote locations and connect via telecommunications lines to a central computer. **Dumb terminals** can send and receive data to and from the main computer; **smart terminals** permit some data to be entered and edited before the connection to the main computer.

postimplementation evaluation In systems design, a formal evaluation of a new system after operation for several months and after systems maintenance has been done to determine if the system is meeting its objectives.

power supply Source of electrical power to components housed in the **system unit** of a microcomputer.

presentation graphics Graphical forms that go beyond simple **analytical graphics** (bar charts, line charts, pie charts); sophisticated presentation graphics software allows the user to function as an artist and combine free-form shapes and text.

Presentation Manager Graphic user interface similar to **Microsoft Windows**, used with **Operating System 2 (OS/2)**.

primary storage *See* **main memory.**

print-chain printer *See* **line printer.**

printer Output device that prints characters, symbols, and sometimes graphics on paper. *See also* **impact printer; nonimpact printer.**

private network Network supporting voice and data communications needs of a particular organization.

procedural language *See* **high-level language.**

procedure In an information system, specific sequence of steps performed to complete one or more information processing activities.

procedures manual Written **documentation** of noncomputerized and computerized procedures used in a computer-based **data processing** system.

processing The computer-based manipulation of **data** into **information**.

processing hardware Circuitry used to process data into information; *see also* **central processing unit, microprocessor, system unit.**

processing phase The second phase of activity in the **computer-based information system**, during which all the number and character manipulation activities are done that are necessary to convert the **data** into an appropriate form of **information**.

processing registers In the **CPU**, the registers holding data or instructions being acted on. Their size determines the amount of data that can be processed in a single cycle.

program Group of related instructions that perform specific processing tasks.

program files Programs stored on magnetic disk or tape.

program flowchart Diagram using standard **ANSI** symbols to show step-by-step processing activities and decision logic needed to solve a programming problem.

program independence Attribute of programs that can be used with data files arranged in different ways—for example, some with the date first and expense items second and others with expense items first and date second. Program dependence means that a separate program has to be written to use each differently arranged data file.

programmable keys *See* **function keys.**

programmable read-only memory (PROM) Type of **read-only memory (ROM)** chip in which data or program instructions are not prerecorded when it is manufactured; thus, users can record their own data or instructions, but once the data has been recorded, it cannot always be changed.

project dictionary Stores all the requirements and specifications for all elements of data to be used in a new system.

proprietary operating system **Operating system** developed for only one brand of computer.

protocol In electronic communications, formal rules for communicating, including those for timing of message exchanges, the type of electrical connections used by the communications devices, error detection techniques, methods required to gain access to communications channels, and so on.

protocol converter Specialized intelligent **multiplexer** that facilitates effective communications between microcomputers and the main computer system.

prototyping In systems analysis and design, the process of building a small-scale working model of a new system, or part of a new system, in order to get feedback from users as quickly as possible. **Report generators, applications generators, DBMS (database management system) software**, and **CASE (computer-aided software engineering)** software may be used as prototyping tools.

pseudocode "Fake" code; programming code not actually entered into the computer that uses modified human language statements (instead of flowchart symbols) to represent program logic. It is more precise in representing logic than regular, idiomatic English human language but does not follow a specific syntax. It uses four statement keywords to portray logic: IF, THEN, ELSE, and DO.

public databank An information service providing users with access, for a fee, to large databases.

public domain software Software entirely in the public domain—that is, it carries no copyrights—and carrying no restrictions.

public network **Network** providing subscribers with voice and data communications over a large geographical area. Also known as *common carrier, specialized common carrier.*

pull-down menu List of command options, or choices, that are displayed from the top of the screen downward when its title is selected from the menu bar. Pull-down menus can be opened by keystroke commands or by "clicking" (pressing) the mouse button while pointing to the title and then dragging the mouse pointer down.

quad(ruple)-density *See* **recording density.**

query language Fourth-generation programming language that allows users to ask questions about, or retrieve information from, database files by forming requests in normal human language statements. Learning the specific grammar, vocabulary, and **syntax** is usually a simple task. The definitions for query language and for **database management systems software** are so similar that they are usually considered to be the same.

QWERTY Term that designates the common computer **keyboard** layout, whereby the first six letters of the first row of lettered keys spell "QWERTY".

RAM *See* **random access memory.**

RAM-resident software (utility) In a microcomputer, software always available to the user because it resides in **main memory (RAM)** at all times.

random access *See* **direct access storage and retrieval.**

random access memory (RAM) The name given to the integrated circuits (**chips**) that make up main memory, which provides **volatile** temporary **storage** of data and program instructions that the **CPU** is using; data and instructions can be retrieved at random, no matter where they are located in main memory. RAM is used for storing **operating system** software instructions and for temporary storage of **applications software** instructions, input data, and output data. *See also* **internal command instructions**.

raster scan rate Measure of number of times per second the image on a video display screen can be refreshed—that is, "lit up" again. Because the phosphors hit by the electron beam do not glow very long, the beam must continuously sweep the screen. With a low raster scan rate, the screen will seem to flicker.

read-only memory (ROM) Type of memory in which instructions to perform operations critical to a computer are stored on integrated circuits (chips) in permanent, **nonvolatile** form. The instructions are usually recorded on the chips by the manufacturer. *Compare* **electrically erasable programmable read-only memory; erasable programmable read-only memory; programmable read-only memory; random access memory (RAM).**

read/write head Recording mechanism in magnetic storage devices that "reads" (accepts) the magnetic spots of data and converts them to electrical impulses and that "writes" (enters) the spots on the magnetic tape or disk. Most disk drives have two read/write heads to access the top and bottom surfaces of a disk simultaneously.

real-time processing Immediate processing; each transaction is fully processed when input, and there is immediate feedback (action can be taken right away). All related computer files affected by the transaction are updated immediately, and printed output can be produced on the spot. *Compare* **batch entry.**

record Collection of related fields. *See also* **data storage hierarchy**.

recording density Number of **bits** per inch (bpi) that can be written onto the surface of a magnetic disk. Disks and drives have three kinds of recording densities: (1) single-density, (2) double-density, or (3) quad-density. The higher the density number, the more data a disk can hold.

reduced instruction set computing Earlier microprocessor design that uses only a relatively small set of instructions; slower than **CISC.**

register Temporary storage location within the **CPU** that quickly accepts, stores, and transfers data and instructions being used immediately. An instruction that needs to be executed must be retrieved from **main memory (RAM)** and placed in a register for access by the ALU (**arithmetic/logic unit**). The larger the register (the more **bits** it can carry at once), the greater the processing power.

relational database model Type of database organization in which many tables (called *relations*) store related data elements in rows (called *tuples*) and columns (called *attributes*). The structure allows complex logical relationships between records to be expressed in a simple fashion. Relational databases can cross-reference data and retrieve data automatically, and data can be easily added, deleted, or modified. Data can be accessed by content, instead of address, which is the case with **hierarchical database** and **network database models**.

relational operation Operation comparing two elements of data to determine if one element is greater than, less than, or equal to the other.

removable media Diskettes, hard disk cartridges, and optical disk cartridges that can be removed from their drives.

report file Data file in a small computer system that stores information for reports for later transfer to a special computer system for printing.

report generator Fourth-generation language similar to **query language**, which allows users to ask questions of a **database** and retrieve information from it for a report. The user cannot alter the contents of the database file but has great control over the appearance of the output.

request for proposal Part of the systems requirement report of phase 2 of the systems development life cycle; companies going outside their own organizations for help in developing a new system use it to request bids from vendors for prices of software, hardware, programs, supplies, and/or services.

resolution Clarity of the image on the **video display screen**. Three factors measuring resolution are number of lines of resolution (vertical and horizontal), **raster scan rate**, and **bandwidth**.

retrieving In **word processing**, obtaining previously created documents from a storage device and placing them in **main memory (RAM)**.

RGB (red/green/blue) monitor Device for viewing text and graphics in various colors. It has three **electron guns**, and the screen is coated with three types of phosphors: red, green, and blue. Each **pixel** is made up of three dots of phosphors, one of each color, and is capable of producing a wide range of colors. *Compare* **monochrome monitor.**

right justification Words at the right margin of a document are evenly aligned.

ring network Electronic communications **network** in which messages flow in one direction from a source on the loop to a destination on the loop. Computers in between act as relay stations, but if a computer fails, it can be bypassed.

RISC *See* **reduced instruction set computing.**

robot Automatic device that performs functions ordinarily ascribed to humans or that operates with what appears to be almost human intelligence; in the field of **artificial intelligence (AI)**, produced to assist in industrial applications, such as **computer-aided manufacturing (CAM)**.

ROM *See* **read-only memory.**

root directory In the hierarchy of the **MS-DOS directory structure**, when a microcomputer program is **booted**, the first directory displayed is the root directory. This contains subdirectories, which can in turn contain sub-subdirectories. The root directory is similar in concept to the filing cabinet.

root record In a **hierarchical database model**, the record at the highest level or top of the "tree." Root records, which are the key to the structure, connect the various branches.

rotational delay In a disk drive, the time required for the disk to revolve until the correct **sector** is under or over the **read/write heads.**

RPG (report program generator) High-level programming language designed to help small businesses generate reports and update files easily. It can be used to solve clearcut and relatively simple problems.

satellite system In electronic communications, a system that uses solar-powered satellites in stationary orbit above the earth to receive, amplify, and retransmit signals. The satellite acts as a relay station from microwave stations on the ground (called *earth stations*).

saving Activity of permanently storing data from a microcomputer's **main memory (RAM)** (primary storage) on disk or tape (**secondary storage**).

scanner (scanning device) Hardware device that "reads" text and graphics and converts them to computer-usable form; scanners "read" copy on paper and transmit it to the user's computer screen for manipulation, output, and/or storage.

schema Describes organization of **relational database** in its entirety, including names of all data elements and ways records are linked. A **subschema** is part of the schema.

screen *See* **monitor.**

screen utility Applications software utility, **RAM-resident**, used to increase the life of the computer video screen.

scrolling Activity of moving text up or down on the video display screen.

search and replace In **word processing**, the activity of automatically searching for and replacing text in a document.

secondary storage Any storage device designed to retain data and instructions in permanent form. Secondary storage is **nonvolatile:** data and instructions remain intact when the computer is turned off. Also called *auxiliary storage. Compare* **primary storage.**

second-generation language *See* **assembly language.**

sector One of several wedge-shaped areas on a hard disk or diskette used for storage reference purposes. The point at which a sector intersects a **track** is used to reference the data location. *See* **hard-sectored disk; soft-sectored disk.**

seek time In a disk drive, the time required for the drive to position the **read/write heads** over the proper **track**.

selection (if-then-else) control structure In **structured programming**, the **control structure** that allows a condition to be tested to determine which instruction(s) will be performed next.

semiconductor Material (often silicon) that conducts electricity with only a little ("semi") resistance; impurities are added to it to form electrical circuits. The integrated circuits (**chips**) in the **main memory (RAM)** of almost all computers today are based on this technology.

semistructured decision Decision typically made at the **middle-management** level that, unlike **structured decisions**, must be made without a base of clearly defined informational procedures.

sequence control structure In **structured programming**, the **control structure** that specifies that all events take place in sequence, one after the other.

sequential file organization (storage) Method of file recording and storage in which data is retrieved one record at a time in the sequence in which it was recorded on the storage medium; to find one particular record, the system must work through all preceding records.

setting time In a disk drive, the time required to place the **read/write heads** in contact with the disks.

shadow mask In a **CRT (cathode-ray tube)**, a shield with holes to prevent dispersion of the beam from the **electron gun** so that only a small, precise portion of the beam is allowed to reach the screen. The distance between any two adjacent holes in the shadow mask is referred to as *dot pitch*.

shareware Software distributed on request for an evaluation period, after which the user pays a registration fee or returns the software. After the user pays the registration fee—or licensing fee—he or she is usually sent documentation, and, in some cases, additional support and notification of updates.

sheet-fed scanner Scanner that uses mechanical rollers to move the paper past the scanhead.

Shift key Computer **keyboard** key that works in the same way that a typewriter Shift key works: when pressed in conjunction with an alphabetic key, the letter appears uppercase.

simplex transmission mode Communications transmission in which data travels only in one direction at all times.

single-density disk *See* **recording density.**

single-sided disk Diskette that stores data on one side only.

smart card Credit card-sized personal transaction computer that can be inserted into special card-reading **point-of-sale terminals**. Smart cards have memory chips containing permanent records that are easily updated each time the card is used. The transaction data stored on the card can later be read into the computer to update the user's bank records.

smart terminal Terminal that can be used to input and retrieve data and also do some limited processing on its own, such as editing or verifying data. *Compare* **dumb terminal; intelligent terminal.**

softcopy Output produced in a seemingly intangible form such as on a video display screen or provided in voice form. *Compare* **hardcopy.**

soft-sectored disk Disk that is marked magnetically by the user's computer system during **formatting**, which determines the size and number of **sectors** on the disk. *Compare* **hard-sectored disk.**

software Electronic instructions given to the computer to tell it what to do and when and how to do it. Frequently made up of a group of related programs. The two main types of software are **applications software** and **systems software.**

software package **Applications software** and **documentation** usually created by professional software writers to perform general business functions.

software piracy Unauthorized copying of software disks for personal use.

source code Program written in **high-level programming language**. Source code must be translated by a **language processor** into **object code** before the program instructions can be executed by the computer.

source document Document such as an order form on which data is manually recorded for later entry in computer-usable form.

specialized common carrier *See* **public network.**

spelling checker In **word processing**, programs that check a document for spelling errors.

spreadsheet-based graphics *See* **analytical graphics.** *Compare* **presentation graphics.**

spreadsheet software Software program enabling user to create, manipulate, and analyze numerical data and develop personalized reports involving the use of extensive mathematical, financial, statistical, and logical processing. The user works with an electronic version of the accountant's traditional worksheet, with rows and columns, called a *spreadsheet.*

star network Electronic communications **network** with a central unit (computer or **file server**) linked to a number of smaller computers and/or terminals (called *nodes*). The central unit acts as traffic controller for all nodes and controls communications to locations outside the network.

start-stop transmission *See* **asynchronous transmission.**

status report Management report used to supply data and information on the state of something, such as the number of items in inventory; it is a form of output.

storage hardware Devices that accept and hold computer instructions and data in a form that is relatively permanent, commonly on magnetic disk or tape or on optical disk.

storage phase Phase of activity in the **computer-based information system**, during which data, information, and processing instructions are stored in computer-usable form, commonly on magnetic disk or tape or on optical disk; stored data can be processed further at a later date or output for the user in **softcopy** or **hardcopy** form.

strategic decision maker Manager in **upper management** who makes **unstructured decisions**—unpredictable and long-range, not just about past and/or current activities. Such decisions tend to be directed toward strategic planning, allocation of resources, and policy formulation.

streaming tape Storage method in which data is written onto a tape in one continuous stream, with no starting or stopping, no **IBGs (interblock gaps)** or **IRGs (interrecord gaps).** Streaming tape cassettes are often used as backup storage for hard disks.

structure chart In systems analysis, a chart for diagramming the breakdown of **modules** in a program. Also known as *hierarchy chart.*

structured decision Predictable decision that can be made about daily business activities by following a well-defined set of routine procedures; typically made by **operating management.**

structured design A **top-down design** system to ensure that agreement is reached as early as possible on major program design decisions. Its goals are simplicity, refinement by level, and modularity. *See also* **module.**

structured programming Method of programming using **top-down design** and three **control structures** (that is, **sequence, selection, iteration**) to break down main functions into smaller **modules** for coding purposes.

structured walkthrough In programming, the method whereby a group of programmers meets to review a program designed by another programmer in order to identify what is not clear or workable.

stub testing Process by which several high-level **modules** in a program are tested before the program is designed for the rest of the lower-level modules; the objective is to eliminate as many errors as possible without having to write the whole program first. A stub is an unprogrammed module.

subdirectory Second level in the **MS-DOS** directory hierarchy; equivalent to a file drawer in a file cabinet (root directory), it can contain sub-subdirectories.

subschema Part of the **schema** of a relational database; it refers to the way certain records are linked to be useful to the user.

sub-subdirectory Low in the hierarchy of the MS-DOS directory structure, it is contained within a subdirectory of the **root directory**. A sub-subdirectory resembles a file folder.

summary report Report for **middle management** that reviews, summarizes, and analyzes historical data to help plan and control operations and implement policy formulated by **upper management**. Summary reports show totals and trends.

supercomputer The largest and most powerful computer; it is about 50,000 times more powerful than a **microcomputer** and may cost as much as $20 million. Supercomputers are housed in special rooms; the next most powerful computer is the **mainframe**.

superconductor A not-yet-developed material to be used for integrated circuits (**chips**); this material would conduct electricity faster (with less or no resistance) and with less heat output than semiconductors.

supermicro A very powerful **microcomputer**.

super video graphics array (VGA) Expansion card plugged into **expansion slot** in **system cabinet** that allows compatible monitor to display **bit-mapped graphics** in color; must be used with appropriate software; displays up to 256 colors at a very high **resolution**.

supervisor The "captain" of the **operating system**, it remains in a microcomputer's main memory and calls in other parts of the operating system as needed from **secondary storage** and controls all other programs in the computer. In a **multitasking** environment, a supervisor coordinates the execution of each program. Also known as *control program.*

supervisory management *See* **operating management.**

surge suppressor Device that protects electrical equipment from being damaged by surges of high voltage; the computer is plugged into the surge suppressor, which is plugged into the wall socket.

switched line **Point-to-point** communications **line** that is disconnected when transmission is finished.

synch bits Header and trailer bytes inserted as identifiers at beginnings and ends of blocks of coded data; used in **synchronous transmission**.

synchronous transmission Form of transmitting groups of characters as blocks with no start and stop bits between characters. Characters are sent as blocks with header and trailer bytes (called **synch bits**) inserted as identifiers at the beginnings and ends of blocks. Synchronous transmission is used by large computers to transmit huge volumes of data at high speeds. *Compare* **asynchronous transmission.**

syntax Rules and patterns required for forming programming language sentences or statements that tell the computer what to do and how to do it.

syntax error   In programming, an error resulting from incorrect use of the rules of the language the program is being written in.

system board   *See* **motherboard.**

system cabinet   *See* **system unit.**

systems development life cycle (SDLC)   Formal process by which organizations build **computer-based information systems.** Participants are users, information processing staff, management of all departments, and computer specialists. The SDLC is used as a guide in establishing a business system's requirements, developing the system, acquiring hardware and software, and controlling development costs. It is generally divided into six phases: (1) analyze current system; (2) define new system requirements; (3) design new system; (4) develop new system; (5) implement new system; and (6) evaluate performance of and maintain new system.

systems flowchart   Systems development modeling tool used to diagram and document design of a new system and present an overview of the entire system, including data flow (points of input, output, and storage) and processing activities.

systems maintenance   The phase after a new system has been implemented when adjustments must be made (correction of minor processing errors).

systems requirement report   Report concluding the second phase of the **systems development life cycle**; it enables managers to determine the completeness and accuracy of the new system requirements, as well as the economic and practical feasibility of the new system; it may also include a request for proposal for prices of software, hardware, supplies, and/or services from vendors.

systems software   Programs that are the principal interface between all hardware, the user, and applications software; comprise **internal command instructions, external command instructions**, and **language processor.**

systems test   Phase of testing all programs and related procedures for operating a new system.

system unit   Main computer system cabinet in a microcomputer, which usually houses the power supply, the motherboard, and some storage devices.

tactical decision maker   Member of **middle management** who generally deals with **semistructured decisions.**

Taligent   New microcomputer **operating system** being produced through a joint IBM and Apple venture. With this operating system, IBM and Apple hope to challenge Microsoft for leadership in computer operating systems. Microsoft DOS runs on Intel microprocessors, whereas the Macintosh operating system runs on Motorola microprocessors. Taligent runs on both IBM and Macintosh computers. Before Taligent becomes widely used, however, applications software must be written for it.

TB   *See* **terabyte.**

teleconferencing   Electronic linkage of several people who participate in a conversation and share displayed data at the same time.

terabyte (TB)   One trillion bytes.

terminal   Input/output device; it typically consists of a **video display screen**, a **keyboard**, and a connecting cable. A dumb terminal is entirely dependent for all its capabilities on the computer system to which it is connected; it cannot do any processing of its own. A smart terminal is able to do some editing and storage of data without interacting with the central computer system, but it cannot be used for programming. An intelligent terminal can input and receive data, as well as allow users to edit and program.

THEN   *See* **pseudocode.**

thermal printer   **Nonimpact printer** that uses heat to produce an image. The print mechanism heats the surface of chemically treated paper, producing dots as characters. No ribbon or ink is used.

thesaurus   Software program that provides a list of words both similar to and opposite from the meaning of a selected word in a document.

thimble printer   Letter-quality **impact printer** similar to **daisy wheel printer**, except that the spokes curve upward instead of lying flat.

third-generation language   *See* **high-level language.**

timesharing   System that supports many user stations or terminals simultaneously. A **front-end processor** may be used to schedule and control all user requests entering the system from the **terminals**, enabling the main computer to concentrate solely on processing.

token ring network   Electronic communications **network** in which each computer obtains exclusive access to the communications channel by "grabbing" a "token" and altering it before attaching a message. This altered token acts as a message indicator for the receiving computer, which in turn generates a new token, freeing up the channel for another computer. Computers in between the sender and the receiver examine the token and regenerate the message if the token is not theirs. Thus, only one computer can transmit a message at one time.

top-down design   In **structured programming** and systems design, the act of identifying the main functions of a program and then breaking them into smaller units (**modules**).

touch screen   **Video display screen** sensitized to receive input from touch of a finger.

Touch-Tone device   Input device hooked up to the telephone line for the purpose of running credit card checks; the device sends data to a central computer, which then checks the data against its files and reports credit information back to the store. Also called *card dialer* or *card reader.*

track   (1) On **magnetic tape** a channel of magnetic spots and spaces (1s and 0s) running the length of the tape. (2) On **disks**, a track is one of the circular bands.

trackball   Essentially an upside-down **mouse**. The ball is held in a socket on the top of the stationary device; instead of moving the ball by rolling the device around on the desktop, the user moves the ball with his or her fingers.

track density   Number of **tracks** on magnetic medium. Common track densities are 48 tracks per inch (tpi) and 96 tpi. Track density affects capacity.

transaction file   Temporary storage file in which data is stored in computer-usable form until needed for processing. *Compare* **master file.**

transaction log   Complete record of activity affecting contents of a **database** during transaction period. This log aids in rebuilding database files if they are damaged.

transaction processing system (TPS)   Information system supporting day-to-day business operating activities or transactions; usually the first and most important objective of an information system. A computer-based transaction information system operates at the lowest level of a business and usually within only one functional area of a business—marketing, accounting and finance, production, or research and development. Also called an *operations information system (OIS)* or an *electronic data processing (EDP) system.*

translator   *See* **language processor.**

tree network   *See* **hierarchical network.**

TRS-DOS   **Disk operating system** for some Tandy/Radio Shack microcomputers.

turnaround document   Computer-produced output document forwarded to a recipient, who records any additional data on it and returns it to the sender.

twisted-pair cable   Insulated pairs of wires twisted around each other; they are often packed into bundles of a thousand or more pairs, as in telephone lines.

Typeover mode   In **word processing**, the mode of inserting text in which existing text is typed over as new text is typed in. *Compare* **Insert mode.**

Unicode New standard binary code that encompasses all written human languages and that may become the equivalent of **ASCII** in the world community. Unicode uses 16-bit character sets instead of 8-bit sets. Although Unicode is not yet used much, many software developers hope it will become the international standard for encoding data.

uninterruptible power supply (UPS) Equipment used to protect your computer hardware from power surges; in addition, if the power goes out, a UPS will keep the system running for around 8-30 minutes, providing time to save work and shut the system down.

UNIX **Operating system** initially created for **minicomputers**; it provides a wide range of capabilities, including **virtual storage**, **multiprogramming**, and **timesharing**.

unjustified text Text with an unaligned (ragged) margin.

unstructured decision Decision rarely based on predetermined routine procedures; involves the subjective judgment of the decision maker and is mainly the kind of decision made by **upper management**. Unstructured decisions are supported by management information systems in the form of highly summarized reports covering information over long time periods and surveying activities outside as well as inside the company.

upper management The level of management dealing with decisions that are broadest in scope and cover the longest time frame. Top managers include only a few powerful people who are in charge of the four basic functions of a business: (1) marketing, (2) accounting and finance, (3) production, and (4) research and development. A manager at this level is also known as a *strategic decision maker*. *Compare* **middle management**; **operating management**.

user Person receiving the computer's services; generally someone without much technical knowledge who makes decisions based on reports and other results that computers produce. *Compare* **computer professional**.

user acceptance test Test of the workability of a newly devloped system by people who will be using the system.

utility *See* **applications software utility**.

video display screen Device for viewing computer output. Two main types are **cathode-ray tube (CRT)** and **flat screen**.

video graphics array (VGA) Expansion card plugged into **expansion slot** in **system cabinet** that allows compatible monitors to display **bit-mapped graphics** in color; must be used with appropriate software; displays 16 colors at a resolution higher than EGA (enhanced graphics adapter).

virtual memory **Operating system** element that enables the computer to process as if it contained almost an unlimited supply of **main memory**. It enables a program to be broken into modules, or small sections, that can be loaded into main memory when needed. Modules not currently in use are stored on high-speed disk and retrieved one at a time when the operating system determines that the current module has completed executing. Also known as *virtual storage*.

virtual storage *See* **virtual memory**.

virus Bugs (programming errors) created intentionally by some programmers, usually by "hackers," that consist of pieces of computer code (either hidden or posing as legitimate code) that, when downloaded or run, attach themselves to other programs or files and cause them to malfunction.

visual table of contents (VTOC) Part of a **hierarchy plus input-process-output (HIPO) package,** it includes a **structure chart**, a short description of the contents of the program, and a legend that provides any necessary explanations of symbols used in the **overview diagram** and the **detail diagram,** also parts of the HIPO package.

voice input device Input device that converts spoken words into electrical signals by comparing the electrical patterns produced by the speaker's voice to a set of prerecorded patterns. If a matching pattern is found, the computer accepts it as a part of its standard "vocabulary" and then activates and manipulates displays by spoken command. Also known as *voice recognition system*.

voice mail Electronic voice-messaging system that answers callers with a recording of the user's voice and records messages. Messages can be forwarded to various locations; local telephone companies provide voice mail services; voice mail systems are also used within companies.

voice output Computer-synthesized "spoken" output.

voice recognition system *See* **voice input device.**

volatile storage Form of memory storage in which data and instructions are lost when the computer is turned off. *Compare* **nonvolatile storage**. *See also* **random access memory (RAM).**

wand *See* **bar code reader.**

window Most **video display screens** allow 24-25 lines of text to be viewed at one time; this portion is called a *window*. By moving (scrolling) text up and down the screen, other windows of text become available.

Windows *See* **Microsoft Windows**.

word processing Preparation of text for creating, editing, or printing documents.

word processing software Program enabling user to create and edit documents: inserting, deleting, and moving text. Some programs also offer formatting features such as variable margins and different type sizes and styles, as well as more advanced features that border on **desktop publishing**.

wordsize The size of a **register** is referred to as *wordsize*. In general, the larger the register, the more bits can be processed at once.

word wrap In **word processing**, when the **cursor** reaches the right-hand margin of a line it automatically returns (wraps around) to the left-hand margin of the line below and continues the text; the user does not have to hit a key to make the cursor move down to the next line.

workstation A sophisticated and powerful microcomputer used by one person at a time for specialized applications such as **computer-aided design** and **computer-aided engineering.**

WORM (write once, read many) **Optical storage** disk whose data and instructions are imprinted by the disk manufacturer but whose content is determined by the buyer; after the data is imprinted, it cannot be changed. *Compare* **compact disk/read-only memory (CD-ROM); erasable optical disk**.

write-protect notch On a **diskette**, a notch in the protective cover that can be covered to prevent the **read/write head** from touching the disk surface so that no data can be recorded or erased.

WYSIWYG (what you see is what you get) **Page description software** that allows the user to see the final version of a **desktop publishing** document on the screen before it is printed out. *Compare* **code-oriented.**

yoke In a **cathode-ray tube (CRT)**, the cylinder placed in front of the **electron gun** that can generate a controlled magnetic field (like a directional magnet). The yoke directs the electron beam of the electron gun across the screen horizontally and vertically.

Index